Question	Answer(s)	See Pages
How do I research a topic?	Begin with general reference works (encyclopedias, almanacs, handbooks); use bibliographies to locate books; use periodical indexes to locate periodicals. Take notes on 4 × 6 cards; prepare 3 × 5 bibliography cards for each source used.	195–205
How do I document my sources?	Follow the formats recommended by the Modern Language Association or by your instructor.	493–505
How do I conduct an interview?	Make an appointment; prepare a set of questions; be direct but not excessively formal.	205–208
How do I revise my work?	Utilize basic revision strategies: deletion, addition, substitution, rearrangement, reperception, and proofreading.	343–348
How can I strengthen my sentences?	Check for opportunities to embed; subordinate; use periodic, cumulative, and balanced patterns; use parallel constructions; vary sentence length.	264–281
How can I improve my paragraphs?	Check to see that supporting sentences relate logically to the topic sentence; avoid cluttering the paragraph with extraneous material.	295–303
How can I improve my word choice?	Strive toward clarity (use unfamiliar expressions correctly; be concise; use terms consistently); watch out for clichés and euphemisms; use your dictionary often.	312–319, 323–328

The Writer's Art
A PRACTICAL RHETORIC AND HANDBOOK

The Writer's Art
A PRACTICAL RHETORIC AND HANDBOOK

Fred D. White, 1943−

Santa Clara University

Wadsworth Publishing Company
Belmont, California
A Division of Wadsworth, Inc.

English Editor: John Strohmeier
Special Projects Editor: Judith McKibben
Production Editor: Jane Townsend
Designer: MaryEllen Podgorski
Print Buyer: Barbara Britton
Copy Editor: Lisa Danchi
Compositor: G&S Typesetters, Inc.
Cover: Paul Klee. *Vocal Fabric of the Singer Rosa Silber*, 1922. Gouache and gesso on canvas, 20¼ × 16⅜ in. Collection, The Museum of Modern Art, New York. Gift of Mr. and Mrs. Stanley Resor. Photograph © 1986 The Museum of Modern Art, New York.

© 1986 by Wadsworth, Inc. All rights reserved. No part of this book may be reproduced, stored in a retrieval system, or transcribed, in any form or by any means, electronic, mechanical, photocopying, recording, or otherwise, without the prior written permission of the publisher, Wadsworth Publishing Company, Belmont, California 94002, a division of Wadsworth, Inc.

Acknowledgments are listed on p. 524.

Printed in the United States of America

1 2 3 4 5 6 7 8 9 10—90 89 88 87 86

ISBN 0-534-06084-6

Library of Congress Cataloging in Publication Data
White, Fred D., 1943–
  The writer's art.
  Includes index.
  1. English language—Rhetoric. 2. English language—Grammar—1950–   I. Title.
PE1408.W5797   1986   808'.042   85-22578
ISBN 0-534-06084-6

To Beverly

Brief Contents

Part One	**The Writing Experience** 1	
Chapter 1	What Is Good Writing? 3	
Chapter 2	Reasons and Incentives for Writing 17	
Chapter 3	A Practical Method of Writing 29	
Part Two	**Principles and Projects** 55	
Chapter 4	Principles of Development: Aiming to Express 57	
Chapter 5	Projects in Expressive Writing 71	
Chapter 6	Principles of Development: Aiming to Inform 85	
Chapter 7	Projects in Informative Writing 99	
Chapter 8	Principles of Development: Aiming to Persuade 121	
Chapter 9	Projects in Persuasive Writing 157	
Chapter 10	Principles of Research 189	
Chapter 11	Research Paper Projects 217	
Part Three	**Tools of the Trade** 257	
Chapter 12	Building Sentence-Writing Skills 259	
Chapter 13	Shaping Paragraphs 293	
Chapter 14	Exploring Words and Meanings 309	
Chapter 15	Revising Your Work 343	
Part Four	**Special Topics** 355	
Chapter 16	Maintaining a Journal 357	
Chapter 17	Getting the Most from Your Conference Tutorial 363	
Chapter 18	Participating in Classroom Workshops 367	
Chapter 19	Composing on a Computer 371	
Chapter 20	Writing Essay Exams 375	
Part Five	**Handbook** 379	
	Rhetorical and Grammatical Principles 381	
	Glossary of Usage 437	
	Punctuation 469	
	Spelling 483	
	Manuscript Formatting/Proofreading and Notetaking Marks 487	
	Documentation Formats 493	
	Reference Works in Major Subject Areas 507	

Contents

Part One

The Writing Experience   1

Chapter 1 — What Is Good Writing?   3

Writing and Thinking   3
Communicating to an Audience   4
Developing Your Audience Awareness   5
The Four Pillars of Good Writing   7
Distinguishing Between Good and Weak Writing   9
Summary   12
For Discussion   12
For Writing   14
- Computer Writing   15

Chapter 2 — Reasons and Incentives for Writing   17

Why Write?   17
Writing as Role Playing   19
Writing as "Re-creation" and Recreation   21
Summary   25
For Discussion   25
For Writing   26
- Computer Writing   27

Chapter 3 — A Practical Method of Writing 29

Making Writing a Habit 30
Writing Rituals 31
Creating the Right Environment for Writing 31
The Writing Process 32
    Invention 33
        Brainstorming 34
        Free-writing 38
        Talk-writing 39
    Gathering and Planning 40
        The 5Ws and the H Grid 40
        Background Reading 42
    Organizing and Outlining 42
        Organizing with an Outline 43
    Writing a First Draft 44
    Revising 45
Kinds of Essays 46
Summary 50
For Discussion 51
For Writing 51
■ Computer Writing 53

Part Two

Principles and Projects 55

Chapter 4 — Principles of Development: Aiming to Express 57

The Range of Expressive Writing 58
    Narration 59
    Description 61
Common Problems in Expressive Writing 63
    Lack of Clear Purpose 64
    Overcomplicated Language 64
    Wordiness 65

Summary   66
For Discussion   67
For Writing   68
- Computer Writing   69

Chapter 5 — Projects in Expressive Writing   71

Writing an Extended Description of a Setting   71
Writing an Extended Description of a Person   74
Writing a Personal-Experience Narrative   76
Summary   79
For Discussion   79
For Writing   82

Chapter 6 — Principles of Development: Aiming to Inform   85

Presenting Information   85
Defining   86
Classifying and Dividing   87
    Classifying   87
    Dividing   88
Narrating in an Explanatory Context   89
Describing in an Explanatory Context   89
Analyzing   91
How the Rhetorical Devices Interact   93
Summary   94
For Discussion   95
For Writing   96
- Computer Writing   98

Chapter 7 — Projects in Informative Writing   99

Writing an Extended Definition   100
    Basic Writing Techniques   103
Writing an Advisory or Instructional Feature   104
    Suggestions for How-to Writing   108
Writing an Analytical Feature   111

Summary 112
For Discussion 113
For Writing 118

Chapter 8

Principles of Development: Aiming to Persuade 121

Reasoning: The Basis of Argument 123
    Classifying Reasoning 123
        Logic-Based Reasoning 123
        Emotion-Based Reasoning 124
        Authority-Based Reasoning 125
    Applying the Three Appeals 126
Common Problems in Argumentation 127
    Confusing Opinion with Argument 127
    Identifying Errors in Logic-Based Reasoning 128
        Question-Begging 128
        Overgeneralizing 128
        Faulty Generalizing 129
        Faulty Deductive Reasoning 131
    Identifying Errors in Emotion-Based Reasoning 136
    Identifying Errors in Authority-Based Reasoning 137
Building an Effective Argument 138
Summary 143
For Discussion 143
For Writing 145
- Computer Writing 146

Special Topic: Mass-Media Persuasion 147
Mass-Media Persuasion: Topics for Discussion 149

Chapter 9

Projects in Persuasive Writing 157

The Opinion Essay 157
The Pro-Con Essay 160
The Problem-Solving Essay 167
Summary 172
For Discussion 172
For Writing 174

Contents   **xi**

Special Topic: Writing Reviews   177
Writing Reviews: Topics for Discussion   181
For Writing   183

Special Topic: The Textual Explication   183
The Textual Explication: Topics for Discussion   187
For Writing   187

Principles of Research   189 — Chapter 10

Your Library   190
A Sampling of Important Reference Works   191
Your Library's Card Catalog   192
    The Dewey Decimal System   194
    The Library of Congress System   194
Getting Involved with Your Topic   195
Gathering Information Systematically   196
    Three Kinds of Note-Taking   196
Incorporating Quotations Gracefully   200
Conducting a Library Research Task   201
Researching Outside the Library   205
    Interviews   205
    Questionnaires   208
    Printed Information Sources Outside the Library   210
    Plagiarism   211
Using a Computer Database   212
Summary   214
For Discussion   214
For Writing   215
- Computer Writing   216

Research Paper Projects   217 — Chapter 11

Project One: Researching a Scientific or Technical Subject   219
    Student Research Paper: Structured Programming: Its Development and Importance, by Jeff Brown   224

Project Two: Researching a Social Sciences Subject   235
   Student Research Paper: Gradually Adjusting to Retirement: Facing the Change, by Ron K. Rock, Jr.   236
Project Three: Researching a Fine Arts Topic   246
   Critical Essay: Henry Tanner's Contribution to Black American Art and Culture, by Ellwood Perry   247
Summary   253
For Discussion   253
For Writing   254
■ Computer Writing   255

Part Three

Tools of the Trade   257

Chapter 12

Building Sentence-Writing Skills   259

What Is a Sentence?   260
   Sentence Skills Checkpoint A: Fragments, Run-ons, and Whole Sentences   263
Writing Strong Sentences   264
   Unity   265
   Sentence Skills Checkpoint B: Unity   267
   Coherence   267
      Misplaced Modification   267
      Lack of Parallelism   269
   Sentence Skills Checkpoint C: Coherence   271
   Development   272
      Embedding   272
      Coordination and Subordination   273
   Sentence Skills Checkpoint D: Development   275
   Variety   276
      Four Common Methods of Achieving Sentence Variety   277
   Sentence Skills Checkpoint E: Variety   280
Toward Syntactic Virtuosity   281
   Analysis of Maya Angelou's Syntax   282
   Analysis of John McPhee's Syntax   283

Special Topic: Combining Sentences 284
    Sentence Combining: Part One 284
    Sentence Combining: Part Two 286
    Sentence Combining: Part Three 287
Summary 288
For Discussion 289
For Writing 289
- Computer Writing 291

Chapter 13

Shaping Paragraphs 293

The Well-Made Paragraph 295
    Paragraph Skills Checkpoint A: Paragraph Coherence 297
Common Problems in Paragraphing 297
    Paragraph Skills Checkpoint B: Amplification 298
    Paragraph Skills Checkpoint C: Cluttering 300
Paragraphing in Relation to Discourse Mode 300
    Analysis 302
Experimenting with Paragraphs 303
Summary 305
For Discussion 305
For Writing 307
- Computer Writing 308

Chapter 14

Exploring Words and Meanings 309

Denotation and Connotation 310
    Diction Skills Checkpoint A: Denotation and Connotation 312
Toward Maintaining Clarity in Diction 312
    Diction Skills Checkpoint B: Consistent Use of Terms 313
    Diction Skills Checkpoint C: Tense Shift 314
    Diction Skills Checkpoint D: Accurate Word Choice 317
    Diction Skills Checkpoint E: Conciseness 318
Metaphorical Language 319
    Diction Skills Checkpoint F: Metaphor 322
Euphemisms and Clichés 322
    Euphemisms 323

Clichés   323
  Diction Skills Checkpoint G: Euphemisms and Clichés   324
The Dictionary and the Writer   324
  Ways to Use a Dictionary   325
    Spelling   325
    Syllabication   325
    Pronunciation   325
    Part-of-Speech Classification   325
    Definition   325
    Grammar and Usage Data   327
  Diction Skills Checkpoint H: Etymology   328
Levels of Usage   328
General and Specialized Diction   331
  Diction Skills Checkpoint I: Specialized Language   333
A Method of Efficient Vocabulary Building   333
Words and Imagination   336
Summary   337
For Discussion   338
For Writing   341
- Computer Writing   342

Chapter 15

Revising Your Work   343

Elements of Revising   343
Anatomy of a Revision   348
Summary   352
For Discussion   352
For Writing   352
- Computer Writing   353

Part Four

Special Topics   355

Chapter 16

Maintaining a Journal   357

Entry Suggestions for Your Journal   360
Journal Writing on the Computer   361

Contents

Chapter 17
Getting the Most from Your Conference Tutorial   363

Chapter 18
Participating in Classroom Workshops   367

Chapter 19
Composing on a Computer   371

Chapter 20
Writing Essay Exams   375

How to Study for an Essay Exam   377

Part Five

Handbook   379

Rhetorical and Grammatical Principles   381
Descriptions and examples of one hundred twenty-nine rhetorical and grammatical principles, presented alphabetically, with short exercises following most entries.

Diagnostic Exercises: Rhetorical and Grammatical Principles   428

Glossary of Usage   437
One hundred eleven common usage problems, presented alphabetically, with exercises and examples following most entries.

Diagnostic Exercises: Glossary of Usage   466

Punctuation   469
Major marks of punctuation, presented alphabetically, with accompanying short exercises.

Diagnostic Exercises: Punctuation   482

Spelling   483
Common causes of difficulty in spelling, with suggestions for improving spelling, along with a list of one hundred twenty commonly misspelled words.

Manuscript Formatting/Proofreading and Notetaking Marks   487

Manuscript Formatting   487
Proofreading and Notetaking Marks   491

Documentation Formats 493

Footnote Format 494
New MLA Style ("In-Text") Documentation Format 498
Bibliography ("Works Cited") Format 500
A Brief Note on APA Style 504

Reference Works in Major Subject Areas 507

General Reference Works 507
Reference Works in Philosophy, Psychology, and Religion 511
Reference Works in History 513
Reference Works in Geography, Anthropology, the Social Sciences, and Economics 514
Reference Works in Political Science 516
Reference Works in Education 517
Reference Works in Music and the Visual Arts 518
Reference Works in Language, Literature, Theater, Film 520
Reference Works in the Sciences and Technology 521

Acknowledgments 524
Index 526

Index of Readings

ARRANGED BY SUBJECT AREA

Note: Many of the following selections are under five hundred words. Those marked with a dagger (†) are complete works or self-contained excerpts from longer works. Selections marked with an asterisk (*) are student essays.

Architecture
Tom Wolfe, *From Bauhaus to Our House*   80

Agriculture
*†Evan Elliot, "The Salinity Problem in Crop Irrigation"   111

Art
Erwin O. Christensen, *A Pictorial History of Western Art*   88
†Ellwood Perry, ["Henry Ossawa Tanner"]   247
Susan Sontag, *On Photography*   278

Astronomy
E. L. Schatzman, *The Structure of the Universe*   96

Athletics
†Norman Cousins, "Who Killed Benny Paret?"   170
†Andy Rooney, "The Problem With Soccer . . ."   159
*Mike White, ["Running in the Foothills"]   65

Biological Sciences and Chemistry
†Isaac Asimov, *Words of Science*   327
Anthony Huxley, *Plant and Planet*   89
Robert Jastrow, *Until the Sun Dies*   6
I. S. Shlovskii and Carl Sagan, *Intelligent Life in the Universe*   7

Computer Science
*†Jeff Brown, "Structured Programming: Its Development and Importance"   224
†"How to 'Write' Programs" (from *Time* magazine)   220
Tracy Kidder, *The Soul of a New Machine*   332

xvii

Communication
Jeremy Campbell, *Grammatical Man* 95
*†Anita Lee, "How Do I Rate Thee? Let Me Count the Ways" 141
†Myra Mannes, "Television: The Splitting Image" 149
†George Plimpton, "How to Make a Speech" 109

Driver Education
†Kim Garretson, "How to Figure Fuelishness" 105
*†Marie Noble, ["How to Drive a Manual Transmission"] 113

Ecology/Environment
†"Ban This Poison Before It Poisons Us" (from *USA Today*) 139
†U.S. Fish and Wildlife Service, *Saving the Whooping Crane* 199

Economics/Labor
†Russell Baker, *So This Is Depravity* 96
†Kim Garretson, "How to Figure Fuelishness" 105
*†Tom Wade, ["Working in a Service Station"] 113

Ethnic Studies
Maya Angelou, *I Know Why the Caged Bird Sings* 281
James Baldwin, "Equal in Paris" 59
Dee Brown, *Bury My Heart at Wounded Knee* 200

Geology/Geography/Natural History
David Alt and Donald Hyndman, *Roadside Geology of Northern California* 92
†Beth Doxee, "Learning Years" 47
Colin Fletcher, *The Man Who Walked Through Time* 301
†Denise Graveline, "Advice for Would-be Wayfarers" 49
"Haleakala National Park, Hawaii" (from *America* magazine) 72
†John McPhee, *Basin and Range* 282
†John Muir, *The Mountains of California* 21
Anaïs Nin, *Diary* 63
Henry David Thoreau, *Walden* 62

Health/Nutrition
†Phyllis Lehmann, "More Than You Ever Thought You Would Know About Food Additives" 302

History
Dee Brown, *Bury My Heart at Wounded Knee* 200
Jefferson Davis, ["Speech of Resignation from the U.S. Senate"] 329
A. R. Meyers, *London in the Age of Chaucer* 296

Home Economics/Parenting
†Dixie Brown, "Baby's Baldness at 18 Months Is a Growing Concern"   303

Human Behavior/Psychology
Julia Alvarez, "El Doctor"   61
†Francis Bacon, "Of Suspicion"   216
†Elise Chisholm, "Breast-Feeding in Public Gets a Nod"   175
†Anne Frank, *Diary of a Young Girl*   59
Erich Fromm, *The Art of Loving*   91
†Ellen Goodman, "Social Nibbling"   81
*†Thomas Hogendijk, "Confessions of a Doorman"   77, 348
Karen Horney, M.D., *The Neurotic Personality of Our Time*   103
*JoAnn Lambkin, ["Videogame Player"]   68
†Laurie Lee, "The Essence of Charm"   101
B. F. Skinner, *Beyond Freedom and Dignity*   301
†David Stansbury, "Cooling Burnout"   115
Thomas S. Szasz, *The Second Sin*   130

Law Enforcement/Crime
†L. Moore, ["Handguns"] (letter to the editor)   158
†Gore Vidal, "Drugs"   167

Language and Literature
†Matthew Arnold, "Dover Beach"   184
†Isaac Asimov, *Words of Science*   307
†James Dickey, "Arnold: 'Dover Beach'"   185
†Emily Dickinson, ["Two Poems"]   338
Joan Didion, "Why I Write"   63
Ralph W. Emerson, "Gifts"   307
†Abby Goldman, "Jean M. Auel" (interview)   206
†Paul Gray, "The Nightmare and the Dream" (review of *Loon Lake*)   178
Patricia Hampl, *A Romantic Education*   75
Ernest Hemingway, "Big Two-Hearted River"   274
Gerard Manley Hopkins, *Notebooks*   63
Henry James, "London"   67
†Denise Levertov, "The Obligation of the Poet"   172
*†Christine Long, "Fear and Trembling and Sick of English"   23
†Nickie McWhirter, "Just a Word Makes All the Difference"   339
Herman Melville, *Moby Dick*   337
George Orwell, "Why I Write"   25
Eugene O'Neill, *The Moon of the Caribbees*   329

†William Safire, "Easier to Start a War Than Consult a Dictionary" 315
Henry David Thoreau, *Walden* 62
†Mark Twain, *Roughing It* 276, 330
John Updike, "Flight" 79
John Hall Wheelock, *What Is Poetry?* 329
Raymond Williams, *Keywords* 104
Virginia Woolf, "The Death of the Moth" 279

Medicine
Richard Selzer, *Mortal Lessons: Notes on the Art of Surgery* 319
†Gore Vidal, "Drugs" 167

Military
†James Fallows, "Why This Country Needs It" (essay on the draft) 162

Music
†Marshall Stearns, *Jazz and West African Music* 93

Physics
Albert Einstein, *Relativity: The Special and the General Theory* 92

Religion/Mythology/Supernatural
Ingri and Edgar D'Aulaire, *Book of Greek Myths* 6
Robert Graves, *The Greek Myths* 6
Washington Irving, *The Sketch Book* 95
W. B. Yeats, "Magic" 198

Social Sciences
*†Don Ballew, "The Danger Zones" (journal) 360
*†Ron K. Rock, Jr., "Gradually Adjusting to Retirement: Facing the Change" 36

Theater/Film
†Richard Corliss, "The Fantasy Film as Final Exam" 180
*†Tom Gough, "Martin Landau's *Dracula* Could Use a Mild Transfusion" 181

Preface to the Student

You have probably been told many times that writing is a basic skill, one that is necessary for success in the real world as well as in college, regardless of the field of study you wish to pursue. You may have accepted this truism, though perhaps skeptically, especially if you are planning a career in, say, medicine or electrical engineering. An important aim of this book, in addition to helping you become a better writer, is to give you a sense of how writing contributes to any kind of learning—as well as to the thinking process itself.

Writing helps us to understand ourselves, our ideas, and our feelings, fully and accurately. Certainly, we often verbalize our thoughts, which can be helpful and often necessary; but writing gives us the added advantage of allowing us to see those thoughts materialized on paper. This process in turn allows us to double-check our statements, to alter them slightly or to remove anything we didn't really want to say, and to make them even more persuasive by adding better examples to support our assertions. Writing makes our thoughts more communicable to other people as well as to ourselves. Because we live in a multicultural society with many value systems, knowing how to communicate our thoughts accurately is more than a necessity—it is a survival tactic.

A textbook on writing can be no more than a guide. It cannot be a "training manual" that will teach you all you need to know about how to write. It functions much like a librarian who can do no more than show you the library and explain the basic procedures for using its resources; which resources you care to use, and why, must be your judgment alone. This particular textbook, certainly, will reveal much about the art and craft of composition and about the principles that underlie all good writing; but it refuses to force your hand and say, "You must do it like this."

The concept "good writing" is meaningless until it is considered within a particular situation. Mark Twain produced "good writing"; so did J. D. Salinger, Ernest Hemingway, Franz Kafka, and Virginia Woolf. But what do these writers share in common? They all knew enough about language to be able to reproduce on paper what was churning about inside their hearts and minds. They knew how to involve and delight their readers—and yet, could one of them have imposed his or her style of writing upon the others? Hardly.

Learning to write well takes time. Even if you have a burning desire to be a writer, you must be as patient as you are persistent. When you are learning to write you are actually learning to think and observe more acutely. You are also learning to interact with the human community and to draw from the resources of others as a way of shaping your own original ideas. You cannot acquire a skill of this depth and richness in a week or two, nor even by the end of your freshman year. But you, as well as this textbook, will succeed if the wheels are set in motion; for learning to write is ultimately a self-guided task. Once you understand the scope of that task and have learned to distinguish between good writing and bad—in your own work as well as in others'—you will have gained the most prized benefit that this book can hope to offer.

Preface to the Teacher

In writing this textbook I have aimed high. I have tried to create a book that students could read with as much pleasure as edification. I have tried to give students, who are often filled with great expectations, a deep-rooted awareness of writing's central importance to education. I want to place in their hands a textbook that clearly shows them how to transform ideas and sensory impressions into words on paper, and how skill in writing enhances comprehension of what is being written about.

The Writer's Art provides several valuable and innovative elements not likely to be found together in a single rhetoric text:

- *A thorough introduction to the dynamics of composing, with options* (there is no such thing as "the" composing process). Emphasis is on the actual habits of working writers. For example, the chapter on sentences includes sections on creating syntactic variety and moving toward syntactic virtuosity; the chapter on paragraphs looks at paragraph structure in relation to the whole discourse, and it includes a section on alternatives to the "well-made" paragraph.

- *Numerous models by both student and professional writers*, covering topics across the curriculum—topics that young men and women in their first year of college will enjoy reading and will learn from.

- *Imaginative "computer writing" exercises for most chapters, plus a chapter on the basics of composing on a personal computer.*

- *A complete guide to research, both in and out of the library*, including techniques of conducting an interview, searching a computer database, and designing a questionnaire. This chapter aims to generate *enthusiasm* for research as well as to introduce the fundamentals of information gathering/assimilating.

- *Three model research papers from three principal disciplines*—physical science, social science, and fine arts. Each research paper is annotated and discussed.

- *Both new and old MLA documentation formats.*

- *Extensive guide to major reference works across the disciplines.*

- *Special topics:* mass-media persuasion • sentence-combining • writing book/performance/film reviews • explications of literary texts • maintaining a journal • preparing for conference tutorials • participating in classroom workshops • writing essay exams.

- *Thorough handbook that includes sections on:* rhetorical and grammatical principles • usage • punctuation and mechanics • spelling • manuscript formatting. All sections include exercises, along with a diagnostic test at the end.

Throughout the book, writing projects are presented separately from the rhetorical principles usually associated with those projects. These "projects" chapters are, in effect, extended writing assignments. Not enough attention has been paid in composition texts to the importance of presenting writing assignments to students; these chapters will fulfill this long-overlooked need.

Rhetoricians sometimes bemoan the "writing in a vacuum" syndrome that can plague the composition course. How can a teacher set up "real" rhetorical situations, working from genuine exigencies? The problem is not as serious as it may seem at first. Certainly one ingredient for making a writing assignment challenging and beneficial is imagination. The directions to the assignment should not only be clear enough to appear "do-able," but they should also engage students enough to encourage them to *participate*—by willing suspension of disbelief or otherwise—in the exigency introduced. In other words, the assignment should *motivate* the student to write. The assignments throughout this text have been carefully designed to achieve these important objectives.

Finally, *The Writer's Art* is an intediscplinary textbook. Because writing is, by its very nature, an interdisciplinary activity—as vital to electrical engineers, painters, and economists as it is to literary scholars and poets—a textbook on writing ought to draw from as many disciplines as possible. I disagree with the notion that students from a given major field of study should concern themselves only with writing that is relevant to that discipline. Students must gain insight into the way that writing is important to all disciplines. Freshman composition is the ideal place for them to discover this. Indeed, *The Writer's Art* was conceived as a vehicle for demonstrating the extent to which this is true.

Preface to the Teacher

Acknowledgments

It is my pleasure to acknowledge those persons who have helped to bring this enormous project to fruition. I am indebted to professors Chris Anderson, University of North Carolina, Greensboro; Patricia Grignon, Saddleback College South; Susan Betts Landstrom, University of North Carolina, Chapel Hill; Stephen Lynn, University of South Carolina, Columbia; Thomas Moore, University of Maryland; Elizabeth Penfield, Univeristy of New Orleans; Susan Petit, College of San Mateo; David Rankin, California State University, Dominguez Hills; Ken Risdon, University of Minnesota; Laurel Sutton; and Nancy Walker, Southwest Missouri State University, for reviewing the manuscript in its various stages of completion and for providing me with invaluable suggestions.

I am also grateful to my Santa Clara colleagues, Professor Mary Ann Aschauer, Professor James P. Degnan, Professor Diane E. Dreher, Professor Helen Moritz, and Professor Richard H. Osberg, for their valuable responses to various chapters.

To my chair, Reverend Charles T. Phipps, S.J., and to my dean, Professor Joseph Subbiondo, I express my gratitude for the reduced teaching load granted me during a critical stage of composition.

To Santa Clara's academic vice president, Reverend Paul Locatelli, S.J., my heartfelt thanks for a university computer grant to study the effects of writing with a microcomputer, and for the indefinite use of an IBM Personal Computer. It was this research, and the use of this equipment, that enabled me to prepare the material relating to composing on a computer, as well as the computer-writing activities presented throughout the book.

For their many hours of assistance with the preparation of the manuscript—with typescript before I received my computer, as well as with innumerable printouts of later drafts—I want to express my thanks to Patty Dionne, Lathell North, and Jo Anna Watt.

I would also like to pay homage to those students who have supplied me with their fine essays, every one of which is an indispensable asset to this book: Don Ballew, Jeff Brown, Evan Elliot, Tom Gough, Thomas Hogendijk, JoAnn Lambkin, Anita Lee, Christine Long, Marie Noble, Ron K. Rock, Jr., and Mike White. A note of thanks also goes to Professor Jane Honeycutt, University of Santa Clara, for calling my attention to her student, Jeff Brown, and his research paper on computer programming.

No author could have been more fortunate than I in working with an editorial staff like Wadsworth's. For his complete faith in me and my work at a time when there wasn't too much to go on, I extend my deepest thanks to Kevin Howat, executive editor. I also thank my production editor, Jane Townsend, and editors Cedric Crocker, John Strohmeier, and

Judith McKibben for their warm support and inexhaustible stream of sage advice. Designer MaryEllen Podgorski, marketing specialist Joy Westberg, marketing manager Terry Baxter, regional field manager Tina Allen, and permissions editors Peggy Meehan and Virginia Phipps have all been wonderfully supportive; I am indeed grateful for their wise counsel and their friendship.

A special note of thanks goes to Lisa Danchi, copy editor, for her keen perception in spotting stylistic flaws and problems with formatting, and for calling my attention to several concepts needing further elaboration or clarification.

And finally, unceasing thanks to my family—to my daughter Laura and my son Michael for their willingness to respond to chapter sections and writing exercises, and to my wife Beverly, to whom I dedicate this book, for her years of selfless devotion.

Santa Clara, California
October 1985

The Writing Experience

PART ONE

What Is Good Writing?

CHAPTER 1

We have come a very long way from grunting at each other across the campfire, ever alert for beasts that could rip us apart. Before civilization began, communication was mainly a survival mechanism: keep the fire going; don't make any noise; find more food; search for a lake on the other side of that hill.

Communication is still necessary for our survival, but the need has become more complex. There are billions of us now, not just thousands. We are a global society, not scattered, isolated tribes. And thanks to that mode of communication known as writing, our thoughts and visions, our urgent messages, can be reproduced, preserved, and put to any use.

Writing and Thinking

Another special quality of writing is its capacity to extend the range of human consciousness. When you sit down to write, you are engaging in several acts of consciousness, not just one. Imagine, for example, that you are writing an article on how to develop your own photographs. Many different types of thoughts will be spinning around in your head, including the following four examples:

Content thoughts — What can I say about the topic at hand? What *should* I say? What are the best examples to use? How specific should I be (e.g., discuss the chemical reactions of developer on film emulsion; the reaction of the fixer on the newly developed images)?

Organization thoughts
How should I begin? with an anecdote? with a "pep talk" on the joys of developing one's own film? Should I use a step-by-step format? What step should I present first? Should I divide each section with subheads? with a numbering system? What should I say in the conclusion?

Style thoughts
Should I use a technical vocabulary? with or without parenthetical definitions? Should I adopt a formal level of word usage? a witty, informal one?

Purpose thoughts
Who is my audience? Beginning photographers? adults? young people? What points do I want to emphasize accordingly? Do I want the article to be purely informational? Do I want to argue for a certain technique of film developing?

Communicating to an Audience

Let's consider further the purpose thoughts relating to audience, to the people who are going to read what you write. Audience awareness is one of the most crucial aspects of learning to write well, and one of the easiest to overlook. Any kind of writing, except perhaps private notebook jottings, is public communication. Whenever you put words on paper, you are almost always writing for a readership of some kind, large or small, general or specialized. The larger the audience, the more *public* the communication needs to be; that is, you need to present your thoughts in a manner that is acceptable and comprehensible to most readers, regardless of their backgrounds. Writing for a general audience means that you must adopt a standard of usage, of correctness, of organization. Such a standard might, for example, compel you to use and spell words according to established dictionary definitions and spelling conventions. This does not mean that writers addressing a general audience cannot bypass the rules; it simply means that writers are expected to follow the rules unless they have a good reason not to, a reason they would share with their readers. To illustrate the importance of adhering to a standard, consider the following example of a letter addressed to an old friend, and notice the abundance of phrases and references that outsiders would not understand:

Dear J:

    Bill's still riding high in Dallas. I keep hoping he'll forget about batting 1,000 and remember that there are fish to catch and lakes to sail on.

    How's the tribe these days? Does Angie expect further output from Old Trusty? I'm in a bind trying to get out the specs for our latest brainchild, but am looking forward to a week of "Reno sunshine," if you catch my meaning.

    Take care!

    Yours,

    S.

No one but the receiver of that letter would understand the cryptic references. Who is "J" and what is his or her relationship to the writer? What do the expressions "riding high" and "batting 1,000" mean in this context? Are they used in a literal or a figurative sense?* And if figurative, what is the author alluding to? Who or what is "Old Trusty"? And so on. Such coded language occurs frequently between close friends and relatives; it reveals the creative range and color and the capacity for playfulness possible in language.

Don't be mistaken: Language intended for a general audience can be colorful, but not at the expense of clarity. This is the special challenge of writing for a general audience: Color, mood, and inventiveness are important, but they must somehow enhance the information, not obscure it. Consider this passage by Loren Eiseley, a distinguished anthropologist, essayist, and historian of science:

> Some men are daylight readers, who peruse the ambiguous wording of clouds or the individual letter shapes of wandering birds. Some, like myself, are librarians of the night, whose ephemeral documents consist of root-inscribed bones or whatever rustles in the thickets upon solitary walks. (Loren Eiseley, *The Unexpected Universe*)

Eiseley might have said, "Some scientists engage in observing daytime phenomena, others in observing nocturnal phenomena." His intention, however, was not merely to relate bare facts to his audience, but to stimulate their imaginations as well.

Developing Your Audience Awareness

An important step in acquiring audience awareness is knowing what kind of readers you want to reach through a given piece of writing. Your decision will greatly influence the approach you take to your topic and

---

*See the Handbook, "Rhetorical and Grammatical Principles," Figures of Speech.

the style in which you present it. Do you want to address children or adults? If adults, do you want to reach specialists in your chosen subject, or laypersons? Would your topic be of interest mainly to men or to women? And so on.

Restricting our discussion here to child/adult and layperson/specialist audience types, let us take a look at the following examples.

First, compare the differences in style and content between two descriptions of the sea god Poseidon; one example is slanted for children, the other for adults:

A

Poseidon, lord of the sea, was a moody and violent god. His fierce blue eyes pierced the haze, and his sea-blue hair streamed out behind him. He was called the Earthshaker, for when he struck the ground with his trident, the earth trembled and split open. When he struck the sea, waves rose mountains high and the winds howled, wrecking ships and drowning those who lived on the shores. But when he was in a calm mood, he would stretch out his hand and still the sea and raise new lands out of the water. (Ingri and Edgar Parin D'Aulaire, *Book of Greek Myths*)

B

Poseidon, who is equal to his brother Zeus in dignity, though not in power, and of a surly, quarrelsome nature, at once set about building his underwater palace of Aegae in Euboea. In its spacious stables he keeps white chariot horses with brazen hooves and golden manes, and a golden chariot at the approach of which storms instantly cease and sea-monsters rise, frisking, around it. (Robert Graves, *The Greek Myths*, I)

Both examples aim to depict the character of Poseidon colorfully and imaginatively. Example A, aimed at a pre-teenage audience, is limited in scope and depth of analysis. Notice, too, the simpler sentence structure compared to that of Example B.

Now compare Examples C and D, which both describe the possible chemical origins of life on earth. It is easy to tell, is it not, which example is aimed at a lay audience and which is aimed at a more specialized audience:

C

A thunderstorm lashes the surface of the planet. The panorama is illuminated sporadically by flashes of lightning; in each electrical discharge, the gases of the atmosphere—methane, ammonia, water, and hydrogen—fuse together to form strange new combinations of atoms. . . . Those groups of atoms are the molecules known as amino acids and nucleotides.

The appearance of amino acids and nucleotides marks the first step along the path to life. These molecules are the building blocks of living matter. . . .

Gradually the amino acids and nucleotides drain out of the atmosphere into the ocean, creating a rich soup of organic matter, like a chicken broth, but more concentrated. (Robert Jastrow, *Until the Sun Dies*)

D

During storms, lightning bolts traverse the atmosphere; during the day, some ultraviolet light from the sun penetrates through the atmosphere and is absorbed in the ocean. The atmosphere is composed of methane, ammonia, water, and very small amounts of hydrogen. Soon the ammonia will become dissolved in the oceans, where it forms ammonium hydroxide (NH_4OH), which will tend to make the oceans alkaline. . . . We can imagine the origin of primitive nucleic acids by the spontaneous polymerization of ultraviolet-synthesized nucleotide triphosphates in a primeval body of water which contained some mineral catalyst such as magnesium. (I. S. Shlovskii and Carl Sagan, *Intelligent Life in the Universe*)

Clearly, Example C is directed to a lay audience, one unfamiliar with the technical vocabulary and principles of organic chemistry; Example D is directed to a relatively specialized audience—not to professional biochemists, but to individuals familiar with organic chemistry.

It is important to note that Example D is not difficult in any absolute sense. The authors aim to inform—as precisely as possible—an audience interested in the origins of life; this audience has already acquired the sense of fascination that the author of Example C is trying to stimulate by using colorful and familiar language ("lashes the surface"; "creating a rich soup of organic matter").

The Four Pillars of Good Writing

Writing is more than public communication; it is a way of thinking. Ordinary thinking is often fragmentary and even more cryptic than the letter to "J" discussed earlier. But writing—*good* writing—is a product of careful thinking and incorporates the following four characteristics: (1) the appeal to a target audience, (2) a coherent structure, (3) a smooth, detailed development, and (4) an appropriate style. Let us consider each of these four pillars of good writing in turn:

1. *The appeal to a target audience.* The writer has identified a problem, or has seen something in a new light, and feels that it is worth sharing

with others. He or she feels the idea is worth publishing, in the word's root sense of "making public." If one discovers, let us say, a technique to extend the life of flowers prepared for indoor display, one might want to publish an article on the subject, as many people would probably want to read about it.

2. *A coherent structure.* For any writing to work, it has to have some kind of organizational scheme. You are probably familiar with one such scheme, the so-called five-paragraph essay: one paragraph to introduce the topic, three to discuss three different aspects of it, and one to summarize and conclude. Here is what an outline of such an essay might look like:

Title:	How to Improve Your Reading Habits
Introduction (Paragraph 1):	Many bright people become frustrated with learning because they have poor reading habits. (Typical example) But it is surprisingly easy to get rid of these poor habits by practicing three techniques. (1......; 2.......; 3.......)
Body (Paragraphs 2, 3, 4):	Description of Technique 1 Description of Technique 2 Description of Technique 3
Conclusion (Paragraph 5):	Importance of practicing regularly so that the good habits can become ingrained. It is easy once you set your mind to it.

Despite its elementary, rather artificial formula (experienced writers simply do not mold their prose according to a set quantity of paragraphs), this scheme can give one a quick sense of how an essay *might* be structured in terms of beginning, middle, and end. The scheme can also serve as an introduction to subtler organizational strategies.

3. *A smooth, detailed development.* Not only does a piece of writing have a framework, a skeleton, but it has meat on the bones as well. To build onto the framework, you need to expand upon an idea by raising the general points and discussing them in detail. You will need to analyze complex matters, provide vivid examples, and perhaps refute opposing ideas and name names. For instance, if you are going to write about improving reading efficiency, you want to *describe* in detail how learners actually apply the techniques you recommend rather than be content merely to recommend that they "read whole phrases rather than individual words at a glance." You would proceed to illustrate this technique, say, by circling phrases in a given passage, starting with three- or four-word phrases at first, then progressing to five- or six-word phrases later on.

4. *An appropriate, well-articulated style.* The language you use to get your important, well-developed idea across should be as accurate and appropriate as possible. This means being able to choose the right words, to find the most suitable level of usage,* and to use no more words than are necessary to convey the intended idea. It also means being able to construct sentences that allow your idea to be transmitted in a crisp, readable manner with minimal interference, such as uneven, ambiguous, or unnecessarily complicated wording. Style, or the art and craft of well-articulated thought, is vital to effective writing, as are the other three pillars.

Distinguishing Between Good and Weak Writing

Along with knowing the abstract principles of audience appeal, structure, development, and style that uphold good writing, it is a good idea to learn to identify the elements that distinguish good writing from not-so-good writing. They include *expressiveness* (color, drama, sharpness of detail and sensory impressions), *viewpoint* (the writer's attitude toward or opinion of the subject), and *style* (the combination of word choice and sentence and paragraph structure that contributes to the writer's individual voice). Let us take a look at the way these elements interact.

Imagine that two writers, A and B, have been asked to capture the excitement of a recent basketball game in just one paragraph. Their respective paragraphs are printed below. Which writer, in your opinion, has done the better job?

WRITER A

The basketball game that the Broncos played in last Friday was truly an exciting one, in my opinion. The crowd was huge and lively. Some of the best action I had ever seen took place in this game. Norman Bell, the team's most talented player, scored twice from across the basketball court. I thought that most of the team members handled the ball really well. They played like pros every minute of the game.

WRITER B

A hush comes over the crowd as Normal Bell rushes down the court, freezes, does a quick fake, then throws a behind-the-back pass to Arturo Sanchez. Sanchez nods, rocks back and forth on his toes, then whips the

---

*See the Handbook, "Rhetorical and Grammatical Principles," Usage, Levels of.

ball to Earl Robinson who is wide open in the corner. Robinson pumps from sixteen feet . . . woosh! clean through the hoop. The crowd goes wild. "Great play!" a fan screams.

Chances are that you did not hesitate to name Writer B as the better writer. But can you explain *why* you chose B over A? Take a moment to scribble down some notes before reading on.

- *Expression*: Writer A tells us that the game was exciting but does not *show* us the excitement. Remember that the particular details (of physical surroundings as well as of the action) of an event are what bring that event to life in your reader's mind. Summary writing has its uses, as we shall see, but in the context of expressing action, it does little more than bore your readers.

- *Viewpoint*: Writer A refers to herself unnecessarily with the expressions "in my opinion" and "I thought that." Such explicit references to oneself should be used sparingly. This does not mean "keep yourself out of your writing." Writer B is present in her narrative, although implicitly, through her expressiveness. The sentence, "I thought that most of the team members. . . ." does not differ one whit in meaning and clarity from "most of the team members. . . ." The second version reveals just as clearly the presence of authorial opinion. The big difference is that the first sentence is made wordy and amateurish by the explicit inclusion of "I think that. . . ."

- *Style*: Each writer's individual way with words and sentences is another important point to consider. Good writers strive to find the most accurate or vivid words to communicate their intentions; they also strive to communicate them in the most readable manner, and that is why good sentence construction is so important. Let's look at the word choice and sentence construction of Writers A and B.

- *Word Choice*: Notice how quickly Writer B caught your interest and established suspense with her use of the word "hush."

   A hush comes over the crowd . . .

   No such mood is generated by Writer A's opening. Then notice also B's strong action-words: "Norman *rushes* down the court . . . *does a quick fake*. . . . Sanchez *nods* . . . *rocks* . . . on his toes." These words do not generalize the action the way a statement such as "Sanchez moved expertly" would. Instead the words come as close as possible to what the players were actually doing.

- *Sentence Construction*: Read Writer A's version over again, this time paying close attention to the construction of the sentences. Now compare this to the construction of B's sentences. Do you detect a difference in quality? A's sentences are somewhat monotonous—that is, they are structured too much alike. As a result, they lack energy and therefore fail to stimulate energy in you, the reader. B's sentences, by contrast, are lively and rhythmic. More information is conveyed in less space, and there is also greater reader involvement. Thus, instead of dreary, ho-hum sentences like:

Norman Bell, the team's most talented player, scored twice from across the basketball court.

we have sentences like:

Sanchez nods, rocks back and forth on his toes, then whips the ball to Earl Robinson who is wide open in the corner.

It is clear how much more effective the use of specific details and a little sentence "choreography" can be.

Now let us turn to another pair of writers. These student essayists—we'll call them C and D—were asked to express their opinions on whether a tract of neglected nineteenth-century Victorian houses in the community should be torn down to construct a badly needed shopping center. While both writers take the same viewpoint, one is more convincing than the other. Which one is it, and why?

WRITER C

Six Victorian houses, complete with gables and towers, weather vanes and tiffany windows, are about to be torn down. By this time next year a grocery, several boutiques, a liquor store, and—oh yes—a fast-food restaurant and several acres of parking lot will fill this space instead.

    Not a bad trade-off, some of you might think. Useless, abandoned relics for a badly needed, economy-boosting (four hundred jobs are expected to open) shopping center.

    The only problem is, these old houses are a legacy. They are constant reminders of an ever-changing society. Once they are restored, we could walk alongside them, or inside them, marvel at the oak woodwork, the balustrades, the ornate masonry, and relive a bygone age. Photographs are not enough to do the trick.

    When it comes to discarding our past, we are trigger-happy. Let bygones be bygones, we say. So down with Victorian houses! Long live McDonald's and Liquor Barn!

WRITER D

When I was a kid, I loved visiting my grandparents. They lived in an enormous Victorian house with a musty attic. There was also a basement. I loved that house. I get very angry when I hear that the city wants to tear down those beautiful old houses in order to build a shopping center. This city is full of shopping centers. Do we really want another one? Victorian houses have a character all their own, and should be preserved. I'm just one person, though. If enough people feel the same way I do, we ought to sign a petition.

Both writers make their opinions clear. Writer C, however, makes his more convincingly because he evokes specific images. Writer D relies too heavily on generalities ("I loved that house. . . . Victorian houses have a character all their own. . . ."). While Writer C also uses generalities ("these old houses are a legacy"), he manages to summon particulars to convince the readers of that generality: "Once they are restored, we could . . . marvel at the oak woodwork, the balustrades, the ornate masonry, and relive a bygone age."

Notice also that readers have a stronger sense of Writer C's personality. Whereas Writer D says she's angry, Writer C succeeds in showing his anger, especially through the use of irony* in the closing paragraph.

Summary

Writing is public discourse, and for that reason it should be worthwhile, well organized, sufficiently developed to accomplish its intended purpose, and clearly and effectively written. The act of writing is also an act of sharing new ideas—or old ideas with a new perspective—with the human community. To write means to put our favorite or most important thoughts forward, to unveil a line of thinking too elaborate to communicate through conversation. Putting our thoughts on paper not only "fixes" them, like verbal photographs, for anyone at any time to read; but it also allows for repeated and in-depth perusal, which is so often necessary for thoughts too rich and complex to be absorbed in one reading. Finally, any act of writing is influenced by three variables: the intended readership, the writer's motives, and the nature of the subject matter.

FOR DISCUSSION

1. Distinguish between the strong and the weak student writing examples that follow. Be prepared to explain your decisions. Do any of the examples reveal a mixture of both strong and weak characteristics? If so, explain.

---

*See the Handbook, "Rhetorical and Grammatical Principles," Irony.

a. If I hoped to fit into the Vista Beach scene I couldn't give the tourists a break, even if I was a tourist myself. It didn't matter that they brought in a lot of revenue. They asked silly questions, they caused traffic jams, they left trash on the beach. And so I acted haughty, giving as little information as possible. I went out of my way to act like a real resident whenever I shopped.

b. Bob was the handsomest boy I knew, and the most courteous. I loved the way he smiled at me when he saw me. It would send chills up and down my spine. He really had a great personality.

c. The music started and the mannequins flourished with life. The dancers were not the only spectacle. The people! There were old people, young people. "That's my daughter, the blonde one!" a proud father cried out. The middle-aged man slapped his buddy on the back as he pointed at a young woman on stage, his voice a husky bellow; he then pulled out a handkerchief and quieted himself in modesty. A pudgy, bald man busily cleaned his plate of cabbage roll in order to devote his full attention to the dancing.

d. In today's society there is a tendency in people to mistrust anybody who looks out of the ordinary. For example, if somebody has their hair dyed a strange color, the tendency is to think that this person is some kind of weirdo. A lot of people jump to too many conclusions just by judging by external appearances.

e. I believe my first date was with a guy I'll call Sweetkins. Short, round, and murky-eyed Sweetkins stood, but I adored him. His head always appeared lopsided because the strands of that rusty-colored hair always flipped over to one side. The remaining short pieces fell straight down resting over his left ear. And guess who wore a size thirteen shoe, a grinning smile, plus a blue baseball cap? Good God, it was Sweetkins. Together we sure did make a pair.

f. Cancer and leukemia patients receive many standard whole-blood transfusions during the course of their illnesses. These are supplied by regular volunteer donors, who donate whole blood at most four times a year. These donations are typed only by the A,B,O system and given to any patient with A, B, or O type blood. These donations are very helpful and life-sustaining, but sometimes after receiving many transfusions, the patient's body starts to react adversely to blood that is not his exact type.

2. Discuss the differences between writing for children and writing for adults, and between writing for laypersons and writing for specialists. Is one audience type more difficult to write for than another? Explain.

3. What do we mean when we say that writing involves several acts of consciousness, not just one?

4. Describe any wording problems you observe in each of the following examples. Suggest a way of rewording the awkward passages.

   a. Cooking is an activity that can stimulate your imagination as well as be a test of your ability to follow directions with exactitude.

   b. It was with utmost expectancy that I entered the lecture hall, eager to listen and learn from the famous woman who was going to lecture.

   c. Wood-carving is a really enjoyable hobby. It gives you a chance to be creative and it allows you to make interesting things with your bare hands.

   d. Many animals are without homes. People don't seem to realize that dogs and cats can suffer too. They need both love and shelter. Something needs to be done about animal abuse. It is especially serious in this city.

5. Dig up some old letters you've received from friends and relatives. Would strangers be able to understand them fully? What words or phrases can you single out as evidence that the author was limiting his or her readership to you alone? Report your findings to the class, or summarize them in a few paragraphs.

FOR WRITING

1. Study the following excerpt from an essay on cigarette smoking. What could the author do to strengthen the passage? Rewrite it accordingly.

   Smoking is a habit that is bad for your health. It is also annoying to nonsmokers. The laws that are supposed to protect nonsmokers from smokers are not severe enough. Nonsmoking tables are often right next to smoking tables. Lots of times I am in a nonsmoking section and getting smoke in my face.
   Smoking is a habit that can cause all sorts of health problems, not just cancer, although cancer certainly is the most serious problem. Laws should be passed to protect people from inconsiderate smokers. Punishment should be severe for anyone violating these laws.

2. Choose one of the following topics and write three opening paragraphs about it: one slanted for children, another for an adult lay audience with no knowledge of the topic, and the third for an adult lay audience with some knowledge of the topic.

   a. the first automobile

b. the latest dancing craze

c. why the dinosaurs became extinct

d. a profile of Sitting Bull

e. the myth of Echo and Narcissus

f. techniques of skateboarding

g. learning to write on a computer

Which paragraph did you enjoy working on most? Which was easiest to write? the most difficult? Hold on to these paragraphs; you may wish to develop them into full-length essays later on.

COMPUTER WRITING *

1. You may already be aware that revising one's writing on the screen is a lot less time-consuming, a lot less arduous, than revising the old-fashioned way, which includes a complete retyping. Practice getting used to on-screen revising by displaying a portion of the rough draft in the top half of the screen, reworking it in the bottom half, then comparing the two versions to see if you've improved it to your satisfaction. If your word processing program doesn't have split-screen capability, simply revise directly underneath the passage in question; the remaining text will simply move downward proportionately. Then delete the faulty passage or recopy it into another file.

   Until you grow accustomed to revising on a computer, it's better to do one thing at a time. First, concentrate on strengthening your sentences. Look for wordiness, choppiness, misuse of passive voice, weak verbs, and the like. If, for example, you see "A bottle of beer that still had some beer in it was thrown onto the field, aimed directly for the umpire, hitting him right on the head," you would replace it with "Someone in the bleachers hurtled an almost-empty beer bottle, striking the umpire on the head," or something to that effect. Revising on the computer means that you can experiment with different wordings as often as you like, knowing that you'll never have to waste hours retyping everything later.

2. Working with another student in a personal computer laboratory, compose a paragraph depicting an action scene. Afterwards, copy your paragraph onto your partner's work disk, have your partner do the same, and then revise each other's paragraphs.

---

*See Chapter 19, "Composing on a Computer."

Reasons and Incentives for Writing

CHAPTER 2

There are many writers in the world who will tell you that writing is darned hard work, tougher than anything else they can think of, and yet who will also tell you that they would sooner stop eating than stop writing.

Paradoxical? Maybe not. Maybe these people have discovered something about writing that beginning writers need to discover. What, you might ask, triggers the impulse, the motivation to write? Is it a set of mental tricks? Is it divine inspiration? Or is it perhaps a commitment, a promise to meet a deadline no matter what? In this chapter, you will discover that the answer to this question is not as perplexing as you might think.

We'll look into the matter by first asking a very fundamental question:

Why Write?

This question is not as easy to answer as the question, "Why speak?" although the answers are not dissimilar. Both involve communicating, or sharing, knowledge.* Much of the speaking we do, however, is spon-

---
*The word *communication* comes from the Latin *communis*, in the sense of "communal" or "shared." For more about etymology, see Chapter 14, "Exploring Words and Meanings."

taneous, noncomplex, linked to the particular situation at hand. And, speech is ephemeral: It is gone as soon as it is uttered. In some cases, that is just as well, for everyday chitchat often contains very little worth preserving; such talk is never *composed*, nor is it organized, developed, or carefully articulated. Speeches, sermons, lectures, debates, and other formal oral presentations do, however, follow the standards of good writing; in fact, these discourses are often written out before they are delivered.

When we write, our aims are usually more ambitious and complex than when we engage in casual conversation. In addition, writers and public speakers generally communicate matters of more lasting value than do casual speakers—matters that demand close analysis and that sometimes even demand an alteration of existing knowledge to allow for a new discovery or insight. Through the act of writing about a subject, we come to understand that subject better. Writing is a *synthesizing* force; that is, through writing, one discovers relationships between ideas and observations that might otherwise remain unconnected. The more such connections we find, the more understanding we acquire. Writing, therefore, is not only an important learning goal, it is itself a means of learning.

Knowing how to write is important from a purely practical standpoint as well. Here are three cases in point:

Writing can improve your academic performance. Because writing is a way of learning, you can actually achieve deeper insight into any subject, from calculus to criminology, by writing out your thoughts. Most unexpressed thoughts are insufficiently developed, but writing them out allows you to see where further development is needed and to examine details you would not otherwise have thought twice about. This process is ideal preparation for exams, especially essay exams.*

Writing allows you to create and maintain a marketable image of yourself in the eyes of potential and current employers. Good writing skills suggest a logical mind, an ability to interact with a wide public (crucial in business-related fields), and a knack for comprehending complex situations in depth. Moreover, in virtually every career requiring a college education, your ability to write well can increase your opportunities for promotions.

Writing enhances personal and community relationships. Whether you need to persuade or to inform, writing can help you reach your goals more effectively. Some of these activities may include: corresponding with politicians, family, and friends; persuading your community (via letters to the editor) to resolve a controversial issue in a certain way; preparing memoranda or newsletters for church and social groups; writing publicity releases for benefit concerts or lectures.

---

*See Chapter 20, "Writing Essay Exams."

Writing as Role Playing

People are motivated to present themselves on paper for another reason—one that takes us into the depths of human nature. *We write to widen our range of experience*, which, in fact, is also the reason we read. In other words, we read and write not just to receive and convey ideas, but also to interact with circumstances we might not normally encounter if we did not actively seek them.

Because most of the writing you do in college is assigned, you have a rich opportunity to encounter a great many circumstances. Many professional writers, such as journalists and technical writers, write on assignment as well. Although these writing assignments may seem artificial at first, they offer writers the opportunity to try out a new "role" and to discover a new way of interacting within a situation. All of us, by virtue of being human, have the capacity to extend ourselves (our *selves*) this way. Think for a moment about the way you behave in various situations, and the way you use language depending upon whom you are with. You alter your mannerisms to some degree, and you adjust your vocabulary, usage, and tone of voice almost without thinking. You may even sometimes wonder, Just when am I *really* myself? The answer is, always!

In the context of writing, to role-play means to see yourself not just as a writer but as a participant in the *rhetorical situation** you have set up for yourself. The British educator and writing theorist James Britton discovered that the way writers envision their target audiences affects the way they shape their own roles as writers to meet the demands of each audience. "If [a writer] sees them as interested but informed laymen, he becomes an obliging expert. If they are seen as equals sharing a community of interest or concern, he speaks as a peer."

One can apply this theory to a specific writing task. If a female student is writing about the danger of nuclear radiation to pregnant women, she might want to assume the role of mother-to-be. By acquiring the role of the expectant mother facing radiation hazards, she will be more inclined to assume a different *perspective* on the subject.

Now imagine that a few days later this student finds herself examining radiation, not from the perspective of its danger to pregnant women, but of its containability. She might ask herself, Is there a way to block radiation to such an extent that it does not contaminate the environment at all? This rhetorical situation invites the student to role-play as a physicist, or as a nuclear engineer.

---

*Four elements comprise a rhetorical situation: the *subject* to be discussed, the *occasion* for the discussion, the *audience* to be addressed, and, of course, the *writer*, who is presenting it.

Role playing is challenging and fun; we naturally enjoy projecting ourselves beyond the limited view of what we ordinarily imagine ourselves to be. Moreover, role playing is important to our conceptual lives, for by housing a "wardrobe of selves" we are better able to acquire a mature perspective. Our insight into the world, into ourselves, and into other people increases when we apprehend from more than one point of view.

Good writing, therefore, means more than well-constructed sentences on paper. Good writing involves the whole person with the world; it reveals the whole person performing on paper.

Here are some creative role-playing tips to use whenever you are assigned any kind of a writing task:

1. See yourself directly involved in the subject about which you are writing, perhaps as a professional—an expert on the subject.

2. Imagine that you have a widespread readership, and that there are thousands of readers out there who are eager to read anything you have to say.

3. Assume that you are a *good* writer, and that you are able to stir feelings and stimulate new ideas through your writing.

Take a moment now to apply these role-playing tips to the following hypothetical situation: You have been invited to speak your mind on the art and business of fortune-telling. The issue is as follows: Should fortune-tellers be allowed to do business, even though many people assert that the services of fortune-tellers are fraudulent? Now begin some role playing:

First, assume that you are a Better Business Bureau investigator. Imagine that you have been asked to inspect the operations of various seers, palmists, clairvoyants, and tea-leaf readers in your area, and to compile a report of your findings. How would you handle the project? What tone of voice would you adopt? What facts would you emphasize?

Now change roles. This time you will be a fortune-teller, out to defend the honor of the profession. How would you go about doing that? As a fortune teller, what facts would you emphasize?

Role playing is a pleasurable and instructive way to get a handle on both sides of an issue, and that can be valuable when doing almost any kind of informative or persuasive writing.*

---

*See Chapter 6, "Principles of Development: Aiming to Inform," and Chapter 8, "Principles of Development: Aiming to Persuade."

Writing as "Re-creation" and Recreation

To "re-create" means to give fresh life to something. Whenever someone paints a picture or writes a poem or even expresses an opinion, that person is using his or her imagination to see the world a little differently than anyone else sees it. This is one of our most human impulses. We are naturally impelled to interpret an event or an experience—to say what an experience means to us personally.

Calling attention to an event or object means investing it with meaning, perhaps with a meaning it did not previously have. Think about walking leisurely along the beach and suddenly encountering thousands of dead or dying fish and seabirds, mired in the sludge of an offshore oil spill. How do you communicate the horror and disgust you feel? How do you express your thoughts so that others, too, will share in your outrage? Writing is the means by which *your* world view, your choice of what to focus on and give urgent emphasis to, becomes a shared experience. Moreover, the heightened awareness sparked by your observations is the very kind of mental stimulus you need to transfer what you feel into words. As psychologist Rollo May explains in *Creativity and Its Cultivation*, "The deeper aspects of awareness are activated to the extent that the person is committed to the encounter."

Writing can also give both emotional and aesthetic pleasure; this we might call the *recreational* as well as the "re-creational" aspect of writing. All of us experience moments of intense feeling, and we often grope in frustration for words to express those feelings. If we persevere, though, we might be surprised how close we can come to the perfect expression. We might even discover feelings we never knew we had.

Intellect and emotion, matter and spirit: such is the range of human communication; and if you are an enterprising writer, you will find new ways to combine thought and feeling.

The great naturalist and conservationist John Muir was very good at achieving that kind of synthesis. Throughout his wonderful book *The Mountains of California* (1894), he was able to be "scientific" and "poetic" in the same breath, revealing that the two spheres of perception may be more closely intertwined than people realize. In the following passage, Muir describes the effects of a windstorm in a Sierra forest:

> I heard trees falling for hours at the rate of one every two or three minutes; some uprooted, partly on account of the loose, water-soaked condition of the ground; others broken straight across, where some weakness caused by fire had determined the spot. The gestures of the various trees made a delightful study. Young Sugar Pines, light and feathery as squirrel tails, were

bowing almost to the ground; while the grand old patriarchs, whose massive boles had been tried in a hundred storms, waved solemnly above them, their long arching branches streaming fluently on the gale, and every needle thrilling and ringing and shedding off keen lances of light like a diamond. The Douglas Spruces, with long sprays drawn out in level tresses, and needles massed in a gray, shimmering glow, presented a most striking appearance as they stood in bold relief along the hilltops. The madronos in the dells, with their red bark and large glossy leaves every way, reflected the sunshine in throbbing spangles like those one so often sees on the rippled surface of a glacier lake. But the Silver Pines were now the most impressively beautiful of all. Colossal spires 200 feet in height waved like supple goldenrods chanting and bowing low as if in worship, while the whole mass of their long, tremulous foliage was kindled into one continuous blaze of sun-fire. The force of the gale was such that the most steadfast monarch of them all rocked down to its roots with a motion plainly perceptible when one leaned against it. Nature was holding high festival, and every fiber of the most rigid giants thrilled with glad excitement.

John Muir, *The Mountains of California*

Muir's aim here is to give his readers a basic understanding of the nature of these splendid Yosemite trees while at the same time transmitting something of their aesthetic qualities. These days, writers usually do one thing or the other, but not both. That makes good sense *most* of the time; because there is so much to learn scientifically about a subject, trying to be poetic at the same time could easily confuse the reader. Even so, writers like Muir are important reminders that the two realms of understanding are essentially inseparable, and that they ought not stray too far from one another.

A great deal of intellectual stimulation is in store for you as a college student, but along the way there are bound to be some frustrations. The necessary partitioning and subpartitioning of subject matter is likely to be one of them. As a writer, though, you are determined not to let these frustrations get the best of you; instead, you will transform them—"re-create" them—in such a way that they become significant to you, as well as to anyone who reads your writing. That was certainly John Muir's goal in his Yosemite writings (which helped to establish Yosemite as a national park, by the way).

Such, too, is the manner in which college senior and English major Christine Long transformed one of her anxieties into a compelling narrative.* Note that the writer chooses to let her viewpoint emerge dramatically by *showing*, rather than nondramatically by merely *telling*.

---

*See Chapter 4, "Principles of Development: Aiming to Express," for a discussion of narrative writing.

FEAR AND TREMBLING AND SICK OF ENGLISH

Typewriters blasted tiny machine-gun fire from the floor below. Kurt escaped up the narrow stairway. In his right hand he clutched his latest essay: an explication of Flaubert's *Madame Bovary*. He looked down at it, at the hemorrhage of angry red marks, and especially at the words "Please See Me!!" written in large, pompous script. Those words, adorned with exclamation points, stuck in him like daggers, made him suddenly want to be an engineer, made him feel the same way he felt when sitting in class, where the professor would stand looking down on them, hurtling questions out like lightning bolts. He asked questions so fast and frequently that students had no time to take cover, let alone answer them. And yet they were scholarly questions, and lofty; for he was Zeus, with silver hair and booming voice.

Kurt hoped, as he ascended the stairs, that he would not be too lost in the clouds of Mount Olympus. He felt like Sisyphus: getting nowhere; or, he was one of the lost souls waiting for Charon to ferry him across the Styx. *Who is the one approaching? Who, without death, dares walk into the kingdom of the dead? . . .*

He turned and ascended [more] stairs. *Because I do not hope to turn again, because I do not hope to turn.* He turned on the third floor, then sat down on the floor outside the professor's office to wait. He listened to the fragments of conversations, a poem with no images:

"Your transitions here . . ."
"What you want the reader to feel . . ."
". . . direct focus because only . . ."
". . . specific audience in order to . . ."
". . . is in apposition . . ."
". . . no, it's meant to modify . . ."

Oh the busy, sad music of humanity. He looked again at the paper in his hand and noticed the small callus on his middle finger. A little Mount Parnassus, a monument to all-nighters, rewrites, rewrites, rewrites . . .

The professor carried an impressive leather briefcase and always walked around campus like Zeus kicking over clouds. In class he would balance the textbook delicately on his fingertips, tilt his head and ask: "What think you of this passage?" Or sometimes, to impart wisdom on the students he would begin a soliloquy with "verily I say unto you . . ."

Oh my God I am most heartily sorry . . . Kurt looked down to the other end of the hall where a professor with patches on his elbows carried a steaming cup of coffee into his office. Students sat in chairs outside of doors, bookbags in their laps . . .

He did not want to go in there. He turned his head to look out the window; he listened to the wind against the panes, listened to it between the leaves. *A motion and a spirit, that impels all thinking things, all objects and all thought. And rolls through all things.*

"I don't think you understood the assignment," Zeus was thundering at him now. Kurt surveyed his office. He was awed by the stacks of books, and a little depressed. *Books! 'Tis dull and endless strife . . .* Two blond-haired kids sat smiling in a frame on the desk. They looked as if they knew Old English, as if they could have rattled off *The Canterbury Tales* at the snap of a finger. With a pen Kurt picked at a loose thread in the patches of his jeans and heard the somber pigeons cooing, and the wind flapping through the leaves.

"I said, I think you misunderstood the assignment."

If I were a dead leaf, which thou mightest bear; if I were a swift cloud to fly with thee . . .

"Your maladroit essay connotes an exorbitant amount of error and lack of perception, not to mention imagination. It's obvious you didn't spend much time on this."

"Yeah, no, well," Kurt said, looking into the professor's eyes, thinking of the night he and some friends talked the security guard into letting them stay late in one of the buildings . . .

"Your point here is well-taken, yet you could improve this simply by stating how the antithesis is contained within the synthesis in Flaubert's imagery."

"Oh, I see," Kurt responded, afraid to say more. He saw his words as only big black heavy letters with too many hyphens and ellipses. He had no style; and he felt the fragile structure of his ideas crumbling . . .

"I think it would help if you were more attentive to Flaubert's use of details, as well as to my instructions. I asked for an in-depth character sketch of Emma Bovary, but instead you have expounded on Flaubert's style."

Kurt squinted his eyes and looked out the window with a semiconvincing air of contemplation. He was thinking whether or not he should show this man his little Mount Parnassus.

And my ending is despair, unless I be relieved by prayer.

He was remembering especially one night, late, when the black blocks of letters seemed to lift off the page and he had slipped gently into them. It was like passing through a keyhole into a room he had never before been in. And he had known then how Emma Bovary felt, trapped on earth with a heart continually beating to be free, like a bird batting its wings against a cage. And he felt also, Flaubert's unrest, his unending struggle to transcend the little words and create a truth . . .

The professor looked at his watch. Kurt got up to leave.

"Thank you."

Zeus smiled slightly . . . "Well," he said, "keep struggling. You know, it amazes me that although I have taught you everything I know, you still know so little. Keep trying, though. And never hesitate to come in and talk."

Christine Long

Long, you will probably agree, has succeeded in communicating a private frustration—a sense of entrapment resulting from a need to receive personal attention from her teacher, but getting only the motions of personal attention. Rather than discuss this frustrating predicament by relying on mere generalities (e.g., "Professors should care more about their students' feelings"), Long chose instead to transform the experience into a story, using the character of Kurt to convey her viewpoint.

The resulting "re-creation" of experience offers readers not only insight into a very real problem faced by many students at one time or another, but it offers pleasurable reading at the same time.

Summary

Writing is a basic skill. It is integral to the learning process and indispensable for business and interpersonal communication beyond everyday informality. Writing can be seen as a kind of role playing: All of us play a variety of roles in life—we "wear different hats," as the saying goes. When we wish to communicate with an audience, we can best do so by thinking consciously about the appropriate roles we wish to assume. Role playing can improve our writing by allowing us to think deeply about issues from contrasting points of view. Finally, by writing about an experience we invest that experience with meaning. We give the experience a shape, a design, that makes for pleasurable, instructive, and memorable reading.

FOR DISCUSSION

1. In looking back on your own experiences as a writer, what roles did you play? How did you communicate those roles in your writing? Was it through word choice? tone of voice? reference to personal experiences? Finally, did you assume the role before you started writing, or did it come to you during the composing process?

2. George Orwell, in his essay, "Why I Write," suggests what he calls "four great motives for writing":

    (1) *Sheer egoism.* Desire to seem clever, to be talked about, to be remembered after death, to get back at grownups who snubbed you in childhood. It is humbug to pretend this is not a motive, and a strong one.

    (2) *Aesthetic enthusiasm.* Perception of beauty in the external world, or in words and their right arrangement. Desire to share a valuable experience.

    (3) *Historical impulse.* Desire to see things as they are, to find out and store facts for posterity.

    (4) *Political purpose.* Desire to push the world in a certain direction, to alter other people's ideas of the kind of society that they should strive after.

Discuss the validity of Orwell's list. Do you agree with his choices? Remember: He is asserting that those four motives exist in *all* writers, not just in himself. What other motives can be added, in your opinion?

3. How do you currently feel about writing? It is important to be candid with your instructor as well as with yourself. In class or at a private conference, try to pinpoint the causes of your likes, dislikes, or even indifference to writing. Here are a few possibilities: the opportunity or lack of opportunity to write in junior high or high school or at home; teachers who praised your writing and encouraged you to write for extra credit; teachers who were too rigid by overemphasizing grammar and syntax, forcing you to follow outlines and paragraph formulas to the letter, or penalizing you for superficial errors so you approached each writing task with dread; prejudices that suggest writing is only for loners, too intellectual, bad for your posture, irrelevant to the real world, escapist; a feeling of respect from friends who admired your facility with words, and the sense of personal satisfaction and accomplishment you felt after creating your own compositions.

4. Examine career opportunities in your major or probable major, and see if any of these careers involve writing. Even when no writing activities are mentioned, can you still see where writing could tie in to the career in question?

5. What is the central idea behind Christine Long's narrative, "Fear and Trembling and Sick of English"? Where does her viewpoint emerge most clearly? Is Kurt a fair representation of most students in a similar course? And does the professor seem typical of most professors, as you've thus far experienced them? What, if anything, might the author have exaggerated or misrepresented? Finally, do you agree or disagree that this dramatization is the most effective means of conveying the main idea?

FOR WRITING

1. Review Orwell's four motives for writing, and then write your own essay entitled, "Why I Write." Be sure you give your own personal reasons for writing, however irrational they may seem. You may then, like Orwell, proceed to compare your motives to what you consider to be the motives of writers in general. Keep in mind, too, that the use of humor with this topic is possible.

2. Recall a frustrating encounter you once had with an instructor. Dramatize that encounter, using Christine Long's narrative as a model.

3. For group writing: Write a letter to a famous (or notorious!) personality, praising or criticizing this person's behavior, appearance, or activities. Take either a straightforward or a humorous or satirical approach.

   Next, exchange letters with a classmate. Become the personality to whom your classmate's letter is addressed and write a return letter. Here are some famous personalities you might consider "trying on":

Barbra Streisand	Dolly Parton
Charles Bronson	The President of the United States
Howard Cosell	The Premier of the Soviet Union
Barbara Walters	Woody Allen
Bruce Springsteen	Mr. Rogers
Steve Martin	Bill Cosby
Mr. T	Sylvester Stallone

4. Write a paragraph on any topic in Column A using one of the roles suggested in Column B. Next, choose a second role and write another paragraph on the same topic. Finally, choose a different topic and write a third paragraph, using whatever role you wish.

Column A	Column B
problems with dieting	recognized authority on the topic
secrets of successful dating	parent
ways to throw a successful party	comedian
preparing for exams	high school senior
experiences with learning a new dance	athlete
ways to get rich quickly	

COMPUTER WRITING

1. Open five separate files on one disk, naming each file after a well-known personality you admire. Choose names from the list in Exercise Three of "For Writing," if you wish. Use code names that only you can decipher. Then write each name on a separate slip of paper, fold each slip so you cannot see the name, and choose a slip. As soon as you see the name, log on to that file and begin writing anything from the point of view of that celebrity. Your task is not just to be-

come these different personalities, but to be able to "sound" like them as well. Whenever you feel like it, exit the file, choose another name, and do the same thing. Finally, print out the files and see if any of your classmates or your instructor can guess which personality is which, just from the writing.

2. For students working in pairs: Student A opens a file called NEWSFILE, or some similar name, and records the headline and a one-sentence statement of content for several news items from a single issue of a newspaper or news magazine. Student A then gives Student B his or her disk. Student B loads NEWSFILE onto his or her own system and selects a news story to use as a springboard—a motive or impulse—for generating an essay on the larger issue of which the news story is an example. If, say, the news item reports the collapse of a hospital during a moderate earthquake, the larger issue, which could become the topic for an essay, might be, "Building Codes—How Earthquake-Safe?" The authors of such a story would likely want to use the news item of the damaged hospital as an attention-getting anecdotal opening for the essay.

A Practical Method of Writing

CHAPTER 3

The late novelist John Gardner was once asked to describe his method of writing. "Well," he said, "I begin at the top left side of the page, write across until I get to the right margin, then go to the next line and do the same thing." That is Gardner's tongue-in-cheek way of saying that the best way to write is simply to sit down and *write*, working to make one's words match one's thoughts.

In the best of all worlds, that would be fine advice; but for many, including those who truly do love to write, the business of putting words together to create a meaningful essay is difficult work. Because writing recruits several fundamental skills, such as observing, expressing, reasoning, and organizing, one needs to practice writing constantly. Cicero, one of the great rhetoricians and orators of the ancient world, said it best in *De Oratore*: "The chief thing is . . . to write as much as possible. The pen is the best and most eminent author and teacher of eloquence."

In this chapter, you will learn a method of composing that will remove much of the frustration that arises when one faces a blank sheet of paper with no clear sense of what to do first. *Method* refers not only to the writing itself but also to the overall behavior of the writer, and particularly to the cultivation of the writing habit.

Making Writing a Habit

You may find the idea of writing a lot very intimidating. But there is a simple secret to being productive: you write *regularly*. The amount you write at a single sitting is not the problem. The problem is facing the typewriter or word processor, not to mention facing those dreaded blank sheets of paper—or blank screen and naggingly blinking cursor—on a regular basis. And when you are learning the craft, "regular basis" should mean "daily basis." An ideal repository for your daily writing, by the way, is a private journal or notebook. There you can record your observations and thoughts, and experiment with new ideas and ways of expressing yourself, free of external restraints.*

How much writing do you suppose you can complete, say, in one month? If you were to write one 750-word (three typewritten, double-spaced pages) essay a week for four weeks, you would be writing 3,000 words (twelve finished, typewritten pages) in less than a month. That's not too bad.

Let's consider your possible output in rough-draft pages. Twelve pages of rough-draft writing every month may seem like a large amount, especially if you've never been too terribly fond of writing. However, if you have been diligently writing in your journal every day—let's say one page (a quantity that many students can produce in twenty minutes, working at a casual pace)—then you can produce thirty pages of manuscript that month, or well over one hundred pages by the end of the semester.

Prodding yourself to produce a predetermined quantity of writing on a regular basis is the single most important step you can take in learning to write. Determine your comfortable *output per sitting* (one-half page? one page? two pages? four pages?) and *stick to it*. You must be honest with yourself: An unreasonably high quota will only encourage you to drop the whole idea after the second day; an unreasonably low quota will not be enough of a challenge.

Why place all this emphasis on quotas and writing habits? Writing is, to a limited degree, a self-correcting skill. The more you write, the sharper your ability becomes to discern stylistic, organizational, and mechanical weaknesses. And there's another very pleasant bonus, too: The more you write, the more you want to write, or the more you feel inwardly motivated to write. That explains why many professional authors, who have long ago cultivated their writing habits, insist that their biggest problem is getting *away* from the writing desk. (May each of you be blessed with that problem!)

However, you may be wondering what you should write *about*.

---

*See Chapter 16, "Maintaining a Journal."

Should you write just for the sake of filling pages? Shouldn't you write with a purpose in mind? The answers are: no, and certainly! But keep in mind that *purpose* can be whatever you want it to be. Work on the kinds of writing you can have fun with: wild fantasies for a dream journal, opinions you can develop into persuasive essays, story ideas, manifestos to change the world. The more motivated you are to write, the more time you will spend doing it.

Writing Rituals

Inherent in the habit of writing is a certain amount of ritual, which may be defined as habitual activity performed for reasons of faith or superstition, or more simply, "to get the ball rolling" as quickly and painlessly as possible. Just as, in baseball, persons at bat may unfailingly rub dirt on their hands, tip their hats, and take any number of practice swings before accepting the first pitch, so too will many writers perform any number of activities that, from an outsider's point of view, do not seem to relate to writing itself. Some writers will go through a pencil-sharpening routine (even though they do all of their composing on a computer!), and some will feel compelled to read for a while, perhaps to get into the right mood. Still others will compose fanciful or spontaneous sentences, doodle furiously, or do pushups before they feel psychologically ready to write their daily quotas. Rituals can bite into one's writing time if one is not properly disciplined, so be careful, without abolishing ritual altogether.

Creating the Right Environment for Writing

Let's face it, writing is rough going even when it's fun. As with all serious study, writing requires intense concentration for extended periods. It makes sense, therefore, to create an appropriate writing environment for yourself. First, choose a comfortable, *quiet* location. Noise—even music—may seem tolerable, but tends to lower your level of concentration, no matter how subtle the sounds may seem. Next, make sure the room has adequate lighting so you can avoid headaches or eye fatigue. Be mindful of your posture; slouching can fatigue you. Also, keep all your writing materials (paper, notes, dictionary, pens, etc.) together, and within easy reach.

As a corollary to maintaining a good working environment, here's another important point to remember: Stick to a few commonsense matters of self-discipline that will give your writing habit a better chance of thriving. For example, allot a specific amount of time for each writing session and hold to it as closely as you can. Resist breaking into your allotted time on a whim, such as a sudden urge to buy a snack in the student union, or an aimless stroll for inspiration. These interruptions wreak havoc with concentration and momentum—skills you're trying to develop. Also, maintain good posture while you're writing. Keep yourself upright, not slouched. Bad posture will wear you out fast. And above all, be patient with yourself! Developing the ability to write well takes time. Don't let impatience disable your capacity for self-criticism. If your writing doesn't come out right the first time (it seldom does), keep reworking it until you are satisfied. Of course, when you're writing in your journal, your goal is not to create a finished piece of work, but rather to capture raw ideas quickly.

The Writing Process

By dividing a complex activity like writing into stages, you will be able to begin mastering it more readily. You may, understandably, forget about these composing stages once you become more skilled at writing; until then, however, you will probably find them very useful in learning the writing process.

To give a simple example, when you learn to bowl, you might divide the delivery into the following stages:

1. Getting into position behind the foul line.

2. Gripping and aiming the ball properly.

3. Beginning the four- or five-step approach to the foul line.

4. Controlling the backswing, slide, and release maneuvers.

5. Finishing with a smooth "follow-through."

These stages continue to be useful for practice sessions, for example when working on your backswing or on controlling the ball's trajectory. But during an actual game, delivery becomes a unified, seamless action.

Although writing, too, may be conveniently seen in stages, the stages are highly variable and overlapping. The manner in which a writer proceeds from initial "spark" to finished manuscript depends a great deal on his or her mental habits. The following list, then, is a *likely* breakdown of composing stages. Once you get a sense of your own inclinations, you may wish to make adjustments.

1. *Invent.* Engage in "mind-play" (brainstorming, free-writing, talking it out) to discover a topic, the important details about the topic, and what you mainly want to say about it.

2. *Gather and Plan.* Retrieve details about the topic from your memory or from background reading.

3. *Organize and Outline.* Tentatively map out your idea in terms of beginning, middle, and end; devise a working (trial) outline to maintain coherence and a thorough development.

4. *Write a First Draft.* Develop your idea, concentrating more on content than on style or correctness.

5. *Revise.* Rework your draft to improve accuracy, readability, and development. Revision can take place whenever you want it to, but the most efficient time for it to occur is after you have completed a preliminary draft.

It is possible for beginning writers to pay no attention to procedures and simply to follow their instincts. What's the rationale? Writing an essay, unlike following a recipe, does not have to proceed in a step-by-step fashion. Although adding an ingredient before bringing another ingredient to a boil could be disastrous for a particular recipe, writing a first draft before writing an outline may not be so serious; in fact, it may prove beneficial for some writers, depending on temperament. By writing a rough draft, then outlining in detail, and then writing a second draft, some writers exercise better control over their material. Writers must be aware of the difference between varying the stages and being totally unaware of the stages in their own writing.

The stages of the composing process identified here may or may not be adopted in the order given; keep in mind, however, that many inexperienced writers will have an easier time completing an essay assignment by following this procedure. If you're doubtful, try the procedure at least once, just to see how well it fits your temperament.

Invention

Any involved activity has its preparation stage: Actors rehearse for a show; artists make preliminary sketches, or "studies," for the paintings or sculptures they envision; businesspeople set up committees to, say, report on the feasibility of a proposed project. Writers need to prepare for their projects too. This preparation is called *invention*.

Even writers who say they don't really prepare to write, who simply sit down and begin writing, most likely toss a few ideas and organizational strategies around in their minds beforehand, then continue to develop and refine their topic by discovering ideas as they go along. Often a word or sentence will pop into mind and trigger a new idea. The author will scratch out a passage and begin it anew, revising to accommodate the new insight. This is an example of *draft writing* as part of the invention process.

Many writers, though, need to do considerable planning before beginning the first draft. If this sounds like you, then you will want to familiarize yourself with the various techniques of *prewriting*, also part of the invention process. The prewriting techniques of brainstorming, free-writing, and talk-writing help you overcome that aggravating I-can't-think-of-anything-to-say slump known as *writer's block*.

Perhaps the greatest cause of writer's block is the inability to retrieve information or to conjure up new ideas quickly and thoroughly, in detail. We might sit for hours lamenting that we have nothing to say, pen poised over a blank sheet of paper or eyes riveted to a blinking cursor on a blank computer screen. The truth of the matter is that we have more to say than we realize. As the American novelist Flannery O'Connor once pointed out, our having survived our childhoods means that we have enough to write about for a lifetime!

Then why does writer's block occur? One possible explanation may be that we are afraid of sounding stupid, or of not saying anything worth writing down, or of making some mistake in grammar or punctuation. The best way around this obstacle is to assure yourself that the greatest of writers rarely get it right the first time (Tolstoy rewrote *War and Peace* seven times). Writing, by its very nature, is a process of discovery, followed by refinement and elaboration, followed by more discovery, and more refinement and elaboration.

Another reason for the block may be the lack of any system of thought retrieval. Such a system is called a *heuristic*, from the Greek word *heuriskein*, to discover. Here we will examine three heuristic devices: brainstorming, free-writing, and talk-writing.

Brainstorming

Brainstorming may be done individually or in groups, although it seems to work much better as a group activity. You and your classmates might arrange an oral brainstorming session and simply toss ideas around freely. This was what brainstorming originally referred to in the 1930s, when the industrialist Alex Osborn used it as a means of quickly generating solutions to business-related problems. Another way to brainstorm is in writing—on paper or on the chalkboard—and there are dozens of methods to use.

One effective method, developed by Professor Gabriele Rico and presented in her book, *Writing the Natural Way*, is known as *clustering*. In a very brief period—two to ten minutes—the student free-associates with a *nucleus word* that is placed in the middle of a page and circled. By radiating lines from the nucleus, the student spontaneously records images, feelings, and abstractions, placing each term in its own circle. Each of *those* terms, in turn, can trigger new sets of associations. In seconds, the student is astonished to discover the tremendous detail that can be incorporated into an essay, poem, or story. Here is how one of Rico's students, Lavelle Leahey, clustered the nucleus word "airplane":

A Practical Method of Writing

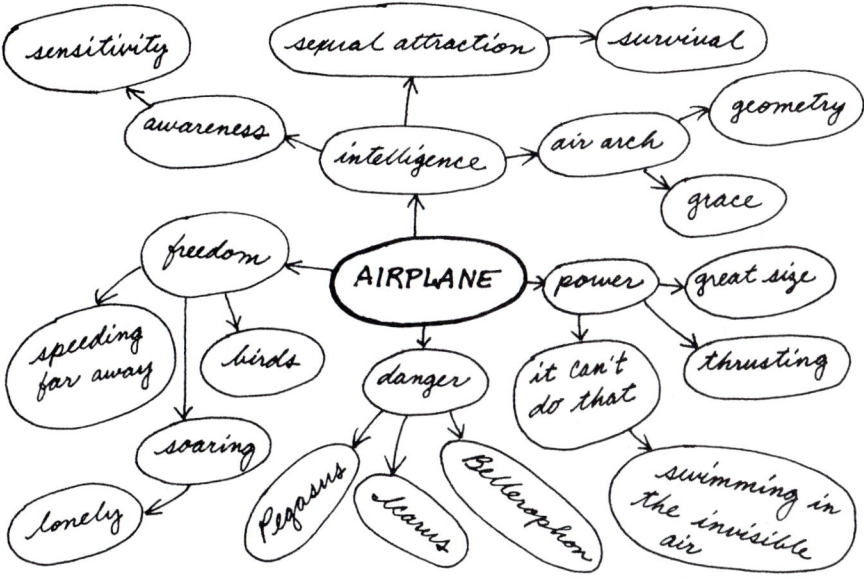

Lavelle then used her clustering exercise as a springboard for developing the following prose passage:

> A huge silver jet airplane is making a graceful arch in the light blue morning sky, material evidence, to me, of the human mind. It is intelligence and courage thrusting above environment, at home with the impossible, powerful proof of the attraction of intellect in natural selection, as sensual as a strip tease.

Clustering works so well, produces such rich results, because it encourages people to use their mental capacities more fully. You may have heard about the "divided-brain" theory of consciousness, which holds that the two halves of our brains carry on different mental processes. The theory suggests that the left hemisphere of our brains specializes in analytical, sequential, linear, and abstract thinking. This kind of thinking is essential for language and mathematics, for reasoning, and for seeing the parts of a whole. The other half, the right hemisphere, specializes in visual perception, in imagination, and in relationships between things. Most of the activities we encounter in daily life are either "left-brain" or "right-brain" activities; but clustering seems to stimulate both sides of the brain at once. To cluster is to use language in a visual way. The effect of this is to break through writer's blocks that often result from trying to get the analytic left brain to do the work of the creative, image-oriented right brain.

Let's take this kind of brainstorming one step further and use it to set up a strategy for a full-length essay. Assume that you have been asked to write a travel piece of sorts, focusing on an interesting place you once visited. First, write down your nucleus word—the name of the place you visited:

Monterey

Now you begin clustering . . .

As your thoughts soar in a dozen directions at once, you might feel a tug for something in particular, say, for Cannery Row. Pay attention to those tugs! They're good indicators that you've stumbled into an area you'd really love to explore. You now let your clustering center around that new nucleus . . .

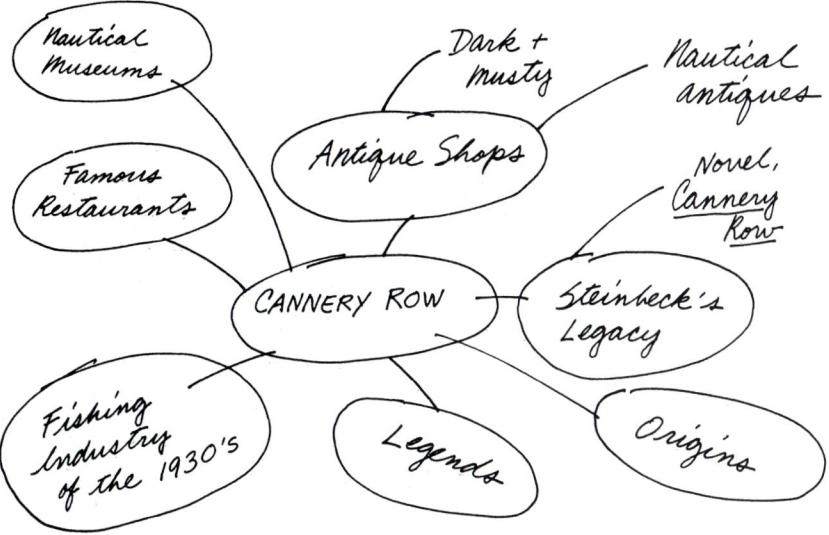

Suddenly, you feel another tug: You'd really like to devote your essay exclusively to the antique shops of Cannery Row. You choose this subject not just because it is a more manageable, narrowed topic, but because it is a topic that gives you a chance to sink your teeth into a lot of intriguing particulars.

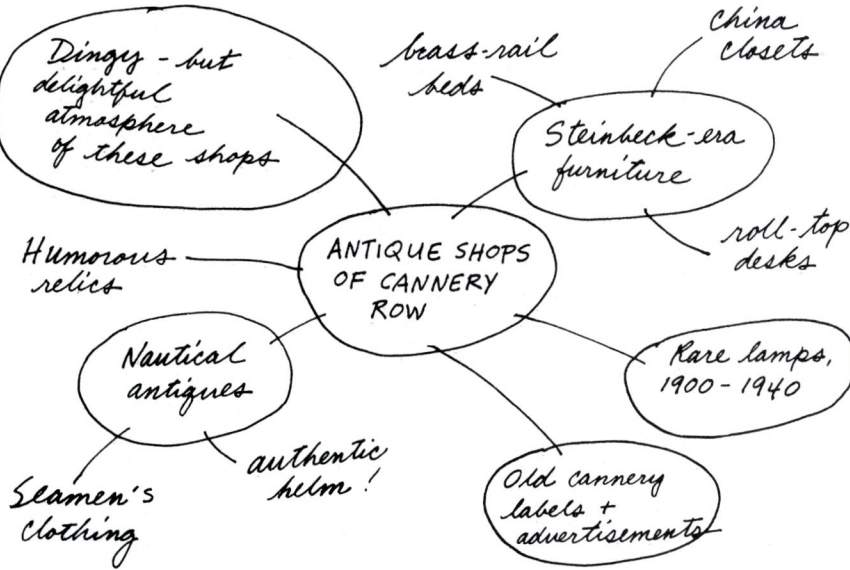

Had you remained content with a sweeping topic such as "Aspects of Monterey," your essay would most likely have consisted of a collection of uninteresting generalities, *unless* your purpose was to write a tourist-type feature on Monterey. Remember that a topic may be categorized as too broad or too narrow only in relation to the author's purpose.

Free-Writing   To free-write means to sit down with pen and paper, or at the typewriter or computer terminal, and to begin writing *without ever hesitating* about anything that comes to mind. If nothing comes to mind, you write: "My mind's a complete blank; my mind's a complete blank," or something to that effect. Inevitably, something will come to mind.

A fifteen-minute free-writing stint might begin like this:

> My head's swimming with ideas but not one is willing to hold still so I can look at it. Reminds me of trying to sketch my dog she wouldn't sit still long enough for me to capture her expression. Now what do I write? guess I just gotta force a thought to hold still but which one? thank God I dont have to worry about spelling or punctuation or any of that other junk teachers used to shove down my throat (maybe thats what I should write about. I remember how Pete hated English but he was a mathematical genius. Both of us were nature lovers and we used to love exploring the Mojave desert, was a great opportunity to—to what? my mind's blank again. Why can't I think of the word But I've got to keep writing Came across a lot of weird critters out there, blue lizards and tortoises I even stumbled onto a tarantula once nearly scared the crap out of me not knowing at the time they were very gentle spiders.

This writer has obviously abandoned style, mechanics, and sense of direction—all those things that bog a writer down during the preparation stage. The idea behind free-writing is to generate content rapidly as well as to accustom oneself to the physical act of putting words down on paper spontaneously, naturally, as a kind of informal conversation. Because free-writing opens the floodgates of memory, there is no end to what you can generate. The above free-writing passage contains several ideas that could be developed into essays; for example, you might write an essay on the behavior of tarantulas or on the origins of deserts. What other topic ideas do you see in that passage?

Another type of free-writing, for those who feel uncomfortable producing uninhibited streams of not-too-intelligible prose, is sometimes paradoxically referred to as controlled free-writing. Instead of opening a floodgate, the writer opens a single tap—one topic only—and writes only on that topic. This kind of free-writing is valuable for anyone intending to examine a topic deeply or extensively; it can also quickly gauge the extent of one's existing knowledge on the subject, and indicate gaps that will need to be filled by subsequent research.

One student with an interest in sailing decided to do some free-writing on that topic before thinking specifically of shaping her thoughts into an essay. Here is what she wrote:

> The language of sailing is as colorful as sailing itself—tiller and rudder, mainsail and jib, boom and mast, halyards, sheets, and guys (the running rigging). And there's much beauty in sailing, too: picture a sloop running downwind, its red-and-blue spinnakers billowing, cutting furrows of whitewater as it traverses the harbor. Oh to be out on the water now, feeling the wind, studying it, rigging the ship for action, launch from the pier ("Cast off!" "Toss line and marker!" "Put tiller to windward!"), trim jib and main, take bearings, feel yourself become one with the wild sea.

Professor Peter Elbow, in his book *Writing with Power*, refers to free-writing as "pushups in withholding judgment," thus enabling students "simply to *get on with it* and not be held back by worries about whether these words are good words or the right words." Whenever you face a writing task, free-writing (uninhibited or controlled) can loosen you up and get the "word-adrenaline" flowing quickly so you need not suffer anxiety attacks about content, structure, and style prematurely. Free-writing can help make writing a pleasurable experience.

Talk-writing Have you ever wondered why we can generate language so spontaneously when we talk, but freeze up the moment we have to write something down? One reason is that we talk so *much*, hour after hour, every day, ever since we first learned to speak. We are simply experts at it. Another reason is that our topics of conversation are often sparked by pressing matters, concerns of the moment; we seldom bother to explore these matters with the same degree of complexity when we write about them. The third reason is perhaps the most revealing: We speak at the speed of thought, but when we write we must slow down our thought processes considerably, and that can be as awkward as trying to ride a bicycle at a snail's pace.

Talk-writing can be seen as a technique to help you grow accustomed to the slower speed of thought needed for composition. It works like this: You get together with one or two persons who can help you discover a possible topic. You should keep a notebook handy; you'll be surprised at how many ideas start to flow as you try to answer questions put to you in conversation. One question might be, "What was the last thing that angered you (or embarrassed you, or frightened you)?" First you talk about the experience, then you scribble down what you've just uttered, coming as close to verbatim as you can. Eventually, the fluency of your oral responses will be transferred to your written responses.

Gathering and Planning

Once you have used one or more techniques of invention to corner your topic, your next step is to gather together as much as you need to know about that topic as possible. Many particulars will come to you as you begin a first draft, but the preliminary gathering of data can be a real time-saver. Writer's block can strike when, even though you may be enthusiastic about a topic, you do not have a sufficient foundation of data upon which to begin shaping the essay.

The 5Ws and the H Grid Students who prefer an efficient system for gathering together what they already know, or what they need to know, about their topic might consider using the famous "5Ws and the H" grid that journalists have been using for years. It works because the questions it generates (What, Where, When, Why, Who, and How) provide a wraparound understanding of the topic.

To make the best use of this heuristic device, take a sheet of paper and make six horizontal columns; label them *What*, *Where*, *When*, *Why*, *Who*, and *How*. Divide the columns into *General* and *Specific*, as follows:

5Ws and the H Grid		
Q	General	Specific
What?		
Where?		
When?		
Why?		
Who?		
How?		

The virtue of this grid is that it allows you to think in two directions at once: *horizontally* (the major facets of the topic) and *vertically* (the specific attributes of each facet). Here is an example of how it can work: Imagine that you have been assigned the topic, "Photographing Insects," and that you are not quite sure what you can say about it. You draw your grid, then you gradually fill in the blanks:

5Ws and the H Grid

Q	General	Specific
What?	Scope of insect photography	Scientific and artistic applications, insects best suited to be photographed
Where?	Countryside, desert, one's own backyard	Habitats of specific insects, e.g., of beetles: under rocks, of spiders: between bushes
When?	Spring, summer	Specific times of day or night, depending on insect, weather conditions
Why?	Educational, relaxing, lucrative	Good for biology projects, as a hobby, for teaching
Who?	Experts in insect photography	Specific profiles and tips of experts
How?	Equipment needed; step-by-step procedures	35mm camera, macro lenses, fast film

Now that you have all this information tabulated, your inevitable question is, "How can I use it for my essay?"

First, here are a few words on how *not* to use it: Do not mechanically turn the data into sentences and then connect the sentences together to form your essay. Your writing will sound like robot speech. It's much better to leave the data in tabulated form.

Remember that this grid works in two ways, at two different times: when you put the grid together, thereby reinforcing your command of the material by asking and answering questions about it; and when you return to the grid to review the material, which supplies the spark you need to begin writing your essay.

Thus if you are just beginning to write an essay on how to photograph insects, you may have gotten your spark by mentally combining your data from the *What* and *Where* slots. The opening sentences of your rough draft might go something like this:

> After several minutes of shuffling through weeds and brush you finally find one: a beautiful, extra-large, black-and-yellow garden spider—and luckier still, he is in the midst of constructing his web. You quickly raise your camera, adjust the focus and shutter speed, and begin shooting.

Background Reading Another way to retrieve information about a topic is to start reading about it. Assume that the topic you're writing about is "A Hike Through the Badlands of South Dakota," which you've earlier whittled down from "Outdoor Activities" during a clustering session. You visit your library and "get a feel" for the topic by reading a few articles about the Badlands in a general encyclopedia, such as *Collier's*. Remember that this is informal research; your aim is to get a stronger sense of the topic, not to investigate an issue fully for a formal research paper.

In addition to consulting encyclopedias, consider using the following reference works for background research:

1. The library card catalog (especially the subject headings).

2. Books cited in the bibliography at the end of many encyclopedia entries.

3. Unabridged and specialized dictionaries (for clarification of terms peculiar to a given field).

Organizing and Outlining

The first point to make about organizing is that it does not differ too much from inventing and information-gathering. To organize something means to arrange its components in a sensible and pleasing manner. Often, when we are thinking about *what* to include in an essay, we are simultaneously deciding *where* to include it. But the more involved the writing task, the more likely you will want to organize as a separate step. Some writers, it is true, compose like blue blazes without ever stopping to organize. For them, main points, supporting points, and examples just fall into place. If this describes your experiences, consider yourself blessed. Then again, you may *think* you can work this way—and probably have done so on occasion, if you are the procrastinating type who dashes off four-page essays the night before they're due. But 99 percent of the time you will forget something important, or you will be a lot less clear and coherent than you realize at the time. Organizing in advance will help you retain large chunks of information.

Organizing with an Outline If you shudder when you hear the word "outline," you may once have had a teacher who would brand a huge "F" on your essay because paragraph seven did not correspond to anything on your outline, submitted a week earlier. This is the outline-as-blueprint approach, and it rests on the fallacy that writers are supposed to know everything they want to say before they begin saying it. This premise simply isn't true; but resist adding fallacy to fallacy by rejecting outlines altogether.

Outlining a scheme for an essay follows a natural human tendency to structure our ideas once we conjure them up. We all have a natural aversion to formlessness. While some of us thrive more on structure than do others, nobody likes to drift aimlessly through even a single day. Schedules are invaluable for getting things done.

An outline should be much more like a schedule than like a blueprint. Blueprints are fine for designing houses. Nobody would consent to live in a house constructed by builders who organized as they hammered and sawed; one can't quite revise a house the way one can a piece of writing. But schedules lay out a *general sequence* to be followed; they don't elaborate too much. The best outlines merely lead you along the path of your essay. Here is an example: a writer contemplating an essay on waterskiing as a hobby might jot down something like this:

   I. Attention getter: thrill of cutting water for the first time
  II. Brief historical note about the sport (originated at Lake Pepin, Minnesota, in the 1930s, etc.)
 III. Most important points a beginner must know about waterskiing
  IV. Getting ready for your first try (step by step)
   V. Summary, concluding remarks

There you have a perfectly usable outline. It isn't substantial (writers call a brief outline like this a *scratch*, or *working*, *outline*), but it's ideal for getting started on a first draft. Did you notice how the five sections may easily be divided into introduction, body, and conclusion? Sections I and II will introduce waterskiing to your readers and whet their appetites, encouraging them to read further. Sections III and IV will constitute the heart of the essay, beginning with the key points about waterskiing the beginner must understand, and then continuing with the nuts-and-bolts, step-by-step procedures for the beginner to follow.

Once you are deeply into your subject, however, you may want to work out a more elaborate outline.* If your subject is complex enough to require a detailed outline, this is the best time to do it.

---

*See the Handbook, "Rhetorical and Grammatical Principles," Outline.

The way you organize your essay depends considerably on the type of essay you plan to write. The organization of a narrative that dramatizes an experience you had on water skis would differ substantially from the organization of an essay that explains how to waterski. Notice that in this textbook, organizational strategies are discussed in the context of particular kinds of essays, and not as absolute principles applicable to any kind of essay. You may want to browse through Chapters 5, 7, 9, and 11 to see how different kinds of essays require different principles of organization.

Writing a First Draft

First drafts can be intimidating. Many writers will spend excessive amounts of time taking notes or doing other kinds of prewriting to avoid taking the plunge—synthesizing all those ideas and notes into a composition. Here are a few suggestions that will make life a bit easier when you face writing your first draft.

Begin your first draft when you feel the need to do so. If Writer A likes to brainstorm, then outline, and then begin the first draft, that doesn't mean you must follow that same sequence. The aim of any prewriting activity is to get you to the first-draft stage more readily; but if you can get there before completing a prewriting activity, all the better. You may even want to go from prewriting to first-draft writing and back to prewriting. If it works, then *do it*.

Write for content more than for organization or style. This is only the *first* draft—a preliminary draft—not a final draft. The most important thing at this stage is to get the particulars of your topic down on paper. These are the specific facts that support your assertions—the matters that must be raised in relation to your topic. If you are arguing a highly debatable point, then you must include your opposition's point of view. When writing a first draft, you don't really have time to worry about matters like sentence structure and word choice, and whether the third paragraph should precede the fourth. However, if your train of thought is aided by transposing a paragraph, then do it. *You* must make the rules that will best suit your needs.

Refer to your prewriting materials often. The best reason to engage in prewriting activity is to make the actual composing of a first draft proceed smoothly. Whenever you reach a momentary stall in the first-draft stage, review your free writing, your brainstorming clusters, your library notes, and your 5Ws and the H grid. This material will spur you on, reinforce your sense of purpose, and prevent those long lapses of time that often lead to frustration.

Keep your reader in mind at all times. Once you forget that you are writing for other people, you risk lapsing into stilted, overly convoluted or simplistic, or insufficiently developed prose.

After you consider the first-draft suggestions, you may nevertheless say to yourself, "But I *still* freeze whenever I try to begin a first draft, even when I'm eager to get started." This is a common problem, even among seasoned writers.

If you get stuck, try this: Write down a *single phrase* that relates to the subject you have chosen. If your subject relates to your experience as a waiter in a fancy restaurant, for example, you might write down a phrase such as:

fussy customers

Then ask a key question about the fussy customers—something like, "How were they fussy?" A more manageable question, one that could spur you to write more readily, might be, "What was one of those fussy customers like?" The second question is more manageable than the first because it leads you to think specifically about a single individual rather than generally about several.

Once you have formed your question, you can proceed to answer it:

One of my steadiest customers—I'll call him Tubsy (since he was shaped like a watermelon)—is sure to keep me running without a stop. Nothing is ever right the first time: The potatoes are cold—*Heat them until they're piping hot*; the coffee is too weak—*I want it stronger.* And where is my bread? *Get my bread now, and it'd better be freshly baked . . .*

As you can see, getting a first draft underway needn't be an ordeal. By asking simple, pointed questions about your subject, you can tap quickly into the heart of your topic.

Revising

Revising is an important stage in the composing process. Unlike informal conversation, where nobody would dream of revising what was uttered off the cuff, essays do require reworking. They are written to last, and to be referred to at any time.

Revising is more *art* than *craft*: What to revise and how to revise it are often difficult matters to determine objectively. However, we can isolate some basic principles:

Once you have completed a draft, let it cool. Do something else for the next several hours, or even longer, so you will see your writing in a more objective light.

*Read your draft through as though you were a member of your target au-

dience. This is a variation on the very important write-for-your-readers theme. Look for any passages you could make clearer, easier to read. You might restructure or reword sentences, rearrange the sequence of sub-topics, add an additional or more effective example to illustrate a generalization, or tighten up wordy passages.

Double-check the assignment guidelines to ensure that the draft has accomplished all that the assignment demanded. Look for key phrases like "describe in detail"; "refute opposing views" (demonstrate how views opposing your own are wrong or limited); "explain the procedure carefully" (break down the procedure into a sequence of steps and explain each step clearly, trying not to overlook anything). Be sure to ask your instructor to clarify anything in the assignment's directions that is not clear.

Proofread. To proofread means to check for mechanical errors—errors in punctuation or manuscript format, in grammar, in spelling, and in usage. Use the appropriate sections of the Handbook in this textbook when proofreading.

Familiarize yourself with revision strategies frequently used by experienced writers. Keeping in mind that every writer's habits of revision are different to some degree, we can isolate common practices.* Keep in mind that revising often means adding or rearranging sentences and paragraphs, rewording and deleting, and generally *reseeing* the whole draft in light of what you aim to accomplish.

You mustn't be discouraged if you find yourself revising two, three, or even four or more times before the essay seems to be good enough to hand in. The more demanding you are, the better your ability for self-criticism will be, which is crucial for anyone who wants to master the honorable art of writing.

Kinds of Essays

Your method of composing will be influenced to some extent by the kind of essay you choose to write. As with speech, writing can be categorized according to the author's principal reason for communicating with others. The three basic categories are the expressive essay, the informative essay, and the persuasive essay.

1. *The Expressive Essay.* The author wishes to entertain others with an interesting experience, real or imagined. Essays about real experiences are called narratives, personal-experience stories, or simply

---

*See Chapter 15, "Revising Your Work."

personal essays. When imaginary experiences are used, the writing is called fiction. Such expressive writing is characterized by vivid descriptions and by a storytelling method of relating events.

2. *The Informative Essay.* The author wishes to explain an idea, a phenomenon, or a procedure. To achieve this goal, he or she will use various techniques to ensure clarity and comprehension. These techniques include definition, classification, comparison, and analysis. Even though the author is mainly concerned with conveying information, he or she will still want readers to be interested in the material and to enjoy reading about it. Thus, *entertainment* elements in the broadest sense of the term are relevant here as well.

3. *The Persuasive Essay.* The author wishes to argue a debatable issue and to change the readers' minds, or at least to help them understand the issue better. Among the persuasive techniques are: appealing to the audience's perceived sense of values, demonstrating false or defective reasoning on the part of the opposition, and providing reliable evidence. Again, we cannot separate argument entirely from explanation or expressiveness: factual information and vivid description can also be important ingredients in a persuasive essay.

Below are three short essays, each of which focuses on what college graduates actually do, can do, or should do with their time immediately following graduation. Essay A is primarily expressive; essay B, informative; and essay C, persuasive. As you read each essay, see if you can determine what specifically gives it its expressive, explanatory, or persuasive nature.

ESSAY A

My friend Sara was spending her last night aboard the *Clearwater*. As the 106-foot sloop headed into New York harbor under full sail, she and I climbed the mast and sat together on the crosstree, high above the murky water. A brightly lighted Manhattan stood confidently before us, the office towers dwarfing everything else in sight. There were only a few cargo vessels anchored in the harbor that warm July night, which helped reduce the usual craziness that accompanies keeping an alert bow watch. From the crosstree we watched the headlights of cars as they traveled over the Brooklyn Bridge. The *Clearwater* moved steadily through the harbor to its berth at South Street Seaport. Sara played her flute.

Then came the five-minute silence that's customary at the close of every *Clearwater* sail. We listened to the sounds of the water and the background noises from the city. After a time, two other crew members, Al and Steve, brought their guitars on deck and sang. Sara and I climbed down from the crosstree, and a moment later the topsail was dropped. We worked together to take in the jib and the mainsail. Dock lines were made ready to cast. The crew stood at the gunwales with tires, ready to cushion the boat in case it scraped against the pier.

Sara had been on board with us during the past week performing as a folk singer. We had often listened to her sing late at night as we sailed past the shadowy Palisades and on up the Hudson. The *Clearwater* is a replica of the 18th-century Hudson River packet sloops that provided upriver transportation back then. She's owned by an environmental group, and in reality she's a public-relations vehicle used to spread ecological awareness in communities up and down the Hudson.

As the boat neared the dock on Sara's last night with us and we all stood together on deck to say our goodbyes, she remarked that it was a shame how quickly the time had passed. So why couldn't she just stay with us longer, I wanted to know. That seemed like an easy enough thing to do. But she answered that staying on board would be too easy—she was afraid of getting sidetracked. "Music is my work, after all," she explained, "and the way I see it, work should be like a straight, long road. If you have too many sidetracks from your work, you'll never achieve the goals you set for yourself."

This hit me somewhat like a sledgehammer, because in the two years since I left the University of Vermont, whatever course I have followed could not exactly be described as a straight, long road. I've been hiking in Alaska, winter camping in Wyoming's Wind River Range, and caving in Big Horn, Montana. And I've spent a whole summer aboard the schooner *Bill of Rights* as a messmate. A lot of that time I was washing the ship's collection of pewter plates while she sailed along the New England coast out of Newport, Rhode Island. I have even "boat-sat" aboard someone's power cruiser. Boat-sitting is like babysitting except that the boat doesn't talk back. You also get paid much better, and you get a free room and sometimes free meals. Aboard the *Clearwater* I've learned all about plankton, fish life, and water chemistry, and I've taught these same things to the hordes of grade school kids who come on board for our daily five-hour educational sails.

Between excursions, I've worked at a Long Island bookstore, allowing myself timeout periods that have been a perfect way to regroup my senses and replenish my finances before another urge makes me set out for someplace new. The bookstore manager is kind enough to take me back for a few weeks or months whenever I need such a respite, and the people there provide what I'd call a safety net—something that's invaluable to anyone considering this kind of haphazard travel.

Looking back on the two years that have passed since graduation, I'd say that "haphazard" is a good label to give my series of sporadic starts and abrupt finishes. All the while I've put aside any thoughts of settling in somewhere and getting serious about a career. This sort of attitude has its drawbacks, I'll admit. Our society, for better or worse, exerts pressure on people to follow straight, long courses. My high school and college friends are mostly immersed in their careers. Several are married; others have finished graduate school. They have their first apartments, dishwashers, and savings plans. Sometimes I think these are things I might also be looking for without having realized it yet.

In any event, my friends usually react to my lifestyle with a mixture of envy and suspicion. My parents, I'm happy to say, don't try to impose their wishes on me, but sometimes I think about settling down just for the sake of their peace of mind. Then again, whenever this kind of internal debate starts overtaking me, I try to put it all out of my mind. At the risk of sounding like a gushing romantic, I'd really much rather take in a deep-red sunset over the ocean than worry about how I might be measuring up against the apparent progress of everyone else.

 Beth Doxsee, "Learning Years"

ESSAY B

Don't be fooled by the folks who say that the only time in your life to "stop out" is while you're still in college. More and more parents, executives, and others are taking a year or more from their established lives to change careers, have children, travel, rest, or simply contemplate the course they've taken.

 Still, the college years are undeniably the most flexible ones of your life. There's no career to worry about yet; you're young; and you're eager to travel. Most college admissions offices are willing to grant leaves of absence, so you have something waiting for you upon your return. Your options are all open, in other words. Sound good so far?

 Here are some suggestions on how to make the most of the experience:
Set goals for yourself. Time is money, but time off doesn't have to mean money lost if you use the time wisely. Even seemingly minor goals (to see one new place, to take a solo road trip) will help you focus your activity so that you won't feel that you've wasted time when the year is up.

Arrange for a safety net—and then forget it. Speaking of self-reliance, that's probably the greatest reward you can get from a learning year. But just in case you end up in a situation that makes the scenario from a traveler's-check commercial pale by comparison, have a safety net set up to depend on in emergencies. It could be a separate savings account, help from your parents, or a job (or admission to grad school) that you've arranged to have waiting upon your return. And then forget it (you don't want to use it unless you *have* to).

Tidy up any loose ends. Though you may be off on an exciting series of adventures, the rest of the world will continue on its steady, practical course. Before you leave, make sure your transition from resident to romantic wanderer is a smooth one. Be sure to vacate or sublet your apartment properly. Touch base with your school's office of admissions. Pay any outstanding utility bills or gambling debts, and arrange for your mail to be forwarded somewhere. For your own good, determine what your medical and accident insurance needs might be, and then arrange for proper coverage.

Don't hesitate. If you're still longing to take off but are wavering, rest assured that the job/college/family/friends will all be waiting for you when you get back. Stop thinking and go.

 Denise Graveline, "Advice for Would-be Wayfarers"

ESSAY C

I always hear about how important it is to set career goals early, to prepare carefully by taking the most "relevant" courses, by not passing up any opportunity to do "odd" jobs that can show a super-employer some of the skills I'm supposed to have learned.

I cannot deny the level-headedness of that advice; but I disagree with its larger narrow-mindedness. That advice overlooks one very important thing: there is more to education than formal education. Oh sure, many will say, hands-on experience with the world itself is very important; but I say that it is too important to put off until several years into your career.

The best time to embark on journeys to those far-off places of your dreams is as soon after graduation as it takes to get your passport and work out your itinerary!

Look: you've *earned it*; but more importantly, you can put a good deal of your classroom experience to immediate use. Your book knowledge of the ancient Greeks and Romans can be reinforced more by walking amid the dusty ruins of the Acropolis and the Forum than by rereading your lecture notes.

Take it from one who waited too long. Like marriage, a career is something to settle into slowly—at least not before you have given yourself a summer of soul-charging excitement.

(unpublished student essay)

Summary

Writing should be approached neither haphazardly nor rigidly. Even though a method of composing should be in keeping with the writer's temperament, a few suggestions should be heeded by all writers. First, cultivate the habit of writing regularly. Next, try different techniques of brainstorming, free writing, and "talking it out" to discover ideas and what to say about them. Use the 5Ws and the H Grid to generate information; then, map out a possible beginning, middle, and end for your idea. Finally, approach writing as a multidraft process. It is important that you develop a system that works best for *you*.

Writers not only concern themselves with what to say and how best to say it, but also with their reasons for saying it. Purpose, or aim, helps determine the shape and character of an essay. Will it describe or dramatize an experience (expressive essay)? Will it explain a concept or process (explanatory essay)? Will it persuade readers to accept one point of view over another with regard to a debatable issue (persuasive essay)?

FOR DISCUSSION

1. Make an inventory of everything you do to start writing. Do you merely sit down and begin, or do you perform certain "rituals" such as sharpen pencils, fix a snack, daydream, free-associate, read? Do you consider these activities helpful, or merely nervous compulsions?

2. Try to pinpoint the obstacles you face when attempting to write. How, if at all, do you overcome those obstacles?

3. Visit the library and see what you can uncover about the writing habits of various successful authors. Many authors have written about their "creative processes." Your instructor will help you locate useful sources. Prepare a summary of the working habits of two writers, preferably writers whose working habits are dissimilar. Report your findings to the class.

4. Discuss the advantages of writing "with both sides of the brain" rather than merely with the analytic left side or the artistic right side. What kinds of activities besides clustering might improve bi-hemispheric activity?

5. Defend, or in some way qualify, Cicero's assertion that "the pen is the best . . . teacher of eloquence."

FOR WRITING

1. Write an essay on your current writing habits. You may take a humorous approach to this assignment, but try to be as detailed—and as honest!—as you possibly can. It's important you don't overlook what might seem like trivial details. You might want to imagine yourself as a famous but eccentric writer with millions of readers who are curious to learn how you go about putting words on paper to create your own special style. Consider using clustering to generate details about your writing habits.

2. Go sleuthing in the library to see how much information you can gather in an hour on one of the following topics. List each source you consult.
    a. Navajo folklore
    b. History of [your favorite sport]
    c. Poisonous spiders
    d. Diamond mining
    e. Musical instruments of the Middle Ages

    f. History of labor-management relations in the United States
    g. Origins of superstitions
 3. Contemplate one of the following photographs for a few minutes. Then:
    a. Free-write for fifteen minutes, using the photograph to trigger ideas.
    b. Reread what you have written and extract at least one topic idea.
    c. Generate essay content by using the 5Ws and the H heuristic and/or clustering.
    d. Prepare a scratch outline.
    e. Compose the first draft of a short essay, using the technique of asking/answering simple questions about the subject to overcome initial writer's block.

    Again, use the photograph to trigger an idea. Refrain from only describing superficially what you "see" in the photograph.

Figure 3-1

Anonymous, "His First Refusal" (1909)

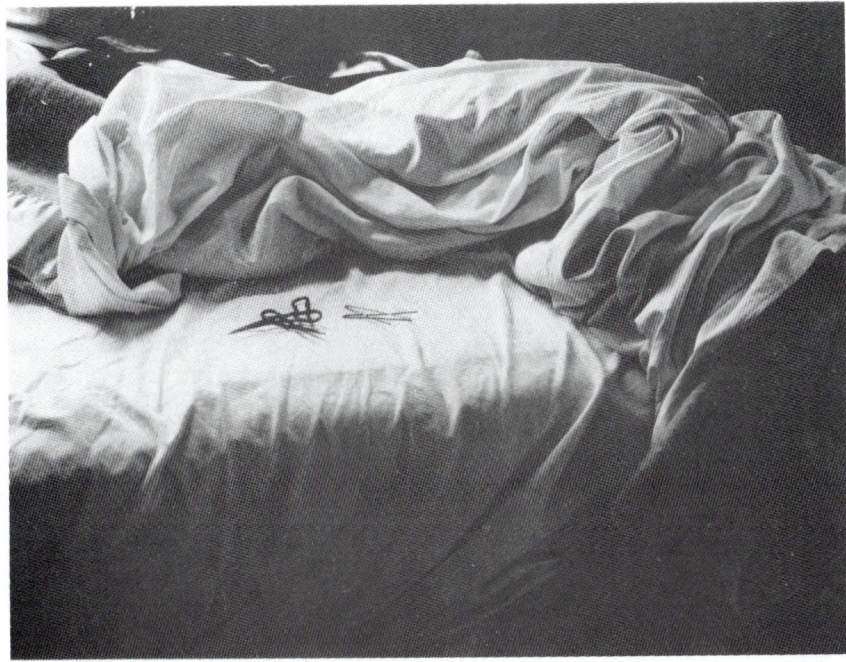

Figure 3-2

Imogen Cunningham, "The Unmade Bed" (1957)

4. You will recall that the three essays on the subject of life after graduation represent the principal aims of writing: to describe or dramatize, to explain, and to persuade. Think of a topic you could approach in this threefold manner. Write a paragraph that reflects each aim.

COMPUTER WRITING

1. Experiment with brainstorming: First, free-write. Fill the screen with whatever words come to mind, with no thought to grammar or mechanics, or even to coherence. The goal is to see how quickly you can fill the screen with words and ideas, and how flexible and unrestrained your mind can be. Second, dim the monitor until you cannot see the words, and continue composing in this manner (known as invisible writing). At first you will feel frustrated and disoriented, but push ahead and try to concentrate—not on the words you are using, but strictly on the idea you are trying to get across. After you've written for as long as you can without becoming too frustrated, turn up the monitor and be surprised.

2. For students working in pairs: Student A writes a paragraph on any topic. Student B revises A's paragraph immediately underneath. Student A studies the revision and writes his or her own revision of that paragraph. Students A and B then discuss which revision is best. Finally, the procedure is reversed: Student B writes a paragraph and Student A revises it, and so on.

3. For students working in pairs: Student A thinks of a fascinating setting, exterior or interior, and lists sensory impressions and concrete details associated with that place. Student B then composes a paragraph or two based on the details and impressions that Student A listed. Finally, Student A reviews Student B's writing, checking for accuracy, and revising as needed. Then, the procedure is reversed.

4. For word processing programs with windowing or split-screen capability: List (horizontally rather than vertically on the screen) everything you do when you write, from sharpening pencils to reviewing notes to rearranging your desk. Keeping this list on your screen, begin writing the essay on your writing habits described in the first exercise in "For Writing." The idea here is to let the raw data work as a prompt to help you develop your essay.

Principles and Projects

PART TWO

Principles of Development:
CHAPTER 4
Aiming to Express

You are writing expressively whenever you succeed in capturing feelings, or emotions, with words. This is no slight task, which is why many of us often find ourselves making statements like, "Words can't express the way I feel right now," or "I love you more than words can say." These are clichés perhaps, but they are usually voiced with sincerity.

The words *are* there though, somewhere, and one of the pleasure-pain experiences of being a writer is struggling to find the right words to do justice to the cauldron of feelings rumbling inside. We are fortunate as a species to have such language capabilities; people who do not bother to use language as an outlet for their feelings tend to find less-desirable ways to communicate their points, such as by throwing a tantrum or by punching someone in the mouth.

By now you may be wondering, Isn't expressing emotion the aim of *creative* writing, such as poetry and short stories? What does emotion have to do with the writing expected of students in freshman composition courses? This chapter aims to answer that question.

The Range of Expressive Writing

Although nearly all writing is fundamentally expressive to some degree, our communicative aims vary according to circumstance. Sometimes we want to emphasize facts and to present unambiguous, useful information to our readers. We call this kind of writing explanatory, or *informative*,* rather than expressive, even though we do "express" these facts in our own ways. When we speak of *expressive* writing, we are talking about writing that is bent on evoking a mood and stirring one or several emotions; fiction, poetry, and nonfiction all fall into this category.

Let's dwell upon the term *emotion* for a moment. The word often carries a negative connotation ("There he goes, getting all *emotional* again"). Actually, there's a very thin line between emotion and intellect, and the more we learn about the ways in which emotion and intellect interact, the more successful our efforts will be to narrow the gap between the experience and the way in which we capture that experience on paper. Emotions complement rather than contradict rationality; they can also trigger rational understanding.

Emotions, more so than rational thought, tend to be spontaneously generated; they occur effortlessly. In fact, it takes a good deal of effort to suppress an emotional response ("Try to control your emotions!"). And it is important for writers to know that emotions can be fascinatingly complex beneath the surface. We observe a person laughing and conclude that he or she is happy. But the laughter could also be spurred by a sense of bitterness or embarrassment, by some absurd situation (not necessarily a funny one), or by a combination of realizations. Often an experience, whether actual or vicarious, can produce a cluster of different emotions, some of them contradictory like pleasure and pain, delight and fear, joy and sorrow.

Any writer wishing to evoke a strong emotional response in readers must become a student of emotions, learning not only to appreciate the range of emotional response but also to manipulate language to trigger the appropriate emotions.

Now let's look closely at two modes of expressive composition, both to understand the nature of expressive writing and to explore ways to integrate it into one's own writing. These two modes are *narration* and *description*.

---

*See Chapter 6, "Principles of Development: Aiming to Inform."

Narration

One of our primal human instincts is that of storytelling. Although writing may seem unnatural—at least until it becomes a part of our lifestyle—storytelling is instinctive. Likelier than not, you've already told several stories since you got up this morning: about how your roommate uses his quadraphonic sound system for an alarm clock; or how the eggs you were served at breakfast were indistinguishable from the melted butter they were supposedly scrambled in; or how you managed to convince your history professor that her penalizing you for a late paper so early in the semester would cause you such distress that it would ultimately lead you to change your major. When you tell stories, the principal technique you use is *narration*; that is, you present the stages of an incident in more or less chronological order, and you answer the question, *What happened?* Here is a famous example:

> Yesterday evening at eight o'clock I was setting with Peter on his divan; it wasn't long before his arm went around me. "Let's move up a bit," I said, "then I don't bump my head against the cupboard." He moved up, almost into the corner, I laid my arm under his and across his back, and he just about buried me, because his arm was hanging on my shoulder.
> Now we've sat like this on other occasions, but never so close together . . . He held me firmly against him, my left shoulder against his chest; already my heart began to beat faster, but we had not finished yet. He didn't rest until my head was on his shoulder and his against it. When I sat upright after about five minutes, he soon took my head in his hands and laid it against him once more. Oh, it was so lovely, I couldn't talk much, the joy was too great. He stroked my cheek and arm a bit awkwardly, played with my curls and our heads touching most of the time. . . .
>
> Anne Frank, *Diary of a Young Girl*

As you can see, Anne Frank's narrative develops chronologically, although most narratives are not as specifically time-conscious as this one is. She establishes the exact time of the incident, and then presents each of its facets in a clear sequence, most likely to emphasize the importance, indeed the preciousness, of this encounter in her otherwise dismal life in hiding.

Narration can also move backward as well as forward in time. Anne Frank does this briefly at the beginning of the second paragraph. Sometimes writers will open a narrative with a present situation, and then "flash back" to events leading up to the present, as in this example:

> On the 19th of December, in 1949, when I had been living in Paris for a little over a year, I was arrested as a receiver of stolen goods and spent eight

days in prison. My arrest came about through an American tourist whom I had met twice in New York, who had been given my name and address and told to look me up. I was then living on the top floor of a ludicrously grim hotel on the rue du Bac . . .

James Baldwin, "Equal in Paris"

To involve his readers quickly in the narrative, Baldwin discloses the central incident—the arrest—before anything else, and then uses the *flashback* technique to present those events that led up to the arrest. Whenever you want to make an event in your story's past come to life, use this versatile flashback technique. After a carefully phrased transition (in the Baldwin passage above it's the sentence that begins with "My arrest came about through . . ."), you can smoothly make the past event the story's new present.

Another very important property of any narrative is something we might call *buildup*; fiction writers will refer to it as "plot-thickening." Instead of just relating a series of events in time, the writer of a narrative will move in a definite direction along a rising curve of conflict or tension, and eventually reach a climactic moment—a showdown.

Assume that you are about to write a narrative based on the harrowing experience you had riding the rapids of the Colorado River. Your main concern is not what to write about—the details of the adventure are as vivid as can be in your memory—but how to present those details so your readers will be able to relive the experience vicariously, in their imaginations. (That relived experience, indeed, is the reason people love to read narratives in the first place.) After you have done some brainstorming to gather up the particulars of the experience, you will want to plan your buildup by working out a rising curve of narrative action. If you were actually to draw out the curve, it might look something like this:

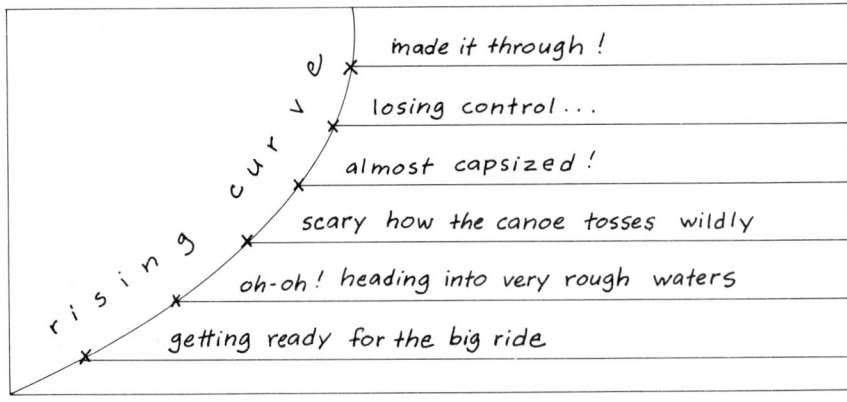

As you can see, the narrative not only unfolds, but its drama intensifies, which is what storytelling is all about.

Focus on the important word *drama*: It means showing action directly instead of telling about it indirectly. Writers sometimes forget that merely telling about or summarizing an event is not nearly as interesting to readers as dramatizing (depicting) it because drama involves readers in the action; the reader becomes a spectator, an eyewitness. Think of the difference between watching a football game as it is occurring and being told the highlights of that game after it has occurred. When composing a narrative, place your readers directly inside the arena, so to speak.

Notice the difference in effect between the direct and indirect approaches in the following two examples. In the first one, the action is summarized nondramatically, and it's no surprise we react to it in a ho-hum fashion. However, the second example, taken from Julia Alvarez's "El Doctor," presents more than just a mere *summary* of an action; it presents *direct* action.

1

My father liked to speak in parables because he felt that he could make his point more convincingly. It usually worked.

2

"I'm going to take this dollar," [my father] showed me, holding a bill in one hand and a flickering lighter in the other, "and I'm going to set fire to it." He never actually did. He spoke in parables, he complained in metaphor because he had never learned to say things directly. I already knew what he meant, but I had my part to play.

"Why would you want to do something like that?" I asked.

"Exactly! Why burn up my money with all these lights in the house!"

Narration, then, is *chronological*; it often makes use of *flashback* and *buildup* techniques, and it works most effectively when a sense of *drama* is conveyed, accomplished by the use of a *direct* approach (showing instead of telling). Let us now turn our attention to the other basic ingredient in expressive writing, description.

Description

A description is a drawing in words. If the aim of narration is to help your readers experience an incident, then the aim of description is to help your readers *see* the objects, persons, and sensations you present. As you might guess, description is important for all rhetorical aims, not just for expressiveness. A science writer, for example, will describe the shape of an airplane wing to help *explain* to readers how mechanized flight is possible.* An attorney might describe the damage done to a bedroom window to help prove forced entry and thereby *persuade* the jury that the accused committed burglary.†

But to return to expressive aims, remember that the aim of description for expressive purposes is to allow readers to "re-create" the experience—particularly the sensory pleasures of that experience—in their own minds, thereby enhancing their delight in the subject at hand. When Thoreau describes the thawing of Walden Pond after a long, cold winter, he does so not for the sheer pleasure of writing descriptively, but to demonstrate (as he does throughout *Walden*) the animated quality of nature and how its processes are more complex and beautiful than nonobservers can realize.

> Every morning . . . the shallow water is being warmed more rapidly than the deep . . . and every evening it is being cooled more rapidly until the morning. The day is an epitome of the year. The night is the winter, the morning and evening are the spring and fall, and the noon is the summer. The crackling and booming of the ice indicate a change of temperature. One pleasant morning after a cold night . . . I noticed with surprise, that when I struck the ice with the head of my axe, it resounded like a gong for many rods around, or as if I had struck on a tight drum-head. The pond began to boom about an hour after sunrise, when it felt the influence of the sun's rays slanted upon it from over the hills; it stretched itself and yawned like a waking man with a gradually increasing tumult.

Thoreau's description is spare but striking, based on close observation. We are delighted by the imaginative comparisons: a single day like a year in miniature; the booming resonance of the ice, the way it seemed to yawn and stretch like someone just awakening. Observing natural phenomena through such creative perception can, if we are looking for purely pragmatic reasons for expressive description, teach us to enjoy and value our environment more than we normally tend to do.

Description is a lot of fun and worth doing for its own sake, for as Thoreau's passage demonstrates, it teaches writers the very important skill of close observation. Naturally, when you are trying your hand at description you would rather not have to worry about a lot of dos and don'ts. Short, well-detailed descriptions of specific objects and persons make ideal journal or notebook entries, and they are perfect starting points for larger writing tasks. For instance, a description of an interesting person could easily lead to a short story or essay. In her essay "Why I

---

*See Chapter 6, "Principles of Development: Aiming to Inform."
†See Chapter 8, "Principles of Development: Aiming to Persuade."

Write" Joan Didion recounts how she began to write a novel after dwelling on the mental "pictures" triggered by observing a woman in a Las Vegas casino:

> A young woman with long hair and a short white halter dress walks through the casino at the Riviera in Las Vegas at one in the morning. She crosses the casino alone and picks up a house telephone. . . . Who is paging her? Why is she here to be paged? How exactly did she come to this? It was precisely this moment in Las Vegas that made *Play It As It Lays* begin to tell itself to me.

Shall we peek into other writers' notebooks? The great nineteenth-century poet-priest Gerard Manley Hopkins filled many volumes with keen observations. Here is a morsel, written in April 1864:

> Moonlight hanging or dropping on treetops like blue cobweb. Also the upper sides of little grotted waves turned to the sky have soft pale-coloured cobwebs on them, the undersides green. Note that the beaded oar, dripping, powders or sows the smooth [surface] with dry silver drops.

In April 1936, diarist Anaïs Nin recorded these intriguing impressions of Morocco:

> One Arab is asleep over his bag of saffron. Another is praying with his beads while selling herbs. . . . Little boys are beating copper trays with small hammers, beating a design into them. . . . The women are veiled. They are going to the mosque, probably. At a certain hour all selling, all work ceases and they all go to the mosque. But first of all they wash their faces, their feet, their sore eyes, their leprous noses, their pockmarked skins at the fountain. . . . A choking stench overwhelms me. . . . It is the smell of excrement, saffron, leather being cured, sandalwood, olive oil being used for frying, nut oil on the bodies, incense, muskrat, so strong that at first you cannot swallow food. . . .

Common Problems in Expressive Writing

Beyond the rough-draft or journal-writing stage, though, you will want to think about making your expressive writing as effective as possible. This means keeping an eye out for three common problems associated with descriptive writing: lack of clear purpose, straining for effect, and wordiness.

Lack of Clear Purpose

It is easy to go off on a tangent when writing descriptively. As previously mentioned, this is to be expected in spontaneous, rough-draft composing where your major concern is to let your ideas flow freely and copiously without fear of saying the wrong thing, or of overwriting. But once you are preparing a manuscript for the eyes of others, you must begin to cut whatever does not contribute to the composition's central image. If, for example, your central image is that of a cathedral's interior, you'll want to delete any stray references to the cathedral's exterior; you may, however, decide to present a comparison between external and internal architecture, in which case these references would be appropriate. If you are writing an extended description of a severe oil spill at a coastal drilling site, you will want to avoid digressing into a description of the various species of seabirds that inhabit the region, unless you intend to make a clear connection between the two. In the following passage the author did not make a clear enough connection:

> The thick black sludge, expanding before our horrified eyes, spread like a tumor across the bright blue cresting sea. Oil drillers rushed to deploy containment equipment; but with each passing minute the spill appeared less and less containable. Already giant gobs of the crude were washing onto the white-sand beach. Sea gulls circled overhead, the ever-amusing sandpipers hopped crazily along the surf. These lovely birds restored our optimism.

Readers could probably guess what the author was up to when he included the sentences about the birds; but the author needs to make a more explicit connection to the oil spill to avoid distracting and annoying readers. After he was alerted to the problem, the author revised the passage as follows:

> The thick black sludge, expanding before our horrified eyes, spread like a tumor across the bright blue cresting sea. Oil drillers rushed to deploy containment equipment; but with each passing minute the spill appeared less and less containable. Already giant gobs of the crude were washing onto the white-sand beach, endangering the seabirds—the gracefully circling gulls and the ever-amusing sandpipers—searching for food along the surf.

Overcomplicated Language

In descriptive writing, *more is less*. Try to avoid whacking your readers over the head with heavy-handed, blatant "purple prose" that calls more attention to itself than to the subject you want to describe:

Principles of Development: Aiming to Express 65

> The sad-looking, disheveled clown, oblivious to the raucous, derisive, mocking laughter of the ridiculously dressed happy-looking clowns, waddled clumsily and lugubriously across the circus's center ring.

This author, in his enthusiasm to communicate the right image to his readers, nearly obliterates the image with unnecessarily abstract and convoluted modifiers. Had he cut away the excess prose, the image would have come across quickly and vividly to readers, as in the following example:

> The sad-looking, disheveled clown staggered across the circus's center ring, ignoring the hooting and hissing happy clowns.

The description is much more readable this time, now that the author has gotten rid of needlessly complicated terms like *lugubriously* and *oblivious to*. These expressions are not intrinsically bad (expressions are never *intrinsically* bad), but they are wrong for the context.

Wordiness

Wordiness is the most common problem writers have in descriptive writing. Actually, it is a compound problem because there are two kinds of wordiness: using more words than are necessary to create a desired impression (often called *redundancy*), and simply adding too much description (which may or may not be intrinsically redundant).

Let's take a look at both kinds of wordiness in an essay-in-progress. When freshman Mike White, a long-distance runner, was encouraged to describe what it was like to train on miles of rugged terrain, he plunged enthusiastically into a first draft, a section of which reads as follows:

> My tightened legs and pumping arms moved me over the crest of the hill atop the mile-long winding road. The tall, golden grass was bent against the warm August breeze that followed me as I made my descent to the base of another upgrade.
>
> By the time my descent was complete, the taut muscles of my legs had recovered from their mile-long climb. I looked ahead of me to see a dragonfly hovering over a patch of foxtails beside the crumbly black dirt trail. When I made my way past the dragonfly, as I pushed up the hill, he fluttered into a vanishing form amidst the shade of scattered sagebrush. . . .
>
> As the sun ascended higher and higher in the sky its heat intensified. The blazing sun highlighted the beads of sweat on my arms. Sweat streamed from my soggy hair, down the lines of my forehead, and dripped to the dry and dusty path.

The intensity of Mike White's descriptions and his choice of details suggest a genuine enthusiasm for the topic. Some of his sensory impressions—the tightening leg muscles, the heavy perspiring, the particular vegetation and insect life of the mountainous terrain—make the experience real to us.

Nonetheless, the example contains verbose expressions that could interfere with the reader's concentration. For instance, although the opening sentence of the first paragraph is packed with important scene-setting information, the sentence could still be more concise, and the action would be strengthened at the same time: "Leg muscles tightening, arms pumping, I scaled the crest of the hill," perhaps. In fact, the sentence would be even more concise with the word *hilltop* instead of *crest of the hill*. But remember that conciseness is rarely a virtue in itself; there's such a thing as cutting *too* much and spoiling the image. "Crest of the hill" is simply more evocative than "hilltop" is and therefore should be retained in this context.

Let's look further to the second sentence of the first paragraph. Here, some condensing would improve the writing: "Now I was surrounded by tall, golden grass that swayed in the dry August breeze" would enhance the image as well as reduce the excess verbiage. Similarly, in the second paragraph, the phrasing could be more economical. "By the time my descent was complete" could be shortened to "By the time I descended"; "the taut muscles of my legs had recovered from their mile-long climb" could be condensed to "my taut leg muscles had recovered from the ordeal" or simply "my taut leg muscles had recovered."

Your goal in writing good descriptions is to generate sensory impact with economical and vivid language. Practice by writing short, descriptive passages frequently in your journal, and by testing them for the common problems described here.

In Chapter 5 you will learn ways to organize and compose different kinds of essays that aim primarily at expressiveness. Once again, keep in mind that expressive writing appears in nearly all types of discourse, not just in "expressive" essays.

Summary

Expressive writing emphasizes emotional responses, rather than intellectual responses, to experience; but it does not necessarily *counteract* intellectual responses. Expressive writing allows readers to experience vicariously what the author experienced firsthand. Fundamental to expressive writing is narration, or storytelling, which dramatizes an incident in chronological stages and answers the question, "What happened?"

Description is "picture-language": It allows readers to see objects, persons, and activities in the mind's eye. For this reason it is a vital ingredient in many narratives.

Good narratives will unfold along a rising curve of action; the story will increase in tension until it reaches a climactic moment, after which it will resolve.

Good expressive writing will be free of the three problems often associated with it: lack of clear purpose, overcomplicated language, and wordiness.

FOR DISCUSSION

1. Identify the strengths and weaknesses of the narration and description in the following examples, and comment on how these aspects affect the writing's impact on the reader. Suggest possible ways to improve expressiveness and narrative development.

   A

   The Washington Monument seemed at once futuristic and ancient; quintessentially American and utterly alien; a strange, proud, obelisk-shaped spike at the far end of the Mall. I loved it most at sunrise, walking toward it with the Capitol in the pink, hazy distance like a vision of utopia out of a Thomas Cole painting. (student)

   B

   It takes London to put you in the way of a purely rustic walk from Notting Hill to Whitehall. You may traverse this immense distance—a most comprehensive diagonal—altogether on soft, fine turf, amid the song of birds, the bleat of lambs, the ripple of ponds, the rustle of admirable trees. . . . In Hyde Park I should follow the waterside, or the Row, or any other fancy of the occasion; liking best, perhaps, after all, the Row in its morning mood, with the mist hanging over the dark-red course, and the scattered early riders taking an identity as the soundless gallop brings them nearer. (Henry James, "London")

   C

   He glared at the flashing screen. One hand gripped a round knob while the other pounded on a white button. The boy's small frame was balanced in an arched position, the knees slightly bent. He kept his feet planted firmly apart, moving his hips with the rhythm of his hand, back and forth, left and right.

   He guided the plane expertly, avoiding obstacles, making it soar and dip. It dropped bombs on vases. Spaceships were released and fired at the plane. The plane fired back. Spaceships blew up; vases shattered. He moved the plane a fraction of an inch too close to the mountains, and it exploded.

Running his fingers through his stringy, blond hair, he licked his lips and waited for the next plane. (JoAnn Lambkin, unpublished student essay)

2. Discuss the range of applications, practical or otherwise, for expressive writing. Is one application of greater value or importance than the others?

3. Establish your own distinction between expressive and nonexpressive writing. Find examples in newspapers or magazines that will support your views.

4. Test your ability to describe a person accurately, on the spot, by describing aloud the facial characteristics of a classmate. (Do not look at the person while you're doing the exercise.) Then see how quickly the class can identify the person you have just described.

FOR WRITING

1. Imagine you are the videogame player in JoAnn Lambkin's brief narrative ("For Discussion," Exercise 1). Revise the narrative, making yourself the central character playing your favorite videogame, and including or deleting anything else in the example to make it your own.

2. Build one of the following story kernels into an expressive, three-paragraph mininarrative:

A

The ancient, supposedly dormant volcano began to rumble ominously when we were halfway to its summit.

B

The stranger leaped out of nowhere and, flashing a switchblade, ordered the man to hand over his wallet.

C

How could I ever forget the night my brakes gave out when I was driving back from my cabin in the high Sierras?

D

Have you ever imagined what it would be like to be a brontosaurus?

E

At the sound of the bell that marked the beginning of the eighth round, the two weary fighters staggered toward each other.

3. Involve yourself in one of the following hypothetical scenarios and write a vividly detailed, 150–250-word description of it.

Principles of Development: Aiming to Express   69

A

Having sneaked into Dr. Jekyll's laboratory in the dead of night, you find yourself witnessing the horrifying transformation of Jekyll into Hyde. Because the newspaper for whom you are working is offering a free luxury-liner cruise around the world for the most descriptive news story of the week, you whip out your notebook (frightened as you are), and begin to write. Share your blood-curdling description with the class.

B

Unbelievable as it sounds, you have been invited to accompany NASA astronauts on the next space shuttle orbital mission. The mission: to retrieve a damaged satellite and secure it inside the cargo hatch. Write a three-part description of the mission, including (1) the lift-off from Cape Canaveral and the attainment of Earth-orbit; (2) the view of the Earth from orbit, two hundred miles up; and (3) the astronauts' experiences working in space to retrieve the damaged satellite.

COMPUTER WRITING

1. Open a file with the name NARRATE and begin with the words "Once upon a time . . ." Using a combination of free writing and directed writing, tell a story to an audience of your choice. Do not pause to think about where the narrative is heading; you will very likely discover that your free-writing narrative will proceed much faster with a personal computer than with a pen, or even with a typewriter. Let the story unfold spontaneously; in other words, don't worry at this stage if everything fits. If you have trouble along the way, return to the beginning and review what you have written. If that doesn't work, spend a few minutes inserting additional descriptions of the characters you have thus far introduced; or develop your descriptions of the interior and exterior settings of your story.

2. As in Exercise 1, write a brief narrative as rapidly as you can, but this time develop the story that follows a rising curve of action. For example, imagine two people in a serious predicament—their automobile skidded off the road and is dangling over the edge of a precipice, let's say. To maintain suspense, dramatize the couple's struggle to figure a way out of the predicament while the predicament worsens at the same time. Finally, bring the narrative to a climactic moment.

3. For students working in pairs at adjoining terminals: Student A mentions a well-known setting; Student B composes, on the spot, a one-sentence description of that setting. Student B then mentions a setting while Student A composes a description of it. Later, each student edits the other's description directly on the screen.

Projects in Expressive Writing

CHAPTER 5

In an expressive essay, fiction and nonfiction merge. Expressive essays such as personal-experience narratives, character portraits, and descriptive pieces borrow some of the techniques associated with fiction, as we learned in Chapter 4. Along with understanding a viewpoint and an attitude, which in fiction is commonly known as a *theme*, readers want to reexperience in their imaginations the original perceptions of the author. This suggests that the author has to be *evocative*—to find words and phrases that will produce the right pictures in readers' minds. Expressive writing is writing that creates an image; it is photographing with words.

In this chapter you will have a chance to compose detailed descriptions of settings (such as landscapes, cities, and the exteriors and interiors of buildings) and people. You will also have a chance to try your hand at narrative writing. Even more important, you will see how description and narration interact within a single discourse.

Writing an Extended Description of a Setting

To write vivid descriptions—that is, to transmit the images in your mind to your reader's mind—with minimal loss of precision, you should keep three basic principles in mind:

1. *Emphasize the objects or events in themselves over your own reaction to them.* Don't tell your readers that the Petrified Forest was strange and colorful; instead, zero in on the *details*: the craggy, translucent scarlet and umber swirls on the exposed cross sections of the petrified logs; the fantasy-like appearance of entire tree trunks turned to stone, toppled over each other as if they had just been uprooted yesterday instead of thirty million years ago. Let the details reveal the strangeness and the colorfulness of the place.

2. *Speak in your own voice, using your own manner of description and your own choice of descriptive phrasing.* Granted, this is tricky advice. You don't want to be original for the sake of being original—there's certainly no virtue in that! On the other hand, you don't want to exhume worn out descriptions and cliché expressions* that you yourself would find boring. You have your own way of seeing things, and you want your language to reflect that uniqueness. This special quality is what readers look for in a piece of writing.

3. *Make sure your description has a sense of purpose.* Your readers should not only enjoy the description in itself, but they should also know why you have bothered to present it. Perhaps you want them to know what to expect when they visit the place you have described. Or maybe you want them simply to acquire some insight into the nature of a given region.

As you read through the following feature about Haleakala National Park, Hawaii, try to determine how well the author has incorporated these three staples of descriptive writing:

Ten thousand feet above the shoreline of Maui, the crater-topped mountain Haleakala is usually enfolded in a thick layer of isolating clouds. In late afternoon you can sometimes see your shadow cast against a wall of mist and surrounded by a rainbowlike aura. But when the clouds part as you're standing on the crater's rim, you can gaze out on 19 square miles of utter volcanic desolation, a scene that evokes the world after a holocaust or *The Martian Chronicles.*

The surface of the crater floor, 3,000 feet below, is covered with sand and finely ground stones colored red, yellow, gray, and black. The flat ground rises here and there to form cinder cones shaped like giant boils; the largest is 600 feet high.

The area is nearly devoid of vegetation save for a bizarre plant called

---
*See Chapter 14, "Exploring Words and Meanings," Euphemisms and Clichés.

ahinahina, or silversword, which grows on the sides of cinder cones and resembles a fiber-optic light sculpture. With its daggerlike, silver-hued leaves, the plant can reach a height of eight feet over a period of 20 years. Then it blooms for the first and only time, spreading thousands of seeds across the harsh volcanic sands.

The silversword's rigid life cycle is a kind of metaphor of the formation of the island. Hot magma rose from the earth's core like steam escaping from a pressure cooker and broke through the fragile crust, erupting through the ocean floor. Over the millennia, the volcanic mound that would eventually be called Haleakala grew higher and higher, breaking the ocean's surface and rising to its present height of 10,023 feet. The last recorded eruption was in 1790, and scientists now describe the volcano as dormant.

Elsewhere on the island, seeds carried by birds and by ocean currents took root, resulting in an incredible diversity of species. This diversity is graphically illustrated on the volcano's eastern slope, whose tropical rain forest receives 250 inches of rain annually. Mirrorlike pools connected by a series of waterfalls stand amid dense growths of mangoes, guavas, and bamboo. Strange pictographs painted by the early Polynesians are found on rocks throughout the forest.

Hiking is rugged in Haleakala because of the high altitude and the steepness of the trails. Ascents from the crater floor are especially rigorous, so be sure to make frequent stops and hike at a moderate pace. . . .

The Halemauu Trail (the best hiking trail) starts off just 3.6 miles from park headquarters at an altitude of 8,000 feet. Follow it one and a half miles over low hills to the crater rim. The descent into the crater is another steep two miles. Inside the crater, the terrain levels out again as the trail winds among the towering cinder cones. After a total distance of 10 miles, the Halemauu Trail terminates at a spot where there are backcountry campsites and rustic cabins. Stop here for the night; you'll need the rest.

America, Spring 1984

Did you notice how the author has incorporated each of the three staples of descriptive writing? First he places emphasis on the objects themselves by evoking particulars—for example, the crater's surface being "covered with sand and finely ground stones"; the "cinder cones shaped like giant boils." The author is also speaking in his own voice; a personality seems to be present behind the phrasing, as in this sentence: "In late afternoon you can sometimes see your shadow cast against a wall of mist and surrounded by a rainbowlike aura." Finally, we can sense the author's aim—to make readers want to visit Haleakala National Park—through his emphasis of the strange and exotic, of the great diversity of life forms and natural phenomena.

Writing an Extended Description of a Person

One of the most pleasurable writing activities is the *character sketch*, or *profile*. Somehow we never seem to be at a loss for ideas when choosing possible subjects. Our families and acquaintances, even complete strangers, quickly come to mind.

Because every human being is like every other human being in some ways, and very different in others, we're always intrigued by people. We love to observe them, to make their acquaintance, to interact with them, and we love to read and write about them, too. Almost instinctively, we scrutinize an individual's physical characteristics, alert for possible clues to the personality lurking underneath. But although any rational connections between, let's say, someone's deep and intense almond-dark eyes and that person's passionate (or compassionate) personality will forever be conjectural, we continue to make those assumptions anyway—perhaps because we love to fantasize and to make our own personal associations. We may also say of some persons that they have "cruel mouths," or that they strut around with "aloof expressions." When it comes to extreme emotional responses, however, the message is usually unmistakable; most of us are quite familiar with the look of, say, anger or shock that can register in a person's face.

There is something truly magical about capturing someone's character in words, which is why this kind of writing can be so rewarding. We love to read about people because nothing can stir our emotions the way people can. We do not exaggerate one bit when we say of characters in great literary works—characters like Huck and Jim, Romeo and Juliet, and like Emma Bovary and Willy Loman and Ralph Ellison's invisible man—that they are unforgettable.

What should you keep in mind when writing about a person or persons, real or fictional? Above all, keep the person firmly in mind while you are writing about him or her. To spur your memory, and to avoid omitting anything important, prepare a character inventory sheet. On this sheet you should list the following vital statistics: name, age, sex, ethnic background, education, employment history, and marital status. Include also important details of physical appearance, starting from the head and working downwards, as well as personality characteristics. For example, is he or she quick-tempered? moody? selfish or generous? whimsical? intellectual? unpredictable? fun to be around? weird?

But remember, try not to let your character sketch read like your inventory sheet! Don't even look at your inventory sheet unless you reach a snag in your writing and need a cue to spur you on. Furthermore, don't be content to present a static description of your subject. Dramatize as well. Show the character(s) involved in some activity, and let that activity reveal even more about his or her nature. Patricia Hampl illustrates this concept in the following provocative description of her grandmother:

> My grandmother worked at her prettiness even as a very old woman. Sunday was the day of great dinners; it was also the day for beauty, when she went to church. . . . She usually wore a print dress of definite, not subtle, color. She always wore a hat. A serious one, too formidable for her small, round self. It was often a dark, two-layer cake of a hat with a net veil, which she turned up over the crown like a pouf of meringue. . . . The veil gave an incongruous dash of airiness to the solid helmet, which she wore dead center, pulled down carefully over a forehead, which, she said as she pulled on the hat, "was too high and had to be lowered," as if the body were a problem for an architect to resolve.
>
> She walked proudly, her short legs perilously bowed; she'd had rickets as a child. . . . Her face, with the exquisite skin that was made more perfect rather than ruined by its map of wrinkles, had been rouged and powdered with a dusty puff before we left the house. Her mouth looked like two mouths, superimposed. One was the larger, thin-lipped undermouth of mauve flesh; the other was a surprised little red mouth of lipstick set on the first like a cartoon kiss. This red mouth never stayed long, faded gradually, but it was always bright and fresh as we began our walk.
>
> Patricia Hampl, *A Romantic Education*

Patricia Hampl has presented a dynamic rather than a static image of her grandmother. From the first sentence, "My grandmother worked at her prettiness, even as a very old woman," your interest is snagged. The strong phrasing, "worked at her prettiness," is the key. Observe how this author intertwines description with narration in a sentence like, "She walked proudly, her short legs perilously bowed; she'd had rickets as a child."

What's the best way to involve your readers quickly? to work that magic that so intrigues readers? to make your characters come to life? The secret is to use vivid language. Keep your senses alert for slack, anemic phrasing; for weak verbs, such as forms of the verb "to be"; and for lifeless expressions. With this idea in mind, consider the following passage:

> Antonio was an extremely handsome young man in his late teens. He had curly jet-black hair and intense black eyes that seemed to pierce right through you when he looked at you. He sprouted a thin moustache, which added to his eighteen years. Antonio was as much a practical joker as he was a serious student (he was majoring in economics), concerned about his

future. He was politically conscious, too, and could hold an audience's undivided attention as he spoke eloquently about the inadequate Chicano studies programs at those few universities that even had them.

Antonio sounds like a fascinating person, but we have to squint through the thin, unenthusiastic description of him to realize that. What might the author do to strengthen the writing? First of all, she needs to be less dependent on weak verbs: Antonio *was* an extremely handsome young man; he *had* curly, jet-black hair; he *was* politically conscious. Second, she should try to avoid weak expressions and generalities. Instead of announcing that Antonio is a handsome young man, why not describe the particular facial characteristics that contribute to his handsomeness? Finally, the example is a static summary from beginning to end; we do not see Antonio in action.

Writing a Personal-Experience Narrative

Every one of us can probably recall experiences that would be of interest to others and therefore worth writing about. Beginning writers sometimes have a difficult time thinking of an appropriate experience to write about because they too hastily pass over an experience as trivial: One such writer might think, Let's see, I visited the farming town where I was born. . . . Who'd want to read about a bunch of smelly barnyard animals, or about some of the gross things you have to do to keep a farm running smoothly?" The answer is, *lots* of people, provided that the writer allows the experience to shed light on some central point or theme. If a writer wants to develop a narrative about revisiting a farm of one's childhood, he or she might choose as a theme the human need for a more intimate contact with the earth, with animal life—a relationship so often lost to city dwellers.

College senior Thomas Hogendijk once worked as a doorman for an orchestra hall. If you think that such a line of work wouldn't offer much material for a personal-experience narrative, you may well have second thoughts when you finish reading the essay.*

---

*Compare this draft of the narrative with an earlier draft, which appears in Chapter 15, "Revising Your Work." Note how changes in wording and tone can affect the mood and thematic direction of the work. Keep in mind that these changes do not always improve the work. As you compare the two versions, decide for yourself which changes are effective and which are not.

CONFESSIONS OF A DOORMAN

I pulled on my gloves, dabbed a spot from my coat for the third time, and checked my tie. White tuxedos are funny—they seem to glow. I glowed at curbside, between two glowing white urns.

A few of the symphony staff stood among the mezzanine railing, just above a billowing tassled banner announcing the gala opening. The sweet odor of stewed tomatoes from a nearby Hunt's Bottling Company mixed with the warm August breeze and the brassy cadences of a Corelli quintet. I tugged at my vest and forced myself to stand up straight and to look serious.

I liked to watch my hands flash through the dark, opening long, black doors. "Good evening," I would say and turn my hand demurely to accept the palm of a lady.

You're supposed to tip me . . . jerk! I would think, directing just that soured gaze of annoyance at the escort. No, San José's rich lack the knowledge of etiquette concerning their social subordinates. Oh, they act the part well enough, but were more often than not surprised at me, so much so as to giggle nervously and to forget my tips altogether.

A Datsun pulled up to the curb. Do I have to open the doors of Datsuns? The woman inside shielded herself with her purse as I opened the door. She jumped back, pushed herself back into her seat. Did she think I was going to rape her? Her husband, seemingly afraid of a similar fate, reached over her, slammed the door, and sped off.

San José tried hard to be San Francisco. Mink, sable, chinchilla (I think); diamonds and sapphires and emeralds, silk handkerchiefs, hairpieces, and this year's face-lift.

I tried hard to ignore the old man. Dressed in rags, he walked very slowly along the curb, then stopped just next to one of the urns and leaned against the worn handle of his shopping cart, smiling. It was stuffed with tattered Safeway bags filled with old clothes, crushed aluminum cans, and dirty 16-ounce bottles of Pepsi. In the little basket in front was propped a gold box filled with long-stemmed yellow roses. He started moving things around and seemed at once to feel my face. He looked up, grinned and turned his head to one side, like the RCA dog.

I was startled by his clear eyes. "Uhh . . . good evening!" *My God, I said to myself, what is happening? I just said good evening to a bum!* I coupled my hands behind me, thrust out my chest and turned to the street, ignoring him. He'd go away, I was certain.

"Oh, and a very good evening to you too sir!" His voice cut through me, high-pitched, yet not harsh or crass. It had an elegance of modulation, as if this raggedy street vendor were a gentleman in disguise.

A Mercedes pulled up. I opened the door, ignoring the old man. But he suddenly wheeled his cart up to us, thrusting out a rose to the woman, saying with his head tilted just that way, "Here, Miss, a beautiful flower for a beautiful lady!" Her escort pushed the rose and extended arm of the old man away, repulsed, and rushed the woman away. Unfortunate beast, I thought to myself, dusting my lapels, hoping he would go away.

But he did not go away, and I was getting angry. "I just love it," he continued. "Everybody looks so nice, I just love it, and you look so nice too, you must love it too!"

I ignored him.

He stepped closer. I couldn't help smelling his breath, warm, pungent, and sweet with wine.

"Maybe this town will get some class after all," he whispered, leaning close to my ear, breaking quietly into a wheezing chuckle.

I just kept looking down the street at an imaginary limousine.

"Here," he said, "give this to your girlfriend, or your mother—to anybody who is beautiful. . . ." He tilted his head, and I could feel his eyes, deep and clear, staring. ". . . anybody beautiful!"

I accepted the rose, thinking it would shut him up and that he would leave.

I stood twirling the rose between my fingers, some dirt from the stem getting on my gloves. A car pulled up. "Good evening!" I exclaimed, opening the door, helping the woman onto the sidewalk. The old man pushed his cart across the red carpet, rang his bicycle bell, and bowed very deeply in a grand sweep, saying, "Good evening! Oh, good evening very beautiful lady!" The couple paused and looked nervously at him, then walked quickly in a large arc around him, shaking their heads.

Thomas Hogendijk

Mr. Hogendijk has managed to take what on the surface appears to be a rather uneventful situation and develop it so a theme emerges. The narrative reveals interesting insights about the way one class of people regards another class. The affluent people attending the concert are contemptuous of the doorman, perhaps because he is not "one of them," even though he is dressed like them. The doorman, in turn, is contemptuous of them because of their arrogance. Ironically, he is just as arrogant as they are—something we discover when he responds to the bum, a flower vendor who refuses to put people into classes, but instead innocently, perhaps naively, regards them all as beautiful.

Did the author think through the theme carefully before he began writing? Most likely he recorded a subconscious response to the situation as he actually experienced it—the experience of encountering a shabby flower vendor amidst formally dressed concert goers. To develop a narrative work, the author must reshape the raw experience by highlighting specific details and omitting others, and then think in terms of the rising curve of development mentioned in Chapter 4. How would you describe the rising curve in Thomas Hogendijk's narrative?

Summary

Expressive essays are rarely purely expressive, just as informative essays are rarely purely informative. An essay is primarily expressive when it uses techniques traditionally associated with fiction: narration, or storytelling, and description, a way to make an actual incident or phenomenon come alive in the reader's imagination. While an author is depicting the subject, he or she is also conveying an attitude, which is sometimes referred to in fiction or poetry as a *theme*. The two principal types of expressive essays are the *narrative* piece, which tells a story and builds suspense or intrigue and then culminates in a climactic moment; and the *descriptive* piece, which may concentrate on a particular setting or person(s), or both. Character portraits not only depict an individual's physical characteristics and personality, but they often provide readers with insight into human nature.

FOR DISCUSSION

1. What did you find most memorable about the description of Mt. Haleakala? Identify the details that work best for you, those that allow you to envision the setting. Which details, if any, did not work quite as well? How might they be strengthened?

2. Browse through several issues of a travel magazine such as *Travel and Leisure*, the travel section found in the Sunday edition of your local newspaper, or any of the in-flight magazines published by the major airlines. Read two articles, and then determine the similarities and differences between the two authors' techniques of description.

3. Discuss the use of description and narration in any one of the examples presented in this chapter or in Chapter 4. Keep in mind the three problems common to descriptive writing discussed on pp. 63–66.

4. Evaluate the uses of description and narration in the following passages. What could each author do to strengthen the descriptive and narrative passages, if anything?

A

At the age of seventeen I was poorly dressed and funny-looking, and went around thinking about myself in the third person. "Allen Dow smiled a thin, sardonic smile." Consciousness of a special destiny made me both arrogant and shy. Years before, when I was eleven or twelve, just on the brink of ceasing to be a little boy, my mother and I, one Sunday afternoon—my father was busy, or asleep—hiked up to the top of Shale Hill, a child's mountain that formed one side of the valley that held our town. There the town lay under us, Olinger, perhaps a thousand homes . . . blocks of brick houses, one- and two-family, the homes of my friends, sloping down to the pale thread of the Alton Pike, which strung together the high school, the tennis courts, the movie theatre, the town's few stores and gasoline stations, the elementary school, the Lutheran Church. . . . It seemed the entire county was lying exposed under a thin veil of haze. I was old enough to feel embarrassment at standing there alone with my mother, beside a wind-stunted spruce tree, on a long spine of shale. Suddenly she dug her fingers into the hair on my head and announced, "There we all are, and there we'll all be forever." She hesitated before the word "forever," and hesitated again before adding, "Except you, Allen. You're going to fly." (John Updike, "Flight," from *Pigeon Feathers and Other Stories*)

B

In arriving [in Paris] from other countries one is struck with a certain want of dignity in the French face. I do not know, however, whether this is anything worse than the fact that the French face is expressive; for it may be said that . . . to express anything is to compromise with one's dignity. . . . As regards the lower classes, at any rate, the impression I speak of always passes away; you perceive that the good looks of the French working-people are to be found in their look of intelligence. These people, in Paris, strike me afresh as the cleverest, the most perceptive, and intellectually speaking, the most human of their kind. The Paris *ouvrier*, with his . . . expressive, demonstrative, agreeable eye, his meagre limbs, his irregular, pointed features, his sallow complexion, his face at once fatigued and animated, his light, nervous organisation, is a figure that I always encounter again with pleasure. In some cases he looks depraved and perverted, but at his worst he looks refined; he is full of vivacity of perception, of something that one can appeal to. (Henry James, *Portraits of Places*)

C

Le Corbusier was a thin, sallow, nearsighted man who went about on a white bicycle, wearing a close-fitting black suit, a white shirt, a black tie, round black owl-eye glasses, and a black bowler hat. To startled onlookers, he said he dressed in this fashion so as to look as neat and precise and anonymous as possible, to be the perfect mass-producible wire figure for the Machine Age. He called the houses he designed "machines for living." Le Corbusier traveled to Germany and Holland and was well known in all the compounds and at all the congresses . . . and panel discussions, wherever the insistent beat of the manifesto, the song of the compounds was heard: *We declare—! We declare—! We declare! We declare!* He was intense, he was riveting, he was brilliant. (Tom Wolfe, *From Bauhaus to Our House*)

D

The lower part of the castle was hollowed into several intricate cloisters; and it was not easy for one . . . to find the door that opened into the cavern. An awful silence reigned throughout those subterraneous regions, except, now and then, some blasts of wind that shook the doors [Isabella] had passed, and which, grating on the rusty hinges, were re-echoed through that long labyrinth of darkness. Every murmur struck her with new terror. (Horace Walpole, *The Castle of Otranto*)

5. In the following essay, Ellen Goodman sketches the faddish dining habits of a modern couple. Goodman's aim is clearly humorous and satirical. What specifically can you point to in her descriptive style that produces this effect?

SOCIAL NIBBLING

They were sitting under the fern next to mine. I began fern-dropping.

The woman ordered Perrier on the rocks with lime. The man wanted his straight up. Ah yes, it would be another three-Perrier lunch during which business would be discussed under properly misted hanging plants, over tastefully appointed tables with white plates and green napkins, sprinkled by yard-long pepper mills.

That is the way it goes now at urban lunch spas that stretch under some giant greenhouse from one coast to the other.

The menu was nothing if not discreet. The fare it offered with such artistic flourish was, of course, restrained. Modest. No roast beef would ever bloody its plates. No french fry would grease its side dishes.

The platters were lean enough to pose for the camera; the luncheon menu so light that it cost more per ounce than caviar.

When the woman's soup came to the table, it was a clear broth with six discreet rings of scallion floating on the top. The man and woman glanced at the French bread the waiter brought, as if it were a gate crasher. Too polite to kick the interloper out, they merely ignored it.

Finally, the lunch arrived. His was spinach with a smattering of mushrooms and a sprinkling of egg whites. Hers was watercress and Boston lettuce with a modest touch of Stilton.

They nibbled through the pasture of choice greens, talking enthusiastically about their health regimens. Placing the watercress neatly into the lean frame under the silk shirt, she shared the wonders of running. Filling his European-cut body with spinach, he talked about his stationary bicycle and his universal exercise machine and the assorted pushups and downs of his mid-life.

I, sitting under my own fern, began wondering if pieces of the plant would be macheted and arranged charmingly under a dressing on a platter in front of me. I wanted to tell the waiter that F. Scott Fitzgerald once recommended giving up spinach for Lent.

Suddenly, I had an urge for a hot oven-grinder with a side of onion rings and ketchup, hold the hot peppers. Suddenly I longed for coconut pie; I hate coconut pie.

It occurred to me that to order anything more massive than the five-inch square of blue fish offered to me would be to commit a social gaffe of urban enormity. The bouncer would, no doubt, get rid of me.

It occurred to me, furthermore, that the right sort of people do not eat food in public anymore. They merely graze and water themselves.

Self-control, we call it, with a straight face. In the middle of international chaos, we manage to worry about staying in shape. When everything is out of control, we try to control our waistline. Self-discipline chic.

If I had called a halt to all the munching, and polled the people under the ferns, I would surely have found ethical relativists and psychical absolutists. I would have found uncertain people in an insecure environment who maintain food regimens and exercise—religiously.

Their hair shirts would be warmup suits and their Ten Commandments would begin with "Thou Shalt Not Eat Pasta." They would arrive at the morning weigh-in as if the scale were an alter offering proof of their virtue.

The grandparents of urban life in a safer time competed with overindulgence, orgies of oysters. Now, in stress, we compete with underindulgence, twigs of watercress: from excess of feasting to excess of fasting. We whip ourselves in shape and are still called hedonists, flagellate ourselves for what we eat and are still labeled narcissists. We regard the sins of the flesh as inches that must be worked off. Maybe we are Me-sochists. Who knows.

The man and woman finished their tea and, ducking the fern, arose, lean and hungry, from the luncheon fast. Another challenge won.

My own leaves arrived. I forked them and thought about what A. A. Milne once wrote: "What I say is that if a man really likes potatoes, he must be a pretty decent sort of fellow." I'll nibble to that.

Ellen Goodman, February 1980

FOR WRITING

1. Over the next few days, prepare a verbal sketchbook of character descriptions, all set roughly within a single environment, such as in a classroom, at a sporting event, or in a concert hall, zoo, or hospital. It is important that you be physically present in this environment. Next, shape a narrative that will shed an interesting light on this environment. Include in the narrative at least half of the characters you've described earlier.

2. Think about an interesting place you've visited recently—a historical landmark, a little-known museum or recreation area, or perhaps an unusual eating place or lodge chanced upon when driving down a back road—and take detailed notes. Then write a travelog, targeting it toward an audience of travelers who are looking for easily accessible, out-of-the-ordinary places to visit.

3. Write a personal-experience narrative in which a single incident or encounter plays a central role. The incident or encounter need not resemble a TV sit-com, but it ought somehow to help you elucidate a theme, a central point. Here are some possibilities to help jog your memory: an embarrassing moment at work, at a social event, or with close friends; a frightful moment; a strange encounter with someone; and a mystical or inspirational experience.

   Remember to visualize your characters and to describe them in enough detail to allow your readers to visualize them as well. Also try to begin the narrative on a note of intrigue, and to follow a rising curve of development.

Principles of Development:
CHAPTER 6
Aiming to Inform

Most of the world's writing tries to inform—to disclose facts, to explain principles and procedures, to clarify confusing matters, and to analyze. When writing to inform, you share with readers what you have learned about a given topic.

Why share? Well, aside from the fact that information is a high-demand commodity, the very effort you expend to write about a subject develops your expertise in that subject. Becoming an expert means more than acquiring information; it also means knowing the techniques for presenting that information to others. In this chapter you will learn about those techniques.

Presenting Information

Think of a microscope. What can you say about the microscope that others would regard as information? First, you can *define* what a microscope is. Then you can extend your definition—*classify* the different kinds of microscopes that exist and *divide* the microscope into its constituent parts. Then you can *describe* its appearance and its function, briefly *narrate* the microscope's history, and then *analyze* the effectiveness, say, of certain laboratory applications of the microscope.

We have just isolated five techniques for presenting information in an essay: defining, classifying and dividing, narrating, describing, and analyzing. Let's take a closer look at each of them.

Defining

The root meaning of "define" (from the Latin *definire*) is to set boundaries or limitations. In a categorical, or dictionary, *definition*, an item to be defined is first identified as belonging to a certain class and is then distinguished from other members of that class. Here, for example, is an *American Heritage Dictionary* definition of "microscope":

> An optical instrument that uses a combination of lenses to produce magnified images of small objects, especially of objects too small to be seen by the unaided eye.

Notice that the definition first introduces the class to which the microscope belongs (optical instruments); then it describes how a microscope differs from other members of that class (from other optical instruments).

As you know, dictionary definitions tend to be impersonal, detached, succinct. They are starting points for writers aiming to interest as well as to inform the reader. If you wanted to write an essay about microscopes, for example, you might begin with a dictionary definition; then you might quickly proceed to include additional meanings and associations drawn from your own experience and which you consider to be necessary to convey an accurate understanding of what a microscope really is. This is known as *stipulative definition*. By stipulating a definition, the writer departs from the *general* meaning of the subject to include *particular* insights or applications based on the writer's own experience or reasoning.

Here is a stipulative definition of a microscope. Try to identify the words or phrases that extend or alter the standard definition:

> When I use the term "microscope" I want it to refer to more than the physical instrument itself, to more than the usual connotation of coldly scientific precision, seeking only to reduce the physical world to its atomistic parts. Rather, I want "microscope" to signify the creative searching for and exam-

ining of fundamental parts that inevitably will lead to a greater comprehension of the whole.

Stipulative definition places emphasis on the writer's individual insights and experience with the subject in question. By doing this, the writer not only elucidates a concept but illuminates it as well.

Another kind of definition, one frequently used by writers in the qualitative sciences and the quantitative sciences alike, is known as *operational definition*. Instead of defining what a term *is*, the writer defines what the term *does*. The following is an operational definition of water erosion adapted from *The Way Things Work Book of Nature*:

> First, water drops disperse soil particles downhill; once water saturation sets in, the ground matter begins to flow. Sedimentation occurs at the foot of the slope, and water (carrying more sediment) runs from the small rills that the sediment-flow gouged, making the gouges ever deeper.

If we wish, we could convert this explanation to a categorical definition: "Water erosion is a process of dissolution whereby sediment is washed away along rills gouged into a slope by water that had saturated the soil."

One more type of definition commonly used when introducing an unfamiliar term is known as *lexical definition*, whereby the writer examines the nature of the word itself, supplying its etymology (theoretical or known origin) and possibly the evolution of its usage. A lexical definition of microscope would call attention to its derivation from the Latin word *micro* (Greek, *mikros*), meaning "small"; and from the Latin word *scopium*, which was derived from the Greek word *skopein*, meaning "to see."

Classifying and Dividing

In a sense, classifying and dividing comprise two additional ways of defining; when we determine the appropriate category in which to place our subject and examine its constituent parts, we provide additional insight into its nature.

Classifying

You will recall that a traditional dictionary definition places the term you are defining into a class, or category, before it goes on to distinguish the term from other members of that class. But when writers concern themselves with the rhetorical device of classification, they are interested in the logical principles that reveal why the item in question belongs to one category and not to another. In your biology courses, for example, you may have learned about the great eighteenth-century botanist, Carolus Linnaeus, who advanced the state of modern science with his system of taxonomic classification. His method classified every living organism into kingdom, phylum, class, order, family, genus, and species. Such a classification scheme simultaneously identifies an organism by its genus name and its species name (e.g., *Homo sapiens*—human beings; *Lumbricus terrestris*—earthworms), and demonstrates its relationship to other organisms.

Now let's see how classification can be useful to writers in dealing with any kind of subject matter. Someone writing about the vases of ancient Greece, for example, might want to introduce the topic as Erwin O. Christensen has done in *A Pictorial History of Western Art*:

> Vases of historic Greece fall into four major styles: geometric (900–700 B.C.), often called eighth-century style; orientalizing, also called early black-figured (700–550 B.C.) or seventh-century style; black-figured, also called later-Attic black-figured (550–480 B.C.) or sixth-century style, corresponding to archaic sculpture; [and] red-figured (525–300 B.C.).

After setting up his classification scheme, the author then discusses each category; it is at this stage that the opportunity for division arises.

Dividing

If classifying means forming logical categories of entities, then dividing means breaking up those logical categories into their constituent parts. An organism, such as a tree, may be *classified* by species, such as oak, maple, palm, or pine; a single species may be classified according to its subspecies, such as Norway pine and ponderosa pine. But a tree is *divided* into parts: leaves, trunk, root system. Similarly, in his discussion of ancient Greek vases, Erwin O. Christensen frequently uses the division technique to help his readers envision the characteristics of each variety. For example, he says the following of the geometric-style vases:

> In this first truly Greek geometric vase the shape itself partakes of an organic quality that in the later Doric style of architecture comes to its full maturity. This organic sense relates to the structure of the human figure, where each member is shaped to carry out its function. Though tentative and uncertain, the base is emphasized as a separate part to stand on, like a foot. The neck meets the body with a determined break; like a real neck, it comes to a halt before the shoulders slope off.

Notice that the author alludes to the parts of the vase to demonstrate the *interrelationship* of parts into an organic whole. Division is thus valuable in providing readers with insight into the way parts interact to form a coherent whole, and is not used merely to reduce an entity to its lowest terms.

Narrating in an Explanatory Context

You'll recall from Chapter 4 that narration means storytelling. Remember also that storytelling is both true, based on personal experience, and fictional, put together from invented experiences that are often based on fact, or that at least give the impression that they *could* be true. But narration plays a vital role in informational writing, too. It is the rhetorical technique that conveys the history of the subject at hand. The very word "history" is derived from the French word *histoire*, meaning story. Since every subject has a history, historical narration is relevant to every subject, without exception. Here's an example, taken from Anthony Huxley's *Plant and Planet*, of how narration may be used in a botanical context:

> The forests began to diminish and the grasslands to spread in the Miocene [approximately 10–25 million years ago], as the grazing mammals became more important. In this period many entirely new plant families make their appearance. Among the plants were many modern prairie grasses, bulrushes, and a host of familiar deciduous trees: beeches, maples, walnuts, oaks, Sweet Gum, Sour Gum, Judas Tree, Mock Orange, and so on. Conifers persisted, pines, redwoods and cedars, for instance, being plentiful.

The information derived from this narrative example could easily and quickly be picked up from a chart, but there is more to the presentation of information than speed and efficiency. Readers tend to absorb and comprehend more when the material is presented in an absorbing manner, as in a story. Charts are certainly interesting and even absorbing, but they do not offer the same degree of involvement that discourse offers.

Describing in an Explanatory Context

The evocative power of description, the way it enhances a reader's involvement with the material, makes it an important rhetorical technique for conveying information. Notice how the nineteenth-century American historian, Francis Parkman, in his book *France and England in North America* uses description in this manner to elucidate a bizarre ritual practiced by the Huron Indians—the Feast of the Dead:

> The corpses were lowered from their scaffolds, and lifted from their graves. Their coverings were removed by certain functionaries appointed for the office, and the hideous relics arranged in a row, surrounded by the weeping, shrieking, howling concourse. The spectacle was frightful. Here were all the village dead of the last twelve years. The [Jesuit] priests, connoisseurs in such matters, regarded it as a display of mortality so edifying, that they hastened to summon their French attendants to contemplate and profit by it. Each family reclaimed its own, and immediately addressed itself to removing what remained of flesh from its bones. These, after being tenderly caressed, with tears and lamentations, were wrapped in skins and adorned with pendent robes of fur. In the belief of the mourners, they were sentient and conscious. A soul was thought still to reside in them; and to this notion, very general among Indians, is in no small degree due that extravagant attachment to the remains of their dead, which may be said to mark the race.

Description may also be used to enhance our understanding of a natural phenomenon or process. Here, for example, is a description of earthquake movement:

> During an earthquake the earth moves in two ways: it shakes and it rocks. The shaking hurls groceries off of shelves, cracks or shatters plate-glass windows, and sends plaster falling from the ceiling. The rocking is what seems to turn the ground (and human stomachs!) to jelly, and what sends skyscrapers weaving like hula dancers.

Description can also include *comparison*.* How is *A* similar to *B*? How is *A* dissimilar? Description that answers these questions contributes to a broader understanding of the phenomenon at hand. When you travel, for example, it is only natural to compare one country or city with another. If you are a car buff, you probably enjoy comparing different makes and styles of automobiles. Likewise, gourmets compare the way two chefs prepare shrimp scampi; music lovers examine the differences and similarities between the impressionistic techniques of Ravel and Debussy; sports fans note the contrasting boxing styles of Ali and Fraser, or the tennis serves of McEnroe and Connors; and students of modern literature compare the prose styles of Vonnegut and Updike.

Let's look at an interesting application of the technique of compari-

---

*"Comparison" is used here to mean comparison of similarities *and* dissimilarities. The term "contrast" is sometimes used to indicate dissimilarities only.

son. In his famous book *The Art of Loving* psychoanalyst Erich Fromm compares motherly love to fatherly love—a comparison that, while of debatable accuracy, is nonetheless clearly orchestrated:

> Mother loves the newborn infant because it is her child, not because the child has fulfilled any specific condition, or lived up to any specific expectation. . . . The relationship to father is quite different. Mother is the home we come from, she is nature, soil, the ocean; father does not represent any such natural home. He has little connection with the child in the first years of its life, and his importance for the child in this early period cannot be compared with that of the mother. But while father does not represent the natural world, he represents the other pole of human existence: the world of thought, of man-made things, of law and order, of discipline, of travel and adventure.

When comparing *X* with *Y*, you have a variety of organizational strategies to choose from. You may first present all of *X*'s traits, then all of *Y*'s, then summarize *X*'s and *Y*'s traits in a single concluding paragraph. Another approach is to compare *X* with *Y* throughout the essay, examining one trait at a time. Erich Fromm uses this second strategy in another section of *The Art of Loving*:

> The child, after six, begins to need father's love, his authority and guidance. Mother has the function of making him secure in life; father has the function of teaching him, guiding him. . . .

When conducting your own comparisons, however, concentrate more on the ideas you are trying to get across than on the organizational pattern. Writers who are too concerned about pattern during the more creative first-draft stage run the risk of overlooking insights. Concentrate on organizational matters during the more critical second-draft stage.

Analyzing

You are analyzing something when you are probing its nature to determine *how* or *why* it works. A phenomenon may be defined and classified, its appearance and function described, and its historical background summarized, but readers would still not comprehend the phenomenon's process. Let's return to our earlier example of earthquake movement. In that example, the process is described but not analyzed. We are brought to *see* how the earth moves, but we are not led to *comprehend* the causes underlying the appearance. The discussion of cause-effect relationships is what analysis is all about. Here is the way David Alt and Donald Hyndman analyze earthquake activity in their book *Roadside Geology of Northern California*:

> An easy way to visualize movement on a fault is to imagine two thick slabs of soft foam rubber sliding past each other with their cut edges touching. They move hitching along in sharp jerks as the edges of the slabs catch and stick together until the rubber stretches enough to snap them free. Faults move in the same way. Rocks on opposite sides catch, accumulate strain for a while by bending as though they were a giant rubber slab, and then pull free and snap past each other in a sudden jerk releasing the accumulated strain energy all at once as an earthquake.

Did you notice how reader-aware these authors are? They invite the reader to visualize, to imagine the process, which they make imaginable through a most versatile device called *analogy*. An analogy is a comparison between the object or phenomenon to be analyzed, in this case earthquake movement, and an object or phenomenon considered to be much more familiar to the reader, in this case slabs of foam rubber rubbing against each other. Analogy is a way of helping the reader to visualize what is being described.

Another noteworthy facet of an analysis is *vivid diction*, illustrated in the preceding example by the expressions "hitching along," "sharp jerks," and "snap them free," for example. These descriptions both aid understanding and give delight; they are both accurate and colorful. (Resist the fallacy that accuracy and color are incompatible!) The example's most important aspect, however, is its depiction of *cause and effect*: The texture of the edges of the crustal slabs *causes* them to stick together momentarily as they move alongside each other in opposite directions; the act of sticking together *causes* the slabs to snap free, which in turn *causes* the earth to shake.

Albert Einstein had a knack for applying simple analogies to elucidate complex concepts of physics such as space. In the following example from *Relativity: The Special and the General Theory*, he illustrates this talent:

> The idea of space . . . is suggested by certain primitive experiences. Suppose that a box has been constructed. Objects can be arranged in a certain way inside the box, so that it becomes full. The possibility of such arrangement is a property of the material object "box," something that is given with the box, the "space enclosed" by the box. This is something which is different for different boxes, something that is thought quite naturally as being independent of whether or not, at any moment, there are any objects at all in the box. When there are no objects in the box, its space appears to be "empty."

How the Rhetorical Devices Interact

Thus far we have paid individual attention to each rhetorical device—definition, classification/division, description, narration, and analysis. But when people sit down to write, they do not tell themselves ahead of time that they're going to do a definition section followed by a comparison section, or whatever. Writers familiar with these different techniques, however, will have an easier time of deciding how best to develop a given section of their essay-in-progress. They are fairly certain that strategies will come to *them*, rather than the other way around, when the need arises.

The following example will reveal the way in which many of the devices we've examined in this chapter interact.

JAZZ AND WEST AFRICAN MUSIC

What is the connection between jazz and West African music? Perhaps the most obvious similarity is the rhythm—not that a West African tribesman would like jazz because he wouldn't; the blending has gone too far. But take a tribal ceremony in Dahomey: the musicians are playing rattles, gongs, and other percussion instruments, while the tribesmen are dancing, singing, clapping, and stamping. The main instrument, however, is the drum—usually a set of three drums known to musicologists as a drum choir—because the gods speak through the drums, the dancers face the drums, and the tribe forms a circle around them.   *Analysis, Comparison*

Classification

At its peak, the sound may seem like a combination of disordered pneumatic drills. The music is polyrhythmic, that is, two or more separate rhythms are being played at the same time, maybe five or six. A common foundation for West African music is a combination of 3/4, 6/8, and 4/4 time signatures. It's as if an orchestra were playing the same tune as a waltz, a one-step, and a fox trot—all at the same time. And of course the singing, clapping, and stamping add further rhythmic complexities.   *Categorical definition ("polyrhythmic")*

Analogy

To a highly trained classical musician this West African music may sound like chaos. For the West Africans have no written music—they play from memory and by ear—and they don't follow anything as regular as the barlines of our European system of notation. In fact, in terms of one of our measures their rhythms seem to change right in the middle, a great stumbling block to musicologists when they try to write them down. And yet even the untrained listener can feel the power and drive and can somehow sense that the complicated parts of this rhythmic juggernaut fit together.   *Comparison*

By comparison, our jazz rhythms are fairly simple. We've come a long way but we certainly haven't caught up and maybe never will. Down in New Orleans, for example, some of the old-timers are still playing "Didn't He Ramble" on the way back from a funeral, but it sounds like a march. Jazz is traditionally approximated in notation as 4/4 or duple meter—actually it's more complex—and this march rhythm is basic. You can hear it plainly in the music of a New Orleans brass band, but something new has been added—the music *swings*. And it is apparent that this new ingredient didn't come from Europe.

> Operational definition ("jazz")

Theorists tell us that there is no limit to the complexities that can be superimposed upon march rhythm—and that is what jazz is doing. The basis of jazz is a march rhythm but the jazzman puts more complicated rhythms on top of it. He blows a variety of accents between and around, above and below, the march beat. It's a much more complicated process than syncopation, which is usually defined as stressing the normally weak beat, for syncopation sounds unutterably old-fashioned to a jazzman. A regular six-piece band playing in the New Orleans style can create rhythmic complexities which no machine yet invented can fully diagram.

> Categorical definition ("syncopation")

> Narration

At the start of a recording session Louis Armstrong, handkerchief in one hand and trumpet in the other, stands in front of the microphone and stamps out a steady rhythm. As the band picks it up, Armstrong's foot doubles the beat and starts tapping twice as fast. And as he sings and plays the trumpet he stresses accents *around and between* the taps of his foot. Recorded examples show that he has broken the measure down to sixteenths at least, but this is a standard jazz procedure.

Erroll Garner is justly famous for what jazzmen call "fooling around with the beat," because he doesn't seem to let his left hand know what his right hand is doing. In general, his left hand plays a steady 4/4 march rhythm, quite opposite to the modern trend, but his right hand is playing the melody in a variety of changing tempos: first he drags behind and then he more than catches up in constantly varying fractions of the beat. The effect is schizophrenic, like rubbing your stomach in one direction and the top of your head in another. A good example of this is at the beginning of the second chorus of "What Is This Thing Called Love?" by Garner.

> Analysis

> Analogy

> Analysis

Here is a quality that gives jazz some of its appeal. Psychologically, Garner's steady left hand creates and fulfills the expectancy of a continuous rhythm. His lag-along right hand, however, sets up a contrasting tension which is released when, by means of more unexpected accents, he catches up. It's like a sprinter who saves himself from falling on his face by an extra burst of speed. It's also a kind of rhythmic game. The effect on the listener varies: he may want to sing, dance, shout, or even hit somebody. Somehow he wants to express himself.

Marshall Stearns, *The Story of Jazz*

Summary

Conveying information consists of the following techniques: *defining* a term; *classifying* a term by establishing categories into which the various types of the item in question are placed; *dividing* an item or concept into its constituent parts to understand the relationship among those parts;

narrating the immediate and historical background to the issue or phenomenon; *describing* that background to recreate the item or concept in readers' minds; and *analyzing* the subject, determining cause-effect and spatial relationships associated with it, and comparing it with similar or dissimilar objects or concepts to comprehend better the distinguishing characteristics. These techniques of informative writing are seldom isolated from each other. Indeed, much informative writing makes use of all of these techniques to provide a deeper understanding of the underlying raw data.

FOR DISCUSSION

1. Present to the class your own stipulative definition of *information*.

2. Isolate the implicit definition of *information* in the following passage, then speculate on the possible implications of the author's assertions:

   In an ordinary conversation, information is conveyed when the speaker says something that changes the listener's knowledge. This means that the listener is in a state of uncertainty as to what message he will actually hear. . . . It may be highly improbable, and therefore very hard to predict, or it may be extremely probable, in which case the listener could have predicted it with ease. But the message will not be impossible, in the sense that it violates grossly the rules of grammar or meaning; otherwise it could not be called information at all. (Jeremy Campbell, *Grammatical Man*)

3. How is stipulative defining useful? Are there any potential problems associated with stipulating your own meaning for an established term?

4. Identify the essential difference between categorical, or dictionary, definitions and operative definitions. Can you think of examples where the distinction overlaps?

5. Identify the rhetorical device or devices used in the following examples. Have the authors used a dominant rhetorical device in each example?

   A

   It is a pious custom, in some Catholic countries, to honor the memory of saints by votive lights burnt before their pictures. The popularity of a saint, therefore, may be known by the number of these offerings. One, perhaps, is left to molder in the darkness of his little chapel; another may have a solitary lamp to throw its blinking rays athwart his effigy; while the whole blaze of adoration is lavished at the shrine of some beatified father of renown. The wealthy devotee brings his huge luminary of wax; the eager zealot his seven-branched candlestick; and even the mendicant pilgrim is by no means satisfied that sufficient light is thrown upon the deceased unless he hangs up his little lamp of smoking oil. The consequence is that in the eagerness to enlighten they are often apt to obscure. (Washington Irving, *The Sketch Book*)

B

A curious side effect of inflation is the psychological change that occurs in the human attitude toward money. It is as if we have a built-in psychological defense to protect us against the mental ravages threatened by declining currency.

Recently, for example, without even noticing it, I abandoned the habit of carrying all paper money in my wallet and took to stuffing bills of $1 and $5 denominations into my trouser pocket, which in the past had been habitually reserved for items of small value, like coins.

In my rigidly organized psychological system, the wallet was the repository for things of value—paper money, credit cards, permits issued by the more terrifying bureaucracies, lists of clothing sizes of persons who might retaliate if holidays and their birthdays were not observed with gift presentations, instructions for shipment of the remains in case of abrupt demise in some remote location and so forth.

The pants pocket, more easily, more thoughtlessly accessible to the right hand, has always been the place for things whose loss would not be a disaster. Toothpicks collected from the delicatessen counter, coins, chewing gum wrappers, lint and messages to telephone editors, lawyers and press agents immediately. (Russell Baker, *So This Is Depravity*)

C

Photography shows that there are enormous numbers of galaxies, diffuse objects of regular outline. The brightest of them are also the closest to us, and can be resolved into stars. The more remote galaxies cannot be so resolved, even with our most powerful instruments, so they look like dim, nebulous patches.

Even a cursory study of the photographs shows that the galaxies may be divided into two main classes. Some galaxies, rich in blue stars and interstellar gas, are of spiral structure; they are flattened and give clear indications of quick rotation. Others, poor in blue stars, have no spiral structure and are much less flattened, but they give the impression of an ellipsoid in a state of rotation, and are called elliptical galaxies. (E. L. Schatzman, *The Structure of the Universe*)

FOR WRITING

1. Comparisons are fun to do, so you may want to work on this exercise as a warmup before beginning an essay in which comparison would be a dominant rhetorical feature.

Compose one-page comparisons of one of the following pairs; whenever appropriate, use specific examples to support generalizations:

- Varsity football/professional football
- Egyptian pyramids/Aztec pyramids
- Uranium-235/Uranium-238
- Junior high teachers/senior high teachers
- Small town life/big city life
- Feline behavior/canine behavior
- Healthy competition/unhealthy competition
- Impressionism/expressionism in one art genre (e.g., painting, sculpture, literature)
- Two varieties of one musical genre (e.g., rock, country-western, jazz, classical)
- Two of your favorite actors
- Lifestyles of the wealthy/lifestyles of the poor
- Maternal and paternal love (if your views differ from Erich Fromm's)
- Brotherly (sisterly) love/spiritual love/romantic love

2. Compose a one-page analysis of one of the following topics:
   - The relationship between certain methods of study, and the degree of mastery of course material
   - The relationship between painting and photography (or between painting and music; or between painting and poetry)
   - The influence a teacher can have on a student (with regard to a certain subject)
   - How a person's manner of dress and grooming can influence another person's attitude toward that person

3. Select one of the following terms. First, compose a stipulative or operative definition for it; second, establish a classification scheme for it; finally, divide it into its constituent parts and describe each part:
   a. Windmill
   b. Encyclopedia
   c. Tennis racket
   d. Motorcycle
   e. Human bone (or muscle)
   f. Mushroom

g. Sailboat
h. Running shoes
i. Blood

COMPUTER WRITING

1. For students working in pairs at adjoining terminals: Bring your desk dictionary with you into the personal computer lab. Open a new file and name it STIPULAT.DEF, for stipulative defining. Open the dictionary at random and find any familiar word. If you wish, copy the principal definition, and remember to cite the name of the dictionary underneath it. Next, write your own definition of that same term in one paragraph, and instruct your partner to define the same term in his or her own manner. You may choose to be humorous, satirical, or even purely fanciful, but don't let your partner in on your scheme.

    Next, copy your partner's file onto your own file, and vice versa. *Caution*: If you are not sure of the file-copying procedure, read the instruction manual carefully or ask the lab assistant to help you. Now compare your definition of the given word with your partner's and discuss its strengths and shortcomings with him or her.

2. For personal computers with graphics capability: Reproduce a pie chart showing, for example, the disbursement of tax dollars per annum. Next, convert the information into a bar graph. Finally, write a paragraph describing the information you presented graphically.

3. Write an essay, either serious or humorous, comparing your writing habits before you learned word processing skills with your writing habits after you learned word processing skills.

CHAPTER 7
Projects in Informative Writing

When professional writers compose primarily to inform their readers, they have two major concerns. You may think finding something to write about would be one of them, but it's not: When they're not overflowing with ideas, most professional writers find digging up topics easy enough (and fun enough) to keep it from being a chore. Rather, professionals are mainly concerned with (1) gathering all the facts and details they need, or think they need (one isn't always certain early on), to develop their idea sufficiently, and (2) presenting the material so it interests as well as informs.

The gathering together of facts and details is better known as *research*. As explained in Chapter 3, research is important for all writing, not just for research papers and formal, scholarly research.* You do not need to begin an in-depth study of research methodology just to do some basic sleuthing. If you know how to use the card catalog, an encyclopedia, and a periodical index, and if you know how the library's book stacks and bound periodicals are arranged, then you can do research.

Research (or *background reading* or *information-searching*, if the word *research* causes you shortness of breath) is therefore a basic step in any kind of informational writing. This does not mean that you must do the research *before* you write; when the words want to come, let them. They

---

*See Chapter 10, "Principles of Research."

may come while you are examining a general encyclopedia entry, or scanning a bibliography at the end of a book or chapter. Anyone who tells you that you must research everything before you write has not been around writers too long.

This chapter gives you an opportunity to try your hand at three common types of informational writing: the extended definition, the advisory or instructional feature, and the analytical feature. Such categorizing is useful, especially to inexperienced writers, who can benefit greatly by trying their hand at each of them.

Writing an Extended Definition

You learned in Chapter 6 that there is more than one way to define a term. But regardless of the kind of definition you choose—categorical, stipulative, operational, or lexical—you can only reveal so much about the term; and the more complex the term is, the less successful the definition will be in capturing its essence, however skillfully worded it is.

Compelling reasons often exist for devoting an entire essay to a definition of a complex idea or phenomenon. For example, we may want to help people acquire new insight into a concept they *think* they understand but really do not—a concept like *courage, morality, beauty,* or *discipline*. Such concepts, with their subtle nuances of meaning, with their need to be carefully exemplified and analyzed, simply cannot be made sufficiently clear in a short definition.

Let's take the concept of *charm*, a term we're all familiar with but very likely can't quite define with accuracy. The dictionary is always a good place to begin, but this *American Heritage Dictionary* definition may not be very helpful:

> 1. The power or quality of pleasing, attracting, or fascinating. 2. A particular quality or feature that fascinates or attracts.

There's just enough here to make us wonder all the more about human charm. To really understand a concept like this, one has to write an *extended* definition, one that might use more than one definition-type. The extended definition might also include description and narration as well as such explanatory devices as classification and division, comparison, analogy, and description,* all of which can help elucidate the concept.

---

*See Chapter 6, "Principles of Development: Aiming to Inform."

The British essayist Laurie Lee has tackled the concept of charm in his article "The Essence of Charm." Read it twice, first to discover how much more you learn about the concept via extended definition, then to identify the various rhetorical strategies Lee uses to develop the reader's full understanding of the subject:

THE ESSENCE OF CHARM

Charm is the ultimate weapon, the supreme seduction, against which there are few defenses. If you've got it, you need neither money, looks, nor pedigree. It's a gift, given only to give away, and the more used, the more there is. It is also a climate of behavior set for perpetual summer and thermostatically controlled by taste and tact.

True charm is an aura, an invisible musk in the air; if you see it working, the spell is broken. Charm is dynamic, and cannot be turned on and off at will. As to its ingredients, there is no fixed formula. A whole range of mysteries goes into the caldron, but the magic it offers must be absolute—one cannot be "almost" or "partly" charmed.

In a woman, charm is probably more exacting than in a man, requiring a wider array of subtleties. It is a light in the face, an air of exclusive welcome, an almost impossibly sustained note of satisfaction in one's company, and regret without fuss at parting. A woman with charm finds no man dull; indeed, in her presence he becomes not just a different person but the person he most wants to be. Such a woman gives life to his deep-held fantasies by adding the necessary conviction to his long suspicion that he is king.

Of those women who have most successfully charmed me I remember chiefly their voices and eyes. Their voices were intimate and enveloping. The listening eyes, supreme charm in a woman, betrayed no concern with any other world than this, warmly wrapping one round with total attention and turning one's lightest words to gold. Theirs was a charm that must have continued to exist, like the flower in the desert, even when there was nobody there to see it.

A woman's charm spreads round her that particular glow of well-being for which any man will want to seek her out and, by making full use of her nature, celebrates the fact of his maleness and so gives him an extra shot of life. Her charm lies also in that air of timeless maternalism, that calm and pacifying presence, which can dispel a man's moments of frustration and anger and restore his failures of will.

Charm in a man, I suppose, is his ability to capture the complicity of a woman by a single-minded acknowledgment of her uniqueness. Here again it is a question of being totally absorbed, of *really* forgetting that anyone else exists, for nothing more fatally betrays than the suggestion of a wandering eye. Silent devotion is fine, but seldom sufficient; it is what a man says that counts, the bold declarations, the flights of fancy, the uncovering of secret virtues. A man is charmed through his eyes, a woman by what she hears, so no man need to be too anxious about his age: As wizened Voltaire once said: "Give me a few minutes to talk away my face and I can seduce the Queen of France."

But charm isn't exclusively sexual; it comes in a variety of cooler flavors. Most children have it—till they are told they have it—and so do old people with nothing to lose; animals, too, of course. With children and smaller animals, it is often in the shape of the head and in the chaste unaccusing stare; with young girls and ponies, a certain stumbling awkwardness, a leggy inability to control their bodies. But all these are passive, and appeal by capturing one's protective instincts.

You know who has charm. But can you acquire it? Properly, you can't, because it's an originality of touch you have to be born with. Or it's something that grows naturally out of another quality, like the simple desire to make people happy. Certainly, charm is not a question of learning palpable tricks, like wrinkling your nose, or having a laugh in your voice. On the other hand, there is an antenna, a built-in awareness of others, which most people have, and which care can nourish.

But in a study of charm, what else does one look for? Apart from the ability to listen—rarest of all human virtues—apart from warmth, sensitivity, and the power to please, there is a generosity which makes no demands. Charm spends itself willingly on young and old alike, on the poor, the ugly, the dim, the boring, on the last fat man in the corner. It reveals itself also in a sense of ease, in casual but perfect manners, and often in a physical grace which springs less from an accident of youth than from a confident serenity of mind. Any person with this is more than just a popular fellow; he is also a social healer.

Charm, in the end, is a most potent act of behavior, the laying down of a carpet by one person for another to give his existence a moment of honor. It is close to love in that it moves without force, bearing gifts like the growth of daylight. It snares completely, but is never punitive. It disarms by being itself disarmed, strikes without wounds, wins wars without casualties—though not, of course, without victims.

In the armory of man, charm is the enchanted dart, light and subtle as a hummingbird. But it is deceptive in one thing—like a sense of humor, if you think you've got it, you probably haven't.

Laurie Lee

One of the best qualities of this essay, you'll probably agree, is its ability to inform you about the nature of charm without slighting its mystique. In fact, Lee goes to considerable lengths to enhance whatever mystique readers already may have harbored about the subject:

True charm is an aura, an invisible musk in the air; if you see it working, the spell is broken. Charm is dynamic, and cannot be turned on and off at will.

The author is wise in emphasizing mystique first, for by doing so he reinforces the reader's fascination with the subject. Although he reveals very little information, strictly speaking, about charm in the first two paragraphs, Lee nevertheless imparts an aura about the subject that is necessary for readers to understand the fullest sense of the word; charm cannot be understood for its rational qualities alone.

Notice too that when Lee gets down to the more tangible aspects of charm, he doesn't stop paying attention to its magical nature:

> In a woman, charm . . . is a light in the face, an air of exclusive welcome, an almost impossibly sustained note of satisfaction in one's company. . . .

Now let's look at the different rhetorical devices Lee uses in this extended definition essay: how many were you able to identify? Most prevalent, perhaps, is the stipulative definition: "Charm is the ultimate weapon"; "Charm . . . is a most potent act of behavior." Lee also uses classification, although not in any rigorous manner: "Charm isn't exclusively sexual; it comes in a variety of cooler flavors," and he briefly mentions charm in children and in animals, in paragraph seven. Lee also employs narration in this essay in order to convey his personal experience with charm: "Of those women who have most successfully charmed me I remember chiefly their voices and eyes. Their voices were intimate and enveloping. . . ."

This kind of writing, however, cannot be reduced to a formula. Laurie Lee probably did not read about how to write an extended definition before penning "The Essence of Charm." More likely, he spent a long time, years perhaps, thinking about the phenomenon of charm until some experience triggered his need to write about it. Only after Lee felt the impulse to write it, not before, did he most likely begin to do anything resembling research. Researching without the seed of an exciting idea stirring inside and spurring you on can cause problems: You and your work-in-progress can be deprived of vital creative energy.

Basic Writing Techniques

As you follow your creative impulses in creating an extended definition, don't forget to keep a few basic guidelines in mind. These are not rules, but suggested techniques that have worked for writers in the past.

1. *Assume a lively, enthusiastic tone from the very beginning.* You might open with an amusing and relevant anecdote or with some reference to a concrete situation to gain your reader's attention at the most critical time. Here is how one writer—the psychoanalyst Karen Horney (1885–1952)—introduces her comparative definition of fear and anxiety:

    > When a mother is afraid that her child will die when it has only a pimple or a slight cold we speak of anxiety; but if she is afraid when the child has a serious illness we call her reaction fear. If someone is afraid whenever he

stands on a height or when he has to discuss a topic he knows well, we call his reaction anxiety; if someone is afraid when he loses his way high up in the mountains during a heavy thunderstorm, we would speak of fear. (Karen Horney, *The Neurotic Personality of Our Time*)

2. *Explore the concept deeply.* Say something about etymology, about a term's range of usage over the centuries, perhaps. You might include a paragraph about the term's subtle nuances, which tend to be overlooked or misunderstood. Consider this extended definition of the word *manage*:

> The word manage seems to have come into English directly from *maneggiare* (Italian) to handle . . . or train horses. Its earliest English uses were in this context. The [immediate forerunner] is *manidiare* (vulgar Latin)—to handle, from . . . *manus* (Latin)—hand. Manage was quickly extended to operations of war, and from (the early sixteenth century) to a general sense of taking control, taking charge, directing. (Raymond Williams, *Keywords: A Vocabulary of Culture and Society*)

3. *Give special emphasis to one or two especially noteworthy aspects of the definition, and provide strong examples.* The idea here is to narrow the reader's field of concentration in order to reinforce mastery of the concept. Notice how Jeff Brown uses this strategy of emphasis when defining a method of program designing known as stepwise refinement.*

4. *Try to end on a provocative note.* A closing anecdote or an overall judgment will make the essay memorable. A good example is the concluding paragraph of Laurie Lee's "The Essence of Charm," p. 102.

Writing an Advisory or Instructional Feature

The how-to-do-it or here-is-what-I-advise writer is a teacher of sorts, one who takes on the role not only of expert on the subject at hand, but of a patient and caring guide as well. Your writing will more likely achieve its instructional purpose if you are aware of this dual role. If you're relating a step-by-step sequence, you'll need to keep your readers' needs in mind when you decide what kind of advice or what set of instructions to include, and how to phrase it so your readers will not misunderstand a

---

*See Chapter 11, "Research Paper Projects."

single step. Your readers, of course, put your writing to the ultimate test by actually doing what you tell them to do.

Perhaps you are saying to yourself, Wait a minute—how can *I* write a how-to feature? I'm not an expert in anything . . . yet. But the truth is that you *are* qualified to write an intelligent instructional essay on one or maybe even several areas of activity, even if you don't consider yourself an expert in those areas. How-to writing usually focuses on very limited-range topics. You do not have to be a geologist, for example, to write a useful feature on how to get started in fossil hunting and collecting, or on how to make jewelry out of agates. You do not have to be a professional athlete to write authoritatively on efficient ways to improve your bowling score. You can be a relative newcomer to, let's say, cross-country running, and still know (from grim personal experience) what other runners can do to avoid stress fractures or dehydration when working out during the summer. And you do not have to be a mechanic to advise readers on how they can cut fuel costs when driving.

We are now going to look at an interesting example of each kind of how-to feature: the important-advice type and the follow-the-steps type. In both cases, the author makes a special effort to generate enthusiasm for the subject, to make the reader want to *participate* in the activity, and, above all, to maintain clarity and simplicity throughout, but without oversimplifying.

First, read the essay the way any curious reader would. Then ask yourself, Has this essay taught me anything useful? Can I quickly summarize the key points in my own words?* Next, reread the essay and ask yourself, How did the author get his or her ideas across clearly and interestingly enough to have gotten through to me?

HOW TO FIGURE "FUELISHNESS"

You have to be an ever vigilant motorist to keep your car from being a "fuelish" gulper of today's high-priced gasoline. Here are some of the sneaky ways your car can waste precious fuel. Some of the losses may sound minuscule, but added together they can represent a heap of dollars spewing from the exhaust pipe of your car.

What goes in your car?

According to the Highway User's Federation, every 100 pounds you add to your car (including passengers' weight) costs you between one-tenth and four-tenths miles per gallon. The smaller and lighter your car and the more

---

*It's always helpful to write a summary of any important reading you do. See Chapter 10, "Principles of Research."

stop-and-go driving you do, the more the extra weight cuts your mileage. How can you cut the load? One way is to stop using your trunk to store snow tires, golf clubs, and other equipment. Another is to usually carry only one-half tank of fuel for city driving, thus lightening the load by 30 to 60 pounds. In winter, snow and ice on the roof, trunk, and hood, and in fender wells, can add up to 100-plus pounds.

The engine's condition

It's estimated that about 60 percent of the cars on the road need a tune-up. If your car is among them, your fuel costs can be about ten percent higher than normal, even if your car is still running OK. If the need is acute and the car is running roughly, it's probably burning about 20 percent more fuel than it should. What causes these losses? A misfiring spark plug can cut miles per gallon by about two miles; a sticky carburetor by about three miles; and a dirty air cleaner by about one mile.

The tires' friction

Underinflated tires can cut one or more miles from your car's mpg. Driving on gravel roads reduces mileage by about 35 percent compared to driving on smooth, paved roads. Improper front-end alignment can cut mpg by about one-third mile. Snow tires and studded tires also increase friction; they should be removed as soon as the weather permits. Radial tires, on the other hand, can boost your mileage by about six percent.

Your car's accessories

When you flick on the air conditioner while traveling down the highway, your car's mpg immediately drops by about ten percent; when you do the same in heavy stop-and-go traffic, the decrease can fall to 20 percent. If you've opted for power steering, it's cutting mileage by about one mile. Other accessories such as lights, heater, defroster, radio, etc., consume extra fuel and shouldn't be used needlessly. One option that might not cost you as much as you might think is automatic transmission; in some cases your loss can be less than one-half mpg. However, if you do the bulk of your driving on city streets, automatic transmission can cost you up to eight percent more in mileage over a properly shifted manual transmission. Letting up slightly on the accelerator each time the automatic transmission shifts into a higher gear can decrease this loss somewhat. If your car has standard transmission, keeping the car in the lower gears too long can be costly; a car running in second gear uses about 45 percent more fuel than in fourth gear.

Speed

Driving at a steady speed instead of speeding up and slowing down a lot (which tailgating usually requires) can save as much as four miles per gallon. And if that steady speed is 55 mph instead of 70, you'll increase mileage by about 20 percent. But even if you drive at a steady speed, your mileage will drop dramatically when you encounter wind resistance or uphill grades. Traveling 50 mph into a 20-mph headwind consumes the same amount of fuel as traveling 70 mph with no wind. And just a four-percent grade produces the same result—a fuel consumption of 70 mph while traveling only 50 mph.

The way you drive

Short trips are one of the biggest gasoline gulpers. Because the engine usually can't warm up to its full efficiency, a short trip can require up to 70 percent more gasoline per mile than a longer trip. Other contributing factors are the extra stops and starts the inefficient engine must face. Obviously, it's wise to combine short trips into longer ones.

Warming up the car in winter is another wasteful practice; your car always consumes a few ounces of gasoline during starting and about half the starting amount of each minute of idling. Driving slowly for the first couple of miles is a much better way to warm up the car. And if you pump the accelerator repeatedly before starting, you might be wasting as much as an extra gallon of gasoline a week. Depressing the gas pedal just once before starting is all most cars require.

Jackrabbit starts also gulp gas; they can burn twice as much fuel as smooth, steady starts. Likewise, hard braking, instead of smooth, steady pressure on the pedal, makes your engine work harder and burn more fuel.

Kim Garretson, in *Better Homes and Gardens* magazine

You are on the mark if you judged this feature to be a fine example of clarity, coherence, and stylistic control. The introductory paragraph captures the reader's attention at once, doesn't it? Notice the strong, informal, but not overly slangy, word choice: "Here are some of the sneaky ways your car can waste precious fuel." Even small losses "added together . . . can represent a heap of dollars spewing from the exhaust pipe of your car." In just a few words, the author has managed to win the audience's rapt attention.

Notice what the author does next: She not only organizes the discussion into discrete sections, each devoted to one common cause of gasoline waste, but she titles each section as well. These titles are known as *subheads*, which are versatile devices in how-to pieces. Subheads provide the reader with a bird's-eye view of the organizational layout, and they also help the reader review the information.

What about the author's organizational strategy? Can you figure out why she discussed one thing before another? Does it matter, from a rhetorical standpoint, that extra weight in the trunk be discussed before the engine's condition—and that the engine's condition be discussed before proper tire inflation? We can't be absolutely sure about this, but doesn't it make sense to begin with problems that can be easily solved, if only to encourage the audience to continue reading? If the author had started with the thorny problem of poor driving habits, she might have lost a lot of readers who could have been thinking, Don't preach to me, or, Hey, there's nothing wrong with the way *I* drive.

Finally, take a good look at the author's tone of voice. He uses a friendly and conversational tone throughout; he speaks directly to you using the second-person point of view. The voice informs without putting you to sleep, and without condescending to you either. The author has carefully targeted his audience—the average driver with little or no knowledge of auto mechanics:

> It's estimated that about 60 percent of the cars on the road need a tune-up. If your car is among them, your fuel costs can be about ten percent higher than normal, even if your car is still running OK.

Take a look, now, at a follow-the-steps how-to feature: George Plimpton's "How to Make a Speech," on pp. 109–110. As you read the article, keep in mind once again that the ultimate test of any step-by-step discussion is the reader's ability to follow the author's directions with ease. Also, as with the previous how-to feature, decide whether Plimpton has succeeded in stimulating your interest in the subject.

Suggestions for How-to Writing

The following suggestions will help you plan your own successful how-to feature:

1. Address your readers directly, and consider the possibility that they may know absolutely nothing about the topic, but are eager to learn. Meet their enthusiasm with your own. Never talk down to your readers, though ("Now, boys and girls, if you'll simply pay attention there is no reason why you can't learn these steps . . ."). At the same time, do not rush through things, or readers will become confused and frustrated. Consider using visual aids if you think they will improve clarity.

2. If the project involves the use of several tools and a variety of materials, it is a good idea to introduce these first before turning to the step-by-step procedure. For example, you might write, "Before you begin dissecting your frog, make sure you gather together the following: . . ."

3. Determine the most logical breakdown of the procedure. You should have a clear reason for discussing Point A before discussing Point B. Note the logical order Plimpton uses to present the topic of speechmaking: He begins by discussing the benefits of acquiring this skill. Plimpton knows that learning a skill proceeds more efficiently if the learner understands *why* the undertaking is worthwhile. Plimpton then suggests a way to arrive at a speech topic and how to research and organize the speech; he then devotes the second half of the fea-

How to make a speech

By George Plimpton

International Paper asked George Plimpton, who writes books about facing the sports pros (like "Paper Lion" and "Shadow Box"), and who's in demand to speak about it, to tell you how to face the fear of making a speech.

One of life's terrors for the uninitiated is to be asked to make a speech.

"Why me?" will probably be your first reaction. "I don't have anything to say." It should be reassuring (though it rarely is) that since you were asked, somebody must think you do. The fact is that each one of us has a store of material which should be of interest to others. There is no reason why it should not be adapted to a speech.

Why know how to speak?

Scary as it is, it's important for anyone to be able to speak in front of others, whether twenty around a conference table or a hall filled with a thousand faces.

Being able to speak can mean better grades in any class. It can mean talking the town council out of increasing your property taxes. It can mean talking top management into buying your plan.

How to pick a topic

You were probably asked to speak in the first place in the hope that you would be able to articulate a topic that you know something about. Still, it helps to find out about your audience first. Who are they? Why are they there? What are they interested in? How much do they already know about your subject? One kind of talk would be appropriate for the Women's Club of Columbus, Ohio, and quite another for the guests at the Vince Lombardi dinner.

How to plan what to say

Here is where you must do your homework.

The more you sweat in advance, the less you'll have to sweat once you appear on stage. Research your topic thoroughly. Check the library for facts, quotes, books and timely magazine and newspaper articles on your subject. Get in touch with experts. Write to them, make phone calls, get interviews to help round out your material.

In short, gather—and learn—far more than you'll ever use. You can't imagine how much confidence that knowledge will inspire.

Now start organizing and writing. Most authorities suggest that a good speech breaks down into three basic parts—an introduction, the body of the speech, and the summation.

Introduction: An audience makes up its mind very quickly. Once the mood of an audience is set, it is difficult to change it, which is why introductions are important. If the speech is to be lighthearted in tone, the speaker can start off by telling a good-natured story about the subject or himself.

But be careful of jokes, especially the shaggy-dog

"What am I doing wrong? Taking refuge behind the lectern, looking scared to death, shuffling pages, and reading my speech. Relax. Come out in the open, gesture, talk to your audience!"

variety. For some reason, the joke that convulses guests in a living room tends to suffer as it emerges through the amplifying system into a public gathering place.

Main body: There are four main intents in the body of the well-made speech. These are 1) to entertain, which is probably the hardest; 2) to instruct, which is the easiest if the speaker has done the research and knows the subject; 3) to persuade, which one does at a sales presentation, a political rally, or a town meeting; and finally, 4) to inspire, which is what the speaker emphasizes at a sales meeting, in a sermon, or at a pep rally. (Hurry-Up Yost, the onetime Michigan football coach, gave such an inspiration-filled half-time talk that he got carried away and at the final exhortation led his team on the run through the wrong locker-room door into the swimming pool.)

Summation: This is where you should "ask for the order." An ending should probably incorporate a sentence or two which sounds like an ending—a short summary of the main points of the speech, perhaps, or the repeat of a phrase that most embodies what the speaker has hoped to convey. It is valuable to think of the last sentence or two as something which might produce applause. Phrases which are perfectly appropriate to signal this are: "In closing…" or "I have one last thing to say…"

Once done—fully written, or the main

(continued)

points set down on 3″ x 5″ index cards—the next problem is the actual presentation of the speech. Ideally, a speech should not be read. At least it should never appear or sound as if you are reading it. An audience is dismayed to see a speaker peering down at a thick sheaf of papers on the lectern, wetting his thumb to turn to the next page.

How to sound spontaneous

The best speakers are those who make their words sound spontaneous even if memorized. I've found it's best to learn a speech point by point, not word for word. Careful preparation and a great deal of practicing are required to make it come together smoothly and easily. Mark Twain once said "It takes three weeks to prepare a good ad-lib speech."

Don't be fooled when you rehearse. It takes longer to deliver a speech than to read it. Most speakers peg along at about 100 words a minute.

Brevity is an asset

A sensible plan, if you have been asked to speak to an exact limit, is to talk your speech into a mirror and stop at your allotted time; then cut the speech accordingly. The more familiar you become with your speech, the more confidently you can deliver it.

As anyone who listens to speeches knows, brevity is an asset. Twenty minutes are ideal. An hour is the limit an audience can listen comfortably.

In mentioning brevity, it is worth mentioning that the shortest inaugural address was George Washington's—just 135 words. The longest was William Henry Harrison's in 1841. He delivered a two-hour 9,000-word speech into the teeth of a freezing northeast wind. He came down with a cold the following day, and a month later he died of pneumonia.

Check your grammar

Consult a dictionary for proper meanings and pronunciations. Your audience won't know if you're a bad speller, but they will know if you use or pronounce a word improperly. In my first remarks on the dais, I used to thank people for their "fulsome introduction," until I discovered to my dismay that "fulsome" means *offensive* and *insincere*.

"Why should you make a speech? There are four big reasons (left to right): to inspire, to persuade, to entertain, to instruct. I'll tell you how to organize what you say."

On the podium

It helps one's nerves to pick out three or four people in the audience—preferably in different sectors so that the speaker is apparently giving his attention to the entire room—on whom to focus. Pick out people who seem to be having a good time.

How questions help

A question period at the end of a speech is a good notion. One would not ask questions following a tribute to the company treasurer on his retirement, say, but a technical talk or an informative speech can be enlivened with a question period.

The crowd

The larger the crowd, the easier it is to speak, because the response is multiplied and increased. Most people do not believe this. They peek out from behind the curtain and if the auditorium is filled to the rafters they begin to moan softly in the back of their throats.

What about stage fright?

Very few speakers escape the so-called "butterflies." There does not seem to be any cure for them, except to realize that they are beneficial rather than harmful, and never fatal.

The tension usually means that the speaker, being keyed up, will do a better job. Edward R. Murrow called stage fright "the sweat of perfection." Mark Twain once comforted a fright-frozen friend about to speak: "Just remember they don't expect much." My own feeling is that with thought, preparation and faith in your ideas, *you* can go out there and expect a pleasant surprise.

And what a sensation it is—to hear applause. Invariably after it dies away, the speaker searches out the program chairman—just to make it known that he's available for next month's meeting.

Today, the printed word is more vital than ever. Now there is more need than ever for all of us to *read* better, *write* better, and *communicate* better.

International Paper offers this series in the hope that, even in a small way, we can help.

If you'd like to share this article with others—students, friends, employees, family—we'll gladly send you reprints. So far we've sent out over 15,000,000 in response to requests from people everywhere.

Please write: "Power of the Printed Word," International Paper Company, Dept. 9V, P.O. Box 954, Madison Square Station, New York, NY 10010. ©1980 INTERNATIONAL PAPER COMPANY

INTERNATIONAL PAPER COMPANY
We believe in the power of the printed word.

ture to the actual delivery: how to sound spontaneous, how to keep the speech concise, how to overcome stage fright.

4. Add special cautionary emphasis to any instructions that, if not properly followed, could ruin the project or cause injury (e.g., "WARNING! Never work with these substances near a flame; they are extremely flammable.").

5. Conclude by offering suggestions for application of the newly learned task, or by congratulating your readers for having completed the procedure. Sometimes this can be built into the final step in very short features.

Writing an Analytical Feature

Like the instructional or advisory feature, the analytical feature presents a dynamic whole, subdivided into discrete parts that are comprehensible to the reader. Unlike the instructional feature, though, the analytical piece does not provide a step-by-step procedure for completing a task. Instead, it typically identifies and describes the parts, and then it shows how the parts interact to create the whole. For example, an essay that aims to show how glass is made would likely begin with a definition of glass, then proceed to identify the basic ingredients of glass (silica [e.g., sand] + oxides [e.g., sodium oxide, calcium oxide, lead oxide]), then show how the ingredients are mixed and fused together.

As with other kinds of informational writing, it is very important to know your audience when planning an analytical piece. If you are interested in writing about how the human eye perceives color, your style, tone of voice, emphasis, diction, and even your organizational strategy can differ considerably, depending on whether your intended readers are curious sixth-graders or first-year medical students.

In the following example, a college senior with some agricultural experience describes a serious irrigation problem known as salinization. An audience of freshman or sophomore geography students, or of any concerned laypersons, is anticipated.

THE SALINITY PROBLEM IN CROP IRRIGATION

Crop irrigation is a blessing for farmers the world over: it can transform arid landscape into lush fields of grain, fruit and vegetables. However, irrigation can also poison the landscape.

How does this happen? The answer is salinization, a process whereby excess or mismanaged irrigation causes underground water to become salty, therefore harmful to plants.

The process works like this:

1. Minute quantities of dissolved mineral salts, present in all water, do not evaporate, so that as water evaporates or is used by plants, the salt concentration of the remaining water increases. Irrigation water unused by plants and not absorbed by the air percolates down to the underground water table which, in turn, may become increasingly salty over time.

2. If natural or artificial drainage of an irrigated area is insufficient, the water table may rise, approaching the surface. Seepage from floods and unlined canals also contributes to the water-table rise.

3. If the water table rises to within four feet of the surface, it meets the irrigation water seeping down from above. When these waters meet, the whole area becomes a brackish marshland, and even if the salt does not damage plants, the omnipresent water will suffocate crops for lack of aeration.

4. If the water table rises still farther and nears the surface, it begins to evaporate, leaving a thin deposit of salt behind. By this stage, successful cultivation is difficult, if not impossible.

Today, the effects of salinization are widespread. Vast areas of southern Iraq glisten with encrusted salt; five million acres of Pakistan's Indus Basin lie waterlogged; and California's Central Valley is showing signs of salinization. The main problem for all of these areas is lack of drainage, and possible solutions are two: artificial drainage and tubewells.

Artificial drainage involves the use of perforated plastic or polyethylene pipes, roughly ten feet in length, placed two or three feet beneath the surface. Into these pipes flows fresh irrigation water, which is carried away from the field and drained into canals or ponds.

The other alternative, less expensive and more popular than drainpipes, is the tubewell—a cylindrical well driven into the ground to tap the water table. When placed in strategic spots throughout the affected area, these tubewells draw relatively pure water from underground, thus lowering the water table. Furthermore, this well water is then used for irrigation, and it often replaces river water brought in for irrigation. The less water that is brought in from outside, the less water to waterlog a given area.

Evan Elliot

Summary

Three kinds of essays intended to convey information are the extended definition, the directional how-to piece, and the analytical how-it-works piece. An extended definition typically probes the origin and past- and present-day use of the term in question, then emphasizes a particularly intriguing facet of that use. A how-to piece typically introduces the task

Projects in Informative Writing

to be performed in a way that stimulates the audience's interest in and willingness to participate in the activity, then presents the task as a series of easy-to-follow steps. Necessary ingredients and tools are mentioned; cautionary remarks are emphasized. An analytical piece often introduces the phenomenon by defining it, then by identifying and describing each part, then by discussing how the parts interact to create the whole.

FOR DISCUSSION

1. The following advisory piece, here in a first-draft stage, was written by a college freshman. Critique the piece, focusing on its content, method of development, organizational strategy, and writing style. Point to the draft's strong points and suggest ways in which it could be improved:

   One problem you will encounter while working at a gas station is that you occasionally get robbed. Since you can't prevent these robberies, you must know how to deal with them. Here are some guidelines to follow.

   1. Keep calm. If you're not, the robber won't be, and he'll blow your head off.
   2. Be as observant as you can. Try to get the best description of the robber that you can, so that the police can catch him more quickly.
   3. Don't try to stop the robber yourself. Odds are that you'll lose your life.
   4. Give him the money quickly. The quicker you give him the money, the less chance he will blow your head off.

   If you follow these tips, odds are that you will live to see tomorrow. (Tom Wade, from Gene Krupa, *Situational Writing*)

2. Discuss the organizational strategy Evan Elliot uses in his feature on salinization. How easily were you able to follow along? What else besides organization helped you grasp the content? Is there anything Elliot could have done to improve clarity? Finally, if the author were asked to rewrite the feature for an audience of, say, seventh graders, what changes would he need to make?

3. Read the following first draft of a how-to feature by a college junior:

   Learning to drive a manual transmission ("stick shift") can be a very frustrating experience. At some point you will probably feel like giving up. But with a little time and patience you will eventually find yourself shifting with ease and enjoying the pleasures of driving.

   Assuming you are driving a standard "H" transmission:

   I. Before starting the car, press the clutch to the floor with your left foot. The clutch disengages the gears so they can be changed. The gear shift creates an "H" formation with reverse in the upper left of the "H", first gear in the lower left, neutral in the horizontal bar, second in the upper right, and third in the lower right.

    Move the gear shift into neutral. Take your foot off clutch.

II. Turn the key and give the car a little gas by pressing lightly on the accelerator.

III. Once the car is started, place the clutch to the floor again. This time you want to put the car in first gear. Move the gear shift to the lower left of the "H". Begin to ease your foot up on the clutch while slowly and steadily pressing down on the accelerator. When the clutch is released and the gears become engaged again, it is essential that you are giving the car enough gas.

IV. The car will begin to move forward. Continue to accelerate.

V. When the car is moving forward you will begin to hear the engine "straining"; it will sound very loud. You are ready to change to second gear. Shifting to second is much easier because you are already moving. Gently push your left foot down onto the clutch, and at the same time slowly release your right foot from the accelerator. Once the clutch is down, move the gear shift to second gear, into the upper right of the "H", then slowly release the clutch while giving a little gas. You are now in second.

VI. Again the car will sound as if it is straining. You are ready to move into third gear. The procedure is exactly the same as moving from first to second. Release foot from accelerator, push clutch to floor, pull gear shift back into third, ease up on clutch while pushing lightly on accelerator.

VII. When preparing to stop, push down on clutch and place gear shift in neutral. When the light turns green, put the shift back into first gear, ease up on the clutch and supply gas.

You are now driving a manual transmission! (Marie Noble)

Assuming that you do not know how to drive a vehicle with this kind of manual transmission, how easily could you follow Marie Noble's directions? Has she skipped any necessary details—either an entire step, or part of a step? How effective is the author's overall organization? Is her diction appropriate? How do you rate her opening paragraph?

4. In the following essay, David Stansbury devotes much attention to a definition of *burnout*—a common affliction among college students. How effectively does Stansbury capture the essential meaning of burnout, in your opinion? Compare his technique of defining with that used by Laurie Lee in "The Essence of Charm." Is there any-

thing that Lee or Stansbury could have done, rhetorically speaking, to strengthen their respective definitions?

Finally, discuss the overall strategy used in Stansbury's essay. Is it well organized? Is it concise? Does the topic unfold clearly, logically, and interestingly? How effective is the introductory segment (the first five paragraphs)?

COOLING BURNOUT

Sophomore slump is only the start. Burnout can strike anytime, anywhere, and for any number of reasons. But you can *fight back.*

Presented for your approval—three average college students, each a victim of the same disease. A disease that can take any form, any shape. A disease that can appear suddenly and without warning, to wreak havoc with its victims' lives. These students have just stepped into . . . the Burnout Zone.

Sally's a great girl. She's a premed major with a 3.81 GPA. She's the majority whip of the Student Senate and an active member in Young Republocrats. She spends at least eight hours a week working with disenfranchised Lhasa apsos. She has a steady boyfriend and was awarded two scholarships recently. She cries a lot for no apparent reason.

Alex never gets up before noon, and he never goes to bed before the national anthem. Lately he has switched from a filter cigarette to one that tastes more like old socks. He is notorious on campus for not leaving his dorm room except to buy more pork rinds at the nearest convenience store. He has recently been put on scholastic probation and no longer has a measurable GPA. When Alex was a freshman, he thought he was going to enjoy college. That was a long time ago.

Chuck has always planned to work in his father's real estate agency. His grades are average, and he works 15 hours a week at the local Madras 'n' Stuff clothing outlet. He goes out regularly, either on dates or with fraternity brothers. He has just two more semesters before graduation. He's thinking of dropping out of school.

While the circumstances and symptoms are different in each case, these students are all burned out on school and don't know it. There's something amiss in their lives that's causing them to be depressed. If they fail to acknowledge the burnout symptoms, their problems will almost certainly increase, perhaps irrevocably.

What Is Burnout?

You are a good candidate for burnout if you follow a tedious routine that makes you feel trapped. When you feel trapped, you feel anxious. Anxiety drains your emotional, intellectual, and physical resources quickly and extensively. As you weaken and tire, you begin to give up. You become one of the walking dead. Well, maybe not dead. You become a walking potato-head.

To control burnout, you need to know what causes it. Unfortunately, the list of contributing factors encompasses everything that is part of your life:

family, friends, lovers, school, work, success, failure, ambition, indolence, opportunity, competition, self-esteem, and the pace of modern life. What's more, burnout can hit over- and under-achievers alike.

Any combination of factors can cause burnout. In fact, the only thing you can count on is that you'll have succumbed to this condition at least once before graduation. As a college counselor, I often see predictable patterns of burnout develop. Your freshman year is filled with the excitement of new challenges to be met and new frontiers to be explored. Most of the time you're so busy trying not to act like a freshman that you don't have time to get caught in a soul-deadening routine. Often the toughest problem you face is figuring out where to buy a *College Blue Book*.

By sophomore year—the time of the legendary sophomore slump—you're comfortably ensconced in the campus community. You know the ropes and you can play the game. Surviving registration lines, bargaining for extended deadlines, and avoiding the cafeteria's meat loaf are old hat. Now you must deal with the realization that you're facing another two or three years of this same damn game.

Sophomore year also marks the time when you experience the sharpest divergence between you and your parents and between your new values and the values of your adolescence. High school certainties—you were destined to be a lawyer, or you'd postpone sex until marriage—start to fade away, and you're left to make your own rules. It's at this point that you find yourself debating whether to spend your available cash on a mohawk haircut or a subscription to *The Wall Street Journal*.

The momentum picks up again during your junior year. You're into the thick of your major studies, and you're either handling it or trying frantically to develop study habits. At any rate, the end of your academic travails no longer seems that far away. In fact, this may be the first time you can give people a straight answer when they ask what your major is.

In your senior year, however, you might become a lame duck looking for crutches. You're almost done with college, so why bother with studying? At the same time, you dread the "real" world beyond campus. It's too late to retreat into childhood; it's too early to start acting like a middle-aged adult (checking into insurance policies and going to bed by 10). All you can do is wait until graduation, with maybe a GRE or a few job interviews to relieve the tedium.

Symptoms of Burnout

So how do you know if you're turning to toast?
- You're ready for bed at six-thirty every night. None of your classes start before noon. Even with 16 hours of sleep, you feel as if you've been lifting houses all day.
- You've cut so many classes that you've forgotten how to get to campus from your apartment.
- You're ill more often than usual. You're constantly touching your forehead to see if you have a fever.
- You recently spent an entire weekend living on beer and Twinkies. The last vegetable you ate was a burrito.

- You blame everyone else for your problems. When your roommate is so stupid, and your parents are so pushy, and your professors are so boring, and your friends are so insensitive, how could anyone expect you to concentrate on school?
- You blame only yourself for your problems. Maybe if you weren't so lazy, maybe if you weren't so dumb, maybe if you weren't such total scum, you'd be able to concentrate on school.
- You realize that your work is slipping, so you decide to give it your all. You study until 3 a.m. every night and take your homework to parties. It doesn't help.
- Your favorite songs are "King of Pain" and "Burning Down the House," and you listen to them constantly instead of working.

Tips for Getting Better

The most dangerous aspect of burnout is its tendency to intensify the more you worry about it. If you try to suppress it by working harder, then you just burn out faster. If you ignore it, insidious burnout will just keep hammering away until you crumble under its assault.

If you're suffering from burnout, the first thing you must do is seek perspective. You should definitely talk about the problem. Friends, teachers, and family members may be able to help, but you really need to talk to someone who's not putting any kind of pressure on you. Campus counseling centers usually employ professionals who can help you recover from burnout. These people have seen burnout in all its various forms; they know how to help. If you don't hit it off with a particular counselor, feel free to move on to another one. In short, talk to the people who actually seem to be doing you some good by listening.

More Tips and Free Advice

- Remember, you won't be in college forever. A case of burnout is not the end of the world—though it may feel like it.
- Change your routine. Don't blow everything off. Instead, rearrange your schedule so that it is more to your liking—or just different. Don't go for long periods of time without leisure, and conversely, don't let schoolwork pile up into an interminable string of all-nighters.
- Do something that relaxes and pleases you when you do have some time off. That may sound simplistic, but think about the ways you spend your leisure time. You'll probably discover that you do a lot of things out of habit. For example, going out for a beer with the same old crowd may have lost its thrill months ago. If so, it's time to develop some new interests.
- Establish short-term goals with concrete rewards. Finish one assigned book this week, then buy yourself a banana split. Do exactly four hours of library research over the weekend, then treat yourself to a movie. Promise yourself at least one quiet evening alone every week.
- Respect yourself. Your mother was right. You should clean up your room, take your clothes to the cleaners, and eat foods that require a knife and fork. Indulge rather than debauch yourself.

- Plan a trip. Even if it's only for the weekend, do something besides take your dirty laundry to your parents' house.
- Stop out. Take a semester off. Work, travel, try a different way of life. This can be an excellent opportunity for you to evaluate your options. In a new location, without the pressure of a daily grind, you may be able to focus on the direction you'd like your life to take. You might decide to completely change your life—or just your major. Or you might decide that you just needed a break and are, in fact, on course and eager to start moving again.
- Change your plans; take a risk. Burnout often indicates a dissonance between your work and your values. If you have chosen a major that doesn't match your talents and dreams, then no wonder you feel alienated, tired, and frustrated.
- Learn to say no. Don't think you have to do what everyone wants you to do. You can accomplish a lot without carving yourself up like a brisket at an Elks' picnic.
- Finally, don't take life—or the occasional case of burnout—too seriously. A little humor and imagination can help you over the hump when the camel gets angry.

David Stansbury

FOR WRITING

1. You have just been appointed expert-in-residence at an academy devoted to the activity you are most familiar with. Your students know nothing about this activity, but they are very eager to learn. Because these students are also avid readers, you decide to prepare (1) an extended definition of one or more key concepts associated with the activity; (2) a how-to piece that will illuminate one phase of the activity (think twice about taking on the entire activity in one short feature!); and (3) an analytical piece that will satisfy your students' curiosity about how one of the pieces of equipment important to the activity actually works.

    Here is an example. Let's say that you love to sail, and that you have been appointed sailing expert-in-residence at the American Academy of Sailing. Your first job will be to write a two- or three-page extended definition of a sailing principle, such as "seamanship," or of a pair of related principles, such as "running" and "reaching."

    After you complete your extended definition, you then take a breather (maybe take your sailboat out on the lake for a while, or do some free-writing),* then you return to your desk and pound out a how-to piece related to sailing. Because your audience consists of

---

*See the free-writing sample on sailing in Chapter 3, "A Practical Method of Writing."

beginners, perhaps you will want to write an article titled "How to Maintain a Sailboat," "How to Sail Safely in Strong Winds," or, more ambitiously, "How to Get Started in Sailing."

Your last task is to explain how something works. A likely topic for sailing would be, "What Makes a Sailboat Go," "How a Compass Works," or "Tide Dynamics."

Feel free to reinforce your explanations with visual aids.

2. Write an informational essay in which comparison is your main, but not exclusive, rhetorical technique. You may choose one of the following topics, or use one of your own:

   a. Student personality traits; you might compare, humorously perhaps, two or more distinct types of students—say, the "party-types," the "nerds," the "jocks."

   b. Smart things to do versus stupid things to do when you're out on a date.

   c. Bosses in your life: good and bad, or sane and insane.

   d. A time when learning is exciting compared to a time when learning is dull.

Principles of Development: Aiming to Persuade

CHAPTER 8

This chapter will introduce you to the principles of sound reasoning and organization. An understanding of these principles is necessary if a writer wishes to convince readers of a certain point of view through argumentation.

In everyday talk, an argument means "having it out" with someone. "Jeannie and Jason have one argument after another; they *never* get along." But in rhetoric, *argument* refers to a method of carefully reasoned and supported discussion that takes a stance on some issue that cannot be easily resolved by objective fact alone. If you wanted to identify and describe the nutritional content of several kinds of baby food, your principal aim would be to inform. But if you wanted to call attention to the fact that a nutrient you consider important to babies was missing from most baby foods, and that it should be included, then your principal aim would be to persuade—the goal of argument.

Let's consider another situation: Assume that while researching infant nutrition you come across two articles on breast-feeding. In one article, the author writes that the nutrients in mother's milk have been identified and can be reproduced in formula milk; therefore it makes no difference whether a mother nurses her baby or not, as long as the baby receives the proper nutrients.

In the next article, by another nutritionist, you find quite a different point of view. This second author asserts that nursing is preferable, and for two reasons: It supplies nutrients to the baby that cannot be reproduced in, say, canned milk, with the same high quality as that of mother's milk; nursing also satisfies the infant's psychological need for maternal, physical contact. That is, nutrition should not be the sole criterion used in choosing between breast-feeding and bottle-feeding.

As you can see, we have moved from the realm of mere fact into the realm of argument. Facts are used to support arguments, but the arguments themselves are not facts—universal truths—such as, "Milk contains vitamin D and calcium," or "Mammoth Cave is a limestone cavern in central Kentucky." Instead we are dealing with options that we judge to be sound or unsound, depending on our personal values.

We need to delve more deeply into this business of values. What are they really? Values are principles that individuals or groups of individuals hold dear. Why can't they be objective and factual? First of all, values are formed not from a single idea, but from complex interpretations of personal conduct, belief, taste, habit, and upbringing that shape our perceptions of objective truth. Values are shaped by experience, and not necessarily by scientific, empirical observation. Someone may oppose the use of animals in medical research not because he or she is against medical research, but because that person wants to stop what he or she considers to be cruelty. There is no scientific basis for the assertion that implanting a malignant tumor in a rat is or is not an act of cruelty. A judgment, not a fact, is asserted; a personal value is thus voiced.

Does this mean that values cannot be supported by evidence? Quite the contrary: The more controversial the value judgment is, the more compelling the evidence must be to support it. The word *evidence* in this context does not mean indisputable proof; instead it refers to data used to illuminate the reasoning behind an assertion. In the courtroom, eyewitness testimony is considered evidence even though it does not constitute *indisputable* proof; testimony can be regarded as *sufficient* proof in helping to determine the innocence or guilt of the defendant.

No matter how skillful the argument is or how compelling the supporting evidence is, debatable matters that involve values can never be resolved for all time. Laws may be passed, not passed, or rescinded based on compelling evidence that supports a value judgment, such as with the fifty-five mile-per-hour speed limit, school prayer, abortion, draft registration, the sale of fireworks or alcoholic beverages, or the minimum drinking age. One can assert as part of one's argument that the evidence presented is indisputable (as with the evidence of Holy Writ), but as long as evidence can be used to refute a point of view, that point of view is not indisputable.

Reasoning: The Basis of Argument

To be able to argue effectively, you need first of all to examine that uniquely human activity of the mind known as reasoning. Reasoning refers to a system of mental procedures that allows you to make sense out of problems, to establish judgments, and to use those judgments to solve the problems. Asserting a point of view without bothering to reason it out logically, in detail, is said merely to be "expressing an opinion"; the negative connotation usually ascribed to the word *opinionated* indicates that most people do not favor the shirking of responsibility toward reasoned support of one's opinions. By exercising reason, on the other hand, you are engaging in the prime responsibility for truth: detailed, logical support for your assertions, necessary for convincing others of that truth.

Classifying Reasoning

Reasoning may be classified, following the tradition of Aristotle, according to its goal in communication. These categories are logic-based reasoning (*logos*), emotion-based reasoning (*pathos*), and ethical- or authority-based reasoning (*ethos*). In strong, well-developed arguments, all three kinds of reasoning—or *appeals*, as Aristotle called them—will interact, although one appeal will usually dominate.

Let's look closely at the particulars of each type:

Logic-Based Reasoning This type of reasoning involves the use of objective, step-by-step analysis. Your aim is to be objective, letting the facts speak for themselves as much as possible. There are two varieties of logic-based reasoning: *induction* and *deduction*. You reason *inductively* when you try to form a generalization, such as a blanket assertion, based on the observation of particular clues. Say, for example, that you are curious about whether students with well-developed writing skills obtain higher-paying jobs than do students with undeveloped writing skills. To find out, you must make specific inquiries: You interview recent college graduates who have just landed various types of jobs, and college graduates who have not found jobs after, say, six months of searching. You should try to gather as many testimonies as possible: The more you get, the better, especially when you have an even distribution of responses.

In most cases, fewer than a dozen will be insufficient to back any kind of argument. When you think you have enough to support a generalization, you must then draw your conclusion based on those testimonies—that is, make your "inductive leap": "Strong writing skills *do* [or *do not*] contribute to the likelihood of a college student landing a high-paying job immediately after graduation."

When you reason *deductively*, you proceed in the opposite direction: You accept a generalization—a premise*—as indisputably true, and you then apply that generalization to specific cases. You are thinking deductively when you reason in the following manner: "I know for a fact that my having good writing skills will improve my chances of getting a high-paying job immediately after graduation; *therefore*, if I am to get a high-paying job when I graduate, I must sign up for another course in composition before I graduate."

Notice how both inductive and deductive reasoning, formal as their methodologies are, carry a central element of faith. You act on faith when you make an inductive leap after gathering what you hope is a sufficient number of clues. You also use faith when making a reliable deduction or application of a general principle in a specific instance.

Emotion-Based Reasoning You might ask yourself, How can one reason with emotions? Are not the heart and the brain mutually contradictory? Isn't the attempt to persuade an audience by stirring emotions bound to be deceitful? And after all, isn't history filled with grim reminders of instances where emotional appeals outweighed sound judgment? But reconsider: Why must emotions necessarily be kept separate from intellect? Emotional appeals *do* play a valid part when your aim is to persuade, but the guideline to keep in mind is this: Use an emotional appeal only when a logical framework is apparent (e.g., "the disadvantages of handgun control"), or when a logical framework is not possible (e.g., "why viewing Picasso paintings fills me with pessimism for the future of civilization").

In arguing against the banning of handguns, you might decide to appeal to your audience's need for family security. However, it is altogether too easy to exploit this appeal to security by offering fearful scenarios of families being assaulted and robbed at knifepoint. But when you *add* the emotional appeal to security to your logical, deductive argument (e.g., "Burglaries have increased 75 percent in the community despite handgun-control measures; therefore, there is a greater likelihood that *your* home will be burglarized, since it is a part of the community"), then your emotional appeal reinforces the believability of your stance.

---

*A premise is an assertion, assumed to be true, from which a conclusion is to be drawn.

Along with the appeal to security are several other emotion-based appeals: the appeal to primary drives such as love—including sexual love—and appetite; the appeal to secondary drives, like self-esteem, youthfulness, and power; and the appeal to freedom.

Authority-Based Reasoning   Perhaps you are familiar with this slogan for highway safety:

> 55 mph
> It's not only a good idea . . .
> It's the law.

The belief that this proposition is "a good idea" is derived from logic-based reasoning. For example, one could allude to the significant decreases in traffic fatalities since the fifty-five mile-per-hour speed limit went into effect. But to say that it is "the law" is to appeal to authority—in this case, to a law-enforcing authority empowered to prosecute violators. All authority- or ethical-based appeals are "short cuts" in the sense that their logical or emotional validity has been previously established.

Here is another authority-based argument:

> Vote for me, Jane Doakes, for governor; I have *proven* my leadership ability.

The claim carries its own invitation to explore a logic-based reason: "Look at my public record as mayor (or whatever) and see for yourself how responsible I am." Of course, success as mayor does not guarantee success as governor; but at least there is a limited, logical analogy to be made.

To argue successfully using authority-based reasoning, keep the following suggestions in mind:

1. Beware of relying on vague groups as authority sources (e.g., "Nutritionists the world over recommend Munchies for breakfast") unless you immediately refer to the particular claims of particular nutritionists in different countries.

2. Be sure you have a logical premise for assuming that the authority you refer to is indeed an authority on the subject you are writing about. If you are writing about dieting, for example, you might want to cite an author whose credentials are more than just that of "free-lance journalist" or "experienced dieter." Reference to an author with an advanced academic degree in nutrition or health, or to an author who is a medical doctor, will carry much more authority.

Applying the Three Appeals

Assume that you have been assigned the topic "Astrology is [or is not] a pseudoscience" and you must argue convincingly one way or the other. Assume also that, after a day or two of preliminary reading and contemplation, you decide to argue that astrology *is* a pseudoscience. You begin by listing as many reasons as you can to support your thesis, and you then categorize them according to the Aristotelian appeals of logic, emotion, and authority, as follows (If you are genuinely interested in this topic, make up your own list for comparison before reading on):

LOGIC-BASED REASONS

Astrology is a pseudoscience because its claims cannot be empirically tested.
Astrology is a pseudoscience because there is no central and consistent governing theory to support its claims.
Astrological foundations that are still recognized today were established long before the rise of modern empirical science.
Astrologers, and the horoscopes they produce, contradict each other.
Astrologers' predictions are too generalized to be testable.

EMOTION-BASED REASONS

Taking astrology seriously can interfere significantly with one's sense of reality by tempting one to accept oversimplified, not-to-be-challenged ideas instead of empirically based ideas in the spirit of challenge.
Astrology can be dangerous to one's physical as well as mental health (e.g., following astrology-based diets; becoming so fatalistic as to ignore rational approaches to business, conduct, and human interaction).
Astrological thinking is basically prejudicial and discriminatory ("Oh, I don't associate with Geminis; they're all so two-faced!").

AUTHORITY-BASED REASONS

Highly educated persons in all disciplines tend to reject astrology as a valid form of knowledge.
Many churches denounce astrology because of its intimate link with the occult.
My nightmarish experience with astrology has convinced me that such obsessions with the occult can undermine one's own sanity.*

As you look over your list of appeals, you suddenly realize that it can serve as a possible organizational strategy, or at least as a working outline

---

*In this example, the author becomes an authority because of once having been pro-astrology until something caused a change of heart.

for your paper. You might begin the essay with a logic-based discussion to establish the necessary foundation of logic,* then appeal to your readers' emotions, and end by appealing to authority.

Common Problems in Argumentation

Skill in argumentation, like skill in other kinds of writing, needs to be studied and, above all, practiced. Get into the habit of scrutinizing arguments—your own and others'—so you will be able to distinguish readily between forcefulness and flimflam.

First you should learn to identify four kinds of problems that occur in persuasive writing: (1) confusing opinion with argument, (2) making errors in logic-based reasoning, (3) making errors in emotion-based reasoning, and (4) making errors in authority-based reasoning.

Confusing Opinion with Argument

When we argue a point orally, informally, we often give short shrift to our lines of reasoning, mainly because the audience (usually one or two people) is satisfied with a generalized reason. Or, the audience is often curious only about the opinion rather than the reasoning behind it:

>Moe: What do you think of Smith's job as mayor so far?
>
>Flo: I think he stinks.
>
>Moe: Why is that?
>
>Flo: 'Cause he keeps vetoing important bills.
>
>Moe: I see.

What Moe sees is Flo's *opinion*, not her line of reasoning (some people regard analytical reasoning as inappropriate for coffeebreak conversation). Now if Flo decides to write an essay evaluating Mayor Smith's accomplishments, she runs the risk of transforming her informal, unsubstantiated argument into print, forgetting that the purpose of written argument is to present an intelligent line of reasoning fully and explicitly, anticipating the readers' questions, such as:

>In what way were the vetoed bills important?
>What were Mayor Smith's reasons for vetoing them?

---

*See "Identifying Errors in Logic-Based Reasoning," pp. 128–136 of this chapter.

Which municipal authorities agreed or disagreed with the mayor's decisions, and why?

What was the overall public response to the vetoes?

Identifying Errors in Logic-Based Reasoning

There are four common error types in logic-based argumentation: question-begging, overgeneralizing, faulty generalizing, and faulty deductive reasoning.

Question-Begging * To "beg" the question means to assume that an idea can be accepted as true or unquestionable when, in fact, it cannot be so accepted. In the statement, "Another of the president's militant speeches is scheduled for this evening," the writer is assuming that readers will accept the charge that the president's speeches are militant. For alert readers, at least two questions come to mind: How are the speeches militant? What evidence exists that this evening's speech is going to be militant?

Learning to spot question-begging is important for two reasons: The error occurs often (not always intentionally), and the hidden assumption may be of greater consequence than the explicit one. In the statement, "Unfair insurance companies such as Golden Fortress should cut their deductibles in half," does the assertion "unfair" relate to the companies' high deductibles or to another matter (failure to settle claims promptly, if at all; unkept promises for certain kinds of coverage; too high premiums)? There is no way of knowing just by reading the statement, hence the question goes begging. Moreover, what is left unsaid raises a more serious issue than does the explicit assertion.

Overgeneralizing To overgeneralize means to make an inductive leap prematurely. Imagine a young boy who picks a green apple off a tree, bites hungrily into it, and immediately spits it out, grimacing. He then finds a red apple, bites into it, and finds it sweet. His conclusion: All green apples are sour, and all red apples are sweet. "No, no," his parents explain. "You're jumping to a conclusion [overgeneralizing]; you did not try enough green and red apples." And they hand the boy a golden-delicious apple and a crabapple to prove their point.

Many people, alas, rely on overgeneralizations for a very clear reason: It is much easier to deal with the world when everything is arranged into neat categories. Exceptions are often merely ignored or devalued. It is easy to see the danger in overgeneralizing: It leads to a

---

*See also the *missing premise fallacy* later in this chapter.

refusal to acknowledge anything that does not "fit the picture." By making the effort to suspend belief of statements that seem too neatly conclusive we can better develop a healthy tolerance for exceptions to supposed rules and a greater respect for the category-defying complexity of life. Perhaps the best way to develop this kind of tolerance is to consider a generalization's *opposite*. If someone says, "Minnesota winters are miserable and unbearable," immediately rephrase it in your mind as "Minnesota winters are fun and entirely bearable," then see if you can support the new assertion. In this case, you might well have come up with: "Minnesota, with its snowmobiling, skiing, ice-fishing, ice-skating, and winter carnivals, is a sportsperson's dream come true."

Overgeneralizing directed at human beings and animals is known as *stereotyping*:* "Of course Dominic can sing—he's Italian!" and "Those Irish—they have all the luck" are a couple of the less harmful examples of stereotyping. As with other forms of overgeneralizing, stereotyping can do much harm. When we realize that a major reason for writing is to communicate the complexity of the human condition, the stereotype is an especially odious error in reasoning. It tends to make caricatures out of human beings, and it tends to promote prejudicial thinking. Good writing, by its very nature, is an anti-stereotyping activity.

Faulty Generalizing While overgeneralizing results from drawing conclusions prematurely, faulty generalizing results from poor or misguided reasoning. Consider, for example, the *post hoc fallacy*, taken from the Latin phrase *post hoc ergo propter hoc*, which means "after the fact, therefore because of the fact." Probably all of us have fallen prey to this fallacy; it is the basis for superstition. It means simply that when two unrelated incidents occur closely together, like walking under a ladder and then tripping and falling, a cause-effect relationship is automatically established between them. To the naive, events that happen in proximity must somehow be causally connected. For example, if an eclipse takes place, then any good fortune or misfortune immediately following must have been *caused* by the eclipse.

Another kind of faulty generalization is the *oversimplified* or *vague assertion*, in which a complex concept or event is so radically simplified that it becomes seriously distorted. Here's an example:

"Computers are dehumanizing society."

Does the writer mean that computers *themselves* are dehumanizing society or is he or she referring to the *use* of computers? If the latter is

---

*Consult your dictionary for the fascinating etymology of *stereotyping*.

the case, wouldn't it be more accurate to say that *people* who use computers are dehumanizing society? The answer to this question raises further questions: Are all computer users doing this? These days, that would include virtually everyone! Just some computer users, then? What criteria would one use to single them out? Their obsessiveness with computers? What does that mean?

The most serious potential for the distortion of truth, though, lies in the use of the word *dehumanizing*. The meaning seems clear, but reconsider: Does the writer mean the word literally? In other words, does society actually lose its humanity? And what might that possibly mean? Compassion for fellow human beings? What about that word *society*? Does it refer to American society? The global society? The society of computer users?

Have you noticed that the questions raised in critical response to the previous assertion filled two paragraphs? Imagine how much writing would be necessary to provide clear, fully developed answers to those questions.

Another kind of faulty generalization is the *flawed comparison*, or *flawed analogy*: an unjustifiable or too restrictive comparison between seemingly identical situations in different categories or contexts. Here is an example:

> To discipline a dog, one must be ready with the stick to punish any disobedience, and ready with treats to reward good behavior. Children, likewise, must be disciplined along the same principles of reward and punishment.

The writer is forgetting that the presence of similarities does not exclude the possibility of differences. For example, when comparing a human being of any age to an animal, the writer neglects the fact that the differences may dramatically outweigh the similarities.

The analogy is clearly an important persuasive device, provided that the author is aware of its inevitable limitations. An analogy, in other words, can be carried only so far. In the following example taken from Thomas S. Szasz's *The Second Sin*, the author uses analogy responsibly. See if you can explain why.

> The struggle for definition is veritably the struggle for life itself. In the typical Western, two men fight desperately for the possession of a gun that has been thrown to the ground: whoever reaches the weapon first, shoots and lives; his adversary is shot and dies. In ordinary life, the struggle is not for guns but for words: whoever first defines the situation is the victor; his adversary, the victim. . . . [Consider] the apocryphal story about Emerson visiting Thoreau in jail; Emerson asks: "Henry, what are you doing over there?" Thoreau replies: "Ralph, what are you doing over there?" In short,

he who first seizes the word imposes reality on the other: he who defines thus dominates and lives; and he who is defined is subjugated and may be killed.

Szasz restricts his analogy between manipulating a person with a gun and manipulating a person with a definition by adding the reminder, "In ordinary life, the struggle is not for guns but for words." The gun analogy is effective because it creates in the reader's mind a vivid, concrete image, which the reader is then invited to carry over to a more abstract situation: controlling a person's life by categorizing that person. Szasz, who is a psychiatrist by profession, succeeds with an analogy meant to criticize the way some of his colleagues label patients too readily as "schizophrenic," "manic-depressive," and so on, without realizing how unfair and injurious such labels can be.

The *false dichotomy*, or the *either-or fallacy*, is one of the most common types of faulty generalizing: "Anyone who invests in stocks will either get rich or lose everything"; "If you are not in favor of our policy, then you must be against it." The writer of such a generalization is neglecting the possibility that there may be more than two ways to respond to a given issue. Does the absence of war mean we are at peace? Only in terms of official declaration. Few people would agree that the numerous international tensions, acts of terrorism, and uprisings that describe the general state of global affairs are indicative of peace.

Faulty Deductive Reasoning

Many errors in deduction exist, but we will examine the six that seem to crop up most frequently in argumentative essays: the valid-but-unsound fallacy, the undistributed middle fallacy, the affirming-the-consequent fallacy, the four terms fallacy, the missing premise fallacy, and the evading-the-issue fallacy.

Valid-but-unsound fallacy: Remember that to reason deductively means to begin with a premise you assume to be true, and then to use that premise to test particular situations. Assume, for example, that you accept the premise that extracurricular activities on campus are important to the college experience. You now learn that one such extracurricular activity, skateboarding, has been criticized by the dean of students, and measures have been taken to prohibit skateboarding. You are angered by this because skateboarding, in your opinion, is among those activities that make college life pleasurable. When asked to explain your reasoning, you present a syllogism—a formal pattern of deductive logic consisting of a major premise, a minor premise, and a conclusion:

Major premise: Campus-based extracurricular activities are important to the college experience.

Minor premise:	The skateboarding competition is a campus-based extracurricular activity.
Conclusion:	Skateboarding is important to the college experience.

The conclusion reached is valid, that is, according to one of the principles of logical deduction—the transitive relationship—which may be expressed mathematically as follows:

$$\begin{aligned} \text{if} \quad & A = B, \\ \text{and} \quad & C = A, \\ \text{then} \quad & C = B. \end{aligned}$$

The principle of the transitive relationship holds that if the relation is true between the first element and a second and between the second element and a third, then it is also true between the first and third elements. In this example, A is campus-based extracurricular activities, B is the college experience, and C is skateboarding and its related activities.

But even though a line of reasoning may be valid, it may not necessarily be sound; when an argument is *sound*, the truth and conviction of the assertions are implicit in the major premise. Take another look at the preceding syllogism, and consider these questions: Is it really true that extracurricular activities in general, and skateboarding in particular, are important to the college experience? Is such an assertion always true for all circumstances? When testing for soundness, one must look to particulars. In this example, what provoked the dean of students to criticize skateboarding in the first place? Were several students injured while attempting dangerous stunts? Was the activity conducted in unsafe areas, such as on a parking ramp? Was the activity interfering to a marked degree with academic obligations? Such questions point to one concern: the importance of qualifying the meaning of "extracurricular activity."

Undistributed middle fallacy: A term is "distributed" when it is used to represent the whole class to which it belongs. That is, if the term in question is *ape*, then it must represent all apes whenever the term is used. The term is a "middle" term when it appears in the major premise (the large, sweeping assertion), or the minor premise (the case in point), but not in the conclusion.

The following example illustrates a syllogism with a distributed middle term:

All apes are mammals.
Washoe is an ape.
Therefore, Washoe is a mammal.

The middle term, *ape*, is indeed distributed because it represents all apes in both premises: *Every* ape is a mammal; Washoe is such an ape.

But now examine the following syllogism:

All apes are mammals.
All human beings are mammals.
Therefore, all apes are human beings.

It isn't necessary to analyze the syllogism to be convinced that it is ludicrously flawed. But it's important to know how to analyze the error just the same. The syllogism is invalid because the middle term, *mammals*, is not used to represent the whole class of mammals, a class which includes both apes and human beings. The syllogism fails to reveal that apes and human beings are separate and distinct *members* of the class of mammals; thus, *mammals* is not distributed. The following Venn diagram* will clarify this concept:

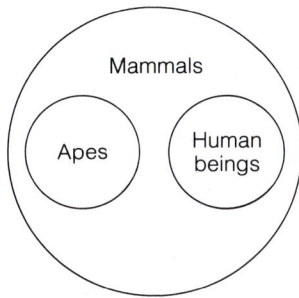

Affirming-the-consequent fallacy: Whenever you set up a hypothetical syllogism (if . . . then), your line of reasoning can become confused if you aren't careful. But first you need to understand the terminology. In a hypothetical syllogism, the first clause in the first line—the "if" clause—is called the *antecedent*; the second clause in the first line—the "then" clause—is called the *consequent*. Your aim here is to affirm the antecedent, as shown in the following example, or to negate the consequent, but not the other way around:

    Antecedent   *Consequent*

If you hear an air-raid siren, it means we are being bombed.
We hear an air-raid siren.
We are being bombed!

---

*The Venn diagram was named after the English logician John Venn (1834–1923), who devised this system of circles to depict categorical relationships.

This hypothetical syllogism is logical. The antecedent has been affirmed, therefore the conclusion is valid, although the syllogism itself is not necessarily true, because the air-raid siren could be a test.

Now take a look at this one:

> If it snows, school will be cancelled.
> It was just announced that school has been cancelled.
> Therefore, it is snowing.

This is an illogical syllogism. Affirming the "then" clause—the consequent—cannot lead logically to such a conclusion. You may be thinking, How could any intelligent person make such an error in reasoning? You'd be surprised; most situations we encounter daily tend to be more complicated than the one in the above example. Read the following syllogism, and this time, make your own brief analysis before you go on:

> If that student keeps cutting class, he will fail.
> That student failed.
> Therefore he continued to cut class.

Again, the consequent is affirmed, and the line of reasoning is invalid; the student could have failed for other reasons. A careless thinker might accept the invalid line of reasoning only because it seems *most likely*, based on what is known about that student's predicament, that the result of cutting class would be failure. But likelihood is one thing, and the logical inevitability indicated in the syllogism's conclusion is quite another.

Just as we cannot affirm the consequent, we cannot deny the antecedent either:

> If Archibald keeps cutting class, he will fail.
> Archibald has stopped cutting class.
> Therefore, Archibald will not fail.

Both affirming the consequent and denying the antecedent are fallacies indicative of reasoning that overlooks the possibility of additional options.

Four terms fallacy: We often substitute one expression for another, assuming that they are interchangeable when in fact there is no logical basis for doing so. That substitute expression is called the *fourth term*—an automatic fallacy because there can be only three terms in a syllogism: the major term (appearing in the major premise), the minor term (appearing in the minor premise), and the middle term (appearing in both the major and the minor premises). The following syllogism illustrates the position of these three terms:

     Middle   *Major*
All rattlesnakes are poisonous.

       Minor   *Middle*
The diamondback is a rattlesnake.

          Minor   *Major*
Therefore, the diamondback is poisonous.

Now study this syllogism:

All irresponsible students are nonachievers.
Gloria is an avid party-goer.
Therefore, Gloria is a nonachiever.

The author of this syllogism has incorrectly used "avid party-goer," the fourth term, interchangeably with "irresponsible."

Missing premise fallacy: Often when presenting our viewpoints we omit a premise because we think it is obvious enough to be a given. This omission is valid insofar as the missing premise is indeed implicit; such a syllogism is called an enthymeme. "That tree will not change color in the fall because it is an olive tree" contains a minor premise and a conclusion, but no major premise ("Olive trees never change color in the fall") because it can be readily deduced from the stated premise and conclusion. Now take a look at the following statement. What is the missing premise?

Ann is an honor student because she studies hard.

The omitted major premise is, "All students who study hard are honor students," which cannot be a given; many students who study hard are not honor students. Thus, it is not a valid enthymeme.

Evading-the-issue fallacy: This error might also be called the *curve-ball fallacy*. The writer introduces an irrelevant issue into the argument and proceeds to build around that issue instead of around the issue that was actually raised. For example, assume you are arguing against the construction of a domed stadium downtown because it would, you claim, result in severe traffic jams during sports events. Someone then counterargues that the stadium *should* be built because the city needs the kind of revenue the stadium can generate. That person has *evaded the issue* you have raised—the traffic problem. This error is sometimes known as the *red herring*, so named from the practice of using red herrings to throw hounds off a scent.

Identifying Errors in Emotion-Based Reasoning

One time or another, all of us have probably resorted to the most popular of emotion-based persuasive tactics, the *ad misericordiam fallacy*—pulling on the heartstrings of others. The motive here is to allow emotions to substitute for, rather than to supplement or amplify, reason. How many of the following *ad misericordiam* situations do you recognize?

> Please don't give me a ticket, officer; my mother's in the hospital, and I've just been laid off.
>
> If you give me a "D" in this course, I'll lose my financial aid. Do you want that on your conscience?
>
> Won't you please give me a dollar for a sandwich? I have not eaten a thing in two days.

Another emotion-based error, one that is particularly odious and all too persuasive, is the *ad hominem fallacy*, which attempts to discredit an individual's professional views or qualifications by attacking his or her person. "Marlis Mouthy should not be elected student body president; she swears too much," is a typical *ad hominem* (literally "toward the man") *fallacy*. The fallacy can also work in reverse: "On the other hand, Priscilla Pious should be elected student body president; she is known to attend church regularly."

A third fallacy that plays on the emotions is the *ad populum fallacy*, used often in advertising and in politicking. It entails appealing to the greatest wants and needs, to the idealized self-image, of an entire people, as shown in the following example:

> The decent American people will no longer tolerate the sale and distribution of books containing obscene material.*
>
> Being the upholders of flag and family that you are, surely you will not allow civil rights activists to speak in our midst.

Similar to the ad populum fallacy is the widespread *bandwagon fallacy*, which persuades one to purchase a product or take action because

---

*Note that this example also begs the question, What is meant by "obscene"?

EVERYONE ELSE is doing so. "People everywhere are switching to Hi-Blast Bourbon"; "Don't be the only family in your neighborhood without a Maxiview VCR!"

Identifying Errors in Authority-Based Reasoning

In arguing from authority you are using character—your own or that of another individual or group—to establish the truth or falsehood of an assertion. The trick is to make sure that the authority figure is specifically suitable for substantiating your claims. A vague authority, or a vague use of authority, made to appear specific and substantial to the audience, is known as *hypostatization*. Because of its frequent use in advertising, hypostatization can filter into your argumentative technique if you are not careful. Here are a few typical examples of hypostatized claims:

> Religious leaders everywhere oppose the draft.

How many religious leaders does this claim suggest? Ten? Ten thousand? What kind of leaders does it refer to? Leaders of established religions, or of the newly formed group of koala bear worshipers? And what is the nature of the opposition? Peaceful protest? The vandalism of draft-registration headquarters?

> Four out of five nurses recommend Ajax bandages over any other.

How many nurses are represented in the total sample? One million or just five? Are they registered nurses or less qualified nurses? What are they recommending the bandages *for*?

> Science tells us that a devastating earthquake will strike California during the next lunar eclipse.

What exactly is meant by "science"? And even if the writer meant "scientists," what kind of scientists would they have been? Seismologists? Botanists?

Another authority-based error is the reference to the *wrong authority*. If you are attacking the use of pesticides on crops grown for human consumption, quoting the views of, say, a supermarket manager would not be relevant—unless that supermarket manager also happened to be a biochemist who was researching the toxicity levels of the pesticide found on the produce in question.

Keep in mind that both of these misapplications of authority-based reasoning can easily create the *illusion* of authenticity. As a result, they can deceive the unwary.

Building an Effective Argument

It is time now to veer our attention from avoiding the common errors of argument to harvesting its strengths. Anyone who is aware of all that is going on in the world has a complicated assortment of opinions and attitudes, with considerable uncertainties, unassimilated facts, and half-truths added to the mixture. And you might wonder, Is there some general procedure one can follow that can bring order to chaos? The answer is yes.

Examine any well-developed persuasive essay and you are likely to uncover a common framework, arranged something like this: introduction (leading to thesis), qualification of thesis, evidence, refutation of opposing views, and recommendations and conclusion. This framework is as old as the law courts of ancient Rome, and has not lost its effectiveness over the centuries. Let's take a closer look at each section:

The topic is presented in an engaging manner in the *introduction* and a thesis idea is stated, or at least inferred. The opening sentence is especially important as an attention-getter.

The next stage focuses on *qualification of thesis*. Events leading up to and associated with the problem are presented. Facts, statistics, and individuals or groups associated with the problem are narrated or described and put into perspective.

Logical proofs, testimonies, laws, and facts are then introduced as *evidence* to support the thesis. The evidence must be as complete and as verifiable as possible, or else the thesis may be easily refuted.

Next, any contradictory arguments are analyzed and shown to be inadequate or false; this is the *refutation of opposing views* process. Many times arguments fail to convince readers because authors do not investigate differing views carefully enough. Authors must also try to avoid perceiving their audience as an opponent just because they adhere to a contradictory viewpoint. As it is only natural for the reader to resist an author's attempt to present a viewpoint that contradicts a deep-rooted belief, the author must take pains to work in harmony with the reader's feelings. This means taking the time to establish a common ground with readers—in other words, to demonstrate how readers' views, however different they seem to be, reflect many of the same values that the author holds. Authors should also try to point out that the differences in opinion stem from additional new knowledge perhaps, or from an overlooked premise, which, if articulated, would easily convince the audience. The kind of persuasive writing that reflects this kind of concern and respect for the audience's views is sometimes referred to as *Rogerian argument* (named after the humanist/psychologist Carl Rogers, who was among the first to articulate the need for this rhetorical stance).

The *recommendations* and *conclusion* are presented last: The highlights of the argument are summarized, the thesis restated (usually with a different emphasis), and a conclusion drawn, with recommendations, if relevant.

Read the following newspaper editorial twice, first to get the gist of it, and then to analyze it in terms of the above argumentative framework.

BAN THIS POISON BEFORE IT POISONS US

Thesis stated in headline

The story is disgustingly familiar. Scientists warned government officials more than 10 years ago that a pesticide used since the '50s on U.S. citrus crops and grain posed an extreme cancer risk for exposed workers.

Attention-getting opening sentence

Introduction, quickly establishing seriousness of the problem

Tests on laboratory animals show a pesticide you probably never heard of—ethyline dibromide, or EDB—is the worst carcinogenic chemical around. It causes birth defects and miscarriages in test animals, and scientists say it could do the same to humans.

Evidence

Workers and researchers asked the Occupational Safety and Health Administration to restrict the amounts of EDB workers were exposed to. Back then, OSHA said exposure levels didn't warrant stricter standards.

The Environmental Protection Agency wanted to ban EDB in 1980, saying that virtually every worker exposed to legal limits for a career could expect to die of cancer. But when growers and chemical manufacturers promised to reduce exposure levels instead, EPA dropped the matter.

Narration, emphasizing historical background

Today, a decade later, citrus fruits and grains are still fumigated with EDB to destroy insects. At least 100,000 workers are exposed to the deadly chemical every year.

And now, traces of EDB have shown up in water wells in California and Florida and in fruits, vegetables, meat, milk and baked goods in those states, plus Hawaii and Georgia. There is no evidence that such traces endanger humans.

Narration, emphasizing current situation

Fearing the worst, Florida officials on Saturday banned growers from injecting EDB into the soil around citrus trees for at least 60 days.

And the EPA doesn't want to take any more chances. This month it plans to ban agricultural use of EDB. OSHA also has admitted that the health risks appear far greater than for any work hazard it has ever regulated. That agency wants to dramatically slash permissible exposure levels from 20,000 parts per billion in the air to 150 parts. And it wants employers to initiate tests to protect workers.

Narration, emphasizing immediate plans

Those measures come late. The health and safety of human workers have been hanging in the balance for a decade, while OSHA and the EPA have

> done little. OSHA says, even now, that new safety rules won't be ready for six months.
>
> *Refutation*
>
> Not everybody in government acknowledges the threat. The Department of Agriculture agrees with growers and chemical industry officials who say there are no pesticide alternatives as cheap or effective as EDB.
>
> *Conclusion, reemphasizing seriousness of the problem; recommendation; restatement of thesis.*
>
> That is true. But none is so deadly either. Researchers must find other methods of controlling insects. But in the meantime we can't continue endangering workers or allowing this cancer-causing chemical to be pumped into our food chain and water supply. EDB must be banned. Pesticides were meant to kill pests, not us.
>
> *USA Today*, September 20, 1983

Now that you can observe the framework in practice, you may be able to understand better why it works. An introduction is necessary, first of all, because it orients the reader to the issue quickly and efficiently; the introduction also sparks that very important ingredient, *interest*—preferably immediate interest. When writing introductions of your own, you would be wise to think of your typical reader as someone who is in a hurry, with many matters competing for his or her valuable time. This impatient reader (you remind yourself) is going to give you one or two minutes to get his or her interest kindled.

Look at the opening sentence of this editorial: "The story is disgustingly familiar." The reader is hooked at once. But the job of introducing the topic is not over yet. The potential seriousness of pesticide contamination is quickly articulated. The reader now wants to know the background details, the evidence to support the thesis, and the kinds of counterarguments that might exist. Whether you choose to discuss any one of these elements before the others is largely a matter of style, or a sense of what might work best for the topic at hand.

The last chore the editorial writer must face is a hard-hitting wrap-up—a conclusion. Notice the writer's strategy: He or she has chosen to impart a sense of urgency—an emotion-based argument, emphasizing the appeal to security—while reemphasizing the thesis:

> Researchers must find other methods of controlling insects. But in the meantime we can't continue endangering workers or allowing this cancer-causing chemical to be pumped into our food chain and water supply. EDB must be banned.

The author of the preceding editorial presents the points firmly, and makes little effort to find a common ground with those who share contrasting opinions about pesticide contamination of water supplies. Perhaps the nature of the topic or the urgency of the message would make a Rogerian approach ineffective; or perhaps there can be no plausible common ground. A Rogerian strategy works best when value systems are being argued; when the evidence is less objectively demonstrable.

In the following essay on the usefulness of movie ratings, freshman Anita Lee attempts to establish a common ground with readers whose views differ from hers. As you read the essay, ask yourself how well Lee's Rogerian strategy works. Might she have represented contrasting views more accurately? More sympathetically? *Less* sympathetically?

HOW DO I RATE THEE? LET ME COUNT THE WAYS

"The motion picture industry's rating board nearly slapped an X rating on Al Pacino's movie *Scarface* as too violent and unfit for youthful eyes," writes Mary Jane Hunter in *USA Today*. . . . That really scared the producers out of their Calvin Kleins, for, according to Ms. Hunter, the youngsters are their best customers. Because the producers feared financial disaster, they pressed an appeal and won a less restrictive R rating. These days, most moviemakers will do almost anything to avoid either a G or an X rating, both considered catastrophic at the box office. The G is looked on as too childish. And many theaters will not show movies rated X; neither will many television stations and newspapers advertise or review them. Many parents fear that their children will be exposed to PG movies that ought to be rated R or X, and as a result, they tend to mistrust the rating system.

Some people feel that the rating system has been so manipulated by the industry that it (the rating system) has become meaningless, and it should be discarded. They might feel that way because they misunderstand and misjudge what the rating system really intends to do and what it should not and cannot do. First, the rating system has one objective: to give some advance cautionary information to parents so they can make their own decisions about which films their children should or should not see. That is the sole reason for the rating system. Second, the rating system cannot act as a second parent. If parents do not care what their children are viewing, or if they are only casually involved in knowing more about a film, then the system is of little worth, if any.

Sure. The rating system has its flaws. It is subjective. There are no precise, fixed lines of demarcation between the G, PG, R, and X ratings, nor do I think there can be. No matter how often people try to tamper with the system, their discontentment with specific ratings will never be eliminated. Although the ratings draw no particular boundaries, each of them bears significant implications. "G" means "general audiences admitted," with nothing that parents would find offensive for their children. It does not mean "a film for children." "PG" means "parental guidance suggested," which in turn means that parents should not allow their children to see the PG-rated movie without learning more. It will contain some language, or sensuality, or violence, but at a level most parents would find acceptable for their children. "R", or restricted, means adult material present in the film, and those under the age of seventeen will be admitted only with a parent or adult guardian. The film will contain violence, sometimes harsh and hard; or sensuality, though not in a totally explicit way; or strong, tough language. "X" means explicit adult material and no one under seventeen is admitted. "X" does *not* mean pornographic, because films are also rated X for their violence or brutal language. This rating system, according to Jack Valenti, president of the Motion Picture Association of America, works as a guide for parents.

Believe it or not, more parents feel satisfied with the movie ratings the way they are now. In 1983, 65 percent of parents with children under eighteen found the rating system very useful or fairly useful, and 27 percent said that it was not very useful. This is the highest affirmation in seven years, according to statistics from the Opinion Research Corporation. Pam Bush, 37, cheerfully says, "I'm satisfied with the movie ratings the way they are now. Trying to describe the content of every movie that's released would be endless and futile." Parents are not the only ones who have a voice in this subject. When I go to R-rated movies, I have to go with an adult. I do not mind at all, though, because I realize that some restrictions need to be set on what kids see on the screen. My parents do not really mind what movie I go to see, as long as it is not triple-X. But what about the unsatisfied parents and moviegoers?

Jim Vanderbeek, 35, says, "Movie ratings don't describe what is taking place on the screen. They're not descriptive enough." It is this major outcry against the rating system that brought the motion picture industry's rating board together to set up the latest rating classification—PG–13. This new rating emphasizes parental guidance for children, especially for those who are under the age of thirteen. PG–13 is more descriptive since it specifies the need for guidance for children of a specific age and under.

Should parents let their children see a movie based on its rating alone? The answer is no. Although the rating system possesses a durable integrity, it does not describe exactly what is on the screen. This is where parents need to step in. There are reviews in the daily newspaper briefly summarizing what the movie is about, giving the industry's rating and its own narrative rating. On one of television's most popular review stations "At the Movies," critics Roger Ebert and Gene Siskel express their popular and not-so-popular opinions to the audience while showing a preview of the movie. Many other sources of movie reviews can be found whether they are in *The Moviegoer* magazine or on television. The main point is that neither parents nor moviegoers are limited to finding out what a movie is like just by the movie industry's rating system. They should take the time and responsibility to be alert for movie reviews, and not just depend on the rating system. The rating system is not perfect, but it is honest. It represents the sanest attempt I know to fulfill the obligations of the film industry to all the moviegoers of this country.

Anita Lee

Principles of Development: Aiming to Persuade

Summary

Arguments are discussions of viewpoints that usually require the careful use of logic-, emotion-, and authoritative-based reasoning as well as empirical data to be convincing. Writers should take care to represent contrasting views accurately, keeping in mind that *argument* need not be *opposition*. The special effort to establish a common ground with the audience is known as Rogerian argument. Arguments often fail to convince because of one or more reasoning errors. These may be outlined as follows:

   I. Errors in logic-based reasoning
      A. Question-begging
      B. Overgeneralizing
      C. Faulty generalizing
         1. Post hoc fallacy
         2. Oversimplified or vague assertion
         3. Flawed comparison or analogy
         4. False dichotomy or either-or fallacy
      D. Faulty deductive reasoning
         1. Valid-but-unsound fallacy
         2. Undistributed middle fallacy
         3. Affirming-the-consequent fallacy
         4. Four terms fallacy
         5. Missing premise fallacy
         6. Evading-the-issue fallacy
  II. Errors in emotion-based reasoning
      A. Ad misericordiam fallacy
      B. Ad hominem fallacy
      C. Ad populum fallacy
      D. Bandwagon fallacy
 III. Errors in authority-based reasoning
      A. Hypostatization
      B. Wrong authority

FOR DISCUSSION

1. Discuss the kinds of experiences you have had when arguing controversial topics with relatives, associates, and friends. You may have discovered that many people are reluctant to bring up reasons for believing this way or that. Sometimes you sense that a friendship could be ruined by attempting to argue out what you consider to be erroneous reasoning on the part of your friend.

   But the great Renaissance essayist and father of the essay, Michel de Montaigne, is somewhat more optimistic: "When anyone contradicts me, he arouses my attention, not my anger; I advance towards the man who contradicts me, who instructs me. The cause of truth ought to be the common cause of both." ("On the Art of Conversing") What might we do, in our conversations, to encourage Montaigne's noble attitude?

2. How do logic-based, emotion-based, and authority-based arguments differ from each other? Suggest topics for which one argument would be preferable to the other two. Can you also suggest a topic for which all three arguments could be equally applicable?

3. Review the discussion of role playing and writing in Chapter 2. How can role playing be particularly useful in persuasive writing?

4. Lead a class discussion that focuses on how the following opinions might best be developed into persuasive essays. Take note when any terms ought to be defined.
    a. You need a college degree to get a good job these days.
    b. When people skip breakfast, they're not as energetic or alert as when they do eat breakfast.
    c. Police officers are always speeding, even with their sirens off, so why should anybody else obey the speed limit?
    d. Lab tests on rats demonstrate that large doses of saccharin can cause cancer; therefore, people should be cautious of their saccharin intake.
    e. Women are weaker than men.
    f. Excessive television viewing can undermine reading ability.
    g. As a safeguard against preadolescent boys becoming effeminate, parents should make sure that their sons get involved in sports, and that they don't get too involved in things like cooking or housecleaning.

5. What attitude toward argument is conveyed by the use of Rogerian strategy? Referring to any of the essays in this or the following chapter, determine whether their persuasiveness would be increased or decreased by the use or elimination of Rogerian strategy.

6. Each of the following contains at least one error in reasoning. Describe the error in your own words, then identify each *type* of error represented. For example, if it's a logic-based error such as faulty deductive reasoning, identify the type of faulty deduction—undistributed middle fallacy, affirming-the-consequent fallacy, and so on. Or it might be an emotion-based error, such as *ad misericordiam*, or an authority-based error, like hypostatization.

a. I was told that if I observed hundreds of fish floating belly-up, it would mean that the Pine Lake is contaminated. Well, I know for a fact that Pine Lake has been contaminated, so when I arrive at the lake I will definitely see hundreds of fish floating belly-up.

b. It doesn't make sense that we must give a speech without notes. Professional speakers are always free to use notes if they choose.

c. Since drinking alcoholic beverages is part of adulthood, and young people must prepare for adulthood, young people should be permitted to drink alcoholic beverages.

d. If A is a part of B, and C is a part of B, then A must be a part of C.

e. I'm never going to eat at the Grizzly Inn again; the last two times I was there the service was poor.

f. I just knew that as soon as I began watering the lawn it would start raining.

g. Scientists claim that because nuclear power safety regulations are so thorough and so carefully enforced, the danger of a radiation accident is negligible.

h. Intellectuals prefer chess to dancing, so it follows that Maria, who just made the dean's list, will turn me down when I ask her to accompany me to the sophomore ball.

i. Un-American organizations like the Urban Renewal League should be placed under careful surveillance.

j. Sean Honcho doesn't deserve an academy award because he was arrested for possession of peyote.

k. Please won't you adopt one of these homeless kittens? They are starved for love and traumatized by having been abandoned by their former masters.

l. God has determined all that has been, is, and ever shall be; therefore it is useless to try and change the future.

m. It is important to eat as little meat as possible. I know, because even though I've never studied nutrition, the less meat I eat, the healthier I feel.

n. You really ought to get away from the books over the weekend; nobody else in our class spends weekends studying.

FOR WRITING

1. Write your own newspaper editorial on any environmental issue, such as pesticide contamination—the topic used in the previous editorial; or, choose one of the following topics:

a. Nuclear-waste disposal hazards
b. Mercury contamination, especially in fish
c. Effects of industrial pollutants on vegetation or animal life
d. Effects of smog on respiratory ailments, or on temperament*

2. Select one of the largely unquestioned assumptions you've encountered somewhere along the line and challenge its validity. A statement like "Cats are aloof," or "A liberal arts degree is useless in today's job market," or "Flowers will grow better if you talk and sing to them" would work fine. Prepare a fact sheet on which you will substantiate, qualify, or negate the claims in question. Finally, prepare a three- to five-page essay entitled, "The Truth About _____," or something to that effect.

3. Outline a logic-based, emotion-based, and authority-based argument for each of the following:
   a. Voluntary prayer in public schools should (or should not) be permitted.
   b. Cities should (or should not) adopt a law that would ban handguns.
   c. Parents should (or should not) have a say in determining the educational policies for their elementary school children.
   d. The FCC should (or should not) ban commercials aimed at children under eight years of age.

4. You have been asked to serve on a committee to reassess the national fifty-five miles-per-hour speed limit. Should the speed limit become a matter for state legislation? Should it be retained as is and enforced? Retained but not enforced? Changed? To what? Or should there be no imposed speed limit at all for highway driving? Present your case as clearly and as convincingly as you can, using the elements of argumentation described in this chapter.

COMPUTER WRITING

1. For students working in pairs at separate terminals with networking capability: Student A assumes the role of irate citizen and writes a brief but nasty letter to Student B, who assumes the role of a corporate executive responsible for the cause of Student A's grievance. Student B responds as diplomatically as possible.

---

*You may want to do some background reading on the smog problems in large metropolitan areas, especially Mexico City and Los Angeles.

2. For students working in pairs at a terminal: Student A expresses, in one paragraph, his or her stance on a debatable topic. Student B asks questions or voices a counterargument. Student A then elaborates, rephrases, or refutes accordingly. One student should keep track of the kinds of changes made, including the particular commands used to edit the text.

Special Topic: Mass-Media Persuasion

Advertising is very much a part of all our waking lives and nearly impossible to avoid. Billboards hawk at us from the highways, radio and TV commercials douse our ears and eyes with repetitive messages, and magazine and newspaper ads worm their way into our consciousness as we read. These all constitute a powerful legion of persuasive force upon our judgment.

It's not surprising that mass-media advertising is immensely successful, and that a good deal of its success is due to thorough research into consumer psychology. Advertisers, like politicians, are aware of their audiences—aware of our deepest human drives, fantasies, and fears. Advertising, like politics, can sometimes be exploitative; it can manipulate language to arouse our inner longings only to increase product sales.

Understanding advertising strategies, by way of analyzing the persuasive elements of printed ads and TV and radio commercials, can increase public awareness of exploitative devices. Students learning about persuasive strategies can put commercials and ads to the test by examining them for errors in reasoning and for unwarranted associations between the product and a basic drive that is irrelevant to that product.

The elements of a typical magazine ad, shown in Figure 8-1, include the *headline*, the *art* or *image*, the *copy* or *text*, and the *logo* (emblem or trademark).

The format is ideal for conveying messages quickly and effectively. The headline and the art work together to grab the reader's immediate attention, which is then secured by the sparse, strongly worded text.

Advertising copywriters arouse a variety of appeals in their ads. Here are a few of them:

1. *Basic drives.* Some ads appeal to such basic human needs as sex, appetite, security, love, self-esteem, and maternal and paternal instincts. An ad for brandy with the heading "Share Your Golden Moments" depicts a couple snuggled together by the fireplace on a cold winter night.

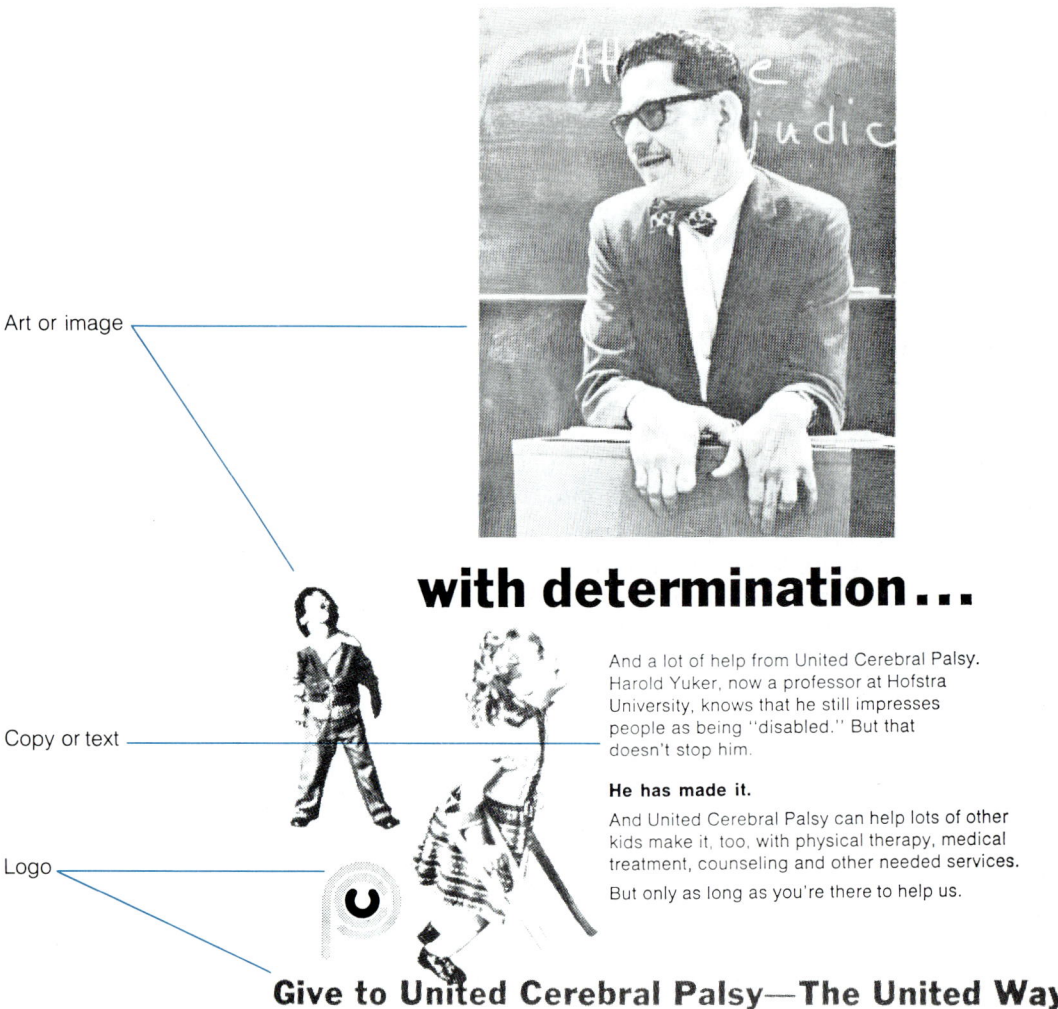

Figure 8-1

2. *Nostalgia.* "Bring back the joys of childhood; drink Kool Aid."

3. *Authority.* Mr. X, an Olympic gold-medalist, eats Wheaties for breakfast.

4. *Fantasy and intrigue.* An automobile ad asserts, "Test drive a Jaguar and enter an exciting new world of high performance."

5. *The five senses.* "The warm, soft look of steel . . ." begins an ad for contemporary office furniture.*

Once again, some ads exploit these appeals in an irresponsible manner, but most do not. In one of the exercises below, you will have an opportunity to analyze and evaluate several ads in terms of manipulative strategies.

MASS-MEDIA PERSUASION: TOPICS FOR DISCUSSION

1. Attack or defend Marya Mannes's attitude toward TV commercials in the following excerpt from her essay "Television: The Splitting Image."

TELEVISION: THE SPLITTING IMAGE

A bride who looks scarcely fourteen whispers, "Oh, Mom, I'm so *happy*!" while a doting family adjusts her gown and veil and a male voice croons softly, "A woman is a harder thing to be than a man. She has more feelings to feel." The mitigation of these excesses, it appears, is a feminine deodorant called Secret, which allows our bride to approach the altar with security as well as emotion.

Eddie Albert, a successful actor turned pitchman, bestows his attention on a lady with two suitcases, which prompt him to ask her whether she has been on a journey. "No," she says, or words to that effect, as she opens the suitcases. "My two boys bring back their soiled clothes every weekend from college for me to wash." And she goes into the familiar litany of grease, chocolate, mud, coffee, and fruit-juice stains, which presumably record the life of the average American male from two to fifty. Mr. Albert compliments her on this happy device to bring her boys home every week and hands her a box of Biz, because "Biz *is* better."

Two women with stony faces meet cart to cart in a supermarket as one takes a jar of peanut butter off a shelf. When the other asks her in a voice of nitric acid why she takes that brand, the first snaps, "Because I'm choosy for

---

*This is also a good example of *image reversal*—creating positive associations toward a product that traditionally has had less appealing associations; steel traditionally suggests a cold, hard image.

my family!" The two then break into delighted smiles as Number Two makes Number One taste Jif for "mothers who are choosy."

If you have not come across these dramatic interludes, it is because you are not home during the day and do not watch daytime television. It also means that your intestinal tract is spared from severe assaults, your credibility unstrained. Or, for that matter, you may look at commercials like these every day and manage either to ignore them or find nothing—given the fact of advertising—wrong with them. In that case, you are either so brainwashed or so innocent that you remain unaware of what this daily infusion may have done and is doing to an entire people as the long-accepted adjunct of free enterprise and support of "free" television.

"Given the fact" and "long-accepted" are the key words here. Only socialists, communists, idealists (or the BBC) fail to realize that a mass television system cannot exist without the support of sponsors, that the massive cost of maintaining it as a free service cannot be met without the massive income from selling products. You have only to read of the unending struggle to provide financial support for public, noncommercial television for further evidence.

Besides, aren't commercials in the public interest? Don't they help you choose what to buy? Don't they provide needed breaks from programming? Aren't many of them brilliantly done, and some of them funny? And now, with the new sexual freedom, all those gorgeous chicks with their shining hair and gleaming smiles? And if you didn't have commercials taking up a good part of each hour, how on earth would you find enough program material to fill the endless space/time void?

Tick off the yesses and what have you left? You have, I venture to submit, those intangible but possibly high costs: the diminution of human worth, the infusion and hardening of social attitudes no longer valid or desirable, pervasive discontent, and psychic fragmentation.

Marya Mannes, *Saturday Review*, Nov. 1970.

2. Discuss Marya Mannes's persuasive strategy in the preceding example. How closely does she follow the classical argumentative framework? Do you detect any flaws in her argument? What are the strongest elements?

3. Discuss the persuasive strategy at work in each of the following magazine ads. Identify as many different persuasive appeals as you can. Which appeals, if any, seem inappropriate? What additional appeals might the advertiser have used to persuade readers of the product's value?

Introducing the most powerful, value-packed business solutions in their field. We call 'em...

WORKHORSES

Don't be left behind in the stampede towards small business computers. Get your hands on a workhorse from ALTOS,® one of the three leading U.S. suppliers.*

For starters, Altos systems provide the truly integrated computer solutions businesses demand. Solutions that can be easily modified, upgraded and expanded to fit your growing needs.

Unlike most computers, a powerful 16-bit Altos multi-user microcomputer system lets up to a half dozen people share computer resources simultaneously. One computer, for example, can quickly perform order entry, accounting, inventory control and financial planning applications—all at the same time.

Altos systems come with many advanced features built-in. You can easily add more data storage and peripherals, or team up other Altos workhorses in a reliable and flexible low-cost network.

Altos Software Availability Program lets you choose from over 100 packages including a wide range of industry business applications.

Prompt nationwide service is available from the Customer Service Division of TRW, Inc.** with ongoing support from your qualified Altos dealer.

Now's the time to hitch your wagon to our team of powerful, value-packed, field-proven workhorses. Your Altos dealer can harness a complete business solution that's just right for you. For an appointment, call, write or return the coupon today.

Packed with more value for business

☐ Please tell me more about the workhorses from Altos.
☐ My application is _____
☐ Have an Altos dealer contact me for an appointment.
Name _____ Title _____
Company _____ Phone _____
Address _____
City/State/Zip _____
Mail to: Altos Marketing Services, 2641 Orchard Park Way, San Jose, CA 95134
TISF-1

Call: 800-538-7872
(In Calif., 800-662-6265)

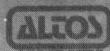

*Source: DATAQUEST, 7/25/83. Estimated U.S. Market Shares of Leading Very Small Business Computer Suppliers. (IBM, Tandy & Altos—ranked 1, 2 & 3. **TRW—continental U.S. DATAFORCE—Canada. ALTOS—a registered trademark of Altos Computer Systems. ©1983 Altos Computer Systems.

Principles and Projects

This year, The Smart Sets from Zenith have more smart, new features than ever before.

There are models that put a 25-inch diagonal picture in a 19-inch space.

There are remote controls that let you switch from VCR to cable to games to regular TV.* Some remotes have Parental Control that lets you lock out channels you don't want. Some even control both the TV and a Zenith VCR.

Here's another brainy idea: all Smart Set models are stereo-adaptable. Some are ready now with built-in stereo decoders, amplifiers and multiple speakers.

And every Smart Set has the new Chromacolor Contrast Picture Tube for more dramatic contrast.

Advanced System 3. The Smart Sets from Zenith. There's only one way to describe them. Brainy.

The quality goes in before the name goes on.®

*With optional accessory.

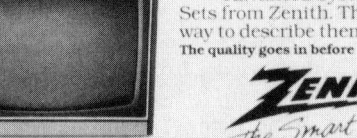

We don't buy just any seats. We design them.

GM begins with detailed studies of the human body. Biomedical research. The kind of comprehensive investigation of anatomy da Vinci undertook in the 1500s.

As a leader in the field of Human Factors Engineering, we design interiors scientifically to minimize the possible distractions from your driving.

It may take us two years and countless clay models to arrive at a more comfortable, durable seat for new GM cars and trucks. But we think it's worth it.

And we believe old Leonardo would have thought so, too.

We believe in taking the extra time, giving the extra effort and paying attention to every detail. That's what it takes to provide the quality that leads more people to buy GM cars and trucks than any other kind. And why GM owners are the most loyal on the road.

That's the GM commitment to excellence.

Chevrolet • Pontiac • Oldsmobile • Buick • Cadillac • GMC Truck

Leonardo da Vinci gave us a great idea for bucket seats.

Let's get it together. Buckle up.

Nobody sweats the details like GM.

Persuasive Writing Projects

CHAPTER 9

The impulse to take up pen and paper is seldom stronger than when we witness someone grinding a cherished idea or value of ours into mincemeat. Our immediate reaction may not be mentionable in polite society, but eventually our "higher" faculties take over and we sit down to write, calling to task all we know about persuasive strategy.

At this very moment, with pen poised, we need to decide which kind of persuasive essay we want to produce. This chapter will introduce you to the basic techniques for composing three common types of essays designed to persuade: the opinion essay, or *feature* in journalism; the pro-con, or position, essay; and the problem-solving, or investigative, essay.

The Opinion Essay

Opinion pieces range from letters to the editor to lively newspaper essays, which are commonly referred to as *columns*. They are relatively short, usually 750–1,000 words, and are fun to write as well as to read. They are often easy to attack or defend because their arguments do not require much time to analyze thoroughly; nor is it their purpose to do so. But if that is the case, what determines their quality? The *liveliness of the writing* is one key characteristic. It determines whether, say, the writer's anger, resentment, or enthusiasm is vividly transmitted, or whether the eloquence and cleverness of the piece is immediately apparent. Another aspect that affects the essay's quality is *a logical, coherent unfolding of a debatable point of view*.

Consider L. Moore's letter to the editor of the *San José Mercury* in light of these criteria:

> Instead of banning handguns, we should ease the requirements granting women licenses to carry them. If most women in exposed jobs (nurses, waitresses, etc.) were armed, the scum that laughs its way through our justice system might think twice before their casual assaults against women.
>
> I can hear the gun-banners deploring the innocent victims (overly amorous) who might get injured. I have a hunch, however, that in the balance, there might be a lot fewer innocents being raped and assaulted, such as at _____ Pancake House.
>
> If anyone ever makes a move on my daughter as she goes from car to apartment, or forces her car from the road as she drives alone, may his soul rest in peace, because he's dead meat.

After the thesis is clearly stated in the first sentence, what follows is vague conjecture rather than anything resembling logical support of that thesis: ". . . the scum . . . might think twice. . . . I have a hunch . . . there might be a lot fewer innocents being raped. . . ." And what other than emotional free association links the last paragraph to the other two? The letter's single redeeming attribute is expressiveness, but expressiveness counts very little when at least a minimal degree of reasoning is absent.

Now examine this letter from a football enthusiast for liveliness and coherence:

> I was delighted by the gigantic front-page headlines proclaiming our team's Super Bowl victory, and by the full-color photograph of loyal, jubilant fans throwing their hats and their Cracker Jacks into the air and hugging each other. But then I noticed, in the lower left-hand corner, that ugly story about the famine in Ethiopia. I mean, good heavens, are you people trying to depress us? Are you trying to ruin our fun? Super Bowl Sunday comes only once a year, so why spoil things? Here I was enjoying my steak and lobster dinner when my eye slipped from the Super Bowl coverage down to that awful story. Needless to say it spoiled my appetite.
>
> Shame on you people! Another tactless mistake like that and I'll cancel my subscription!

Here the writing is crisp—and bitingly ironic. The thesis, that it is irresponsible for newspapers to give front-page importance to an athletic event, even a major one, when people are dying of starvation in massive numbers, emerges through the very reversal of that stance. The thesis is supported by the attitude of ridicule that the irony generates. Now if the author of this letter wished to demonstrate convincingly the view that insufficient emphasis on news about human crises can seriously interfere with emergency food drives, for example, he would then be obliged to exemplify his assertions. The author might call attention to several front-page spreads that had been published during times when such crises were taking place, or allude to the opinions of media experts as well as of famine-relief fundraisers.*

One of the most popular kinds of opinion pieces is the *syndicated column*. Here a high premium is placed on sustained wit, on cleverness, and on the overall character or personality (*ethos*) of the columnist. Columnists are often outspoken and at the same time they are virtuosos of style, so that you love reading them even though they may infuriate you. Andy Rooney is a case in point:

THE PROBLEM WITH SOCCER IS . . .

The United States ought to have a team in the World Cup matches every four years, even if we finish last. It's a great international sporting event, and we ought to play in it even though it's not our game.

One of the problems for us is that we don't know what to call it. They call it "football," but as every red-blooded American knows, we have the only real football game, even though we don't play it with our feet much of the time. We call their kind of football "soccer."

A New York Times reporter wrote his story about Italy's recent World Cup victory without ever mentioning the name of the game. The official governing body is called the Federation Internationale de Football Association, but the reporter didn't want to be technically wrong by calling the game "soccer," and he probably didn't want to irritate and confuse American football fans by calling it "football."

This was the first year American television covered the World Cup games, and there was a lot of talk about when soccer will become as popular here as it is in Europe and South America. I think a safe guess for that time span might be never. Many schools now have soccer teams, and there's no doubt that soccer is growing in popularity, but it always has been.

The reason soccer isn't as popular here as football is that it isn't as good a game. People who like soccer and don't like football say that football is too slow because the ball isn't in play enough of the time. That's like saying golf is a dull game because golfers are only hitting the ball a small percentage of the time they're on the course.

My complaint about soccer is that the ball is always in play, but it isn't usually going anywhere in particular. The person the ball is kicked to doesn't usually get it, and often when a goal is scored it appears to be at least half luck.

---

*See the next section, "The Pro-Con Essay."

Soccer, unlike football or baseball, doesn't give you much time to anticipate the next play or savor the last one. People who like baseball enjoy thinking about what the next play will be, and the football fan uses the pause between plays to participate in the game, to a certain extent, by planning what ought to be done next. Football isn't just a lot of mindless milling around by people in short pants kicking at a ball.

My chief reservation about soccer is its most basic rule. It seems artificial to make a game dependent on a rule that says you can't touch the ball with your hands. It's too much like a card trick or a three-legged race. Hitting the ball with your head instead of throwing it with your hands seems silly. It's an intervention of rules over good sense that I can't get used to.

It's hard to understand why some national games have international appeal in some places, but not others. Baseball has made enormous progress in Japan. Soccer has made progress in the United States, but it's most popular here with people who came from someplace else recently. For some reason, Europeans have never taken to baseball the way they've adopted basketball. Even in Russia, you see kids playing basketball in the parks.

The best thing about soccer and the reason it will become more popular is that all a kid needs to play it is a ball and a pair of short pants, and he doesn't have to be tall and heavy. Soccer is a nice little game for people who, for one good reason or another, can't play or watch real football.

I will now pause briefly while people in the stands throw things at me.

Andy Rooney, from the *San José Mercury*, July 20, 1982

As you can see, Rooney's evidence for his thesis that "soccer isn't as popular here [in America] as football" because "it isn't as good a game" is subjective, based on personal taste. He suggests that "the ball is always in play, but it isn't usually going anywhere in particular. . . . Soccer, unlike football or baseball, doesn't give you much time to anticipate the next play or savor the last one." He could just as easily praise soccer for being more spontaneous and less structured and slow-going than are baseball and football—but he doesn't. Rooney himself acknowledges his biased views in his concluding paragraph. But that's exactly why we read his columns—for his biases, which are clearly and colorfully related—not to discover subtle, objective truths about the subjects he writes about.

The Pro-Con Essay

The goal of any pro-con essay is to convince your audience that the stance you take on a controversial issue is more sensible, more beneficial, and more ethical perhaps than the position taken by those with opposing views. This does not necessarily mean that the opposing views are completely in error. Complex issues are rarely all bad or all good; as your concern to get at the truth outweighs your desire to win your audience over, you, the arguer, are willing to examine impartially the strengths and weaknesses of both sides.

Most pro-con essays will follow the classical argumentative framework we examined in Chapter 8:

1. The stage is set in the *introduction*: The issue is described and put into context. Its importance, timeliness, and its immediate and far-reaching consequences are emphasized. Of particular importance is the *occasion* that prompts the essay. In a writing class, the occasion would simply be the assignment, and ideally students would respond to the issue in question as though they were self-motivated free-lance writers. For a professional writer, the occasion would be a particular incident that the author would focus upon in the introduction and then use as a springboard for the larger idea. Say, for example, that a self-appointed "anti-smut" group in your community managed to persuade public libraries to remove and destroy all copies of *Grimm's Fairy Tales* on grounds that a children's story depicting anything as perverse as wolves devouring grandmothers is immoral. You might well use that incident as the foundation for an essay against censorship of all kinds.

    The introduction also usually leads up to the *thesis*: the central idea of the essay—the statement reflecting the author's point of view on the issue.

2. Sometimes the thesis needs immediate *qualification*: potentially ambiguous terms need to be carefully defined. Misreadings of authorial intent should be anticipated. Background details relevant to both the issue and the thesis are then given. Special repercussions are examined.

3. The *evidence* for the thesis is provided in the next step. This may include a logical analysis of a specific system of values shared by author and target audience.

4. Following the presentation of the evidence is the *refutation*: Contrasting views are raised, any sensible aspects of those views are acknowledged, and points shown to be inadequate or false are discarded.

5. Finally, the *conclusion* reaffirms the strength of the thesis and ends the essay with some sort of dramatic assertion or *recommendation*. Perhaps an appeal is extended to the audience to undertake some action, or to envision future consequences stemming from the adop-

tion or rejection of the thesis. Mere summations of main points covered in the argument usually fall flat and can even weaken the enthusiasm generated earlier.

We will now take a look at one writer's handling of a frequently debated issue: the peacetime draft. Before you begin reading James Fallows's essay favoring the draft, you may want to clarify your own stance on the issue in a journal entry.

THE DRAFT: WHY THE COUNTRY NEEDS IT

> Attention-getting lead: emotion-filled letter to the editor revealing a common antidraft sentiment. This gives author an opportunity to show that his prodraft stance is not necessarily antagonistic to an antidraft stance (see Fallows's opening sentence following letter).

*I am more than angry. I did not give birth to my one and only son to have him snatched away from me 18 years later. My child has been loved and cared for and taught right from wrong and **will not** be fed into any egomaniac's war machine.*

Our 18- to 25-year-olds have not brought this world to its present sorry state. Men over the age of 35, down through the centuries, have brought us here, and we women have been in silent accord.

*Well, this is one woman, one mother, who says **no**. I did not go through the magnificent agony of childbirth to have that glorious young life snuffed out.*

Until the presidents, premiers, supreme rulers, politburos, senators and congressmen of the world are ready to physically, as opposed to verbally, lead the world into combat, they can bloody well forget my child.

Unite mothers! *Don't throw your sons and daughters away. Sometime, somewhere, women have just got to say **no**.*

No. No. No. No. No. Never my child.

Louise M. Saylor, from the *Washington Post*, January 28, 1980

> Brief explanation of situation, leading to thesis statement.
>
> Thesis statement.

Nor my child, Mrs. Saylor. Nor either of my mother's sons when, ten years ago, both were classified 1-A. But *whose*, then? As our statesmen talk again of resisting aggression and demonstrating our will—as there is talk, that is, of sending someone's sons (or daughters) to bear arms overseas—the only fair and decent answer to that question lies in a return to the draft.

I am speaking here not of the health of the military but of the character of the society the military defers to. The circumstances in which that society will choose to go to war, the way its wars will be fought, and its success in absorbing the consequent suffering depends on its answer to the question Whose sons will go?

> What history can teach us about draft resistance and about draft alternatives during a war.

History rarely offers itself in lessons clear enough to be deciphered at a time when their message still applies. But of all the hackneyed "lessons" of Vietnam one still applies with no reservations: that we wound ourselves gravely if we flinch from honest answers about who will serve. During the five or six years of the heaviest draft calls for Vietnam, there was the starkest class division in American military service since the days of purchased draft deferments in the Civil War. Good intentions lay at the root of many of these inequities. The college-student deferment, the various "hardship" exemptions, Robert McNamara's plan to give "disadvantaged" youngsters a chance to better themselves in the military, even General Hershey's intelligence test to determine who could remain in school—all were designed to allot American talent in the most productive way. The intent was to distinguish those who could best serve the nation with their minds from those who should offer their stout hearts and strong backs. The effect was to place the poor and the black in the trenches (and later in the coffins and the rehabilitation wards), and their "betters" in colleges or elsewhere far from the sounds of war. I speak as one who took full advantage of the college-student deferment and later exploited the loopholes in the physical qualification standards that, for college students armed with a doctor's letter and advice from the campus draft counseling center, could so easily be parlayed into the "unfit for service" designation known as 1-Y. Ask anyone who went to college in those days how many of his classmates saw combat in Vietnam. Of my 1200 classmates at Harvard, I know of only two, one of them a veteran who joined the class late. See how this compares with the Memorial Roll from a public high school in a big city or a West Virginia hill town.

For all the talk about conflict between "young" and "old" that the war caused, the lasting breach was among the young. In the protest marches on the Pentagon and the Capitol, students felt either scorn for or estrangement from the young soldiers who stood guard. What must the soldiers have felt about these, their privileged contemporaries who tormented them so? To those who opposed the war, the ones who served were, first, animals and killers; then "suckers" who were trapped by the system, deserving pity but no respect; and finally invisible men. Their courage, discipline, and sacrifice counted for less than their collective taint for being associated with a losing war. . . . Most veterans knew the honor they had earned, even as they knew better than anyone else the horror of the war. They came to resent being made to suppress those feelings by students who chose not to join them and who, having escaped the war without pain, now prefer to put the whole episode in the past. Perhaps no one traversed that era without pain, but pain of the psychic variety left arms, legs, life intact and did not impede progress in one's career. For people of my generation—I speak in the narrow sense of males between the ages of twenty-eight and thirty-six or thirty-seven—this wound will never fully heal. If you doubt that, sit two thirty-two-year-olds down together, one who served in Vietnam and one who did not, and ask them to talk about those years.

Unfairness of past draft policies exemplified further.

At least there was theoretical consistency between what the students of those days recommended for others and what they did themselves. Their point was that no one should go to war, starting with them. It should also be said that their objection to the war, at least in my opinion, was important and right. . . .

I hear little of that tone in the reaction to President Carter's muted call for resumption of draft registration. Within a week of his request in the State of the Union address, I spent time at two small colleges. At both, the sequence of questions was the same. Why is our defense so weak? When will we show the Russians our strength? *Isn't it terrible about the draft?*

Senator Kennedy, who so often decried the unfairness of the draft during Vietnam, won cheers from his college audience for his opposition to draft registration, in the same speech in which he suggested beefing up our military presence in the Persian Gulf. Kennedy did go on to argue that we should not shed blood for oil, which is more than most anti-draft groups have done to date. It would have been reassuring to hear the students say that they oppose registration *because* they oppose a military showdown in the Persian Gulf. Instead many simply say, We don't want to go. I sense that they—perhaps all of us—have come to take for granted a truth so painful that few could bear to face it during Vietnam: that there will be another class of people to do the dirty work. After seven years of the volunteer Army, we have grown accustomed to having suckers on hand.

> Weak aspects of reasons underlying some students' decisions to resist the draft.

That the volunteer Army is another class can hardly be denied. The Vietnam draft was unfair racially, economically, educationally. By every one of those measures, the volunteer Army is less representative still. Libertarians argue that military service should be a matter of choice, but the plain fact is that service in the volunteer force is too frequently dictated by economics. Army enlisted ranks E1 through E4—the privates and corporals, the cannon fodder, the ones who will fight and die—are 36 percent black now. By the Army's own projections, they will be 42 percent black in three years. When other "minorities" are taken into account, we will have, for the first time, an army whose fighting members are mainly "non-majority," or, more bluntly, a black and brown army defending a mainly white nation. The military has been an avenue of opportunity for many young blacks. They may well be first-class fighting men. They do not represent the nation.

> Refutation of volunteer Army alternative.

Such a selective bearing of the burden has destructive spiritual effects in a nation based on the democratic creed. But its practical implications can be quite as grave. The effect of a fair, representative draft is to hold the public hostage to the consequences of its decisions, much as children's presence in the public schools focuses parents' attention on the quality of the schools. If citizens are willing to countenance a decision that means that *someone's* child may die, they may contemplate more deeply if there is the possibility that the child will be theirs. Indeed, I would like to extend this principle even further. Young men of nineteen are rightly suspicious of the congressmen and columnists who urge them to the fore. I wish there were a practical way to resurrect the provisions of the amended Selective Service Act of 1940, which raised the draft age to forty-four. Such a gesture might symbolize the desire to offset the historic injustice of the Vietnam draft, as well as suggest the possibility that, when a bellicose colulmnist recommends dispatching American forces to Pakistan, he might also realize that he could end up as a gunner in a tank.

> Consequences of ethical transgressions of unfair draft policy.

> Ways to compensate for past unfairness.

Perhaps the absence of a World War II-scale peril makes such a proposal unrealistic; still, the columnist or congressman should have to contemplate the possibility that his son would be there, in trench or tank. Under the volunteer Army that possibility will not arise, and the lack of such a prospect can affect behavior deeply. Recall how, during Vietnam, protest grew more broad-based and respectable when the graduate school deferment was eliminated in 1968. For many families in positions of influence, the war was no longer a question of someone else's son. How much earlier would the war have ended had college students been vulnerable from the start?

Those newly concerned families were no better and no worse than other people at other times; they were responding to a normal human instinct, of the sort our political system is designed to channel toward constructive ends. It was an instinct that Richard Nixon and Henry Kissinger understood very well, as they deliberately shifted the burden of the war off draftees and finally off Americans, to free their hands to pursue their chosen course. Recall how fast protest ebbed with the coming of the volunteer Army and "Vietnamization" in the early 1970's. For this reason, the likes of Nixon and Kissinger might regard a return to the draft as a step in the wrong direction, for it would sap the resolve necessary for a strong foreign policy and introduce the weakening element of domestic dissent. At times leaders must take actions that seem heartless and unfair, and that an informed public would probably not approve. Winston Churchill let Coventry be bombed, because to sound the air-raid sirens and save its citizens would have tipped off the Germans that Britain had broken their code. But in the long run, a nation cannot sustain a policy whose consequences the public is not willing to bear. If it decides not to pay the price to defend itself, it will be defenseless. That is the risk of democracy.

What kind of draft? More than anything else, a *fair* one, with as few holes as possible to wriggle through. "Fairness" does not mean that everyone need serve. This year 4.3 million people will turn eighteen, 2.2 million women and 2.1 million men. For the last few years, the military has been taking 400,000 people annually into the volunteer Army—or, in raw figures, only one in ten of the total available pool. Using today's mental and physical standards, the military knocks off 30 percent of the manpower pool as unqualified, and it excludes women from combat positions. When these calculations are combined with the diminishing number of young men—only 1.6 million men will turn eighteen in 1993—the military projects that it will need to attract one of every three "qualified and available men" by the end of the 1980's.

Read another way, this means that a draft need affect *no more* than one in three—and probably far fewer. To make the draft seem—and be—fair, the pool of potential draftees should be as large as possible, even if only a few will eventually be picked. Those who are "disabled" in the common meaning of that term—the blind, paraplegics—should be excluded, but not the asthmatics and trick-back cases who are perfectly capable of performing non-combat military jobs. The military's physical requirements now assume that nearly all men must theoretically be fit for combat, even though only 14 percent of all male soldiers hold combat jobs. The proportion of draftees destined for combat would probably be higher, since those are the positions now most understrength; if actual fighting should begin it would be higher still. But combat will never represent the preponderance of military positions, and its requirements should not blindly dictate who is eligible for the draft. Instead, everyone without serious handicap should be eligible for se-

Analysis of thesis: what author means by a "fair" draft.

Analysis and justification of thesis (evidence).

lection by lottery—men and women, students and non-students. Once the lottery had determined *who* would serve, assignments based on physical classifications could determine where and how.

> Special concern raised by thesis: women's service.

The question of women's service is the most emotionally troubling aspect of this generally emotional issue, but the progress of domestic politics over the last ten years suggests that the answer is clear. If any sexual distinctions that would deny a woman her place as a construction worker or a telephone pole climber have been forbidden by legislators and courts, what possible distinction can spare women the obligation to perform similar functions in military construction units or the Signal Corps? If women are drafted, they have an ironclad case for passage of the Equal Rights Amendment. If they are not, their claim for equal treatment elsewhere becomes less compelling. At the same time, it is troubling to think of women in combat, or of mothers being drafted, and a sensible draft law would have to recognize such exceptions.

There should be no educational deferments except for students still in high school, and possibly in two other cases. One would be for college students who enroll in ROTC; like their counterparts in the service academies, they would be exchanging four years of protected education for a longer tour of duty as an officer after graduation. The other exception might be for doctors, possessors of a skill the military needs but cannot sensibly produce on its own. If potential doctors wanted to be spared all eligibility for the draft, they could enter a program like the Navy's V-12 during World War II, in which they could take a speeded-up college course and receive a publicly subsidized medical education, after which they would owe several years' service as military doctors. Except in the most far-fetched situations, "hardship" cases should be taken care of by compensation rather than by exemption. If these are permitted, they become an invitation to abuse: who can forget George Hamilton pleading hardship as his mother's sole supporting son? Instead, the government should offset hardship with support payments to the needy dependents.

One resists the idea of lottery, because it adds to the system the very element of caprice and unfairness it is so important to remove. But since only a fraction of those eligible to serve are actually required, there seems no other equitable way to distribute the burden. With a well-established lottery, every male and female might know at age eighteen whether he or she was near the top of the list and very likely to be called, or near the bottom and almost certainly protected. How far the draft calls went down the list would depend on how many people volunteered and how many more were needed.

> Concluding remarks: reemphasis of need for a draft in light of what has been argued.

None of these concerns and prescriptions would matter if the volunteer Army were what it so often seemed in the last few years—a stand-in, a symbol, designed to keep the machinery running and the troops in place, not to be sent into action for any cause less urgent than absolute survival. But now we hear from every quarter that the next decade will be a time of testing, that our will and our strategy and our manpower will be on the line. The nature of this challenge, and the style of our response, are what we should be thinking and talking about now. Our discussions will never be honest, nor our decisions just, as long as we count on "suckers" to do the job.

James Fallows, from *The Atlantic*, April 1980

The Problem-Solving Essay

Problem-solving arguments may be divided into two categories: those that begin with the solution and proceed to argue for its acceptance, and those that begin with the problem and progress toward a solution and a rationale behind that solution. The author of the first type of essay does not acknowledge a need to discuss the nature of the problem, assuming that awareness of the problem is common knowledge. For example, if you were an expert on United States/Soviet relations writing to your colleagues on the issue of bilateral weapons-systems deployment, you would probably begin by introducing your possible solution, in light of other possible solutions perhaps. However, you would not want to waste your audience's time by introducing the problem itself—that bilateral weapons-systems deployment is a difficult diplomatic strategy to execute successfully.

The author of the second kind of problem-solving essay, on the other hand, *does* feel obliged to examine the problem carefully—mainly because he or she realizes that the audience is unfamiliar with the problem, or that the problem needs to be articulated with greater clarity than it has been until now. Let's use the previous example once again: If you suspected that the very concept of bilateralism—whether applied to trade, defense, or to scientific research—has never been clearly understood by anyone (including the experts comprising your audience), then you would certainly want to open your essay with a description of the problem.

The following article by Gore Vidal will exemplify the first strategy:

DRUGS

It is possible to stop most drug addiction in the United States within a very short time. Simply make all drugs available and sell them at cost. Label each drug with a precise description of what effect—good and bad—the drug will have on the taker. This will require heroic honesty. Don't say that marijuana is addictive or dangerous when it is neither, as millions of people know—unlike "speed," which kills most unpleasantly, or heroin, which is addictive and difficult to kick.

For the record, I have tried—once—almost every drug and liked none, disproving the popular Fu Manchu theory that a single whiff of opium will enslave the mind. Nevertheless many drugs are bad for certain people to take and they should be told why in a sensible way.

Along with exhortation and warning, it might be good for our citizens to recall (or learn for the first time) that the United States was the creation of men who believed that each man has the right to do what he wants with his own life as long as he does not interfere with his neighbor's pursuit of happiness (that his neighbor's idea of happiness is persecuting others does confuse matters a bit).

This is a startling notion to the current generation of Americans. They reflect a system of public education which has made the Bill of Rights, literally, unacceptable to a majority of high school graduates (see the annual Purdue reports) who now form the "silent majority"—a phrase which that underestimated wit Richard Nixon took from Homer who used it to describe the dead.

Now one can hear the warning rumble begin: if everyone is allowed to take drugs everyone will and the GNP will decrease, the Commies will stop us from making everyone free, and we shall end up a race of Zombies, passively murmuring "groovie" to one another. Alarming thought. Yet it seems most unlikely that any reasonably sane person will become a drug addict if he knows in advance what addiction is going to be like.

Is everyone reasonably sane? No. Some people will always become drug addicts just as some people will always become alcoholics, and it is just too bad. Every man, however, has the power (and should have the legal right) to kill himself if he chooses. But since most men don't, they won't be mainliners either. Nevertheless, forbidding people things they like or think they might enjoy only makes them want those things all the more. This psychological insight is, for some mysterious reason, perennially denied our governors.

It is a lucky thing for the American moralist that our country has always existed in a kind of time-vacuum: we have no public memory of anything that happened before last Tuesday. No one in Washington today recalls what happened during the years alcohol was forbidden to the people by a Congress that thought it had a divine mission to stamp out Demon Rum—launching, in the process, the greatest crime wave in the country's history, causing thousands of deaths from bad alcohol, and creating a general (and persisting) contempt among the citizenry for the laws of the United States.

The same thing is happening today. But the government has learned nothing from past attempts at prohibition, not to mention repression.

Last year when the supply of Mexican marijuana was slightly curtailed by the Feds, the pushers got the kids hooked on heroin and deaths increased dramatically, particularly in New York. Whose fault? Evil men like the Mafiosi? Permissive Dr. Spock? Wild-eyed Dr. Leary? No.

The Government of the United States was responsible for those deaths. The bureaucratic machine has a vested interest in playing cops and robbers. Both the Bureau of Narcotics and the Mafia want strong laws against the sale and use of drugs because if drugs are sold at cost there would be no money in it for anyone.

If there was no money in it for the Mafia, there would be no friendly playground pushers, and addicts would not commit crimes to pay for the next fix. Finally, if there was no money in it, the Bureau of Narcotics would wither away, something they are not about to do without a struggle.

Will anything sensible be done? Of course not. The American people are as devoted to the idea of sin and its punishment as they are to making money—and fighting drugs is nearly as big a business as pushing them. Since the combination of sin and money is irresistible (particularly to the professional politician) the situation will only grow worse.

Gore Vidal, from *Homage to Daniel Shays: Collected Essays*

Although Vidal's argument probably raises more questions than it answers, its strengths are clear: The proposal is lucid and incisive; a possible solution to a devastating social problem is unveiled in a ten-word sentence. Moreover, Vidal prefaces that solution with the word *simply*. He dramatizes his notion that serious problems such as drug addiction remain unsolved because of wrongheaded ideas stubbornly maintained. Vidal is trying to cut through that wrongheadedness by bluntly calling attention to it.

Reread Vidal's essay to determine its basic structure. A moment's reflection will reveal that it, like the pro-con essay before it, follows the classical argumentative framework fairly closely.

Vidal first provides a clear context for his proposed solution: "It is possible to stop most drug addiction in the United States within a very short time." This statement is quite an attention-getter, even though we may be uncertain about just how short "a very short time" is supposed to be. Now instead of describing the severity of the problem, he takes for granted that his readers are quite aware of this, and so he presents his proposed solution: "Simply make all drugs available and sell them at cost."

Next, Vidal presents his refutation with greater wit than thoroughness:

> Now one can hear the warning rumble begin: if everyone is allowed to take drugs everyone will and the GNP will decrease, the Commies will stop us from making everyone free, and we shall end up a race of Zombies, passively murmuring "groovie" to one another. Alarming thought. Yet it seems most unlikely that any reasonably sane person will become a drug addict if he knows in advance what addiction is going to be like.

Does Vidal's argument offer anything that can pass as evidence to support his proposal? In the first paragraph we read: "Don't say that marijuana is addictive or dangerous when it is neither. . . ." Since this assertion is not supported by medical evidence, it can scarcely stand as evidence. In the second paragraph, Vidal tells us that he has tried "almost every drug and liked none, disproving the popular Fu Manchu theory that a single whiff of opium will enslave the mind." Can any one person's experience with drugs prove or disprove anything about the effects of drugs on others?

Vidal comes closest to supplying evidence when he tries to show how selling drugs at cost will put the black market out of business; but once again, we see more clever turns of phrase than convincing support.

Finally, in the conclusion, Vidal unleashes his satiric wrath for all it's worth: "Will anything sensible be done? Of course not." If Vidal had intended to be more straightforward, how might he have conceived his concluding remarks? Perhaps he could have appealed to his audience to help stop the destruction of young lives at the hands of narcotics pushers by writing to their congresspersons. But such an approach would probably not work for Vidal; he is a satirist. His satirical bite, not his depth of analysis, is the persuasive element.

Let us now proceed to the more common type of problem-solving essay—the kind that begins with a discussion of the problem and then moves toward a solution. In the following example, Norman Cousins wants his readers to reconsider with whom the responsibility of the death of a talented prizefighter truly lies.

WHO KILLED BENNY PARET?

Recently a young man by the name of Benny Paret was killed in the ring. The killing was seen by millions; it was on television. In the twelfth round he was hit hard in the head several times, went down, was counted out, and never came out of the coma.

The Paret fight produced a flurry of investigations. Governor Rockefeller was shocked by what happened and appointed a committee to assess the responsibility. The New York State Boxing Commission decided to find out what was wrong. The district attorney's office expressed its concern. One question involved Mr. Paret's manager; did he act in time to stop the fight? Another question had to do with the role of the examining doctors who certified the physical fitness of the fighters before the bout. Still another question involved Mr. Paret's manager; did he rush his boy into the fight without adequate time to recuperate from the previous one?

In short, the investigators looked into every possible cause except the real one. Benny Paret was killed because the human fist delivers enough impact, when directed against the head, to produce a massive hemorrhage in the brain. The human brain is the most delicate and complex mechanism in all creation. It has a lacework of millions of highly fragile nerve connections. Nature attempts to protect this exquisitely intricate machinery by encasing it in a hard shell. Fortunately, the shell is thick enough to withstand a great deal of pounding. Nature, however, can protect man against everything except man himself. Not every blow to the head will kill a man—but there is always the risk of concussion and damage to the brain. A prizefighter may be able to survive even repeated brain concussions and go on fighting, but the damage to his brain may be permanent.

In any event, it is futile to investigate the referee's role and seek to determine whether he should have intervened to stop the fight earlier. This is not where the primary responsibility lies. The primary responsibility lies with the people who pay to see a man hurt. The referee who stops a fight too soon, from the crowd's viewpoint, can expect to be booed. The crowd wants the knockout; it wants to see a man stretched out on the canvas. This is the supreme moment in boxing. It is nonsense to talk about prizefighting as a test of boxing skills. No crowd was ever brought to its feet screaming and cheering at the sight of two men beautifully dodging and weaving out of each other's jabs. The time the crowd comes alive is when a man is hit hard over the heart or the head, when his mouthpiece flies out, when blood squirts out of his nose or eyes, when he wobbles under the attack and his pursuer continues to smash at him with poleax impact.

Don't blame it on the referee. Don't even blame it on the fight managers. Put the blame where it belongs—on the prevailing mores that regard prizefighting as a perfectly proper enterprise and vehicle of entertainment. No one doubts that many people enjoy prizefighting and will miss it if it would be thrown out. And that is precisely the point.

Norman Cousins, *Present Tense*

Norman Cousins does not describe each potential cause of Paret's death—the referee, the attending physicians, the manager, Paret's opponent—as thoroughly as he might have. Had he done so, the argument might have lost its momentum and become too ponderous. The thesis is nevertheless compelling in the way it brings into uncompromising focus something we already darkly suspect about human nature. The fault could not have been with the referee or the physicians; a sudden violent blow to the head can be lethal. Obviously, then, Paret's *opponent* must have been responsible; but the responsibility of the opponent in the ring, Cousins insists, is inseparable from the audience's, for the audience demands this sort of entertainment. Cousins proves his case by placing dramatic emphasis on what we already inwardly acknowledge about the bloodthirsty ringside crowd when the physical brutality of the fight reaches its peak:

> The time the crowd comes alive is when a man is hit hard over the heart or the head, when his mouthpiece flies out, when blood squirts out of his nose or eyes, when he wobbles under the attack and his pursuer continues to smash at him with poleax impact.

This passage is both the climax of the essay and the most dramatic answer to the essay's main question: *All* of us, by approving of boxing as a legitimate sport, have killed Benny Paret.

Summary

There are three common types of persuasive essays. The opinion piece, or feature, is read more for entertainment than for information. The pro-con position paper often springs from a recent newsworthy incident; in this type of essay the writer takes a clear stance, supportive or critical (although not necessarily an *unqualified* pro or con stance), on a debatable topic. The problem-solving investigative essay may begin by introducing the solution and then proceed to an argument for its acceptance, or it may begin by introducing the problem and then proceed logically toward the solution.

FOR DISCUSSION

1. What is the meaning of the word *evidence* in the context of a persuasive essay? How does the meaning change, if at all, from one type of persuasive essay to another?

2. Identify the basic similarities and differences between an opinion essay and a problem-solving essay. You might compare Rooney's essay with Vidal's as a case in point.

3. What additional evidence could Norman Cousins have used to support his thesis that the audience must share in the responsibility for Benny Paret's death? Would this have improved the essay?

4. Read the following excerpt from Denise Levertov's essay "The Obligation of the Poet," and defend or attack the author's assertion that a writer is obliged "to take personal and active responsibility for his words . . . and to acknowledge their potential influence on the lives of others." How convincingly does Levertov support this assertion in her essay?

THE OBLIGATION OF THE POET

The author begins by addressing the issue at once: she first makes clear what she doesn't mean by obligation. *This rhetorical strategy increases reader involvement by making the reader wonder, What, then,* is *the poet's obligation?*

The obligation of the poet (and, by extension, of others committed to the love of literature, as critics and teachers or simply as readers) is not necessarily to write "political" poems (or to focus attention primarily on such poems as more "relevant" than other poems or fictions). The obligation of the writer is: *to take personal and active responsibility for his words, whatever they are, and to acknowledge their potential influence on the lives of others.* The obligation of teachers and critics is: *not to block the dynamic consequences of the words they try to bring close to students and readers.* And the obligation of readers is: *not to indulge in the hypocrisy of merely vicarious experience, thereby reducing literature to the concept of "just words," ultimately a frivolity, an irrelevance when the chips are down. . . .* When words penetrate deep into us they change the *chemistry of the soul, of the imagination.* We have no right to do that to people if we don't share the consequences.

People are always asking me how I can reconcile poetry and political action, poetry and talk of revolution. Don't you feel, they say to me, that you and other poets are betraying your work as poets when you spend time participating in sit-ins, marching in the streets, helping to write leaflets, talking to people about capitalism, imperialism, racism, male chauvinism, oppression of all kinds? My answer is no; precisely because I am a poet, I know, and those other poets who do likewise know, that we must fulfill the poet's total involvement in life in this aspect also. "But is not the task of the poet essentially one of conservation?" the question comes. Yes, and if I speak of revolution it is because I believe that only revolution can now save that earthly life, that miracle of being, which poetry conserves and celebrates. "But history shows us that poets—even great poets—more often fulfill their lives as observers than as participants in political action—when they do become embroiled in politics they usually write bad poems." I answer, good poets write bad political poems only if they let themselves write deliberate, opinionated rhetoric, misusing their art as propaganda. The poet does not *use* poetry, but is at the service of poetry. To *use* it is to *mis*use it. A poet driven to speak to himself, to maintain a dialogue with himself, concerning politics, can expect to write as well upon that theme as upon any other. He can not separate it from everything else in his life. But it is not whether or not good "political" poems are a possibility that is in question. What is in question is the role of the poet as observer or as participant in the life of his time. And if history is invoked to prove that more poets have stood aside, have watched or ignored the events of their moment in history, than have spent time and energy in bodily participation in those events, I must answer that a sense of history must involve a sense of the present, a vivid awareness of change, a response to crisis, a realization that what was appropriate in this or that situation in the past is inadequate to the demands of the present, that we are living our whole lives *in a state of emergency* which is—for reasons I'm sure I don't have to spell out for you by discussing nuclear and chemical weapons or ecological disasters and threats—unparalleled in all history.

When I was seven or eight and my sister sixteen or seventeen, she described the mind to me as a room full of boxes, in aisles like the shelves of a library, each box with its label. I had heard the term "gray matter," and so I visualized room and boxes as gray, dust-gray. Her confident description impressed me, but I am glad to say I felt an immediate doubt of its authenticity. Yet I have since seen lovers of poetry, lovers of literature, behave as if it were indeed so, and allow no fruitful reciprocity between poem and action.

"No ideas but in things," said William Carlos Williams. This does not mean "no ideas." It means that "language [and here I quote Wordsworth] is not the dress but the incarnation of thoughts." "No ideas but in things," means, essentially, "Only connect." And it is therefore not only a craft-statement, not only an aesthetic statement (though it is these things also, and importantly), but a moral statement. *Only connect. No ideas but in things.*

Notice how Levertov makes it clear that those who teach the poet's work, as well as those who read the work, have similar obligations.

The author now introduces opposing views, one at a time.

Here the author responds to those opposing views.

Levertov refutes the common misunderstanding that the poetic representation of ideas as aesthetic objects is contrary to an active involvement with the world.

She concludes with a deeply felt wish.

The words reverberate through the poet's life, through *my* life, and I hope through your lives, joining with other knowledge in the mind, that place that is not a gray room full of little boxes. . . .

Denise Levertov, "The Poet in the World"

5. What evidence would you use to defend or attack the following debatable topics?
   a. Iron Curtain countries should automatically be banned from the Olympic Games.
   b. Gambling should be legalized throughout the United States.
   c. Required foreign-language instruction should begin in elementary school. (This has a built-in secondary issue: What language(s) should be taught at this grade level?)
   d. Writing courses in college should be taken pass/fail only.

FOR WRITING

1. Find a news story in your daily newspaper that triggers in you a strong reaction. Express your sentiments in a letter to the editor. Later, edit it for clarity and coherence—but don't "tame" its charged-up tone. Mail a copy of the letter to the newspaper's editor!

2. Imagine yourself a nationally syndicated columnist à la Erma Bombeck, Art Buchwald, Andy Rooney, Miss Manners, Russell Baker, Ellen Goodman, Sydney Harris, or anyone else who comes to mind. Spend a few days gathering ideas on two or three of your favorite topics. Then write three 500-word columns, each on a well-focused topic, each reflecting your personality and biases as much as possible.

3. Over the next couple of weeks, read and gather up letters to the editor from a variety of periodicals. Arrange them according to quality, from poor to satisfactory to outstanding, making sure that you are able to establish clear criteria for each category. Finally, compose an essay in which you defend your "standards for excellence in editorial letters."

4. Write your own essay supporting or opposing the peacetime draft. You may want to allude to situations that have arisen since Fallows's essay first appeared (April 1980), as well as to situations Fallows could have mentioned, but didn't.

5. Determine your stance on one of the following issues:
   a. Genetic research should (or should not) be regulated by a bioethics review board consisting of nonbiologists as well as biologists.

b. "There is no such thing as a moral or an immoral book. Books are well written, or badly written. That is all." (Oscar Wilde, preface to *The Picture of Dorian Gray*, 1891)

c. College students in business and engineering programs should take more courses in literature, philosophy, and history than the current minimum "core" requirements provide.*

Find someone in your class whose stance on one of the above issues contrasts with your own. Debate the issue orally, taking notes. Then compose a formal position-essay on the issue.

6. As the mayor or chief of police of a large city, you are disturbed by the heavy increase of assaults against citizens in public places, such as in parking lots, bus and subway stations, and parks. Moreover, you have been noticing that vigilantism—private citizens taking the law into their own hands and counterattacking their alleged assailants with deadly weapons—is also on the rise, and that many condone, even praise, their actions.

Think about this issue carefully and write an essay arguing for or against vigilantism in light of one or more specific incidents you have read about or witnessed. To help determine your stance, you might consider the following case in point:

On December 22, 1984, a man gunned down four teenagers on a New York subway train after one of them demanded money. The man, Bernhard Goetz, pulled a gun and shot them as they fled. Two of them were hit in the back, and one of them was paralyzed for life. The incident made national headlines and the vigilante was given a hero's praise by many. Some, however, called the incident racially motivated; Goetz was white, and the youths were black. Goetz was acquitted of attempted murder, but found guilty of illegal possession of a handgun.

7. Write an essay attacking or defending Elise Chisolm's attitude toward breast-feeding in public as she presents it in the following column:

BREAST-FEEDING IN PUBLIC GETS A NOD

So a mother says she was tossed out of a restaurant called C.J.'s because she was breast-feeding her baby. She believes she was discriminated against, and the incident has spawned a lot of debate.

A spokesman for La Leche League International, a group that promotes breast-feeding as the best way to feed the newborn, says the restaurant position is ridiculous and that courts and human rights commissions nationwide

---

*Use your own college requirements as an example.

are acknowledging the rights of mothers to breast-feed their infants in public.

But an assistant state's attorney in Baltimore County says the restaurant owner may be right because indecent exposure laws prohibit the exhibition of private body parts in public. The mother, Eva Whitley, has filed a formal complaint against the restaurant.

OK, while they work this out, I want to say this: I think Eva Whitley should have been able to nurse her baby in C.J.'s. If I had seen her, I wouldn't have minded. After all, C.J.'s is a family restaurant and "family" means children.

There is talk that parents may not want their children exposed to such a thing. But I have to say that if I'd had a seven-year-old with me, I would rather he see a female breast in this context than the breasts he might see [as he was] giggling his way furtively through *Penthouse* magazine.

What I object to in restaurants are parents who bring in badly behaved children who scream, cry, or spill things. They make the whole meal a wretched experience for my family and me and everybody else in the place. If you've ever watched a four-month-old slowly spit his spaghetti onto his high chair, you'd not mind a mother suckling her infant.

And to tell you the truth, I see much more of the anatomy when a woman comes in wearing a low-cut dress, halter or tube top, or tight pants.

OK, OK. Would I have done it when I was raising infants? Well, probably not. For one thing, we didn't go out to eat with our babies. I am also very modest, and I can't help the way in which I was brought up. But that doesn't mean others shouldn't do it.

Ours is one of the few cultures in which women don't nurse babies in public. I just can't see why a mother should have to go to a bathroom to nurse her baby. That is dumb and unsanitary.

A mother nursing her baby is, to me, the same as feeding him or her with a bottle.

Secondly, I am not sure the breast is a private part anymore. Watch television for a few hours and you'll see we have made it a very public part.

I think the trouble lies in sexism. Men—the so-called macho men at least—have perceived the female breast as something sexy and something to joke about.

From the more explicit slang words to "stacked," "loaded," and "built," there is a preoccupation with bosoms. And women have gone right along, showing off their breasts and trying to enlarge them.

That's why people are embarrassed to see a breast in public; it has come to mean sexual stimulation instead of a beautiful part of the anatomy that was put there for a reason.

When we learn to put less emphasis on the breast and more on the brain, we will have evolved.

Elise T. Chisolm, from the *San José Mercury*, October 10, 1982

8. Write a problem-to-solution or cause-to-effect essay based on one of the following situations:

a. Think back on a difficult problem that you eventually managed to solve successfully. Perhaps it was finding a way to overcome a handicap that threatened a lifelong goal. Perhaps it was working out a way to get along with someone you really cared about but could not reach out to because of some misunderstanding. Allow your readers to see why the solution you arrived at was superior to other alternatives.

b. Work out a possible solution to a seemingly unresolvable issue in today's world: attaining a bilateral nuclear freeze; resolving the conflict in the Middle East; putting a stop to the slaughter of endangered wildlife species such as the sea cow or the humpback whale. Hold your readers' attention by saving the key idea for last.

9. Write a historical problem-to-solution essay. That is, dramatically relate the steps taken over a number of years, or perhaps centuries, in an attempt to solve a baffling problem. Here are some possible topics:

   a. The search for the Loch Ness monster
   b. Unraveling the mystery of Easter Island
   c. Humanity's search for the perfect aphrodisiac
   d. How the human brain was mapped
   e. How geologists have determined the age of the earth

Special Topic: Writing Reviews

Evaluative essays pass judgment on a work or performance; unlike reports, they are meant to entertain as well as to inform—using *entertain* in the broadest sense of "holding in the mind" in addition to "giving delight." A strong evaluative essay is energetically written; it "speaks out" the way a letter to the editor speaks out, except that a reviewer will put his or her views more carefully into context. In a book review, this can mean relating the work in terms of content, style, or theme to other books the author has written, or to similar books by other authors. Or it can mean relating the work to the author's personal life as well as to both immediate and overall society, to which it may draw attention.

Paul Gray's review of *Loon Lake*, a novel by E. L. Doctorow, may not do all that a review is capable of doing, but it comes close.

THE NIGHTMARE AND THE DREAM

LOON LAKE by E. L. Doctorow

> Introduction: Doctorow's past literary achievement (specifically, the stunning success of *Ragtime*).

Author E. L. Doctorow's *Ragtime* (1975) was one of the cultural happenings of the past decade. The novel received largely rhapsodic reviews; its fictional use of such historical figures as Henry Ford and J. P. Morgan prompted reams of analysis. Commercial success accompanied the critical welcome. Paperback rights went for $1.9 million, a record at the time, a film deal was struck, and *Ragtime* became a bestseller. As the cash register continued to jingle, though, a number of literati began backing and filling from their earlier praise. If Doctorow is that good, so the argument ran, how come he is making so much money? The question is flawed, of course; the fact that many bad books sell well does not mean that all good ones are quickly remaindered. But having prospered a trifle too handsomely in the eyes of the purists, Doctorow created a skeptical, show-me audience for his next work of fiction.

> Transition leading to thesis statement.
> Thesis statement.
>
> Evidence supporting thesis.

That is too bad, because the author's new novel demands some patience and cooperation from readers before its effects begin to take hold and grip. Gone is the spare, metronomic prose that made the inventive plot of *Ragtime* so accessible and entertaining. The written surface of *Loon Lake* is ruffled and choppy. Swatches of poetry are jumbled together with passages of computerese and snippets of mysteriously disembodied conversation. Narration switches suddenly from first to third person, or vice versa, and it is not always clear just who is telling what. Chronology is so scrambled that the aftereffects of certain key events are described before the events occur. Such dislocations are undeniably frustrating at first, but they gradually acquire hypnotic force. Reading the book finally seems like overhearing bits of an oddly familiar tune.

> Interpretive remarks.
>
> Overview of plot.

Doctorow is indeed playing a variation on an old theme: the American dream, set to the music of an American nightmare, the Depression. Much of the book's plot is generated by a single gathering of characters in 1936. A group of gangsters and their girlfriends travel to Loon Lake, the 30,000-acre Adirondack retreat of their host, millionaire F. W. Bennett. The Mob runs an industrial service, which actually means spying, strikebreaking and union busting, and Bennett has been having more than a spot of trouble with the workers at his Indiana auto-body plant. The two sides make a business agreement, and the head crook generously gives his moll Clara to Bennett to sweeten the bargain.

Also present at Loon Lake are Bennett's wife Lucinda, a world-famous aviator, and Warren Penfield, a drunken poet whom she keeps on as a pet and confidant. And an uninvited guest arrives: a young hobo named Joe, who wanders onto Bennett's property and is nearly killed by a pack of vicious dogs. As he recuperates, a young woman employee on the estate explains his accident: "Those are wild-running, those dogs. It's the fault of the people who own them and can't feed them any more. And then they go off and forage and breed wild and hunt in packs."

The novel is framed by this startling juxtaposition: starving dogs amid baronial splendor. When Joe decides to help Clara escape from her involuntary servitude, he steals a 1933 Mercedes from Bennett and starts driving through a landscape of blighted hopes and lives. He fears pursuit by Bennett; he is also worried that Clara's gangster friend may want her back. The last place Bennett would look, Joe decides, is at his own auto plant. But does Joe really take a job there of his own free will, as he believes? Or have the enormous forces of wealth and crime conspired to crush him?

Joe's story calls up some eerie echoes. Imagine *The Great Gatsby* set a decade later, told by its ambitious hero while he was on the make. Joe survives and triumphs through a combination of luck, animal cunning and absolute recklessness. And his tutor, ironically, is the very man he robbed. Joe never forgets his first sight of F. W. Bennett: "All the intelligence I had of him, from his house and his lands and his train and his resident poets, had not prepared me for the impersonal force of him, the frightening freedom of him." The race, Joe decides, is to the feral.

Doctorow may try to do too much in *Loon Lake*. When the poet Penfield reminisces about his experiences in Japan, for instance, he seems to belong in a different novel. But the author's skill at historical reconstruction, so evident in *Ragtime*, remains impressive here; the novel's fragments and edgy, nervous rhythms call up an age of clashing anxiety. *Loon Lake* tantalizes long after it is ended. As Penfield writes about the bird that gives its name to the Bennett estate, "The cry of loons once heard is not forgotten."

Paul Gray, from *Time*, September 22, 1980

> Interpretive and critical remarks arising from plot overview.
>
> Conclusion: overall assessment. Imaginative close: passage from novel used to describe novel itself.

Performance reviews, that is, reviews of musical events, stage plays, and films, are somewhat tougher to write because the reviewer often does not have the opportunity to see the performance over again in the time available. All of the action unfolds in two or three hours, and it's not easy to take notes and to pay close attention to the stage or screen simultaneously.

The following suggestions may help you when you are preparing a performance review:

1. *Regard yourself as simply another member of the audience, not as a "reviewer" with a specially trained eye.* You are not out to capture the Absolute Essence of the performance, but only to say something interesting from the viewpoint of an audience member who may or may not have any substantial background information on the performance. Adopting this frame of mind will help prevent you from sounding pompous or elitist.

2. *Have faith in your memory.* Take notes during intermission and immediately following the performance, not during (when you'd risk missing part of a key scene).

3. *Do background reading on the performers and, if applicable, on the playwright or filmmaker, the director, the cinematographer, the special-effects person, and so on.* Such background information can do much to

enhance your reader's understanding and appreciation of a performance.

4. *Write colorfully and vigorously, exploiting your personal tastes.* Reviews are more than just "service pieces." They are essays in their own right! Notice in the following film review how the author's lively tone adds to the flavor of the judgment.

THE FANTASY FILM AS FINAL EXAM

DUNE *Directed and Written by David Lynch*

Science fantasy is an act of subversion disguised as a fairy tale. In primal imagery and orotund cadences it sets the young imagination on a children's crusade against malevolent power. It describes a vicarious rite of passage through bloodshed and anarchy to heroic manhood; it upends the prevailing social order to establish a new moral equilibrium. For the generation of budding revolutionaries in the 1960s, Frank Herbert's *Dune* was a magical mystery trilogy that, along with *The Lord of the Rings* and the *Gormenghast* books, galvanized the spirit like a Disney *Das Kapital*. In *Dune*, rival masters from four planets battled for control of "mélange," an addictive spice that conferred powers of prophecy and transcendence. Here was an intergalactic Colombian drug war, with a stash of celestial LSD waiting to be harnessed by a teen-age messiah—Holden Caulfield maturing into Che Guevara.

Well, the '60s are prehistory now, and nothing ages as fast as futurism. So it seems anachronistic for David Lynch, the gifted eccentric whose only previous features were the $20,000 *Eraserhead* and the $5 million *The Elephant Man*, to spend some $50 million (not another one!) bringing Herbert's mammoth fantasia to the screen. And more than a little confusing to those mortals who have not memorized the book. For Herbert devised not just a teeming universe but the rudiments of several new languages, and Lynch works hard to squeeze the novel's richness and oddness into 2½ hours. *Dune* begins with an animated lecture—leaving a mass of factoids swimming through the moviegoer's brain—and ends with the cry "For he is the Kwisatz Haderach!" So inward and remote does the movie seem, it might have arrived in a time capsule from one of the four warring planets. Most sci-fi movies offer escape, a holiday from homework, but *Dune* is as difficult as a final exam. You have to cram for it.

And why not? the host of *Dune* bugs might ask. Who decreed that fantasy films must be as simple and simple-minded as *Porky's Goes to Arrakis*? Nobody did; and one can admire the world Herbert and Lynch have created even as one feels like an illegal alien visiting it. At the very least, *Dune* provides a bizarre bestiary of characters. One such, the Navigator, is a giant walrus-like creature that rules the universe while floating inside a liquid cage. The Harkonnens are the comic villains of the piece. These red-haired nasties with a taste for drinking human blood and baroquely torturing farm animals are led by the pustulous, airborne Baron Vladimir (Kenneth McMillan) and his aide-de-camp Feyd (the rock star Sting), in gold-leaf bathing suit resplendent. The Guild Spokesman, an imperial messenger, has a bald head cracked on one side and oozing like a soft-boiled egg. Then there are the 1,000-ft. worms of Arrakis, the universe's longest phallic symbols, which hold within themselves the secret of mélange.

The worm, then, is a sort of Moby Python, and young Paul Atreides (Kyle MacLachlan) is an Ahab with a happy ending. MacLachlan, 25, grows impressively in the role; his features, soft and spoiled at the beginning, take on a he-manly glamour once he assumes his mission. Like most of the other cast members, MacLachlan delivers his speeches as incantations from an old, old testament. The actors seem hypnotized by the spell Lynch has woven around them—especially the lustrous Francesca Annis, as Paul's mother, who whispers her lines with the urgency of erotic revelation. In those moments when Annis is on-screen, *Dune* finds the emotional center that has eluded it in its parade of rococo décor and austere special effects. She reminds us of what movies can achieve when they have a heart as well as a mind.

Richard Corliss, from *Time*, December 17, 1984

WRITING REVIEWS: TOPICS FOR DISCUSSION

1. Search the current periodicals for at least three different reviews on one book. *The New York Times Book Review, The New York Review of Books, The New Yorker, The Christian Science Monitor,* and the Sunday editions of nearly all metropolitan newspapers are easily accessible sources. Take notes on the differences in writing style, emphasis, and kinds of evidence used to support assertions; then present your assessment to the class.

2. Conduct a survey to determine the percentage of persons who read reviews. Of those who do, what motivates them to read them? To determine whether it's worthwhile to read a book or to attend a concert? To learn about the work without having to read it or attend a performance? Or simply to enjoy the witticisms or unique writing style of the reviewer? Report your findings to the class.

3. Evaluate the following student-written theater review in terms of its liveliness, diction, level of usage, emphasis, and method of development.

A THRILLER, AFTER FIRST ACT

Martin Landau's Dracula Could Use a Mild Transfusion

Count Dracula. The Prince of Darkness. That dapper, fanged gent whose slumber hours somewhat resemble a college student on weekends and whose sinister atrocities have been (pardon me) sucked up by many generations of film audiences in many contrasting renditions.

Recently, the touring stage play "Dracula" sank its teeth into the San

José Center for the Performing Arts for two celebrated performances January 11–12.

The script and story were deliciously classic Dracula, incorporating every imaginable vampire myth—he sleeps at sunrise, alters his appearance to a bat in a blink, is repulsed by crosses and wolfbane. The list goes on. Unfortunately, the compelling story needed to crutch this slightly limping performance. The overall production was about as steady as the intramural field after a giant rainstorm.

The plot is old hat; we've seen it infinite times, but that matters little. It is still enjoyable. A mysterious gentleman moves into the neighborhood, in this case from Transylvania, and perplexing abnormalities begin to plague the area.

The new neighbor seems to take a liking to a voluptuous lass next door whose behavior lately has been notably odd. Slowly her combination mentors and detectives, father, fiancé and family acquaintance puzzle the clues and legends together until the malady is deduced. Then appropriate action is taken to extinguish the unwelcome evil visitor.

The second and third acts were so saturated with suspense and anxious tension—I really wish I'd seen this with a girl, for obvious reasons. The most engrossing and masterful scenes are those in which Van Helsing, the wise friend of the family, first confronts Dracula with his suspected identity and in which Lucy, Dracula's prey, recounts the living dead man's recent attack. However, the entire play was not this biting; the first act was more like . . . gumming.

Director Dennis Rosa injected potent doses of corny humor which, granted, were funny, but completely inconsistent with the rest of the play. Aided by spastic lighting, this gross contrast between the melodrama of act one and the sobering suspense of acts two and three was annoying for it created two entirely different moods. It was like watching another show all together.

Martin Landau, of Mission Impossible fame, was disappointing in the title role, especially considering that he received top billing. Although his performance was generic, he looked the part—every middle-aged woman in the audience was swooning—and he carried the riveting parts with sly grace. But he completely lacked the mystery and romantic horror of the Prince of Darkness, playing the seductive demon like a foppish traveling salesman.

Humbert Allen Astredo as Abraham Van Helsing, the very German, very wise main nemesis of Dracula, commanded the stage convincingly with his colorful portrayal of the stout nationalist. However, nearly half of his dialogue was lost in the troubled sound system which could not clearly project his heavy accent .

Mary Dierson (Lucy Sewald) differentiated the real Lucy with the one under the Count's spell. She, in her own subtle way, kept the performance glued together in moments of dilemma.

Lucy's fiancé Jonathan Harker, played by Tom Galantich, was a spineless kiss-up who developed some guts as the story progressed. Galantich meant well and tried hard, but he didn't offer much. His portrayal was about as fresh as the avocado dip left in the unplugged refrigerator over winter break.

Michael Nostrand kept the play from becoming too heavy as the insect-munching, psychopathic patient of Dr. Sewald. This fit Danny DeVito clone was a one-man circus as he continuously escaped from his heavily guarded cell in undetectable ways.

Dalton Dearborn (Dr. Sewald), Laura Kenyon (Miss Wells), and G. B. Riche (Butterworth) rounded out the cast competently.

A standing ovation must go to Edward Gorey's Tony-Award-winning sets. Bats are subtly included in the scenery's configuration, giving a gory cartoon effect, especially Lucy's bed which had a white satin bat for a canopy looming 30 feet above it.

Once "Dracula" recovered from the first act, it produced a solid night of thrilling theatre. I think the grandeur of the Performing Arts Center swallowed much of the intimacy this show longed for. A smaller theater would have been much more enticing.

Overall, though, it was a worthy performance. Acts two and three had the house cringing down to their corpuscles, but the first was definitely stricken with a blood disease.

Tom Gough, from *The Santa Clara*, January 17, 1985

FOR WRITING

1. Keep abreast of campus activities and make it a point to attend three of the following events during the current term: an art exhibit; a musical performance; a stage play; a film; or a lecture, debate, or symposium. Write a review for each performance you attend.

2. Read a newly published book in your major, or proposed major, field of study. Write a 750-word review of it for the campus newspaper.

Special Topic: The Textual Explication

Similar to the review, only more thorough and detailed in its analysis and more restricted in its scope, a textual explication commonly includes the following elements:

1. An introduction and/or conclusion that mentions the work's impact on readers, or its contribution to the genre of which it is a part

2. An original thesis on which the detailed interpretation is based

3. A minutely detailed interpretative reading of the work, with ample reference to specific words, phrases, sentences, and literary devices that support your thesis

4. The highlighting of a particularly fascinating or disturbing element that is raised by your interpretation

As a rule, short explications will not include the following elements:

1. Discussion of previous scholarship on the work

2. Discussion of the author's entire corpus of work, although very brief generalizations are appropriate at times

3. Discussion of the author's personality or personal life

Now read the famous poem, "Dover Beach," written in 1867 by Matthew Arnold. Read it through several times, not just to comprehend and enjoy it, but to form an attitude toward what it seems to be saying. Only after you have done so, read James Dickey's explication that follows. Study the way Dickey incorporates the elements of explication discussed here.

DOVER BEACH

The sea is calm to-night,
The tide is full, the moon lies fair
Upon the straits;—on the French coast, the light
Gleams, and is gone, the cliffs of England stand,
Glimmering and vast, out in the tranquil bay.   5
Come to the window, sweet is the night-air!
Only, from the long line of spray
Where the sea meets the moon-blanch'd land,
Listen! you hear the grating roar
Of pebbles which the waves draw back, and fling,   10
At their return, up the high strand,
Begin, and cease, and then again begin,
With tremulous cadence slow, and bring
The eternal note of sadness in.

Sophocles long ago   15
Heard it on the Aegean, and it brought
Into his mind the turbid ebb and flow
Of human misery; we
Find also in the sound a thought,
Hearing it by this distant northern sea.   20

The Sea of Faith
Was once, too, at the full, and round earth's shore

Lay like the folds of a bright girdle furled.
But now I only hear
Its melancholy, long, withdrawing roar, 25
Retreating, to the breath
Of the night-wind, down the vast edges drear
And naked shingles of the world.

Ah, love, let us be true
To one another! for the world, which seems 30
To lie before us like a land of dreams,
So various, so beautiful, so new,
Hath really neither joy, nor love, nor light,
Nor certitude, nor peace, nor help for pain;
And we are here as on a darkling plain 35
Swept with confused alarms of struggle and flight,
Where ignorant armies clash by night.

ARNOLD'S "DOVER BEACH"

"Dover Beach" has been called the first modern poem. If this is true, it is modern not so much in diction and technique—for its phrasing and its Miltonic inversions are obvious carry-overs from a much older poetry—but in psychological orientation. Behind the troubled man standing at the lover's conventional moon-filled window looking on the sea, we sense—more powerfully because our hindsight confirms what Arnold only began to intuit—the shift in the human viewpoint from the Christian tradition to the impersonal world of Darwin and the nineteenth century scientists. The way the world is seen, and thus the way men live, is conditioned by what men know about it, and they know more now than they ever have before. Things themselves—the sea, stars, darkness, wind—have not changed; it is the perplexed anxiety and helplessness of the newly dispossessed human being that now come forth from his mind and transmute the sea, the night air, the French coast, and charge them with the sinister implications of the entirely alien. What begins as a rather conventional—but very good—description of scenery turns slowly into quite another thing: a recognition of where the beholder stands in relation to these things; where he *really* stands. It is this new and comfortless knowledge as it overwhelms for all time the old and does away with the place where he thought he stood, where his tradition told him he stood, that creates the powerful and melancholy force of the poem.

In statement, "Dover Beach" goes very easily and gravely, near prose and yet not too near. It has something of the effect of overheard musing, though it is addressed, or half addressed, to someone present. Its greatest technical virtue, to my mind, is its employment of sound-imagery, particularly in the deep, sustained vowels of lines like "Its melancholy, long, withdrawing roar." The lines also seem to me to *break* beautifully. ". . . on the French coast, the light / Gleams, and is gone." I have tried many times to rearrange Arnold's lines, and have never succeeded in doing anything but diminish their subtlety, force and conviction.

> Emphasis on a disturbing element in the poem raised by Dickey's thesis.

The one difficulty of the poem, it seems to me, is in the famous third strophe wherein the actual sea is compared to the Sea of Faith. If Arnold means that the Sea of Faith was formerly at high tide, and he hears now only the sound of the tide going out, one cannot help thinking also of the cyclic nature of tides, and the consequent coming of another high tide only a few hours after the present ebb. In other words, the figure of speech appears valid only on one level of the comparison; the symbolic half fails to sustain itself. Despite the magnificence of the writing in this section, I cannot help believing that it is the weakest part of the poem when it should be the strongest; the explicitness of the comparison seems too ready-made. Yet I have the poem as it is so deeply in memory that I cannot imagine it changed, and would not have it changed even if I knew it would be a better poem thereby.

> Continuation of explication with paraphrased or direct quotations from the poem.

In the sound of waves rolling pebbles, an eternal senseless motion, unignorable and meaningless, Arnold hears—as we ever afterwards must hear—human sadness, the tears of things. It links us to Sophocles and to all men at all times who have discovered in such a sound an expression of their own unrest, and have therefore made of it "the eternal note of sadness." Yet our sadness has a depth that no other era has faced: a certainty of despair based upon our own examination of empirical evidence and the conclusions drawn by our rational faculty. These have revealed not God but the horror and emptiness of things, including those that we cannot help thinking beautiful: that *are* beautiful. By its direct, slow-speaking means, the poem builds toward its last nine lines, when the general resolves into the particular, divulging where *we* stand, what these things mean to *us*. The implication is that if love, morality, constancy and the other traditional Western virtues are not maintained without supernatural sanction, there is nothing. The world that lies before us in such beauty that it seems to have come instantaneously from God's hand does not include, guarantee or symbolize the qualities that men have assumed were also part of it. It is beautiful and impersonal, but we must experience it—and now suffer it—as persons. Human affection is revealed as a completely different thing than what we believed it to be; as different, in fact, as the world we were mistaken about. It is a different thing but also a new thing, with new possibilities of terror, choice and meaning. The moment between the lovers thus takes on the qualities of a new expulsion from Eden: they tremble with fear but also with terrible freedom; they look eastward. The intense vulnerability of the emotional life takes place in an imperiled darkness among the sounds of the sea and against the imminence of violence, wars, armies blundering blindly into each other for no

> Conclusion that recaps points raised earlier and closes on a startling note.

reason. Yet there is a new, fragile center to things: a man and a woman. In a word, it is love in what we have come to call the existential predicament. Nearly a hundred years ago, Arnold fixed unerringly and profoundly on the quality that more than any other was to characterize the emotion of love in our own century: desperation.

James Dickey, from *Master Poems of the English Language*

THE TEXTUAL EXPLICATION: TOPICS FOR DISCUSSION

1. Were you able to anticipate any of Dickey's views on "Dover Beach" in your own assessment of the poem? Which of his points came as a surprise?

2. Compare James Dickey's explication of Arnold's poem with Paul Gray's review of Doctorow's novel. Describe the differences in style and in the use of evidence to support assertions.

FOR WRITING

1. Write your own explication of "Dover Beach." Be sure to support your points thoroughly, and to stimulate your reader's interest in the poem as well as in your own response to it.

2. Write an explication of your favorite poem or short story. Remember to quote appropriate passages from the text to support your thesis.

Principles of Research

CHAPTER 10

At the mere mention of the word *research*, some students will groan as they imagine themselves spending the finest hours of their young lives awash in indexes and bibliographies, or wandering through the stacks in search of elusive books, or transcribing endless notes until the main thread of meaning seems lost, or, worst of all, struggling to arrange all those notes into some meaningful sequence to form a worthy enough thesis. . . .

Although a little exaggerated, that scenario may seem uncomfortably real to a student who has not taken the time to learn the basic principles of research. Research is a fundamental skill, a fact of life for anyone wishing to write authoritatively on important issues and ideas. There is no reason why it should be drudgery. Nearly all writing involves some kind of research, even if it goes no further than background reading. If you were planning to write an essay about grooming a cat, for example, you might feel inclined to browse through previously published articles on cat-grooming to gain a fuller perspective of your own ideas. Your ideas will inevitably differ from those who've written before you, but frequently you will want to *allude* to what others have said to build a strong, informed presentation for your readers. Such allusions to the ideas and discoveries of other authors requires careful annotation—a topic we will explore later in this chapter.

The first step toward mastering the principles of research is to become acquainted with the resources of your college library. Such acquaintance offers you access to more knowledge than you could ever assimilate in a hundred lifetimes. Easy-to-learn activities such as checking periodical indexes, locating any book or article quickly, or finding bibliographies will channel you into the mainstream of global knowledge covering three millennia of human thought and endeavor.

Of course, learning to do research is one thing; learning to transform a pile of notes into a ten-page paper that presents an original idea in an engaging and convincing manner—that's something else again.

Your Library

Your college library is truly the heart and soul of academia, for here resides the legacy of the human mind. You may have instant access to any of it just by learning the techniques we are about to examine.

For those of you who have taken a library tour during orientation and retained little—don't despair. To become comfortable with the library's resources you must plan on making several visits and learning just a few things at a time. Trying to take in everything at once could lead to the erroneous impression that libraries are more complicated than they really are.

Take yourself on a tour of your college library—not only to familiarize yourself with some of the basic research tools, but to acquire a feel for the place as well. Be like the child who enters a museum for the first time, awed by all he or she encounters. Awe provides a strong foundation on which to build important skills; it tends to make the more tedious facets of research more bearable, even enjoyable.

Here's what you can do: First ask someone at the front desk for a copy of the library's floor plan. Also inquire about any exhibits currently on display. Next, visit the "stacks"—the floor(s) where all the books are shelved according to *call numbers* (the Library of Congress classification number or the Dewey Decimal number) listed in the card catalog. Sooner or later you'll be busy in the stacks locating books for actual research papers; but for now, take a leisurely look around, maybe examine one or two interesting-looking volumes. Curiosity is a precious feeling to experience inside a library! After you're through marveling at the stacks, visit the special collections, such as the rare books and manuscripts room, the archives, the art and map collections, and the regional books collection.

Now visit the periodicals room; this is a fun place to browse! Here you will find current magazines and journals and back issues of periodicals bound into large volumes. You might enjoy looking at the issues of *Life* magazine that appeared during World War II. Notice the advertisements!

Before you leave the periodicals room, it might be a good idea to browse among the periodical indexes. We'll be examining these versatile research tools in just a moment; but for now, just try to get a general sense of how they're set up. Locate, for example, the *Education Index* and pull any volume. Now choose a topic, say, *minority education*, and survey the many articles listed. Note that the periodical in which each article appears is listed in abbreviated form and followed by the issue date. Take a look at the abbreviation key at the beginning of the volume, and then see if you can locate one of the articles.

Your last stop on this self-guided tour will be the reference room. Books in this room never leave the library; they all exist to aid researchers in speedy fact-gathering tasks and to serve as points of departure for more in-depth inquiry. Here you will find two types of encyclopedias: the general kind, such as the *Encyclopaedia Britannica*, and the topical kind, such as the *Encyclopedia of Computer Science and Technology*. You will also find book-length bibliographies and indexes, collective biographies, atlases, concordances, dictionaries, and even bibliographies of bibliographies, which are exceptionally useful tools.

A Sampling of Important Reference Works

Make it a point to become familiar with some key library references, such as the following periodicals classified according to function.*

General Encyclopedias Encyclopedias differ greatly in depth of coverage and readability, as you'll readily discover when you examine the following sources:

- *Encyclopedia Americana*, 30 vols., 1983
- *The New Encyclopaedia Britannica*, 30 vols., 1981
- *The New Columbia Encyclopedia*, 1 vol., 1975

Unabridged Dictionaries An easy work to take for granted, an unabridged dictionary describes and defines every word in the language.

- *The Oxford English Dictionary* (O.E.D.), 13 vols., 1933
- *Webster's Third New International Dictionary*, unabridged, 1 vol., 1966

---

*For a more thorough list of reference works, classified according to subject matter, see the Handbook, "Reference Works in Major Subject Areas."

The O.E.D., fifty years in the editing, is one of the most astonishing reference works in any language. In this vast dictionary you will find a historical profile complete with etymology, history of spelling and pronunciation, and quotations that demonstrate every known usage *for every word in the English language.* Webster's, while not as ambitious as the O.E.D., is a more up-to-date dictionary of American and British English.

Periodical Indexes Indexes are your key to the incredibly vast body of journal, newspaper, and magazine literature. Here are a few of the most frequently used volumes:

- *The Reader's Guide to Periodical Literature,* 1900–current
- *Applied Science and Technology Index,* 1958–current (formerly *Industrial Arts Index,* 1913–57)
- *Social Sciences and Humanities Index,* 1965–74
- *Humanities Index,* 1974–current
- *The New York Times Index,* 1913–current
- *Education Index,* 1929–current

Collective Biographies Detailed information about thousands of persons living or dead may be found in these valuable reference books.

- *Celebrity Register,* 1963
- *Current Biography,* 1940–current (monthly supplements)
- *Dictionary of American Biography,* 21 vols., 1928–40
- *Dictionary of National Biography,** 22 vols., 1922; supplements through 1970
- *Notable American Women,* 1607–1950, 3 vols., 1971
- *Who's Who Among Black Americans,* 2d ed., 6 vols., 1978

Your Library's Card Catalog

Although you probably know how to use a library card catalog, you may not be completely familiar with all of its features. The most important thing to remember is that there are three types of catalog cards: author card, title card, and subject card. Any given item will have more than one

---

*This dictionary refers researchers to British biographies only.

Author Card (Main Entry Card)

① **Carney, Louis P.**
②   Corrections, treatment and philosophy / Louis P.
③ Carney.—Englewood Cliffs, N.J.: Prentice-Hall, c1980.
④   xiv, 352 p.: ill.; 24 cm.
    Includes bibliographical references and index.
⑤   ISBN 0-13-178236-3

⑥   1. Corrections.   2. Corrections—United States.   I. Title.
⑦ HV9275.C36   ⑧ 364.6   79–22444
                                                 MARC
Library of Congress   79

Key to Card Elements

① Author or editor
② Book title
③ Publication data
④ Technical description of book: prefatory pages, main text pages, "illustrated" pages, size, inclusions
⑤ Book number (used when ordering or purchasing a copy)
⑥ Subject "tracings" that describe book's content
⑦ Library of Congress classification number
⑧ Dewey Decimal number

Title Card

① **The Correlates of War**/edited by J. David Singer.—New York:
③ Free Press, c1979-   ②
    v.; 25 cm.
④   Bibliography: v. 1, p.: 363–394.
    Includes index.
    CONTENTS: v. 1. Research origins and rationale.
⑤   ISBN 0-02-928960-2

⑥   1. War.   2. International relations.   I. Singer, Joel David, 1925-
⑦ U21.2.C67   ⑧ 327′.11   77–18431
                                                 MARC
Library of Congress   78

Subject Card

⑥ Photography, medical
② **Biomedical photography:** a Kodak seminar in print.—1st
③ ed.—Rochester, N.Y.: Eastman Kodak Co., 1976.
④   128 p.: ill.; 28 cm.—(Kodak publication; no. N–19)
⑤   ISBN 0-87985-183-X: $10.00

⑥   1. Photography, medical.   I. Eastman Kodak Company.
TR708.B56   616.07′54   76–27101
                                                  MARC
Library of Congress   77

Figure 10-1

Elements of library catalogue cards.

card, but only one will be the *main entry card*, indicated by boldface print. Familiarize yourself with the contents of each type of card as shown in Figure 10–1. Also take note that your library uses one of two book-classification systems: the Dewey Decimal system or the Library of Congress system.

The Dewey Decimal System

The Dewey Decimal system is actually a combination of two systems: the Dewey classification number and the Cutter author number—the first and second rows of the call number respectively. For example, *The Machine in the Garden* by Leo Marx has the following call number:

    917.3   Dewey number
    M.39   Cutter number

This system has ten major divisions:

000–099	General Works	500s	Pure Science
100s	Philosophy and Psychology	600s	Applied Science; Technology
200s	Religion	700s	The Fine Arts
300s	Social Sciences	800s	Literature (all languages)
400s	Language	900s	History

The Library of Congress System

As knowledge becomes more specialized and as new disciplines evolve, the classification system must become flexible enough to accommodate that added complexity. The Library of Congress system, with its twenty-one major categories, was designed with this objective in mind. The major categories are as follows:

A	General Works		G	Geography/Anthropology
B	Philosophy, Psychology, Religion		H	Social Sciences
			J	Political Science
C	History/Auxiliary Sciences		K	Law
D	History/Topography (excluding America)		L	Education
			M	Music
E	History: America		N	Fine Arts
F	United States History (local)/Latin, Central, South America		P	Language/Literature
			Q	Science
			R	Medicine

S   Agriculture/Plant and Animal Industry
T   Technology
U   Military Science
V   Naval Science
Z   Bibliography/Library Science

To give you an example of how these major categories are subdivided, let's break down the science category:

Q   General Science
QA   Mathematics
QB   Astronomy
QC   Physics
QD   Chemistry
QE   Geology
QH   Natural History
QK   Botany
QL   Zoology
QM   Human Anatomy
QP   Physiology
QR   Bacteriology

Studying these classification systems will give you quick insight into the way knowledge is formally organized and thus make library terrain less alien. You will probably agree, however, that there is a big difference between knowing what library materials are available to you and knowing how to go about researching a topic. Without a clear procedure for gathering and utilizing information, or an understanding of what to do with the information once it is gathered, a student may experience a severe case of writer's block. Before we look closely at various research procedures, let us consider an important preliminary concern: *involvement*.

Getting Involved with Your Topic

"Getting involved," in this context, means learning as much as you can about a topic, which means absorbing more than you're likely to use for your paper. This degree of familiarity is necessary to build a foundation for your own authority. As you prepare to convey an original view on a topic that has been analyzed many times before, you need to have a clear sense of that topic's boundaries. This doesn't necessarily mean that you must read *everything* on the topic; but it does mean that you ought to have read a representative sampling of the relevant scholarship.

To help you reinforce your familiarity with the topic, prepare an *inventory sheet* consisting of the following: points about the topic with which you're already familiar; questions about the topic about which you're uncertain and which you'll hope to uncover during subsequent research; and matters about which you have varying opinions. This preliminary research will also give you a sense of how best to *restrict* your topic; you're not gathering data for a doctoral dissertation, nor for a mere editorial.*

Gathering Information Systematically

The word *systematic* is sometimes mistakenly thought to mean inflexible, but *efficient* would be a much more accurate definition. Systematic information-gathering, or *note-taking*, allows you to obtain the information you require as quickly as possible. In this stage of the research process, index cards are your best tools: The four-by-six-inch size is just about right; three-by-fives are commonly used for bibliography entries; five-by-eights give you more space than you really need. Index cards can be shuffled, organized and reorganized to your heart's content, and conveniently stored in a purse or jacket pocket for frequent review anywhere.

Three Kinds of Note-Taking

The most common kinds of notes you'll be taking are verbatim quoting of a passage, paraphrasing, and summarizing. Let us examine each kind:

Verbatim quoting refers to copying passages word for word. When quoting verbatim, don't forget to double-check what you've written with the original; it's very easy to misread an unfamiliar word, or to skip entire phrases, especially when you've been poring over books and articles for the last five hours! A frequently used device for verbatim quoting is the *ellipsis*, indicated by three dots with a space between each one to replace words or phrases that you wish to delete from the original passage. Four dots with the first one placed close to the last word would indicate an omitted whole sentence. The author, for example, might have alluded parenthetically to a topic discussed earlier in a previous chapter or paragraph; you would need to leave out this portion of the passage as it would make no sense to the reader. Also, you would want to delete phrases that originally served as transitions from one point to another.

Let's say you want to quote verbatim from the following passage taken from G. Lowes Dickinson's *The Greek View of Life*:

> Primarily, then, Greek sculpture was an expression of the national religion; and therefore, also, of the national life. For, as we saw, the cult of the gods

---

*See Chapter 3 for the discussion on narrowing and focusing a topic.

was the center, not only of the religious but of the political consciousness of Greece.

You should use the following notecard format, substituting ellipsis points for any words you choose to omit:

G. Lowes Dickinson, *The Greek View of Life*, p. 136.

Primarily . . . Greek sculpture was an expression of the national religion; and therefore, also, of the national life. For . . . the cult of the gods was the center, not only of the religious but of the political consciousness of Greece.

And just as you may omit unnecessary words, you may also add a word or phrase to make a quotation more intelligible. Let's say that you want to quote a passage that begins with the sentence, "His novels were attacked by critics when first published." You know from the preceding sentences in the original that the author is referring to William Faulkner, so you merely insert Faulkner's name in brackets in that opening sentence:

His [Faulkner's] novels were attacked by critics.

[Faulkner's] novels were attacked by critics.

Because you must reproduce a passage precisely as found whenever quoting directly, you may wonder what to do when you find an obvious error, such as a misspelled word or a factual or typographical error. When this happens, you simply insert in brackets the Latin word *sic* (literally "thus") immediately following the questionable word or phrase. Your readers will then understand that you have reproduced the passage exactly as found.

None of Jupiter's moons have [sic] an atmosphere.

Paraphrasing means to use different words to express the same idea. Paraphrasing is a useful form of note-taking for two reasons: It allows the writer to comprehend a point more fully by expressing it in his or her own particular manner; and it allows the writer to capture a point more concisely.*

Paraphrasing, however, can be a bit tricky. Always be certain that your rewording does not distort the meaning of the original passage. Of course you could rightfully assert that any rewording is a distortion to

---

*Sources of paraphrased passages must be fully cited, either in a footnote or within the text.

some degree. But we're concerned with the difference between significant and insignificant distortion relative to the point of the quoted passage.

Read this fascinating passage from "Magic" by W. B. Yeats. Then decide which of the paraphrases that follow it are acceptable, and which are not:

> I believe in the practice and philosophy of what we have agreed to call magic, in what I must call the evocation of spirits, though I do not know what they are, in the power of creating magical illusions, in the visions of truth in the depths of the mind when the eyes are closed; and I believe in three doctrines, which have, as I think, been handed down from early times, and been the foundation of nearly all magical practices. These doctrines are: (1) that the borders of our mind are ever shifting, and that many minds can flow into one another, as it were, and create or reveal a single mind, a single energy; (2) that the borders of our memories are shifting, and that our memories are a part of one great memory, the memory of Nature herself; (3) that this great mind and great memory can be evoked by symbols.

PARAPHRASE A

W. B. Yeats, for one, believes in magic, although he dislikes that term, preferring instead "evocation of spirits," "creating magical illusions," and "visions of truth." Specifically, Yeats believes in three doctrines: that our minds are forever shifting and flowing into each other; that our memories are likewise shifting and are really a part of nature; and that both our minds and our memories can be evoked by symbols.

PARAPHRASE B

In his essay on magic, Yeats expresses his personal belief in what he prefers to call "evocation of spirits," "the power of creating magical illusions," or "visions of truth in the depths of the mind when the eyes are closed." Yeats believes that our minds flow into one another, creating a single mind, a single energy; that our memories are part of one great memory—that of Nature; and that this great mind and great memory can be evoked by symbols.

The author of Paraphrase A has distorted the original passage in a rather irresponsible manner. Yeats did not say—nor did he even imply—that he disliked the term *magic*. And notice the distortion in the second sentence: The author of the paraphrase has omitted Yeats's assertion that our combined minds flow together to become a single mind; that our memories become one great memory, that of Nature herself. The author of Paraphrase B, on the other hand, was careful not to omit any of Yeats's key points. Moreover, the author of the second paraphrase managed to preserve the enthusiastic tone of the original.

Summarizing an article or chapter from a book or newspaper trains you to concentrate on and retain key information from a given source. When you research a topic, you'll depend heavily on this important basic study skill. And, since you will have to consult a large number of sources, and will very likely want to return to some of them, summary-writing can prove to be a useful tool indeed. Summaries will offer you a better basis to judge which sources to incorporate into your research paper and which to exclude, or to merely refer to parenthetically.

Before you write your summary, the first thing you must do, of course, is *read the material* you want to summarize. Try not to skim too much, or else you may lose the central thread of the argument and thus make the summary difficult to write accurately or quickly. Next, *scribble out a paragraph* that describes a rough gist of the idea. Don't worry if you stumble a bit here, because you'll have a chance to revise later. Then, *reread*, scouting for gaps in your comprehension. If the material belongs to you, or if you photocopied it, underline key passages. And finally, *rewrite your rough summary* on a four-by-six notecard, correcting inaccuracies.

Read the following example about the whooping crane as if you planned to summarize it afterwards; remember to read carefully enough to retain the important points:

SAVING THE WHOOPING CRANE

Once flourishing in grassy marshlands and bogs, the whooping crane almost disappeared as people's croplands and cities altered its natural habitat.

In the late 1940s, only one flock of fewer than twenty whooping cranes was left in the world. No one knew where the whooper went to lay its eggs, but after a long search, scientists found the whooping crane's nesting grounds in Canada's remote Wood Buffalo Park in 1954. It was a crucial discovery, enabling biologists to begin a comprehensive program to save the great white birds.

Efforts began to protect the crane's habitat, from its Canadian nesting grounds through key stopover points along its migration route to its wintering grounds at Aransas National Wildlife Refuge on the Gulf Coast of Texas, 2,600 perilous miles away. An education program was launched to alert farmers and hunters to the bird's endangered status.

Wildlife biologists then set about building up the whooping crane population. They began a program to breed the cranes in captivity. The female crane usually lays two eggs, but generally only one chick survives. Canadian and American wildlife scientists took some of the "extra" eggs from the nests in Wood Buffalo Park and flew them to the Patuxent Wildlife Research Center in Laurel, Maryland, where they were incubated. The whooping cranes hatched at Patuxent make up a captive flock. These birds have now reached maturity and some are producing chicks. (United States Fish and Wildlife Service, Department of the Interior, from "Endangered Species")

To write an accurate summary of this item, you will first want to capture its essential point as concisely as possible. If you feel unsure about that central point, reread the article, underlining key phrases as you go along, and then base your "nutshell statement" on those key phrases. Here's an example:

> Wildlife biologists then set about <u>building up the whooping crane population</u>. They began a <u>program to breed the cranes</u> in captivity. The female crane usually <u>lays two eggs</u>, but generally only <u>one chick survives</u>.

Next, you will need to write out your nutshell statement as follows:

> When whooping cranes are bred in captivity, only one chick for every two eggs laid will survive, generally.

Before reading on, take a few minutes to write a summary of the entire article.

Incorporating Quotations Gracefully

A common problem that writers face when composing a research paper is the difficulty of maintaining readability. Even the most dedicated scholar will grow impatient with papers that introduce quotations rigidly and monotonously, or that flood the page with excessive documentation, particularly at the expense of the author's own original insight.

Remember that there are no strict rules for presenting quoted material; many variations exist, and the more variations you become familiar with, the better. Consider the way Dee Brown is able to "texture" his original observations with quotations in the following passage from *Bury My Heart at Wounded Knee*:

> General Howard and his lumbering army arrived to reinforce Miles, and [Chief] Joseph knew that his dwindling band of warriors was doomed. When Miles sent truce messengers to arrange a battlefield council, Joseph went to hear the general's surrender terms. They were simple and direct: "If you will come out and give up your arms," Miles said, "I will spare your lives and send you to your reservation."
>
> Returning to his besieged camp, Joseph called his chiefs together for the last time. Looking Glass and White Bird wanted to fight on. . . . They had struggled for thirteen hundred miles; they could not quit now. Joseph reluctantly agreed to postpone his decision. That afternoon . . . a sharpshooter's bullet struck Looking Glass in the left forehead and killed him instantly.
>
> "On the fifth day," Joseph said, "I went to General Miles and gave up my

gun." He also made an eloquent surrender speech . . . and in time it became the most quoted of all American Indian speeches: "Tell General Howard I know his heart. What he told me before I have in my heart. I am tired of fighting. Our chiefs are killed. Looking Glass is dead. . . . The old men are all dead."

You will notice that Brown's style is smooth and readable; he introduces quoted material in more than one way, and he introduces each quotation in a graceful manner.

Conducting a Library Research Task

No two researchers will conduct their business exactly alike; but as with any multifaceted activity, it always helps to cut your teeth on a suggested method, knowing that you can adapt it to your own style later on.

Whether you have a strong, a general, or just a vague notion of what you want to investigate for a research project, your first order of business is to involve yourself in the topic. You can determine your familiarity with the subject by preparing an inventory sheet, or by doing some clustering exercises.* The sooner you tend to this, the better; students who plunge into note-taking and writing too soon risk reaching a dead end or ending up with a hopelessly diffuse, superficial treatment of a topic that had not been carefully researched beforehand.

Let's assume that you are interested in sculpture and would like to investigate some aspect of this topic for a research paper. Even before you begin an inventory sheet, you might want to obtain a quick overview of *topic possibilities* in this area. The best place to go for this is not the card catalog but the Library of Congress Subject Headings (LCSH), those two fat, red volumes near the card catalog. Here you will discover how a subject is indexed and what subtopics to any given subject are available. Here are some of the subtopics listed in the LCSH under "Sculpture":

Alabaster sculpture	Cement sculpture
Animal sculpture	Ceramic sculpture
Bas relief sculpture	Driftwood sculpture
Brasses	Effigies
Bronzes	Gem carving
Cardboard sculpture	Glass sculpture
Carving (art industries)	Granite sculpture

---

*See Chapter 3, "A Practical Method of Writing."

Ice carving
Indians—sculpture
Indians of Central America—sculpture
Indians of Mexico—sculpture
Iron sculpture
Ivory carving
Kowars (sculpture)
Latex sculpture
Marble sculpture
Masks
Metal sculpture
Mobiles
Modeling
Models (e.g., clay, plaster)
Monuments
Paper sculpture
Photo sculpture
Plaster casts
Plastic sculpture
Portrait sculpture
Proportion
Relief (sculpture)
Sand sculpture

If it occurred to you that such a list of subject headings could make an ideal brainstorming tool, you're right! But before you begin researching one of the specialized areas, whet your appetite on a *survey article* on sculpture. Also, make a point of looking over the bibliography at the end of the article, as shown in Figure 10–2. Jot down these bibliography entries and return to the card catalog to see if these books are in the stacks.

Dockstader, Frederick. *Indian Art in America*. Burns and MacFachen, 1962.
Dockstader, Frederick. *Indian Art in Middle America*. New York: New York Graphic Society, 1964.
Laude, Jean. *Arts of Black Africa*. Berkeley, CA: University of California Press, 1961.
Linton, Ralph, and Paul S. Wingert. *Arts of the South Seas*. New York: Museum of Modern Art, 1946.
Mason, J. Alden. *Ancient Civilizations of Peru*. New York: Penguin Books, 1966.
Wingert, Paul S. *Primitive Art*. New York: Oxford University Press, 1962.

Figure 10-2

Typical bibliography following a general encyclopedia article or article section. This particular bibliography follows Section Five of *Encyclopedia Americana*'s article on sculpture (history—African, Oceanian, Pre-Columbian).

> Introduction
>> The Indian Artist at Work
>> The Problem of Chronology
>> Kings, Emperors, and Cociques
>> When the White Gods Came
>> Gold, Graves, and Scholars
>> The Surviving Arts
>
> Maps
>
> Plates and Commentaries
>
> Bibliography

Figure 10-3

Table of contents to Frederick Dockstader's *Indian Art in Middle America*. New York: New York Graphic Society, 1964.

If so, hunt them down. For each book you locate, study and take notes on the book's table of contents (see Figure 10–3), the book's bibliography, if any, and the book's introduction. You will likely find yourself immersed in a fascinating topic—in this case Indian sculpture in Middle America—in a very short time.

The next step is to prepare a prospectus. Because of the many discoveries you will make regarding your topic, it is almost inevitable that the background reading will modify your sense of what you'll want to investigate. So, prepare a prospectus *after* your background reading, rather than before.

Your prospectus should include your restricted topic, your statement of purpose (thesis statement), a working (tentative) title, and a working bibliography.

A prospectus for a research paper on Indian sculpture in Middle America might look something like this:

1. Restricted topic: Idol sculptures of the ancient Aztecs.
2. Statement of purpose: To demonstrate the extraordinary craftsmanship and range of styles the ancient Aztecs used in sculpting religious idols.

3. Working title: "Idols of the Ancient Aztecs."
4. Working bibliography: Blom, Franz, and Oliver LaFarge. *Tribes and Temples*. 2 vols. Tulane, Louisiana: Middle American Research Institute, 1926.
   Brenner, Anita. *Idols Behind Altars*. New York: Payson and Clarke, 1929.
   Caso, Alfonso. *The Aztecs: People of the Sun*. Norman, Oklahoma: University of Oklahoma Press, 1958.
   Dockstader, Frederick. *Indian Art In Middle America*. New York: New York Graphic Society, 1964.

Once your prospectus is written, it's time to roll up your sleeves and dig in. Your working bibliography will lead you to books that in turn will lead you to more books via their own bibliographies. For each book that seems even marginally suitable to your needs, prepare a three-by-five bibliography card, or "bib card," like the one in Figure 10–4.

In addition to writing the main bibliographic heading (top lines of card), include a brief note (middle line) to remind yourself of the most important reason for consulting the book in the future. And just to speed up the relocating process, write in the book's library call number (last line). One aspect of intensive research not to be slighted is *serendipity*, or lady luck as it's called in gambling circles; it's not something to shrug off as unprofessional by any means. Allow yourself to be open to chance findings! If nothing else, this makes research a little more fun and adventurous. Thus, when you locate a book on your working bibliography, take a few minutes to browse through some of the adjacent

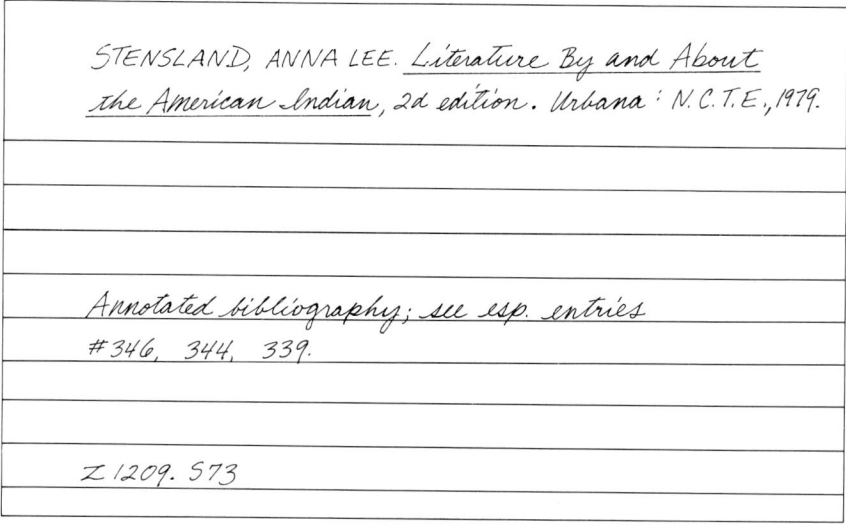

Figure 10-4

Three-by-five card for a working bibliography.

books on the shelf; likelier than not, you'll stumble upon another book highly suited to your needs.

Remember to consult reference librarians when you are confused. These librarians are trained to help student researchers and will be eager to help you; but make sure you adhere to the following suggestions when you do consult them:

1. Seek a librarian's assistance only after you have made an attempt to solve the problem on your own.

2. Show enthusiasm and respect for your research project.

3. Be clear and specific in phrasing your questions. Instead of asking, "What do you have on Indians?" ask, "Could you help me locate material on Aztec religious sculpture?"

4. Be willing to share your work-in-progress. Librarians can supply you with many suggestions when they have some sense of what you are trying to accomplish.

Researching Outside the Library

If you are researching a local topic, such as alcoholism on your campus or the dating habits of first- and second-year college students in your community, much of your research will likely be conducted outside the library. Even with more library-oriented topics such as "Walt Whitman's Concept of Democracy," an awareness of information sources beyond the library walls can be an important asset. For example, state historical societies, the New York Historical Society in particular, would be helpful in researching popular concepts of democracy in the nineteenth century.

Most information outside the library is obtained through interviews, questionnaires, and other printed sources such as privately published ("in-house") documents, and catalogs and brochures from museums and historical societies. Let's take a look at each of these sources.

Interviews

Any college is a community of specialists representing virtually every field of knowledge. These scholars are often willing to be interviewed by students, provided that students set up appointments well in advance. The same holds true for specialists off campus, such as public officials, business executives, scientists and physicians, attorneys, city planners, athletes and athletic directors, managers and supervisors, curators, theatrical producers and actors, counselors, clergy, and so on. Request interviews with off-campus people by letter, explaining clearly and concisely who you are, why you want the interview, and how long the interview should take.

Interviewing is fun, but you must be well prepared. Work out a detailed set of questions and the most appropriate sequence for them. Review the questions several times before the interview begins; there's no need to memorize them, but a thorough review will help you remember your general line of inquiry during the interview, especially when unexpected matters crop up, and they often do.

Should you use a tape recorder, or take notes? Because listening to playbacks is time-consuming, careful note-taking actually results in a more economical use of time; besides, you'll never have to worry about decoding inaudible or garbled sections of the tape, not to mention worrying about the defects that frequently occur in the tape cassettes themselves.

Think of the interview as a directed conversation: well planned and paced, and with a clear purpose in mind. But "directed" does not mean excessively formal. Liveliness and a reasonable amount of informality are just as important in encouraging the interviewee to speak fluently and in a way that you, the interviewer, can comprehend.

Furthermore, liveliness and continuity together are worth attaining not just to ensure a good yield of information, but also to make the interview interesting as a feature in its own right; an interview with a celebrity or with a person whose activities have been newsworthy would be good material for a possible feature. Abby Goldman's interview with the novelist Jean Auel demonstrates how a combination of carefully posed questions plus a smooth, conversational style can yield valuable information—in this case, insights into the working habits of a highly successful author. A carefully planned and smoothly executed interview will most likely also be interesting enough to work as a feature for a wide readership.

THE WEST INTERVIEW: JEAN M. AUEL

Before her phenomenal best seller, Clan of the Cave Bear, *the only writing Jean Auel had done was some "closet poetry." She'd been too busy raising a family. But at 40, she quit her credit-management job and started* Clan—*the first of six* Earth's Children *novels about life in the Ice Age. Both* Clan *and her second novel,* The Valley of Horses, *were among the top 20 best-selling books of 1983. Now 47, Auel is writing* The Mammoth Hunters *and helping draft plans to turn the earlier books into films. She talked to* West *between 20-hour bouts with a word-processor at her home on the Oregon coast.*

Q. You married at age 18 and had five children by age 25. When did you first wonder if homemaking was enough?

A. I guess I was about 28. I'd gone through a kind of personal revolution and decided I wanted to go to college. That's what Betty Friedan's book did for me, *The Feminine Mystique*. It gave me the feeling that I could do what I wanted to do. My husband, Ray, was going to school, and I decided it was my turn. I went to night classes, taking algebra, analytical geometry, four terms of calculus, some electronics. I never got a degree. You don't have time, taking one class per term.

Q. But you eventually got an MBA?

A. I was working at Tektronics—a corporation that builds oscilloscopes and computer peripherals. They had a special MBA program, so my husband and I both did that. I was writing term papers, learning how to research in a library and doing a little poetry on the side. I got the MBA when I was 40, in May of 1976. By that time, I'd worked my way up in the company to credit manager, and I quit—because the job wasn't what I wanted to do. I didn't know what to do; I had absolutely no idea in my head about writing a book.

Q. Then how did it occur to you?

A. It was just a fluke. It was late one night, and this idea was just going through my head. It was of a girl or a young woman who was living with these people who were different, physically less developed. But they were looking at her as if *she* were different. It was a kind of twist. And I thought, "Hey, I'm not doing anything right now. Why don't I see if I can write a short story?"

Q. Some short story. Your research into prehistory impressed even the veteran anthropologists. You studied herbal lore, spent nights in stone caves, read hundreds of books.

A. I think it's a wonderful way to learn. Research is a kind of Pied Piper; it just leads you on. And, yes, I've gotten really good responses from the scientific community. The view that the general public has of cave man dragging mates around by their hair is such a distorted view, and there's such a gap between that and what scientists know.

Q. How do you answer criticism that your characters are too modern?

A. Once you have taken a tough old hairy deer hide that's been dried for three years, and you go through this whole three-day process and what you come out with at the end is the softest, most velvety buckskin you have ever felt, you gain a tremendous appreciation for the intelligence that had to figure that process out. You begin to have an appreciation for the fact that they were not grubbing in the dirt for an existence. They had control of their lives.

Q. Some say you took things a bit too far in *The Valley of Horses*. There are a couple of pretty steamy love scenes, which prompted *People* magazine to call the book a "primordial ooze opera."

A. *People* can call it what it likes. The point I'm trying to make is that their emotional responses were the same as ours. These people had the exact same skeletons as we do. So they had to have the same ability, the same range of intelligence, the same psychological traits. I've seen the cave paintings in Lascaux, and I defy anyone to tell me that the people who put those paintings on the walls were any less capable of love, of language, of any emotional response than anyone today.

Sexuality is absolutely essential to the story. I was trying very hard to write innocent sex. Innocent, erotic sex. Innocent of shame and "dirtiness." Many people today seem to think that we invented sex. That earlier people didn't know anything about it. I mean, we're here! They've known how to do this for a long time! We didn't invent sex. What we invented is obscenity, repression.

Q. You're hoping to finish the third novel so it can be published this fall. Like George Lucas, you've promised your fans a series of adventures, but he has been known to complain of burnout. How are you holding up?

A. I'm still excited, still having fun with this. I hope that it'll stay with me for all six books, because I *will* write all six books.

Q. Did your life change much with the money you made from the novels? With success?

A. It makes it easier. I went to Europe and talked to some of the best-known anthropologists in the field. I've held in my hand the actual artifacts. It's been a wonderful experience. If I want to, at Christmastime, I can say, "Hey, kids, come on home. I'll give you an airline ticket." I can build a house on the coast and look out the window and watch the whales migrate. I'm having *more fun.*

Q. You've become something of a local hero. When *Clan* was published, Portland proclaimed "Jean Auel Day." In New York City, nobody would have batted an eye.

A. Somebody asked me one time, "How can you stand being so far away from where everything's going on?" When I'm writing, I need to be alone. I can't run out for an evening, come home and get myself back 30,000 years ago.

There are not that many best-selling authors in the Northwest—Ruth Hill (*Hanta Yo*) lives up here, and Tom Robbins. But more writers seem to be moving in this direction. You get a certain perspective in the West; your world isn't just New York. Your world really does enlarge. Maybe the *New York Times* doesn't give you such a great review, but you can live with that. You say, "Maybe the *Scapoose Times* will like me!"

Q. Any words of advice for budding middle-aged novelists?

A. You know, there are a lot of people who say "research the market" and do this and do that. If I had researched the market, I would never, ever, have written a story about cave men. If you've got a story and you want to tell it, just *do* it. If you were to ask all of the people on top of the best-selling list—Steven King or Robert Ludlum or any of those people—they'd tell you they're writing what they love to write. That's what you have to do.

Abby Goldman, from *West*, February 19, 1984

Questionnaires

Collecting data via questionnaire, whether mailed or hand-distributed, is risky business. You will not receive responses from everyone; in fact, you will be lucky if half of the recipients return the questionnaire filled out. On the other hand, this is a relatively efficient way to determine community response on a given issue, provided you design your questionnaire judiciously.

Let us say that you are conducting a study of drinking among students who are under the legal drinking age. Your aim is to find out just how serious this problem is and what, if anything, might be done about it. Your questionnaire, to be distributed to the entire university community, might look like this:

Dear Member of the Xanadu State College Community:

I am a Xanadu College freshman investigating the possible problem of alcohol abuse by underage students on this campus. Please answer the following questions as accurately as you can. Return the completed form to me, Joan Smith, via campus mail. My address is Box 150, Xanadu College.

1. Are you a student _____ faculty member _____ administrator _____ other (please specify) _____?

2. If a student, are you a freshman _____ sophomore _____ junior _____ senior _____ graduate student _____ attending full-time _____ part-time _____?

3. Is your age: under 18 _____ 18 _____ 19 _____ 20 _____ 21 _____ over 21 _____?

4. Do you or do you not consume alcoholic beverages? _____

5. If you do consume alcoholic beverages, how often do you do so?
   _____ rarely (only on special occasions, like weddings)
   _____ infrequently (once a week)
   _____ regularly (whenever I unwind)
   _____ frequently (more than once a day)
   _____ very frequently (several times a day)

6. When you drink, what is your amount of consumption at a given time?
   _____ very slight (less than one-half ounce hard liquor or one-half glass wine or beer)
   _____ light (one ounce hard liquor or one glass wine or beer)
   _____ moderate (two ounces hard liquor or two glasses wine or beer)
   _____ heavy (four ounces hard liquor or four glasses wine or beer)
   _____ very heavy (five or more ounces hard liquor or five or more glasses wine or beer)

7. Have you ever been involved in an alcohol-related incident on campus? _____
   Describe the incident: _____
   _____

8. Have you ever witnessed drunken behavior in the dorms or in the classroom? _____
   Describe a typical occurrence: _____
   _____

9. In your own judgment, is there a problem of alcohol abuse on this campus? _____
Explain what the college ought to do about it, if anything: _____

Thank you very much for your cooperation.

Note that the above questionnaire is effective for a number of reasons. The questions are specific and therefore relatively easy to answer. Also, the questions that require the most time for reflection are saved for last. Many respondees would otherwise be tempted not to bother with them. Finally, the questions are designed to yield useful information. Always be sure that your questions aren't vague, that they don't yield useless information, and that they don't "load the dice" by implying an attitude that could prejudice an answer (e.g., "Are you for or against continued aggressive use of missiles?"). Here are a few such ineffective questions:

What do you think of the alcohol problem on campus?

The question assumes what the aim of the questionnaire is supposed to help determine. Moreover, any what-do-you-think-of question is very difficult to answer.

Are you a heavy drinker or a light drinker?

The options are not defined; neither are they sufficient. Any kind of an answer to such a question could not yield useful or accurate information.

Describe what you consider to be the principal psychological reasons behind student drinking.

Such a question would be appropriate for a dissertation, not for a questionnaire!

Printed Information Sources Outside the Library

You may be surprised to discover that a wealth of documents is obtainable from sources other than your college or community library. Some of the major information sources include the following:

1. Local chambers of commerce
2. Local Internal Revenue Service offices

3. Large corporations*

4. State historical societies

5. City, county, university, and private museums

6. State boards of education

7. The United States Government and its agencies†

There are also hundreds of government agencies to whom you can write for information. The sourcebook for all such addresses is *Information U.S.A.*, edited by Matthew Lesko (New York: Viking Press, 1983).

Plagiarism

When you are collecting data from printed sources, you must be aware of the distinction between the use of reference materials and plagiarism (from the Latin *plagiarius*, "kidnapper").

To plagiarize means to use willfully as one's own the words and ideas, published or unpublished, of another. Plagiarism is a kind of theft, not merely dishonesty; it is illegal when one is writing for publication as it violates federal copyright laws. Many colleges have a plagiarism policy, whereby offenders could be punished with an automatic "F" in the course, or even expulsion from school.

Because of the potential seriousness of the offense, students should make an effort to understand plagiarism. There are three kinds:

1. Total plagiarism: an entire article is lifted verbatim

2. Partial plagiarism: sentences or paragraphs are lifted verbatim from an article

3. Idea or paraphrase plagiarism: original ideas of another are reworded

To avoid plagiarism, always acknowledge the source of a direct quotation, paraphrased material, or idea. Understand the difference between common-knowledge information and attributable information. Common knowledge refers to the body of *factual* information (as opposed to interpreted information) on a given subject. Statements such as

---

*Examples of these are Eastman Kodak in Rochester, New York, for information on cameras, film, or photographic processes; and Atari in Palo Alto, California, for information on computer videogames.

†Your library most likely has a government publications room, but you can obtain material directly through the United States Government Printing Office by writing to them at: United States Government Printing Office, Public Documents Division, Washington, D.C., 20402.

"Galileo was the first astronomer ever to use a telescope"; "Joseph Smith founded the Church of Jesus Christ of Latter Day Saints in 1830"; or "Rugby is the British form of football that was created at Rugby School in Warwickshire" are examples of common knowledge. You would not document their sources even if you did not possess this knowledge beforehand. When in doubt about whether certain information is common knowledge, acknowledge the source or consult your instructor.

Using a Computer Database

Even in this age of technological miracles, computer "on-line" database systems boggle the imagination. Before your very eyes, vast stores of data on virtually any subject can be retrieved. What is more, conducting a *search*, as it is called, is easy and in most cases inexpensive.

Before conducting your first search, you should became familiar with databases. Companies that provide databases are known formally as on-line information services. One such company, perhaps the largest and best known, is Lockheed's DIALOG service. DIALOG subscribes to more than one hundred databases, which together contain a staggering forty million records. In Figure 10–5 you will see a page from the January 1985 DIALOG database catalog. Notice that each database entry lists the number of records in its files, the frequency of updating, a description of the file contents, and the cost per hour of connect time. Even if your research project does not require an investigation that is thorough enough to require the services of a database network, it makes sense to learn the procedure now, and to conduct an actual search on a topic you're familiar with already. The avalanche of additional data you would receive could provide you with a great many ideas for essays.

To conduct a database search, you'll need to first ask your librarian for a *search request form*. On this form you will be asked to indicate your search needs, and to provide a list of important concepts and key words, including synonyms. These enable the computer to retrieve the information most relevant to your needs. Also, you will most likely be asked to include the names of any relevant authors.

You will then present your search request form to either the librarian or a computer operator, who will then bring you to the database computer and "log on"; that is, the computer will be "patched" (linked) into the database network. This process is made possible by a telecommunications system, which converts computer signals into telephone signals, and vice versa at the other end. Thus, computers are able to "talk" to each other across great distances. You or the operator will enter the key

METADEX (METALS ABSTRACTS/ALLOYS INDEX), 1966–present (Alloys Index, 1974–present) 497,000 records, monthly updates (American Society for Metals, Metals Park, OH)

The *METADEX* database, produced by the American Society for Metals (ASM) and the Metals Society (London), provides the most comprehensive coverage of international literature on the science and practice of metallurgy. Included in this database are *Review of Metal Literature* (1966–67), *Metals Abstracts* (1968 to present), and since 1974, *Alloys Index*. *Metals Abstracts* include about 30,000 citations each year from about 1,100 primary journal sources. *Alloys Index* supplements *Metal Abstracts* by providing access to the citations through commercial, numerical, and compositional alloy designations; specific metallic systems; and intermetallic compounds found within these systems. In addition to specialized topics (including specific alloy designations, intermetallic compounds, and metallurgical systems), six basic categories of metallurgy are covered: materials, processes, properties, products, forms, and influencing factors. Each month about 2,500 new documents related to metals technology are scanned and abstracted for the ASM database, with intensive coverage of appropriate conference papers, reviews, technical reports, and books. These sources are international in scope, including the U.S.S.R. and Eastern European nations among the 43 countries covered.

SDI: $6.95/update

$80 per online connect hour, 15¢ per full record printed offline, 10¢ per full record typed or displayed online   **File 32**

METEOROLOGICAL AND GEOASTROPHYSICAL ABSTRACTS, 1972–present, 94,000 records, irregular updates (American Meteorological Society and NOAA, Washington, D.C.)

METEOROLOGICAL AND GEOASTROPHYSICAL ABSTRACTS provides current citations in English for the most important meteorological and geoastrophysical research published in worldwide literature sources. Over 200 sources, including technical journals, monographs, proceedings, reviews, and annual publications are scanned for relevant literature. Subject coverage includes meteorology, astrophysics, physical oceanography, hydrosphere/hydrology, environmental sciences, and glaciology. Abstracts are included for records from 1972–1973 and 1976 to the present.

$95/hour database connect charge, 15¢ per full record printed offline   **File 29**

MICROCOMPUTER INDEX™, 1980–present, 13,000 records, quarterly updates (Microcomputer Information Services, Santa Clara, CA)

The *MICROCOMPUTER INDEX* is a subject and abstract guide to magazine articles from over 21 microcomputer journals. Included are general articles about the microcomputer world, book reviews, software reviews, discussions of applications in various milieu, descriptions of new microcomputer products, and more. Publications indexed include *Byte, Interface Age, InfoWorld, Personal Computing, Softside, Dr. Dobb's Journal,* etc. Each record includes a short abstract and complete bibliographic information plus assigned descriptors. *MICROCOMPUTER INDEX* corresponds to the printed work of the same name.

$45 per online connect hour, 15¢ per full record printed offline   **File 233**

MILLION DOLLAR DIRECTORY*, current, 121,000 records annual reload (Dun's Marketing Services, Parsippany, NJ)

The *MILLION DOLLAR DIRECTORY (MDD)* comprises comprehensive business information on 121,000 U.S. companies from the three-volume *Million Dollar Directory Series*. Listings are limited to companies with a net worth of $500,000 or more, and include hard-to-find information on businesses that are privately held, as well as publicly-owned companies. These business establishments, which account for over one trillion dollars in sales, may be headquarters, subsidiaries, or single locations. The *MDD* records contain full address including county and SMSA, primary and secondary SIC codes, annual sales, number of employees, and name of chief executive officer. The *MDD* file records can also include the names of the top financial, sales, and purchasing executives. Also recorded in this file are the stock exchanges and the ticker symbol for public companies as well as indicators for companies that import and/or export. For coverage of even more companies, *DUN'S MARKET IDENTIFIERS** *10+* is available as File 516. The *MDD*, File 517, is available to U.S., Canadian, and Japanese users only.

$100 per online connect hour, $1.50 per full record typed or displayed online or printed offline   **File 517**

MLA BIBLIOGRAPHY, 1970–present, 469,000 records, annual updates (Modern Language Association, New York, NY)

The *MLA BIBLIOGRAPHY* database provides the first online access to the distinguished and comprehensive bibliography of humanistic studies produced annually by the Modern Language Association. The *MLA BIBLIOGRAPHY* indexes books and journal articles published on the modern languages, literature, and linguistics. Detailed coverage is provided of English, American, medieval and neo-Latin, and Celtic literatures and of folklore; as well as of European, Asian, African and Latin American literatures. Comprehensive coverage of the fields of theoretical and descriptive linguistics and comparative and historical linguistics is also provided as well as information on specific languages including composite and derivative languages and other communicative behavior.

$55 per online connect hour, 15¢ per full record printed offline   **File 71**

Modern Language Association Bibliography (See MLA BIBLIOGRAPHY)

Monthly Catalog (See GPO MONTHLY CATALOG)

MRIS Abstracts (See TRIS)

National Criminal Justice Reference Service (See NCJRS)

Figure 10-5

Sample page from DIALOG's database catalog (January 1985). Reprinted, with permission, from DIALOG Information Services, Inc.

information described earlier, and you will wait for the data to appear. You may obtain a printout of the data at a slight additional cost.

Summary

The first step in acquiring good research skills is to familiarize yourself with the resources of your college library. First embark on a self-tour or guided tour using the library floor plan, available at the circulation or information desk, to help you. Take the time to browse through the reference room, the periodicals room (where newspapers, magazines, and scholarly journals are kept), the microfilm room, the government documents room, the special collections, the stacks (the general book collection), and the card-catalog room.

Next, learn to use key reference tools: periodical indexes for locating relevant articles in the periodicals room; bibliographies for finding relevant books in the stacks or in special collections; general and specialized encyclopedias; handbooks; yearbooks for obtaining quick overviews of your topic; and the card catalog, not just for locating a particular book, but for finding out basic information about the book, such as its publication data and its table of contents.

Then begin your systematic information-gathering. Take notes by means of paraphrases, summaries, and direct quotations on index cards, and prepare accurate bibliography cards for every item you consult.

Finally, learn the fundamentals of information-gathering outside the library. This includes conducting interviews, designing and administering questionnaires, and obtaining published documents from private sources such as corporations and historical societies.

FOR DISCUSSION

1. Describe your current library research methods to the class. Do you follow any procedures that differ from the procedures described in this chapter?

2. What aspects of library research have you found to be excessively time-consuming or frustrating? What might be done to save time and to reduce frustration?

3. Recall the last time you interviewed someone. If the interview went well, what contributed to its success? If it did not go well, what would you do differently next time?

4. Make a list of printed materials not likely to be found in your college library. Discuss the possible usefulness of these materials.

5. Conduct a computer database search on a subject of your choice; report your experience to the class.

FOR WRITING

1. For each of the following reference works, prepare a half-page report. Describe the work's principal contents and its "working parts," that is, cross-references, bibliographies, illustrations, indexes, and the like.
   a. *The New Grove Dictionary of Music and Musicians*, 20 vols., 1980
   b. *Guide to Reference Books*, 9th ed., 1976
   c. *Encyclopedia of World Art*, 15 vols., 1959–68
   d. *Encyclopedia of Bioethics*, 4 vols., 1978
   e. *McGraw-Hill Encyclopedia of Science and Technology*, 15 vols., 1982
   f. One additional reference work of your choice from the Handbook, "Reference Works in Major Subject Areas"

2. Locate each of the following periodical indexes:
   a. *Art Index*
   b. *Applied Science and Technology Index*
   c. *Education Index*
   d. *Bibliography Index*
   e. *New York Times Index*

   Then locate three articles using three different indexes from the preceding list. Write a half-page summary of each.

3. Read the following excerpt from an essay by Francis Bacon. Then prepare:
   a. Two four-by-six notecards, one containing a direct quotation of one passage, the other containing a paraphrase of that same passage
   b. A three-by-five bibliography card
   c. A summary of the whole essay from which the excerpt shown here is extracted (try to locate the essay on your own before requesting assistance)

OF SUSPICION

Suspicions amongst thoughts are like bats amongst birds; they ever fly by twilight. Certainly they are to be repressed, or at least well guarded: for they cloud the mind; they leese* friends; and they check with business, whereby business cannot go on currently and constantly. They dispose kings to tyranny, husbands to jealousy, wise men to irresolution and melancholy. They are defects, not in the heart, but in the brain; for they take place in the stoutest natures, as in the example of Henry the Seventh of England. There was not a more suspicious man, nor a more stout. And in such a composition they do small hurt. For commonly they are not admitted, but with examination, whether they be likely to or no? But in fearful natures they gain ground too fast. There is nothing makes a man suspect much, more than to know little; and therefore men should remedy suspicion by procuring to know more, and not to keep their suspicions in smother. (Francis Bacon, *Essays*)

4. Prepare a questionnaire of no more than two pages for an investigation of a campus-related issue.

5. Compose an essay, serious or humorous, on the joys and frustrations of doing library research.

COMPUTER WRITING

Practice your interviewing skills by interviewing a fellow student at your personal-computer workstation. Keep the keyboard, if it is detachable, on your lap while you converse. Enter into the computer whatever notes you deem necessary, but try to keep your eyes on your interviewee as much as possible. You may also wish to dim the screen or to keep the monitor facing only you so your interviewee will not be tempted to read your notes. Immediately after the interview, review your notes and make whatever additions, deletions, rearrangements, and rephrasings are necessary to make the interview as readable as possible. Then print it.

---

*alienate

Research Paper Projects

CHAPTER 11

If you browse through this chapter briefly before you begin studying it methodically, you'll notice that the so-called research paper can refer to more than one kind of project. You will also learn that not all research papers are written on the same level of formality, which contradicts a popular belief that they represent the highest level of formality possible in writing. This doesn't mean that research papers should be written in a casual, colloquial style; but some papers are geared for a general audience, and should not allow readability to be sacrificed for technical minutiae.

At this point, we should take a careful look at our term *research paper*, which seems to imply that some papers are in fact not researched; this is a fallacy based on a misunderstanding of the term *research*. We ought instead to use the term professionals use that makes explicit reference to outside sources: the *scholarly paper*, or *scholarly article*. Research is a basic ingredient in virtually all writing, whether it be novels like *Gone With the Wind* or *Moby Dick*, or a humorous piece on the foibles of Washington politics, or a personal-experience essay on the Grand Canyon. A novelist researches a topic such as the American Civil War not just to inject background detail into a story, but to recreate the reality of that time: the overall mood, the mannerisms of individuals, and the social conventions. The novelist aims to be convincing about the times. The writer of personal essays, likewise, often must do considerable background reading to generate interest and emotional response in his or her readers.

Furthermore, as you've learned in Chapter 10, not all research is conducted in the library. If you plan to write an essay on the social impact of political assassinations and you ask your parents to describe their reactions to John Kennedy's assassination, you are conducting research. Such information may not be formally documented in your paper, but it is researched information nonetheless.

Research is also the element that turns you into an expert in your own right. You do not write a research paper simply to regurgitate facts and to record the opinions of experts. Rather, you uncover what others have said about a topic to assimilate that information into your own point of view. You write a research paper when you want to "show your hand," that is, to let your readers in on who said what, specifically *how* they said it, and *where* they said it.

But why are these facts so important? Why do people bother to read research papers? There are two reasons: One, a reader may need to consult the sources you have used to obtain more detailed information, perhaps for a research project he or she is undertaking; and two, the research-paper format suggests a spirit of scientific rigor, occurring when the truth of an argument is established as unambiguously and demonstrably as possible. "Here is my evidence," the researcher is saying implicitly to readers. "Consult my documentation and go check out the facts for yourself."

This chapter aims to guide you through some typical research paper projects. You will get a clear picture of how to make that sometimes tricky transition from notes and outlines to the first draft. You will also learn what it means to make your paper *readable*, not just referable. In most research papers, a vigorous and colorful writing style is just as important as are clarity, coherence, and accuracy.

The model research papers you will study here represent varying academic disciplines. As an undergraduate, you will discover that familiarity with research methods in more than one discipline will benefit you in a number of ways. For one thing, the disciplines are much more *interactive* than they've ever been. For example, chemists have much to offer to and learn from social scientists; if you add knowledge of organic chemistry to that of drug abuse, you may uncover new ways to combat one of our greatest social problems.

Each discipline offers you a unique way to perceive the world. The more points of view you encounter, the more mature your assimilated world view will become. One of the best ways to acquaint yourself with these differing points of view is to conduct research in each major discipline. The projects and exercises in this chapter will help you toward that goal.

Each of the following research projects represents a major academic discipline; and yet, each is "interdisciplinary" in the sense that it is relevant to an academic discipline outside its own. Study these papers carefully, even though you may have already decided upon a major field of study. It certainly makes good sense to prepare a research paper on a topic most relevant to your major, or proposed major, field of study; but keep in mind that the similarities of material and research methodology among different subjects outweigh the differences.

One possible way to proceed is to superimpose your major area of interest upon that of another area. If, for example, you are an English major, think about literature in relation to, let's say, medicine, and you might come up with a topic like "Physicians and Surgeons in the Modern Novel." If you're a music major, think about music in another context, like music and language, music and mathematics, or music in relation to the other arts, such as "Musical Analogues of Cubism."

Project One: Researching a Scientific or Technical Subject

Now that we have considered the idea of superimposing one area of inquiry upon another, let's apply it to the subject of computers, which lends itself ideally to interdisciplinary study. Almost every academic subject has subdisciplines for which computers can be very helpful. Computer art is one example; engineers and architects often depend on computer-generated drawings in their work. Literary scholars use computers with ever-increasing frequency to compile bibliographies, indexes, concordances. Word processing also improves the efficiency of writers and editors everywhere.*

Before you examine one student's research into computers, why don't you whet your own appetite in this challenging area? Take a moment or so to glance over the following list of topic possibilities:

- Computers That Talk: Frivolity or Necessity?
- Computers in the Home: Effects on Family Relations
- Using Computers to Combat Crime
- New Approaches to Fighting Computer Crime
- Systematizing Computer Programming
- How Computers Are Helping Young Children Learn to Read Better
- Biochip Technology and the Computers of the Future
- Computers and Books: Adversaries or Allies?

---

*See Chapter 19, "Composing on a Computer."

- Music by Computer
- Electronic Mail: Its Impact on Personal Correspondence
- The Computer in Science Fiction

An especially intense interest in a particular topic is an excellent motive for research. Imagine, for example, that you have always been baffled by the problems of programming a computer. You would probably want to take this opportunity to research the topic and to discover once and for all what it's all about.

When student Jeff Brown decided that he would like to do his research project on programming, he began to do some basic background reading. He searched not only for articles and books related specifically to programming, but also for those on computer technology in general to get a thorough grasp of the material so he would be able to see particulars in relation to the larger context. Even though Jeff was quite familiar with programming methodology, it was worth his time to review introductory articles on the subject, especially if they were written in a provocative manner, such as the following piece, published in January 1983 in *Time* magazine. By the way, if you are not familiar with computer programming, be sure to read this piece before turning to Jeff's research paper.

HOW TO "WRITE" PROGRAMS

Hardware is not difficult to understand. It is nuts and bolts and microchips. But what is software? Perhaps the easiest way to think of it is in terms of a simple analogy: hardware is to software as a television set is to the shows that appear on it. Computer programs, rather like those aired on TV, are a man-made effort to turn lifeless hardware into something one might want to spend some time with.

Programs, like television scripts, are "written"—not in English, but in English-like commands that vary from machine to machine. BASIC, for example, is a "language" most desktop computers are wired to understand.

In the past, computer owners had to write their own software. Today thousands of prewritten programs are on the market, ranging from games to accountants' tools. Running these software packages, as opposed to writing them, is no more difficult than playing a record or a videotape. Just find the appropriate disc, put it in a disc drive and push a button. In a matter of seconds the computer is programmed and set to do the job at hand—from balancing the books to finding misspelled words to playing a video game.

Making the programs, however, involves grueling and painstaking work, most of it done by a software engineer, also known as a programmer. Just what is it that a programmer does and how does he do it?

The first step is to decide what you want the computer to do—play blackjack, manipulate text, juggle figures? Once the task is clearly defined, the programmer lays out a step-by-step procedure for executing that task. Think of these procedures as roughly akin to cookbook recipes. The recipe for playing blackjack, for example, might go something like this: "Get a deck of cards. Shuffle the cards. Deal two cards to each player. Ask the first player if he wants another card. Did the face value of that third card put his total over 21? If not, ask if he wants another card . . ."

Once the task is set and the recipe spelled out, the programmer sits down at a computer and translates each step into commands that the machine can understand. A typical command might say: PRINT "DO YOU WANT ANOTHER CARD?"

The computer, interpreting commands one word at a time, recognizes the word PRINT and the quotation marks that follow it. It has been wired to gather up messages that appear between quotation marks and translate them, character by character, into sequences of numbers. These numbers, in turn, are translated into a corresponding sequence of electrical signals. These signals are sent to an electron "gun" housed in the vacuum tube behind the computer's video screen. This gun, following the sequence of signals, fires bursts of electrons at the back side of the screen. The electrons strike bits of phosphor that coat the screen and energize them, lighting up a pattern of dots. These dots form the shape of alphabetic characters, spelling out the message: DO YOU WANT ANOTHER CARD?

Thankfully, the programmer does not have to worry about every electron and phosphor dot. He has enough on his hands typing his commands into the computer and testing them to see if they do what he meant them to do. Even a program for playing blackjack can quickly grow to be hundreds of lines long, each line densely packed with convoluted commands and alphanumerical characters. If there is even one character out of place in those hundreds of lines, chances are the program will not work properly. These software "bugs," as programming mishaps are called, can take weeks to find. One bug in an AT&T program knocked out all long-distance telephone service to Greece in 1979. It was months before Ma Bell's programmers pinned down the problem.

When the programmer has thoroughly tested and corrected his work he stores it on a magnetic tape or disc, much as someone might use a tape recorder to store a noteworthy speech. A particularly useful or entertaining computer program might be accepted by one of the growing number of software publishers. They will copy the program onto blank discs and send them to computer stores around the country.

When a user slips his brand-new blackjack program into a disc drive and turns on his computer, the drive starts spinning the disc at a rate of hundreds of revolutions per minute. As the disc spins, a record-playback head moves across its surface, picking up the original programmer's typed instructions and loading them onto the computer's memory. When the disc stops spinning—presto!—an exact replica of the program will be imprinted on the machine's temporary memory, all debugged and ready to deal the cards. Or, depending on the disc, proofread the term paper, balance the books or tell you to sell the hogs.

Jeff's next task was to draw up a prospectus, or proposal, for his research project. You'll remember from Chapter 10 that a prospectus should consist of a statement of purpose, an outline divided into introduction and conclusion, a working title, and a working bibliography.

PROSPECTUS

Statement of Purpose

My purpose in writing this research paper is to trace the development of structured programming and to discuss its importance in today's computer movement. I will begin with the historical origins of structured programming and move into some ideas and methods that have been implemented. I will close with the benefits of structured programming and its necessity in modern computing.

Synopsis

Introduction. Imagine the resulting difficulties and confusion in communication if the English language lacked a set of established grammatical rules. A similar situation exists today in computer programming. The newest machines allow someone with little computer experience to operate them: at the same time, much larger and more complex computers are being developed. The complexity of programming and the large scale it encompasses have brought about the need to develop a method to ease the task of designing and writing programs. The past ten years point to the development of a revolutionary method called structured programming.

Conclusion. The structured programming revolution has brought about a method of program development that produces more readable, more understandable programs. As concepts of structured programming are accepted and implemented by more and more programmers, the finished product of a programming project will be a program that will leave its makers proud and its buyers appreciative. If at a later date a programmer decides to read the program out of duty or curiosity, he or she will find it easy to follow and will be able to communicate what the program does and how it does it.

Outline

I. Origins
   A. Need for larger, more complex programs
   B. Bohm and Jacopini's control structures
   C. Dijkstra's famous letter to the editor

II. Characteristics of structured programming
   A. Construction of programs
      1. Minimal "gotos"
      2. Control structures
         a. Sequence
         b. Decision
         c. Iteration
         d. Case

B. Style
      1. Comments
      2. Indentation
III. Methods of implementation
   A. Stepwise refinement ("top-down")
      1. Pseudocoding
      2. Segmenting
   B. Chief programmer team
      1. Chief programmer
      2. Assistant programmer
      3. Librarian
IV. Benefits of structured programming
   A. Readability
   B. Maintenance
   C. Reliability
   D. Efficiency
      1. Cost
      2. Time
V. Conclusion

Working Title

"Structured Programming"

Working Bibliography

Bohm, C., and G. Jacopini. "Flow Diagrams, Turing Machines and Language Rules with Only Two Formation Rules." *Communications of the Association of Computing Machinery* 9 (1966): 366–71.

Dahl, O. J., E. W. Dijkstra, and C. A. R. Hoare. *Structured Programming*. New York: Academic Press, 1972.

McCracken, Daniel. "Revolution in Programming: An Overview." *Datamation* 19 (1973): 50–52.

Yeh, Raymond T., ed. *Current Trends in Programming Methodology*. Englewood Cliffs, NJ: Prentice-Hall, 1977.

Let us now turn to the fruits of Jeff's labors: his finished research paper. As you read through it, pay attention to the notes in the margin; they will remind you of the several kinds of mental gymnastics involved in composing a research paper. Take a look, too, at some of Jeff's many notecards (Figure 11–1).

English 002
Professor Jane Honeycutt
March 1, 1984

Structured Programming: Its Development and Importance
by
Jeff Brown

Brown's opening paragraph is designed to ease his lay audience painlessly into the subject of programming by indicating its place in the context of computer technology. He makes no assumptions about the reader's familiarity with programming jargon.

The key term "structured programming" is introduced. Note how Brown adds to the comprehensibility by including a relevant and interesting historical background.

Notice the way Brown varies his manner of introducing outside sources.

Because the computer industry is relatively young, new advances are common in every aspect of computing. Software (the instructions that tell a computer what to do) is no exception. In today's highly competitive computer market, the importance of software stands out. However, in the past, advances in software technology have tended to lag behind the breakthroughs in computer hardware. It is important that software keep pace with hardware, for programming is the communication link between humans and computers.

Imagine the resulting difficulties and confusion in communication if the English language lacked a set of established grammatical rules. A similar situation has plagued the field of computer programming. The complexity of programming, along with the large scale it encompasses, has brought about the need to develop a method to ease the task of designing and writing programs. The experiences of the past ten years point to the development of a revolutionary method called structured programming. Structured programming was born out of a crisis—programming methods had to change. In the early years of software development, programmers were forced to code in highly efficient—but unfortunately much too cryptic and difficult to read—segments because of the limited memory of early computers (Miller and Boyd 28).

James Donaldson, in an article printed in a special issue devoted to structured programming in <u>Datamation</u> in 1973, described the term "structured programming" as "a manner of organizing and coding programs that makes the programs easily understood and modified" (Donaldson 53). The method has its roots in the latter half of the 1960s and gained recognition in the mid-1970s.

As programs came to demand more in terms of complexity, programmers were forced to divert attention from program design and concentrate their thoughts on confusing details. When unforeseen problems arose, a programmer could simply add a couple of gotos and corresponding statement labels to remedy the situation. The result of the use of gotos, which allow branching to anywhere in a program, clouded the original logical intentions (Miller and Boyd 31). Edsger Dijkstra, the father of the structured programming revolution, claimed, "The quality of programmers is a decreasing function of the density of goto statements in the programs they produce" (Dijkstra 147).

> Brown explains the problem that arises in nonstructured programming: excessive use of "gotos"—statements that undermine the program's logical intentions.

In 1966, Corrado Bohm and Giuseppe Jacopini published a paper in the Communications of the Association of Computing Machinery. The paper presented proof that any program could be constructed using three control structures, namely sequence, selection, and iteration (Bohm and Jacopini 366–71).

> The assertion made in paragraph four is reinforced by the quotations from Bohm and Jacopini and from Dijkstra.

Most programmers agree that Edsger Dijkstra's now famous letter to the editor of Communications of the Association of Computing Machinery, which was published in the March issue of 1968, started the structured programming revolution. The letter, titled by the editors "Goto Statement Considered Harmful," pointed out that the superfluous use of goto statements in programs had to be stopped. In Dijkstra's own words, "The goto statement as it stands is just too primitive; it is too much an invitation to make a mess of one's program" (Dijkstra 147).

So the foundations of structured programming had been set. Large programs were new, and as Dijkstra put it, "Widespread underestimation of the specific difficulties of size seems one of the major underlying causes of the current software failure" (Dijkstra 2). Programs of greater length and complexity had created problems for programmers, and the best solution seemed to be the quickest solution. Good habits programmers had developed over the years were being replaced by haphazard programming methods. The work of Bohm, Jacopini, and Dijkstra proposed a way of making programs easier to create, read, and understand (McCracken 50–51).

> Brown discusses additional virtues of structured programming. Observe here and elsewhere how the author's skillful use of transitional phrases at the beginning of each paragraph helps the topic move forward smoothly and interestingly.

Since the initial publications on the subject, structured programming has gained acceptance as it developed into an effective method of program design and development. Over the years, the term has come to mean more than just the minimal use or total elimination of gotos. Structured programming is also characterized by the use of the control constructs described by Bohm and Jacopini. The constructs allow a certain structured style, which makes the program code unambiguous.

> Operational definition, a key rhetorical technique for explaining a process, is put to good use in this paragraph.

The constructs presented by Bohm and Jacopini were a sequence mechanism, a selection mechanism, and an iteration mechanism. The sequence mechanism simply dictates that the program code appear in the same order that it is to be executed in. The selection mechanism involves a choice of action that depends upon the evaluation of a Boolean expression, which appears in most programming languages as an "if-then-else" expression. If the Boolean expression is evaluated as true, the "then" action is executed; otherwise, the "else" action is carried out in favor of the "then" action. The iteration mechanism involves the idea of a loop, and is implemented with either a "while," which causes execution while a condition is true, or with a "repeat," which executes until a condition is false.

Other control structures have proven valuable to structured programmers in recent years. Among these are the "case" and the "for" structures used in Pascal. Pascal is a programming language that has gained popularity recently because it provides for use of the constructs necessary to write structured programs. A "case structure" is a decision mechanism whose choice of action depends on the value of an expression. A "for structure" is a looping mechanism used when a definite number of iterations is desired.

> Brown provides a categorical definition of "case structure."

While the control structures are important in that they minimize the need for branching in a program, a programmer must exhibit style to realize the full benefit of the structures. Two important elements of style are indentation and the use of comments. Indentation makes logical relationships readily apparent, since the statements indented are those that occur within the scope of control structure (Miller and Boyd 28–33). Because the constructs are isolated in this way, when the time comes for maintenance on a program, the indented program is much easier to read and understand (Richardson et al. 4).

Inserting comments within a program is an on-line form of documentation. It involves providing comments within a program to provide a description of what the program does. Good documentation makes the maintenance chore much easier, but the comments should not necessarily be measured quantitatively. If a program is not commented sufficiently, a program's user is left to find quirks hidden in the code (Urdaneta et al. 114). But if overused, comments can cause more harm than good (Reilly, Jr. 1447). When documenting program code, care must be taken to make the comments simple and self-explanatory. Comments explaining entire program segments are considered more helpful than single comments for each statement in a program (Urdaneta et al. 114).

> Here is the implicit support of Brown's opening analogy between computer language and human language.

Structured programs are characterized by certain features that include minimal branching, use of logical constructs, and the use of explanatory comments. These are all-important to structured programming, yet without a method to integrate and implement them, they mean nothing to the structured programming process. Stepwise refinement is a method of program design and development that is based on structured programming notions. The method involves breaking down functions of a programming project into further subfunctions, and these subfunctions into further subfunctions, etc., until they are refined to a level that parallels the programming language being used for the project (Jensen 47). The complexities of a program are broken up by this technique. James Welsh and Michael McKeag, coauthors of <u>Structured System Programming</u>, evaluate stepwise refinement as follows:

> The author introduces "stepwise refinement," which is the breaking down of complex functions of a program into more manageable subfunctions.

> In this way, a complex program structure is built up in a systematic fashion, and the complexity which the programmer has to face at any moment is limited to the component currently being refined (Welsh and McKeag 7).
>
> At each stage of refinement, a programmer is faced with decisions which, once made, should be clearly defined as to reduce the accumulation of complexities (Wirth 221).
>
> *Brown carefully explains the specific practices associated with stepwise refinement.*
>
> One of the main practices involved with stepwise refinement is pseudocoding. Pseudocoding is a tool to provide for easy transition between a programmer's native language and the programming language being used (Jensen 42), thereby providing a description of the general organization of a program without the complexities that arise from confusing details. The pseudocode identifies the control structures with indentation normally used in the appropriate programming language (Jensen 43). It should easily be understood by people besides the programmer (Richardson et al. 8). The pseudocode is valuable in that it makes the conversion to a high-level language easy (Miller and Boyd 7). Even more significantly, it is valuable as a means of documentation in the developing stages because of the lucid description that it provides (Jensen 42).
>
> The other major practice associated with stepwise refinement is the segmenting of programs into short modules. The segments are "small structured programs" that provide straightforward logic and ease in reading (Linger and Mills 120). Usually less than a page in length and designed for a specific function, the modules allow easier debugging of the individual modules and, eventually, the final product (Miller and Lindamood 56). Besides providing easier debugging, each completed segment can be used as a guideline to follow in the work toward the completion of a project (Linger and Mills 127).
>
> *Here we learn about the benefits of teamwork in the more complex programming projects.*
>
> Structured programming techniques are implemented in large-scale projects by what is known as a "chief programmer team." F. Terry Baker first demonstrated the success of the team concept in the produc-

tion of the information bank of The New York Times in 1971. The team completed the project with production 500 percent higher than the normal programming production standards of the time (Baker and Mills 58–61). Because structured programming techniques were used, the code produced proved very reliable. Many large projects since have enjoyed similar success, including the testing and preparation operations of the Skylab project. Despite budget cuts, which weakened manpower, use of the chief programmer team allowed 400,000 lines of program code to be completed on time.

The chief programmer team is an advancement in programming using managerial and structured programming techniques. The team consists of a chief programmer, an assistant to the chief programmer, and various other programmers and data processing technicians (Richardson et al. 8). Working as a unit on specialized assignments, the team is able to handle large undertakings.

A chief programmer has been referred to as the "chief architect" of the chief programmer team (Richardson et al. 8). Working as technical manager, the chief programmer designs and writes the important segments of the program code and oversees the work of all others working on the project (McGowan and Kelly 151). Alongside the chief programmer is the backup programmer, who must be available to assume the responsibilities of the chief if necessary. The backup programmer assists the chief with the details that are involved in the development of a project (McGowan and Kelly 151).

The author describes the role of the chief programmer on a programming team.

Perhaps the most important aspect of the chief programmer team is its use of what is known as a development support library. The library maintains the program status by providing a place where all program segments being developed, complete with documentation, can be stored in an orderly fashion. This procedure allows programmers working on the jobs to see the progress of the entire project so their segments will interface correctly with the other segments (Baker and Mills 58). The "librarian" keeps the library organized and performs clerical work. Rather than spending time on secretarial work, programmers can then complete their tasks more quickly and efficiently (Baker and Mills 58).

Using managerial techniques, the chief programmer team is able to utilize structured programming techniques, providing an environment in which high levels of production are possible. Without such a vehicle, structured programming would not be what it is today. Structured programming has become a standard in the software industry. Introductory programming courses teach structured programming practices to provide future programmers with a proven method of software development to guide them.

> Now Brown turns his attention to the larger impact of structured programming on the computer industry.

The structured programming revolution has made great contributions to the growing software industry. Programs must first serve their purpose by doing what they are supposed to do. After this is accomplished, programmers can begin to look for ways to make their programs better. The idea of a better program has changed, as Donaldson states:

> Where at one time, secondary emphasis was placed only on software efficiency, that is, core and time required, today three other factors are recognized as requiring special emphasis. These factors are reliability, maintainability, and extensibility (Donaldson 52).

Structured programming aids in each of the departments, all of which came about because of economical reasons. The results from the use of structured programming techniques are programs that are rapid, efficiently developed, readable, easily maintained, and reliable.

Structured programming accomplishes the task of making programs readable in the various ways summarized above. Among these are the short segments appearing on a single page, a format that makes the logic paths easy to follow (Otto and Butler 30). Another is the reduction of branching through use of control structures and the elimination of gotos; the result is simplified logic paths, and easier reading and understanding (Miller and Boyd 31). It follows that a program that is easier to read and understand is more easily maintained and modified.

Understandable code is now preferred over efficient code because of the resulting ease. Donald Knuth, a well-known author of programming texts and a Stanford professor, reported, "Premature emphasis on efficiency . . . may be the source of most programming complexity and grief" (Knuth 190).

Rather than actual program efficiency, software developers are now more concerned with efficiency in terms of the time and cost involved in the development of a project. Using structured programming techniques, productivity has increased from two to sixty lines of program code per man-day (Richardson et al. 4). In terms of cost, clear, understandable code is necessary because of the enormous outlays that software companies make toward program debugging. An article in Electronics Design that appeared in 1982 stated:

> With the haphazard approach to programming now in use, the cost of debugging the software is running three times higher than the cost of writing it (Urdaneta et al. 107).

The author discusses the influence of structured programming on productivity.

Through the use of structured programming, these costs can be by "goal-oriented planning, program modularity, and total control over finished program modules" (Urdaneta et al. 107).

The structured programming revolution has brought about a method of program development that produces more reliable, highly understandable programs. As concepts of structured programming are accepted and implemented by more and more programmers in their work, the software industry may soon see comprehensible programs that keep both programmers and software consumers happy.

Jeff concludes by returning to the broad view he used in his introduction, but this time in the context of the achievements of structured programming.

In the past decade, computers have become part of nearly everyone's lives. New machines are being built that allow one with little computer experience to operate them. At the same time, much larger and more complex computers are being developed.

Why not alleviate the belief in the dehumanizing social aspect that has been attributed to the computer? A computer is only as good as its programmer. With the proper tools and training, there is no reason why a programmer should not produce code worthy of being read and understood by others. E. D. Reilly, Jr. describes the aesthetic quality of computer programming:

> Carefully structured programs can be creative works of sufficient literary merit to deserve being read by humans and not just computers (1451–52).

> Because Brown introduces the author in the paragraph that precedes the quotation, it is not necessary to repeat the author's name in the citation.

Works Cited   [new page]

Baker, F. Terry, and Harlan D. Mills. "Chief Programmer Teams." <u>Datamation</u> 19 (1973): 58–61.

Bohm, Corrado, and Giuseppe Jacopini. "Flow Diagrams, Turing Machines and Language Rules with Only Two Formation Rules." <u>Communications of the Association of Computing Machinery</u> 9 (1966): 366–71.

Dijkstra, Edsger W. "Goto Statement Considered Harmful." <u>Communications of the Association of Computing Machinery</u> 11 (1968): 147–48.

Dijkstra, Edsger W. <u>Structured Programming</u>. New York: Academic Press, 1972.

Donaldson, James R. "Structured Programming." <u>Datamation</u> 19 (1973): 52–54.

Jensen, Randall W. "Structured Programming." <u>Computer</u> 14 (1981): 31–48.

Knuth, Donald E. "Structured Programming with Go To Statements." <u>Current Trends in Programming Methodology</u>. Ed. Raymond T. Yeh. Englewood Cliffs, NJ: Prentice-Hall, 1977, 140–94.

Linger, R. C., and H. D. Mills. "On the Development of Large Reliable Programs." <u>Current Trends in Programming Methodology</u>. Ed. Ray-

> The "Works Cited" page conforms to the new MLA style (*MLA Handbook for Writers of Research Papers*, 2nd ed. New York: Modern Language Association, 1984).

mond T. Yeh. Englewood Cliffs, NJ: Prentice-Hall, 1977, 120–39.

McCracken, Daniel D. "Revolution in Programming: An Overview." Datamation 19 (1973): 50–52.

McGowan, Clement L., and John R. Kelly. Top-Down Structured Programming Techniques. New York: Petrocelli Charter, 1975.

Miller, Edward F., Jr., and George E. Lindamood. "Structured Programming: Top-Down Approach." Datamation 19 (1973): 55–57.

Miller, Floyd, and Sandra Boyd. "Structured Programming Techniques: Part I." Journal of Systems Management 30 (1979): 6–12.

Miller, Floyd, and Sandra Boyd. "Structured Programming Techniques: Part II." Journal of Systems Management 30 (1979): 28–33.

Otto, Robert, and James Butler. "Structured Programming." Instruments and Control Systems 48 (1975): 27–30.

Reilly, E. D., Jr. "Structured Programming." Encyclopedia of Computer Science and Engineering. Ed. Anthony Ralston. New York: Van Nostrand, 1983.

Richardson, Gary L., Charles W. Butler, and John D. Tomlinson. A Primer on Structured Programming. New York: Petrocelli Books, 1980.

Urdaneta, Nelson, Christopher Chui, and John Robinson. "Structured Programming Cuts GPIB Software Costs for ATE." Electronic Design 30 (1982): 107–14.

Welsh, James, and Michael McKeag. Structured System Programming. London: Prentice-Hall, 1980.

Wirth, Niklaus. "Program Development by Stepwise Refinement." Communications of the Association of Computing Machinery 14 (1971): 221–23.

Yeh, Raymond T., ed., Current Trends in Programming Methodology. Englewood Cliffs, NJ: Prentice-Hall, 1977.

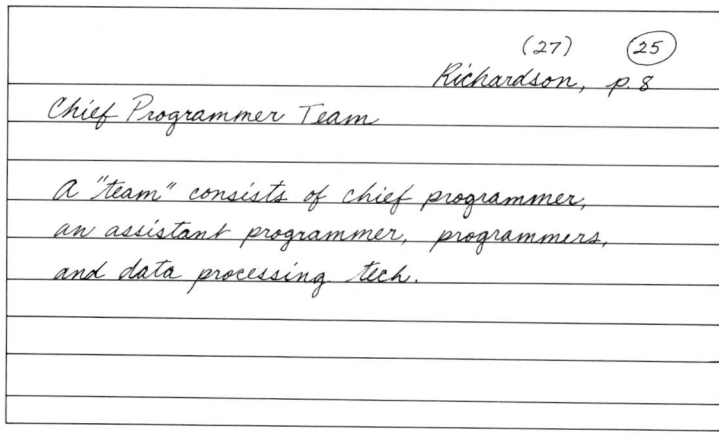
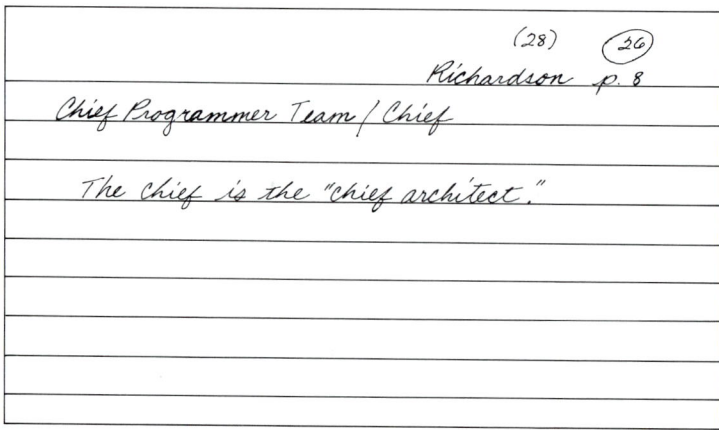
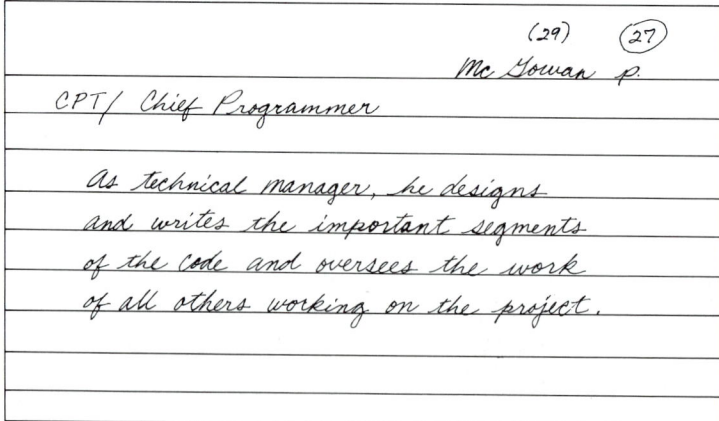

Figure 11–1

Notecards for Jeff Brown's research paper, "Structured Programming"

Project Two: Researching a Social Sciences Subject

The social sciences encompass the fields of psychology, urban life, criminology, social work, popular culture (including mass media and film), labor and leisure, the sociology of aging, ethnicity, and so on; these areas of study provide students with a wealth of topics for research. Like computer science, the social sciences have established ties with virtually every other discipline, making it easy for students to investigate a topic of importance to their major fields. The following list of topics might provide some interesting subjects for research:

1. Criminology
   Rehabilitative Versus Nonrehabilitative Punishment
   Neighborhood "Watch" Programs: Are They Effective?
   Pornography and Crime

2. Psychology
   Toward a More Accurate Definition of "Intelligence"
   Competition, Good and Bad
   Handwriting and Personality: Is There Really a Link?
   Effects of TV on Pre-Kindergarten Children
   Effects of TV on Male-Female Relationships

3. Urban Life
   A Study of Adolescent Recreation in the Inner City
   Needed: A Higher Priority for Old-Building Preservation
   "Shakespeare in the Streets" Programs: Why They Work

When Ron Rock, Jr., a freshman at the University of Santa Clara, was asked why he chose to do his research paper on work opportunities for people past retirement age, he replied, "I get upset when I see how society tends to put people in age categories. I've seen a lot of bright and energetic old people lose their spirit because they suddenly find themselves useless after mandatory retirement. It's time to speak out."

Let Rock's motive for researching his topic remind you that you need not be an expert in a given subject. A strong interest and an urge to get involved can carry you a long way; this is how people become experts in the first place! Your strong views on the subject will provide you with the impetus you need to gather further information.

You will notice as soon as you begin reading Rock's paper that his style is vigorous and lively, and that he manages to present a great deal of factual information (including information derived first-hand through interviews) without sacrificing interest or readability.

English 002
Professor White
Nov. 28, 1984

Gradually Adjusting to Retirement:
Facing the Change
by
Ron K. Rock, Jr.

Outline

Thesis

Instead of regarding the elderly (more respectfully termed "senior citizens") as burdensome and unproductive, we should, by expanding and making better use of existing programs such as flexible retirement and volunteer work, actively integrate them into society.

   I. Flexible retirement
      A. Shorter hours until full retirement is wanted
      B. Transition from paid employment to volunteer employment
      C. Career change

  II. Volunteer work
      A. Place of past employment
      B. Hospital
      C. Church

 III. Social integration
      A. Community organizations
      B. Programs to restrict stagnation
      C. Programs to retrieve shut-ins

IV. Old involved with the young
   A. Special relationships
   B. Places for volunteering

V. Conclusion

Retirement is supposed to be a time in senior citizens' lives when they can relax and enjoy the fruit of their labor. Unfortunately, many of our senior citizens grow old and lose the admiration they received from those who once respected them. Being retired and enjoying the rest of one's life hardly resembles what it used to be.

Rock's introduction reminds us that our society has not been sensitive to the needs of its senior citizens.

Today senior citizens appear to take a back seat when it comes to how we treat them. A recent survey showed that the will to live among elderly people, on a point scale of 1 (greatest will to live) and 2 (least will to live) is 1.34 for those involved with society and its activities, and 1.65 for those uninvolved (Hunter and Linn 210).

Society has determined the retirement age to be sixty-five. Although no set laws state that one must retire at this age, this seems to be the pattern among the work force. Because workers have been within the job market for over forty years, engaged in full-time employment, the sudden withdrawal from this livelihood causes some difficulties. Among the programs that are being instituted to cope with these problems are flexible retirement, voluntarism, community organizations, and young-old relationships.

The scope of this paper is made clear: Rock describes each of these programs, and shows how they help the elderly to cope with their retirement years.

Flexible retirement helps to keep senior citizens in the work force as a productive part of the community. Because of the dramatic change from work to leisure, the elderly need time to adjust. Gerontologist Joseph F. Quinn stated that "these changes are made more smoothly when workers choose a gradual withdrawal from the labor force—a transitional period of partial retirement between full-time work and a complete retirement" (Quinn 634). This program allows older employees to continue working in a manner that fits their abilities and interests as well as the company's needs. Quinn discovered that 26.4

The first program, flexible retirement, is described. Note the way the author introduces authoritative support for his assertion; note also his manner of documentation.

percent of the male population between the ages of fifty-eight and sixty-three are "partly retired" (Quinn 636). Once they reach sixty-five, senior citizens are eligible for full retirement. But because of economic and/or social factors, they desire to continue working to receive supplementary income and/or to stay involved within the community. Out of that 26.4 percent of partly retired workers, 29.5 percent are "very happy," 49.4 percent are "pretty happy," and 21.1 percent are "not very happy" (Quinn 641).

One form of flexible retirement is the reduced work week. Retirement of this kind is accomplished through limiting either the number of hours worked per day or days worked per week. Payment is usually kept the same depending on the management policies involved. Other ways of adjusting senior citizens to a life without work involve longer vacation periods, leaves and sabbaticals, part-time work, or volunteer positions at the place of past employment. Each of these subprograms is designed to acclimate the older workers into the retirement period of their lives. These latter programs leave the workers with quite a bit of free time, to which they grow accustomed with ease. Through the use of this flexible, or gradual, retirement plan, the elderly worker has a chance to ease out of the once rigid system.

The old adage, "You can't teach an old dog new tricks," does not apply to the average older person. Simply because senior citizens have worked at certain occupations for forty years or more is no reason to assume that they cannot change careers. Experts also note that cutting back gradually on the amount of time worked can ease elderly people into volunteer positions that potentially benefit many sectors of the community (Parker 123).

The volunteer system within the aged community is growing considerably. National statistics show that "22 percent of people 65 and over regularly volunteer, while an additional 10 percent said they would like to volunteer" (Johnson and Williamson 71). Retired workers, with their vast talents and wisdom, can develop into an integral part of the community. There is certainly no shortage of institutions where volun-

---

The second program, voluntarism, is now introduced. Note the many examples Rock cites to demonstrate the effectiveness of volunteer programs. Particularly interesting are the comments

teer activity is needed: thrift shops, hospitals, schools, and churches are all places of potential volunteer employment that are popular among senior citizens. Kerry Allen points out that the myriad corporations that are in the United States could significantly help in integrating our elderly volunteers into specific programs (Allen 22).

As senior citizens grow older, a major counterproductive attitude develops, one of uselessness and unwantedness. This idea, equated with getting old, proves to be a mistake. In an area study, Abraham Monk and Arthur Cryns concluded that "voluntarism or doing things for others may be then considered as an indicator of successful resolution of the crises of this last stage of the life cycle" (428). In their study comparing volunteers and nonvolunteers, K. I. Hunter and M. W. Linn found no significant differences within religion, education, age, sex, or widowhood, but the main areas of difference fell in the categories of hospitalization, daily medication, and sensory-motor impairment (208). Their survey covered a six-month study. Volunteers remained in the hospital 0.77 days, compared to nonvolunteers who remained for 3.80 days. Volunteers took on the average of 1.18 medications per day, when nonvolunteers took 2.22 medications per day. Lastly, on a scale of 3 to 14, with 3 equaling least impairment, the degree of sensory-motor impairment among volunteers was 5.08, versus that of nonvolunteers at 5.94 (209). The study points out that the volunteer is in better physical and mental status than the nonvolunteer.

As stated previously, examples of elderly volunteers are those within hospitals, churches, senior citizen centers, and convalescent homes. Because hospitals have such a voracious appetite for volunteers, elderly people fit well into this realm of employment. According to Mercy Hospital administrator Sister Mary Joanne Devencenzi, S. M., "hospital costs would skyrocket if they had to pay a salary for what each volunteer does" (1983). Their jobs entail running the gift shop, assisting admitted patients to and from their rooms, or delivering flowers and mail. Sister Devencenzi concluded that because of the fast-

made by those who work closely with the elderly in these programs. The author obtained this information through the invaluable research strategy, the interview.

Rock was dissatisfied with the first-draft version of this paragraph. Here is what it looked like:

The volunteer system within the aged community is growing considerably. National statistics show that "22 percent of people sixty-five and over regularly volunteer. An additional 10 percent said they would like to volunteer (Johnson and Williamson 71). The retired workers can develop into an integral part of the community. Thrift shops, hospitals, schools, and churches are all places of popular employment among the elderly. Kerry Allen points out that the myriad of corporations that are in the United States could significantly help in integrating our elderly volunteers into specific programs (Allen 22).

The problem, Rock realized, was readability: The sentences were flat, structured too much alike. Note how the author's injecting greater emphasis into *the point he is making, plus the adding of transitional elements, has improved the paragraph in the final draft.*

paced action a hospital constitutes, senior citizens are kept involved with constant human interaction (1983). The churches that elderly volunteers involve themselves with sponsor quite a few programs. For example, at St. Martin's Parish in San José, senior citizens help with child care and nursery school, sewing for the missions, and visiting shut-ins within the parish community (O'Brien 1984). Monsignor Timothy O'Brien, pastor, stated that senior citizens "really do it all for themselves. We just enable them, through our programs, to do for others. It is their choice to get involved or not. This keeps them active, alive, and young at heart" (1984).

Interaction between the elderly also helps in their mental attitudes toward aging. After speaking with a convalescent home nurse, it was clear to me that weekly visits by the elderly volunteer to these homes bring positive results by generating a will to live and bringing back many memories of special times that both the volunteer and the infirm may have shared (Gallagher 1984).

Monk and Cryns, in an article on volunteering, reported that a mature personality stems from actively being involved within and contributing to the society (428). The report aids in abolishing the stigma that has been attached to growing old. Many assume that older people become susceptible to psychological breakdown and loss of identity because of role loss and lack of appropriate feedback. Even the word "elderly" has come to connote fragility or an imminent breakdown of mental capabilities. Because of the lack of feedback, older people sense that they are useless and obsolete. If they accept this dependent role, they will act useless when in fact they are as useful as before. The way to defeat this implanted negative attitude is to emphasize the value of senior citizen involvement for all of us. For example, they possess skills learned through the roles they filled not only on the job but in the family, community organizations, and the church.

A prime example of an older person leaving the work force only to find a void in her life is that of Miss Grace Barrett. After leaving her job with the United States Navy as a nurse, she settled next door to our family. For the five years preceding her retirement, Miss Grace was actively involved in the everyday lives of my brother and me. We eventually moved to a different town and Grace began to feel very alone. After about a year of boredom, she started volunteering at our old grammar school. This revitalized her spirits; she felt better about herself and was helping children in the process.

Steps can be taken to liberate senior citizens from the mistaken idea that certain behavior is inappropriate over age 65. Irving Rosow states that "people are tied into their society essentially through their beliefs, the groups that they belong to, and the positions that they occupy" (9). These bonds are set during the mid-years of their lives and if disrupted when they grow older can cause a permanent halt in their social integration (9). Restructuring the skills and values of work, through age-appropriate opportunities and volunteer roles during the mid-years, proves effective with the social integration of older persons. Old age is a different, but valued, time. Through this action, the negative attitudes of and toward older persons can be destroyed.

Volunteering is becoming a prestigious social role for senior citizens as many agencies and organizations incorporate older volunteer positions and programs into their formal structures. A new and rapidly developing older volunteer activity involves the organization and operation of community centers that plan, coordinate, and provide social support services for senior citizens. According to Rose Glaser, an employee at the Senior Center of Santa Rosa, "the goal of these centers is to sustain older people in their home community and engage these older residents in activities which give purpose to life" (1984). Much of the work at these centers is done by older volunteers. An interviewer working for K. I. Hunter and M. W. Linn received statements from elderly volunteers such as, "When I come here, I see how bad off others are and I feel like I'm pretty lucky," or, "When I come here I have to do my work and there isn't time to think about my usual aches and pains," and, "Volunteering

Notice the smooth manner in which Rock introduces the third program, community centers.

changed my whole life. I was really as good as dead before, but now I feel like I'm alive . . . I feel like I have some purpose" (211–212). These people constitute prime examples of how most socially integrated senior citizens feel: appreciated, useful, and enriched.

A study found that older persons make up 12 percent of our population and will most likely increase to 20 percent within a generation (McCarthy 396). Kurt Wolff, tracing the sociological aspects of aging, seems to agree that the population is growing older faster and sees future problems with older domination in politics and the work force (Wolff 37). Within politics, older people lay a strong lobby for pension, and through the ever-changing technological society, it would be hard to keep an aging work force abreast of the latest advancements (Wolff 37). With this rapid increase of older people in our society, there must be a better way to keep them active, and these senior centers prove to be a good answer.

Senior citizens are removed from their communities to institutions where they become greatly disoriented. Because of living in the same area for years, these people, whether on the verge of senility or not, are disrupted when relocated. Using the alternatives already stated, rather than institutionalization, will enhance our ability to integrate senior citizens into our society.

And society is producing better and better ways to help those who are unable to leave their homes without assistance. Glaser conveyed that many who go to these centers are brought on a daily basis by such organizations as Volunteer Wheels (1984). Some other programs to help aid the shut-in residents of communities are brought into focus by Elizabeth S. Johnson and John B. Williamson. They state that "the development of community programs, such as Meals on Wheels, day care, home care, and congregate living help senior citizens to remain in their communities" (139). Unless these programs become cost-effective, they will be cut out entirely, leaving the handicapped senior citizens to be rounded up and institutionalized without even a look at their personal attitudes (Johnson and Williamson 139). This whole rash movement, pitting money against lives and the quality of living, will defeat the integration effort.

Johnson and Williamson point out that "there are certain factors which contribute to the likelihood that a person will enter a nursing home. Perhaps the most critical is environmental support, which, if absent, can shorten an older person's residence in the community" (141). The integration factor depends completely on environmental support; without it there will be a complete lack of older people within the community. Statistics show that people infrequently check out of a nursing home. Patients are rarely released except to a hospital or funeral home; 85 percent of institutionalized elderly die within the institution (Johnson and Williamson 140). Because our older citizens live longer lives, the nursing homes are becoming extremely overcrowded, thus making the integration factor more complex and in need of greater attention.

It is widely accepted that the elderly and youth are very distinct groups, yet when integrated, the outcome is marvelous. Monk and Cryns, when talking about whom older people wished to serve on a volunteer basis, stated that "there was a marked tendency among them to select both the young and the old as desirable target groups" (428). The older volunteers even know who they can work with best. Rosow makes comments on the relationship between the young and the old, and points out that such a relationship is greatly needed. In essence he is concluding that as senior citizens increase in age and lose their major responsibilities, they begin to have greater rapport with young people (Rosow 23). This is accomplished through volunteering at schools or youth organizations. The youths who respond to this assistance develop a bond of friendship with senior citizens and enjoy the time shared together.

There is nothing more valuable than the wisdom of the elderly. Their long lives with their wide-ranging experiences, both good and bad, can be of great use to us all. Moreover, they are willing to share their joys and warn us of the pitfalls if we would only let them, and show

---

The final program, youth-elderly interaction, is described. How effective is the author's coverage of this program, in your judgment?

Rock's concluding paragraph gave him problems. Here is his earlier version:

There is nothing more valuable than the wisdom of the elderly. Their lives have witnessed a myriad of encounters, some good and some difficult. They are willing to share their joys and warn us of the pitfalls if we would show them that we care. Oftentimes we see a need, but rush over it because of "more pressing business." The elderly, like everyone else, have specific needs that must be fulfilled. Without our efforts, a tragic schism will continue to widen within society, effectively separating the elderly from youth, and thus a valuable resource will continue to go untapped.

In addition to the choppiness of the first few sentences, the phrasing near the end is uneven and wordy. How well did the author improve this concluding paragraph?

them that we care. Often we see a need, but rush over it because of "more pressing business." Older persons, like everyone else, have specific needs that must be fulfilled. Without our efforts, a tragic schism will continue to widen within society, separating old from young, and thus a valuable resource will continue to go untapped.

Works Cited [new page]

Allen, Kerry K. Worker Volunteering: A New Resource for the 1980's. New York: American Management Associations, 1980.

Devencenzi, Sister Mary Joanne, S. M. Personal interview. August 15, 1983.

Gallagher, Noreen, R. N. Personal interview. Santa Rosa, CA, May 11, 1984.

Glaser, Rose. Personal interview. May 29, 1984.

Hunter, K. I., and Margaret W. Linn. "Psychological Differences Between Elderly Volunteers and Non-Volunteers." International Journal of Aging and Human Development 12 (1980–81): 205–13.

Johnson, Elizabeth S., and John B. Williamson. Growing Old: The Social Problems of Aging. New York: Holt, Rinehart, and Winston, 1980.

McCarthy, Abigail. "Fruit of Their Years." Commonweal July 16, 1982: 396–97.

Monk, Abraham, and Arthur G. Cryns. "Predictors of Voluntaristic Intent Among the Aged." Gerontologist 14 (1974): 425–29.

O'Brien, Msgr. Timothy E. Personal interview. May 16, 1984.

Parker, Stanley. Work and Retirement. London: George Allen and Unwin, 1982.

Quinn, Joseph F. "The Extent and Correlates of Partial Retirement." Gerontologist 21 (1981): 634–43.

Rosow, Irving. Social Integration of the Aged. New York: The Free Press, 1967.

Wolff, Kurt. The Biological, Sociological, and Psychological Aspects of Aging. Westport, CT: Greenwood Press, 1959.

Project Three: Researching a Fine Arts Topic

Students with a special inclination toward the visual or performing arts (for example, music and dance; theatre, film, and TV production; painting, sculpture, engraving, and calligraphy), will find research in this area to be doubly challenging and rewarding. Not only will they examine published documents, but they will also almost inevitably examine the works of art firsthand, whether in the theatre, the art gallery, or the museum. A student preparing a research paper on, say, "Techniques of Realism Among Renaissance Religious Painters," will have an opportunity to visit the appropriate museums and to scrutinize priceless original art treasures. He or she might view an original masterpiece such as Caravaggio's glorious "The Supper at Emmaus" (ca. 1598), depicting the newly risen Jesus absorbed in table conversation with three animated villagers. Or the student might have the chance to see Leonardo da Vinci's "The Benois Madonna" (1478), in which a laughing Mary is playing with the infant Jesus on her lap. By observing such masterpieces up close, the student is able to draw his or her own conclusions about the artist's techniques.

The essay that follows focuses on one of the first black American artists, Henry Ossawa Tanner (1859–1937), to gain recognition as a painter. As you read the piece, notice the author's skillful use of documentation and close description of the paintings in question. These aspects support his thesis that Tanner succeeded in raising black consciousness as well as in improving the image of black people in the eyes of whites when attitudes toward blacks were essentially what they were before the abolition of slavery.

Henry Tanner's Contribution to Black American Art and Culture*
by
Ellwood Perry

As a Black man with light skin, possessing deep religious convictions in addition to an artist's sensitivities, Henry Ossawa Tanner ... faced many obstacles at the start of his career. The first difficulty was in obtaining a decent art education. In 1880, at age 21, he applied to the Pennsylvania Academy of the Fine Arts, where Thomas Eakins was the Professor of Painting. He was accepted on the strength of some samples of his work; no one knew what he looked like until he arrived. There was no rule at the Academy "excluding people of color from the schools," but the timid Chairman of the School Committee felt that it was wise to put the matter to a vote in the Antique and Life Classes for Men. None of the students objected—at first.

"The advent of the Nigger," according to Joseph Pennell, who was a pupil at the Academy at exactly the same time (1880–1881), became one of the great excitements of the year, nearly surpassing the frequent faintings of the female models. The following account comes from Pennell's autobiographical <u>Adventures of an Illustrator</u> (1925). Tanner is never mentioned by name in this outrageously bigoted passage, but the factual parts of the description seem to fit. The remainder of Pennell's report drips with condescension at best; and, at its worst, it reveals the kind of prejudice and racial insult that Tanner had to endure on this side of the Atlantic:

> He came, he was young, an octoroon, very well dressed, far better than most of us. His wool, if he had any, was cropped so short you could not see it, and he had a nice moustache. He worked at night in the Antique, and last of all, he drew very well. I do not think he stopped long in the Antique—the faintest glimmer of any

_{Notice how Perry, in this first paragraph, quickly and concisely informs readers of Henry Tanner's background, particularly his struggle to become accepted in the art world of the 1880s.}

_{Here Perry reveals the bigotry that pervaded academia, particularly through art student Joseph Pennell's account. Firsthand accounts such as this one deepen the reader's involvement with the subject.}

---

*From Ellwood Perry, *The Image of the Indian and the Black Man in American Art*. New York: George Braziller, 1974, 163–68.

artistic sense in a student, and he was run into the Life [class by Eakins]. He was quiet and modest, and he "painted too," it seemed, "among his other accomplishments."

We were interested at first, but he soon passed almost unnoticed, though the room was hot. Little by little, however, we were conscious of a change. I can hardly explain, but he seemed to want things; we seemed in the way, and the feeling grew. One night we were walking down Broad Street, he with us, when from a crowd of people of his color, who were walking up the street, came a greeting, "Hullo, George Washington, house yer getin on wid yer white fren's?" Then he began to assert himself and, to cut a long story short, one night his easel was carried out into the middle of Broad Street and, though not painfully crucified, he was firmly tied to it and left there. And this is my only experience of my colored brothers in a white school; but it was enough.[1]

Tanner was obviously caught between his birthright as a Negro and his aspirations as an artist, belonging to neither group completely in America. It is no wonder that he found Paris, the cosmopolitan center of the art world, a far more congenial place in which to work. After living in Atlanta, Georgia, where "he had charge of the Art Department in Clark University for several years," Tanner finally had the opportunity in 1891–1892 of going to Paris and studying at the popular Académie Julian. There, his considerable talent, his warm, though rather quiet personality, and his total dedication to his art could be appreciated without racial bias or prejudgment.

In a letter of 1894 Tanner summarized, using a formal third-person voice, the major events of his career to that point. Understandable pride glows beneath the surface of these soft-spoken words; and all the difficulties of his life were simply omitted from this brief history:

[1] Joseph Pennell, Adventures of an Illustrator, Boston, 1925, pp. 51–52.

Henry Ossawa Tanner, the subject of this sketch, is the oldest son of Bishop B. T. Tanner of the African Methodist Episcopal Church. His family removed from Pittsburgh, his birthplace, to Phila., early in his childhood and he has resided there most of the time since that period. Studied at the Pennsylvania Academy of the Fine Arts, afterwards in Paris under Jean-Paul Laurens and Benjamin-Constant. While in Paris at the celebrated "Académie Julian" he received [a] prize for [the] best composition made in a given number of hours, also a prize from the American Art Association in [the] same city. When leaving for America he received a letter of commendation from his masters, Jean-Paul Laurens & Benj.-Constant.[2]

Paris was later to become Tanner's permanent home, but he occasionally felt compelled, it seems, to return to the United States, as he did in 1893–1894 and again in 1902–1904 when Eakins painted his portrait. . . . During the 1893–1894 period, Tanner painted some of his best-remembered works which found permanent homes. The Banjo Lesson, . . . for example, was donated to the Hampton Institute by his patron, Robert Ogden, in 1894. Another canvas, using the same older man as a model and inscribed The Thankful Poor, . . . was recently rediscovered in storage at The Pennsylvania School for the Deaf in Philadelphia; it was presented to that institution in 1894 by John T. Morris, one of the trustees.

In addition to these Negro genre subjects—remarkable for their spiritual qualities—Tanner also made another sort of contribution to Black consciousness and to the study of American art at that time. According to his own biographical sketch, "He also read a paper on 'The American Negro in Art' before the World's Congress on Africa in Chi-

Perry now focuses attention on his chief concern, the particulars of Tanner's artistic contribution.

---

[2] From an undated autobiographical letter by Tanner in the collection of the Pennsylvania School for the Deaf, Philadelphia.

Figure 11-2

Henry Ossawa Tanner (1859–1937), *The Banjo Lesson*, 1893. Oil on canvas, 48 x 35 inches.

cago."³ Even without knowing exactly what Tanner said at that meeting in Chicago—which was undoubtedly held in connection with the Columbian Exposition of 1893—it is easy enough to tell what he was thinking by looking at his pictures, especially the two reproduced here. Fortunately, as an added guide to his intentions, we do have his own brief description of the work he was doing in 1893–1894:

> Since his return from Europe he has painted many Negro subjects, he feels drawn to such subjects on account of the newness of the field and because of a desire to represent the serious, and pathetic side of life among them, and it is his thought that other things being equal, he who has most sympathy with his subject will obtain the best results. To his mind many of the artists who have represented Negro life have only seen the comic, the ludicrous side of it, and have lacked sympathy with and affection for the warm big heart that dwells within such a rough exterior.⁴

In the clear light of this statement of principles, The Banjo Lesson . . . has to be read as a sobering antidote to sixty years of minstrel shows in America, sixty years of White entertainers in Blackface and Black clothes performing borrowed dances (Jump Jim Crow) and borrowed songs in Negro dialect (My Old Kentucky Home, Carry Me Back to Old Virginny) for the delight of their audiences. When it was put on public display in Earle's Galleries, Philadelphia, in 1893, a reviewer for the Daily Evening Telegraph recognized the profound essence of the picture, and yet he could not free himself completely of years of stereotyped thinking. The minstrel show tradition and images of the comic side of Negro life . . . were in his mind as he described the figures in Tanner's work: "An old Uncle Ned, bald and venerable, has a bare-footed little darkey of seven or eight years between his knees, and is ear-

Notice how the assertions of the above paragraph are exemplified through particular paintings of Tanner's.

³ Ibid.
⁴ Ibid.

nestly instructing the youngster how to finger the strings of an ancient banjo."⁵

On the more positive side, this same newspaper critic was deeply pleased by the firm modeling of these two figures and the way in which they were enveloped in space by a sense of atmosphere, each occupying his own place and each bearing the stamp of individuality. For special praise, he cited the treatment of hands and faces, and his remarks this time have no trace of condescension: "The hands are especially well drawn, that of the child being a study Mr. Tanner may well be proud of, and the faces are formed with intelligence and expression."⁶

Precisely the same artistic virtues can be found in The Thankful Poor . . . a year later—along with some of the same props. The table in the background of The Banjo Lesson, set with a few dinner plates and a water pitcher, has now become the major object in the foreground. The venerable grandfather figure on the left appears to be the same model that Tanner used for The Banjo Lesson; his face is partially hidden in shadow, but the light reveals (in the strongest passage of the painting) the way he holds his head, his shoulders, and his hands clasped in prayer before a meager meal. No sound, no plucking at a banjo, disturbs the profound, also melancholy silence of the scene. In this quiet is Tanner's commentary on the White images of Negro family life and religious practices that rarely rose above the anecdotal. In place of picturesque details, The Thankful Poor conveys a sense of the real privations of poverty (for those with hardly enough to eat) and the sustaining power of humble prayer. By being so much closer to his subjects, Tanner was able to deliver what he promised. His figures are handled with a degree of sympathy and affection that was far beyond the abilities of most White painters.

⁵Quoted from the Philadelphia Daily Evening Telegraph by Marcia Matthews, Henry Ossawa Tanner, American Artist, Chicago, 1969, pp. 70–71.

⁶Ibid., p. 71.

Perry's elaborate discussion of "The Thankful Poor" painting serves to re-emphasize Tanner's artistic genius as well as his great compassion for the people he painted.

Collection of Dr. and Mrs. William H. Cosby, Jr. Photo: Philadelphia Museum of Art.

Figure 11-3

Henry Ossawa Tanner (1859-1937). *The Thankful Poor*, 1894. Oil on canvas, 45 × 35½ inches.

Summary

"Research papers" vary considerably in style, content, and level of formality. They are essentially critical essays more than reports in that they attempt to present a new perspective on the subject in question, based upon the evidence brought to light. A research paper is *not* a mere compilation of facts. As in other kinds of essay writing, the author's viewpoint governs the piece, determines what is to be emphasized or de-emphasized, what constitutes evidence and what doesn't.

Supporting data must be formally documented in a research paper because the audience is presumed to consist of fellow researchers who would be interested in examining the reference sources used by the author—not so much to "check up" on the author as to pursue the topic in greater depth.

FOR DISCUSSION

1. How, if at all, could the author of "Structured Programming" improve his paper? Respond to the question on three levels: content, organization, and style.

2. Describe the principal stylistic differences that you detect among the three research papers. Do you suppose the differences have something to do with the subject matter? the author's intended audience? the author's personality? other factors? Finally, which style did you find most effective, and why?

3. Examine each author's technique of alluding to outside authority. Are the quotations or paraphrases smoothly or awkwardly introduced? Do they always contribute essential evidence to support the thesis? Do any of the authors at times seem to rely too heavily on the views of others?

4. Assume that you were asked to research the influence of senior citizens on young people. What aspect of that topic would you be inclined to examine in depth? What kinds of primary and secondary sources would you anticipate using?

5. Present a progress report on your own research. Are you proceeding in distinct stages? Is the nature of your project such that you find yourself having to do some things simultaneously, like outlining and writing a first draft? Be as detailed as you can, and invite your classmates to offer suggestions if you have trouble.

6. Prepare a detailed commentary, either individually or as a group, on the organization, development, and style of Ellwood Perry's "The Image of the Black Man in American Art."

FOR WRITING

1. Prepare a rough draft of your research-project prospectus, solicit criticism from your classmates, and offer your own criticism of their prospectuses. One of the first questions you want to answer with complete conviction is, Am I sufficiently intrigued by this topic to want to spend two months investigating it and writing about it?

2. Write out a more detailed version of your present outline. If you currently have a topic outline, expand it to a sentence outline; if you have a sentence outline, expand it to a complete synopsis. Look for weak spots or conceptual gaps that could emerge as a result, and rework your outline or synopsis accordingly.

3. If you are unable to find a research-paper topic to your satisfaction, don't worry. Just guide yourself through a good brainstorming session. Here's what you can do:
    a. Go someplace where you can relax for an hour, perhaps a dark corner of the library, and do some "clustering" around a subject

you naturally enjoy. Don't think about the research paper just yet. If you can't think of any good subjects for clustering, try one of these:
- Athletic competitions (grueling? breeds bad habits in people? absolutely necessary in our tense society?)
- Traffic congestion in your community (ways to solve the problem?)
- Saving endangered species from extinction (focus on one species, like the American bald eagle or the blue whale)
- Horror films
- Latest special-effects technology
- Freezing embryos: the ethical implications
- Inner-city recreation programs that reduce crime

b. Now write a one-paragraph overview of your possible paper, drawing clues from your clustering.

c. Does your overview reveal a statement of purpose? If not, write one.

d. It's time to do a little sleuthing around the library. First locate a general article on your topic in one of the encyclopedias. Take notes. Now find a book or periodical article, possibly one in the encyclopedia article's bibliography, and take more notes.

e. Write your prospectus. If the topic is right for you, the prospectus should practically write itself!

---

1. In preparing to write a first draft of your research paper on the computer, consider the following suggestion for what might be called a proto-draft:

    COMPUTER WRITING

    a. Once your research is more-or-less completed and you have worked out a fairly well-detailed outline, copy the outline into a new file.

    b. Gather all of your notecards together and arrange them to correspond to the sequence of your outline.

    c. Copy the contents of each notecard under the appropriate subhead of your on-screen outline. *Triple*-space to allow for revisions by hand on the printed copy.

    d. Print the file.

    You now have, in effect, a sequence of topic sentences (outline subheads), each topic sentence followed by supporting evidence.

With your printed draft before you, work in your own discussion and transitional passages.

2. With your edited proto-draft before you, prepare the first draft of your research paper in a new file. This time concentrate on the smooth, logical unfolding of your thesis idea. Enter appropriate in-text documentation of all quotations and paraphrases.

After you have completed the draft, scroll through it, checking for clarity, strong sentence construction and variety, precise word-choice, consistent level-of-usage. Use the critiquing checklist in Chapter 18 for additional reminders. Finally, scroll through once more to proofread: Check for errors in spelling, punctuation, and mechanics.

Tools of
PART THREE
the Trade

The heart of this section of *The Writer's Art* lies at the heart of writing itself: rewriting. No matter how much attention writers give to their first drafts, no matter how much control and sense of direction they may have over their ideas or writing style, their initial drafts will require additional work. Compared to spontaneous conversation or even letter writing, essays reflect a greater complexity of thought, and this in turn requires more concentrated reworking, refining, and polishing for the essay to have its intended impact on readers.

A writer's revising technique is largely dependent on his or her individual temperament and on the particular problems that arise in a given essay. However, the general principles provided in the next four chapters will offer a starting point from which writers may develop their own individual styles of revision. Part Three opens with a chapter on the art of making sentences clear and forceful; the focus then shifts to the arts of paragraphing and diction with the same goals in mind: clarity and forcefulness. Finally, the elements of the revision process itself are examined in the last chapter.

Building Sentence-Writing Skills

CHAPTER 12

One of the many ways to define the composing process is as follows: One merely writes down one sentence after another and makes sure that each sentence builds toward a central idea, stems clearly and logically from the sentence before it, prepares the reader for the sentence to follow, *and*, while doing all these things, also manages to hold the reader's attention. This, of course, is easier said than done.

The aim of this chapter is to guide you through a wide range of sentence development activities to strengthen this aspect of the composing process. Because weak syntax often means weak writing, careful attention to each section of this chapter is bound to help you strengthen your writing. Even if you feel that you've already mastered a particular syntactic skill, study it anyway, and work through the accompanying exercises. The review will most likely help you enhance your knowledge of that skill.

By the time you finish this chapter, you should be able to detect an improvement in your ability to construct sentences. And just as important, you should be able to detect and successfully revise unsatisfactory sentences.

What Is a Sentence?

A sentence is the smallest unit of discourse. Typically, it is a train of words (subject, predicate, and any number and variety of subject-and-predicate modifiers) that are organized according to the grammatical principles of the language in which they are written, and that convey a grammatically independent unit of discourse.* Thus, a single word all by itself is not a sentence, because no grammatically independent discourse unit is transmitted. The following single word is not a sentence:

> tomorrow

But it can become what grammarians call an *elliptical sentence* if a clear enough context is provided:

> "When is your dentist appointment?"
> "Tomorrow."

Here, *tomorrow* functions as a grammatically independent discourse unit because the words needed to make the sentence meaningful ("is my dentist appointment ") are clearly understood. It's fortunate that we have this kind of flexibility; we might sound like robots otherwise:

> "What kind of ice cream are you going to buy?"
> "I am going to buy chocolate chip ice cream."
> "Is chocolate chip ice cream your favorite variety of ice cream?"
> "Yes, chocolate chip ice cream is my favorite variety of ice cream."

But, you may be wondering, what about sentence fragments? They certainly do occur; but it is important to distinguish between the "understood" sentence, which only superficially resembles a fragment, and the true fragment, which cannot hold its own as an independent sentence.

> Tennis challenges me more than any other sport. Because it requires speed and coordination.

The second utterance is a true fragment because it is grammatically tied to the first utterance. The first utterance is an *independent*, or *main*, *clause*; it is independent because it can stand alone as a separate sen-

---

*For a grammatical description of a sentence and a discussion of sentence types, see the Handbook, "Rhetorical and Grammatical Principles," Sentences, Kinds of.

tence. The second utterance is a *dependent*, or *subordinate*, *clause*. Its opening word, *because*, is known as a subordinating conjunction, or simply subordinator, which signals that the clause it introduces can only modify some part of the independent clause; in this case, the verb *challenges* is modified.*

There is more than one way to slip that dependent clause into the independent clause:

1. Tennis challenges me more than any other sport does because it requires speed and coordination.

2. Because it requires speed and coordination, tennis challenges me more than does any other sport.

3. Tennis, more than any other sport, challenges me because it requires speed and coordination.

Other fragments, such as infinitive phrases, cannot stand by themselves as bona fide sentences:†

When I saw the strange black box I grew curious. To see what was inside.

In this case, the *infinitive phrase* should be incorporated into the first sentence. No internal punctuation is needed, as the two utterances together represent one continuous thought; a pause is not necessary between "curious" and "to see." The most common reason fragment errors are made, in fact, is just that: The writer senses a pause where one should not exist. Here is a similar fragment error, but with a *participial phrase*:

Tanya was late for her piano lesson. Running as fast as she could up the music building stairs.

One way to eliminate the fragment is to insert the participial phrase immediately after the noun it modifies:

Tanya, running as fast as she could up the music building stairs, was late for her piano lesson.

Another solution is to turn the first statement into a subordinate clause using the word *because*, and to replace the participial phrase with a clause in the simple past tense:

---

*See the Handbook, "Rhetorical and Grammatical Principles," Clauses.
†See the Handbook, "Rhetorical and Grammatical Principles," Phrases.

> Because she was late for her piano lesson, Tanya ran as fast as she could up the music building stairs.

This last expression is probably what the writer intended to say in the first place. Inexperienced writers often use participial phrases when they really want to express a cause-effect relationship.

Similar to the participial phrase fragment is the *gerund phrase* fragment, which looks like this:

> George became dizzy. His constant somersaulting.

The gerund phrase is easily combined with the main clause to form the intended complete sentence:

> George's constant somersaulting made him dizzy.

As in the earlier example, a more explicit cause-effect relationship might be what the author is really after here. A subordinate clause instead of a gerund phrase would then be the preferred choice:

> Because George was constantly somersaulting, he became dizzy.

Fragments are not the only kinds of "nonsentences," however. The *fused*, or *run-on*, *sentence* occurs when the writer meshes together two independent clauses or sentences without using an appropriate conjunction or punctuation mark:

> Fourteen-year-old girls *can* fall deeply in love it happened to me.

Adding a comma will only create another type of run-on sentence, called a *comma splice*:

> Fourteen-year-old girls *can* fall deeply in love, it happened to me.

Clearly, some pause is needed to separate the two independent clauses, but the comma does not register a sufficient pause. The writer has three possibilities. He or she may use a semicolon instead:

> Fourteen-year-old girls *can* fall deeply in love; it happened to me.

The writer may also use an appropriate coordinating conjunction preceded by a comma:

> Fourteen-year-old girls *can* fall deeply in love, for it happened to me.

Or the writer may decide to create two separate sentences, one from each independent clause:

> Fourteen-year-old girls *can* fall deeply in love. It happened to me.

Is one option better than another? Not in any absolute sense. It all depends on the kind of rhythm, emphasis, and tone the writer wishes to convey. If you compare the three options, you will notice that the minor differences between each of the expressions alter these stylistic elements subtly. Such subtle changes, as you will see later in the chapter, can sometimes alter the shape, and therefore the perceived meaning, of a sentence quite dramatically.

Sentence Skills Checkpoint A:
Fragments, Run-ons, and Whole Sentences

Directions: Circle each sentence fragment or run-on sentence and either change it into a whole sentence or work it into the sentence preceding or following it. Be careful not to confuse fragments with elliptical sentences.

1. The English department sponsored a composition prize. That was open to freshmen only.
2. Jet lag upsets my biorhythms, sometimes it takes me two days to overcome it.
3. Ned, who never had any faith in his writing ability, won first prize in the essay contest. Having written about poverty in Guatemala.
4. After she devoured twenty-two bananas in a banana-eating contest Marlis became violently ill. No wonder!
5. According to a mysterious and ancient legend, which evolved sometime during the Middle Ages, a link between vampires and werewolves.
6. Of all the novels Hemingway has written I love *The Sun Also Rises* best it is a disturbing novel the struggle for love and the meaning of life in a postwar world.
7. Several of the children in the neighborhood missed school. Because they all had the flu, the principal called the health department to inquire about flu vaccines.
8. Eddie Shimitzu had one goal in life. To become a great architect.
9. The notion that dinosaurs became extinct because they were stupid is a myth, they existed on earth ten times longer than did human beings.

10. Wow! Do you see that whale it must be the size of a battleship.

11. Whenever I get a craving for food in the middle of the night I force myself to eat—not pie, not a turkey sandwich, not ice cream. But yogurt. It takes a lot of self-discipline, though.

Writing Strong Sentences

The way we put our sentences together has as much to do with our individual personalities as with our knowledge and skill. Writing style begins here. Do you enjoy keeping your readers in suspense, anxious for the punch line? If so, then you will enjoy composing *periodic sentences*, wherein the main clause (the "punch line," so to speak) appears at the very end:

> Aiming carefully, adjusting her footing, and displaying an intensity of concentration her boyfriend never knew she had, Phyllis whacked the ball out of the sand trap.

Or, if you are more inclined to get the main point across as quickly as possible, the *cumulative sentence* might work for you:

> Phyllis whacked the ball out of the sand trap, a solid and precise hit, her club lifting in a perfect arc, sand scattering everywhere.

You might even choose to use a middle-of-the-road approach called a *balanced sentence*, in which the main clause is somewhere in the middle, with modifiers on either side:

> Aiming carefully, adjusting her footing, and concentrating as hard as she could, Phyllis whacked the ball out of the sand trap, her club lifting in a perfect arc, sand spattering everywhere.

The point is simple: Sentences can be practically anything you want them to be; and the possible permutations and combinations of elements can make any writing enthusiast dizzy with delight.

But first things first. Before you can become a virtuoso of English syntax, you need to be well-grounded in the basics. The basics of good sentence construction include the following:

- *Unity*. Does the sentence center on one main point, or does it try to squeeze in too many points at once?

- *Coherence.* Are the sentence parts smoothly and logically arranged for maximum clarity and readability?

- *Development.* Are the opportunities for conveying sufficient information via coordinating and subordinating elements fully utilized?

- *Variety.* Do your sentences interact well? Do they engage the reader and highlight the key points? Is their rhythm pleasing to the ear instead of monotonous? Is the tone appropriate to what is being discussed?

Let us examine these basics individually.

Unity

A sentence builds around a single point. When a writer tries to pack in too many separate points, or so many modifiers that the central point is obscured, then the sentence is said to lack unity.* You will most likely agree that such is the case with the following sentence:

> The new generation of computers, the "reasoning machines," are coming, and computers already process information thousands of times faster than any human being can.

Do you see what the problem is? The author has a double focus: (1) the new generation of computers, and (2) the efficiency of current computer technology. We cannot assume that the two points connect together logically; we only know that the author failed to make that connection and tried to say too much, too quickly.

    The author, then, has two options: to establish the link, or to simplify the sentence. If the author chooses the first option, though, she must still decide whether the connection could be established better through a series of sentences rather than through one elaborate sentence. What do you think? Consider the options:

- *Option One: an elaborate single sentence with improved unity.*

  > The new fifth-generation computers, the "reasoning machines," are coming, and they will have ten times the speed and versatility of the most sophisticated computers now on the market, an astonishing fact when you consider that existing computers are capable of completing hundreds of

---

*Compare this discussion of sentence unity with that of paragraph unity in Chapter 13, "Shaping Paragraphs."

tasks per second, and can process data thousands of times faster than any human being can.

- *Option Two: a cluster of short, separate sentences, each with its own internal unity.*

    The new fifth-generation computers are coming. These "reasoning machines" will have ten times the speed and versatility of the most sophisticated computers now on the market. That is an astonishing fact when you consider that existing computers are capable of completing hundreds of tasks per second, and can process data thousands of times faster than any human being can.

You might say to yourself that you like the simpler sentences in the second option, but something still isn't right. The sentences seem a bit wooden and monotonous.* So, you proceed to the next possibility:

- *Option Three: sophisticated yet readable sentences that yield a large amount of information.*

    The new "fifth-generation" computers are coming—"reasoning" machines with ten times the speed and versatility of the most sophisticated computers now on the market. This fact is astonishing, considering that existing computers are capable of completing hundreds of tasks per second, and can process data thousands of times faster than any human being can.

Lack of sentence unity is often a symptom of a more fundamental problem: the failure to think through a point completely. The points get "short-circuited" in the sense that the author perceives the implicit connection but neglects to make the connection clear to the readers. Let's look at another sentence that lacks unity:

> Working himself into a frenzy, the lead guitarist shocked everyone by smashing his guitar to pieces against the stage, a growing trend in hard rock these days, and the drummer began dancing spasmodically.

You can almost feel the author's impatience here; he just couldn't wait to begin a new sentence, if not a new paragraph, about the "growing trend" in hard rock. He might have expressed his message more effectively in the following manner:

> Working himself into a frenzy, the lead guitarist shocked everyone by smashing his guitar to pieces against the stage. The drummer, catching his bug of madness, began dancing spasmodically. Such activity is typical of a growing trend in hard rock these days.

---

*The section on variety later on in the chapter discusses ways to avoid sentence monotony.

Notice that the author has made the first two sentences cases in point for the third sentence, which now emerges as the main idea. Not only does each sentence possess unity, but the three sentences together also represent one unified, continuous thought.

Sentence Skills Checkpoint B: Unity

Directions: Decide which of the following sentences or sentence clusters lack unity, and why; then revise accordingly.

1. The orthopedist, well-known for her skill, examined my wrist and told me it was broken, yet another example of my having become accident-prone.

2. Tornadoes are frightening as well as dangerous, and I recall how scared of lightning I used to be as a young child.

3. After much planning and years of saving, the Andersons built a mountain cabin amid pine trees, career success never being one of their priorities.

4. Euclid systematized the study of geometry as well as the very principles of deductive reasoning, so it is no exaggeration to say that the ancient Greeks laid the foundation for logic.

5. Professor Bierman's geology lectures are colorful in more ways than one in that he likes to sketch rock layers using different-colored chalk, and he likes to dress colorfully.

Coherence

Coherence means *sticking together logically*. On the sentence level, it means placing modifying elements as close as possible to the words they modify, and maintaining a grammatical symmetry among those elements.* Coherence is disrupted when a word or phrase and its modifiers are not in clear relationship with one another; the modifiers, in this situation, are "misplaced." Coherence may also be disrupted when sentence elements do not adhere to a common pattern of phrasing; in this case, the sentence would be said to "lack parallelism."

Misplaced Modification   One type of misplaced modification is known as the *dangling modifier*, whereby the modifier "dangles" in front of the wrong object of modification:

---

*Compare this discussion of coherence with that in Chapter 13, "Shaping Paragraphs."

> Running with my net, the swallowtail butterfly managed to evade me.

Unless butterflies have suddenly learned to run with nets, the author would be wise to clarify her intended meaning. A quick realignment of sentence parts and some word changes will do the trick:

> Running with my net, I failed to catch the swallowtail butterfly.

Here's another possible solution:

> The swallowtail butterfly managed to evade me as I ran with my net.

Sometimes the dangling modifier is difficult to spot, which results in a possible misunderstanding of the author's intended meaning. Such is the case with the following sentence:

> After another mile of hiking we finally caught up with our friends, exhausted and famished from the journey.

Who is exhausted and famished? "We," "our friends," or both? The sentence is constructed so that any one of those possibilities could be the case.* By linking up the modifier with the intended object, the confusion is easily cleared up:

> After another mile of hiking, exhausted and famished from the journey, we finally caught up with our friends.

The sentence could also be reconstructed so that the word *friends* is modified:

> After another mile of hiking, we finally caught up with our exhausted and famished friends.

Or, here's another possibility:

> After another mile of hiking, we finally caught up with our friends; they were exhausted from the journey, as were we.

A less conspicuous type of misplaced modification occurs when the modifier is separated from the object of modification by a phrase or clause:

---

*When more than one possible meaning is generated, the meaning is said to be *ambiguous*. See the Handbook, "Rhetorical and Grammatical Principles," Ambiguity.

The bagpiper stopped performing and took a few deep breaths on occasion.

The words *on occasion* are intended to modify the verb phrase *stopped performing*, not the verb phrase *took a few deep breaths*. Here is the correct way to express the intended meaning:

The bagpiper stopped performing on occasion and took a few deep breaths.

Lack of Parallelism   Another disrupter of sentence coherence, lack of parallelism, refers to the absence of symmetry within a single sentence or from sentence to sentence. Such symmetry involves the repetition of verbal patterns and of individual words. The longer your sentences are, the more likely you will need parallel structures to hold the meaning together and to maintain the flow and readability of the sentences. Notice the parallelism at work in this lovely sentence taken from Ann Morrow Lindbergh's *Gift From the Sea*:

I walked far down the beach, soothed by the rhythm of the waves, the sun on my bare back and legs, the wind and mist from the spray on my hair.

The two sets of parallel elements, (1) "the waves," "the sun," and "the wind and mist" and (2) "on my bare back and legs" and "on my hair," make this an easily readable as well as elegant sentence. The author somehow captures the rhythm of the sea in these parallel structures.

However, Lindbergh could have overdone the parallelism in this sentence, as this device is sometimes deceptively easy to overuse. If she had, the sentence might have looked like this:

I walked far down the beach, soothed by the rhythm of the waves, enraptured by the sun on my bare back, on my bare legs, spellbound by the wind, captivated by the mist from the spray on my hair.

Here the parallelism is redundant, and it also spoils the sentence by calling far too much attention to itself. Parallelism in writing works best when it works inconspicuously and when it contributes to the readability of the sentence, thus assisting the reader in making quick connections. The following sentence, for example, would be more coherent with parallelism:

Truthfulness enriches not only your own character but others.

Here, the parallelism clarifies the meaning of the sentence without disturbing the readability:

Truthfulness enriches not only your own character but also the character of others.

Another problem writers sometimes have with parallelism might be called *incomplete parallelism*, which happens when a writer starts off with a parallel pattern but fails to follow through with it. This error usually occurs when writers are not consciously aware of the patterns they are generating:

Our school librarian, Ms. Wood, is stern yet kind, highly self-disciplined yet fun-loving, and an interesting person.

That last noun phrase just doesn't fit the parallel sequence of adjective clusters, "X yet Y." For the parallelism to work in this sentence, another "X yet Y" adjective cluster should be substituted for the noun clause, perhaps something like this:

Our school librarian, Ms. Wood, is stern yet kind, highly self-disciplined yet fun-loving and interesting.

So far we have limited our consideration of parallelism to the boundaries of a single sentence. Let us now examine the way parallelism can extend over two or more sentences as a means of reinforcing the author's thread of meaning. Read the following examples with the idea of an extended parallelism in mind:

Any law that uplifts human personality is just. Any law that degrades human personality is unjust. (Martin Luther King, Jr., "Letter from Birmingham Jail")

The event of brain formation is an important step in the development of life. Before this event, a living unit and its reactions to the outside world are completely determined by chemical structure. After the event, the reactions of the unit depend not only upon its structure but also upon its previous experience. (Victor F. Weisskopf, *Knowledge and Wonder*)

In the King example, note how perfectly symmetrical the contrasting sentences are:

| Any law that | uplifts | is just. |
| Any law that | degrades | is unjust. |

This symmetry results not only in a graceful and readable style but in a *memorable* one as well, giving the passage the quality of a proverb:

> A penny saved is a penny earned.
>
> To be great is to go on;
> to go on is to be far;
> to be far is to return. (Lao Tzu)

King, we could readily assume, is implicitly urging his readers to commit his point to memory.

In the Weisskopf passage, we see parallelism used to enforce comprehension. The author employs the commonly used "before . . . after" pattern as a means of driving home his point about the emergence of the brain. Because Weisskopf is explaining sophisticated scientific concepts to an audience of young people, it is important that every part of the discourse connects well with every other part.

Finally, parallelism is sometimes used for dramatic emphasis, especially in persuasive discourse such as sermons or political campaign speeches. Note the difference in emphasis between the two sentences that follow:

> The government should stop lending money to other nations until it can eliminate poverty and hunger among our own people.
>
> Until we can feed our hungry, until we can decently house and clothe our poor people in this nation, we cannot continue to permit our government to lend money to other nations.

The second version, through parallelism, generates a greater degree of emotional involvement than does the first.

Sentence Skills Checkpoint C: Coherence

Misplaced Modification

Directions: Realign the modifier with the object of modification wherever necessary in the following examples.

1. Did dress rehearsal go smoothly, when you're usually the most nervous?

2. Dawn could only bring herself to write fiction when she felt inspired.

3. Hammering the last shingle into place, Walter's feeling of relief at completing an enormous job was intense.

4. Before straying significantly off course, the guidance system will correct the rocket's flight path.

5. The Treaty of Versailles was signed at the end of World War I after being negotiated in Paris between Germany and the Allied Nations.

Parallelism

Directions: Look for asymmetrical patterns in the following sentences and revise to make them symmetrical, or parallel.

1. People grew disoriented, fearful, and they were nervous too, during the blackout.

2. Not only is the Great Salt Lake growing saltier, its size has increased considerably.

3. To read is to discover; to discover is to have a happy life; to live happily is to know what beauty and love are.

4. Henryk received the gold award, Donald the silver one, Juanita the platinum, and Allison the bronze award for excellence in public debate.

5. We are neither planning to back down on our demands, and are not going to compromise them either.

Development

Sentence development refers principally to the methods writers use to make the sentence yield more information without becoming more difficult to read or understand. In fact, well-developed sentences are generally quite easy to digest; they process information more economically than do weaker, less concise sentences.

Writers use three main techniques of sentence development: embedding, coordination, and subordination. Let's examine each one.

Embedding Imagine that one day a friend of yours starts talking to you like this:

> Hank has a pet. The pet is an armadillo. The armadillo's name is Sam. Hank found Sam. He found him on a desert. The desert is in New Mexico.

Naturally, this is an exaggerated example because people generally do not speak in such short, abrupt sentences that offer only a tiny morsel of information. It would seem ridiculous to use such a sentence pattern in writing. *Embedding* is the process that allows us to avoid this problem by packing together many separate units of information into a single sentence, resulting in increased readability and comprehension. So, realistically, your friend probably would have expressed herself like this:

> Hank found Sam, his pet armadillo, on a New Mexico desert.

We all unconsciously carry out this embedding process when we speak. However, when we try to juggle complex ideas while writing essays, we sometimes do not embed enough, and this can result in wordy, weak, and therefore insufficiently informative sentences. Embedding accomplishes two important tasks simultaneously: It allows for the rapid development of ideas and it results in more concise writing.

Study the following passage and think about how it could be improved through embedding:

> The world is full of insects. All of them are strange and interesting. Some insects are harmful. Examples of harmful insects include termites, aphids, and locusts. But many other insects are beneficial. The ladybug is an example. Ladybugs eat aphids. Another example is the honeybee.

Clearly, the author missed several opportunities for embedding. Notice, for example, the second sentence: Why devote a separate sentence to the modifiers *strange* and *interesting* when these words could easily be embedded in the first sentence as single adjectives preceding the noun *insects*? Notice, too, that the fourth sentence could be embedded in the third, and that the sixth sentence, along with the last sentence, could be embedded in the fifth one. The result? A more compact and digestible version, reduced from forty-five to twenty-eight words, with no information loss.

> The world is full of strange, interesting insects. Some, like the termites, aphids, and locusts, are harmful; others, like the aphid-eating ladybugs and the honeybees, are beneficial.

Coordination and Subordination *Coordinate elements* are those that carry equal grammatical weight in the sentence; each element is part of an independent clause, which, with a few minor mechanical adjustments, could function as a separate sentence. Here's an example:

> Insects have six legs but arachnids have eight.

In this sentence, *insects* and *arachnids* are coordinate elements, and their clauses, *insects have six legs* and *arachnids have eight [legs]*, are independent. *But* is the coordinating conjunction linking the two clauses together and making explicit the contrast that is already implicit between them.

Coordination is an ideal way to present strings or sequences of ideas and impressions; it is a highly useful narrative device, as the following passage from Ernest Hemingway's "Big Two-Hearted River" indicates:

> Nick dropped his pack and rod-case and looked for a level piece of ground. He was very hungry and he wanted to make his camp before he cooked. Between two jack pines, the ground was quite level. He took the ax out of the pack and chopped out two projecting roots. That leveled a piece of ground large enough to sleep on. He smoothed out the sandy soil with his hand and pulled all the sweet fern bushes by their roots. His hands smelled good from the sweet fern.

Only three of the seven sentences (the third, fifth, and seventh) are *simple sentences*. The others are coordinate clause sentences, or, as they are more commonly known, *compound sentences*.* The proportion seems just right; a long uninterrupted string of compound sentences would call too much attention to itself and impede the lean, narrative flow for which Hemingway is famous. Consider the way compound sentences are used in this example:

> The sky darkened ominously and Al decided to close the windows. It began to rain just then, and the wind began howling fiercely. Al knew that he should bring in his garden tools, but he did not want to get wet. He lay down on the sofa instead, and began reading a magazine.

All the sentences are compound, causing a monotonous rhythm. Not only that, the author does not emphasize relationships between clausal elements. To do this, the author needs to use *subordinate clauses*, as in the following two examples:

> *After the sky darkened ominously,* Al decided to close the windows.

> Al decided to close the windows *because the sky was darkening ominously.*

The words *after* and *because* are the subordinators, or subordinating conjunctions, which signal the relationship to be made between the clauses they introduce and the main clauses in their respective sentences.

We may group subordinators and the clauses they introduce into five categories: temporal, causal, circumstantial, spatial, and relational. (See Table 12-1.) Therefore, from the preceding example, *after* signals a temporal relationship and *because* signals a causal one.

---

*See the Handbook, "Rhetorical and Grammatical Principles," Sentences, Kinds of.

Table 12-1 Categories of Subordination

Category	Typical Subordinators
Temporal	after, as, before, during, once, since, until
Causal	because, in order to, owing to, on account of
Circumstantial	although, even though, if, unless
Spatial	where, wherever
Relational	who, which, that, whose

Sentence Skills Checkpoint D: Development

Embedding

Directions: For each of the following, embed the short sentence clusters into a single coherent and unified sentence.

1. My older sister likes to sneak her dates into the house. She does this late at night. She thinks everybody is asleep.
2. Jas-purr is the name of Clare's cat. He was once stuck in a tree. That happened when he chased a squirrel. The squirrel had dashed up the tree.
3. Avery's desk is a hopeless mess. Avery is a poet.
4. Eventually the sun will consume all of its energy. It will bloat out to ten times its current size. Then it will shrink to a black cinder. This will happen fifty billion years from now.
5. Some people think the moon influences people's moods. Is it the moon itself? Perhaps they worry about it too much. Then their moods really do change.

Coordination and Subordination

Directions: Transform each of the following sentence pairs into a compound sentence (two independent clauses), then into a subordinating sentence (one independent and one dependent, or subordinate, clause). Use a different type of subordinator each time.

1. Eunice and Candice passed their bar exams. They threw a wild party at the Chalice.
2. Gloria got a chance to see the planet Jupiter through a giant telescope. She is an astronomy enthusiast now.

3. The Department of Health and Human Services was established in 1980. It exists to protect and improve the health of the American people.

4. Benjamin Franklin began writing his autobiography in 1771. The book did not appear in print in America until 1818.

5. People have always dreamt of paradise. It's not surprising that some of our greatest literature is utopian.

Variety

We turn now from the techniques of developing sentences internally to the techniques of developing sentences in the context of surrounding sentences. You might be a master at building absolutely dazzling sentences, but unless you vary the syntax, your readers will abandon you in a hurry.

But what does *vary* mean in this context? It means constructing sentences that are pleasingly rhythmic (as opposed to monotonous), that stress key points at the beginning or the end of the sentence, and that reflect a tone of voice appropriate to the point of view. Let's begin with an example. Read the following paragraph and see if you can detect any stylistic problems:

> My salary was increased to forty dollars a week. I seldom drew it. I had plenty of other resources. Two broad twenty-dollar gold pieces were nothing to a man who had his pockets full of such. I had a cumbersome abundance of bright half-dollars besides.

The sentences, patterned too much alike, give the reader a bumpy ride and therefore are distracting. Compare the passage with the original version from Mark Twain's *Roughing It* and try to identify the improvement:

> My salary was increased to forty dollars a week. But I seldom drew it. I had plenty of other resources, and what were two broad twenty-dollar gold pieces to a man who had his pockets full of such and a cumbersome abundance of bright half-dollars besides?

First of all, in Twain's original version, the sentences are not all the same; that is, their rhythms differ, making them seem like conversation, thus engaging the reader more readily and making the narrator seem more realistic and interesting. In the first version, the monotone has just the opposite effect: It prevents the reader from becoming fully involved with the situation described by the narrative.

We can be even more analytical. Note how the opening *but* of the second sentence is just enough to dispel the flat tone of the first version. However, Twain could have used other devices, such as combining the first two sentences to create a compound sentence:

My salary was increased to forty dollars a week, but I seldom drew it.

Or, Twain could have written a complex sentence, using subordination:

Although my salary was increased to forty dollars a week, I seldom drew it.

Twain, we surmise, preferred beginning a new sentence with *but* simply because that word provided just the right rhythm he wanted—as if to make us readers imagine the narrator pausing a bit and rubbing his chin before continuing.

Twain then made the next sentence *interrogatory*—a rhetorical question in this case.* Notice how effectively the rhythm produced by the interrogatory sentence contrasts with the others. This last sentence is also considerably longer than the preceding two. And while the others are both simple sentences, the last is a *compound-complex sentence*: two main clauses linked by the coordinator *and*, followed by the subordinate clause (a *relative clause*† in this case) *who had his pockets full of such*, followed by another independent clause. The sentence is grammatically complex, yet much more readable than its grammatically simple, but weak, counterpart.

The best way for you to master the art of syntactic variety is to study the common types of variation presented in the following discussion. Then do Part Three of the sentence combining exercises near the end of this chapter. And even more important, rework the sentences from your own essays, not so much to improve them as to develop a working familiarity with syntactic variables.

Four Common Methods of Achieving Sentence Variety

Remember that any method of syntactic variety must reflect the context, or the rhetorical situation, in which you the author are involved. Study these methods carefully, as your familiarity with them will make it easier for you to manipulate your own syntax accordingly.

---

*See the Handbook, "Rhetorical and Grammatical Principles," Rhetorical Question.

†"Relative clause" = a dependent (subordinate) clause beginning with a relative pronoun such as "who" or "that." Example: We met the economist *who had just won the Nobel Prize.*

1. *Vary the arrangement of your phrases and clauses.* Monotonous sentences are caused by using the same phrase and clause structures in the same places from sentence to sentence. Try to develop an ear for monotony to avoid this very common problem. Of course, some monotonous passages are more noticeable than others:

> I have just broken up with Lucy. She kept kicking me in the shins whenever I said something she disliked. She never once enjoyed a movie I took her to see. She refuses to eat in fast-food restaurants. She says it's beneath her dignity.

All but the first sentence begin with *she*, which is a sufficient enough cause for monotony. But more than that, the predicates (verbal elements) are all in the same position (*have just broken up with*, *kept kicking*, *never once enjoyed*, and so on). The problem, though, is easy to remedy. Shift a phrase or two and alter the wording to produce a livelier rhythm:

> I have just broken up with Lucy. Why, you wonder? She kept kicking me in the shins whenever I said something she disliked, that's why. And not once did she enjoy a movie I took her to see. She even refused to eat at fast-food restaurants, insisting that they were beneath her dignity.

Sometimes the cause of a monotonous passage isn't as easy to determine. Where, do you suppose, does the problem lie in the following passage?

> Contemporary photographers often fail to exorcise the specter of art. Professionals sometimes object to having their photographs printed to the edge of the page in books or magazines. They are invoking the model inherited from painting in this instance. Painters put their paintings in frames. Photographers "frame" their photographs with white space.

Every sentence is syntactically almost identical to every other: subject, verb, object, and object complement. Here is the original passage as it was actually published:

> Despite the efforts of contemporary photographers to exorcise the specter of art, something lingers. For instance, when professionals object to having their photographs printed to the edge of the page in books or magazines, they are invoking the model inherited from another art: as paintings are put in frames, photographs should be framed in white space. (Susan Sontag, *On Photography*)

No one sentence is structured quite the same as any of the others. Notice how the original opening sentence is made more dramatic through the use of a subordinate clause. Also notice how the transitional *for instance* creates a welcome rhythmic variation. Reread that final sentence. Again, as in the Twain example, the grammatical complexity simplifies comprehension and increases readability, mainly due to effective use of parallelism.

2. *Vary the word order of your sentences.* The most common word order shifts occur when we follow a *declarative* sentence with an interrogative one:

Greg was in a hurry to get home. Can you guess why? He knew his parents were going to surprise him.

Aside from shifting from a statement to a question, it is possible to change the normal word order without breaking any grammatical rules. This technique should be used sparingly, however. Study the following inversions:

a. We've succeeded in solving some of the unemployment problems. *All the problems, though, we'll never solve.*

b. Use your eyes as if *tomorrow you would be stricken blind.* (Helen Keller)

In both of the preceding examples, the variation in the customary word order allows the main point to have greater impact. Without the inversions, these sentences would fall flat, as they do here:

a. We've succeeded in solving some of the unemployment problems. We'll never solve all the problems, though.

b. Use your eyes as if you would be stricken blind tomorrow.

3. *Vary the length of your sentences.* The way you control sentence length has a considerable effect on your writing style. But controlling sentence length depends greatly on the nature of your subject as well as on the natural rhythms of your own voice. As with any of the suggestions relating to syntactic variation, there can be no rules to follow. The best advice is to be mindful of the way good writers control their sentence length, and then to see what you can assimilate into your own style. And remember, it's important to experiment.

Observe the way Virginia Woolf, in her essay "The Death of the Moth," generates a pleasant rhythmic texture by varying her sentence length:

The same energy which inspired the rooks, the ploughmen, the horses, and even, it seemed, the lean bare-backed downs, sent the moth fluttering from one side of his square of the windowpane. One could not help watching him. One was, indeed, conscious of a queer feeling of pity for him. The possibilities of pleasure seemed that morning so enormous and so various that to have only a moth's part in life, and a day moth's at that, appeared a hard fate, and his zest in enjoying his meagre opportunities to the full, pathetic.

Here is a schematic representation of the relative lengths of Woolf's sentences:

Sentence One: _____ (thirty-two words)
Sentence Two: _____ (six words)
Sentence Three: _____ (twelve words)
Sentence Four: _____ (forty-three words)

Was Woolf conscious of her sentence length and the rhythm it produced? Most likely she was aware of it to *some* degree. But if a writer were to become too conscious of it, the effect would be something akin to being overly conscious of every dance step on a ballroom floor: The dancer would surely begin to stumble.

4. *Use transitional expressions.* A *transition* is a word or phrase that bridges, or smoothly connects, one point to another, whether in the same sentence, between sentences, or between paragraphs. Such transitional expressions, like the first word in the sentence you are now reading, may interlock one sentence with the one preceding it; or, they may interlock one phrase or clause with a preceding one within a single sentence, as in the following passages:

When swimming in the ocean, remember to keep close to shore at all times, and to be alert for breakers that could rough you up pretty badly; but even more important, test the underwater surface for sharp rocks and sudden drop-offs.

Astronomy is an ideal pursuit for young people because of the way it stimulates their sense of wonder about the whole universe; and that sense of wonder, needless to say, is vital to learning.

But heed one note of caution here. It is easy to use transitions in a mechanistic way. They must come naturally, as the need arises. As the following example clearly illustrates, the mechanistic use of transitions also causes monotony:

Mountain climbing is loads of fun. *However*, you have to think about literally every step you take. *Nevertheless*, the fun element prevails, *and what is more*, you can have an experience to last a lifetime. *However*, before we discuss the fun, we must discuss the safety rules.

Sentence Skills Checkpoint E: Variety

Directions: Improve the variety of the following sentence clusters.

1. The Middle Ages began to wane throughout the fourteenth century. By 1400, Europe was no longer church-dominated. Classical learning was being revived and idealized. The spirit of exploration was high.

2. Emily Brontë lived a very sheltered life. She lived in a large house with her three sisters and brother in a village near the desolate York-

shire moors. The Brontë sisters (Charlotte, Ann, and Emily) spent much of their time telling stories. Eventually they began writing down some of them.

3. Gustave Courbet, the nineteenth century French painter, began a painting by sketching in human figures and other details with a weak brown pigment. Then he applied base colors with a knife. Then he worked up the human figures with brushes. He created leaves on trees with a tightly wadded, paint-covered rag.

Toward Syntactic Virtuosity

This chapter thus far has introduced you to the fundamentals of sentence building. By studying these fundamentals and by experimenting with syntactic structures you will develop your own "sentence sense" considerably. All of this cannot be done over one weekend, of course; you must be patient.

Inevitably your own distinctive voice will emerge in your writing. Why "inevitably"? Because you are already a distinctive individual in so many ways: Nobody else on earth thinks *exactly* the way you do; nobody else has quite your preferences for this or that; nobody has quite the same goals in life. Similarly, your way of using language, once you're in control of the basics, differs from everyone else's; no two persons express their ideas or fashion their sentences in the same way. *The possibilities for variation are virtually infinite*, which is what makes writing so exciting, and sometimes even frightening, yet so very human.

Let us examine the sentence artistry of two American essayists, Maya Angelou and John McPhee. Read each example twice: first for comprehension and enjoyment, and then for the sentence building technique.

> The missionary ladies of the Christian Methodist Episcopal church helped Momma prepare the pork for the sausage. They squeezed their fat arms elbow deep in the ground meat, mixed it with gray nose-opening sage, pepper and salt, and made tasty little samples for all obedient children who brought wood for the slick black stove. The men chopped off the larger pieces of meat and laid them in the smokehouse to begin the curing process. They opened the knuckle of the hams with their deadly looking knives, took out a certain round, harmless bone ("it could make the meat go bad") and rubbed salt, coarse brown salt that looked like fine gravel, into the flesh, and the blood popped to the surface. (Maya Angelou, *I Know Why the Caged Bird Sings*)

Near the far side of Utah, the flats turned blinding white, corn-snow white, and revolving winds were making devils out of salt. Over the whiteness you could see the salt go off the curve of the earth. When the drivers of jet cars move at Mach .8 over the Bonneville Salt Flats, they feel that they are always about to crest a hill. Dig into the salt and it turns out to be a crusty white veneer, like cake icing, more than an inch thick—an almost pure sodium chloride. Below it are a few inches of sand-size salt particles, and below them a sort of creamy yogurt mud that is the color of blond coffee. (John McPhee, *Basin and Range*)

Analysis of Maya Angelou's Syntax

You may have noticed that each sentence opens with the subject: *the missionary ladies*, *they*, *the men*, and *they*. Yet the pattern does not strike us as monotonous because of the author's keen ear for internal sentence rhythm, resulting principally from variations in phrase-clause patterns and in sentence length.

Angelou's first sentence is a simple sentence, grammatically speaking, but with some complex embedding. Attached to the sentence base, *the ladies helped Momma*, are two subject modifiers, *missionary* (the adjective) and *of the Christian Methodist Episcopal church* (the prepositional phrase), and an elaborate predicate modifier, *[to] prepare the pork for the sausage*. Were this information presented without embedding, it would have to appear something like this:

> The ladies helped Momma. The ladies were missionaries. They belonged to the Christian Methodist Episcopal church. They helped prepare the pork. The pork was for the sausage.

The second sentence is structurally very different: a compound-complex sentence consisting of three consecutive independent clauses plus a subordinate clause (the relative clause, *who brought wood for the slick black stove*). The third sentence is a compound sentence consisting of two independent clauses; the predicate of the second clause is modified by a prepositional phrase, *in the smokehouse*, and an infinitive phrase, *to begin the curing process*. The last sentence, considerably longer than the others, is a masterful example of syntactic orchestration and clever embedding, and is worth examining in closer detail. There are four consecutive independent clauses, each with its own distinct modifying elements:

- *Clause One*. The base, *they opened the knuckle*, has two predicate modifiers: *of the ham* and *with their deadly looking knives* (both prepositional phrases).

- *Clause Two.* The base, *[they] took out a bone*, has two predicate modifiers; *certain round, harmless* (an adjective cluster) and *"it could have made the meat go bad"* (a cleverly embedded dialogue-sentence).*

- *Clause Three.* The base, *[they] rubbed salt*, has one elaborate subject modifier: *coarse brown salt that looked like fine gravel* (the appositive).†

- *Clause Four.* The base, *the blood popped*, has one predicate modifier: *to the surface* (the prepositional phrase).

- Finally, a schematic representation of the relative sentence lengths would look like this:

  Sentence One: _____ (seventeen words)
  Sentence Two: _____ (thirty-seven words)
  Sentence Three: _____ (twenty words)
  Sentence Four: _____ (forty-seven words)

Analysis of John McPhee's Syntax

McPhee, in contrast to Angelou, likes to begin his sentences with prepositional phrases: *near the far side of Utah*, *over the whiteness*, and *below it*. The third sentence opens with a subordinate clause, which contains two prepositional phrases: *when the drivers of jet cars move at Mach .8 over the Bonneville Salt Flats*. The fourth sentence seems to begin with a main clause, *dig into the salt*, but it is actually a truncated subordinate clause. He is really saying, "If you dig into the salt [you will discover that it turns out to be a crusty white veneer]." This interesting construction works well toward sustaining McPhee's conversational tone, while at the same time keeping the language terse.

McPhee, too, is a master of the art of embedding accurate, technical detail into a predominantly impressionistic description, as we observe in his first sentence:

> Near the far side of Utah, the flats turned blinding white, corn-snow white, and revolving winds were making devils out of salt.

The last two sentences in the passage have similar intent.

---

*A more conventional way of presenting this would have been: "They took out a . . . bone because, according to one of them, it could have made the meat go bad." But this expansion would have made the whole sentence unmanageable.

†Even the appositive, as you can see, is complex. It contains a subordinate (in this case, relative) clause, *that looked like fine gravel*.

Like Angelou, McPhee has a musician's ear for rhythmic variation. You may want to read the passage aloud to get a better sense of this.

Finally, here is a schematic of McPhee's relative sentence lengths:

Sentence One: _____ (twenty-two words)
Sentence Two: _____ (fifteen words)
Sentence Three: _____ (twenty-six words)
Sentence Four: _____ (twenty-seven words)
Sentence Five: _____ (twenty-six words)

McPhee's sentence length, you may have noticed, does not vary nearly as much as Woolf's or Angelou's; yet, because of rich *syntactic variation*, the sentences are not monotonous.

Special Topic: Combining Sentences

One of the toughest aspects of learning to write well is learning to apply to your own writing the principles discussed in a textbook such as this one. It's like learning to play chess: You can study the clever strategies of the grandmasters, yet when it comes time to play your own game, the models cease to be as useful as you would have hoped them to be. Models will often help you if you study them so thoroughly that you become able to recognize similar situations and recall an appropriate strategy; they will also help you increase your general powers of perception as a result of continuous study. The key, however, is *immersion*: complete involvement in the activity you are determined to master.

The aim of combining sentences is to give you as many opportunities as possible to try out new syntactical strategies. The reason? Syntax is intimately connected with meaning; the way you shape your sentences will influence the substance of what you are saying. Doing sentence combining exercises will not only help you develop and control your style, but it will also sharpen your ability to express ideas and to convey meaning. As the rhetorician Francis Christensen asserts in *Notes Toward a New Rhetoric*, "the mere form of the sentence generates ideas."

Sentence Combining: Part One

Directions: Turn each of the following sets of statements into one sentence. Your objective is to *embed* in a single sentence bits of information that should not be isolated in separate sentences. Embedding helps you to be more concise; you are giving your readers more information to assimilate in a single breath, as it were. Your next step is to rewrite the new sentence in a different manner to become familiar with the variety of syntactic possibilities.

Example: Jean Smith is a champion skater.
She is expected to make it to the Summer Olympics.
She won a dozen competitions.

Jean Smith, a champion skater who won a dozen competitions, is expected to make it to the Summer Olympics.

Having won a dozen competitions, champion skater Jean Smith is expected to make it to the Summer Olympics.

1. My brother is an artist.
   His name is Vincent.
   Vincent likes to paint weird animals.

2. Jonathan Swift is the author of *Gulliver's Travels*.
   Gulliver's Travels is a brilliant and caustic satire.
   The novel satirizes human pride, greed, and vanity.

3. Carolyn feeds and waters her plants.
   She really loves doing this.
   She has many plants.
   Her plants include ferns, parlor palms, and jades.

4. Cory is a poet.
   Cory's poems are rich in sensual imagery.
   Cory is the kind of poet who inspires other poets.

5. There are seven wonders of the ancient world.
   The Great Pyramid of Cheops is one of them.
   The Great Pyramid is in Egypt.
   It was erected by thousands of slaves.
   It took twenty years to build.

6. Last night I dreamt I was an eagle.
   This was the third time in a row I had this dream.
   I had golden wings and razor-sharp talons.

7. Jeff has a fascinating collection of rocks and minerals.
   His collection includes a huge geode filled with amethyst crystals.
   His collection also includes also a specimen of malachite.
   The malachite is bright green.

8. Computerized landing simulations are vital to the Space Program.
   They play a key role in training astronauts.
   They train astronauts to practice complicated landing maneuvers.

Sentence Combining: Part Two

Directions: Turn each of the following sets of statements into one sentence, as you did in the preceding section. This time, however, you are going to include one subordinate clause in your new sentence. Finally, present the new sentence in a different way by shifting the subordinate clause to a new position.

Example: Delilah cut off Samson's hair.
Samson lost all his strength.

After Delilah cut off Samson's hair, Samson lost all his strength.

Samson, after Delilah cut off his hair, lost all his strength.

1. One of Judith's favorite novelists is James Joyce.
   Her favorite novel is George Eliot's *Middlemarch*.

2. The tomcat climbed the fence.
   It meowed forlornly.
   Someone threw a shoe at the poor cat.

3. I heard that silver is going to double in value soon.
   An investor-friend told me this.
   I've decided to keep all of my old silver spoons.

4. Mr. Sloan is a respected banker.
   His identity as Iceman will never be known.
   As Iceman, he is a notorious diamond smuggler.

5. Laws must be passed to protect the brown pelican.
   It is possible that they could become extinct.
   Their numbers are diminishing rapidly.

6. Astronomers have estimated the age of the earth.
   They say it is four and a half billion years old.
   I immediately wanted to know how they arrived at that number.

7. You seem to have changed in five years.
   Five years ago you loved to tell jokes.
   Now you dislike joking.

8. Marty loved to jump on the hoods of neighbors' cars.
   He also loved to write naughty things on neighbors' windows.
   The neighbors liked Marty.
   I found that unbelievable.

Sentence Combining: Part Three

Directions: Turn the following sets of statements into one, two, or three varied, colorful, and rhythmic sentences. You may add or alter words as you deem necessary.

Example: Outer space is unimaginably vast.
Are there other worlds out there?
Do any of them harbor life?
Could some of that life be intelligent?
Think of the possible implications of making contact.

In the unimaginable depths of space, worlds bearing intelligent life may exist, awaiting our first message. Think of the implications of making such extraterrestrial contact!

1. Do we adults grow up too fast?
   Do we outgrow our need to play like children?
   I sorely doubt it.
   Adults should not feel repressed.
   Many adults feel too repressed.
   They ignore their playful feelings.
   They abandon them forever.

2. Arnold wanted to give a party.
   He invited his best friends.
   He also invited people he hardly knew.
   The party got out of hand.
   The people he hardly knew smashed up Arnold's furniture.
   Arnold got smashed up too.

3. Sandra has a weird way of choosing a subject for a paper.
   She goes to the library.
   She enters the reference room.
   She goes up to the encyclopedias.
   She takes a blindfold out of her purse.
   She puts on the blindfold.
   She reaches for a volume.
   She opens the volume at random.
   She plops her finger down on the page.
   Whatever her finger lands on will be her subject.

4. Imagine living in a space colony.
   The colony would be in orbit around the earth.
   Colonists would live inside an immense cylinder.

The cylinder would be transparent at night, opaque at day.
The weather would be completely controlled.
Exciting new modes of agriculture would be possible.
Exciting new modes of scientific research would be possible, too.

5. According to Fernand Braudel, the population in the fifteenth and eighteenth centuries was unsteady.
Braudel is a French historian.
The population rose and fell.
That is very different from today.
Today the population steadily increases.
The rise and fall of the population in the fifteenth and eighteenth centuries caused the respective rise and fall of commerce.

6. In Plato's ideal state, only "the best" would rule.
This is the origin of aristocracy.
Aristocracy is a compound of two Greek words.
The words are *ariston*, to rule, and *kratos*, best.
Only those who reveal the greatest potential for ruling should be trained to rule.
Plato assumed that this potential was innate.

7. Beethoven inspires Ann to write poetry.
Liszt and Wagner make Manuel want to paint stormy seascapes.
Schubert spurs Naomi into composing her own sonatas.
Great music can stimulate creative thought.
Great music makes us sensitive to harmonic and rhythmic variations.
These elements are possibly at the heart of creativity.

8. In Pueblo Indian society, sunwatching was important.
The Pueblo priests were called Priests of the Sun.
Sunwatching was a sacred act.
It was basic to Pueblo religious rituals.
Sunwatching was also a practical act among the Pueblo Indians.
The sun priest's responsibility was to keep a calendar.
This information about Pueblo Indians can be found in a book by Dr. E. C. Krupp.
The book is titled, *Echoes of the Ancient Skies: The Astronomy of Lost Civilizations*.

Summary

A sentence is the smallest unit of discourse; it is the smallest unit of meaning for communicating an idea. An isolated word or fragment cannot carry such meaning, because it requires a larger context—words or sentences preceding or following it—to establish some kind of relationship between the subject of the sentence and the action or mood it attempts to convey. For sentences to work effectively, they should be as economical as possible while taking advantage of the opportunities for expression that can distinguish a writer's style. Such opportunities include subordinating parts of a sentence to other parts; varying sentence rhythm, emphasis, and tone by way of periodic, cumulative, and balanced structures; and embedding—incorporating unnecessarily separate clauses and phrases and even whole sentences into the kernel sentence.

FOR DISCUSSION

1. Explain the difference between an elliptical sentence and a true fragment. Provide two or three of your own examples.
2. Distinguish between unity and coherence in sentences.
3. Choose a magazine article at random and locate as many examples of sentence parallelism as you can find.
4. Discuss, using your own examples, the difference between embedding and subordination.
5. How does syntax influence a writer's style? Locate two works by two of your favorite authors whose styles differ greatly (e.g., Ernest Hemingway and William Faulkner). Specify the differences in typical sentence construction between the two writers.
6. Describe each of the following sentence varieties; illustrate each variety with two of your own sentences:
    a. periodic
    b. balanced
    c. cumulative

FOR WRITING

1. Transform the following fragments into complete sentences; embed them in the adjoining sentence(s), if appropriate, or leave them as is, if the fragment can pass as an elliptical sentence:
    a. Charlene's immense popularity being why she was elected to the student council.
    b. We enjoyed the flight to Puerto Vallarta. Almost as much as we enjoyed our stay there.
    c. Is Simone satisfied with her new Porsche? As if you couldn't guess.

d. Eerie sounds during the night that seemed to rise from the mist-shrouded swamp.

e. Because of the current rate of inflation. Investors were confused.

2. In each of the following sentences, change one of the coordinate clauses into a subordinate clause.

   a. I waited for hours so I left without you.
   b. Sophia was wagging her tail and I knew she was happy to see me.
   c. You may have this book, but please read it.
   d. The blizzard dumped a foot of snow on us, but I had to go to work just the same.
   e. *Yuppie* and *nerd* are obnoxious expressions, but I find myself using them anyway.
   f. Mathematics is imaginative and fun, yet some teachers make it seem like drudgery.

3. Write a descriptive paragraph about any household item, and use nothing but declarative sentences. Next, rewrite the paragraph using interrogative, imperative, and declarative sentences. Describe the difference in style between the two paragraphs.

4. Expand the following kernel sentences into periodic, cumulative, or balanced sentences as you see fit.

   Example: Helen broke the tape.
   Gasping, lungs burning, her mouth parched, and every muscle in her body screaming in protest, Helen triumphantly broke the tape at the finish line [*periodic*].

   Example: The dancers twirled.
   Upon the gleaming plastic floor, amid flashing lights, the dancers twirled, their bodies like unraveling colored ribbons [*balanced*].

   Example: The waves smashed against the rock.
   The waves smashed against the rock, wild pinnacles of white foam leaping high into the air, spraying mist everywhere [*cumulative*].

   a. The starving man engorged himself.
   b. The hydrogen bomb exploded.
   c. Marlene fainted.
   d. The coyote howled.

e. Darkness fell.

f. We walked through the slums.

g. Professor Meson's laboratory was in shambles.

COMPUTER WRITING

1. For students working in pairs at a terminal: Student A types out a sentence. Student B then revises the sentence by adding or rearranging words and phrases, embedding, subordinating, changing the emphasis and rhythm, and so on. Notice how well the word processing program allows for easy addition and deletion of words and phrases. Student A revises that same sentence once again and then Student B does likewise. This may continue indefinitely. Keep the printer on if you wish to have a record of each phase of revision.

2. Record all the problem sentences from a recent paper into a file named SENTENCE.PRX. Next, rework each sentence several times, trying out as many permutations as you can.

3. Select a short paragraph at random from any published source and try turning the paragraph into a coherent single sentence. Next, do just the opposite: Turn the original paragraph into one that contains twice as many complete sentences.

Shaping Paragraphs

CHAPTER 13

Wrongheaded ideas about paragraphing abound, so our first order of business is to separate fact from fable. To begin with, not all paragraphs are structured the same way, each with its topic sentence at the beginning, followed by two or more support sentences that may be subdivided into primary and secondary support, and brought to an end with a concluding sentence. You will very likely find yourself writing paragraphs like that, but more often your paragraphs will be less formally developed. It all depends on how much support a given point needs, how much emphasis you want to give to that point, how much depth of treatment you sense the point requires, and how distinct a boundary you wish to suggest between one point and another.

The word *paragraph* comes from the Greek word *paragraphos*, meaning "to write beside," and is represented by the familiar sign, ¶, which scribes once placed in the margins of manuscripts to indicate a new section of the discourse, or a new speaker in a dialogue. Discourse unit markings are sometimes still used today, as in elaborately subdivided philosophical or legal treatises. Aside from that, the universal indicator of a new paragraph is the indentation.

Like sentences, paragraphs can be well-developed independent or semi-independent units of discourse, or they can be only one part of an argument or point and completely dependent upon the paragraphs that precede and follow them. They can even be *fragments* such as exclamations or statements to which the author feels a need to give special emphasis:

> Once upon a time there lived a greedy little elf who stole food from children since children were weaker than grown-ups and were more easily frightened into not telling anyone.
>
> Or so he thought!
>
> One day, a hungry little girl . . .

The trick is to know when to use one type of paragraph rather than another. As you study the types of paragraphs that follow, remember that these are *typical* examples. They are not meant to be used as molds for your own paragraphing technique; that would cramp your style!

Paragraphs also have internal as well as external coherence and rhythm as do sentences. If you were to turn to any magazine article and read one of the middle paragraphs, chances are you would find the paragraph to be *context-bound*; that is, its opening sentences would tie in with something that had been discussed earlier.

If every paragraph in an article began in a *context-free* manner, with the topic sentence at the very beginning, the monotonous rhythm would probably become too distracting. Read the following example from a student essay and you'll see why this is true:

> The road to riches in football is a long one. The path is narrow, and only a few survive its length. Those football players who make the trek are those who hunger for success; they are the "scrappers." Their ambitions are much greater than those of the others.
>
> Professional players differ greatly in size and ability. Receivers and backs are fleet-footed highjumpers with soft, nimble hands. Linemen and linebackers are colossal titans with incredible speed of arm and mind. The coaches are offensive and defensive geniuses who try to instill the winning attitude in players who are not experiencing it.
>
> The long journey to success begins in the front yard. Dad and son toss an old football around. Dad gives pointers on throwing a spiral, although his passes resemble a shot duck. The son complies with his father's directions and improves.

The content here is surely interesting; but each of the paragraphs is model-perfect, as though the author were convinced that every paragraph in an essay had to be structured the same way. What agony writing would be if that were true! And the poor reader would doze off from the hypnotic effect of the metronomelike rhythm.

A more serious problem, however, has to do with the paragraph's coherence. There is no clear progression from paragraph one to paragraph two, nor from three to four. Each paragraph reads like a separate, super-condensed essay.

Now let's look at what this same student did to improve the paragraph coherence and rhythm:

> The road to riches in football is a long one. The path is narrow, and only a few survive its length. Those football players who make the trek are the ones who hunger for success; they are the "scrappers" whose ambitions are so much greater than the others.
>
> But aside from their common ambition to endure, professional ball players differ greatly in size and ability. Receivers and backs are fleet-footed highjumpers with soft, nimble hands, while linemen and linebackers, by contrast, are colossal titans with incredible speed for such large frames. The quarterback, with his strong personality, arm, and mind, is the leader. And finally we have the coaches: offensive and defensive geniuses who try to instill the winning attitude in players who are not experiencing it.
>
> How do they acquire that winning attitude, you may wonder? The long journey to success begins in the front yard, where dad and son toss an old football around. Dad gives pointers on throwing a spiral, although his passes resemble a shot duck. But the son nonetheless complies with his father's directions and improves.

You should be able to detect two improvements in the second version. First, there is greater *external coherence*; the paragraphs flow along smoothly, logically, each stemming naturally from the one before it and anticipating the one following it. Note how the opening sentences in the second and third paragraphs bridge the thought emphasized in the first and second paragraphs, respectively, without resorting merely to mechanical transitional markers. Second, a greater degree of readability within each paragraph (*internal coherence*) has been achieved, mainly because of more rhythmic variation from sentence to sentence. We now have the feeling that the author is speaking to us.

The Well-Made Paragraph

Nobody needs to tell you about this kind of paragraph; you've probably had it drilled into your head since the seventh grade. Typically, the topic sentence appears at the beginning and is followed by any number of *support sentences* that elaborate upon, restrict, or otherwise modify the topic sentence. Then, examples that illustrate these elaborations or restrictions of the topic sentence often follow. Finally, a concluding sentence briefly summarizes the paragraph.

The preceding description represents various levels of generality: The topic sentence constitutes the first level; the support sentences constitute the second level; and the illustrations, the third level. The concluding paragraph would belong to the first level. These levels of generality may be diagramed as follows:

1. Topic sentence
   2. Support sentence
   2. Support sentence
      3. Example/illustration
      3. Example/illustration
1. Concluding sentence

This kind of paragraphing most often occurs in explanatory or argumentative writing; it is less common in expressive writing. The well-made paragraph, you must understand, is *not* the preferred model for paragraphing; it is simply one of the many varieties of paragraphing a writer chooses or does not choose to use, depending on what the rhetorical situation suggests.

The following well-made paragraphs open the third chapter of a book on London in the Middle Ages. First, read the example for its information content, and then read it again, this time paying close attention to the author's paragraphing technique.

> It is clear that by Chaucer's day the guild system was of great importance for the whole fabric of London society. This does not mean that all, or even most, of the inhabitants were full members of guilds and enjoyed through them the rights of citizenship. It is very hard to say what was the exact proportion. Let us take the figures from Henry VIII's reign as a start, because these are much fuller than anything available for the fourteenth century, even though inadequate.
>
> In 1537, the total number of freeman householders was about three thousand. If we allow an average of five members to a household, we get a figure for the citizen class of about fifteen thousand, and the total population of London at that time has been estimated at about sixty thousand. The proportion of freemen in the fourteenth century is unlikely to have been greater; indeed, to judge from the comparative number of apprentices, it was probably less. It therefore seems that, at a generous estimate, for every freeman there were in Chaucer's London at least three adult men unenfranchised. The latter were called "foreigns" and were of at least four different kinds.
>
> A. R. Meyers, *London in the Age of Chaucer*

Did you notice how the author begins each paragraph with the topic sentence? But is the style monotonous? Not at all, owing to the conversational flow, to the internal sentence rhythm, and to the participatory attitude conveyed by the author (*it is clear that* and *let us take*). Notice too how every subsequent sentence provides specific discussion and elaboration of the premise introduced by the topic sentence.

Paragraph Skills Checkpoint A: Paragraph Coherence

Directions: Rewrite each paragraph to improve the logical connection between the topic sentence and the primary support sentences, and between the primary and secondary support sentences. You may need to reword some of the sentences.

1. Van Gogh's sunflowers are dazzling creations. Van Gogh used brilliant colors in dazzling, almost hallucinogenic patterns. In one painting, even the night sky is alive with fiercely blazing stars.

2. The fantastic predicaments, the gadgetry, the villains, the amorous affairs between James Bond and the exotic women all *take place* in the real world, but are themselves the stuff of fairy tales. Every James Bond film is a real-world fantasy. These films are sheer escapist fun, never to be taken seriously.

3. The need for creative people in science and industry has increased, not decreased. The notion that growth in science signals a decline in creativity is completely false. Being able to conceive of a new experiment, or of a connection between one phenomenon and another, are just two examples of how creativity works in science. Without creativity there could be no science.

Common Problems in Paragraphing

As you would probably agree from your own experience, the most common problem that occurs with paragraphing is *getting sidetracked*; letting yourself think in great associative leaps that make your paragraphs seem like one big grab bag of topic sentences. Here's an example of a paragraph that displays this type of problem:

> More and more employers in business and industry are insisting that their prospective employees acquire thorough training in writing, math, and computer science. Computer science should be a required class, not an elective. Composition courses ought to include units on writing for business and industry. These days, without a good practical education, it is almost impossible to find a worthwhile job.

Each one of the sentences in this paragraph could be the basis for a separate paragraph, if not a separate essay. Thus, after the first sentence, some *amplification** of the point should follow, as the following paragraph illustrates:

> More and more employers in business and industry are insisting that their prospective employees acquire thorough training in writing, math, and computer science. These areas are basic to all communication in our technological society. Since communication lies at the heart of business and scientific activity, these skills are truly indispensable to any occupation in those fields.

Here's something else to keep in mind: If you tend to compose paragraphs that operate on only one level of generality, it's possible that the fundamental problem lies not with your paragraphing skills, but with your skills in developing ideas.† However, an understanding of the structure of the well-made paragraph can help you learn to discuss a given point thoroughly.

Paragraph Skills Checkpoint B: Amplification

Directions: Amplify where necessary in each of the following passages so that they may function more effectively as paragraphs. It may be necessary to turn a passage into multiple paragraphs.

1. The weather has been stormy every night for a week. Usually, springtime is the mildest time of year, but this year the opposite has been the case. Winters, of course, are just as bad, or worse, than they're rumored to be. During the second half of January, the temperatures stayed consistently below zero.

2. Why is it so difficult for me to keep my room tidy? My roommate is a slob. Of course when coursework piles up, it's impossible to find time to eat.

3. Everyone needs to be alone at times. Some people get very uncomfortable whenever they are by themselves, and that's unfortunate. Solitude shouldn't be equated with loneliness.

Another common paragraph-related problem is *cluttering*. You probably know the feeling: You have so much to say about a particular topic, let's say your roommate, that you want to get it across to your readers all at once. Actually, there is nothing wrong with this manner of composing; it proceeds rapidly, you're enthusiastic about your writing,

---

*That is, a more detailed discussion of the assertion made in the first sentence.
†For a review of the composing process, see Chapter 3, "A Practical Method of Writing."

and you're not worried about the mechanics of the paper. The latter point is important, as worry frequently interferes seriously with the composing process. The problem arises, however, when the writer neglects to reread this grand outpouring later on to make sure that the paragraphs are not overloaded with detail.

A cluttered paragraph causes readers' heads to swim. An overly rapid bombardment does not give your readers the time they need to evaluate matters on their own. As a result, readability and comprehension are lost. Try to keep to the *aim* of your discourse when constructing your paragraphs. For example, are you writing to inform, to entertain, or to persuade? Recall what you need to include and how you may best phrase what you want to say.

Getting back to your roommate, imagine that you want the whole world to know just what kind of slothful, irresponsible, boisterous knave your college roommate really is. With a fiendish gleam in your eye, you happily sharpen your pencil to a fearful point and plunge into your first paragraph:

> My roommate, Darla, is so sweet and proper on the surface, but you can't imagine what she's like inside the room. She never hangs up her clothes, her snacking habits are absolutely disgusting, and she must be nearly deaf because she plays her stereo full blast and thinks it's barely audible.

The readers certainly learn quite a bit about Darla, don't they? Too much too soon, as a matter of fact. They might even find themselves telling you, the author, "Whoa, slow down; let me absorb one thing at a time!" You quite agree, let's say, and proceed to develop her profile more fully, more patiently:

> My roommate, Darla, is so sweet and proper on the surface, you can't imagine what she's like when she is out of the public eye, when she is just with me, in the room I have the misfortune of sharing with her.
>
> If only she would hang up her clothes, or at least keep them in the same pile on the floor. But no: Darla's clothes are *everywhere*. It isn't much fun to look forward to an evening with Johnny Carson and find Darla's pantyhose flung across the TV.
>
> And then Darla likes to snack. Mind you, she doesn't snack like normal people; she gets food all over—pieces of lettuce, chunks of tuna, big splotches of salad dressing and catsup on the chairs, on the bedsheets, even on the walls. And heaven help me if I tell her something funny while she's mashing away on an ear of corn!
>
> Do I need to tell you about Darla's music-listening habits? Not if you live within a three-square-mile radius! The poor girl must be near deaf, because whenever she listens to her, ah, music, she blasts it so that the walls shake. Even though I threaten to reach for her neck, she merely pouts and says, "Jeez, I can hardly hear it as it is."

Paragraph Skills Checkpoint C: Cluttering

Directions: The following paragraphs are overambitiously written. Unclutter them by developing them into two or more paragraphs each.

1. Christmastime is full of sensory delight. Even crowded shopping is fun because of all the lavishly displayed goods in every store. I love the specialty gift shops best because they are always full of unusual gifts like ceramic novelties, contemporary glassware, leather goods, pendants, and the like. What tops my list, though, are the bakeries. Nothing beats the lush aroma of fruitcakes, tortes, Christmas cookies, chocolate truffles, and raisin bread.

2. The last time I visited the museum, I made it a point to study the mummies. The skull of one of them was exposed and you could see some of the mummified flesh still on the cheekbones and neck. Then I visited the insect and spider display, marveling at the giant Brazilian tarantula that was bigger than my hand, and the incredible variety of beetles from all over the world. In the Hall of Minerals, I gasped at diamonds and rubies the size of goose eggs. There were also giant quartz crystals, discovered in a deep cave, that were the size of a human leg.

3. Westerners sometimes overlook the astonishing diversity of African art. Also easy to overlook is the fact that art in Africa is inseparable from daily life. Fetish statuettes, ceremonial cloths like the large *kente* cloth that the peoples of Ghana drape around themselves, and bizarre masks such as initiation and funeral masks are examples of art objects that are equally utilitarian.

Paragraphing in Relation to Discourse Mode

The paragraphs you will create in personal experience writing will usually have a different purpose, and sometimes a different organizational scheme, than that of the paragraphs you will create in explanatory or persuasive writing. The paragraphs will be different because the essays themselves differ in purpose. A personal experience essay aims to recreate an experience vicariously for readers, and this calls for writing that stimulates the senses and evokes an atmosphere or mood. A pro-con essay unfolds a line of reasoning to convince readers of a particular stance on an issue or problem. Sensory experience *could* be an ingredient, but not at the expense of carefully developed logical analysis. In the case of the explanatory essay, the author's main goal is to explain an issue or relate a procedure in a logical sequence. Here again, the author may see fit to introduce sensory experience, especially in a feature on how to prepare some exotic gourmet meal, or to argue an issue, especially if more than one solution is available. But sensory experience would never be included at the expense of the dominant aim: *to convey information*.

Examine the following paragraph clusters representing each of the essay types mentioned here. How do they differ, and how are they similar?

PERSONAL EXPERIENCE (EXPRESSIVE) WRITING

The trail fell steeply. As I walked, dust spurted out from under my boots like jets of water. The dust hung suspended for a moment; then the wind whirled it away. I walked on downward. The trail twisted around an immense rock buttress, cut under an overhang, and swung sharp left.

And then I was no longer walking.

I was standing, alone and cut off and not quite understanding why I had stopped, on a natural rock platform that jutted out over Hualpai Canyon. Rough brown sandstone walled me in, blocking off the wind. I found myself listening. It was so still that there was nothing to hear but silence.

Colin Fletcher, *The Man Who Walked Through Time*

PERSUASIVE WRITING

The application of a science of behavior to the design of a culture is an ambitious proposal, often thought to be utopian in the pejorative sense, and some reasons for skepticism deserve comment. It is often asserted, for example, that there are fundamental differences between the real world and the laboratory in which behavior is analyzed. Where the laboratory setting is contrived, the real world is natural; where the setting is simple, the world is complex; where processes observed in the laboratory reveal order, behavior elsewhere is characteristically confused. These are real differences, but they may not remain so as a science of behavior advances, and they are often not to be taken seriously even now.

The difference between contrived and natural conditions is not a serious one. It may be natural for a pigeon to flick leaves about and find bits of food beneath some of them, in the sense that the contingencies are standard parts of the environment in which the pigeon evolved. The contingencies under which a pigeon pecks an illuminated disk on a wall are clearly unnatural. But although the programming equipment in the laboratory is contrived and the arrangement of leaves and seeds natural, the schedules according to which behavior is reinforced can be made identical.

B. F. Skinner, *Beyond Freedom and Dignity*

EXPLANATORY WRITING

Consumers can tell which foods are fortified because all products with nutrients added must be labeled. Through labeling regulations, the types and amounts of nutrients in foods are also controlled. "Enriched flour" or "fortified milk" must contain specified levels of specified nutrients.

In the past, fortification has been made in staple foods to combat deficiency diseases and to restore nutrients destroyed during processing and storage.

A misconception among some consumers is that addition of vitamins and minerals always makes a food superior to unfortified foods. In fact, adding nutrients already abundant in the diet provides no extra benefit because the body uses only what it needs. There also can be too much of a good thing. Excessive amounts of some nutrients, such as vitamins A and D, or of trace elements, such as copper, zinc, molybdenum and selenium, can be toxic.

Phyllis Lehmann, "More Than You Ever Thought You Would Know About Food Additives"

Analysis

Although none of the above paragraph clusters should be regarded as ironclad models for expressive, persuasive, and explanatory writing, they can serve as reminders that differences in paragraph strategy generally do exist among these modes of communication. The Skinner paragraph cluster, as you no doubt quickly noticed, comes closest to the "well-made" paragraph structure with its leadoff topic sentences and clearly tied-in support sentences. As suggested earlier, this type of paragraphing is ideal for conveying complex information in the clearest manner possible. Skinner makes a key point, explains what he means by it, and provides examples whenever feasible. The deeper you go into a Skinner paragraph, the more detailed the information becomes; if you forget what his main idea was, you need only return to the first sentence in the paragraph to be reminded.

A quite different paragraphing technique is to be observed in Colin Fletcher's passage. Here the author's aim is to recreate an incident for readers to experience vicariously. To make this work, the author needs to set a mood by evoking concrete images and sensory descriptions, such as the steepness of the trail and the spurting of the dust. The way a writer shapes the paragraphs can determine whether those effects, which together make up a great deal of the art of storytelling, are highlighted or clouded.

Finally, Phyllis Lehmann's paragraphing style seems to fall somewhere in between the styles of the other examples. They're not exactly model paragraphs, but neither are they entirely expressive. Lehmann seems rather to cluster her points around three separate yet related concerns regarding vitamin fortification. The first paragraph discusses how consumers can tell which foods are fortified; the second paragraph, the shortest of the three, provides a brief but useful historical note: Fortification was once used to combat vitamin deficiency. This paragraph relates logically to the third and longest paragraph, in which the author discusses a serious misconception held by some consumers that extra vitamins mean extra nutrition for the body to utilize. The author points out, however, that our modern-day eating habits in fact do supply us with sufficient nutrition.

Before you go on to experiment with your own paragraphing style, go back to the preceding examples and look closely at the way each author moves you logically and comfortably from one paragraph to the next. The device they use is known as the *transition*, but it isn't always an explicit tag like *also*, *however*, or *on the other hand*. In fact, be advised that any mechanical use of transitional tags will stand out as the mark of an amateur. Often the transition is, in a sense, built into the logical flow of the argument or discussion. Skinner succeeds in establishing his progression from the first to the second paragraph without need of an explicit transition.

Experimenting with Paragraphs

The paragraph can be a versatile stylistic device, and you are encouraged to experiment with different paragraphing forms in your notebook or journal. Forget about the *topic sentence/support sentence* formula and just concentrate on communicating your thoughts as effectively as you can. Don't be afraid to try new approaches in writing, not for their own sakes, of course, but for the sake of finding your own voice—for being truly yourself on paper. Otherwise, writing will always seem like a chore, something that you do to fulfill someone else's standards instead of your own. *Your own voice* could very well mean writing model paragraphs; on the other hand, it could also mean using very short, journalistic paragraphs to lend a certain kind of rhythm and tone to the piece. Note the way this works in the following amusing feature:

BABY'S BALDNESS AT 18 MONTHS IS A GROWING CONCERN

My baby daughter is incredibly beautiful. But after spending 18 months with her, I have to say she's also incredibly bald.

If you, too, have a bald baby, you may already know that for the world at large, bald babies are of great concern. Complete strangers feel compelled to offer sympathy and advice, to confess their own bald babyhoods or those of their offspring. They'll hail you in the park, confront you in the supermarket, nudge you on buses.

And things get worse over time. If your baby lacks the genetic pizzazz to get reasonably fuzzy-headed by a year (the cut-off point beyond which no passerby will pass you by), give up on anonymity.

Here's a sampling of remarks from last week alone:

From an old lady in a supermarket: "What a beautiful little boy! He should be a girl!"

"He is."

"Honey, why don't you Scotch-tape bows to her head?"

From the father of an equally bald baby at a park: "You know what my pediatrician told me? He said bald babies are healthier, and tend to be more intelligent."

From a pizza-maker: "Hi, Baldie! With that little hair, she's gotta be a girl."

"She is."

"Bingo! I got five daughters. Nothing till they were 3 years old. The pits. But now? Talk about hair!"

And my mother. Her ego is reeling from the blow of a bald granddaughter.

"How's Heidi's hair?" she asked on her weekly phone calls from the East Coast.

"You really want to know?"

"I can't understand it," she whimpered last week. "All my babies had lots of hair. Have you asked John's mother about his hair as a child?"

"I'm afraid to," I said. "What if he was bald until he was 10?"

She ignored me. "Don't you worry. That child's going to have lovely, curly hair."

My mother feels very strongly about curly hair.

Imagine her joy at Heidi's birth. Heidi actually had trace amounts of curly black hair. Then she started shedding, attaining the Yul Brynner Look at six weeks. Having studied my revised Spock, I took this quite well. It helped when Susie, a friend's baby, lost all her hair, too.

But Susie, as it turned out, was a bad baby to know. When it came to hair production, Susie was tops.

Within a few weeks, that girl had black fuzz. After a month, real hair. Heidi, of course, had nothing. But I was brave. Luckily, the general public takes no special interest in bald 3-month-olds.

Around this time, my mother started rooting for curly hair. "All of you had curly hair," she said. "Wait until she's 6 months old."

At 6 months, Heidi resembled a billiard ball. Susie's hair was hanging over her ears. I remained relatively calm. The world still left us in peace.

At a year, when Susie had to have her bangs cut, Heidi had a barely perceptible layer of down. She was beginning to be singled out in supermarkets.

"I can just tell that child is going to have curly hair," my mother said. She had perhaps been studying recent photographs under a microscope.

Age 15 months. Heidi's hair consisted of a few invisible wisps. She was averaging five comments per week in public places.

"How's her hair?" asked my ever-vigilant mother. "Curly yet?"

I confess I snapped at her. "She's got see-through hair, Mom, you know what I mean? A high scalp-to-hair ratio."

"How about hats? Have you tried hats?"

Eighteen months of this kind of harassment, and you start losing your cool. My husband is no help.

"Do you think it could be some kind of vitamin deficiency?" he asked yesterday. "Is she getting a balanced diet?"

"Would you recommend a hair transplant?" I hissed.

Susie Superbaby now has pigtails. Her mother suggested I buy Heidi a wig.

I don't know why I didn't hit her.

Dixie Brown, from the *San José Mercury*, August 2, 1983

Summary

A paragraph can be a self-contained unit of discourse or it can be dependent upon the paragraphs that precede or follow it. In most discourses both types are common; each is a reflection of the author's purpose and style. The "well-made" paragraph (a stylistic option rather than a rule) begins with a topic sentence that reports the main idea, and is followed by any number of support sentences, some of which may, in turn, be followed by illustration sentences. Beginning writers sometimes put too much into a single paragraph, thus giving it a cluttered effect that disrupts clarity. Sometimes the opposite problem occurs: Writers will not develop their paragraphs sufficiently, and every sentence reads like a separate topic sentence—that is, remains on the same level of generality.

For Discussion

1. How much time do you spend thinking about paragraphing strategy in relation to other rhetorical strategies? What particular problems regarding structure, rhythm, content, length, and coherence do you encounter? When does paragraphing begin to concern you most, in the first, second, or final draft stage?

2. What is the relationship between paragraphing and readability? Does readability necessarily increase as paragraph size decreases? Find sample paragraphs to support your assertions.

3. Study each of the following paragraph clusters and identify their strengths and weaknesses in terms of apparent target audience and dominant rhetorical mode.

   a. I recently purchased two T-shirts from your company. They were not cheap in that I am a student and I don't earn much money. After wearing one of them for a couple of hours I noticed a long run in the material and a small hole. These were not present when I purchased the shirt, nor did I do anything to cause these defects. I attempted to return the T-shirts to the store, but was told by one of the salespersons that I had caused the problem. He told me that I could not be allowed to exchange the shirt for another, nor be given a refund.

      Your company has a fine reputation for quality clothing. I hope you can assist me in getting a fair adjustment.

      I have enclosed the damaged T-shirt for you to examine.

      Thank you for your assistance.

   b. We got into our foul weather gear because the latest forecast included a 50 percent likelihood of a squall. We also decided to bring along extra drinking water. Finally we started out under power from the estuary. Almost immediately the wind started to gust heavily and the bay got rougher, with swells reaching eight feet. As I made my way to the bow of the craft to hoist the jib and the mainsail, I got drenched in minutes from the splashing water against the hull of the clipper. Once all the sails had been hoisted, the hard work was finished. Hours later, after several more bouts with the storm, the captain turned the helm over to me. I quickly trimmed the twelve hundred square feet of sail in an effort to pick up more speed.

   c. The time has come: You drive to your girlfriend's house for that very important first date. What's the best way to proceed? First, you try to be calm, self-assured, but not to a fault. Of course you are bound to be nervous to some extent, but she'll be nervous, too. Think about *her* nervousness, not yours. That is, think about what you can do to make her feel at ease. Then, there's the business of good manners.

      You may wonder: In this day of changing male-female roles, will you look stupid opening doors for her, or pulling the chair back for her to sit down at the restaurant?

      The answer is: Absolutely not. Don't confuse good manners with male chauvinism.

   d. Never purchase food in cans that are badly dented or that have bulging lids.

Never eat canned or jarred foods that emit a foul odor. The danger is botulism. Botulism is an often fatal variety of food poisoning caused by the botulin organism. There are several symptoms of botulism you should be aware of.

These symptoms include vomiting, muscular weakness, disturbed vision, and sharp abdominal pains.

FOR WRITING

1. Think about your past employment experiences, pleasurable or unpleasurable, and do the following:
   a. Write a cluster of three or more paragraphs in which you express a moment of frustration or delight at one of your jobs.
   b. Using either the same job or another one as a subject, compose a paragraph cluster in which you advise a newcomer on how to perform a particular task or how to maintain a particular attitude.
   c. Now write a paragraph cluster in which you try to persuade your target audience (e.g., the company's board of directors) to change a long-established but outmoded policy.

2. Rewrite each of the paragraph clusters in the third topic in "For Discussion." Rephrase where necessary to maintain coherence and conciseness.

3. Compose a "well-made" paragraph for each of the following topic sentences. You may use these topic sentences as they are or modify them.
   a. The town I grew up in had some fascinating old buildings in it.
   b. My cat [dog] has a personality all her own.
   c. I've discovered a new way to cook hamburger.
   d. Have you often wondered what it would be like if people could read each other's minds?

4. Read the following paragraph from an essay by Ralph Waldo Emerson titled "Gifts," then divide it into shorter paragraphs, revising as you see fit; you may want to condense it. The goal here is not to improve Emerson's style—that would be presumptuous to say the least—but to adapt his style for an audience more concerned with content than with prose artistry.

   It is said that the world is in a state of bankruptcy, that the world owes the world more than the world can pay, and ought to go into chancery, and be sold. I do not think this general insolvency, which involves in some sort all the population, to be the reason for the difficulty experienced at Christmas and New Year, and other times, in bestowing gifts; since it is always so pleasant to be generous, though very vexatious to pay debts. But the impediment lies in the choosing. If, at any time, it comes into my head that a present is due from me to somebody, I am puzzled what to give, until the opportunity is gone. Flowers and fruits are always fit presents; flowers, because they are a proud assertion that a ray of beauty outvalues all the utilities of the world. These gay natures contrast with the somewhat stern countenance of ordinary nature: They are like music heard out of a workhouse. Nature does not cocker us: we are children, not pets: she is not fond: everything is dealt to us without fear or favor, after severe universal laws. . . .

COMPUTER WRITING

For students working in pairs at a terminal: Student A types a large block of text, perhaps one full page, from a previously completed essay, but does not indicate the original paragraph junctures. Student B then reads through Student A's text and makes the junctures where he or she thinks they are supposed to be. This is done very easily by placing the cursor on the first letter of the first word at the beginning of the presumed new paragraph, pressing the return key, and then indenting five spaces. After comparing Student B's version with Student A's original, the two students change roles and repeat the exercise with a block of text from one of Student B's essays.

Exploring Words and Meanings

CHAPTER 14

Words are atoms of thought, and like atoms of matter, they take on a new character when combined together to form larger structures. A word by itself, without context, however intrinsically beautiful it may sound, has only limited meaning. Take the word *celestial*: we can give it a "simpler" synonym, like *heavenly*, or we can give it a full dictionary definition, "Of or pertaining to the sky or heavens,"* but a definition alone does not constitute full meaning.† For a word to be truly meaningful, it must be placed into a sentence:

- Your eyes, Gladys darling, are *celestial*.
- Yehudi Menuhin creates *celestial* music with his violin.
- Galileo's telescope opened a new era in *celestial* observation.

As you can see, the meaning of the word changes slightly from sentence to sentence, although the general definition remains the same. In the third sentence, *celestial* is meant to be taken literally, referring to the

---

*This definition is taken from the *Funk & Wagnall's Standard Desk Dictionary*.

†When we say, "Look up the meaning of that word," we are using the term *meaning* interchangeably with *definition*. However, definitions have only limited meaning, extracted from customary uses of the word.

heavens. However, in the first two sentences, *celestial* is used metaphorically;* the speaker is reminded of heaven when gazing into Gladys's eyes, or when listening to Yehudi Menuhin perform. Of course the speaker could be speaking ironically, generating a meaning opposite to that which is expressed on the surface if Gladys were, say, a frog, or if Yehudi Menuhin were a notoriously poor violinist. Unless we have a larger context, though, we would have no way of knowing this.

Understanding the influence of context upon words is important for students of writing. By examining the properties of words—their denotative and connotative values, their capacity to grow into metaphors or wither into clichés, their ability to control an author's level of formality—you will gain insight into the relationship of word to context.

Denotation and Connotation

The simplest way to distinguish between denotation, the literal meaning, and connotation, the associative meaning, is the way of logicians: That which *denotes* points to something, whereas that which *connotes* infers or hints at. The words *that church* in "That church is a thousand years old" refer to a particular church. Of course we could include the name of the church: "Reims Cathedral is a thousand years old." Both *church* and *Reims Cathedral* are denotative in this context.

For a term to be *connotative*, it must invoke the whole concept with all its possible objective (rational) and subjective (emotive) meanings. In the sentence, "Churches stir the soul," *churches* is connotative. The word doesn't single out any specific church or type of church, but it asserts what is assumed to be elemental to all churches.

But the uses of denotation and connotation are not as separate and distinct as the preceding definition may suggest; sometimes words acquire both literal and associative values. The literal, denotative value, formulated as a universal definition, would be the standard dictionary definition. However, the associative, connotative value would be an unestablished personal meaning, which may or may not be formulated as a definition, depending on how widespread the association becomes. For example, the term *rainbows* is clearly denotative in the sentence, "Rainbows are caused by the refraction of light passing through water droplets," but it is both connotative and denotative in the sentence, "May your life be filled with rainbows." In the last sentence, the word denotes

---

*See pp. 319–322 of this chapter.

not actual rainbows but events long hoped for. *Rainbows* is thus a metaphor for these hoped-for events, but it is still denotative in the sense that this meaning has been established for virtually everyone. On the other hand, *rainbow* is connotative in this same context: It evokes associations that cannot quite be formulated as a standard definition. Think of what goes through your mind at the mention of *rainbow* in such a context: child fantasies? Dorothy in the land of Oz? romance? The associations are rich and varied. A writer wishing to take advantage of the connotative resources of *rainbow* might come up with a passage like this:

> Joan noticed the rainbow that had formed just above the mountains in the direction in which she was driving. The sense of dread she felt whenever she thought of returning home gradually began to fade. Maybe things would be different. She increased her speed and wondered just how long the rainbow would last.

Here the connotations of *rainbow* are more subtle and numerous, mainly because an entire paragraph is used to develop the association, not just one sentence. As you might guess, the connotative dimension of language is what makes symbolism* possible.

Many words trigger either favorable or unfavorable connotations when their original denotative meanings are transplanted to another context. The word *mob*, for example, denotes a disorderly crowd: "The mob was controlled by riot police." But when used in a different context, "The mob of teenagers cheered the rock group," the author wishes either consciously or unconsciously to equate *teenagers* with *disorderly crowd*, and so triggers a negative connotation.

Sometimes we can supply either a positive or a negative connotation to a term, depending on the context into which we place it. The words *lecture* and *smart* have this potential:

Positive: The Shakespeare scholar presented a fascinating *lecture* on the theme of betrayal in *King Lear*.

Negative: I got a big *lecture* from my mom when I came home at 4:00 A.M.

Positive: Joe made a *smart* move by sacrificing his pawn.

Negative: You think you're *smart*, throwing spitballs at passersby, don't you?

In general, though, we keep a repertoire of words for triggering predictable positive or negative connotations, or for ensuring that no connotative values will be generated. Here is a sampling:

---

*See the Handbook, "Rhetorical and Grammatical Principles," Symbol.

Neutral	Positive	Negative
female	woman	broad
male	man	brute
mechanic	automotive technician	grease monkey
lavatory	restroom	toilet
writer	essayist, novelist	hack
police officer	law enforcement officer	copper

**Diction Skills Checkpoint A:
Denotation and Connotation**

Directions: For each of the following neutral words, supply a word that can carry a negative connotation and one that can carry a positive connotation. Then compose an appropriate sentence for each of the three words.

1. Neutral: obese
   Negative: _____
   Positive: _____
   Neutral sentence: _____
   Negative sentence: _____
   Positive sentence: _____

2. Neutral: computer programmer
   Negative: _____
   Positive: _____
   Neutral sentence: _____
   Negative sentence: _____
   Positive sentence: _____

3. Neutral: physician
   Negative: _____
   Positive: _____
   Neutral sentence: _____
   Negative sentence: _____
   Positive sentence: _____

Toward Maintaining Clarity in Diction

We have an obligation, as writers, to use the full resources of our language. We also have an obligation to be as clear as possible in conveying meaning. Clarity, though, should not be confused with complexity.

A writer can express simple and complex ideas clearly by choosing words that are both accurate and economical, and by choosing modes of expression and explanation that are appropriate to the target audience.

Let us now consider a few commonsense guidelines for revising to improve clarity of expression:

1. Use your terms consistently.
2. Avoid inadvertent tense shifts.
3. Use expressions that are sufficiently accurate for the context.
4. Use unfamiliar words correctly.
5. Be as concise as the rhetorical situation allows.

Use your terms consistently. When composing our first drafts, we sometimes use different terms for the same concept, which can easily confuse the reader. Consider this example:

> Rex is facing several emotional predicaments. His problems, though, are common among teenagers.

Do the words *predicaments* and *problems* refer to the same, or to different, referents? The sentence gives us no clue. Here is a possible revision:

> Rex is facing several emotional problems. These problems, though, are common among teenagers.

Or, here's a more concise version:

> Rex is facing several emotional problems common among teenagers.

Diction Skills Checkpoint B: Consistent Use of Terms

Directions: For each passage, reword where necessary to improve the consistency of terminology.

1. Whenever we develop effective procedures, it's necessary to explain each step in these methods to all personnel.
2. Adults should always treat young people with as much respect as they pay to other older people. Teenagers are guaranteed the same basic rights as seniors.
3. The solar system consists of nine worlds. All of these planetary bodies are inhospitable to life except our own planet earth.

Avoid inadvertent tense shifts. When putting a narrative down quickly on paper in a rough draft, we can easily forget about tense and unwittingly shift from present to past, or vice versa:

> The huge waves tossed our boat around wildly and threatened to topple us over. I am suddenly panic-stricken, and try to row toward shore. But nothing I could do helped. The things got even worse, it seems.

The reader is as tossed around chronologically as the narrator is physically. What is present action and what is past action? Most likely, everything takes place in what is called "the literary present": the past tense of a narrative is used merely as a storytelling device. Some modern authors use the present tense for narrating to create a heightened sense of immediacy. But inexperienced writers may find this an uncomfortable way to narrate and inevitably slip back into the more natural past tense. This is, incidentally, one of the most common causes of tense shifting. The preceding passage ought to be revised as follows:

> The huge waves tossed our boat around wildly and threatened to topple us over. I was suddenly panic-stricken, and tried rowing toward shore. But nothing I did helped. Then things got even worse, it seemed.

Diction Skills Checkpoint C: Tense Shifts

Directions: Check each of the following passages for unwarranted shifts in tense. Revise where necessary.

1. It's fun taking time off to trek in the mountains, an activity I always enjoyed doing as a child.
2. Todd mounts the bridge's guardrail and did a handstand before the horrified spectators.
3. After packing all their belongings, they begin their journey across the country. After three days, they decided that they had traveled far enough.
4. Sandra could not decide which turnoff to take to get to her uncle's ranch, so she takes a wild guess, and luckily it turned out to be the right one.
5. Even though union leaders and company executives are debating the retirement benefits issue, nobody felt that they would reach an agreement by contract expiration time.

Use expressions that are sufficiently accurate for the context. We sometimes like the sound of certain words to the point of using them without regard to the level of usage we have already subconsciously adopted:

Well guys, I gotta zoom out of here in approximately five minutes.

Why use a mouthful of syllables like *approximately* when *about* would work just fine in this context?

> Ladies and gentlemen, I regret to inform you that our distinguished speaker cannot appear with us tonight, as a result of his having suddenly gotten sicker than a dog.

The audience, too, would quickly grow ill hearing that.

Use unfamiliar words correctly. Often when we have had too little experience with a word (for example, it is in our reading vocabulary but not in our writing vocabulary), we may confuse that word with another similar-sounding word. A student once talked enthusiastically about the *concubine* of knowledge that a liberal arts education can offer. When questioned about this usage, he replied innocently, "But isn't that just another word for the horn of plenty?" The teacher explained that the word he was trying to think of was *cornucopia*, and that it would be in his best interest to study carefully the difference in meaning between the two words. In the following essay, William Safire brings this point home vividly:

EASIER TO START A WAR THAN CONSULT A DICTIONARY

"I thought they taught English at the Naval Academy," writes Charles Maechling, Jr. of the Carnegie Endowment for International Peace in Washington. He attached a clipping quoting a letter written by Gen. Robert Barrow, commandant of the Marine Corps, to the Secretary of Defense.

Barrow was complaining to his civilian chief about incidents involving U.S. Marines serving in Lebanon. He contended that the episodes had been "timed, orchestrated and executed for obtuse Israeli political purposes," which the Israelis promptly denied.

What did the general mean by the word obtuse? A Marine Corps spokesman, asked this question, replied as if by the numbers: "The letter speaks for itself."

The harassed spokesman looked up the dictionary definition: "blunt, dull, insensitive." From that, he ventured a tentative interpretation: that the Israelis had taken a bold, blunt move.

That didn't add up; a "political purpose" is a phrase that demands a modifier imputing deviousness, not dullness. Besides, the only man who knew for certain what Barrow meant was Barrow. I went on up the line, and a higher-level spokesman, Lt. Col. Walt DeForest, sent word to the general that a language columnist wanted his definition of the word "obtuse."

Crisp as a command barked out on a drill field came the definition from Barrow: *Obtuse* to him meant "vague, unclear, difficult to understand."

The general may be the only one to give the word that meaning. To most of the rest of the English-speaking world, obtuse means "blunt and insensitive," not "vague and unclear."

My purpose was not to make fun of a brave officer who evidently had been asked, for political purposes, to write a letter to the Secretary of Defense. On the contrary, my job is to be helpful. What word was he reaching for that sounds like obtuse?

Obscure means "vague, murky, not easily perceived"; that was part of what he had in mind, since it nicely modifies "political purposes." But the general's definition included a second meaning, as he reported to me: "hard to understand," which is not precisely the meaning of *obscure*.

For that hard-to-understand shade of meaning, we can turn to *abstruse*, which is rooted in the Latin for "to thrust away" as if to hide. That means "recondite, profound, difficult to comprehend."

I think that the head of the Marine Corps inadvertently took obscure ("vague") and mixed it with abstruse ("complicated") to come up with obtuse. The trouble is that obtuse already has a meaning, which is "insensitive," and is neither "vague" nor "hard to understand." Before using an unfamiliar word to excoriate another government, the Pentagon might try looking it up. The State Department is better at this sort of thing: It may be *obfuscatory* or *obscurantist* at times, but it is rarely obtrusive when heaping obvious obloquy.

Here is a good way to avoid confusion: Obscure and abstruse are usually applied to murky or profound *things*, and obtuse is ordinarily applied to an unfeeling *person*. For example, Eric Conger of New York, writing about a political coinage by my Times colleague Mary Cantwell, asks: "How could you resist pointing out the delicious etymological aptness of the name Cantwell, whose owner we are to credit for coining the phrase 'squeal rule'? Or did you, and am I obtuse?"

He is having fun with the noun *cant*, which comes from the Latin *cantus*, meaning "song," and originally described the singsong dialect of beggars and thieves; it now refers to any insider lingo or argot, and one who uses cant well is apt at coining political phrases. Conger, in asking if he is being obtuse, wonders if his antennae missed anything.

According to "A Dictionary of Soldier Talk," the new lexicon by Elting, Cragg and Deal, the mock-cool reaction to any military blunder is to dismiss the victims profanely "if they can't take a joke." I salute our commandant and his unique modifier for "political purposes"; in years to come, militant solecists may obscure the meaning of obtuse.

William Safire

A word that is used improperly due to its physical resemblance to the appropriate word is called a *malapropism*; the term was named after Mrs. Malaprop, a character in Richard Sheridan's drama *The Rivals* who comically misuses words in this fashion. Here are a few other malapropisms:

Evelyn has a *vicious* (voracious) appetite this morning.
Mr. Crumley is an *antiquated* (antiquarian) bookdealer.
After the funeral, the body was *interned* (interred).

Diction Skills Checkpoint D: Accurate Word Choice

Directions: Decide which word(s) are incorrect for the context, and replace them with more appropriate words.

1. Little Bobby revealed how musically prestigious he was by playing Beethoven's *Appassionata* from memory.

2. My buddies and I, dog-tired from a long haul at the foundry, inferred from each other's lamentations that we were all set for a few beers.

3. The geologist examined the crystalline structure of the volcanic rock and reckoned that a mighty strong pressure had been partially responsible.

4. Dr. Sanders's diagnosis was that the bone would heal completely in two months.

5. The cavern was especially eerie with its long stalactites and stalagmites gleaming like the teeth of Tyrannosaurus rex.

Be as concise as the rhetorical situation allows. Learning to write well is not only frustrating at times, but it can also be downright confusing. Consider the notion of wordiness. Your teachers will tell you in one breath: "Develop your ideas! Go into more detail! This is too cut-and-dried!" Yet in the next breath they will say: "Trim this down! You could have said the same thing in just half as many words! Be concise!" Can any sense be made of these apparently contradictory objectives?

First, we need to be clear about the distinction between *conciseness* and *insufficient development*. This is not always easy to do. Although a passage could be shortened without loss of essential meaning, writers are not always out to transmit ideas like telegraph messages. Consider Macbeth's agonized cry:

> Out, out brief candle!
> Life's but a walking shadow, a poor player
> That struts and frets his hour upon the stage
> And then is heard no more. It is a tale
> Told by an idiot, full of sound and fury,
> Signifying nothing.

This passage could have been condensed to something like, "Life is a furious yet brief and senseless idiot's tale"; but Shakespeare wanted emotional involvement from his audience, a sharing in the unfathomable mystery of human destiny, to be reflected in the words. Thus we could say, *in light of the author's intentions*, the passage is remarkably concise.

Wordiness has many causes, but most often it is a first-draft phenomenon; it's only natural to use more words than one needs during that initial draft, when you are more concerned with content than with style. Another problem is that novice writers sometimes try too hard to impress the reader by using unnecessarily formal or complex language. This usually stems from an uncertainty regarding readers' expectations. Consider this example:

> It was with utmost determination, after considerable hesitation, that the interrogation of his roommate about the missing watch was decided upon by Ellis.

Perhaps the author of this passage doesn't want to impress anyone with his or her vocabulary, but simply does not realize that comprehension is impeded when more words are used than needed to convey an idea. The author needed only to write:

> Ellis decided once and for all to question his roommate about the missing watch.

Notice that the strength of this revision is due not only to the removal of unnecessary words, but also to the word changes that clarify the meaning of the phrase: the noun phrase *the interrogation* becomes the infinitive *to question*; the passive voice in *was decided upon by Ellis*, becomes the active voice, *Ellis decided*.

Diction Skills Checkpoint E: Conciseness

Directions: Revise the following passages to make the sentences more concise. Change or rearrange the word order if necessary.

1. Whenever Jenny and her boyfriend Nelson go out on a date together, they sooner or later get into a needless quarrel as to whether or not they should go see this film or that film, or go to this restaurant or that restaurant.

2. It was mutually agreed upon by the city council last week that a museum of computer technology would be erected once formal and signed approval from the office of the mayor was received.

3. My purpose in this essay is to convey the idea that Nathaniel Hawthorne in his famous novel *The Scarlet Letter* creates the feeling in the

reader's mind that sin and virtue are sometimes unable to be distinguished from one another.

Metaphorical Language

When two outwardly dissimilar concepts are identified with each other, the resulting utterance is called a *metaphor*, from the Greek *metaphora*, "to transfer." The properties of the object forming the comparison, known as the *vehicle*, are "transferred" to the subject, or the *tenor*, as illustrated in the following metaphor composed by Christopher Morley:

New York is the nation's thyroid gland.
   Tenor   *Vehicle*

Metaphors can have considerable impact in our writing, mainly because they present a relationship in a more concentrated form than do ordinary comparisons.* Morley could have conveyed his intended meaning more explicitly, and conventionally, by writing the following: "New York is one of the nation's most important cities because it regulates the economic and cultural metabolism or growth of the whole country in much the same way as the thyroid gland regulates the metabolism of the human body." But the virtue of the metaphorical approach is that it makes a stronger impact on the reader: The metaphor *surprises* us by identifying a city with a gland all in one brief sentence.

Some metaphors are more ambitious than others, such as when the author sustains the metaphorical relationship over an entire paragraph, or even an entire essay. If Morley had continued to write about New York in terms of either glandular functions or other anatomical features (the *bowels* of the Lower East Side, the *spleen* of the Garment District, the *heart*† of Midtown, or whatever), we would say that he was building an *extended metaphor*. Note how, in his book *Mortal Lessons: Notes on the Art of Surgery*, surgeon-author Richard Selzer describes the appearance and function of the human liver by using the extended metaphor *liver cells equals building blocks of a house* to make the description as vivid as possible for his audience of laypersons:

---

*See the discussion of comparison and contrast in Chapter 6, "Principles of Development: Aiming to Inform."

†*Heart* is so overused that it has virtually lost its metaphoric impact. We call such metaphors *dead* or *dormant metaphors*.

Envision, if you will, a house whose stones are living hexagonal tiles not unlike those forming the bathroom floors of first-class hotels. These are the hepatocytes, the cellular units of the liver. Under the microscope they have a singular uniformity, each as like unto its fellow as the antlers of a buck, and all fitted together with a lovely imprecision so as to form a maze of crooked hallways and oblong rooms.

And consider the Reverend Martin Luther King's richly metaphorical "I Have a Dream" speech, wherein King uses images associated with banks and banking as a vehicle for the abstract concept of justice—specifically, for America's constitutional guarantee of freedom for all its citizens:

> America has given the Negro people a bad check; a check which has come back marked "insufficient funds." But we refuse to believe that the bank of justice is bankrupt. We refuse to believe that there are insufficient funds in the great vaults of opportunity of this nation.

Our language is saturated with metaphors. In a sense, it is tough to employ language that is not metaphorical. For example, look again at the sentence you just read: *Saturated*, *sense*, *tough*, and *employ* are metaphors because they have literal meanings other than what is intended here. We may literally saturate ourselves with cookies (the word is derived from the Latin *satur*, "full of food"), but we figuratively saturate our language with metaphors.

The metaphor is an important means of adding color and comprehension to writing—to all writing, in fact, not just to "expressive" writing. The color results from the way metaphors spark our imaginations: We learn to see the similar in the outwardly dissimilar; and the more we think in terms of interrelationships, the more insightful our comprehension becomes.

Imagine, for example, that you are taking a course in introductory astronomy and your professor makes statements such as the following:

- Galaxies are *island universes* in the *ocean* of space.
- The surface of Venus is a *cauldron* of poisonous gases.
- Our solar system includes the *mother* sun and *her* nine *offspring*.

As you will notice, the tenors of each statement (*galaxies*, *Venus*, and *solar system*) are made more comprehensible by the vehicles they receive (*island universes, ocean; cauldron; mother, her offspring*) in the metaphor. The metaphorical elements encourage you to think of a galaxy in space as analogous* to an island in an ocean,† or of Venus's surface as analogous to a great vat of boiling substance, and so on. These metaphor vehicles are more familiar to the audience than are the tenors; thus the vehicles assure quick comprehension.

In their book *Metaphors We Live By*, Professors George Lakoff and Mark Johnson classify metaphors as either orientational, structural, or ontological. Here are some of the examples Lakoff and Johnson provide for each category:

Orientational Metaphors

Concept: Good is up; bad is down.
Examples: Things are looking up; We hit a *peak* last year, but it's been *downhill* ever since.

Structural Metaphors

Concept: Ideas are plants.
Examples: His ideas have finally come to *fruition*; Mathematics has many *branches*.

Concept: Life is a container.
Examples: I've had a *full* life; Her life is *crammed* with activities.

Ontological Metaphors‡

Concept: Inflation as an entity.
Example: Inflation is backing us into a corner.

Concept: Mind as machine.
Example: The *wheels are turning*; I'm a little *rusty* today.

Metaphorical language is the result of metaphorical thinking; before you can add such language to your own writing style, you need to practice thinking metaphorically. To some extent you already do, as you've seen here, but to control your metaphorical thinking better, you need regular practice. One method is to do some metaphorical free-associating. As you face your blank sheet of paper or computer screen, look around you and list what you see. Your list might look like this:

- window
- floppy disks

---

*See the Handbook, "Rhetorical and Grammatical Principles," Analogy.

†The word *galaxy* is itself a dormant metaphor (Greek *gala*, or "milk"). In ancient times the part of our own galaxy visible from Earth reminded the Greeks of milk streams (hence "Milky Way"), and specifically, of the milk flowing from the breasts of the goddess Hera.

‡In ontological (relating to being or existence) metaphors, objects and ideas are treated as tangible entities.

- roommate's tennis racket
- books
- file cabinet
- pile of dirty laundry

Next, think of an abstract concept, such as *freedom* or *college life*, and describe that concept in terms of one or more of the objects you've recorded. Here are some possibilities:

- Freedom is an open window.
- College life is your roommate's tennis racket buried in a pile of dirty laundry alongside a stack of books.
- Books unshackle the mind and spirit.
- I need to reformat my disks (i.e., I need to reorganize my thoughts).
- My brain is an overstuffed file cabinet.
- I've been resorting my thoughts lately.

Exercises such as this will help you integrate metaphorical associations into your normal thought processes.

Diction Skills Checkpoint F: Metaphor

Directions: Use each of the following words, or variations thereof, metaphorically in a sentence:

1. cave
2. hammer
3. sand dune
4. curtains
5. blanket

Euphemisms and Clichés

Sometimes metaphors are used for the wrong reasons or they turn stale from overuse, in which case they are known as *euphemisms*. The word comes from the Greek *eu*, "pleasant" or "good," plus *pheme*, "speech," meaning expressions chosen for their pleasing sound as well as for their pleasing connotations. *Clichés*, from the French word *clicher*, to "stereotype," are by contrast once-original expressions that have become trite.

Euphemisms

First of all, some euphemisms are not a problem. Most of us use the term *bathroom* or *restroom* instead of *toilet* when we are speaking to anyone outside our immediate family. One could argue, though, that expressions such as *powder room* or *little boy's* or *girl's room* sound a bit silly. Similarly, when a loved one dies we hesitate to be blunt, so we use the words *passed away* or *gone to sleep*. Yet we might find distasteful other euphemisms for death, such as *journeyed to the Great Beyond* or *ventured to the Other Side*, even in times of bereavement.

The euphemisms we should make an effort to avoid, though, are the ones that distort truth, often to the point of generating a meaning completely opposite to the real one. Calling a missile armed with a nuclear warhead a *peacemaker* is such a euphemism; saying one is having an animal *fixed*, meaning sterilized, castrated, or spayed, is another. The term coined for such truth-distorting expressions is *doublespeak*.

Clichés

Clichés are rarely acceptable outside of colloquial conversation. The reason is simple: Use of clichés suggests a lack of originality of thought, and that contradicts the very reason for writing in the first place. However, clichés are so numerous it is sometimes easy to use them unwittingly, no matter how original a thinker one may be. But, like spelling and grammar errors, they tend to cast a shadow of amateurishness over the writing.

Most clichés are easy to identify; these are metaphors gone sour, "fad" words, and miscellaneous figures of speech like onomatopoeic expressions. Here is a sampling:

- Shirley's room is *clean as a whistle*.

- Tony seems caught *between the devil and the deep blue sea*.

- *Uptight* from the *hustle and bustle*, we got out of the office *quick as a wink*.

- George is *first and foremost* a *chip off the old block*.

- I've got *an axe to grind* (or *a bone to pick*) with you.

- The cookie thief was caught *red-handed*.

- Their poor behavior was just *the tip of the iceberg*.

- Paula and Frank had a *storybook wedding*.
- Sam would gladly *give you the shirt off his back*.

Many clichés are quotations or allusions to fables, parables, songs, and so on:

- Candace *cried wolf* once too often.
- I have witnessed *the slings and arrows of outrageous fortune*.
- We left the examination *sadder but wiser*.
- *Fools rush in where angels fear to tread*.

Once again, many clichés, even some of the worst ones, are acceptable in casual conversation. "There's a sight for sore eyes," "Our raises are few and far between," and "It's hotter than hell outside" are examples.

**Diction Skills Checkpoint G:
Clichés and Euphemisms**

Directions: Substitute the clichés or euphemisms in the following sentences for more standard expressions, where appropriate.

1. The sky was clear as a bell this morning when, feeling like a million, I showered and hit the road.
2. Priscilla, mad as a hatter, gave her boyfriend her two cents' worth the instant he arrived.
3. Bob, after receiving notice that his services at Anodyne, Inc. were no longer required, decided to fight it come hell or high water.
4. We extended our condolences to Mrs. Edwards, whose sister had just passed away.
5. Sarah was pleased as punch when she discovered that she was far and away the top choice for the new directorship.

The Dictionary and the Writer

You've undoubtedly used a dictionary to look up the meanings of words, to check their spellings, pronunciations, syllabications, and parts of speech, and perhaps to study their etymologies (origins) as well. But you may not be familiar with two particular facts about dictionaries: One, there are several *kinds* of dictionaries, serving a wide range of writers' needs. Two, your dictionary can serve as much more than a reference tool. Let us briefly survey the important reference functions of dictionaries, if only to reinforce what you already know.

Ways to Use a Dictionary

Spelling   Despite the paradoxical situation of having to know how a word is spelled before you can look it up to check the correct spelling, the task is not too difficult. We usually know how to spell most of the word; it is only when we are not sure about the first two or three letters that it can be a problem. *Mnemonic, prerogative,* and *ophthalmologist* are the sorts of words that are hard to locate if we cannot spell them. Keep in mind, too, that some words have variant spellings, like *theater* and *theatre, sceptical* and *skeptical,* and *disk* and *disc.* No matter how descriptive, rather than prescriptive, modern dictionaries claim to be, they will list what *they* consider to be the preferred spelling first. The choice, however, should be your own; but stay with that spelling once you have adopted it.

Syllabication   The sole purpose of dividing words into syllables is to let writers know when and where to hyphenate a word at the end of a line. This can be tricky because the basis for syllable division can be morphological, based on units of meaning (such as the suffix *-ly*), or phonological, based on the manner of pronunciation. Here's one rule of syllabication you can be sure of: *Never hyphenate single syllable words*, such as *thro-ugh.*

Pronunciation   Most dictionaries are careful to make their pronunciation keys broad enough to allow for dialect variation. These pronunciation keys are described in detail in the dictionary's prefatory material, and they appear in a concise format at the bottom of every page.

Students who find themselves turning frequently to the dictionary for spelling, syllabication, or pronunciation may find it useful to purchase a small, pocket-sized "spelling dictionary," which includes no definitions. This type of specialized dictionary can reduce the time it takes to look up a word.

Part-of-Speech Classification   Many words fall into more than one part-of-speech category without changing form. For example, *rain* can be a noun, a verb, and an adjective. Always check to see if a part-of-speech label immediately precedes the definition in question. The standard abbreviations are as follows: n. (noun), v. (verb), adv. (adverb), adj. (adjective), prep. (preposition), conj. (conjunction), and interj. (interjection). Proper nouns—any words in the dictionary that are capitalized, are sometimes not identified as such.

Definition Most dictionaries begin with the definition closest to the etymology and proceed to the most current use. Standard definitions precede specialized ones.

No dictionary can be exhaustive in treating every possible nuance of meaning; any one definition will contain numerous potential "shades of meaning" depending on the context in which the writer places the word. Consider, as an example, any of the four principal definitions of *fortune* in *Webster's New World Dictionary*:

1. the supposed power thought of as bringing good or bad to people; luck; chance; fate: often personified
2. what happens or is going to happen to one; one's lot, good or bad, esp. one's future lot
3. good luck; success; prosperity
4. a large quantity of money or possessions; wealth; riches

We can, inventive writers that we are, do much more with any one of those definitions by generating connotations in our own writing. For example, according to the first definition, we could personify Fortune as one who is as sadistic as she is cruel, or as one who constantly blunders into misfortune herself, if we have a taste for cosmic comedy. And even though Fortune has always been personified as female, nothing can stop us from changing her sex.

In other words, no matter how detailed or seemingly exhaustive a word's definition is, it is never more than a *generalization* of the way the word has been actually used. Occasionally, and this occurs less frequently in desk dictionaries than in unabridged ones, you will see quotations that illustrate the definition in question; still, the context is only hinted at.

Another element of the definition is the *etymology*, the known or hypothetical origin of the word. Besides being fascinating in their own right, etymologies provide you with a good deal of insight into the nature of a word and can shed new (or should we say old) light on its current standard definitions. Take a word like *amateur*, for example. We have come to think of an amateur as someone unskilled, below the level of professionalism. Yet the etymology of the word reveals a very different meaning: *amateur* comes from the Latin *amare*, "to love." An amateur photographer, say, is one who engages in this activity for the *love* of it. By keeping the etymology of this word in mind, we avoid a common prejudice: that unless one can earn money doing a task, one cannot perform the task sufficiently well.

Getting back to *fortune*, the dictionary shows that the word comes from the Latin *fortuna*, "chance." (By the way, in Roman mythology, the goddess of fate was Fortuna—the origin, perhaps, of our "lady luck.") The connection between chance and riches—making "a fortune" in the stock market or having one's "fortune" told—is reestablished by the etymology.

A particularly fascinating book of word origins is Isaac Asimov's *Words of Science*, a collection of short narratives that clarify key scientific and technical concepts by focusing on the words themselves. Let's look at a typical entry—Asimov's story of *potassium*:

> Soap was not known to ancient peoples. The Greeks and Romans used oil as a cleaning agent. This sounds odd to us now, but oil will dissolve grease and help remove grime. Naturally, any substance that would help the oil do this would be much in demand. The ancients showed their desperation in that they sometimes added sand or other gritty material to the oil, for the sake of the scouring action, but that has obvious disadvantages.
>
> A more suitable additive was eventually found in the ash of certain woods. This ash would be stirred in water, which would dissolve out some of the substances in the ash. The water, with the substances dissolved in it, would be poured off into a large pot. The water would then be boiled off and the dry residue heated strongly. The powdery material that resulted was called (in English) *potash*. The two syllables run together in pronunciation so that most people don't notice that it simply means "pot ash." The Arabs, who were the great chemists of the Middle Ages, called the same material "alquili," meaning "the plant ash."
>
> When oil was heated with potash, a kind of soap was formed, so that a new and better cleaning material was developed.
>
> The British chemist Sir Humphrey Davy isolated a hitherto unknown metal in 1807, and, because it occurred in potash, he gave it the Latin-sounding name *potassium*. The Germans, oddly enough, gave it a Latin-sounding name derived from the same substance, but they used the Arabic word and called the metal *Kalium*. For that reason, the chemical symbol for the metal is K, even in those countries that call it potassium.
>
> Potash is one of a group of substances that share properties opposite to those possessed by acids. Such opposite-to-acid compounds are named *alkalis*, a word which obviously descends from the Arabic word for "potash."

Grammar and Usage Data A dictionary tells us much about the grammar and usage level of a word relative to a particular context. Many words, such as *cork*, exist as different parts of speech, in this case as a noun, verb, and adjective. We also learn that the word is used only as a *transitive* verb, which means that the predication action suggested by the verb must be directed toward an object: "Wally could not cork the bottle." The sentence, "Wally could not cork," in which the verb is used intransitively, would be ungrammatical.

A dictionary also provides information on types of word usage.

When the definition of a word, or the word itself, is nonstandard, the dictionary will tell you. Here are a few examples of typical usage indicators:

dial.: regional or ethnic usage (British *lift* for elevator).

slang: substandard, profane, or "in-group" language; self-consciously colorful and vigorous usage (*hooch* for illegal liquor*).

obsol.: obsolete word or definition; rarely used, if ever (*make one's toilet* for bathing, hairdressing, etc., from Old French *toile*, meaning "cloth," which in Middle French became *toilette*, a large protective cloth used for hairdressing and such).

Diction Skills Checkpoint H: Etymology

Directions: Look up the etymology of each word below, noting as much of the words' evolution as you can find; you may need to check more than one dictionary.

1. grammar
2. tragedy
3. bikini
4. denim
5. fornication

Levels of Usage

We usually talk about usage as standard or nonstandard use of language. In the context of standard usage, the term applies to the level of formality or informality. Nonstandard usage, strictly speaking, is neither formal nor informal; it is, rather, a dialect variation such as Black English or Cockney.

We may identify the following levels of standard usage:

1. *Extremely formal*: used in ceremonial speeches, proclamations, and homilies.

2. *Formal*: used in lectures and scholarly texts.

---

*"Hooch" is a shortened form of *Hoochinoo*, the tribal name of the Indians who made crude liquor.

3. *Informal*: used in polite conversation and personal essays.
4. *Extremely informal*: used in casual conversation.

Let's take a look at a sample of discourse from each level:

EXTREMELY FORMAL

I rise, Mr. President, for the purpose of announcing to the Senate that I have satisfactory evidence that the state of Mississippi, by a solemn ordinance of her people in convention assembled, has declared her separation from the United States. Under these circumstances, of course, my functions are terminated here. It has seemed to me proper, however, that I should appear in the Senate to announce that fact to my associates, and I will say but very little more.

    Jefferson Davis, Speech of Resignation from the United States Senate, January 21, 1861

FORMAL

Once we grasp the tremendously important role that words play in poetry, as compared to the role they play in prose, it may help us to arrive at a definition of the difference between the two categories. A poem will result when the genius of a language—its words, their sound and their sense—offers the genius of a poet an opportunity to perform a miracle.

    John Hall Wheelock, *What Is Poetry?*

INFORMAL

    I'm no scientist at all. I'm glad now, though, that I was pressured into becoming a scientist by my father and my brother. I understand how scientific reasoning and playfulness work, even though I have no talent for joining in. . . . I've spent a lot more time with scientists than with literary people, my brother's friends, mostly. I enjoy plumbers and carpenters and automobile mechanics, too.

    Kurt Vonnegut, Jr., *Palm Sunday*

EXTREMELY INFORMAL

The Donkeyman (spitting placidly): Queer things, mem'ries. I ain't ever been bothered much by 'em.

Smitty: No, you wouldn't be.

The Donkeyman: Not that I ain't had my share o' things goin' wrong; but I puts 'em out o' me mind, like, an' fergets 'em.

Smitty: But suppose you couldn't put them out of your mind? Suppose they haunted you when you were awake and when you were asleep—what then?

> The Donkeyman (quietly): I'd get drunk, same's you're doin'.
>
> Eugene O'Neill, *The Moon of the Caribbees*

Any one level of usage is seldom pure; the most formal discourse is occasionally laced with an informal or even an extremely informal witticism or aside. Informal discourse, similarly, will sometimes include a formal, analytic "moment." It's important for you as writer to be in control, to know when you are operating on one level of usage or another, and especially to avoid mixing standard with nonstandard usage. In the following example Mark Twain amusingly depicts the confusion that can result from such a "usage gap"; in this case, the gap occurs between a clergyman and a Nevada frontier "rough," who visits the man of cloth to inquire about a proper burial for his buddy Buck Fanshaw.

> [Scotty] sat down before the clergyman, placed his fire hat on an unfinished manuscript sermon under the minister's nose, took from it a red silk handkerchief, wiped his brow and heaved a sigh of dismal impressiveness, explanatory of his business. He choked, and even shed tears; but with an effort he mastered his voice and said in lugubrious tones:
> "Are you the duck that runs the gospel mill next door?"
> "Am I the—pardon me, I believe I do not understand?"
> With another sign and a half sob, Scotty rejoined:
> "Why you see we are in a bit of trouble, and the boys thought maybe you would give us a lift, if we'd tackle you—that is, if I've got the rights of it and you are the head clerk of the doxology works next door."
> "I am the shepherd in charge of the flock whose fold is next door."
> "The which?"
> "The spiritual adviser of the little company of believers whose sanctuary adjoins these premises."
> Scotty scratched his head, reflected a moment, and then said:
> "You ruther hold over me, pard. I reckon I can't call that hand. Ante and pass the buck."
> "How? I beg pardon. What did I understand you to say?"
> "Well, you've ruther got the bulge on me. Or maybe we've both got the bulge, somehow. You don't smoke me and I don't smoke you. You see, one of the boys has passed in his checks and we want to give him a good send-off, and so the thing I'm on now is to roust out somebody to jerk a little chin music for us and waltz him through handsome."
> "My friend, I seem to grow more and more bewildered. Your observations are wholly incomprehensible to me. Cannot you simplify them in some way? At first I thought perhaps I understood you, but I grope now. Would it not expedite matters if you restricted yourself to categorical statements of fact unencumbered with obstructing accumulations of metaphor and allegory?"
> Another pause, and more reflection. Then, said Scotty:
> "I'll have to pass, I judge."

"How?"

"You've raised me out, pard."

"I still fail to catch your meaning."

"Why, that last lead of yourn is too many for me—that's the idea. I can't neither trump nor follow suit."

The clergyman sank back in his chair perplexed. Scotty leaned his head on his hand and gave himself up to thought. Presently his face came up, sorrowful but confident.

"I've got it now, so's you can savvy," he said. "What we want is a gospel sharp. See?"

"A what?"

"Gospel sharp. Parson."

"Oh! Why did you not say so before? I am a clergyman—a parson."

"Now you talk! You see my blind and straddle it like a man. Put it there!"—extending a brawny paw, which closed over the minister's small hand and gave it a shake indicative of fraternal sympathy and fervent gratification.

"Now we're all right, pard. Let's start fresh. Don't you mind my snuffling a little—becuz we're in a power of trouble. You see, one of the boys has gone up the flume—"

"Gone where?"

"Up the flume—throwed up the sponge, you understand."

"Thrown up the sponge?"

"Yes—kicked the bucket—"

"Ah—has departed to that mysterious country from whose bourne no traveler returns."

"Return! I reckon not. Why pard, he's *dead!*"

"Yes, I understand."

Mark Twain, *Roughing It*

General and Specialized Diction

A casual thumbing through your desk dictionary will reveal that many definitions are arranged according to discipline or profession. Consider the word *neutral*. In *Webster's New World Dictionary* we find, in addition to the general definition of "not taking part in either side of a dispute or quarrel," the following specialized (subject-specific) uses:

Biology: same as *neuter*.

Chemistry: giving neither acid nor alkaline reaction.

Electricity: neither negative nor positive; uncharged.

Phonetics: pronounced with the tongue in the relaxed, mid-central position.

Mechanics: a disengaged position of gears, in which they do not transmit power from the engine to the operating parts.

Some terms are, we might say, highly specialized; they are inevitably the result of highly specialized research, involving a relatively small group of people. Such terminology is commonly referred to as *jargon*.*

Jargon is not really private language, however; it is simply language that has not yet had a chance to become public. It is a kind of linguistic shorthand that is used for two reasons: first, to make the transmittal of information among fellow specialists as economical as possible; and second, to account for principles, objects, and events that do not exist outside the specialized field. Much jargon is metaphorical. In computer technology, for example, we use terms like *chip*, *boot (up)*, *run (a program)*, and *floppy disk*, all of which may have nonmetaphorical and wordier referents. *Floppy disk* refers to a flexible magnetic information storage disk. Because jargon terms are functional, they are used in formal as well as informal contexts. A few terms, however, border on slang: *hacker* for a fanatical computer user; *hot rod* for a super-fast computer; and *kludge* for a sloppily assembled computer. Such terms have a smaller range of appropriate application. Tracy Kidder, in his Pulitzer-Prize-winning account of American computer culture titled *The Soul of a New Machine*, captures something of this strange computer jargon:

> "What goes on here is not part of the real world," [remarked Tom West of Westborough].
> "How so?"
> "Mmmmmmmmmmh. The language is different."
> Some of it was, and a phrase book, such as the *Penguin Dictionary of Computers*, could be useful. *ECO*—each letter pronounced—meant "engineering change order." Hence this remark: "A friend of mine told his girlfriend they had to *ECO* their relationship." *Give me a core dump* meant "Tell me your thoughts," for in the past, when computers used "core memories," engineers sometimes "dumped" the contents of malfunctioning machines' storage compartments to see what was wrong. A *stack* is a special small compartment of memory, a sort of in-box inside a computer; it holds information in the order in which the information is deposited, and when it gets overfull, it is said to "overflow." Hence the occasional complaint, "I've got a stack to overflow." "His mind is only one stack deep," says an engineer, describing the failings of a colleague.

A fascinating aspect of much scientific and technical jargon is that a lot of it filters rapidly into the mainstream. Few people today would refer

---

**Jargon also means language that is purposively obscure or evasive. This meaning is not suggested here.

sub-	below	submerge; subtract
supra-	above	supreme
super	above	supernatural
sur	above	surcharge; surmount

Latin Roots

alt	high	altitude
ann	year	annual; perennial
capit	head	capital; cap
corpus	body	incorporate; corpse
cruc	cross	crucify; crucial
ego	self	egocentric
fac	do; make	factory; artifact
fil	thread	filament; filter
hum	earth; soil	humus; exhume
lac	milk	lactate
mal	bad	malicious; malady
os	bone	ossify
ped	foot	pedestrian; bipedal
sec	cut	bisect; section
sol	sun	solar; solstice
spir	breath	inspire; respiration
terra	earth	terrain
vor	eat	voracious; herbivore
vox	voice	evoke; vocalize

Words and Imagination

"Any word," writes Emerson, "becomes poetic in the hands of a higher thought." That "higher thought" of which Emerson speaks is not so much of genius as it is of alertness, sensitivity, and eagerness to make words capture more of reality and beauty than they ordinarily can. Only by allowing our perceptions to dwell—to incubate—in our minds can we hope to capture the fullest meaning from those perceptions. A strong vocabulary is important, of course, but more is needed.

Let us look at three practical steps aspiring writers can take to develop their perceptions as well as their "word hoard":

Before writing, try to imagine what you want to write about. You'll need to interpret the word *imagine* in the most literal sense of "forming an

Greek Roots

anthropo	man; human	anthropology; philanthropy
bios	living	biology; symbiosis
chroma	color	chromatic
chron	time	chronological
eidos	image; shape	eidetic (memory)
eikon	image; shape	icon
erg	work	energy; erg
gam	marriage	bigamy; gamete
ge	earth	geology
gen	be born	genesis; gene
gramma	write	telegram
graph	write	graphic; telegraph
heli	sun	heliocentric; helium*
id	image; shape	idea; identity
koron	crown	coronation; corona
kosm	order	cosmos; microcosm
lex	speech; word	lexicon; lecture
lith	stone	lithograph; monolith
path	feel	pathetic; sympathy
phil	love	philanthropy
plat	flat	plate; plateau
poly	many	polygamy; polygon
proto	first; primal	proton; protoplasm
psych	mind; soul	psychology; psychic
tele	afar	television; telepathy

Latin Prefixes

bi-	two	bicycle; binocular
co-	together	cooperate; coherence
ex-	out of	exclude
extra-	out of	extraordinary
in-	not	ineffective
post-	after	postpone
re-	back; again	reflex
retro-	back; again	retroactive

Helium is so named because, strangely enough, the element was first discovered on the sun (via spectroscopic analysis) before it was discovered on Earth.

Greek Prefixes

a-	not; without	anemic; atypical
anti-	against	antidote; antifreeze
di-	two	dissect; dichotomy
dys-	not; fail	dysfunction
ec-	out(side)	eccentric
epi-	upon	epidemic; epidermis
eu-	well; good	euphoria; euthanasia
ex-	out(side)	external
pro-	before; ahead	proceed; prognosis
sym-	together; with	sympathy; symphony
syn-	together; with	synthesis

Front

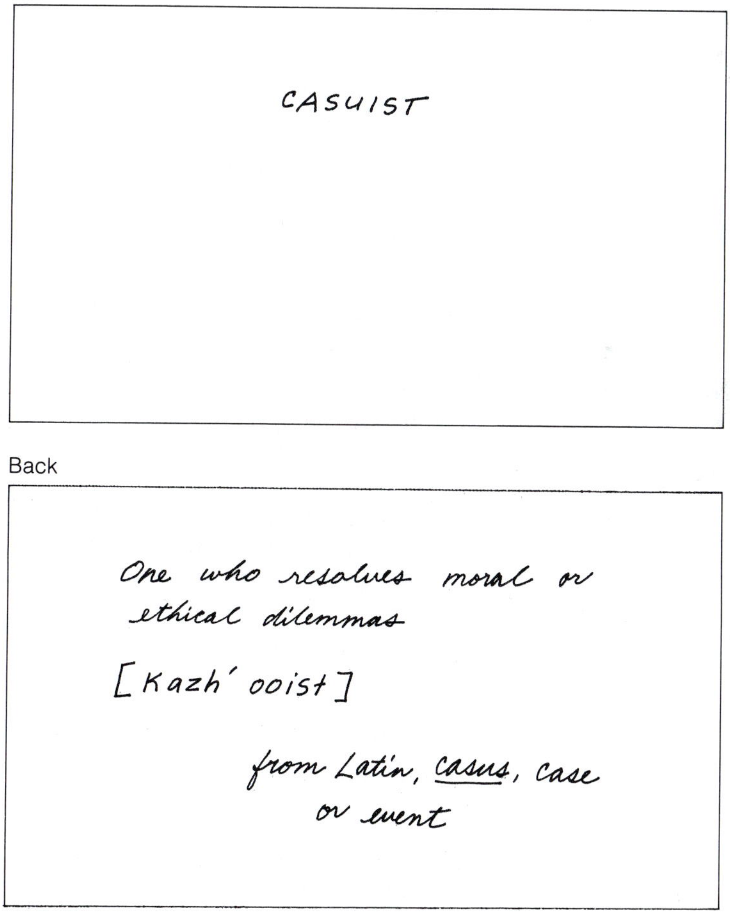

CASUIST

Back

One who resolves moral or ethical dilemmas

[kazh´ ooist]

from Latin, *casus*, case or event

Figure 14-1

Sample vocabulary card

to terms like *laser*, *meltdown*, *printout*, *EKG*, and *videodisc* as jargon.

In your own writing you need to acquire a sixth sense for when and when not to use jargon without an accompanying definition. One can only know so much about one's audience. But when in doubt, define.

Diction Skills Checkpoint I: Specialized Language

Directions: See how many specialized, or subject-specific, uses you can discover for each of the following terms:

1. program
2. flow
3. resolution
4. decay
5. proof

A Method of Efficient Vocabulary Building

An effective way to increase your vocabulary is to increase both the amount and the intensity of your reading. Read assertively; demand of the words and their arrangement on the page that they communicate to you at once. Mark every unfamiliar expression, as if for combat, and return to it later, armed with a dictionary and a stack of index cards (three-by-five cards are recommended). Write each unfamiliar expression on a separate card, alphabetize them, look them up in the dictionary, and write down on the back of the card not only their principal meanings but their etymologies as well. The more attention you pay to etymology, the better you will be able to determine the meanings of new words without having to look them up. Also, if the pronunciation was not familiar, add the pronunciation key as well. A sample vocabulary card is shown in Figure 14-1.

Once you have made up a batch of cards, drill yourself with them frequently, and get into the habit of composing one or more original sentences using each of the newly learned words. If this seems like a lot of work, it is; but it works better than merely memorizing long vocabulary lists. The idea is to assimilate the words into your own vocabulary.

To learn the basics of etymology study, try to memorize the meanings of as many Greek and Latin prefixes and roots as possible. Memorize the following lists, for starters:

image." Allow your mind's eye to zero in on the subject until you can see every minute detail, every movement. Learn also to "see" with all your senses—smell, touch, sound, and taste, as well as sight. Notice how many of your senses Herman Melville is able to arouse in the following harpooning scene from *Moby Dick*:

> Like desperados they tugged and they strained, till the welcome cry was heard—"Stand up, Tashtego!—give it to him!" The harpoon was hurled. "Stern all!" The oarsman backed water; the same moment something went hot and hissing along every one of their wrists. It was the magical line. An instant before, Stubb had swiftly caught two additional turns with it round the loggerhead, whence, by reason of its increased rapid circlings, a hempen blue smoke now jetted up and mingled with the steady fumes from his pipe.

Get in the habit of learning specific terms. Inexperienced writers tend to lapse into vague generalizations simply because they have not developed their curiosity about the little details of life. Take a walk around campus and look closely at the flowers you see. Try to describe them as carefully as possible, as though you were planning to sketch them. Chances are that you will be at a loss for words beyond *stem* and *blossom*. You may not even recognize the species. If your writer's instincts are right, your immediate impulse will be to learn what you cannot put into words.

A quick survey of the word *flower* in any encyclopedia will reveal the following information: The floral-classification section will identify, for example, "simple," "composite," and "tube" flowers; the discussion on identification of parts will introduce, say, the *calyx*, the *stamen*, and the *pistil*, which can be further broken down into *ovary*, *style*, and *stigma*; and the section on flower types will enumerate the glorious profusion of flower varieties: lilies, orchids, gentians, dahlias, and so on.

Find alternatives for sexist language, e.g., *firefighter* instead of *fireman*.*

The more you experience, the more vocabulary you will need in order to make accurate word choices and effectively convey your thoughts and observations to your reader.

Summary

Word meanings are dependent on context and should be used with some understanding of both their objective *denotative* meaning and their possible subjective *connotative* meanings. Another important aspect of language is *metaphorical expression*, evoking concrete images, or word pictures, in readers' minds to help them understand better the abstract

---

*See the Handbook, "Rhetorical and Grammatical Principles," Sexist Language.

concepts suggested by those word pictures. Although metaphorical language is common in fiction and poetry, it is also appropriate to expository writing in making difficult concepts easier to understand. Overuse of metaphorical expressions, however, can have the opposite effect—they become clichés.

Developing one's proficiency with diction takes time and perseverance. It is important to study the dictionary, to learn new words in a methodical fashion, and to become familiar with Greek and Latin roots and prefixes.

FOR DISCUSSION

1. What is the difference between standard and nonstandard usage? Argue for or against the notion that nonstandard usage is just as legitimate as is standard usage.

2. What distinction exists between informal and extremely informal (casual) usage? When, if ever, is casual usage appropriate for written discourse?

3. Visit the library and examine three or four dictionaries. Make note of as many dictionary functions as you can and summarize your findings to the class.

4. Express your candid views on sexist language. Does it make sense to remove gender-specific references from contexts that do not intrinsically involve gender (e.g., *mankind, lady doctor, stewardess,* and *mailman*)?

5. What is your immediate reaction to Emily Dickinson's phrasing and word choice in the two poems that follow? After you've read each poem several times and looked up unfamiliar words, reevaluate your original response.

#479

She dealt her pretty words like Blades—
As glittering they shone—
And every One unbared a Nerve
Or wantoned with a Bone.

#465

I heard a Fly buzz—when I died—
The Stillness in the Room
Was like the Stillness in the Air—
Between the Heaves of Storm—

The Eyes around—had wrung them dry—
And Breaths were gathering firm

For that last Onset—when the King
Be witnessed—in the Room—

I willed my Keepsakes—Signed away
What portion of me be
Assignable—and then it was
There interposed a Fly—

With Blue—uncertain stumbling Buzz—
Between the light—and me—
And then the Windows failed—and then
I could not see to see—

6. What are the connotations of the following words? Do any of them have more than one connotation for you?

    a. tomboy

    b. bashful

    c. party (noun or verb)

    d. cute

    e. aggressive

7. Select a newspaper or magazine article at random and isolate as many metaphors as possible. Did you come across any "dormant" metaphors or trite metaphors (clichés)? Discuss the importance of metaphor use in newspaper or magazine journalism.

8. In the following essay, Nickie McWhirter discusses the negative connotations Americans give to certain jobs they or others hold. Do you agree or disagree with the particular assertions she makes, in light of your own experience?

'JUST' A WORD MAKES ALL THE DIFFERENCE

Americans, unlike people almost everywhere else in the world, tend to define and judge everybody in terms of the work they do, especially work performed for pay.

Charlie is a doctor; Sam is a carpenter; Mary Ellen is a copywriter at a small ad agency. It is as if by defining how a person earns his or her rent money, we validate or reject that person's existence. Through the work and job title, we evaluate the worth of the life attached.

Larry is a laid-off auto worker; Tony is a retired teacher; Sally is a former showgirl and blackjack dealer from Vegas. It is as if by learning that a person currently earns no money at a job—and maybe hasn't earned any money at a job for years—we assign that person to limbo, at least for the present. We define such non-employed persons in terms of their past job history.

This seems peculiar to me. People aren't cast in bronze because of the jobs they hold or once held.

A retired teacher, for example, may spend a lot of volunteer time working with handicapped children or raising money for the Loyal Order of Hibernating Hibiscus. That apparently doesn't count. Who's Tony? A retired teacher.

A laid-off auto worker may pump gas at his cousin's gas station or sell encyclopedias on weekends. But who's Larry? Until and unless he begins to work steadily again, he's a laid-off auto worker. This is the same as saying he's nothing now, but he used to be something: an auto worker.

There is a whole category of other people who are "just" something. To be "just" anything is the worst. It is not to be recognized by society as having much value at all, not now and probably not in the past either. To be "just" anything is to be totally discounted, at least for the present.

There are lots of people who are "just" something. "Just" a housewife immediately and painfully comes to mind. We still hear it all the time. Sometimes women who have kept a house and reared six children refer to themselves as "'just' a housewife." "Just" a bum, "just" a kid, "just" a drunk, bag lady, old man, student, punk are some others. You can probably add to the list.

The "just" category contains present non-earners, people who have no past job history highly valued by society and people whose present jobs are on the low end of pay and prestige scales. A person can be "just" a cab driver, for example, or "just" a janitor. No one is ever "just" a vice-president, however.

We're supposed to be a classless society, but we are not. We don't recognize a titled nobility. We refuse to acknowledge dynastic privilege. But we certainly separate the valued from the valueless, and it has a lot to do with jobs and the importance or prestige we attach to them.

It is no use arguing whether any of this is correct or proper. Rationally it is silly. That's our system, however, and we should not only keep it in mind; we should teach our children how it works.

It is perfectly swell to want to grow up to be a cowboy or a nurse. Kids should know, however, that quite apart from earnings potential, the cattle breeder is much more respected than the hired hand. The doctor gets a lot more respect and privilege than the nurse.

I think some anthropologist ought to study our uncataloged system of awarding respect and deference to each other based on jobs we hold. Where does a vice-president–product planning fit in? Is that better than vice-president–sales in the public consciousness, or unconsciousness? Writers earn diddly dot, but I suspect they are held in higher esteem than wealthy rock musicians—that is, if everybody older than 40 gets to vote.

How do we decide which jobs have great value and, therefore, [which] job-holders are wonderful people? Why is someone who builds shopping centers called an entrepreneur while someone who builds freeways is called a contractor? I have no answers to any of this, but we might think about the phenomenon the next time we are tempted to fawn over some stranger because we find out he happens to be a judge, or the next time we catch ourselves discounting the personal worth of the garbage collector.

Nickie McWhirter, from the *San José Mercury*, March 8, 1982

FOR WRITING

1. Read the following, if you can:

    It has been brought to my attention that certain undesirable elements are attempting to initiate a negative priority initiative within our long-proven system of operation, said elements quite possibly having internal rather than external point of origin. It is doubtless apparent that appropriate and ethically inevitable countermeasures be implemented immediately.

    This is a fictitious, but not exaggerated, example of what can happen to language when it is used solely to manipulate and to camouflage truth. Such doublespeak, like the doublethink of Orwell's *1984*, aims to communicate ideas that will very likely be interpreted in a manner contrary to the underlying thought that brought them forth.

    Write an essay in which you probe the possible motives behind such writing and speaking. You might begin by searching for clues in the above passage (e.g., the use of passive voice, the reliance on abstractions, and the heavy use of polysyllabic terms).

2. Prepare a detailed survey of desk dictionaries, and decide which dictionary you consider to be the best. Here are five dictionaries you ought to examine, among several others:

    - *The American Heritage Dictionary* (1st ed., 1976; 2nd ed., 1982)
    - *Funk & Wagnall's Standard Desk Dictionary* (1980)
    - *The Random House College Dictionary* (Rev. ed., 1975)
    - *Webster's New Collegiate Dictionary* (1977)
    - *Webster's New World Dictionary* (2nd ed., 1979)

3. Compose a scenario in which two or more characters with radically different habits of speech try to communicate with each other. You may take a humorous approach, as does Mark Twain in the passage from *Roughing It*, or you may take a more serious approach.

4. Research (firsthand, if possible) the jargon or slang of a given profession, or of an ethnic or social group. Write a lively essay about these people and their in-group "lingo." Here are some professions or groups to consider:

    a. hairdressers, beauticians
    b. skiers
    c. bowlers
    d. police officers
    e. prisoners
    f. circus performers

5. Research a single word as fully as possible, consulting several dictionaries, including the *Oxford English Dictionary*. Write an essay on this word, focusing on its origins, its historical development, its oddities, and what it reveals, perhaps, about human nature.

COMPUTER WRITING

1. At the top of a new file, list a dozen newly learned words in two columns of six. First, write a dozen sentences, each using one word from the list. Check the dictionary if you are not sure about the usage, but only after you've written your sentence.

    Your next challenge is to write six sentences, each sentence correctly using two of the vocabulary words.

    Then, write a paragraph in which you make use of all twelve words. Keep revising the paragraph on the screen until all the words are used meaningfully. Don't worry about paragraph structure!

2. For students working in pairs at a terminal: Student A names a common object, such as a stone, tree, door, cup, or book, and Student B writes a sentence using the word as a metaphor. For example, Student A says "card," as in playing card, and Student B writes, "I like to associate with honest people who always lay their cards on the table."

    Student A then challenges Student B by writing a different sentence, using the same word in what is hoped will be a stronger example. A third student, or the instructor, should then act as disinterested judge.

Revising Your Work

CHAPTER 15

Revision is a way of life for writers, as necessary as rereading a work of literature to enhance appreciation and comprehension is for college students. It need not be an unpleasant experience; in fact, many writers find that revision is easier on the nerves and not quite as filled with uncertainties as when they are generating prose out of thin air, wondering if they're headed in the right direction or making any kind of sense.

Because writing an essay employs more language skills than you might customarily use, your prose is not likely to come out full-blown just the way you want it to the first time. You will have to add details, eliminate deadwood, reshape sentences, and perhaps find a more precise word or phrase. Much of the time you'll discover what you want to say only by making the effort to say it, which is similar to writing out a word before you can be sure you know how to spell it correctly.

Now let's say you're convinced that revision is necessary, and that ample time for revising your essays must be allotted. But how does one go about revising a manuscript? Granted, every essay will present a different set of revision problems, but are there any general revision guidelines that can make a writer's task easier?

Elements of Revising

First of all, it is important to keep in mind that revision isn't always a discrete stage in the writing process. You revise when you feel a need to revise. It makes sense, naturally, to wait until you have finished a draft before tackling most of the rewriting, but there are times when you know that the paragraph, sentence, phrase, or word you have just brought into existence doesn't work. It would be a mistake to ignore the impulse to improve it on the spot; not only could you forget what you had in mind, but the flawed passage could generate problems later on. If you have already worked through the specific revision strategies for sentence structuring, paragraphing, and diction,* then you have a strong perception of these revision strategies.

Second, get in the habit of rereading your work-in-progress frequently to remind yourself of where you are going, to check if you're leaving anything out, and to determine whether your writing is clear and concise. Don't look specifically for problems; reread your writing as though it were a published piece in a magazine, written by someone else. Some flaws will leap out at you; others will make you feel vaguely uneasy, and you'll have to read the passage over several times before you know what the problem is. And by the way, a word about that vague feeling of uneasiness: don't shrug it off; it is often justified.

Third, become familiar with the six basic revision operations: deletion, addition, substitution, rearrangement, reperception, and proofreading.

1. *Deletion.* Cutting out wordy and redundant passages can be painful, especially if the passages in question are ones you spent hours working on. But if a passage does not contribute to the whole, if it goes off on a tangent, or if it repeats an idea you've already expressed, squeeze your eyes shut and x it out.

   Deletion Example

   Wordy passage   Carla walked over to the refrigerator, opened it and took out the package of cooked ham and the lettuce and made herself two ham sandwiches. She was so extremely hungry that she could have eaten at least one more. But she decided not to eat any more when her boyfriend came over.

   Analysis   The author is using far too many words to convey a simple point. It is not necessary to say that Carla walked over to the refrigerator; in fact, it isn't necessary to refer to the refrigerator at all. Where else would that food be kept? It is also wearisome to point out that Carla *made* the sandwiches. Finally, note how

---

*See Chapters 12, 13, and 14, respectively.

	the idea of "extremely hungry" can be captured by one strong verb, as shown in the revised version:
Revision	Carla wolfed down two ham sandwiches and was just about to devour a third when her boyfriend dropped by.

2. *Addition.* "Develop your ideas!" may be the most frequent criticism directed at writers-in-training. It is one thing to discover the points you need to make during the first-draft stage, but quite another to "flesh out" each point sufficiently at the same time. Perhaps the following situation rings true for you: You're reading through your essay and you discover that nearly every sentence sounds like a topic sentence. This usually means that you have failed to go beyond the generalized assertion. You therefore sit back down at the typewriter and try to discuss or exemplify the main points of your essay.

Addition Example

Undeveloped passage	The circus acrobat astounded us with her spectacular maneuvers. When she completed her act, we all stood up and cheered.
Analysis	Readers will want to know what the acrobat did that is deserving of the word "spectacular"; they will want to be convinced that the standing ovation was justified.
Revision	The circus acrobat astounded us when, unprotected by a net, she leaped from the high platform as though diving into a pool, clasped the swinging bar with one hand, swung practically to the top of the tent and did a backwards flip into the arms of her partner, who had swung out to catch her at the last possible moment. When she completed her act, we all stood up and cheered.

3. *Substitution.* You aren't satisfied with your first choice of a word or phrase, so you replace it with one that is stronger, more colorful, or more accurate.

Substitution Example

Paragraph with weak diction	The girl went into the basement even though it was past midnight and she had a definite fear of ghosts. She absolutely had to know if her brother had really hidden her favorite doll here.

Analysis	The subject matter suggests a tale meant to create intrigue and suspense, but the word choice detracts from that objective. Verbs like *went* and *had* tend to make the tone flat and uninteresting. *Definite* is a tiresome cliché because it is often used redundantly. No difference in meaning exists between "She had a fear of ghosts" and "She had a definite fear of ghosts." The diction in both, however, is not as strong as that in "She feared ghosts," which eliminates the weak auxiliary verb and turns a dreary noun phrase, *a fear of*, into a strong verb.
Revision	The girl crept into the basement, trying not to realize that it was past midnight, or that she feared ghosts more than she feared death itself. She vowed once and for all to find out if her brother had hidden her best doll here.

4. *Rearrangement.* You read through your draft again and this time you discover that point *x* doesn't stem logically from point *y*. It would make more sense, you realize, to discuss point *y* first, then go to point *x*. That is one kind of rearrangement. Another kind is stylistic: You decide that the middle clause of a sentence, if made the opening clause, would strengthen the sentence and get the point across more clearly.

Rearrangement Example

Paragraph not satisfactorily coherent	There are three basic steps to teaching yourself to swim. If you master them, the rest will be easy. Learning to swim takes a lot of patience, and sometimes it's tempting to give up. At any rate the three steps are: (1) . . . , (2) . . . , and (3). . . .
Analysis	The writer announces three steps, but neglects to present them until three sentences later. This disrupts the reader's attention.
Revision	There are three basic steps to teaching yourself to swim: (1) . . . , (2) . . . , and (3). . . . If you master these steps, the rest will be easy. And when you learn to swim, be patient and don't give up.

5. *Reperception.* This means reworking a passage, a large section of an essay, or even a whole essay more or less from scratch. This can be

especially frustrating; no one likes to redo pages of work that may have taken hours to complete. On the other hand, this revision operation more than any other can lead to a dramatic improvement in the work. Doing this kind of revision is an excellent way to train your powers of perception and critical scrutiny. Never assume that the earlier draft was a waste of time for that reason. The greatest of writers, in fact, have "revised from spirit," to quote F. Scott Fitzgerald's term for this kind of revision.

Reperception Example

Insufficiently realized passage (an earlier draft of the preceding paragraph)	*Reperception.* While not exactly starting again from scratch, it's a close second: You've read through the essay and reached the painful decision that it stinks. Rather than beat a dead horse you begin anew, but with a keener sense of what to avoid, and what to give better emphasis to. Don't feel like a loser if you realize your need for this kind of revising. The greatest of writers have "revised from spirit," to quote F. Scott Fitzgerald.
Analysis	The point about this kind of revision was not made clearly or straightforwardly. The level of usage is too "folksy" for the particular context.
Revision	*Reperception.* This means reworking a passage, a large section of an essay, or even a whole essay more or less from scratch. This can be especially frustrating; no one likes to redo pages of work that may have taken hours to complete. On the other hand, this revision operation more than any other can lead to a dramatic improvement in the work. Doing this kind of revision is an excellent way to train your powers of perception and critical scrutiny. Never assume that the earlier draft was a waste of time for that reason. The greatest of writers, in fact, have "revised from spirit," to quote F. Scott Fitzgerald's term for this kind of revision.

6. *Proofreading.* Checking a draft for errors in grammar, mechanics, spelling, and punctuation is called proofreading. Be alert for these common problems, all of which are discussed in the Handbook:

348   Tools of the Trade

      Agreement of subject and verb
      Dangling and misplaced modifiers
      Parallelism errors
      Passive voice (misuse or overuse of)
      Tense (unwarranted shifts in)
      Apostrophes (misuse of)
      Capitalization
      Commas (misuse or overuse of)
      Quotation marks (when to use)

Anatomy of a Revision

Reproduced below is student Thomas Hogendijk's rough draft of "Confessions of a Doorman."* First read the draft through to see how accurately you can identify the substantive problems without looking at the revised version in Chapter 5. Then turn to pages 350–51 and compare your responses with those made by Thomas's instructor.

Confessions of a Doorman (first draft)

    The sky was bright orange and pink over the mountains. How beautiful . . . why smog *is* useful! And the orange and pink turned the great walls of glass into golden mirrors—the whole performing arts center, sitting like a sand castle, its many promenades, spires, and fortifications washed into monstrous curving planes by the sea.
    I pulled on my gloves, dabbed a spot from my coat for the third time, and checked my tie: White tuxedos are funny, seeming to shine, as if they have an inner luminosity of their own—and I glowed at curbside, between two glowing white urns.
    A few of the symphony personnel stood on the mezzanine balcony just above a billowing tassled banner announcing the gala opening. Hunt's Bottling was working late, the sweet odor of stewed tomatoes mixing with the lukewarm twilight breeze and the brassy cadences of a Corelli quintet. I tugged at my vest saying to myself, stand up straight. And I felt my face take a stern attitude. I liked to watch my hands flash bright in the dark, opening long black doors, "Good evening," and extending demurely to accept the palm of a lady. Just don't sit there, I thought, staring with just that hint of stern indignation at the lady's escort—you're supposed to tip me—jerk! No, he would ignore me, or worse than that, smile as if I were an amusing novelty. Of course, that is what I was, like the red carpet, the urns, and that ridiculous music—smothered like so many French fries in ketchup.
    The financial district tried its hardest to shine impressively, yet the Holi-

---

*See Chapter 5, "Projects in Expressive Writing," for the final draft of "Confessions of a Doorman."

day Inn was the most interesting. I watched a woman dress on the eighth floor—third window over just two floors down from the top. A Datsun wagon drove up. Did I have to open the doors of Datsuns? The woman threw herself back into her seat holding her purse over her head as if I were going to rape her. She slammed the door and they drove off.

But the city's wealth was there. Mink, sable, chinchilla, diamonds, sapphires, emeralds, cummerbunds, silk hankies, patent leather, hair pieces, and that year's face-lifts.

I tried to ignore him. He walked very slowly along the curb, leaning against the worn handle of a grocery shopping cart, smiling. He stopped just next to the urn, and started moving things around in his cart. It was clad with oily pieces of cardboard; a bicycle bell hung from the handle by a length of knotted string, and a ragged sleeping bag was stuffed underneath, where we normally put the potatoes and the Clorox. He felt my gaze, and looked up, grinning, and turned his head to one side, like the RCA dog.

I was startled by his very clear eyes. "Uh . . . uh—Good evening." Good evening! My God, saying "Good evening" to a bum! I coupled my hands behind me, thrust out my chest and addressed the street.

"Oh, and a very good evening to you too, sir!" His voice cut through me, high-pitched yet not harsh or crass. It had a distinctive elegance of modulation, as if this bum were possessed of a gentleman. A car approached. I opened the door, ignoring the man.

"A beautiful flower for a beautiful lady!" He held out a long-stemmed rose to the woman as she passed. She looked nervously at him, her escort hurrying her off. What an unfortunate beast, I thought. Why isn't he earning a proper living, instead of corrupting the finer world with his base presence? I became angry, feeling somehow contaminated by him. I jutted my chin out and up a bit more, concentrating on the empty road before me.

"A lovely warm summer's breeze tonight, don't you think?"

The question was clearly directed at me. He was addressing me! Who does he think he is? I don't have to answer, I thought.

"—and everybody looks so nice. It's just lovely, it just is!"

A bum. I'm standing here with a bum!

"Oh . . . I can see that you don't feel like talking." I felt him come near. "It seems that nobody ever feels like talking anymore." His breath was acrid with wine. "I don't know exactly why. Maybe it's because this town is finally getting some class." I stepped away from him, and he followed.

How silly—no, how very idiotic of me; what a jerk! I turned to face him. "Thank you." I even smiled.

"Here," he said. "Give this to your girlfriend, or to your mother—just to somebody beautiful, because beautiful people make beautiful things beautiful."

I stood twirling the rose in my fingers, some dirt from the stem getting on my gloves. A car came. He pushed his cart across the red carpet, and stopping in the middle, rang his bicycle bell, smiling and tipping his head over on one side, saying, "Good evening!" The people from the car walked in a large arc around him, shaking their heads.

Thomas Hogendijk

CONFESSIONS OF A DOORMAN (first draft)

Does this opening really prepare your readers for what follows?

The sky was bright orange and pink over the mountains. How beautiful . . . why smog *is* useful! And the orange and pink turned the great walls of glass into golden mirrors—the whole performing arts center, sitting like a sand castle, its many promenades, spires, and fortifications washed into monstrous curving planes by the sea.

I pulled on my gloves, dabbed a spot from my coat for the third time, and checked my tie: White tuxedos are funny, seeming to shine, as if they have an inner luminosity of their own—and I glowed at curbside, between two glowing white urns.

Consider using a simpler word for this context.

doesn't go with "mezzanine"

Try to make this more concise.

sharp imagery!

A few of the symphony personnel stood on the mezzanine balcony just above a billowing tassled banner announcing the gala opening. Hunt's Bottling was working late, the sweet odor of stewed tomatoes mixing with the lukewarm twilight breeze and the brassy cadences of a Corelli quintet. I tugged at my vest saying to myself, stand up straight. And I felt my face take a stern attitude. I liked to watch my hands flash bright in the dark, opening long black doors, "Good evening," and extending demurely to accept the palm of a lady. Just don't sit there, I thought, staring with just that hint of stern indignance at the lady's escort—you're supposed to tip me—jerk! No, he would ignore me, or worse than that, smile as if I were an amusing novelty. Of course, that is what I was, like the red carpet, the urns, and that ridiculous music—smothered like so many French fries in ketchup.

The financial district tried its hardest to shine impressively, yet the Holiday Inn was the most interesting. I watched a woman dress on the eighth floor—third window over just two floors down from the top. A Datsun wagon drove up. Did I have to open the doors of Datsuns? The woman threw herself back into her seat holding her purse over her head as if I were going to rape her. She slammed the door and they drove off.

But the city's wealth was there. Mink, sable, chinchilla, diamonds, sapphires, emeralds, cummerbunds, silk hankies, patent leather, hair pieces, and that year's face-lifts.

I tried to ignore him. He walked very slowly along the curb, leaning against the worn handle of a grocery shopping cart, smiling. He stopped just next to the urn, and started moving things around in his cart. It was clad with oily pieces of cardboard; a bicycle bell hung from the handle by a length of knotted string, and a ragged sleeping bag was stuffed underneath, where we normally put the potatoes and the Clorox. He felt my gaze, and looked up, grinning, and turned his head to one side, like the RCA dog.

[margin: good detail, but see if you can bring in more of this strange man's physical characteristics.]

I was startled by his very clear eyes. "Uh . . . uh—Good evening." Good evening! My God, saying "Good evening" to a bum! I coupled my hands behind me, thrust out my chest and addressed the street.

[margin: necessary?]

"Oh, and a very good evening to you too, sir!" His voice cut through me, high-pitched yet not harsh or crass. It had a distinctive elegance of modulation, as if this bum were possessed of a gentleman. A car approached. I opened the door, ignoring the man.

[margin: can you simplify?]

"A beautiful flower for a beautiful lady!" He held out a long-stemmed rose to the woman as she passed. She looked nervously at him, her escort hurrying her off. What an unfortunate beast, I thought. Why isn't he earning a proper living, instead of corrupting the finer world with his base presence? I became angry, feeling somehow contaminated by him. I jutted my chin out and up a bit more, concentrating on the empty road before me.

[margin: Consider sharpening focus here; let's see the flower vendor's actions more clearly.]

[margin: Do you feel that this is consistent with the narrator's personality? Consider reworking.]

"A lovely warm summer's breeze tonight, don't you think?"

The question was clearly directed at me. He was addressing me! Who does he think he is? I don't have to answer, I thought.

"—and everybody looks so nice. It's just lovely, it just is!"

A bum. I'm standing here with a bum!

"Oh . . . I can see that you don't feel like talking." I felt him come near. "It seems that nobody ever feels like talking anymore." His breath was acrid with wine. "I don't know exactly why. Maybe it's because this town is finally getting some class." I stepped away from him, and he followed.

How silly—no, how very idiotic of me; what a jerk! I turned to face him. "Thank you." I even smiled.

"Here," he said. "Give this to your girlfriend, or to your mother—just to somebody beautiful, because beautiful people make beautiful things beautiful."

[margin: Try developing this scene a bit more; it seems too abrupt.]

I stood twirling the rose in my fingers, some dirt from the stem getting on my gloves. A car came. He pushed his cart across the red carpet, and stopping in the middle, rang his bicycle bell, smiling and tipping his head over on one side, saying, "Good evening!" The people from the car walked in a large arc around him, shaking their heads.

Thomas Hogendijk

Tom —

You're well on your way toward producing a fascinating "encounter narrative" involving two eccentric and colorful characters; in so doing, you are also giving readers a wry slice of modern urban life. People — and whole cities — are as status-conscious as ever.

Your narrative, so far, has several rough spots, and the point-of-view isn't consistent. Try ironing out these problems in your rewrite — and see if you can bring out the individual natures of the two characters more sharply.

Summary

Revision is not always a discrete stage in the writing process. Writers revise whenever they feel the need to do so, and such a need can occur immediately after a phrase, sentence, paragraph, or page is put on paper. The thorough, methodical revising of a first draft is a separate undertaking, and ought to proceed in light of the six basic revision operations: deletion, addition, substitution, rearrangement, reperception, and proofreading.

FOR DISCUSSION

1. Meet in groups of three and retrace, as candidly as you can, the way you revised your last essay. Be sure to have the drafts of this essay on hand. Don't neglect to mention any revising you did before completing the first draft. Which of the six revision operations discussed in this chapter did you use? Take notes when the other members in your group describe their strategies. Finally compare strategies and decide whose revision was most thorough.

2. Make two copies of an unrevised essay-in-progress. Meet in groups of three, read each other's drafts, then discuss revision strategies.

3. Read up on the working habits of well-known writers (a good source is the multi-volume series *Writers at Work*); report on the revision habits of three of these writers.

FOR WRITING

1. Write a critique of your own, or a classmate's, revising strategies. Discuss the strong points as well as possible strategies that were overlooked and could have been applied fruitfully. Keep the six revision operations in mind as you prepare your critique.

2. Write a personal essay on the joys and frustrations of revising.

COMPUTER WRITING

Bring your work disk containing an essay-in-progress to the computer lab. Obtain a printout of the essay-in-progress if you do not already have one. Then, sitting two to a terminal, critique each other's drafts—in the following manner:

1. Writer A examines the printout of Writer B's draft, offers suggestions to Writer B.

2. Writer B executes the revision on screen; Writer A records the revision on Writer B's printout.

3. Writer B then critiques Writer A's draft; Writer A revises accordingly on screen.

PART FOUR

Special Topics

Maintaining a Journal

CHAPTER 16

Writers learn their craft by writing, and not just when the mood strikes them, but regularly, habitually. Writing is more than completing a project, whether for a class or for yourself; writing is a way of interacting with the world to make better sense of it, of discovering how your deepest thoughts can come to life through poems and stories and essays of all kinds.

Most writers—that is, not just people who write for a living, but people who love to write and want to be good at it—believe firmly that one of their most useful tools is the journal (literally *daybook*), and it isn't hard to see why.

First, writers often must test out their wording of a complex idea, and the journal is an ideal medium for such experimenting. Just because they have a brilliant thought doesn't mean they're going to capture it in precise, vivid language without a struggle! Even after decades of writing, the most eminent of writers do not "get it right the first time." They are hardly slow-witted, however; rather, they make increasingly tougher demands on themselves, insisting upon greater economy of phrasing and greater clarity and color.

But, you may be wondering, isn't this what first-draft writing is for? Yes and no. *Any* kind of a draft has an air of formality about it, and you need a better place to experiment—to play around with an idea unencumbered by the notion that you are "writing an essay." You can talk to yourself in your journal; you can write in fragmentary sentences, leap from one point to another in mid-air, and even draw pictures. The prewriting activities discussed in Chapter 3—brainstorming, free-associating, and the like—are ideal for journals.

Another valuable function for a journal is that of a verbal scrapbook, a reservoir for raw data: statistics; snippets of conversation overheard on your way to class or in the cafeteria; observations of people and of incidents, presented in as much detail as you can perceive; quotations from leisurely or directed reading; and lists! Let's not forget lists. Journals are wonderful for making lists of various items: your favorite films, sports, musicians, foods, fashions, books, and places to visit; your most embarrassing moments; the things you hate, love, or can't understand.

Finally, the journal can be a secret book filled with words intended for your eyes only, with highly personal thoughts that you have an emotional need to objectify through language, but can't bring yourself to share with anyone.

The one kind of entry you should avoid is the what-I-ate-for-breakfast entry. Don't waste time recording routine, uninteresting details unless you sense that they might be useful to you.

Chances are that you still have many questions about the mechanics of keeping a journal. Here are the questions students most often ask:

Q: What's the best kind of notebook to write my journal in?

A: A loose-leaf notebook. You may want to remove some of your more private entries if your instructor asks you to hand in your journal. You can reinsert these pages later.

Q: How long should my entries be?

A: As long as you want them to be. An entry can be a single word or name that can trigger an entire memory. Or it can be several pages long if you're on a hot streak.

Q: How often should I write in my journal?

A: Journal writing is most beneficial when it is done not frequently but regularly. Set aside a certain time during the day, say three or four times a week, to write in your journal; but don't make excessive demands on yourself or else you will quickly grow weary of the task.

Q: How do I develop a journal entry into an essay or story?

A: Reread the entry several times and work out an outline or synopsis of the potential essay or story. Take notes on possible ways to expand the content; for instance, you might use examples to support your generalizations or include additional subtopics. Finally, try to write a first draft with the same enthusiasm you applied to the original entry.

Q: Besides writing a lot, how else can I develop my journal-writing skills?

A: You should come to regard your journal as more than a repository for raw data to be turned into full-length projects; that is, you can enjoy journal writing as an art in itself, and then read as many published journals as you can. Many prominent writers through the ages have published their journals. Some of the most revealing in terms of journal possibilities include those by the following authors:

James Boswell	Henry James
S. T. Coleridge	Anaïs Nin
Fyodor Dostoevsky	Henry David Thoreau
Ralph Waldo Emerson	Mark Twain
F. Scott Fitzgerald	Walt Whitman
Nathaniel Hawthorne	Thomas Wolfe
Gerard M. Hopkins	Virginia Woolf

Just to give you a quick idea of the range of journal entries, a page from the journals of two of these authors is reproduced below. But keep this in mind: Your own journals should reflect your tastes, your personality, and your writing style through and through.

F. SCOTT FITZGERALD

- Her beauty was as poised and secure as a flower on a strong stem; her voice was cool and sure, with no wayward instruments in it that played on his emotions.
- The intimacy of the car, its four walls whisking them along toward a new adventure, had drawn them together.
- Your eyes always shining as if you had fever.

HENRY JAMES

New York, 115 East 25th St., December 20th, 1881. I had to break off the other day in Boston—the interruptions in the morning here are intolerable. That period of the day has none of the social sanctity here that it [has] in England, and which keeps it singularly free from intrusion. People—by which I mean ladies—think nothing of asking you to come and see them before lunch. Of course one can decline, but when many propositions of that sort come, a certain number stick. . . . I have been three weeks in New York, and all my time has slipped away in mere movement. I try as usual to console myself with the reflection that I am getting impressions. This is very true; I have got a great many. I did well to come over; it was worth doing.

Finally, let us look at an excerpt from a journal kept by a college freshman during a visit to El Salvador:

It is 9:40, my first night here. What can I say but new, new, new. Never have I seen or hardly imagined what I have seen since yesterday. Families, lines, guns, soldiers, women washing clothes in rivers, worst poverty I ever imagined and greatest wealth. . . .

Outside [the airport] a little girl, seven or eight, came up to me begging. I would have given her something, but I had American money and it was in my bag. Maybe I should have, I was just in such awe. Anyway, she persisted; I got into the car, she put herself face smashed against car, begging. She was really scary, she didn't look cute or sad and desperate, but like an experienced old hardened prostitute at seven.

In trunk of car, M-16. On floor, backseat handgun, driver with a gun beside him under leg—one in center of where emergency brake is. Four guns.

Friday. Along freeway, out in country one hour from San Salvador. People walking. Ladies with baskets on top of heads with laundry from washing in river, lots of kids. Men with machetes, soldiers with guns. Soldiers here are divided up. Ones in fatigue are not police. The police, they scare me. They stare right at you holding Uzis.

> Don Ballew, "The Danger Zones," *The Santa Clara*, January 10, 1985

Entry Suggestions for Your Journal

Ideally, your journal should become your own private body of writing, containing whatever you want it to, for whatever purposes. But if you are new to journal writing, you may welcome a few suggestions to help get you started. The seven journal entry suggestions that follow—which cover several of the applications mentioned earlier—can be used for your first week of keeping a journal.

Day One   Sentence-development practice. Develop cumulative, periodic, and balanced sentences (see Chapter 12, pp. 264–265) using any or all of the following base clauses:

> She awakened suddenly
> The fire raged uncontrollably
> The creature appeared out of nowhere
> The pain would not go away

Day Two   Word-sketching: People. Find a place where many people convene or pass, and write paragraph-long descriptions of five or six individuals that you see. Include both physical characteristics and mannerisms.

Day Three Word-sketching: Objects. Pay close attention to *everyday* objects—furniture, signposts, jewelry, desktop stuff, kitchen stuff, flowers, insects—and describe each object in the most minute detail possible.

Day Four Lists. Make all kinds of lists:

> Your favorite recreational and athletic activities
> Songs you love; songs you can't bear listening to
> Things that bore you; that excite you
> Your favorite movies
> College courses you like and dislike
> Your worst fears
> Your greatest challenges in life
> Celebrities you would like to meet

Day Five Writing practice: Summaries. Read half a dozen articles (any subject) or short stories and write a half-page summary of each one.

Day Six Letter to an imaginary friend. Write a personal letter to someone imaginary (a fictional/fairy tale hero or heroine, an alien from another world).

Day Seven Personal confessions. Write something very private, for your eyes only!

Journal Writing on the Computer

Personal computers are ideal for keeping a journal for one reason: You can tap out your thoughts quickly because you have no paper or notebooks to fuss with, and no pens to give you writer's cramp. You can write at a pace much closer to the speed of thought, thus reducing the likelihood that a sizable chunk of an idea that suddenly occurred to you will flutter into oblivion. And because you're aware that you can zap out sentences and paragraphs forever with just a flick of the fingers, you can write in a much more uninhibited manner.

Here are a few fun things you can do for your computer journal:

1. Freewrite nonstop on anything that comes to mind. You'll discover that thoughts will flow more freely because you don't have to push a cumbersome pen across the page.

2. Take a mental inventory of everything you know about one of your favorite topics. Write either in fragments or in complete sentences, it doesn't matter. Concentrate on filling the screen with details.

3. Dim your screen until you cannot see the words you type. Now try your hand at some invisible writing! This isn't as crazy as it sounds: If you're unable to see what you're writing, your instincts for coherence may be frustrated, but you can heighten your sense of concentration considerably. Write this way for at least ten minutes, then turn up the brightness and see how you fared.

4. Create ten separate subject files on a single disk. For example, F. Scott Fitzgerald divided his journal into several topics, one for each letter of the alphabet: Anecdotes, Bright Clippings, Conversations and Things Overheard, Descriptions of Things, and so on. Each day, write one entry for at least three files.

Getting the Most from Your Conference Tutorial

CHAPTER 17

Instruction in the art of writing is most effective when it includes individual attention. Although the classroom environment is just as important for the feedback it provides from fellow writers, the private conference is necessary in writing instruction for two reasons: First, you have a unique combination of strengths and weaknesses in your writing that simply cannot be fully addressed in a classroom of, say, twenty to twenty-five students. In the private conference, your regular classroom instructor, writing lab instructor, or specially assigned tutor will be able to concentrate on the troublesome aspects of your general writing style or on the particularly perplexing matters concerning a specific assignment that, to be resolved, require extended discussion. Second, the private tutorial will give you the opportunity to obtain more insight into an essay-in-progress than is usually possible via marginal commentary on a returned paper.

The private conference is the ideal environment for raising questions that could not be satisfactorily answered in class. Such questions might include, for example, "What are some of the things I could possibly say about the topic I've chosen?" or "Can you give me one or two examples of how I could make this incoherent and uninteresting paragraph coherent and colorful?"

If your class is large, chances are that the opportunity to discuss your writing tête-à-tête with your instructor is limited by the number of conferences as well as by the time allotted per conference. Here, then, are a few guidelines that will help you make the most out of the conference time available to you:

1. *Don't wait for your instructor to schedule a conference before seeing him or her if you need to.* Nearly all professors keep scheduled office hours, and they hold them for their students' benefit, not their own. Your writing instructor *wants* you to take advantage of his or her office hours, so don't hesitate to do so.

2. *Whether your conference is scheduled or unscheduled, always come prepared.* Try to formulate specific questions to ask about problems you are having with an assignment or with writing in general. A statement like, "I've read through my first draft and I just can't seem to express my central idea clearly; will you help me identify the problem?" can help you a lot more than if you were to say you're hopelessly confused and you wish you'd never heard of freshman comp. Even if you *do* feel hopelessly confused (is there a college student who isn't, at one time or another?), try plowing through that confusion. Remember that one of your goals in this course is to become as much of your own editor as you can, and that means tasting and fighting frustration now and then.

3. *Bring along all of your assigned essays, in-class exercises, journals, etc., to your conference, even if your instructor doesn't specifically request it.* The problems you are having with your essay-in-progress may have appeared in an earlier piece, and that earlier context might give you or your instructor some insight into how to deal with those problems. Also, teachers like to see as large a sampling of your writing as possible at any one time to be able to detect any identifiable patterns; this concept is akin to a physician's concern about previous illnesses you may have had as a source of possible insight into a present ailment.

4. *If your instructor informs you of the purpose of the conference in advance, then prepare for it.* Will you be discussing your sentence structure? Then review Chapter 12, and perhaps do some of the exercises at the end of that chapter. Will you need to discuss your outline for a research paper? Then review your copy of the outline and try to anticipate the kinds of questions your instructor might ask about it.

5. *Be independently minded!* This does not mean you should disagree with everything your instructor advises. It *does* mean you should feel good about advancing toward the kinds of writing goals you want to set for yourself. If you think of an interesting variation on an essay assignment—one that you would much rather work on—then voice your sentiment during the conference, and feel entitled to a logical explanation if your idea is rejected. If you want to experiment with any of the rhetorical devices you're learning, prepare a few journal entries to illustrate what you have in mind, then show them to your instructor.

6. *Always be on time to a scheduled conference.* Every minute matters during a conference, and your being late will eat into another student's conference time, if not your own.

Participating in Classroom Workshops

CHAPTER 18

The road to becoming your own editor is sometimes a long one. There are many things to look for, rhetorically speaking, in a given essay. You may often sense that something is amiss, but until you actually study the principles of good writing one at a time, the problem can be difficult to identify.

Even after you've studied these principles, you still need to practice evaluating the way they are applied (or not applied), not only in your own essays, but also in the essays of your peers; more often than not, they are wrestling with problems similar to your own. The classroom activity known as *workshopping* is an important instrument for helping you master these editing skills.

Several variations to workshopping exist, but many sessions proceed like this: Your instructor tells you to split up into small groups, usually groups of four. You have come to class already equipped with photocopies of your essay, usually in first-draft form, for each member of your group; or you could have chosen a more economical alternative—that of typing your essay on ditto masters and then having your instructor or the department secretary run off the copies you need. If the workshopping is done in pairs, then you need only exchange papers with your partner.

Now comes the uneasy moment: Other students are going to read your essay, and you haven't even gotten any feedback from the instructor as to how good or bad it is. What if it's embarrassingly bad? you wonder. Oh, if only I had spent more time with it, you lament, as you watch, out of the corner of your eye, your fellow students reading it. . . .

A reaction like this is normal, and, believe it or not, healthy. It shows that you are becoming aware of your audience, which is a fundamental skill that all writers need to cultivate.

The ideal role for students to assume when critiquing papers of their peers is that of the *critical reader*, or more specifically, the critical reader who is especially appreciative of good writing, rather than that of the writing expert. In other words, as you read through your classmate's essay, you react to passages you enjoy, and to passages that confuse you or that seem structurally flawed. You then ask this basic question: What can the writer do to improve the essay?

Now your task seems to get a little thorny. Who am I, you might say to yourself, to criticize another writer's work? The answer to that is, a college student who has been reading material written by professional writers for at least thirteen years! You really do know good writing when you see it. Your task now is to learn *why* it's good, or why it isn't, so you can communicate that information to others as well as to yourself when you read over your own work.

But what specifically do I look for when critiquing a paper? you may be wondering. Three things not to be too concerned about in first-draft editing are punctuation, spelling, and mechanics—unless your instructor directs otherwise, of course. Your principal concerns, rather, should be as follows:

CRITIQUE LIST

Content/Development

1. Is the thesis, or the main point of the essay, clear? If not, what can the writer do to make it clearer?

2. Has the writer covered all aspects of the topic suggested by the thesis? If not, what else does the writer need to include?

3. Did the author use examples to illustrate the generalizations made? Are there enough examples? Are they *interesting* examples? If not, what could you suggest in the way of improvement?

Organization

1. Beginning. Did the writer engage your interest in the opening paragraph(s)? If not, what can the writer do to strengthen that opening? Does the opening sequence prepare the reader for the central idea of the essay?

2. Middle. Is each facet of the main idea discussed in sufficient detail? If not, what details need to be added? Does the writer move smoothly and

logically from one point to the next? If not, try to identify the cause of the unevenness, like the lack of a transitional expression. Are concrete examples used to illustrate important assertions? If not, what kinds of examples would be most suitable?

3. End. Has the writer summarized key points or given special attention to one or two of the most noteworthy items raised? Has the writer offered a conclusion and recommendations, if appropriate?

Style

1. Syntax. Do any of the sentences interfere with the readability? If so, which ones, and why? Perhaps a group of them are patterned too much alike, thus causing a choppy effect. Or perhaps some of the sentences need to be livelier or to emphasize their respective points better.

2. Word Choice and Usage. Is the level of usage (formal, informal, or slangy) appropriate for the writer's intended audience? Is the language concise? If not, how might the writer change the phrasing so that fewer words are used to express the same idea? How precise is the word choice relative to the target audience? Are some expressions unnecessarily formal or complex for the rhetorical situation at hand? Or, conversely, are some expressions vague or ambiguous?

Punctuation, spelling, basic grammar, and mechanics have been omitted from this list, but not because they're unimportant. These topics are actually quite essential, but they are best discussed during a second-draft workshopping session. This does not mean that you must refrain from noticing such errors; go right ahead and make corrections if you're certain of the errors. But don't spend time discussing them now.

As for the actual critiquing procedure, follow this sequence unless your instructor directs otherwise:

1. Read the essay carefully. Don't do any critiquing during this initial read-through.

2. Following the above critique list, pencil in comments like "this isn't clear," "give an example," "wordy and hard to follow," or "try to simplify this paragraph" in the margins.

3. Write a brief "blanket" comment at the end of the essay, giving your honest overall impression.

4. Discuss your comments with the writer.

Don't forget—all of your critiquing is designed for one purpose: to help your fellow writer improve his or her paper, which is a work-in-progress and not a finished essay.

Composing on a Computer

CHAPTER 19

The computer is, along with the automobile and the telephone, a tool of fundamental importance to daily life. We are not more mechanized by a computer culture; on the contrary, we have a chance to become more human than we've ever been before by assigning to these miraculous machines all of our time-consuming, tedious, unimaginative chores.

But how can a computer help us with our *writing*? Over the past few years, many teachers of writing, the author of this textbook among them, have looked into the possible advantages that composing on a computer might have over the old-fashioned ways of writing. These teachers discovered that the advantages can be considerable. Computers can help writing students accomplish the following:

- *Brainstorm a topic thoroughly and quickly.* Ideas can flow more freely; one is less apt to repress ideas, since text can be zapped out forever with one flick of the finger.

- *Stimulate greater involvement with the writing process.* One's writing is, in effect, *on display*; more hand-eye coordination is needed. Writing becomes more of a sensory experience.

- *Make rewriting a much more efficient, swifter, even a more enjoyable operation.* One never feels a sense of dread about revising because nothing has to be retyped.

- *Improve one's ability to manipulate language and information, to gain better insight into their organization, and to improve their retention.* All writers, inexperienced or professional, can benefit from improving their ability to *learn*.

Although this is not the place to provide step-by-step instruction on how to use a personal computer with word processing capability for planning, drafting, and revising essays, some of the broader procedures may be set forth here.

For students of freshman composition, the ideal arrangement is to have unlimited access to a personal computer (PC) system. The PC system includes the CPU (the central processing unit, where all of the computer's memory resides), the monitor (screen), disk drives (to run the software, that is, the programs, such as the word processing program), and the printer. To take advantage of the benefits of composing on the computer, it is important to have easy access to a system.

Let's assume that your college has a PC lab dedicated to freshman composition instruction, or that you have your own PC at home or in your dorm room. Here are four suggestions to help you get started:

1. *Learn the word processing program thoroughly.* This means knowing all the commands necessary for editing your "files."* *Thoroughly* means knowing the commands well enough to keep your attention on what you're writing. Generally, this takes place between one and two weeks of steady practice.†

   Any good word processor will have at least these five capabilities:

   - *Automatic "wraparound."* You just type in the words and the computer begins a new line whenever you reach the pre-set margin. The right margin can be set so that every line of text is the same length, which is called a "justified" margin, or so that the text lines vary from line to line, in a "ragged" margin.

   - *Automatic pagination.* The program automatically begins a new page when you've filled a page. You may also enter a command to begin a new page at any time. The program also automatically numbers each page, both on the screen while you're writing and on the "hard copy" when it's time to print.

   - *Text "block" movement.* If you need to move a passage of from one word to several pages to a different part of the document, you can do so very easily. What might have taken a half hour or longer with scissors and tape, not to mention considerable retyping if the revisions were made on a final draft, takes only seconds on a PC.

   - *Instant deletion of a word, sentence, paragraph, or larger block of text.* No longer will you lose time fussing with whiteout to patch up

---

*Files are what you ask the computer to open for each writing task you embark on.

†Note: Many word processing programs are available, but not all of them are suitable to the needs of college writers. If you must purchase your own word processing program, discuss your needs with an expert first.

corrections. This feature is not only a convenience, but it also encourages you to take risks and to write swiftly, usually at a speed approaching the speed of thought itself.

- *Menu driven.* A "menu" is a display of commands—text movement, cursor movement, spacing, margin adjustment, etc.—that you can call up whenever you need to. Most word processing programs will automatically display a menu of key commands and will give you the option of canceling a command at any time.

2. *Always*—repeat: *always*—*make a backup copy of the disk(s) containing your files.* Keep those backup copies in a safe place, separate from the original copies. If you are working on a long project, such as a research paper, copy your day's work onto the backup copy each day. It isn't much fun to lose a month's worth of brilliant writing as a result of a power failure, or of one of many possible desktop blunders like spilling hot coffee onto your floppy disk before you got around to making backup copies.

3. *Get in the habit of writing at every stage—brainstorming, outlining, preliminary drafting, revising, and proofreading—on the PC.* This takes time, and not every student will be content to work in this manner, no matter how accessible the hardware. But at least give it a try. Chances are you'll increase your fluency and strengthen your style by experimenting with different syntactic structures and phrasing, since it's so easy to zap out false starts and poor wording and then to try again. Your ability to organize and to revise will also improve faster than if you use the "scissors and paste" approach.

4. *Become acquainted with the several writing tutorial programs now on the market.* Some programs can help you plan an essay, develop each key point, and check your word choice, sentence structure, spelling, and mechanics.

Before you start composing on a computer, remember this advice: You must be patient and expect to make mistakes now and then. Practice as often as you can. Make a point of doing all the computer writing exercises at the ends of most chapters in this book. Once you've become familiar with the word processing commands as well as with the experience of composing with phosphorescent words on a screen, you will undoubtedly agree that the advantages far outweigh the disadvantages.

Writing Essay Exams

CHAPTER 20

You will most likely be doing some in-class writing for freshman comp. And you may find it nerve-wracking at first, much preferring to write your essays when you're alone and without any time pressure, or at least without that minute-by-minute time pressure that tends to scramble your thoughts. But in-class writing is important for two reasons: First, it convinces you that you can get a lot of writing done in a relatively short span of time. If the topic has sparked enthusiasm, you could produce a five-hundred-word rough draft in less than one class period, even if you consider yourself a slow writer. You then realize that a five-hundred-word essay sometimes takes you a *week* to write.

The point is this: Learning to organize and to develop a topic on the spot is a useful skill to acquire. When you write under such conditions, you are improving your ability to *think*—to conceptualize, to manipulate abstractions, and to apply them to real situations.

A second reason and more immediate reward is that in-class writing can help you improve your ability to write "bluebook" essay exams. These exams are as integral to the college experience as is a TGIF bash—not as much fun, maybe, but at least just as important.

Just as overcoming your fear of the water is a prerequisite to learning to swim, your first step in learning to write good bluebook essays is to cease being afraid of them. Some students have such anxiety attacks over mid-term and final-exam bluebook essay writing that they literally faint. Other students may not faint, but they get so nervous they lose control of their thoughts and begin scribbling things down wildly. They then wind up with something incoherent.

To become more accustomed to essay exams, simply *practice*; don't wait for in-class writing activities to be assigned. Give yourself topics to write on and do so under strict exam conditions: Ask someone to time you, do not look at books or notes, organize your thoughts quickly, and work quickly without sacrificing self-control. As soon as you feel yourself "freezing up," ask yourself why.

Remember that the principles of good essay writing discussed throughout this book apply to essay exams as well. Do not assume that just because you're writing under pressure, you needn't be concerned about quality.

The most important advice is this: *Know precisely what is expected of you.* Have you been asked to explicate a poem or short story? Then do only that and nothing else. Does the exam question call for your analysis of a topic? Then remind yourself at once what that analysis involves. But no matter what the task of the exam is, the fundamentals of all good writing apply: strong lead-in, explicit thesis statement, logical organization, detailed support of assertions, and clear and concise expression.

The fourth rule—detailed support of assertions—can mean the difference between an "A" and a "D" on an essay exam. Whenever you make a generalization, a parrot should begin squawking inside your head: "Support it! support it! support it!"

Imagine, for example, that everyone has to write an hour-long essay on Walt Whitman's sense of beauty as it is evoked in his famous poem, "Song of Myself." One student writes:

> In my opinion, Walt Whitman had a keen sense of beauty, although it doesn't look that way. For example, he likes to work with images that other poets of his day would have considered ugly, even disgusting. But I think that because of Whitman's enthusiasm for the kind of progress he was witnessing in America, and because material progress suggested an underlying spiritual progress, Whitman even considered machinery beautiful.

The problems with the above example should be immediately apparent: The student did not say anything specific, despite the fact that he went through the motions of doing so ("For example, . . ."). What he thought was specific support of an assertion wound up being only another assertion.

Let's assume that our student spotted his mistake, and that he had the opportunity and the time to revise his essay during the exam. Here is what he might have finally submitted:

> Walt Whitman exhibits an unusual—but undeniable—sense of beauty in "Song of Myself." Whitman truly was a "poet of America" in the sense that he embraced progress (urbanization, scientific exploration, and political and social reform) and found it beautiful. Now *beautiful* is a word we usually associate with color, rural landscape, harmony, serenity, and physical attrac-

tiveness. Whitman found beauty in these, but he did not stop there. As if eager to reinforce the truth behind Keats's famous assertion that "Truth is beauty, beauty truth; that is all ye know on earth and all ye need to know," Whitman set out to celebrate the beauty of the modern human condition. "I am enamored," he writes, "of men who live among cattle or taste of the ocean or woods, of the builders and steerers of ships and the wielders of axes and mauls, and the drivers of horses." In one section of the poem he includes a "catalog" of modern-life scenes—images of factory girls, shoemakers, vagabonds and peddlers, fishermen, prostitutes, the President holding a meeting with his cabinet, janitors, fur traders and farmers.

Progress is beautiful to Whitman because it is *human*. When he writes that "The narrowest hinge in my hand puts to scorn all machinery," he is not putting down technology, but saying that technology must always be seen in terms of human nature. Human nature is a part of *all* nature; it remains beautiful as long as it is not perverted.

How to Study for an Essay Exam

You may have been wondering as you studied the above example how anyone can recall exact lines from a long poem during a closed-book exam. First of all, it isn't usually necessary to quote verbatim; notice the paraphrasing of Whitman's "catalog" passage. Second, if you reread required works several times over a long period of time rather than all at once just before the exam, you will be able to recall specific passages with ease. So the first tip to keep in mind when preparing for an essay exam is this: *Review continually throughout the term.* And the second tip is just as important: *Anticipate possible exam topics and write essays on your own, under exam conditions.* The more you practice spontaneous writing, the more proficient at writing you'll become, and the less nervous you'll be when you take the exam.

Let's take a closer look at the way these exam-preparation strategies might be applied. Imagine that you are studying ancient history and are fairly certain that at least one of the essay topics on the exam will have to do with Sumerian (Mesopotamian) culture. Here is what you can do:

1. Thoroughly review the entire Sumerian period, taking notes in the principal areas of concern; for example:
   agricultural techniques
   language
   religious customs
   technological developments
   art
   political life
   warfare

Ask questions about every observation you record. If you write, "The Sumerians conceived of their cities as the property of a particular god," then ask yourself, What were the larger implications of this? How did it affect their political philosophy?

2. Conduct follow-up reviews by consulting sources other than the required reading. Take more notes, ask more questions. This is how you build up a repertoire of support data to back up any general assertions you may care to make.

3. Formulate your own exam questions—questions that seem to you capable of eliciting students' understanding of major concepts. Here is an example:

   Describe one major technological development of the Sumerians and explain in detail why it was important to their civilization.

   Notice that in addition to the specific content that is called for, a specific methodology is requested. You are to *describe* (not just mention) *one* (not several) *major* (not obscure) *technological* (not artistic or religious) development and then *explain* (not just outline) its importance to Sumerian civilization as a whole (not just to a particular activity).

4. Now write your essay, adhering to strict exam conditions (all books and notes out of sight; write for an allotted time and no longer). Begin by reviewing the demands of the task. Next, either in your head or on scratch paper (during an actual exam you'll want to make sure you are permitted to write on scratch paper), formulate a thesis statement, for example, "One of the most important technological developments of the Sumerians was the use of bronze for warfare." You might also work out a brief outline:

   I. Sumerians were a warring people; had many enemies who were becoming more and more of a threat.

   II. Necessity the mother of invention! Bronze (discovered in 2500 B.C. during time of Sargon) could be used for helmets, shields, spears, thus strengthening both defense and offense.

   III. Sumerians were warring people but not belligerent. Along with their increased military security, applied their metallurgical skills to agriculture and the arts.

5. Finally, after writing your essay, double-check it against the criteria reflected in the directions as well as against the criteria for good writing in general: clarity, conciseness, coherence, detailed support of generalizations.

Handbook
PART FIVE

Rhetorical and Grammatical Principles

This section of the Handbook is intended to provide you with concise and useful information on major grammatical and rhetorical principles with which all writers need to be familiar. To derive maximum benefit from the section, follow these suggestions:

1. Set aside twenty minutes every day to study two or three entries. "Study" includes: (1) reading the entry thoroughly; (2) completing the exercise (if any) at the end of the entry; (3) reading the cross-references (if any) and completing any exercises that may accompany these entries; (4) reviewing the main entry and exercise, and formulating questions you need to have answered to complete your understanding of the concept; (5) presenting these questions to your instructor—but not until you have tried to answer them yourself.

2. Check the drafts of each essay-in-progress for grammatical and rhetorical shortcomings. Before you can perform this task efficiently, however, you need to acquire a general familiarity with the contents of this Handbook section.

3. Be sure to study those Handbook entries recommended by your instructor. If your instructor uses correction symbols such as FRAG, COH, DM, AGR, and the like, use the reference key on the inside back cover of this textbook.

4. About once a week, work through several of the diagnostic exercises at the end of the section.

5. Mark with an asterisk all entries that seem to you particularly difficult to master; review these entries regularly.

Absolute

An absolute is a descriptive phrase that modifies a word, clause, or entire sentence. It consists of a noun or noun phrase plus an adjective, adverb, or participle, and the phrase may precede or follow the clause or clauses it modifies. Absolutes look like sentences with their verbs missing, or in the case of participial absolutes, with their auxiliaries missing. *See also* Phrase, Appositive.

> Alex gripped the rope, *his hands sweaty*. (noun phrase plus adjective)
>
> Alex, *muscles bulging*, lurched upward. (noun plus participle)
>
> *Her competitors far behind*, Sonya was the easy winner. (noun phrase plus adverb)

Exercise: Absolutes

Directions: Combine each pair of sentences by turning one of them into an absolute phrase.

1. The cat leaped onto the fence. Its eyes were aglow.
2. Eileen was the most obvious candidate for the Rhodes Scholarship. Her aptitude test scores were higher than anyone else's at this school.
3. Vern examined the enormous diamond. His fingers trembled.

Abstract Diction

An abstract term is a nonsensory concept that may or may not be followed by concrete, sensory illustrations of that concept. *Discomfort* is an abstraction; *throbbing pain in my leg*, or *dry, blistering lips from the intense heat* are possible concrete illustrations of that abstraction. Both abstract and concrete diction are important, but excessive reliance on abstraction in writing where sensory detail is expected can be unsatisfying to readers. *See also* Details, Use of.

Exercise: Abstract Diction

Directions: For each of the abstractions provide three concrete illustrations.

1. noise
2. peacefulness

3. anger

4. ecstasy

5. drunkenness

Acronym

Acronyms are created by putting together the initial letters of an expression. Examples include DOS for Disk Operating System and MADD for Mothers Against Drunk Drivers. Laser, or *l*ight *a*mplification by *s*timulated *e*mission of *r*adiation, is an example of an acronym that became so commonly used that it was incorporated into the English language and spelled, as any other noun, with lowercase letters.

Active Voice

See Voice.

Adjective

Adjective comes from a Latin word that means "an attribute of"; it refers to any word that describes, or modifies, a noun, pronoun, or another adjective.

> That is a *fine* specimen. (*Fine* modifies the noun *specimen*.)
>
> She is *gorgeous*. (*Gorgeous* modifies the pronoun *she*.)
>
> These are the *most* valuable emeralds in the store; they are *more* valuable than diamonds (*Most* and *more* modify the adjective *valuable*.)
>
> *Most* is known as a superlative adjective; *more* is known as a comparative adjective. *See also* Parts of Speech.

Exercise: Adjectives

Directions: Identify the adjectives, if any, in each sentence.

1. The old woman, bent from arthritis, knelt in prayer inside the empty Gothic cathedral.

2. One of my most memorable surfing experiences took place just last summer, in Honolulu.

3. Little Red Riding Hood's two biggest problems were her gullibility and her poor eyesight.

4. We huddled, freezing, around the feeble campfire.

5. It is always a good idea to carry an ample supply of drinking water when driving through desert country during the summer months.

Adverb

Adverbs modify verbs, adjectives, other adverbs, and sometimes even entire sentences. *See also* Parts of Speech.

> The skydiver tumbled *frighteningly* for nearly ten seconds before opening her parachute. (*Frighteningly* modifies the verb *tumbled*.)
>
> Beverly is *utterly* captivated by Fitzgerald's *eloquently* written short stories. (*Utterly* modifies the predicate adjective *captivated*; *eloquently* modifies the adjective *written*.)
>
> Arlan *very* painstakingly engraved his girlfriend's initials on the back of the locket. (*Very* modifies the adverb *painstakingly*.)
>
> Luckily, we will get a refund.* (*Luckily* modifies the whole sentence, *we will get a refund*.)

Exercise: Adverbs

Directions: Identify the adverbs, if any, in each sentence.

1. The giant beetle crawled sluggishly across the table.
2. Erika has lovely golden hair that glows mysteriously in the dark.
3. Tobias felt bad about his having to miss work again.
4. Evidently, the detour is causing a traffic tie-up.
5. The sun feels good when the humidity is low.

Agreement

Words that relate to each other grammatically are said to "agree." For example, a singular or plural subject takes a correspondingly singular or plural verb:

> The *eagle screeches*.
> The *eagles screech*.

---

*Some adverbs used to modify sentences can cause ambiguity. See the Handbook, "Glossary of Usage," Hopefully.

Rhetorical and Grammatical Principles

A compound subject is essentially a plural subject:

The eagle and her mate are building a nest.

Agreement also exists between a demonstrative and the noun it modifies:

This person adjusted the telescope eyepiece.
These persons placed the optics table on its mount.

Remember that the indefinite pronouns *everybody, everyone, either, neither, each*, etc., are singular, and so take singular verbs as well as singular possessives:

Neither of us *likes* to ski.

Everyone is entitled to take *his* [or *her*] vacation.

Note: Use the singular possessive *his* only when every person in the group is male; use *her* if everyone is female; use *his or her* or *his/her* if the group is mixed. "Everyone . . . their" is incorrect.

Subject-verb agreement is not influenced by prepositional phrases:

Only one *person* among millions *catches* so rare a disease.

See also Sexist Language.

Exercise: Agreement

Directions: Correct any errors in agreement in the following sentences.

1. Jerry and David enjoys scuba diving.
2. One out of every five children hate roller coasters.
3. Neither Pauline nor her mother cares for modern art.
4. Everyone on earth value freedom.
5. Nearly every child remembers his first visit with Santa.

Ambiguity

Any utterance that can have more than one possible meaning is said to be ambiguous. Four common kinds of ambiguity include: (1) an unclear pronoun reference, (2) a misplaced modifier, (3) an ambiguous word choice, and (4) an ambiguous causative agent, resulting from a passive voice construction.

>   **Ambiguous:**   When Renée took her dog, Alicia, to the vet, she said she was getting dizzy from the hot weather.

Who was getting dizzy? Renée, the dog, or the vet? Revise to improve clarity of pronoun-antecedent relationship.

>   *Improved*:   Renée told the vet that her dog, Alicia, was getting dizzy from the hot weather.

>   **Ambiguous:**   Eduardo, a physics major, wants to study at MIT, uncompromising and highly disciplined.

Is Eduardo or MIT uncompromising and highly disciplined? Reposition the misplaced modifier.

>   *Improved*:   Eduardo, an uncompromising and highly disciplined physics major, wants to study at MIT.

>   **Ambiguous:**   Mr. Chang was surprised when someone offered him a thousand dollars for his car.

Since *surprised* can suggest both delight and disappointment, a more precise word needs to be used.

>   *Improved*:   Mr. Chang was appalled when someone offered him a thousand dollars for his Ferrari.

Exercise: Ambiguity

Directions: Revise each sentence to remove any ambiguities.

1. Sandra visited Wendy after she got off work.
2. Before you drive your car into the garage, you'd better clean it first.
3. Every night our cat climbs that rickety fence and caterwauls. Maybe we ought to get rid of it.

Analogy

An analogy is an extended simile of sorts whereby an object or phenomenon is said to resemble a completely different type of object or phenomenon. Writers use analogies mainly to help readers comprehend concepts unfamiliar to them. For example, one might describe the function of the human eye in relation to that of a camera, or one might compare genetic reproduction to telegraph code transmission. *See also* the discussion of comparison in Chapter 6.

Analysis

See the discussion of analysis in Chapter 6.

Appositive

An appositive is a word or phrase that sits next to the noun, noun phrase, or pronoun it defines. *See also* Absolute.

> Cheops, *ruler of all Egypt*, considered himself a god.
>
> We own a red-crowned Amazon parrot, *a beautiful but aggressive bird*.
>
> Send your dues to me, *the treasurer*.

Exercise: Appositives

Directions: Combine each pair of sentences by turning the second sentence into an appositive embedded in the first sentence.

1. Louis knew every square foot of Marsh Lake. Louis was an experienced fisherman.
2. Bruce Henry walked bowlegged. He was an ace rodeo star.
3. That old house at the edge of the cliff is going to be renovated. It is a masterpiece of Edwardian architecture.

Article, Definite and Indefinite

The definite article *the* is principally a demonstrative; in fact, it is descended from the Anglo-Saxon *phat*, meaning "that."

> *The* fire began in the closet.

It can also introduce a generalized statement:

> *The* Native American feels a deep spiritual bond with nature.

The indefinite article, *a* or *an* (descended from *one*), is used as a nonspecific referent:

> Take *a* book from the shelf.

See the Handbook, "Glossary of Usage," A/An.

Article, Nonfiction

Any short piece of nonfictional prose may be called a nonfictional article; this phrase is often used synonymously with *feature*, *piece*, or *essay*. In its more specific sense, an article is an expository prose discourse that focuses on a timely, practical concern. See also Essay; Review.

Auxiliary Verb

See Verb, Auxiliary.

Awkward Writing

The word *awkward* in writing usually indicates a general clumsiness or roughness of style. For example, a sentence could be considered awkward if its modifiers are misplaced, or if it is wordy, or if the main idea does not emerge clearly. An awkward paragraph usually contains sentences that lack coherence or that are simply choppy. *See* Coherence; Style; Wordiness; "Writing Strong Sentences" in Chapter 12, and "The Well-Made Paragraph" in Chapter 13.

Book Review

See Review.

Brainstorming

Brainstorming is a problem-solving technique whereby one or more people freely and spontaneously retrieve known ideas, facts, or details on a given subject area from memory, either to discover what can and ought to be said about a subject, or to discover new ideas or insights. *See* the discussion of brainstorming in Chapter 3.

Case

In grammar, *case* refers to the different forms, or inflections, of nouns, verbs, pronouns, and adjectives that result from their grammatical function in the sentence. The major cases include the following:

Nominative	subject case
Accusative	direct object case
Dative	indirect object case
Genitive	possessive case

Some languages, like Russian, use inflectional forms extensively. However, English words are inflected only in some instances. For example, English has retained a distinct genitive case: When a noun is used as a possessive, it is inflected with a final *'s*:

John has a bike. (nominative case)

It is John's bike. (genitive)

Dative case inflections occur rarely in English; *who* is still inflected to *whom*, as in the following example:

Who is the lucky winner?

To *whom* did you give your lottery ticket?

Other inflected pronouns are *he/him/his*, *she/her/hers*, *they/them/theirs*, and *it/it/its*. Adjectives and verbs do not have distinct case forms in English.

Classification

See Division and Classification.

Clause

A clause (from the Latin *claudere*, meaning "to close") is a group of words that has both a subject and a predicate. Clauses may be *independent*,* which means they are able to stand by themselves as grammatically complete sentences; *dependent*, which means they open with a subordinator that binds them grammatically to an independent clause in the same sentence, or *elliptical*, that is, one of their elements is grammatically "understood." Elliptical clauses can be either independent or dependent. *See* the discussion of coordination and subordination in Chapter 12.

Independent clause	*Enrico is singing today*, and he is eager to perform.

---

*Independent clauses are sometimes called main clauses.

Dependent clause	*Because Enrico is singing today*, he must not abuse his voice.
Elliptical independent clause	Liz is painting the ceiling, *and I the walls*. The words *am painting* are understood.
Elliptical dependent clause	Ramon speaks Spanish better *than French*. The words *he speaks* are understood.

Exercise: Clauses

Directions: Identify the type of clause underlined.

1. Louis loves Andrea more <u>than his other three girl friends</u>.
2. Thunderstorms are rare in this part of the country, <u>but we just might be getting one tonight</u>.
3. Todd came to dinner wearing a suit, but <u>Eric only a pair of swim trunks</u>.
4. <u>After nursing her cubs</u>, the tiger washed them with her huge tongue.
5. Time is running out; <u>we must hurry</u>.

Cliché

Clichés are expressions that have become trite from overuse. Examples: fit as a fiddle; last but not least; macho; out of this world; mind-blowing. See "Euphemisms and Clichés" in Chapter 14.

Coherence

To cohere means, literally, to stick together. Sentences and paragraphs are coherent when their internal parts are logically and consistently arranged. See Chapters 12 and 13 for a discussion of coherence at the sentence and paragraph levels, respectively.

Complement

A noun or adjective that follows a linking verb and that qualifies the subject of the sentence is called a complement. Noun complements are sometimes called *predicate nouns*; adjective complements, *predicate adjectives*. See Object.

Predicate noun complement	Boris is a *daredevil*.
Predicate adjective complement	Boris will be *unsurpassed*.

Exercise: Complement

Directions: Underline the complements; label them either noun complement or adjective complement.

1. Goldfish are funny.
2. Magritte's paintings seem dreamlike.
3. These brass lamps are antiques.
4. Proteus is powerful but moody.
5. Is it true that at this airport SSTs are banned?

Conjunction

The word *conjunction* comes from the Latin *conjungere*, meaning "to join together." A coordinating conjunction joins one independent clause to another, a subordinating conjunction signals that the clause it begins is dependent upon another clause, and a correlative conjunction establishes a correlation between one clause and another.

Coordinating conjunction	Igor barks a lot *but* he never bites.
Subordinating conjunction	We're go for liftoff *even though* a storm is coming.
Correlative conjunction	*Either* we leave now *or* we don't leave at all.

Exercise: Conjunctions

Directions: Change each sentence pair into a single sentence, using the type of conjunction indicated.

1. Bacteria saturate our every pore. Most of them are harmless. (coordinating)
2. Alfonso is a recluse. He does appear in town once in a while. (subordinating)

3. We can walk to the other end of the terminal. We can take a shuttle bus. (correlative)

Connotation and Denotation

Words that trigger emotional, irrational, or symbolic associations are said to be *connotative*. Not all words have connotative value, but all words have *denotative* value, or standardized, objective definitions. Sometimes words acquire connotative value independently of the author's intention. *See also* Figure of Speech; "Connotation and Denotation" in Chapter 14.

Dangling Modifier

See Modifier.

Deadwood

See Wordiness.

Definition

Definition (from the Latin *definire*, "to limit") refers to one or more of several possible methods of isolating the particular characteristics of a term. These methods include the following:

Lexical definition	an examination of the term itself, its etymology, and its usage.
Categorical definition	the term classified and examined in relation to other members of its class (sometimes referred to as *Aristotelian definition*).
Stipulative definition	The term given a special or restricted meaning by the author.
Operative definition	The term defined according to its function or to whatever measurable or observable phenomenon it produces.

See also "Defining" in Chapter 6.

Demonstrative

A demonstrative is a kind of nondescriptive adjective that works like an energetic definite article in that it points directly to the noun it modifies:

Those taxis [outside the hotel] have been waiting for hours.

This coin [I'm holding in my hands] is tarnished.

Details, Use of

Details are the particulars, the parts that make up the larger picture. They may be divided into two sometimes overlapping categories:

1. *Specific points that illustrate or support general assertions*: "Sheila is a generous person [*general assertion*]: She contributes one hundred dollars to each of five charity groups and she volunteers her time at the community hospital [*specific examples that support the generalization*]."

2. *Concrete, sensory, tangible particulars that illustrate abstract, intangible concepts*: "Edgar dresses ridiculously [*abstraction*]; his orange and pink paisley tie seems to shriek aloud, and his wrinkled yellow plaid slacks clash violently with his blue and red Hawaiian shirt [*concrete details that illustrate the abstract concept*, ridiculous dresser]."

See also "Words and Imagination" in Chapter 14.

Dialogue

Dialogue is conversation between two or more persons. In a composition, it is customary to enclose dialogue in quotation marks and to begin a new paragraph when a different person speaks:

"Are you sure we're on the right road?" John asked his wife.
"Yes," she replied. "I double-checked on the map."

See also Discourse, Indirect.

Diction

Diction may be defined as the style or manner of one's wording. *See also* Usage; Connotation and Denotation; Euphemism; Cliché; Abstract Diction; Details, Use of; Wordiness; Syntax.

Direct Object

See Object.

Discourse

Discourse refers to any form of linguistic expression, written or oral.

Discourse, Indirect

If we want to describe what a person has said without actually reproducing his or her words, then we use *indirect discourse*.

> **Direct discourse** Ludwig announced, "Today I shall compose a new sonata."
>
> **Indirect discourse** Ludwig announced that he would compose a new sonata today.

Notice that quotations are not used in indirect discourse. *See also* Dialogue; the Handbook, "Punctuation," Quotation Mark.

Division and Classification

To *divide* means to break down an object or idea into its parts. To *classify* means to gather up like objects or ideas into categories devised according to shared characteristics or classes. *See also* "Classifying and Dividing" in Chapter 6.

Double Negative

Before the nineteenth century, double negation was acceptable usage for emphasis, but today it is considered ungrammatical, even though it is common in colloquial speech.

Double negative (colloquial only)	*Single negative*
Don't you know nothing?	Don't you know anything?
I can't hardly wait to leave.	I can hardly wait to leave.

Embedding

Embedding is a technique of concision whereby the ideas in one or more sentences are combined with a third sentence to form one concise sentence. See "Embedding" in Chapter 12.

> **Awkward** Clyde is a clown. He dresses funny. Clyde likes to stand on his head.

Improved   Clyde, a clown who dresses funny, likes to stand on his head.

Essay

An essay (from the French, *essayer*, "to try," or "to test out") in the original sense of the word is a short literary prose composition that "tests out" the author's personal point of view on a topic. The author's style is generally either informal or semiformal, and the aim is mainly to share wisdom or advice in an entertaining manner. In recent times, the term has come to include articles, reviews, critical and scholarly papers, and even book-length nonfiction. *See also* Article; Exposition; Review.

Etymology

Etymology (from the Greek, *etymon*, or "true meaning of a word") is the study and determination of word origins. *See* "Ways to Use a Dictionary" in Chapter 14.

Euphemism

Euphemisms (Greek, *eu*, meaning "good," plus *phanai*, meaning "to speak") are polite, cosmetic substitutes for words considered too blunt or offensive for certain contexts. Some euphemisms, like *disabled* for *crippled*, are tactful; others border on the ridiculous, like *in a family way* for *pregnant*. *See also* Cliché; "Euphemisms and Clichés" in Chapter 14.

Exposition

Exposition, or expository writing, refers to a manner of presentation rather than to a distinct literary genre; it is any writing that relates facts and detailed information on a topic. Exposition may be a dominant element in a composition, as in an explanatory essay (*see* Chapter 6), or it may serve as evidence in a persuasive essay (*see* Chapter 8). Expository writing may even supply necessary background information in a short story or novel, as in the famous "Cetology" chapter (Chapter 32) of Melville's *Moby Dick*.

Figure of Speech

Figures of speech (or *tropes*, from the Greek, *tropein*, "to turn"; whence "turn of phrase") are words and phrases that add color and vividness to writing by expressing thoughts in a surprising or nonliteral manner.

Among the numerous examples identified by the ancient Greeks are the following:

Metaphor/ Simile	A comparison of superficially dissimilar objects or ideas. Metaphors indicate a complete identification ("I am the good shepherd" [John 10:11] or "We would be sitting ducks if they chose to attack") while similes make a more explicit comparision ("I lead my congregation as shepherds lead their flocks"; "We would be vulnerable, like sitting ducks, if they chose to attack").
Pun	An expression that suggests more than one meaning at the same time, thus generating wit. For example, one might use a word in both its literal and its metaphorical senses: "The nudists gave us the bare facts about their colony."
Periphrasis	The act of replacing a description of a particular kind of conduct or a typical aspect of a person or object with the name of that person or object. "When it came to gaining yardage fast, Tom was another Crazylegs Hirsch."
Synecdoche	The use of one part of a whole to represent the whole. "Tony borrowed his friend's wheels for his date."
Hyperbole	An exaggeration. "You scared thirty years off my life, sneaking up on me like that!"
Litotes	An understatement. "Hollis was pleased to learn that she won ten million dollars in the state lottery." Litotes is sometimes achieved when affirmation is expressed by negating the contrary: "Hearst Castle is not a shabby bit of real estate."

Exercise: Figures of Speech

Directions: Identify the trope that best characterizes each sentence.

1. Ellen, a gifted pianist, was determined to become the next Alicia de la Rocha.

2. The zookeeper was a bit startled to see the rhino burst out of its cage and chase after the visitors.

3. The stockmarket seesawed for a week before leveling off.
4. The hand of the law is more like a fist in some countries.
5. Jamie's bedroom looks like a war zone.
6. That last dentist bill took an awful bite out of my paycheck.
7. Jamie's bedroom is a war zone.
8. Our lives are too often regulated by the clock.
9. Gail, the weather forecaster, had a breezy manner of delivery.
10. A thousand people pushed their way into the elevator before I could get on.

Fragment

Fragments are grammatically incomplete sentences; that is, they are missing a subject or predicate or both. In the passage, "The kids ordered sundaes. For dessert." *for dessert* is a fragment. *See* "What is a Sentence?" in Chapter 12.

Generic Noun

This is a singular noun that on the surface seems to refer to one specific member of a class, but it really refers to any member of that class: "The dog is a lovable animal," instead of the more customary, "Dogs are lovable animals." *Man*, meaning "mankind," or more properly, "humankind," is often used this way: "Man's survival is threatened by the possibility of nuclear war."

Gerund

Gerunds are nouns fashioned out of verbs; they always have the *-ing* stem. Gerunds may be the subject, complement, or direct or indirect object of a sentence.

Loving you is grand. (as subject)

Gus's dream is *sailing* across the world. (as complement)

Jeff listed *running* as his favorite sport. (as direct object)

Ann sacrificed schoolwork for her *swimming*. (as indirect object)

Exercise: Gerunds

Directions: Use each word as the type of gerund indicated.

1. hunting (direct object gerund)
2. exercising (subject gerund)
3. painting (complement)
4. singing (indirect object)

Grammar

In the Middle Ages, grammar (from the Greek, *grammatike*, meaning "literary or writing art") referred to any learning in Latin. Not until centuries later did *grammar* take on its current meaning: a set of principles that describes the way a given language is correctly used. Grammar may be divided into the following specialized areas:

Parts of speech	Words classified according to the way they function in the sentence.
Morphology	The internal structure and inflection of words.
Syntax	The structure and dynamics of sentences.

Grammar is distinguished from semantics, the study of word meanings. *See also* Linguistics.

Idiom

An idiom is a nonliteral informal expression that is peculiar to one language and that cannot be literally translated into another language. "Getting your foot in the door" is an idiomatic expression for *opportunity*. "Good and tired" is idiomatic for *extremely tired*.

Imperative Mood

See Mood.

Indicative Mood

See Mood.

Indirect Object

See Object.

Infinitive

The infinitive form of a verb names the action only. It is the uninflected verb; it is never limited by person, tense, or number: "She likes *to dance*." "They like *to dance*." "We like *to dance*." Finite verbs, by contrast, are influenced by person, tense, or number. The verb *like* in the above examples is a finite verb.

Because the infinitive form of a verb is always two words in English, *to* plus the verb, it becomes possible to create structures called *split infinitives*, which occur when a writer places a word or phrase between the word *to* and the verb: "I like to sometimes dance." Split infinitives should be avoided in formal discourse. *See also* Split Infinitive.

Inflection

Inflection is the change that results in the form of a finite verb when a change in person, tense, or number occurs. Here are some of the inflections of the verb *to go*:

- I go.
- He goes.
- They go.
- We went.
- We shall go.

See also Case; Infinitive.

-ing Words

See Participle; Gerund.

Irony

Writers sometimes create an impression of someone or something in such a manner as to suggest an opposite view. Calling attention, let us say, to a murderer's politeness in public could create a sense of bitter irony, a sardonic incongruity, that could in turn heighten the monstrousness of the murder.

Linguistics

Linguistics is the scientific study of language and its uses, and is divided into the following specialized areas:

	Historical linguistics	the origins and evolution of language.
	Structural linguistics	the way languages work; the grammar of language.
	Dialectology	the study of language variation from country to country, or in different parts of one country.
	Semantics	the study of meaning in language.
	Stylistics	the nature and elements of writing style; the interaction of word choice, syntax variation, tone, and emphasis.
	Psycholinguistics	the relationship of human thought processes to language.
	Sociolinguistics	the study of language as a social phenomenon.
	Phonology	the study of the sounds that constitute oral language.
	Orthography	the study of the written symbols that constitute language (including spelling conventions).

See Grammar.

Linking Verb

See Predicate Adjective.

Main Clause

See Clause.

Metaphor

See Figure of Speech; Mixed Metaphor; "Metaphorical Language" in Chapter 14.

Misplaced Modifier

See Modifier.

Mixed Metaphor

Metaphors are so prevalent in our language that we sometimes forget they are metaphors; this can lead to using metaphors whose literal referents (words receiving the modification) contradict or in some way clash with each other. Here are some examples:

> When Al said he had *a bone to pick* with his neighbor, he was only *scratching the surface*.

> Janice *sailed* through her calculus final faster than a *hot knife through butter*.

Exercise: Mixed Metaphors

Directions: Rephrase each sentence to eliminate the clashing metaphor.

1. The children stampeded through the house like chickens with their heads cut off.
2. Once Chad fired up the boat's engine, it was smooth sailing all the way.
3. The cut-and-dried, sterile wording of the contract simply did not wash with his client.

Modifier

Modifiers (from the Latin, *modificare*, meaning "to limit," "to regulate") are words or phrases that limit the meaning of nouns or of other modifiers. In a sentence such as "Mark is an extremely daring stuntdriver," *daring* is an adjectival modifier of *stuntdriver*, and *extremely* is an adverbial modifier of *daring*.

Problems with use of modifiers include dangling modification, misplaced modification, and squinting modification.

1. A *dangling modifier* is a participle, phrase, or clause whose referent is not apparent:

Dangling modification	Exhausted from a long workout, the shower made her feel much better.
Corrected	Exhausted from a long workout, she felt much better after a shower.

2. A *misplaced modifier* inadvertently modifies the wrong referent:

Misplaced modification	They pruned the rose bush that bloomed lavishly every Thursday. (The rose bush bloomed lavishly every Thursday?)

Corrected — Every Thursday they pruned the rose bush that bloomed lavishly; or, Every Thursday they pruned the lavishly blooming rose bush.

3. A *squinting modifier* obscures the meaning of a sentence because it can modify either the word(s) preceding or following it:

Squinting modification — James reminded his son earnestly to study.

Corrected — James was earnest in reminding his son to study; or, James reminded his son to study earnestly.

Mood

One of four ways in which verbs may be inflected is mood (from the Old English *mōd*, meaning "mind"); the other three ways are voice, tense, and person. There are three moods in English: the indicative, the subjunctive, and the imperative.

Indicative mood — General statement or question of fact.

Our friend *is visiting* us tomorrow.

Is our friend visiting us tomorrow?

Subjunctive mood — Expression of wish or hypothetical situation.

I wish our friend *were visiting* us tomorrow.

If she *were* an inch shorter, she *would not have qualified* for the team.

Imperative mood — Giving a command.

Be quiet.

Narration

Narration is a form of discourse characterized by the dramatic presentation of events in a chronological and/or spatial arrangement. Such an arrangement is often used for the retelling of personal experience and for fictional storytelling, but it is also used in informative and persuasive writing as a means of providing historical background on a topic. *See* "Narration" in Chapter 4; *see also* Exposition.

Nominalization

To nominalize means to use noun forms of words where verb forms would be stronger, more concise.

> **Nominalized** Our *rearrangement* of the furniture was done hastily.
>
> *Predicated* We hastily *rearranged* the furniture.

Exercise: Nominalization

Directions: Turn the unwieldy nominalizations, italicized in the following sentences, into predicates.

1. Our *exaggeration* of the story was done in order to make it more interesting.
2. The *examination* of each of the athletes by the team's physician went quickly.
3. The *implication* of the committee was that additional funds would be needed to complete the project.
4. We did an *assessment* of our property's value.
5. O'Toole's *resignation* from the company took place yesterday.

Noun

A noun may be classified as any word that *names*—either an intangible element, such as an idea, feeling, condition, sensation, or force; or a tangible element, such as a person or object.

Exercise: Nouns

Directions: Identify all the nouns you can find in the following passage.

> Mr. Andrews watched in awe as his son and daughter performed a series of extremely complex skating maneuvers. Afterwards, when he asked them what they felt about their own performance (which received a standing ovation from the judges!), they launched into a ruthless criticism of themselves.

See also Parts of Speech.

Noun Clause

A noun clause is any dependent or subordinate clause that serves the same function as a noun, either as the subject of a verb, as the object of a verb, or as an appositive.

> *Whoever rang the doorbell* ran away. (Noun clause as subject)
>
> Jody hoped *that her friend would find her*. (Noun clause as object)
>
> The possibility *that life exists on Mars* is very remote. (Noun clause as appositive)

Noun Cluster

A group of nouns that function as a single noun, a noun cluster is often a symptom of doublespeak or verbosity. *Waste-storage facility* might be used for *dump*, or *media information dissemination* for news.

Noun Phrase

See Phrase.

Object

Any noun, noun phrase, pronoun, or prepositional phrase that depends upon the action of a verb or preposition for its complete meaning in the sentence is said to be the *object* of that verb or preposition.

> The Johnson family *won* the *Hawaiian vacation*. (noun phrase as object of a verb)
>   V   NP
>
> The search party *rescued them*. (pronoun as object of a verb)
>   V   P
>
> The poodle *swam* across the *neighbor's pool*. (noun phrase as object of a preposition)
>   V   NP
>
> *Note*: The entire prepositional phrase, *across the neighbor's pool* (preposition plus noun phrase), is the object of the verb *swam*. *See* Complement.

Exercise: Object

Directions: For each sentence, locate the object and identify its type.

1. Seamus bit into the enormous strawberry.
2. The coast guard issued a storm warning.

3. Where did you learn aerobic dancing?
4. As for the candy, I cannot find it.
5. The hungry tortoise devoured the entire head of lettuce.

Outline

An outline is an abbreviated summary of key points, often revealing hierarchical relationships, for a proposed writing project. There are two basic types: tentative, or scratch, outlines and finished outlines. A *tentative outline* is one that is drawn up spontaneously in an initial attempt to arrange gathered information about a topic into a logical pattern. These preliminary outlines inevitably change once the first draft of the essay is under way. A *finished outline*, on the other hand, is much more detailed and not as likely to be substantially altered. These outlines are especially useful for long writing projects, such as research papers, to ensure against digressions and to help the pace of the writing proceed more efficiently. Most finished outlines are prepared after a preliminary draft of the essay is under way.

Note the differences between tentative and finished outlines in the following examples:

TENTATIVE OUTLINE: "WHY NUCLEAR POWER IS DANGEROUS" (FIND STRONGER TITLE?)

I. Dramatic opening: near-meltdown conditions at two reactors in the United States within a single year

II. Background: energy needs—how urgent?
Can we get along on alternative resources given sensible conservation and alternative-energy research and development programs?

III. Central focus: principal dangers of nuclear energy
- waste disposal
- radiation leaks
- explosion risk
- contamination of waterways (including reservoirs)
- danger to wildlife
- risk of sabotage (?)

IV. Conclusion (include recommendations?)

FINISHED OUTLINE: "NUCLEAR POWER: DANGEROUS NO MATTER HOW SAFE"

I. Introduction
  A. We almost lost the cities of N—— and P—— when reactors X and Y overheated.

B. Even though the press and the Nuclear Regulatory Commission downplay the problem, reactors are deadly; are a constant threat to our lives and our health.
II. Discussion
  A. How we've come to have such faith in nuclear energy:
    1. Uncertainty of geothermal power, wind power, fusion power.
    2. High cost of solar power, synthetic fuels.
    3. Exaggeration of "foolproof" safety features.
    4. We are already using it; no disasters yet.
  B. Where the greatest dangers lie:
    1. Waste disposal—no satisfactory solution has yet been found.
    2. Instability of the earth's crust:
      a. Diablo Canyon reactor sits on an earthquake fault.
      b. Crustal instability exists everywhere, to some degree; it's only a matter of time.
    3. Constant possibility of terrorist-group sabotage, blackmail.
    4. Dire consequences of radiation leaks, meltdown, or explosion:
      a. to human community
      b. to biosphere
  C. Refutation of opposing views:
    1. "Nuclear energy is safer than most people think."
    2. "Nuclear energy will eventually bring energy costs down, thereby improving the economy."
    3. "Nuclear energy is cleaner."

See also the discussion of organization and outlining in Chapter 3.

Paragraph

A paragraph is a unit of discourse containing any number of sentences. It is called a "unit" for several reasons, including emphasis, change of subtopic, change of speaker (when dialogue is used), and change in continuity. Paragraphing is also a convenience to the reader, allowing for greater readability than do unsectioned "walls" of discourse. *See also* Chapter 13.

Parallelism

The repetition of grammatical elements or single words in a sentence or paragraph is called parallelism, used to facilitate clarity and comprehension. *See* discussion of parallelism in Chapter 12.

Paraphrase

To paraphrase is to reword an original passage to simplify the point or points made in the original. *See* discussion of paraphrasing in Chapter 10; *see also* Summary.

Participle

A participle is the *part* of a verbal element, as the prefix indicates, that functions as both a verb part and a verbal adjective. Present participles carry the *-ing* suffix and past participles the *-ed* suffix, unless the verb is irregular. Perfect participles exhibit the following construction: *having* or *having been* plus a past participle.

	Present Participle	Past Participle	Perfect Participle
Verbal Construction	Joan is *parking* her truck.	Joan has *parked* her truck.	After *having parked* her truck, Jane was ordered to move it.
	I was *singing* in the choir.	I had *sung* in the choir.	
Adjectival Construction	This is not a *parking* zone.	Let's meet by those *parked* cars.	
	Listen to those *singing* kids.	These are the most frequently *sung* hymns.	

Exercise: Participles

Directions: Identify the type of participle used in each sentence: present, past, or perfect; verbal or adjectival.

1. Wanda has mistaken that stranger for her sister.
2. The airline pilots are striking for more than higher wages.
3. Long after having seen the Northern Lights, Denise could envision them with her eyes closed.
4. The working title for my research paper is "Impotence and Criminal Behavior."
5. Ambrose is walking around with clenched fists and looking for trouble.

Parts of Speech

This expression is a not-too-precise reference to the way words function in a sentence. There are generally six functions: *nominative* (noun or pronoun), *predicative* (verbal), *adjectival*, *adverbial*, *prepositional*, and *con-*

junctive (connective). Any word that fits one of the following patterns would be identified accordingly:

Nominative pattern	Any word that fits is a noun or pronoun. The _____ is/are fun. Bill struck the _____.
Predicative pattern	Any word that fits is a verb or linking verb. Mary _____ everything. John _____ here.
Adjectival pattern	Any word that fits is an adjective. Joe is a(n) _____ person. The _____ train just passed.
Adverbial pattern	Any word that fits is an adverb. Alma gazed _____ at the moon. Our dog is _____ friendly.
Prepositional pattern	Any word that fits is a preposition. Sam walked _____ the ladder.
Conjunctive pattern	Any word that fits is a conjunction. Amy took a bus _____ Sandy biked.

Generally speaking, nouns are names of things, ideas, conditions, or persons; they may take a definite or indefinite article, *the*, *a*, or *an*. Pronouns are noun substitutes used for conciseness and to avoid awkward repetition; for example, *we* would be used instead of *Joan, Alice, Ignacio, and I*. Verbs embody the action of the sentence; they are what the noun *does*. Adjectives modify, or restrict the meaning of, nouns and pronouns. Adverbs modify verbs, other adverbs, or adjectives. Prepositions give spatial or temporal orientation to the verb. Conjunctions connect one clause to another. *See also* Adjective, Adverb, Conjunction, Noun, Preposition, Pronoun, Verb.

Exercise: Parts of Speech

Directions: Identify the nominative, predicative, adjectival, adverbial, prepositional, or conjunctive pattern suggested by each of the following:

1. Copeland _____ stirring symphonies.
2. What is the _____ of Puerto Rico?

3. We accidentally drove _____ our turnoff.
4. The miners listened _____ to the sound of falling rock.
5. The _____ books in this cabinet were given to me by my grandfather.

Passive Voice

See Voice.

Person

Person refers to one of four ways in which verbs may be inflected; the other three are *mood*, *tense*, and *voice*.

First person	I am; we are
Second person	you are; you are
Third person	he, she, it is; they are

A common error in narration is the *person shift*; the author begins in, say, the first person, then shifts to the third person. Person, like tense, should be used consistently throughout a narrative.

Personal Pronoun

These noun substitutes refer to persons rather than to things: I, you, they, us, who, and so on. *See also* Reflexive Pronoun; Relative Pronoun.

Phrase

A phrase is a group of words that can serve as the subject or the predicate of a sentence; it can also modify the subject or the predicate of a sentence. A phrase may contain a subject or a predicate, but not both. *See also* Clause; Absolute.

Noun phrases

The priceless Rembrandt painting was stolen. (noun phrase as subject)

Eric was *a sweaty, disheveled mess* after the race. (noun phrase as subject complement)

Long-distance swimming is her forte. (gerund phrase as subject)

Jody's hobby is *horseback riding*. (gerund phrase as subject complement)

Verb phrases	The old man *nearly fell backwards* on the stairs. (verb phrase modifying subject, "the old man")
	Twirling merrily, the ice skater circled the rink. (participial phrase modifying subject, "the ice skater")
	Loren longs *to travel everywhere*. (infinitive phrase modifying predicate, "longs")
Prepositional phrases	Alice flung herself *through the looking glass*. (prepositional phrase modifying predicate, "flung herself")
	The baby began crying *during the wedding ceremony*. (prepositional phrase modifying predicate, "began crying")

Exercise: Phrases

Directions: Locate and classify each phrase in the following passage.

Caroling merrily, the children stomped through the snow. All of them were ruddy-cheeked and beaming with joy. People rushed to their windows to see them.

Plagiarism

Plagiarism is the act of using the words or ideas of another in such a way as to give readers the impression that those words are the user's own. *See* the discussion of plagiarism in Chapter 10.

Point of View

Point of view has two meanings in rhetoric: the external, orientational perspective from which a narrative unfolds (first person, second person, and third person points of view); and the internal, "psychological" perspective, ranging from the objective, or neutral, point of view to the subjective, or involved, point of view. The following definitions of *dog* will illustrate the extremes:

> A dog is a domesticated mammal, varying widely in size, appearance, and temperament from breed to breed. (objective/neutral)

> "If you pick up a starving dog and make him prosperous, he will not bite you. That is the principal difference between a dog and a man." (Mark Twain) (subjective/involved)

Possessive

Possessives are pronouns or pronominal adjectives that indicate ownership or possession. *See also* Pronoun.

	Possessive Pronominal Adjective	*Possessive Pronoun*
First Person	my, our	mine, ours
Second Person	your	yours
Third Person	his, her, its	his, hers
Indefinite	whose	whoever

Exercise: Possessives

Directions: Locate and identify each of the possessives used in the following sentences.

1. Where did you leave your sweater?
2. Whoever finds our lost kitten will receive a generous reward.
3. Has your tree shed its leaves yet?
4. Is it true that San Francisco is everyone's favorite city?
5. That wheelbarrow is theirs.

Predicate Adjective

This type of adjective follows the noun it modifies and is "linked" to that noun by a *linking verb*.

> Eunice   is   ambidextrous.
> noun   linking verb   predicate adjective
>
> The cauliflower   looks   delicious.
> noun   linking verb   predicate adjective

When an adverb fills the predicate adjective's slot, it will, of course, modify the linking verb:

> Robert   looks   appallingly   tired.
> linking verb   adverb   predicate adjective

See also Adjective.

Exercise: Predicate Adjectives

Directions: For each sentence identify the linking verb and the predicate adjective.

1. Gambling is habit-forming.
2. When just above the horizon, the moon seems larger.
3. The last blizzard was unbelievably severe.

Predicate Noun

A noun that follows a linking verb is called a predicate noun; it presents an alternative name or title for the same subject. *See also* Noun.

> Dr. Gonzales   is   the neurosurgeon at this hospital.
> noun   linking verb   predicate noun

Exercise: Predicate Nouns

Directions: Locate the linking verbs and the predicate nouns in the following sentences.

1. Mr. Carter once was our attorney.
2. Gyorgy's grandparents are immigrants.
3. A bully! That's what you are.

Preposition

A preposition is a word that is placed before (*"pre-positioned"*) a noun phrase, thereby establishing a spatial or temporal relationship between the resulting prepositional phrase and the subject or object of the sentence. In the sentence, "The squirrel darted up the tree," the preposition is *up*; the resulting prepositional phrase, *up the tree*, establishes a spatial relationship between *squirrel*, the subject of the sentence, and *tree*. In formal usage, avoid ending a sentence with a preposition. Write, "To whom are you speaking?" rather than, "Whom are you speaking to?" *See also* Parts of Speech.

Exercise: Prepositions

Directions: Identify the preposition in each sentence. Describe the spatial or temporal relationship between the subject or object of the sentence and the resulting prepositional phrase.

1. Susan skillfully maneuvered her canoe around the yacht.
2. The tightrope walker tripped during his act.
3. The old man hid his valuables inside the wall.
4. Before you crawl under the car, make sure your wheels are secured with wooden blocks.
5. "It was like being inside the belly of a whale," said the diver of his venture into the undersea cavern.

Pronoun

Pronouns are economical replacements for nouns and noun clauses. They may be definite, indefinite, absolute, relative, possessive, or demonstrative.

Definite	I, we; you; he, she, it, they (subjective case) me, us; you; him, her, it, them (objective case)
Indefinite	one; anyone; someone; something; everybody; everything
Absolute	nobody; no one; nothing
Relative	who, whom; which; that The relative pronoun *that* is not to be confused with the demonstrative *that*: "The poem *that* I memorized is by Wordsworth." (relative pronoun introducing the relative clause modifying *poem*) "*That* is the poem I just memorized." (demonstrative pronoun)
Possessive	my; our; his, her, its, their
Demonstrative	that, those; this, these *This* and *these* are not to be confused with demonstrative adjectives: "I want *these* books" (demonstrative adjective) "I want *these*." (demonstrative pronoun)

Exercise: Pronouns

Directions: Isolate the pronouns in the following passage and identify types.

Who among us has had enough experience in public speaking to consider himself or herself an expert in it? Even seasoned speakers feel nervous when they reach the podium. The best antidote is practice; this, say experts, is the best anxiety-eliminator. But nothing can eliminate our anxieties completely; any method that is touted as a 100-percent stress reliever is pure hokum. Besides, we need some nervous energy to help us be lively.

Proofreading

See Revision.

Pun

See Figure of Speech.

Quotation

See Discourse, Direct/Indirect.

Redundancy

Redundancy is a type of wordiness wherein a word or phrase is not needed because another word or phrase already contains its meaning. Some examples are "ink pen," "true facts," or "the nurse vaccinated the child with a hypodermic needle"; *with a hypodermic needle* is redundant because one cannot be vaccinated with anything else. *See also* Wordiness; the discussion of conciseness in Chapter 14.

Reflexive Pronoun

A pronoun whose referent is the subject of the sentence is called *reflexive* (from the Latin, *reflectere*, "to reflect [back]"); a reflexive pronoun carries the suffix *-self* (singular) or *-selves* (plural). *See also* Pronoun.

	Singular	*Plural*
First Person	myself	ourselves
Second Person	yourself	yourselves
Third Person	himself	
	herself	themselves
	oneself	
	itself	

Relative Clause

See Relative Pronoun.

Relative Pronoun

These pronouns introduce clauses that modify the noun they represent. *Who* and *whom* are customarily used for human subjects; *that* and *which* for inanimate or nonhuman subjects.

> We gave a dollar to the blind man *who* was selling pencils.
>
> We gazed reverently at the giant redwood *that* is supposed to be seven hundred years old.

Typical relative pronouns are who, whom, that, and which. *See* Clause.

Restrictive/Nonrestrictive Clause

In the sentence, "My computer, *which I keep in the office*, has a color monitor," the clause, *which I keep in the office*, is *nonrestrictive*—the essential meaning of the sentence is not distorted by omitting that clause, which modifies "computer." The author infers that she has only one computer, and that she keeps it in the office.

But in the sentence, "My computer *that I keep in the office* has a color monitor," the clause, *that I keep in my office*, does influence the essential meaning of the whole sentence. The inference is that the author has more than one computer, and that she is speaking only of the one she keeps at the office. The clause in question is therefore *restrictive*.

Notice that nonrestrictive clauses begin with *which*, and are set off by commas; and that restrictive clauses begin with *that*, and are not set off by commas. *See also* That/Which in the Glossary of Usage.

Review

A review is a relatively short composition that evaluates a recent literary work, exhibit, or concert, and that often includes a commentary about the author(s) or artist(s) in question.

Reviews are commonly written for newspapers and commercial magazines; but a more developed, scholarly review (sometimes called a *review-essay*) can be found in academic journals and literary tabloids. *See* the discussion of the evaluative or review essay in Chapter 9; *see also* Essay; Article, Nonfiction.

Revision

Revision is an integral part of the composing process concerned with strengthening a composition, either holistically or in part, and either spontaneously or in planned stages. Revision includes such operations as rewording; rearranging ideas, paragraphs, and sentences; deleting extraneous or weak material; simplifying unnecessarily complicated passages; adding material where development is thin; and proofreading—checking for grammatical, spelling, and mechanical errors. *See* discussion of revision in Chapter 15.

Rhetoric

Rhetoric (from the Greek, *rhetor*, meaning "orator") is the art of speaking and writing clearly and effectively relative to purpose and audience. The formal discipline of rhetoric, designed for the training of orators, evolved in newly democratized Athens in the fifth century B.C. Teachers of rhetoric, called Sophists, emphasized the mastery of persuasive devices; but Plato (ca. 427–ca. 347 B.C.) shifted emphasis to the *ethical* foundations of oratory, holding *truth* to be the highest ideal. Plato's student Aristotle (384–322 B.C.) adopted this view of rhetoric and made it the basis for his great treatise, *Rhetoric*. Aristotle asserted that the aim of rhetoric is not to persuade but "to discover the available means of persuasion in a given case." He also stated that rhetoric, properly used, upholds righteousness and prevents fraud and injustice from taking hold. It was Aristotle who first distinguished between the basic *appeals*, or *proofs*: ethical, persuasive, and logical.

Rhetoric continued to flourish in ancient Rome, where Cicero (106–43 B.C.) and Quintilian (ca. A.D. 35–ca. A.D. 100) produced influential treatises on rhetoric (*De Oratore* and *Institutio Oratoria* respectively), which were read and imitated during the Renaissance.

The Renaissance was also a time when anti-Aristotelian sentiments were high. Laurentius Valla (1407–57), a philosopher/rhetorician who believed that rhetoric was the art of inquiring into essential truth, subordinated logic to rhetoric, in contrast to Aristotle, who regarded logic and rhetoric as "counterparts" of each other). Another philosopher/rhetorician, Petrus Ramus (1515–1572), viewed logic as a reflection of the way the human mind naturally operates. Ramus identified what he called the "loci," or categories, of thought, such as causal relationship, classification, and definition. He then applied these loci to reach conclusions about a given issue. In the late eighteenth century, the Scottish rhetorician George Campbell published his *Philosophy of Composition* (1776), a work which has influenced composition theory to the present day. In this work, Campbell, like Ramus, saw rhetoric as a reflection of mind, and argued that a speech may be seen as having one of four goals or aims, each corresponding to a facet of thought: to please the *imagination*, to aid the *intellect*, to influence *judgment*, and to rouse the *passions*. Nearly a century later, another Scottish rhetorician, Alexander Bain, translated these discourse aims into modes, or forms, in *English Composition: A Manual* (1866); thus Campbell's aim, "to please the imagination," became one or another form of imaginative discourse, such as poetry, for Blair.

In the twentieth century, rhetorical theory has been illuminated by many areas of inquiry, particularly psychology. A few examples include Jean Piaget's work in the language acquisition of children, Carl Rogers's insights into humanistic psychology, and Arthur Koestler's and Jerome Bruner's analysis of the range and nature of creativity.

During the "new rhetoric renaissance" beginning in the late sixties and still continuing, several rhetoricians have made fundamental contributions: Kenneth Burke, Richard Young, and D. Gordon Rohmann for their work in heuristics (invention) theory; Janet Emig, for her research into the actual composing habits of high school seniors; and Mina Shaughnessy, for her study of the nature of errors in the writings of underprepared students. Rhetoricians who have deepened our insights into the nature of discourse include James Kinneavy, James Moffett, and James Britton.

Rhetorical Question

Rhetorical questions are structured grammatically as questions, but rhetorically, they emphasize a point for which the answer is already known.

> An anonymous benefactor is giving me $500,000 to spend any way I please. How can I possibly refuse?

Run-on Sentence

See Sentence, Run-on.

Sentences, Kinds of

Sentences may be classified according to *syntactic options*, *mood options*, and *stylistic options*.

Syntactic options

1. A *simple sentence* consists of one independent clause, containing a subject and verb plus optional subject or verb modifiers.

Phyllis programmed her computer.

Here, *Phyllis* is the unmodified subject and *programmed* is the verb, modified by the noun phrase, *her computer*.

2. A *compound sentence* consists of two or more independent clauses linked by a coordinate conjunction.

    I love collecting books, but I am running out of bookshelves.

    But is the coordinating conjunction linking the two independent clauses.

3. A *complex sentence* consists of one independent clause plus one dependent, or subordinate, clause.

    Even though Dali painted grotesque visions, his paintings are beautiful.

    Here the independent, or main, clause, *his paintings are beautiful*, is qualified, or restricted in meaning, by the dependent clause, *even though Dali painted grotesque visions*. The subordinating conjunction, *even though*, signals the dependency of the clause.

4. A *compound-complex sentence* consists of two or more independent clauses and one dependent clause.

    After the poetry reading, Claudia and Don met one of the poets and enjoyed a long conversation with him.

Mood options

1. A *declarative mood* makes a statement of information.

    Ed is going to reserve a seat on the next flight to Mexico City.

2. An *imperative mood* presents a command.

    Please reserve a seat for Ed on the next flight to Mexico City.

3. An *interrogative mood* poses a question.

    Can you get me on the next flight to Mexico City?

Stylistic options

Emphatic devices, such as the use of inversions, and of cumulative, periodic, and balanced sentences, are included in the stylistic options category.*

---

*See Chapter 12, "Building Sentence-Writing Skills," for a discussion of these emphatic devices.

Sentence, Run-on

A run-on sentence is one in which the writer has joined two complete sentences together without supplying any intervening punctuation.

> Everyone who saw our college's production of *Macbeth* loved it too bad there won't be another performance.

A new sentence should begin with the word *too*, and so a period would need to be inserted after *it*. However, a semicolon or colon would also correct the run-on sentence.

Similar to the run-on sentence is the so-called *comma splice*, in which the writer incorrectly uses a comma where, in fact, a full stop is required. "Virginia City was Nevada's most famous boom town in the 1860s, it is now a virtual ghost town and tourist attraction."

Sexist Language

In recent years we have become aware of the way sex discrimination has, over the centuries, penetrated our language. For example, we have traditionally used the male singular possessive, *his*, to refer to someone who could conceivably be female. For example, sentences like "Has everyone completed his assignment?" should be avoided. The common alternative, "Has everyone completed their assignment?" is ungrammatical, as *everyone* is a singular subject. Here are some possible nonsexist options:

1. "Have all of you completed your assignments?" (The question is recast in the plural.)

2. "Has everyone completed his or her [his/her] assignment?"

Here are other examples of sexist language:

- Gender identification with certain professions: chair*man*, police*man*, steward/steward*ess*, and *lady* doctor (but never *man* doctor). The respective nonsexist equivalents are: chair*person* (or simply *chair*), police *officer*, *flight attendant*, and *doctor* (or *physician*).

- Gender identification with certain behavioral traits: *sissy* and *manly* (instead of modest, emotional, courageous, or aggressive); *old-womanish* (for fussy); *spinsterly* (for celibate).

See Generic Noun.

Exercise: Sexist Language

Directions: Revise each sentence so possible sexist connotations are avoided.

1. All men are equal.
2. Policemen risk their lives daily.
3. Pulling that child out of the deep water was a manly act for her to do.
4. Every public school child received his measles vaccination last month.
5. The stewardess helped us pass the time during the long ground delay.

Split Infinitive

In most languages, infinitives are single words: Latin, *legere*; French, *lire*; German, *lesen*; and Spanish, *leer*. Therefore, these infinitives cannot be "split" by intruding modifiers. But in English, infinitives are always two words (*to read*), and split infinitives can occur easily: "We love to sometimes read in bed." Although split infinitives are technically ungrammatical, they are generally acceptable in informal usage.

Spoonerism

An Oxford warden, Reverend William A. Spooner (1844–1930) had the curious habit of exchanging a syllable in one word with a similar syllable in another word in that same sentence. His famous "spoonerism," as the practice came to be known, was, "It is kisstomary to cuss the bride." *See also* the discussion of malapropisms in Chapter 14.

Squinting Modifier

See Modifier.

Style

Style in writing refers to the interaction of *several* techniques, not to just one technique: A writer's distinctive style is marked by the way he or she uses syntax and word choice, emphasis within a sentence or paragraph, as well as strategies of organization and development. Here are some representative definitions of style:

> Proper words in proper places. (Jonathan Swift)
>
> The manner, as distinct from the matter. (W. H. D. Rouse)
>
> L'homme même. (The man himself.) (Buffon)

The product of an individual personality interacting with the world; . . . how a writer characteristically makes sense of things. (Louis Middleman)

Subject (of a sentence)

The noun, pronoun, or noun phrase that is the agency of the sentence's predication is called the *subject*:

Diane sings.

The Mormon Tabernacle Choir will sing tonight.

Exercise: Subjects of Sentences

Directions: Identify the subject of each sentence.

1. The swallows soon will migrate south.
2. Where do you prefer to study?
3. Avoid the Christmas rush; shop early.
4. Bev's favorite Mexican dish is a beef tostada.
5. When do Tim and his wife plan to have their party?

Subjunctive

See Mood.

Subordinate Clause

See Clause.

Subordinate Conjunction

See Conjunction.

Summary

A summary is a condensed, objective (nonevaluative) restatement of an author's work in another writer's own words, but generally adhering to the original author's organization. Its uses are varied: to train oneself for extracting key information from a source quickly and accurately; to recapitulate an argument in a research paper or persuasive essay; or to transmit needed information to researchers. *See also* the discussion of how to write a summary in Chapter 10; *see also* Paraphrase.

Symbol

A symbol is any object made to represent a rich complexity of ideas or experiences, rather than a single, restricted idea or object such as an emblem (rose equals innocence). Symbols are generally subtle, rather than explicit, rising organically out of a narrative as, let us say, both a part of the story and a metaphysical commentary on the story's theme. For example, in his endless pursuit of Moby Dick, the Great White Whale, Captain Ahab may be said to symbolize pathetic, inherently debilitated humanity in its futile quest for . . . immortality? for the deepest mysteries of Nature? *See also* Figure of Speech.

Syntax

Syntax refers to the arrangement of sentence elements, or the sentence structure. *See* Sentences, Kinds of; discussion of writing strong sentences in Chapter 12.

Tense

Tense (from Middle English, *tens*, meaning "time"; from the Latin, *tempus*, also meaning "time") is one of four ways in which verbs may be inflected; the other three are mood, person, and voice. A verb's tense is its occurrence in time, such as in the past, past perfect, present perfect, present, progressive, future, and future perfect. The verb *go*, conjugated in these tenses, would be as follows:

- *Past*: went
- *Past perfect*: had gone
- *Present perfect*: have gone
- *Present*: go
- *Progressive*: am going
- *Future*: will go
- *Future perfect*: will have gone

Tense, Shift in

A tense shift refers to the unwitting lapse from one tense to another within the same time frame, say, from present to past, as in the following example:

> I get into my Jaguar and zoom out to the beach to meet my buddies. But when I arrived at the designated place, they were nowhere to be seen.

Exercise: Tense Shifts

Directions: Correct the tense shifts in the following passage.

> Monique is taking me on a tour of Monte Carlo, where we spend a lovely time at the famous casino. We also took a tour of the palace, as well as having visited several art museums.

Tone

See Voice.

Transition

A transition is a word or phrase that both links one independent clause, sentence, or paragraph to the next and emphasizes the relationship between them. Transitions are referred to technically as *conjunctive adverbs*. Common transitional expressions include the following:

- also
- moreover
- on the other hand
- as a result
- but even so
- in addition
- nevertheless
- however
- therefore

See also the discussion of transitions in Chapters 12 and 13.

Unity

A sentence, paragraph, or whole discourse is said to have unity when each of its elements contributes directly to a realization of the central purpose—when no extraneous matters are present. If an article focusing on how to pickle beets suddenly started discussing at length the history of beet farming, then unity would be violated. *See* Coherence.

Usage, Errors in

See the Handbook, "Glossary of Usage."

Usage, Levels of

In writing, as in speaking, we adjust our language use according to three variables: the occasion, the subject matter, and the target audience. We may distinguish four general levels of usage (keeping in mind that they often intertwine): slang (or nonstandard), informal, formal, and highly formal. The differences may be roughly illustrated as follows:

Slang	Bless me! Tommy's done flip-flopped like a crazed bullfrog over his sweetie-pie.
Informal	Can you believe that Tommy's fallen for Kathy Sue?
Formal	It seems that Tom has become quite attracted to Kathy Sue.
Highly formal	Thomas has evidently grown infatuated with Katherine Susan.

Exercise: Levels of Usage

Directions: Identify the level of usage in each sentence, then translate it into each of the other levels of usage.

1. The tropical birds are thriving in our new, environmentally monitored aviary.
2. It is to be regretted that external factors have precluded our plans to scrutinize the assembly process.
3. You put a tad more blue in the sky and splash more color in them rocks, and you'll have yourself one mighty fine picture, boy.
4. Don and Peggy are having the time of their lives taking in all the sights on their South American cruise.
5. Let's all pitch in to clean up City Park.

Vagueness

Vagueness is a term synonymous with lack of clarity or ambiguous meaning.

Verb

A verb relates the action or state of existence of the subject, and changes form depending on the *person* (first, second, third), and *number* (singular or plural) of the subject, and the *time* in which the action is occuring (past, present, future tense; complex tenses such as future perfect and present progressive). In the sentence, "Woody loves a good joke," *loves* is the third person, singular, present tense form of the complete verb (infinitive), *to love*. Here are some of the other forms of this verb:

I love a good joke. (first person, singular, present)

We love a good joke. (first person, plural, present)

You will love a good joke. (second person, singular or plural, future)

They loved a good joke. (third person, plural, past)

You and I will have loved a good joke. (first person, plural, future perfect)

She is loving this good joke. (third person, singular, present progressive)

See also Parts of Speech; Tense; Verb, Irregular; Verb, Auxiliary.

Verb, Auxiliary

Some verbs need the assistance of other verbs to help them complete their meanings; these are the auxiliary (or helping) verbs. When they appear by themselves in a sentence, the main verb is always implied. "We should be studying our heads off" contains two auxiliary verbs, *should* and *be*, that complete the meaning of the main verb, *studying*. If someone asks, "Shouldn't you be studying your heads off?" you would probably answer, "Yes, we should be." In this case the auxiliary verbs can stand alone because the main verb is clearly implied.

Other auxiliary verbs include forms of the verbs *to be* (is, was, am, are), *to have* (have, has, had), can, must, would, could, will, shall. *See also* Verb, Linking.

Exercise: Auxiliary Verbs

Directions: Identify the main verbs (as MV) and the auxiliary verbs (as AV) in each of the following sentences.

1. Nobody could explain the magician's strange trick.

2. They must have forgotten our address.

3. Can you walk a straight line with your eyes closed?

Verb, Irregular

These verbs do not follow the usual tense patterns of most verbs, and so they can confuse some writers. The "normal" past tense takes the *-ed* or *-d* stem, as in love*d* or walk*ed*. But irregular verbs change form: see/saw;

lie/lay; hang/hung (when referring to a sweater in a closet; hang/hanged when referring to a lynching). For present tense words ending in *-y*, the *-y* changes to *-i* and *-ed* is added. However, the *-y* remains if a vowel precedes it: apply/applied; *but* bray/brayed. Exceptions to the exception include lay/laid, say/said, pay/paid.

Exercise: Past Tense of Irregular Verbs

Directions: Supply the past tenses of the following verbs, some of which are irregular.

1. rise
2. lead
3. relay
4. drown
5. spring
6. sing
7. seek
8. pin
9. label
10. loan

Verb, Linking

Also called *copulatives*, these verbs identify or link, rather than predicate, the subject to its complement. *See* Predicate Adjective; Predicate Noun; *see also* Verb, Auxiliary.

Predicating verb   Elmer gained weight.

Linking verb   Elmer is fat.

Voice

The term *voice* has two meanings:

1. Voice is one of the four ways in which verbs may be inflected; the other three ways are mood, tense, and person. Voice may be *active*, whereby the subject of the sentence directly causes the action upon the object, or *passive*, whereby the subject of the sentence is the receiver of the action. In the latter instance, the cause of the action may or may not be disclosed.

    Active voice   Smangoland declared war on Ugolia yesterday.

    Passive voice   War has been declared upon Ugolia [by Smangoland].

2. Voice is another way of referring to *tone* or *tone of voice*: Is the author ironic? melancholy? bitter? tongue-in-cheek? angry? Reference to the way a composition comes across to readers as a result of the type of emphases, sentence construction, and word choice he or she utilizes is a reference to voice.

Wordiness

Wordiness is the condition of having used more words in a passage than is necessary to get a point across clearly and effectively. Consider the following sentence:

> It is an obvious fact that, in our day and age, cutting school budgets can only lead to a pronounced reduction in the quality of education for our children.

The sentence is wordy because the same idea could be expressed more concisely—and therefore more effectively:

> Cutting school budgets will inevitably lead to severely reduced quality education.

See also Redundancy; the discussion of conciseness in Chapter 14.

Writer's Block

Writer's block is the common term for being unable, for whatever reason, to continue or to begin work on a writing project. One of the most common causes is the high anxiety that stems from lack of confidence and uncertainty about how to begin: "What can *I* say about X that could possibly be interesting to others?" *See* the discussion of writer's block in Chapter 3.

DIAGNOSTIC EXERCISES: RHETORICAL AND GRAMMATICAL PRINCIPLES

Note: The page reference in parentheses indicates where the rhetorical or grammatical principle is discussed. Answers to the exercises may be obtained from your instructor.

1. Replace each of the italicized abstract expressions with a suitable concrete expression. (382)

    Example   The *flowers* were *colorful*.

    Revised   The *daffodils* were *a brilliant, almost luminous yellow-gold in the late afternoon sunlight*.

    a. *The athlete* decided to *work out*.

    b. "I'm feeling *ill*," the little boy whimpered.

    c. *The route* took us through *spectacular scenery*.

    d. The *campus building* was *unusual*.

2. Identify the absolute phrase, if any, in each sentence: (382)

    Example   *Ever the clown*, Missy did a somersault for her friends.

    a. His temper ablaze, the cook stormed from the kitchen.

    b. The designer, unrelenting in her demands, immediately rejected the plans.

    c. Jo Anna, perplexed, once again dismantled the photocopier.

    d. In Florida the lemon crop, to everyone's surprise, was meager.

3. Transform the second sentence in each of the following pairs into an absolute phrase that you then embed into the first sentence. (382)

    Example   Charley explained the procedure once more. His patience was worn thin.

    Revised   Charley, *his patience worn thin*, explained the procedure.

    a. The driver screeched to a halt. He was clearly drunk.

    b. The eagle soared high overhead. Its wings were long and graceful.

    c. Sidney double-checked his lottery ticket against the list of winning numbers. His heart was pounding.

4. Distinguish between the dependent and independent clauses in each of the following sentences. Not every sentence will contain both types of clauses. Do not confuse clauses with phrases. (389)

   Example   Before I can go home, I must finish my letter.
                   Dependent clause   *Independent clause*

   a. Did anybody phone me after I left the office?
   b. The morning was cool, but the afternoon was colder.
   c. The tiny plane disappeared inside a cloud.
   d. Unless we can raise another million dollars, the program will have to be dropped.
   e. Who among these people knows the secret?
   f. Everyone leaped under the table when the air-raid siren blared.

5. In each passage convert the dialogue to indirect discourse, or the indirect discourse to dialogue, as the case may be. (393)

   Example   "Why are you crying?" the old man asked the child.
   Revised   The old man asked the child why she was crying.

   a. "I'd like to order an extra-large pizza with anchovies, Bermuda onions, green olives, and hot banana peppers," ordered the man who had obviously been drinking.
   b. Bonnie asked her grandmother for a dozen of her prize-winning summer squashes.
   c. When Jerry asked his father if he could jump into the swimming pool from the rooftop, his father told him that he most certainly could not.

6. Some, not all, of the following sentences contain an error in agreement. Revise where appropriate to correct the error. (384)

   Example   Tanya and her friend is having a party tomorrow.
                   [*Tanya and her friend* is a compound subject requiring a plural auxiliary.]
   Revised   Tanya and her friend *are* having a party tomorrow.

   a. The books in this library are badly worn.
   b. Both the clam chowder and the grilled snapper is delicious.
   c. John and Vicky's relandscaping their front yard.
   d. Almost everywhere in Iowa is cornfields.
   e. Everybody has now got to take their seat.

7. Revise each of the following sentences to remove the ambiguous meaning. (385)

   Example The dog brought Jerry his bowl. [Does *his* refer to Jerry or to the dog?]

   Revised The dog brought his bowl to Jerry.
   The dog brought Jerry's bowl to Jerry.

   a. The sergeant approached the new recruit and returned his uniform to him.
   b. Chris asked Ted if Cynthia understood his last lecture.
   c. Gloria asked Sandra if Alice was going to call her this evening.

8. Transform the second sentence in each of the following pairs into an appositive. Then embed it into the first sentence. (387)

   Example Randolph flew all the way from Germany to visit me. Randolph is my uncle.

   Revised Randolph, *my uncle*, flew in all the way from Germany to visit me.

   a. The seismic wave flooded the coastal town. A seismic wave is caused by an earthquake.
   b. Cloris was worried about her cat. Cloris's cat is a fluffy Persian tom.
   c. Marilyn, Suzanne, and Amy graduated from medical school together. They are all first-rate neurosurgeons.

9. Locate the conjunctions in the following paragraph. Then identify their types: coordinating, subordinating, or correlative. (391)

   Example She sang *and* danced. (coordinating)

   Although we were late, we didn't miss our flight. (subordinating)

   Andrew drinks *neither* tea *nor* coffee. (correlative)

   Because of the thunderstorm, we had to cancel our fishing trip and picnic. Whenever I planned an outing this year, either it turned cold and windy or it rained. Perhaps next week or the week after, the weather will improve so I can make new plans.

10. The following passage is an example of indirect discourse. Transform it into direct discourse, that is, into actual dialogue. (393)

Example   Thomas asked Joan if she had planned to attend the Bach recital. Joan replied that she hadn't, but would love to go. (indirect discourse)

"Are you planning to attend the Bach recital?" Thomas asked Joan.
"No," Joan replied, "but I would love to go." (direct discourse)

Howard told Rosalind that he felt like doing something crazy. Rosalind wanted to know what he had in mind. Howard thought that perhaps it would be fun to go hang gliding, that he knew just the cliff to embark from. Rosalind looked at him strangely and asked him if he had another, less crazy suggestion.

11. Replace the euphemisms italicized in the following passage with more standard equivalents. Would your replacements be appropriate in all contexts? (395)

    Example   Mrs. Aldrich appears to be *in a family way*.

    Revised   Mrs. Aldrich appears to be *pregnant*.

    a. Ned excused himself to go to *the little boy's room*.
    b. The Pentagon decided it needed an extra three dozen *peacemakers* for the newly designated launch sites.
    c. Mr. Crumbly announced that the next person who came late to work would be *let go*.
    d. Mr. Sedley packed his *unmentionables* in his overnight bag.
    e. Carl is employed as an *automotive technician* for Lou's Fix 'Em Right Garage.
    f. We are out of *body spray*.

12. Locate and correct the error in modification in each of the following sentences. Then identify the type of error it is: dangling, misplaced, or squinting. (401)

    Example   Walking into the flower shop, my senses were overwhelmed with exotic fragrances. (dangling)

    Revised   Walking into the flower shop, I was overcome by exotic fragrances.

    Example   We visit a church that houses a rare, European pipe organ every time we're in Boston. (misplaced)

    Revised   Every time we're in Boston, we visit a church that houses a rare, European pipe organ.

Example   Jake urged his friend repeatedly to make a contribution. (squinting)

Revised   Jake repeatedly urged his friend to make a contribution.
Jake urged his friend to make repeated contributions.

a. The ham he baked gradually filled the kitchen with a tantalizing aroma.
b. Knowing she was being watched, Darla's fear intensified.
c. As she leaped over the high hurdles, the athlete's energy level increased.
d. The wrestler threw himself against his opponent with a wild look on his face.

13. Change the mood of each of the following sentences from declarative or interrogative to subjunctive. (402)

    Example   Fernando is here. (declarative)

    Revised   I wish Fernando were here. (subjunctive)

    a. Is the guard on duty?
    b. When is Grandfather visiting us?
    c. Leprechauns are real.

14. Locate the nominalizations in each of the following sentences and change them to predicates. (403)

    Example   The guard's *treatment* of the prisoner was harsh. (nominalization)

    Revised   The guard *treated* the prisoner harshly. (verbal)

    a. Lydia's memorization of the script was quick.
    b. The actor's recitation of a monologue from *Julius Caesar* was made with great eloquence.
    c. His examination of the patient was made in less than an hour.

15. Identify the object(s) of the verb(s) or preposition(s) in each of the following sentences. Then decide if those objects are noun phrases, prepositional phrases, or pronouns. (404)

    Example   The soccer team won *the state championship*.
    object/noun phrase

a. The school sponsored a spelling bee, and Terrence won it.
b. Who fed the dog peanut butter?
c. Clarence claims that he saw an oriole in the apple tree.
d. If you need more paper, look inside my briefcase.

16. Provide the equivalent possessive pronoun for each of the following possessive pronominal adjectives. (411)

    Example   My: *mine*

    a. your
    b. her
    c. our
    d. whose
    e. its

17. Replace the following sexist words with nonsexist equivalents; dispute any examples by writing "Okay as is." (419)

    Example   Mailman: *letter carrier*

    a. stewardess
    b. lady doctor
    c. chairman
    d. waiter
    e. Miss
    f. freshman
    g. seamstress
    h. salesman
    i. actress
    j. poetess
    k. housewife
    l. suffragette
    m. co-ed
    n. career girl
    o. mankind
    p. manmade
    q. manpower

18. Choose the verb that agrees with the subject it modifies. (384)

    Example   The circuses (*was/were*) always a lot of fun. (were)

    a. The choir (*sing/sings*) splendidly.
    b. Not everyone (*love/loves*) apricots.
    c. (*Is/Are*) your business transactions settled?
    d. Which of the two puppies (*have/has*) brown spots?
    e. One of several vases in the museum's collection (*was/were*) stolen.

19. Change the following passive voice constructions to the active voice. Can you think of any situations where the passive constructions in any of these sentences would be preferred? (426)

    Example   War was declared. (passive voice)

    Revised   Andorra declared war on Luxembourg. (active voice)

    a. The window was slowly being pried open.
    b. The ball was sent soaring into the bleachers.
    c. Dinner is being served.
    d. Your job has been terminated.

20. Rewrite the following sentences so the elements are parallel. (406)

    Example   The parks in this city are clean, well-maintained, and you're safe in them.

    Revised   The parks in this city are clean, well-maintained, and safe.

    a. The orchestra practiced diligently, carefully, and they were also sensitive.
    b. Freshman orientation can sometimes *disorient* students, and also is intimidating.
    c. The fish in this lake are plentiful, playful, and they grow to enormous size.

21. For each infinitive supply the following tenses for the third person: present, present perfect, progressive, past, past perfect, future, future perfect. (399)

    Example   to run: he runs, he has run, he is running, he ran, he had run, he will run, he will have run.

    a. to be
    b. to swim
    c. to occur

22. Identify the verb and its object in each of the following sentences; then decide whether the object is a noun phrase, pronoun, or prepositional phrase. (404)

    Example   The gardener uprooted the unsightly weeds.
                              verb   object (noun phrase)

Rhetorical and Grammatical Principles **435**

a. The glider soared over the foothills.

b. The dog was whining, but Betsy comforted it quickly.

c. Last week, Vonda purchased a state lottery ticket.

23. Replace the cliché expressions in each of the following sentences with non-cliché expressions. Revise the sentence if you wish. (390)

    Example   Jeanette survived the *acid test* of her oral exam.

    Revised   Jeanette survived the ordeal of her oral exam.

    a. As soon as classes ended we *high-tailed it* to the lake.

    b. Todd *put his nose to the grindstone* and finished his essay by midnight.

    c. The beach on Cape Cod was *pretty as a postcard*.

24. Identify the gerund(s) in each sentence; indicate whether they are the subject, complement, direct object, or indirect object. (397)

    Example   Skydiving is an exciting sport. (skydiving; used as subject)

    Example   Happiness is crocheting. (crocheting; used as complement)

    a. Kim turned to acting for therapy.

    b. The Warners devoted their summer to camping.

    c. Begging will get you nowhere.

    d. Seeing is believing.

25. One of the sentences in each of the following pairs is a fragment. Change it to a complete sentence, or embed it in the accompanying sentence. (397)

    Example   The clown traversed the tightrope. On a monocycle.

    Revised   The clown traversed the tightrope on a monocycle.
    or
    The clown traversed the tightrope. Amazingly, he did so on a monocycle.

    a. Rain has been forecast. For the weekend.

    b. Before we leave. Remind me to turn off the coffeepot.

    c. Zen koans are perplexing. Yet delightful anecdotes that embrace spiritual mysteries.

Glossary of Usage

This glossary contains two kinds of entries. One type offers comparative descriptions of words that are either easily confused, similarly pronounced, or closely synonymous in meaning; for example, the varied meanings and uses of *farther/further*, *complement/compliment*, and *complex/complicated* are explored in terms of these three most common problems, respectively. The second entry type presents descriptions of the preferred uses of terms in a given context; typical assumptions and established rules about words like *approximately*, *etc.*, *quite*, and *so*, for example, are discussed.*

You will probably want to use the Glossary of Usage in two ways: first, as a guide for revising (copyediting) your writing, whether your task is self-directed or conducted under your instructor's direction; and second, as a text for learning any or all of the entries. The glossary has been written to be studied for its own sake, not just to be used as a reference. Browsing through the glossary from time to time and reading whatever catches your attention can be a painless way to increase your command of English usage—and much more effective than memorizing the entries alphabetically.

A/An

These variant spellings of the same indefinite article are influenced by the word immediately following. If that word begins with a vowel sound, then *an* will be used: "The pianist gave *an* exciting performance." If the word following the article begins with a consonant sound, including the

---

*An asterisk before a term signifies ungrammatical usage.

aspirated consonant sound *h*, then *a* will be used: "We witnessed *a* startling performance"; "She usually tells *a* hilarious anecdote at company parties." But when the initial sound of the word is that of the vowel, *o*, because the *h* is silent, then the article *an* will be used: "*An* honorable man is hard to find."

Accept/Except

To accept [verb] is to approve or receive, or both: "I *accept* your proposal"; "Will you *accept* this package for the company?"

Except [preposition] is that which is left out: "All the tests were negative *except* the last."

Exercise: Accept/Except

Directions: Fill in each blank with *accept* or *except*.

1. The judges did not _____ any of the entries _____ the last one.
2. Will you _____ an out-of-town check?
3. "_____ no rides from strangers, ever," the schoolteacher said to his class.

Adopt/Adept/Adapt

To adopt [verb] is to assume responsibility for, to make a part of one's system: "They *adopted* that controversial policy."

Adept [adjective] is skilled, well-trained: "Joan is *adept* at operating an electron microscope."

To adapt [verb] is to adjust, to change to meet an objective or requirement: "Carl *adapted* his essay on tightrope walking for a younger audience."

Exercise: Adopt/Adept/Adapt

Directions: Fill in each blank with *adopt*, *adept*, or *adapt*.

1. Rolf is an _____ tightrope walker who can _____ his technique to any weather conditions.
2. A Hollywood producer plans to _____ that novel for the screen.
3. Students will be less confused by the new documentation format we plan to _____.

Advice/Advise

Advice [noun] refers to guidance, instruction: "Their telling you not to feed the alligators was good *advice*."

To advise [verb] is to give advice: "I *advise* you to invest conservatively until you know the market better."

Exercise: Advice/Advise

Directions: Fill in each blank with *advice* or *advise*.

1. Did the counselor _____ you well?

2. Exactly what kind of _____ did that counselor give you?

3. The defense secretary gave the President crucial _____ about the newest development in space weapons.

Affect/Effect

To affect [verb] is to influence, to interfere with: "Those three highballs *affected* his ability to sit upright."

An *effect* [noun] is a condition resulting from a specific cause or force: "What emotional *effect* did the earthquake have on the community?"

To effect [verb] is to cause, to bring about: "The rash of shark sightings *effected* a reduction in the number of surfers at that beach."

Exercise: Affect/Effect

Directions: Fill in each blank with *affect* or *effect* as nouns, or with the correct form of the verb *effect*.

1. Has the long-range _____ of mercury contamination been studied?

2. Everyone was relieved to hear that the airport _____ a more advanced security system.

3. Judd was surprised to learn that even one glass of wine was enough to _____ reaction time noticeably.

All ready/Already

All ready [adjective] means all set to go: "The kids are *all ready* to begin their Easter egg hunt."

Already [adverb] means by now: "The kids are *already* hunting for Easter eggs."

All right/Alright

All right is an informal way of saying that something is satisfactory: "We did *all right* in the calculus course."

All right is also a synonym for entirely correct: "Jeff got those calculus problems *all right*."

Alright is an incorrect spelling of the same concept; it probably originated via analogy with *all ready/already*. Sometimes, however, a fiction writer, wishing to reproduce gruff-sounding dialogue, may record something like, "Awright, who took a bite outta my chewin' tobacco?"

All together/Altogether

All together is a two-word (adjective plus adverb) compound modifier: "We are finally *all together* for our long-awaited reunion."

Altogether is an adverb meaning entirely: "Tom was altogether wrong in thinking that his mother would eventually get used to his pet tarantula."

Allusion/Illusion/Delusion

An *allusion* is an implied or indirect reference to something: "Did you catch Professor Barfroth's *allusion* to *The Great Gatsby*?

An *illusion* is a visual deception, such as an optical illusion: "When Molly wears her heavy coat, she creates the *illusion* of being overweight."

A *delusion*, by contrast, is a false notion: "Molly has *delusions* about being overweight, when in fact she's skinnier than Twiggy used to be."

Alumna, Alumnae/Alumnus, Alumni

These are college graduates, all. A female graduate is an *alumna* (plural, *alumnae*); a male graduate is an *alumnus* (plural, *alumni*); a graduate referred to without reference to gender is an *alumnus* (plural, *alumni*).

Exercise: Alumna, Alumnae/Alumnus, Alumni

Directions: Fill in each blank with *alumna, alumnae, alumnus,* or *alumni*.

1. Edgar is State's first Native American _____ to be elected to the United States Senate.

2. All the women in our department are City College _____.

3. The twentieth anniversary reunion for Xanadu's _____ will take place this week.

4. Paul, are you an _____ of the University of Paris?

5. Where do the City College _____ like to celebrate their reunions?

Apostle/Disciple

An *apostle* is one who is selected or one who volunteers to teach a master's doctrines (as was the case with the Twelve Apostles, whom Jesus called upon to preach His gospel). The word comes from the Latin, *apostolus*, meaning "messenger." "The guru sent his five *apostles* to America to preach."

A *disciple*, on the other hand, is one who learns from a master (from the Latin, *discipulus*, meaning "pupil"). Disciples often become apostles. "The guru's newest disciples listened intently to their master."

Approximately

If "big" words are to be associated with "difficult" words, then the five-syllable monstrosity, *approximately*, is a glaring exception. For some reason, many people love using this word when *about* or *roughly* would do just fine; "Good evening, shoppers, our store will be closing in *approximately* ten minutes." Actually, any of these words is redundant in most cases. When announcing a closing time, nobody is going to expect a NASA-like countdown! "Shoppers, the store will be closing in ten minutes" says it all. On the other hand, *approximately* works well in formal situations where precision is needed or desired but difficult or impossible to attain: "The radiation level will abate in *approximately* one year." But, when used with other words that already suggest imprecision or uncertainty, *approximately* is redundant: "The radiation level ought to abate in one year," not "The radiation level ought to abate in *approximately* one year."

As

See Like/As.

A while/Awhile

While (of *a while*) is a noun; *awhile* is an adverb. When *while* is preceded by the indefinite article *a*, it is easy to mistake it for the adverb *awhile*, or to assume that no difference exists between them. The difference is small, but distinct.

Will you be in town for *a while*? (indefinite article plus noun)

Will you be in town *awhile*? (adverb modifying *be*)

Exercise: A While/Awhile

Directions: Fill in each blank with *a while* or *awhile*.

1. If you're willing to wait just _____ longer, I can finish the job today.
2. The lovers sat for _____ on the deserted beach.
3. Once in _____ I'll feel like taking a long walk.

Bad/Badly

Both words may follow the noun-plus-verb construction. But the two adverbs differ in meaning as well as in function.

Bad following a linking verb is a predicate adjective that complements the linking verb and refers to an emotional state: "Andrea feels *bad* about yelling at her brother."

Badly is an adverb that modifies a verb and describes the quality of the action indicated by the verb: "Rex speaks *badly* whenever he's nervous."

Exercise: Bad/Badly

Directions: Fill in each blank with *bad* or *badly*.

1. The dentist felt _____ about pulling the wrong tooth.
2. The dentist performed the extraction _____ as well.
3. Does that reproduction look _____ to you?

Being that

Being that is a cumbersome phrase, best to avoid. "*Being that* the party was cancelled Filbert threw a tantrum." Use *because* instead. "*Because* the party was cancelled Filbert threw a tantrum." See also Due to the Fact That.

Beside/Besides

Beside means alongside: "Sir Charles, our pet iguana, likes to sleep *beside* his favorite rock."

Besides means along with, in addition to: "*Besides* our pet iguana, we have a pet boa constrictor too."

Glossary of Usage   **443**

Between/Among

Between refers to two, *among* to more than two: "Steven asked to be seated *between* two nonsmokers"; "Holly sat *among* her five closest friends."

*Between you and I/Between you and me

Since nobody would dream of saying "between I," everyone should equally dread saying "between you and I." Both pronouns are used in the objective case.

Borrow/Lend

You borrow something *from* someone and lend something *to* someone: "I had to *borrow* Mr. Reeve's hacksaw [borrow the hacksaw from Mr. Reeve]." But: "Mr. Reeve *lent* me his hacksaw [lent his hacksaw to me]."

Exercise: Borrow/Lend

Directions: Fill in each blank with *borrow* or *lend*.

1. My brother agreed to _____ me a thousand dollars, provided I _____ him my Lincoln Continental for as long as it takes me to pay him back.

2. When you _____ from that company, make sure you read the fine print very carefully.

3. That company will _____ to anyone for any reason, but their method of collecting delinquent debts is a bit extreme.

Can/May

You may have heard the anecdote about the child who asked her mother, "Can I go out and play?" to which her mother replied, rather snobbishly, "Yes, you *can*, but you *may* not." Keep in mind that *can* means to be able to, and *may* means to be permitted to.

Exercise: Can/May

Directions: Fill in each blank with *can* or *may*.

1. Anyone _____ write a sonnet, and you _____ do so if you wish.

2. Nobody with a weak stomach _____ watch that surgery without passing out.

3. _____ we see your passports, please?

4. Do you think you _____ unclog that drain?

5. The teacher is amazed that some of her kindergarten pupils _____ recite poems by heart.

Can hardly/*Can't hardly

Can hardly is an acceptable expression, but **can't hardly* is a double negative and therefore should be avoided: "We *can hardly* endure the heat when the humidity is high."

Capital/Capitol

A *capital* is a seat of government: "Washington, D.C., is the *capital* of the United States." *Capital* also means money available for investment, a type of crime punishable by death, and the initial letter of a sentence or proper noun.

A *capitol* is a building that houses a state or federal legislature. The word is capitalized when it refers to a particular capitol: "The United States *Capitol* has a majestic dome."

To avoid confusing the two terms, think: capit*o*l (with an *o*) equals d*o*med (with an *o*) building.

Both words originate from the Latin word *kaput*, meaning "head."

Exercise: Capital/Capitol

Directions: Fill in each blank with *capital* or *capitol*.

1. Ms. Ellwood visited the _____, where she hoped to sit in on a Senate meeting.

2. To open a new business one often needs to obtain venture _____.

3. Austin is the _____ of Texas.

Childish/Childlike

Childish is a derogatory term, synonymous with *immature*: "Throwing a tantrum on the floor is a *childish* way for a business executive to behave."

Childlike is always a term of endearment, calling to mind the most treasured qualities of childhood: "Many people love being around my grandparents because of their *childlike* natures."

Christmas/Xmas

The *X* in *Xmas* isn't the English "X" but the Greek "X" (chi), and is a standard Greek abbreviation for Christ (transliterated as Kh/Khristos). *Xmas* is used only informally.

Clue/Cue

Clue is a small piece of information used to guide one toward solving a problem: "The crime was solved on the basis of a single *clue*."

Cue is an auditory or visual signal used as a prompt: "The ringing phone was her *cue* to come on stage."

Compare to/Compare with

To *compare to* is to present the similarity *or* the dissimilarity: "Mr. Reynolds likes to *compare* the pseudo-Tudor architecture of American houses *to* the genuine Tudor architecture of British houses."

To *compare with* is to present the similarity *and* the dissimilarity: "It is intriguing to *compare* the painting style of Rembrandt *with* the styles of the other Dutch masters."

Exercise: Compare to/Compare with

Directions: Fill in each blank with *to* or *with*.

1. Justin learned a lot about farming by comparing one farmer's methods of sowing and harvesting _____ another's.
2. Compared _____ some punk hairstyles, Bo's is really quite attractive.
3. Astronomers were able to classify the newly discovered galaxy after carefully comparing it _____ other galaxies.

Complement/Compliment

That which *complements* something helps bring it to higher realization or completion: "A glass of ice-cold lemonade is the perfect *complement* to a sandwich lunch."

A *compliment* is a statement of praise: "The president of the university *complimented* the students for their exemplary behavior during the homecoming game."

Exercise: Complement/Compliment

Directions: Fill in each blank with the correct form of *complement* or *compliment*.

1. Do you think this pink sweater _____ my orange dress?
2. The Italian provincial china cabinet best _____ our dining room table.
3. We _____ our neighbors for their redecorating suggestions.

Complex/Complicated

A hairline distinction exists between these words. Something is *complex* when its nature possesses many facets: "T. S. Eliot's *The Waste Land* is a provocative and *complex* poem about the sterility of modern life." On the other hand, we say that something is *complicated* when we find it to be too much, or almost too much, for us to understand: " The directions he gave us to their mountain retreat were too *complicated* to follow."

Exercise: Complex/Complicated

Directions: Fill in the blanks with *complex* or *complicated*.

1. Reading the unnecessarily _____ contract gave me a headache.
2. Norris succeeded in making the computer program much less _____ than it was originally.
3. Bach's fugues are deliciously _____.

Concave/Convex

Concave means inwardly or negatively curved, as is the interior of a sphere.
    Convex means outwardly or positively curved, as is the lens of a magnifying glass or the outside of a sphere.

Conscience/Conscientious/ Conscious/Self-conscious

Your *conscience* is your moral or ethical awareness, which you may choose to follow or ignore: "Eleanor was content with herself for following her *conscience* and refusing to testify."

Conscientious has two meanings: It describes one who follows his or her conscience ("Eleanor *conscientiously* chose not to testify"); and one who is careful in monitoring one's behavior: "Mark was *conscientious* in the way he chose his words."

To be awake and aware is to be *conscious*: "Bob remained *conscious* after he was struck on the head with a crowbar."

To be *self-conscious* is to be aware of one's appearance and/or actions to an extreme degree, often uncomfortably so: "Margaret felt *self-conscious* about attending the costume party dressed as Lady Godiva."

Exercise: Conscience/Conscientious/Conscious/Self-conscious

Directions: Choose the most appropriate of the four alternatives for each blank.

1. Protesting apartheid is a noble act of _____.
2. Do you suppose the protesters felt _____ about marching through the heart of downtown?
3. Alex _____ gave each visitor an instructive tour of the archives.
4. After having been comatose for a week, the woman slowly became _____ of her surroundings.
5. The little boy felt a pang of _____ after he poured vinegar into the goldfish bowl.

Continually/Continuously

Something that runs *continually* is subject to regularly occurring interruptions: "Serious athletes train *continually*."

Something that runs continuously occurs without interruption: "The air conditioner runs *continuously* in extremely hot weather."

Here's a memory aid to help you avoid confusing these terms: Continu*al*, *al*low for interruptions.

Exercise: Continually/Continuously

Directions: Fill in each blank with *continually* or *continuously*.

1. The faucet dripped _____.
2. Every chessplayer on the team _____ practices new strategies; some need to listen _____ to music when they do.
3. The baby cried _____ throughout the night.

Could care less/Couldn't care less

"They could care less" means that they can imagine themselves caring less about something they already care about, which is contrary to the intended meaning. Here's an example of the correct usage: "My father loves bow ties and *couldn't care less* that they're out of style."

Could have/*Could of/Could've

Could of is an erroneous construction that has come about because it sounds like *could've*, the contraction for *could have*. *Could've* is a perfectly acceptable informal construction, particularly when used in dialogue: "'I *could've* gone all the way to the top,' the ex-executive muttered into his beer."

Credible/Credulous

It's easy to confuse these two. *Credible* means deserving to be believed: "Her story, backed up by so much evidence, is entirely *credible*."
Credulous means gullible: "The children are ever *credulous* when it comes to stories about the Great Pumpkin."

Criteria [plural]/Criterion [singular]

This term most often appears in the plural: "NASA's *criteria* for astronaut selection are incredibly strict; one *criterion* in particular would probably eliminate 90 percent of the applicants."

Different from/Different than

Unlike comparatives like *fatter* or *richer*, which stress similarities between X and Y ("Taft was fatter than Churchill"; both were fat, but one was fatter), *different* signals dissimilarity. Hence, *different from*: "Swahili grammar is *different from* English grammar." *Note*: *Different* plus a clause beginning with *than* is acceptable: "The wiring procedure was more different than the supervisor had earlier suggested."

Dilemma/Problem

A dilemma is a special kind of problem, as the etymology reveals: *Di* means two; *lemma* means option or proposition. When you face a dilemma, you are facing a fork in the road—a need to choose between just two equally viable options. That is why we have the somewhat clichéd expression, "horns of a dilemma."

Dinner/Lunch/Supper

Once upon a time the main meal of the day, served late in the afternoon, was *dinner*, and the evening meal, something of a snack by comparison, was *supper*. The terms are now roughly interchangeable, particularly in large urban areas. A possible exception is the holiday dinner: "We serve Thanksgiving dinner at 3 P.M." *Lunch* has become our early-afternoon meal, and the word always has an informal ring to it: "Let's grab some lunch over at Woolworth's." Formal early-afternoon meals are called *luncheons*.

Discreet/Discrete

Discreet means tasteful in one's behavior: "Paul *discreetly* refrained from insulting his opponent." The noun is *discretion* (the *c* is pronounced like a *k*, and the *e* is short).

Discrete means separate and distinct: "That bedrock consists of at least ten *discrete* layers."

Exercise: Discreet/Discrete

Directions: Fill in each blank with the correct form of *discreet* or *discrete*.

1. We responded _____ to the controversial question.

2. Researchers detected _____ differences between current and year-old data derived from the same experiment.

3. Sometimes it isn't possible to make _____ comments about certain eccentric sexual customs.

Disinterested/Uninterested

Disinterested is a word we probably wouldn't use even if we did remember how to use it correctly. Like *fulsome* (loathsome), *disinterested* just doesn't *look* right as "objective, neutral": "The *disinterested* judge was completely absorbed in the court battle." It's no surprise that the word is often used the way *uninterested* should be used: as expressing no interest.

Exercise: Disinterested/Uninterested

Directions: Fill in each blank with *disinterested* or *uninterested*.

1. The news commentator gave a(n) _____ report on the new immigration law controversy.

2. Sleepy and uncomfortable, the child seemed completely _____ in the clown's antics.

3. Although Pierre loves painting and sculpture, he is generally _____ in taking courses in those subjects.

Dived/Dove

Dived used to be the preferred usage. These days, either *dived* or *dove* is acceptable. **Doved* is ungrammatical. "Ellen *dived* [or *dove*, but not *doved*] into the pool."

Dominant/Dominate

Dominant (adjective) is the quality of being in control: "Luciano's is the *dominant* voice in the choir."

To *dominate* (verb) is to exert control, to be the most noticeable: "Luciano's voice *dominates* everyone else's in the choir."

Drowned/*Drownded

**Drownded* is ungrammatical. "The kitten would have *drowned* [not *drownded*] if Mom had not dived in to save it." For a similar tense-confusion error, *see* Spay/Spayed/Spayded.

Due to the Fact That

Due to the fact that is verbose. "*Due to the fact that* the main rocket overheated, the shuttle launch was scrubbed." Use *because* instead. "*Because* the main rocket overheated, the shuttle launch was scrubbed." See also Being That.

Effect

See Affect/Effect.

Ensure/Insure

The distinction between *ensure*, to assure, and *insure*, to protect with an insurance policy, has blurred over the past twenty-five years. Nowadays, *insure* serves both meanings, at least in the United States.

Enthused/Enthusiastic

In informal conversation, *enthused* is appropriate since *enthusiastic* is such a mouthful. But the word *enthused* is inappropriate in writing: "At first nonchalant, Marge is now *enthusiastic* [not enthused] about her upcoming trip to Nova Scotia."

Etc.

Etc. (an abbreviation of the Latin *et cetera*, meaning "and so on") should be limited to informal writing. In formal writing, the expression seems to halt commentary prematurely: "Their majestic country estate has a gigantic family room with a brick fireplace, three ceramic-tiled bathrooms, *etc.*" Use *etc.* when you are certain that readers know what is being left out and don't care to have everything itemized.

Evoke/Invoke

To *evoke* is to bring forth, to draw out: "Poe's *The Raven* always *evokes* an air of gloom and mystery for me."

To *invoke* is to call upon, particularly in a ritualistic manner: "Using a long-lost incantation, the mystic *invoked* the ghost of her great-great-grandfather."

Exercise: Evoke/Invoke

Directions: Fill in each blank with the correct form of *evoke* or *invoke*.

1. During the Navajo ceremony, the chief _____ the fertility spirit.
2. Walking through a forest always _____ childhood memories for me.
3. Faust shrunk back in terror after he _____ Mephistopheles.

Evidence/Proof

Evidence is that which is presented to support an assertion or hypothesis: "Newly uncovered documents have supplied additional *evidence* that a merger was planned much earlier than suspected."

Proof refers to virtually indisputable evidence: "While we have some evidence that no life exists on Mars, we'll never have *proof* of that until we actually visit the planet." *See also* the discussion of effective argument building in Chapter 8.

Except

See Accept/Except.

Farther/Further

Use *farther* with reference to distance: "We drove twenty miles *farther* than anticipated before reaching our destination."

Use *further* to indicate "more time" or "to a greater degree": "Study the report *further* before making a decision."

Exercise: Farther/Further

Directions: Fill in each blank with *farther* or *further*.

1. The _____ I get from that city, the more relaxed I feel.
2. Do you need to extend that column _____ down the page?
3. Everyone's hopes were raised after _____ communications were received.

Fewer/Less

When referring to discernible parts, use *fewer*: "We eat *fewer* steaks than we used to."

When referring to a noun that does not consist of discernible parts, use *less*: "I drink *less* water when it's ice-cold."

Exercise: Fewer/Less

Directions: Fill in each blank with *fewer* or *less*.

1. Lenny was pleased to see that he'd made _____ mistakes on his last calculus quiz.
2. The tank showed _____ corrosion than Mary had previously anticipated.
3. McEnroe won _____ games at Wimbledon this year than last.

Figuratively/Literally

Figuratively means metaphorically: "The shoe is on the other foot, *figuratively* speaking." As in this example, the metaphor is often obvious and therefore the expression is redundant; use it only when confusion is likely otherwise.

Literally means what is actually meant at face value: "Meteors are *literally* out of this world." Make sure you don't use this term when you are really speaking figuratively: "My grandfather's age is *literally* Methuselan" means that the grandfather is eight hundred years old.

Flaunt/Flout

To *flaunt* is to display proudly, to show off: "King Henry *flaunted* his jeweled rings."

To *flout* is to be contemptuous of: "The demonstrators *flouted* the approaching riot police."

Exercise: Flaunt/Flout

Directions: Fill in each blank with *flaunt* or *flout*.

1. Peacocks like to _____ their fabulous tails.
2. The antique buff _____ most of the cheaply made lamps of today.
3. Throughout her tour of the Soviet Union, Talia _____ her American-flag pin proudly.

Further

See Farther/Further.

Glance/Glimpse

These are tricky. A *glance* is a brief look *at* someone or something: "Although I only took one *glance* at her, I knew she was my sister." A *glimpse* is a brief sighting *of* someone or something: "I got a *glimpse* of that meteor last night."

Exercise: Glance/Glimpse

Directions: Fill in each blank with the correct form of *glance* or *glimpse*.

1. All the children cheered as soon as they got their first _____ of Wonder Woman.
2. After _____ at the first suspect, the man shook his head.
3. Wilbur took one last _____ at the stunning seascape before returning to his car.

Graduated/Graduated from/Was graduated

The use of *graduated* as a transitive verb, as in "Joan *graduated* college today," is incorrect. Write instead, "Joan *graduated* today"; "Joan *graduated from* college today"; or "Joan *was graduated* from her college today."

Hanged/Hung

The past tense of *hang* in the sense of "lynch" is *hanged*. The past tense of *hang* in the sense of "place on hangers or clothespins" is *hung*.

Hopefully/It is hoped

Hopefully is used correctly when it modifies a verb rather than a whole sentence. "Lana gazed *hopefully* into her mother's eyes."

Hopefully used in the sense of "I/we hope," "it is hoped," or "let us hope" is an informal, although some will say erroneous, construction: "*Hopefully*, the circus will come to town this summer."

Imply/Infer

To *imply* is to suggest: "What were you *implying* by that remark?"

To *infer* is to interpret, to piece together: "I *inferred* from your remark that you were displeased."

Exercise: Imply/Infer

Directions: Fill in each blank with the correct form of *imply* or *infer*.

1. Can anyone _____ from these ancient records what kinds of foods the Babylonians ate?

2. The directions _____ that you need to approach the problem in three stages.

3. The child pointed to her stomach, _____ that she was hungry.

Insure

See Ensure/Insure.

*Irregardless/Regardless

The *-ir* prefix added to *regardless* is ungrammatical, and presumably used for additional emphasis; **irregardless* is similar in nature to double-negative construction. *Regardless* is the correct term: "I'm going to wear my zombie costume to the party *regardless* [not *irregardless*] of what people will think."

It's/Its

It's is the contraction for "it is": "*It's* about time you showed up."

Its is a possessive pronoun: "The whale lashed *its* flukes." Inadvertent misuse of *it's* and *its* is quite common in first-draft composing; keep an eye out for it when proofreading.

Glossary of Usage

Exercise: It's/Its

Directions: Fill in each blank with *it's* or *its*.

1. The spider wrapped _____ prey in a cocoon of silk.
2. Are you sure _____ been a whole year since my last visit to the dentist?
3. _____ a shame you refuse to eat your dinner while _____ hot.

Lay/Lie

Almost everyone has trouble distinguishing between these two words. *Lay* is the present-tense verb meaning to put down: "*Lay* your cards on the table." The past tense would be: "He *laid* his cards on the table." But *lay* is also the past tense of the verb *lie*, meaning to recline: "*Lie* down if you feel dizzy"; "She *lay* on the bed until her headache went away." The following chart should be helpful.

Infinitive	Present Tense	Past Tense	Present/Past Indicative	Present/Past Perfect
to lie	lie, lies	lay	is/was lying	has/had lain
to lay	lay, lays	laid	is/was laying	has/had laid

Exercise: Lay/Lie

Directions: Fill in each blank with the correct form of *lay* or *lie*.

1. While Arthur and David were _____ on the beach at Los Alamitos, two of the most beautiful women they had ever seen _____ down next to them.
2. _____ your toolbox here, where Arnie _____ his.
3. Sharon _____ in the shade of her umbrella and still gets sunburned.
4. Whenever Ken _____ his ice cream on the table, the dog sneaks up and eats it.
5. Once someone with light skin has _____ in direct sunlight for more than half an hour, sunburn is almost inevitable.

Lead/Led

Led is the past tense of *lead*, pronounced lēēd: "The scout *led* the sightseers up the mountain"; "Please *lead* the way."

The chemical element, *lead*, is pronounced led.

Exercise: Lead/Led

Directions: Fill in each blank with *lead* or *led*.

1. Will you _____ the class discussion today?
2. The sergeant _____ his men into battle.
3. Get the _____ out of your feet and move!

Lend

See Borrow/Lend.

Like/As

Use *like* as a preposition indicating resemblance: "She sings *like* a pro."

Use *as* as a conjunction indicating a correlation: "The little boy splashed through the mud, *as* children love to do"; "We guarantee our work, *as* our customers have come to expect." Using *like* instead of *as* in these last two examples is strictly informal.

Exercise: Like/As

Directions: Fill in each blank with *like* or *as*.

1. It takes a makeup artist hours to make someone look _____ a monster.
2. _____ any experienced parent knows, children love having grownups read them stories.
3. Alaska is not as cold _____ most people think.

Loose/Lose

The adjective *loose* means the opposite of tight.

The verb to *lose*, pronounced lōōz, means to misplace.

——ly (at the end of ordinal numbers)

Adding the suffix *-ly* to ordinal numbers, as in *firstly*, *secondly*, and *thirdly*, is redundant. Write instead *first*, *second*, *third*, and so on.

Masterful/Masterly

Masterful means powerful and domineering: "Joan of Arc was a *masterful* soldier."

Masterly means demonstrating the talent of a master: "Rudolf Serkin gave a *masterly* performance of the Beethoven sonata."

Exercise: Masterful/Masterly

Directions: Fill in each blank with *masterful* or *masterly*.

1. After only a year's practice, Laura has learned to play the alto saxophone with _____ skill.
2. General Eisenhower proved to be a _____ leader during the D-day invasion.
3. Karpov played the final chess match in his usual _____ fashion.

Media/Medium

Media, in the sense of mass media, is plural, and therefore takes a plural verb: "The top advertising *media* are TV and radio." Use *medium* for singular constructions: "TV is a controversial *medium* in many ways."

Exercise: Media/Medium

Directions: Fill in each blank with *media* or *medium*.

1. It seems that the _____, in covering these events, are often biased.
2. In some ways, newspapers are a more influential _____ than radio or television.
3. The _____ of television has profoundly affected journalism.

New/Newly

Both *new* and *newly* can be used as adverbs to modify participles; *new* can also be used as an adjective. Use *new* to modify one-syllable nouns or adjectives: "Our *new*-found friend." Use newly for larger words: "We dined at the *newly* remodeled restaurant."

Obsolete/Obsolescent

Something that is *obsolete* is no longer fashionable or in use: "The abacus may be woefully *obsolete*, but some people find it fun to use."

Obsolescent refers to that which, in the writer's opinion, is becoming obsolete: "Computer technology advances so rapidly that some new machines are *obsolescent* even when they first appear on the market."

Oftentimes

This word is best to avoid, as *-times* is redundant. Use *often*.

Passed/Past

Past can be a noun meaning "before the present" ("the earth's remote *past*") or a preposition meaning beyond in position ("We walked *past* the bank"). *Passed* is a verb of motion: "We *passed* the bank on our skateboards."

Persecute/Prosecute

To *persecute* is to mistreat or to oppress: "That gang is notorious for *persecuting* elderly people."

To *prosecute* is to bring legal proceedings against someone: "Shoplifters will be *prosecuted*—even first offenders."

Plus

Outside its mathematical sense, *plus* is strictly informal: "Our poor cat got caught in the tree, *plus* she hurt her paw." In this sentence, *and* would be more appropriate. Here's another example: "Tiling the entry was a real *plus* to the appearance of our house." In this sentence, use *improvement*, or recast the expression as a verbal: "Tiling the entry *improved* the appearance of our house."

Precede/Proceed

To *precede* is to occur or go before: "A benediction *precedes* and follows the graduation ceremony."

To *proceed* is to continue or to begin: "The mutt sniffed the kitten and then proceeded to lick its startled face."

Exercise: Precede/Proceed

Directions: Fill in each blank with *precede* or *proceed*.

1. Please _____ across the intersection, then pull to the curb.

2. Review the instructions in the paragraphs that _____ this one, then _____ to complete the task.

3. Once the astronauts are safely landed, they will _____ to explore the planet's surface.

Prejudice/Prejudiced

The noun *prejudice* means the act of passing judgment beforehand, whether favorable or unfavorable: "Mr. Leer revealed his *prejudice* toward redheads when he doubled Rhonda's and Rena's salaries."

The adjective *prejudiced* describes the application of prejudicial thinking: "Clyde is *prejudiced* against anyone who drives a Chevrolet."

Principal/Principle

You learned in elementary school that your princi*pal* is a *pal*, but that doesn't help you remember the other use of the word *principal*—the adjective meaning main: "Can you describe the *principal* characteristics of cellular meitosis?"

Principle, on the other hand, is always a noun meaning concept, explanation, or moral scruple: "Sarah could explain the *principle* of radioactivity in a clear and fascinating manner"; "They are fierce competitors, but they adhere to high *principles* of fair play."

Exercise: Principal/Principle

Directions: Fill in each blank with *principal* or *principle*.

1. The _____ of this school is known to be a woman of high _____.

2. It seems that one of the _____ obstacles to world peace is one culture's inability to understand the value system of another culture.

3. He violated a basic company _____ when he refused to work with her.

Quite

Quite means to an extreme: "I was quite surprised by your remark."

Avoid using *quite* as an unnecessary intensifier: "The kids are quite excited about going to the circus."

Quotation/Quote

Use *quotation* as a noun without restrictions; use *quote* as a verb, and only informally as a noun: "I used the *quotation* [informal: "quote"] verbatim"; "I decided to *quote* your remarks on foreign policy."

Raise/Rise

Raise is a transitive verb meaning lift: "*Raise* your right hand."

To *rise* is an intransitive verb meaning to move upward: "The sun will *rise* at 5:35 A.M. tomorrow."

Real/Really

Standard usage for *real* is adjectival: "The flowers in that vase are not *real*."

The adverbial use of both terms is strictly informal: "I'm *real* proud of you, son"; "I'm *really* happy to hear from you."

*Reason is because/Reason is that

The standard usage is *reason is that*: "Our *reason* for not attending the lecture *is that* we arrived too late." **Reason is because* is ungrammatical.

Before using this construction, however, consider more vigorous wording. "We did not attend the lecture *because* we arrived too late" is a better way to phrase the above sentence.

Sensual/Sensuous

Confusing these two terms could be embarrassing (assuming that the audience knows the difference), so pay attention. *Sensual* pertains to erotic stimulation. "Salome's *sensual* dance aroused her male audience."

Sensuous, on the other hand, pertains to that which stimulates any or all of the five senses. "The kitchen was filled with the *sensuous* aroma of cinnamon and hot pumpkin pie."

Exercise: Sensual/Sensuous

Directions: Fill in each blank with *sensual* or *sensuous*.

1. The schoolchildren stared in fascination at the _____ sculpture, while their teacher looked away in embarrassment.
2. We were drawn into the bakery shop as soon as we caught the _____ smell of gingerbread.
3. Monet's paintings are filled with the _____ colors of exotic flower gardens.

Set/Sit

Set means "to put down" (transitive verb). "*Set* that Ming vase down very, very gently." Use of *sit* in this context is ungrammatical.

Sit means "to be seated" (intransitive verb). "Please *sit* at the head of the table."

Exercise: Set/Sit

Directions: Fill in each blank with *set* or *sit*.

1. We prefer to _____ in the no-smoking section.
2. _____ a tray of ice cubes in front of the fan for a cooler breeze.
3. Decide where you want to _____, and _____ your books there.

Shall/Will

In American usage, a distinction no longer exists between these two words. In sermonic speech and writing, however, *shall* is used to imply inevitability. "Seek, and you *shall* find." [Luke 11:9] *Will* is appropriate for all future-tense utterances.

So

Learn to distinguish between the formal and informal uses of this word.

Formal (adverb)	"We were *so* anxious to leave that we forgot our suitcases."
Informal (expletive)	"You were *so* rude!"
Informal (implicit subordinator)	"We won two free tickets to Rome, *so* we celebrated." However, the following two alternatives would be better: "When we won two free tickets to Europe, we celebrated"; "We celebrated because we won two free tickets to Europe."

Spay/Spayed/*Spayded

To *spay* is to remove a female animal's ovaries. The past tense of spay is *spayed*. **Spayded* is incorrect; it most likely derived from the mistaken notion that the present tense of the term is *spade* instead of *spay*.

Stationary/Stationery

The adjective *stationary* means held in place: "The weather vane was made *stationary* by two strong metal brackets."
The noun *stationery* means quality writing paper and envelopes. To

avoid confusing the two terms, let the "e" in stationery remind you of the "e" in envelope.

Than/Then

Than is a conjunction used to compare two subjects: "Phoenix has hotter summers *than* Los Angeles."

Then is an adverb that refers to an outcome or to a moment in the past: "If the baby's fever worsens, *then* call the doctor"; "Back *then*, a good steak cost only fifty cents."

Exercise: Than/Then

Directions: Fill in each blank with *than* or *then*.

1. First we'll eat, _____ we'll hit the road.
2. Is it true that fish is more nutritious _____ steak?
3. According to Einstein's Special Theory of Relativity, nothing can travel faster _____ light.

That/Which

In formal English, *that* introduces a restrictive clause:* "We examined manuscripts *that* were suspected of being fakes."

Which is used to introduce a nonrestrictive clause: "The mushrooms, which looked poisonous, were quickly removed."

Also, *which* can substitute for a second *that* to avoid awkward repetition: "The entrée that I ordered which was a "special" turned out to be extremely filling."

That/Who

The relative pronoun *that* properly takes a nonhuman antecedent (noun referent): "The dog *that* just crossed the street was nearly struck by a car." For human antecedents, use *who*: "The woman *who* crossed the street headed toward the corner delicatessen." "The woman *that* . . ." is informal; however, *that* may be used with children or infants: "The nurse rocked the baby *that* had been crying most of the night."

---

*See the Handbook, "Rhetorical and Grammatical Principles," Restrictive/Nonrestrictive Clause.

Glossary of Usage

Their/They're/There

Their is a plural possessive pronoun: "Please carry *their* suitcases." The absolute form is *theirs*: "That suitcase is *theirs*."

They're is a contraction for *they are*: "You take their suitcases; *they're* too heavy for me."

There is an adverb indicating place: "Set their suitcases *there*, beside the desk."

*Theirselves/Themselves

The ungrammatical *theirselves*, as in "The children bathed **theirselves*," probably arose out of analogy with *their* in a sentence like "The children washed *their* faces." The correct reflexive pronoun is *themselves*.

This kind/*These kind

Demonstrative pronouns and nouns must agree: *this kind*; *these kinds*. **These kind* is ungrammatical.

Thus/*Thusly

Thus means as a result or to this extent: "Earthquakes strike there often; *thus* many residents are ever fearful"; "I have come *thus* far; why should I stop now?" **Thusly* is ungrammatical.

Till/Until

Until is slightly more formal than *till*; otherwise, there is no distinction between them.

Unique

Because *unique* means literally "one of a kind," it can rarely be modified. *Very unique* or *somewhat unique* are illogical. However, *definitely unique* makes sense.

Use/Utilize

Utilize is often regarded as a formal substitute for *use*: "Do you know how to *utilize* those components properly?" This sounds pretentious and should be avoided. A more accurate usage for *utilize* is when the meaning "to make very specific use of" is intended: "The boy scouts *utilized* the raw materials of the local junkyard to build a dune buggy."

Weather/Whether

Weather is rain and sunshine and balmy breezes; *whether* is a conjunction indicating a set of alternatives: "I can't decide *whether* to complete my reading assignment or to begin my essay."

Which

See That/Which.

Who/Whom

Although the grammatical distinction between *who* and *whom* has all but vanished from informal usage, it is still observed in formal usage. *Who* can be the subject of either a sentence or a clause: "*Who* will be the lucky winner?" [subject of a sentence]; "I do not recognize the woman *who* is speaking." [subject of a clause]. *Whom* is objective case: "*Whom* did you meet?"

Exercise: Who/Whom

Directions: Fill in each blank with *who* or *whom*.

1. Julie, for _____ I have the highest regard, was accepted into medical school.
2. We accompanied Mr. Aldo, _____ always knows his way around.
3. These kittens are free to anyone _____ will give them loving care.
4. _____ will you ask to the ball?
5. John warmly greeted the golf star, for _____ he had high regard.

Whoever/Whomever

These are the subjective and objective cases of *who* and *whom*, respectively: "anyone *who*"; "anyone to *whom*." Use *whoever* if it is the subject of the sentence or an independent clause: "*Whoever* speaks here must expect an unfriendly audience"; "You will be sure to applaud *whoever* speaks here." (In the independent clause, "whoever speaks here," *whoever* is the subject.) Use *whomever* if it is the object of a sentence or clause: "I will pay my respects to *whomever*."

Exercise: Whomever/Whoever

Directions: Fill in each blank with *whomever* or *whoever*.

1. _____ is a friend of Bugsy's is a friend of mine.
2. The orchestra performed for _____ wished to dance.
3. Disoriented and afraid, the escapee began telephoning _____.

Who's/Whose

Who's is the contraction for *who is*: "*Who's* the wise guy?" *Whose* is the possessive relative pronoun of *who*: "*Whose* side are you on?"

Will

See Shall/Will.

You

In informal usage, *you* can mean *one* or *anyone*: "Sometimes *you* have to say no." This is acceptable usage. But confusion arises when the informal *you* suddenly appears in a passage governed by the third or first person point of view:

> People often become disorderly when they find themselves in crowds. They will push and shove like beasts. You will tend to forget all of your good manners.

The last sentence should read as follows: "*They* will forget all of *their* good manners."

Your/You're

Your is a possessive pronoun: "*Your* ferns need to be watered." *You're* is a contraction for "you are": "If you practice, *you're* bound to improve."

DIAGNOSTIC EXERCISES: GLOSSARY OF USAGE

Note: The page reference in parentheses indicates where the usage principle is discussed. Answers to the exercises may be obtained from your instructor.

1. Choose between *awhile* (adverb) and *a while* (indefinite article plus noun) for each of the following sentences. (441)
    a. I will miss you, knowing that you'll be gone _____.
    b. The president remained in town only for _____.
    c. _____ back, no freeways existed in this area.
    d. Don't stay up; I'm going to work for _____.

2. For the following sentences, choose between *accept* and *except*. (438)
    a. Will you _____ my apologies?
    b. Janet is confident that her employer will _____ her request for a raise.
    c. Who _____ Marlis won't be able to attend tonight's meeting?
    d. Are you going to _____ or decline the invitation?

3. Choose the correct word from each of the pairs that appear parenthetically in the following passages.
    a. (*Can/May*) you (*borrow/lend*) me (*you're/your*) hairdryer?" Harriet asked her brother. "I (*advice/advise*) you to ask me more politely," he answered. (443, 465, 439)
    b. The landlord informed us that we were (*all ready/already*) one week behind on our rent, but we needed to divide that money (*among/between*) four other impatient debtors. (439, 443)
    c. Karen spent the past year training (*continually/continuously*) for the half-marathon, especially because the terrain this time would be much (*different from/different than*) last year's. (447, 448)
    d. The Nobel prize committee invited its newest laureates to an elegant (*lunch/luncheon*), but at least two laureates (*discreetly/discretely*) declined. (449)

4. Choose between *bad* and *badly* in the following passage. (442)

    Ms. Lynch felt _____ about firing her accountant, but she felt that he was doing his work _____.

Glossary of Usage

5. Use *capitol* or *capital* correctly in the following sentence. (444)

   When the Andersons visited the nation's _____, the first thing they did was take a guided tour of the _____ building. The couple live in Albany, which is the _____ of New York.

6. Locate and, if necessary, correct any of the expressions underlined in the following passage. (444, 447, 448, 454, 451, 454)

   The children <u>couldn't hardly</u> concentrate on their reading. For the past ten minutes, air-raid sirens had been whining <u>continually</u>, without so much as a second's interruption. What was worse, the teacher looked frightened. Could anyone be that <u>credulous</u>? Of course, the teacher had pointed out last week that even a test siren should, <u>hopefully</u>, <u>evoke</u> some degree of apprehension among people, <u>irregardless</u> of the annoying sound.

7. Use the correct form of *to lie* or *to lay* as suggested by each context in the following paragraph. (455)

   Sunbathers who _____ in direct sunlight day after day run the risk of getting skin cancer, even when sunscreen lotions are applied. To play it safe, it's best to _____ your blanket in a shaded area where some object is blocking the sun's rays. Once when I _____ my blanket in a shady spot, and _____ there for about twenty minutes, I still got some color.

8. Use *principal* or *principle* correctly where indicated below. (459)

   One of the _____ virtues of Mr. Norman, the school _____, is his genuine interest in young people. And when a child misbehaves, he patiently explains the _____ of good behavior to him.

9. Insert either *than* or *then* in the blanks below. (462)

   Our pet tortoise, Constance, will dig a hole not much larger _____ herself, _____ crawl into it and sleep for hours. Tortoises are more amusing _____ dogs sometimes.

10. Choose between *that* and *who* in the following sentences. (462)
    a. We are the members of the team _____ asked for different uniforms.
    b. Which one of these dogs was the one _____ chased you?
    c. People _____ like to go mountain-climbing are real daredevils.

Punctuation

Punctuation guides the reading of a text: when to pause; how long the pause should be, depending on whether the words that follow modify an earlier idea or begin a new one; and so forth. Imagine reading passages that lacked punctuation:

> in the beginning was the word and the word was with god and the word was god the same was in the beginning with god all things were made by him and without him was not anything made that was made in him was life and the life was the light of men and the light shineth in darkness and the darkness comprehended it not there was a man sent from god whose name was john the same came for a witness to bear witness of the light that all men through him might believe

Most of the rules for punctuation make good sense and are easy to learn; you probably know many of them already. Other punctuation rules, such as when to use a semicolon or colon, or whether a particular phrase or clause needs to be set off with commas, are somewhat trickier. The best way to develop your "punctuation sense" is to do an extra reading of your first draft to check every sentence (with this section of the Handbook at your elbow) for its surface clarity and readability.

Apostrophe '

Apostrophes may be used as follows:

1. To indicate the possessive case of nouns. The apostrophe precedes the possessive stem, -s, of singular nouns: Owen's bike, Mars's thin atmosphere, Mr. Jones's friendly pet scorpion. Likewise, plural nouns (including hyphenated nouns) that do not end in -s take -'s to show possession: children's books, chairmen-of-the-board's annual meeting. However, for plural nouns ending in -s, the apostrophe indicates possession by itself: the trees' leaves.

2. To indicate *common* possession by a pair or series of nouns when only the last noun carries the apostrophe: Frank and Barbara's beautiful home. The apostrophe also indicates *individual* possession when each noun in the series carries an apostrophe: Richard's and Sally's offices.

3. To replace an omitted letter or letters in a contraction: can't for cannot. The apostrophe replaces an omitted figure as well: '46 for 1946.

Exercise: Apostrophe

Directions: Correctly place an apostrophe wherever needed.

1. Ages ago, Earths first mammals were scrawny little creatures in the dinosaurs shadows; but after the dinosaurs died off the worlds domain passed to these strange, warm-blooded, furry animals whose young were born live.

2. Were planning to attend Larrys birthday party tomorrow; hes going to be nineteen, so its probably not a bad idea to buy him some dress clothes, which are on sale at Macys.

Directions: Place the following into possessive form.

1. The estate of Sonya and Karl Lubinski.

2. The bicycles belonging to these children.

3. The haunting beauty of many American deserts.

Braces { }

Braces are used to group a series of items into a set.

1. Single brace:
   $$\left.\begin{array}{l}\text{radium}\\\text{strontium}\\\text{uranium}\end{array}\right\} \text{natural radioactive elements}$$

2. Double brace: Set {a,b,c} is not equal to set {x,y,z}.

Brackets [ ]

Brackets have two standard applications:

1. To contain a parenthetical expression within a parenthetical expression: "The circus acrobats (all of them professional [some were with Barnum & Bailey]) generously performed for our church group."

2. To contain words or phrases not part of an original quotation to make sense of the quotation: "They [the Apollo 11 astronauts] were the first human beings to set foot on another world." *Note*: Newspapers almost always use parentheses for this purpose.

Exercise: Brackets

Directions: Apply brackets where needed; remove brackets that are incorrectly applied.

1. The new commemorative coins (silver, 95 percent pure), produced at the Philadelphia Mint, went on sale today.

2. "He [Smith] said he was only trying to scare him when he aimed the gun at him Edwards."

3. The beaches were crowded with thousands of tourists hoping to get a glimpse of the migrating [blue] whales.

Capital Letters

The following rules apply to the use of capital letters:

1. The first word in a sentence is capitalized.

2. Names and titles of persons, ethnic groups, works, events, ages, and organizations are capitalized: Her Majesty the Queen; the Native American people (*people* is not capitalized because it is not part of the name of this ethnic group); Schubert's *Impromptu No. 2*; the Labor Movement; the Iron Age; the Huntington Library (*Library* is capitalized because it is part of the name of this library; *library* would not be capitalized in the phrase "an American library"); the American Civil Liberties Union, the Federal Bureau of Investigation. But, the following expressions are not capitalized: many labor movements; the great queens of English history; Schubert wrote several lovely impromptus; there are many federal offices.

3. The first word of spoken dialogue is capitalized: "Janet yelled, 'Where are you?'"

4. Nouns and pronouns indicating deity are capitalized: "Then Jesus spoke to His disciples." When no specific deity is mentioned, the word is not capitalized: "The gods of the ancient Greeks had their separate shrines."

5. Holidays are capitalized: Hannukah, Washington's Birthday, Good Friday, Mother's Day, Cinco de Mayo, Independence Day (or Fourth of July).

6. Days of the week and months of the year are capitalized. But centuries and millennia are not capitalized: "The twenty-first century, just around the corner, will begin the third millennium A.D."

7. A.D. (*anno Domini*—Latin for "in the year of the Lord"), B.C. ("before Christ"), and B.C.E. ("before the common era") are capitalized. A.D. *precedes* the date in formal usage: "That Greek city, founded in 100 B.C., fell in A.D. 425."

8. In titles, the definite article, *the*, and the indefinite articles, *a* and *an*, along with short conjunctions, prepositions, and the infinitive marker, *to*, are not capitalized unless they appear at the beginning of the title: Forster's *A Passage to India*; Faulkner's *The Sound and the Fury*; James's *The Turn of the Screw*.

Exercise: Capitalization

Directions: Capitalize where needed; change any incorrectly capitalized words to lower case.

1. the taj mahal in india, built in a.d. 1652 by shah jahan for his wife, agra, is the most beautiful structure I have ever seen on this Planet.

2. The american Author, Henry James, was not only a great Novelist (*Portrait of a lady*) but a great Literary Critic as well.

3. Mission santa clara de asis, founded by franciscan Missionaries six months after the signing of the declaration of independence, became the eighth of california's twenty-one Missions.

4. Mount vesuvius erupted in a.d. 79, destroying the Cities of pompeii and herculaneum, along with all of their Inhabitants.

5. The Sears tower in chicago is the world's *tallest* building, but the world's *largest* is the vehicle assembly building on cape canaveral.

Colon :

The colon says to the reader, "Get ready for a series": "To bake a cake, follow these steps: . . ." The colon also emphasizes one observation or fact: "We have made a discovery based on years of research: . . ."

Don't use a colon where a period could not terminate the sentence: "Jerry has: dark brown eyes, silky black hair, and dimples."

The colon is also used to separate hours, minutes, and seconds, respectively: 11:42:04; 10:00 A.M. (or a.m.).*

---

*When spelling out time of day (as in dialogue), do not use numerals (ten o'clock, not 10 o'clock).

Punctuation

Exercise: Colon

Directions: Use a colon wherever necessary; replace existing punctuation with a colon if necessary; remove any incorrectly used colons.

1. These items are a must for any backpacker. Sleeping bag, waterproof matches, utility knife, dried fruit, insect repellent. It is also a good idea to take along: a first-aid kit and a compass.

2. Look before you leap. A cliché expression: but a nugget of wisdom nonetheless.

3. Follow the directions carefully: or else you may injure yourself.

Comma ,

Welcome to the world's most complicated punctuation mark. Many rules exist; some are outdated. The first rule of comma use is to listen for the natural pause in a sentence that a comma serves to represent. The pause, and therefore the comma, is needed to avoid misreading the sentence. Here are the most frequent applications:

1. To set off items in a series of three or more: "The casting director chose a fat man, a dwarf, and two six-foot women for the film." But, a comma is not necessary here: "The casting director chose a fat man and a dwarf."

2. To separate *coordinate* adjectives, meaning adjective strings whose positions are interchangeable: "Sophie is a sweet, lovable, well-mannered, intelligent dog." *Note*: A comma does not follow the last adjective before the modified noun.
   Do not use commas to separate *cumulative* adjectives, meaning adjectives whose sequence cannot be rearranged: "Judy wore a light blue silk blouse and a genuine eighteen-carat gold necklace."

3. To set off independent clauses: "Edgar looks ferocious, but he's really a sweet and gentle bear." *Note*: (a) The coordinating conjunction (*and*, *but*, *or*) must be present, or else you will write what is known as a comma splice: "Edgar growls menacingly, he's really a gentle bear; and (b) Commas are not used to set off dependent clauses unless ambiguity could result: "After the rainstorm everything smelled fresh." But, the comma in the sentence ensures clarity: "After Phil arrived, home seemed like a happier place.

4. To set off nonrestrictive clauses: "The two Voyager spacecraft, which housed high-resolution cameras, took stunning photographs of Jupiter and Saturn." Note how the meaning of the sentence is

changed when the commas are removed. Without commas, the sentence implies that there are many Voyager spacecraft, but only the two that are mentioned possessed high-resolution cameras; thus, the clause becomes restrictive. With commas, the sentence suggests that there are only two Voyager spacecraft; the clause is therefore nonrestrictive.

5. To set off quotations or dialogue from the rest of the sentence: "The umpire shouted, 'Foul ball!'"

6. To set off the day of the month from the year: *December 7, 1941*. *Note*: No commas are used in the European dating format: *7 December 1941*.

7. To set off appositives:* "Henry, an electrical engineer, is listed in *Who's Who*."

8. To set off introductory phrases and clauses: "To study effectively, silence is necessary"; "Before you leave, turn off the lights."

Exercise: Comma

Directions: Supply commas where needed; remove incorrectly used commas.

1. "Star Trek" fans who go by the name "Trekkies" gather at conventions all over the world hold best-costume awards and often feature members from the original TV series or the films.

2. Our last visit to the zoo included, a trip to the House of Reptiles where we saw, a coral snake, a king cobra and an asp three of the deadliest snakes in the world.

3. Lenore purchased a pair of black satin slacks, and a stylish expensive silk blouse. Afterwards she asked me her best friend to lend her fifty dollars.

4. If you're not sure of the answer proceed, to the next question.

5. Of course going on fad diets can endanger your health.

Dash — and Hyphen -

A dash is a double hyphen; a hyphen is half a dash. Perhaps the best way to remember one from the other is to think, "Dash is Double." Each is used as follows:

---

*See the Handbook, "Rhetorical and Grammatical Principles," Appositive.

Dash: A dash is inserted to interject a word or group of words; it's a kind of self-interruption that can be stylistically effective if not overused. "The leaves—especially the oak leaves—were changing color rapidly." *Note*: No spaces come between the dash and the letters on either side of it.

Hyphen: A hyphen is used to link together some compound words, such as *pro-con*, *post-operative*, and *hunt-and-peck sale*; it also divides a word at one of its syllable junctures when a sentence reaches its marginal limit on the page.

Exercise: Dash and Hyphen

Directions: Supply a dash or hyphen where appropriate.

1. We ran like crazy to get to the supermarket before it closed, and wouldn't you know it they'd just locked the doors when we arrived.

2. I was partly interested in what that self serving egotist had to say, even though his holier than thou attitude grated on my nerves.

3. Wherever we drove no matter what direction the traffic was backed up because of a last minute decision to run on the spot sobriety tests.

Diacritical Marks

These are a series of pronunciation marks, none of which are used in English except for the acute accent and the diaeresis, and these only rarely.

Accent marks (acute ´ and grave `) The acute accent indicates that the vowel it marks is to be pronounced like a long *a*: café; déjà vu. The grave accent indicates that the vowel it marks is to be "flattened": *les élèves*.

Cedilla ¸ Used in French and Portuguese, the cedilla indicates a soft *c*, as in *façade*.

Circumflex ^ The circumflex is not used in English, except with adopted words such as *bête noir*. It indicates a short vowel.

Diaeresis ¨ The diaeresis indicates that the vowel it superscribes is to be pronounced separately: coöperation; the Brontë sisters.

Hacek ˇ   This mark (literally, "little hook") is used in some eastern European languages to indicate that the *c* is to be pronounced [ch]: Karel Čapek (Czech novelist); the word *haček* itself.

Tilde ˜   The tilde is a Spanish and Portuguese diacritical mark indicating that the *n* it superscribes is to be pronounced [nyeh]: *señor*, or that the *a* or *o* it superscribes is to be pronounced nasally: *São Paulo*.

Umlaut ¨   Resembling a diaeresis, the umlaut is used in German, Dutch, and in Scandinavian languages to indicate a change in vowel quality: The pronunciation of *au* in *das Haus* [hawz], the singular German noun for house, changes when the umlaut is added in the plural form, *die Häuser* [hoizer].

Ellipsis Dots . . .

The word *ellipsis* comes from the Greek, *elleipein*, meaning "to leave out." These dots, sometimes called ellipses points, usually appear in groups of three, and are used in a verbatim quotation to indicate that a word or words have been omitted for whatever reason.*

Exclamation Mark !

Use this one sparingly, when a highly significant or surprising point is made, or for explosive utterances (interjections).

> Get out!
>
> I was half-asleep when blam! the heater exploded.
>
> Just as I bent down to drink from the fountain I saw, right next to my foot, a hundred-dollar bill!
>
> Give up? Never!

Double or triple exclamation marks are used for humorous or sarcastic purposes only; they're to be avoided in standard usage.

> You've just misspelled your own name!!

---

*See Chapter 10, "Principles of Research," pp. 196–197.

Exercise: Exclamation Mark

Directions: Add an exclamation mark where appropriate; remove any exclamation marks that seem inappropriate.

1. Cecil spent the whole day writing a two-page essay! Boy, is he ever slow. If I would have spent as much time as he, I probably could have written a *ten*-page essay!

2. Any time you want a favor, just ask me! After all, that's what friends are for.

3. "Let go of me, you creep," Darlene hissed at her ex-boyfriend. "I mean it."

Hyphen

See Dash.

Italics or Underscore

Italics refers to a type style featuring characters that slant upward and to the right. Underscoring a word or phrase in a manuscript means that the word(s) in question would appear italicized in print. Italics are used for the following:

- Titles of books, periodicals, films, and plays (but not of articles from periodicals or chapters from books)
- Especially important words or phrases
- Foreign expressions, except proper nouns

Exercise: Italics

Directions: Underscore any words or phrases that ought to be italicized; remove incorrect underscoring.

1. The lungfish (Protopterus annectens), which possesses both lungs and gills, is described in Mr. Perch's book, Strange Creatures of the Sea.

2. I was impressed by Mr. Barnes's latest essay, <u>Avoiding Pitfalls in Soviet-American Diplomacy</u>.

3. Everyone was more or less pleased with Mr. Stallone's competent, but sometimes weary, performance in Rocky VIII.

Parentheses ( )

Parentheses are used to enclose an aside or a piece of information that would otherwise disrupt the rhythm of the sentence or cause confusion: "Once again the mighty warrior (not so mighty-looking the way he was hopping on one foot) brandished his sword."

Period .

Periods terminate sentences and abbreviations, except for some abbreviations with all capital letters, such as post-office abbreviations for states (NY, TX, etc.). They are used with single letters and numbers in outlines (I., A.) or pagination (p. 15; pp. 35–40), and in decimals (3.8; 2.04).

Exercise: Periods

Directions: Insert a period where needed; remove unnecessary periods, if any.

> Insulating your attic can save one-third on heating costs I never knew that until I talked to an energy expert at the power company. Who referred me to p 35 of their energy-savings booklet.

Question Mark ?

Question marks are most commonly used to terminate an interrogative sentence: "Why are you laughing?" They also may be used less formally within a sentence: "Where did she go, outside? to her room?" *Note*: In this example, the first question mark appears after the first option, *outside*, rather than at the end of the apparent first question, after *go*. In contexts where formal usage is preferred, the sentence should be rephrased so only one terminal question mark is used: "Did she go outside or to her room?" Finally, question marks are not used at the end of an indirect question: "Cindy asked Mindy how she managed to get straight *A*'s."

Exercise: Question Mark

Directions: Supply question marks where needed; remove unnecessary question marks.

1. Vance wanted to know where the coach kept the tennis balls? "Did you check the supply room," Bill asked.

2. "Why do you suppose we're underpaid, or that we have no vacations with pay, or that we have no medical benefits," one of the union members cried out.

3. Check the oil, or did you check it already before you drove the car.

Quotation Marks " " ' '

Quotation marks are placed around dialogue, verbatim passages from an outside source, article and short story titles (book titles, however, are italicized), and words used in an unexpected manner. All take double quotation marks except for quotations within quotations, which require single quotation marks.

Dialogue	"Where are we going?" the little boy asked. "Oh," replied his father, "maybe to the circus."
	Note: The end punctuation falls *inside* the closing quotation mark; also, the first word following a quotation is not capitalized unless that word begins a new sentence. Do not use quotation marks with indirect dialogue: The little boy wanted to know where they were going.
Quoted passage	According to Ben Franklin in his famous *Autobiography*, "Few in public affairs act from a mere view of the good of their country, whatever they may pretend."
Dialogue containing a quotation	"Bob isn't coming today," Tom explained. "His excuse was, 'I just can't get myself to move this morning.'"
Unconventional use of a word	My cat was the "burglar" you heard last night.
Word discussed as such	The expression "zounds" has a fascinating origin.
Title of a short work	"The Pit and the Pendulum" is one of Poe's most famous short stories.
	Note: Product names are capitalized but *not* placed in quotation marks. "She likes to eat Jell-O [not "Jell-O"] for lunch."

Exercise: Quotation Marks

Directions: Insert quotation marks where needed; remove any unnecessary quotation marks.

1. I'm as ready as I'll ever be for my final exam, Arthur grumbled.
2. The maitre d' recommended the house burgundy, "Mountain Vine," but we declined by saying perhaps next time.
3. Are you familiar with Robert Frost's somber short poem, Design?
4. How did you like the way they sang Gershwin's Summertime? Gladys asked.
5. The expression pull the wool over one's eyes goes back to the eighteenth century, when people wore "wigs."

Semicolon ;

This versatile punctuation mark has an undeservedly bad reputation for being difficult to learn. The semicolon is used to join two or more related independent clauses when a stronger pause than that provided by a coordinating conjunction plus comma is desired. A period can always be used in place of a semicolon, but there is a difference. A period terminates the sentence; a semicolon continues it for whatever reason—most commonly, to place greater emphasis on the relationship of parts, or to maintain a particular syntactic rhythm.* Notice how the pauses suggested by the punctuation in each of the following sentences differ:

> The wind whipped the trees fiercely, and for a moment it looked as though they would be uprooted.

> The wind whipped the trees fiercely; for a moment it looked as though they would be uprooted.

> The wind whipped the trees fiercely. For a moment it looked as though they would be uprooted.

Exercise: Semicolon

Directions: Add a semicolon wherever needed; remove any unnecessary semicolons.

1. The orthopedist skillfully bandaged the girl's sprained ankle, he then adjusted her crutches; "You'll only need these for a week"; he said.

---

*See Chapter 12, "Building Sentence-Writing Skills."

2. Thomas Paine; in *The Rights of Man*; called for state support of education, he also advocated pensions for the elderly.

3. Writing letters to celebrities is fun besides; they enjoy receiving fan mail.

Slash /

The slash is used to indicate options: "Answer the following true/false questions"; "A student should think carefully about his/her choice of careers before taking the plunge." This punctuation mark is also used to separate lines of poetry: "Oh, that torment should not be confined/To the body's wounds and sores." In addition, the slash is employed in fractions: "Hand me the 11/32 socket."

DIAGNOSTIC EXERCISES: PUNCTUATION

Note: The answers to these exercises may be obtained from your instructor.

1. Add apostrophes where needed in the following passage:

    Scientists dreams are often as creative as nonscientists. One scientists dreams, for example, include visions of domed cities on the moon, where ones basic needs are cared for by robots. A robots task would typically include preparing its masters meals, tending the botanical gardens, maintaining the colonys life-support systems, and even supplying the colonists entertainment.

2. Add commas and semicolons where needed in the following passages:

    People who speed should be aware of the possible consequences for example if one is cutting through a residential area at let us say fifty miles per hour no matter how alert one drives it is impossible to stop in time for an animal or child who might dart into the street in front of the car.

    Black leather boots wool shirt buckskin jacket and wide-brimmed hat describe old Luke Harwood's wardrobe. Luke one of the finest cattleraisers in Wyoming doesn't like to call attention to himself but nevertheless he loves dressing up like a real cowboy a proud self-image for Luke.

3. Add quotation marks and commas, and if necessary alter the paragraphing where needed, to clarify the following dialogue scene:

    What on earth are you doing with that hedgetrimmer Bob said. Rita answered I'm sick of looking at these overgrown bushes. I'm going to cut them to half their size. Oh no you're not Bob replied. I like them just the size they are. Well Rita snapped back my tastes count just as much as yours so it looks as though we'll have to talk this out more. There's nothing to talk about he yelled back. I'm the breadwinner around here.

4. Capitalize or change to lower case where needed:

    Two Tax Reform Bills will be sent to congress tomorrow (april 20). the president plans to Veto both of them. In the meantime, the federal Tax Laws are being severely criticized in the south, especially in georgia.

Spelling

Poor spelling is not necessarily a reflection of poor writing ability, but unfortunately many people, including teachers, will draw that conclusion. If you find yourself misspelling words regularly, it is worth your while to set aside a short time each day for spelling practice. *Steady practice will make you a better speller.*

The first step is a psychological one: Abandon the notion that your problems with spelling automatically suggest that you are not a good writer. Literary history is filled with authors who were not good spellers.

The second step is to become mindful of the problem areas that cause many spelling mistakes. The most common of these involve either exceptions to the traditional rules of pronunciation, causing spelling confusion; rules that for some reason tend to be forgotten; and carelessness in speech. Let's look at some of the more troublesome examples:

1. The sounds created by a particular arrangement of letters in a word are different from the sounds those letters traditionally represent:

    carburetor: The *e* sounds like *a* as in *rate*, rather than *e* as in *meteor*.

    seize: The *ei* sounds like *ee* as in *breeze*, rather than *i* as in *height*.

    ecstasy: The *sy* sounds like *cy* as in *infancy*, rather than *sy* as in *easy*.

    separate: The first *a* sounds like *e* as in *literary*, rather than *a* as in *carat*.

    traitor: The *or* sounds like *er* as in *writer*, rather than *or* as in *ignore*.

2. Some letters are silent:

    condemn: The *n* is not pronounced.

    resign: The *g* is silent; also, the *s* sounds like [z] rather than [s].

    debt: The *b* is silent.

3. Some letters are dropped when a suffix is added. Remember this rule: When a suffix begins with a vowel and the root ends in a silent *e*, that *e* is dropped; when the suffix begins with a consonant, the final *e* is retained:

shine, shining

lone, lonely

energize, energizer

purpose, purposeful

4. Some words are carelessly pronounced by nearly everyone, and the word thus becomes difficult to spell:

   diaper (often pronounced without the *a*)

   aspirin (often pronounced without the first *i*)

   prerogative (often pronounced "perogative")

   coupon (often pronounced "cyupon")

   disastrous (often pronounced "disasterous")

5. The plural forms of some words are easy to misspell. Remember these rules:

   a. For singular hyphenated compound words, only the first word in the compound is made plural: president-elect / presidents-elect.

   b. For singular words ending in *-is*, the plural is *-es*: thesis / theses.

   c. For singular words ending in *-f*, the plural is *-ves*: scarfs / scarves.

   d. For singular words ending in *-on* or *-um*, the plural is *-a*: criterion / criteria; bacterium / bacteria.

   e. For singular words ending in *y*, the plural is *-ies* if the letter before the *y* is a consonant: rely / relies. But if a vowel precedes the *y*, the plural is *-ys*: tray / trays.

   f. For singular words ending in *-o*, the plural is *-es* for some words and *-s* for others: potato / potatoes; radio / radios; hero / heroes; dynamo / dynamos.

   g. For words ending in *-x*, *-ch*, *-s*, or *-sh*, the plural is *-es*: box / boxes; match / matches; pass / passes; wish / wishes.

6. Numbers are spelled out when used in nontechnical contexts or at the beginning of a sentence. Numerals are used for dates. "Twenty-three persons were indicted on June 4, 1980"; "This 16mm projector is an heirloom"; "The Braves lost to the Twins, 12–10."

The third step toward improving your spelling is to devise a set of drills for yourself. Here are a few suggestions:

1. *Become more "word-conscious."* Before you look up a word, try to spell it correctly first; scribble variations on scratch paper to see which spelling looks accurate. *Then* check the dictionary.

2. *Read for one-half hour each day.* Choose a novel or any other type of reading you enjoy. Underline any words you can't spell as you go along. Go back and copy these words onto a sheet of paper; date the sheet so you can chart your progress. Drill yourself until you can spell these words without hesitation.

3. *Memorize any twenty words at a time from the accompanying list.* Use the following procedure:
    a. Write a complete sentence using each word.
    b. Underline the word.
    c. Ask someone to drill you on the underlined words, preferably using a random sequence.

*Commonly Misspelled Words**

1. conscientious
2. conscience
3. conscious
4. reminiscent
5. shepherd
6. furor
7. conquer
8. amateur
9. achievement
10. seizure
11. excellent
12. excel
13. satellite
14. conceive
15. perceive
16. auxiliary
17. privilege
18. religious
19. sacrilege
20. acquiesce
21. desirable
22. precede
23. proceed
24. occurring
25. occurred
26. occur
27. occurrence
28. liaison
29. ninety
30. ninth
31. forty
32. fourth
33. forthcoming
34. pursue
35. peruse
36. committee
37. committed
38. commitment
39. explain
40. explanation
41. camouflage
42. carburetor
43. corduroy
44. khaki
45. plaid
46. diocese
47. gruesome
48. hemorrhage
49. fluorescent
50. weird
51. seize
52. fiery

---

*This list is organized to highlight spelling similarities and differences among words whose spellings are easily confused.

53. panic
54. panicked
55. usable†
56. plausible
57. arctic
58. alignment
59. feign
60. ecstasy
61. prophecy
62. prophesy
63. nucleus
64. Capitol*
65. capital
66. incapacitate
67. acetate
68. succession
69. minuscule
70. violin
71. plagiarism
72. pituitary
73. daisies
74. calendar
75. cemetery
76. deity
77. deceive
78. grieve
79. recede
80. proceed
81. precede
82. allege
83. allegiance
84. pledge
85. incidentally
86. accurately
87. develop
88. development
89. developes
90. developing
91. embarrass
92. exaggerate
93. accommodate
94. silhouette
95. roulette
96. exalt
97. exhort
98. inevitable
99. feasible
100. until
101. till
102. missile
103. muscle
104. mussel
105. label
106. idle
107. idol
108. role
109. roll
110. boundary
111. foundry
112. temperament
113. regiment
114. patriot
115. expatriate
116. government
117. environment
118. athlete
119. rhythm
120. anthem

*Use lower case when referring to capitols (capitol buildings) in general.
†*Useable* is an alternative spelling.

Manuscript Formatting/ Proofreading and Notetaking Marks

Manuscript Formatting

Although several formatting variations exist, the following recommendations are widely accepted. However, always double-check with your instructor if you have any doubts.

Indentation

The first line of a paragraph is indented five spaces from the left margin. For block quotations, each line is indented ten spaces. If the first line of the quotation represents the beginning of a paragraph, it is indented an additional five spaces.

Line Spacing

Always double-space your manuscripts, unless instructed to otherwise. Correspondence, however, is single-spaced, with double-spacing between paragraphs. Block quotations are single-spaced and set off from the body of the text by three spaces at the top and three spaces at the bottom. Every line is indented ten spaces from the left margin.

Margins

Margins are necessary for neatness—which is important for readability—and for editorial comments. Standard margins should be one inch on all sides. Some manuscripts, such as dissertations, require one-and-one-half-inch margins. Inquire if you're not certain.

If you use a word processor, you have the option of *ragged* or *justified* right margins. With ragged right margins, line lengths will differ from line to line, although none will exceed the margin limit unless you hit the margin release key. The line lengths of justified margins, on the other hand, are all the same; however, the spacing between the words is slightly uneven to compensate for the natural discrepancies in line lengths.

Page Layout: Essays (first page)

```
First name, Last name                           Assignment number
Course number; Section number
Professor's name
Date




                       Title of Essay, Centered and
                           Double-spaced




     Begin your text here, four spaces below the bottom line of the title.
Be sure that your typewriter ribbon is dark, and that the keys are clean
so that your o's, e's, and a's can be distinguished from each other. Keep
at least one-inch margins on all sides.
```

Page Layout: Formal Letters

All types of business letters and cover letters, sometimes called "letters of transmittal," follow a standard format, with minor variations:

1900 Wildcrest Avenue Redondo Beach, CA 90000	Heading
January 10, 1986	Dateline
	Four spaces
Mr. Paul Reynolds Azimuth Computer Systems 100 Disque Drive Silicon, CA 95000	Inside address
	Two spaces
Subject: Defective Monitor	Subject line (optional)
	Two spaces
Dear Mr. Reynolds:	Salutation
	Two spaces
I have had trouble with the resolution of my Azimuth color monitor. At first I experienced just slight fuzziness, but after a week or so, the images on the screen became nearly illegible. I would appreciate your sending me instructions that clearly explain what I can do to improve the resolution.	Body of letter (single-spaced, each paragraph indented five spaces; two spaces between paragraphs)
	Two spaces
Sincerely,	Complimentary close
Owen Filbert	Signature block
	Two spaces
OF:en Encl.	End notations Writer's initials: typist's initials Another document is enclosed

Page Layout: Title Page

Longer projects such as research papers generally require a title page. Here is a suggested layout:

```
                          Title of Essay

                               by

                           Your Name




                      Submitted to Prof. White
                       in Partial Fulfillment
                of the Requirements for English 002.18

                         January 3, 1986
```

Pagination

Always number every page of your manuscript (except the title page or the first page) to avoid confusion if the pages get mixed up.

Place page numbers in the upper right-hand corner, flush with the margin, one line above the first line of text. Another option is to center the number at the very top of the page, with a hyphen on either side of the number. In long papers that include "front matter" such as a table of contents, an abstract, or an outline or list of illustrations, use lowercase roman numerals (i, ii, xiv, etc.) at the bottom center of the page. These numbers are independent of those used for the body of the paper.

Proofreading and Notetaking Marks

Proofreading Marks

Delete word or passage	ℯ	~~fish~~
Transpose word or letter	∩	fs̨ih
Leave as originally intended	Stet	fish
Insert word(s)	∧	Let me tell you a ^fish story.
Capitalize	≡	fish
Use lower case	/	F̸ish
Misspelled word	(SP)	dolfin
Typographical error	×	fishȯ
Close up space	⌒	fi sh
Add a space	#	fresh#fish
Begin new paragraph	¶	... the open sea. ¶Fish from the ocean depths are more bizarre.
Incorporate into above paragraph	↶	... the open sea.⌒Fish from the ocean depths are more bizarre.
Indent (number of spaces)	5	... the open sea. 5⌐Fish from the ocean depths are more bizarre.

Notetaking Marks

Similar to	∼
Not similar to	≁
Parallel to	∥
Greater than	>
Less than:	<
Therefore:	∴
Interacts with:	⇄

Equal to: =

Not equal to: ≠

More or less: ±

Per item: @

Leads to: →

Notetaking Abbreviations

For example: e.g. [*exempli gratia*]

In other words: i.e. [*id est*]

Compare: cf. [*confer*]

Refer to: ref.

Take careful note: N.B. [*nota bene*]

Approximately: c. (or ca.) [*circa*]

Especially: esp.

With: w/

Within: w/n

Without: w/o

And others: et al. [*et alii*]

Born: b.

Manuscript: ms (plural: mss)

Usually: usu.

Documentation Formats

Research papers are time-consuming enough without your having to spend hours memorizing all the various documentation formats, some of which you may not even use anyway. A good idea would be to memorize the most frequently used formats to cite material from books and from journal articles, and to refer to this guide for the others.

Both the traditional (footnote) and the new (in-text) MLA formats are presented here.* The older format is still in use; however, the new format is gradually becoming the standard for scholarly documentation in writing and literature courses. It has more in common with the widely used APA (American Psychological Association) style designed for the social and physical sciences, and thus students and scholars across the disciplines can better understand each other's annotations.

The older tradition makes use of *footnoting*: A superscript numeral is placed at the end of a quoted or paraphrased passage. Then the complete source is cited at the bottom ("foot") of the page, or at the end of the essay on a separate sheet headed "Notes" or "Endnotes."

The newer tradition abandons the footnoting procedure (except in the case of informational footnotes),† and instead uses an abbreviated citation in parentheses at the end of the quoted or paraphrased passage. This abbreviated citation consists of the quoted author's surname and the page number of the passage (e.g., Jones 12), or just the page number if the author's name is already mentioned in the text. The reader

---

*Based on Joseph Gibaldi and Walter S. Achtert, *MLA Handbook for Writers of Research Papers, 2nd ed.* (New York: The Modern Language Association of America, 1984).

†Informational footnotes are brief explanations of a specific point rather than textual citations.

is supplied with just enough information to be able to track down the complete citation in "Works Cited," which appears at the very end of the essay.

Bibliography formats are the same for both documentation styles.

Footnote Format*

Pattern A: Book

Footnote number, raised one-half space; author(s),† first name first; complete title, underlined; translator, preceded by *trans.*; editor, preceded by *ed.*; edition, followed by *ed.*, if other than first; volume number, if work contains more than one volume; publication data in parentheses (city of publication [use city listed first if more than one], publisher, copyright date); and page(s) on which quoted passage appears. The abbreviations for pages, *p.* or *pp.*, are not used.

Examples

¹ Susan Sontag, *On Photography* (New York: Farrar, Straus, and Giroux, 1977) 50.

² William Strunk, Jr. and E. B. White, *The Elements of Style*, 3rd ed. (New York: Macmillan, 1979) 6–7.

³ Mary Ann Frese Witt, et al., *The Humanities: Cultural Roots and Continuities*, vol. 2 (Lexington, Mass.: D. C. Heath and Company, 1980) 192.

⁴ Thomas Mann, *Doctor Faustus*, trans. H. T. Lowe-Porter (New York: Alfred A. Knopf, 1948) 273.

Pattern B: Short Work from Edited Anthology

Footnote number; author(s); complete title of short work, in quotation marks; title of anthology, underlined; editor(s), preceded by *ed.*; publication data (see Pattern A above); and page numbers on which original passage appears.

---

*This is the format used in the model research paper in Chapter 11, pp. 247–252.
†If the book cited has more than three authors, use first author plus et al.

Example

¹ J. R. Cole, "The Language of American Presidents," *The State of the Language*, eds. Leonard Michaels and Christopher Ricks (Berkeley: University of California Press, 1980) 422.

Pattern C: Article from Weekly or Biweekly Magazine

Footnote number; author(s); title of article, in quotation marks; title of periodical, underlined; date of issue (day, month, year); and page(s) on which original quotation appears.

Example

⁴ Lori B. Andrews, "Mind Control in the Courtroom," *Psychology Today* March 1982: 67.

Pattern D: Article from Quarterly, Biannual, Annual Journals

Footnote number; author(s); title of article; name of journal; volume number; issue number (only if each issue is paginated separately rather than continuously [*see* the second example]); year; and page number(s).

Examples

¹ Suzanne Morris, "The Writing of Historical Fiction," *English in Texas* 12.2 (1980): 14.

² William Wresch, "Computers in English Class: Finally Beyond Grammar and Spelling Drills," *College English* 44 (1982): 489.

Pattern E: Article from Daily Newspaper

Footnote number; author(s), if any; title of article; name of newspaper, underlined; date (day, month, year); edition (e.g., *late evening*) if indicated; then a colon, followed by section and page number (e.g., C14).

Examples

² Charles Petit, "Scary Report on a Bay Area Quake," *San Francisco Chronicle*, 13 Oct. 1982: A2.

¹ "Teens Write Own Ticket for Fun and Profit," *San José Mercury*, 25 March 1982, morning final ed.: F1.

¹¹ "Police Corruption Can Damage Us All," editorial, *USA Today*, 17 July 1984: A10.

Pattern F: Article from Encyclopedia or Other Reference Book

Footnote number; author (identified at end of article);* title of encyclopedia, underlined; edition; and most recent year of publication. [*Note*: Page-number reference in encyclopedia citations is superfluous; publication data are not included in the footnote or in the bibliography.]

Examples

¹ Philip G. Altback, "University Reform," *International Encyclopedia of Higher Education*, 1977.

² H[ubert] H[orace] L[amb], "Climate," *The New Encyclopaedia Britannica*, Macropaedia, 1981.

Pattern G: Government Publication

Name of agency; title of publication, underlined; publication data, in parentheses; and page number(s).

Examples

¹ National Institute of Mental Health, *Plain Talk About Dealing with the Angry Child* (Rockville, Md.: United States Department of Health and Human Services, 1978) 1.

² United States Bureau of the Census, *Statistical Abstract of the United States*, 102nd ed. (Washington, D.C.: United States Government Printing Office, 1981) 186.

Pattern H: Review (With or Without By-Line)

Footnote number; author, if given; title of review, if any; *rev. of* (plus title of work reviewed; *by* plus author of work; title of periodical in which review appears, underlined; date of review (day, month, year); and page number(s).

Examples

⁴ Jack Miles, "An Inventor Visits Nature to Reinvent His Life," rev. of *The Pathless Way: John Muir and American Wilderness*, by Michael P. Cohen, *Los Angeles Times* 19 Aug. 1984: book review section 2.

---

*Sometimes only the author's initials are given at the end of the article. (See the second example.) In that case, you must locate the author's full name, listed elsewhere. (In *The New Encyclopaedia Britannica*, the list of authors appears in the Propaedia.)

¹"Exploring a Lost Continent," rev. of the Waverly Consort [performers], *Time*, 18 Feb. 1980: 57.

³Rev. of *Max Perkins: Editor of Genius*, by A. Scott Berg, *New Yorker* 31 July 1978: 79.

Pattern I: Published Interview

Footnote number; name of person interviewed; title of interview, if any, in quotation marks; *interview*; *with* plus interviewer's name; title of periodical; volume number; date (day, month, year); page(s).

Example

³Frank Herbert, interview, with Mary-Ann Bendel, *USA Today*, 4 Dec. 1984: A9.

Pattern J: Personal Interview

Footnote number; *Personal interview with*; name of person interviewed; date (day, month, year).

Example

¹Personal interview with Neil Sedaka, 20 Jan. 1984.

Pattern K: Lecture

Footnote number; name of lecturer; title of lecture, in quotation marks, name of program sponsoring the lecture, if any; location; date (day, month, year).

Example

⁵Carol Berkenkotter, "A Context-Based Theory of Revision," Conference on College Composition and Communication, New York, 30 March 1984.

Miscellaneous Footnote Information

1. *Additional footnote from a given work*: The last name of author (no intervening punctuation) and page number(s) are included. The Latin abbreviations, *op. cit.* and *ibid.*, are rarely used these days. For lectures, repeat the title; for interviews, add *interview* following the name.

2. *Informational footnotes*: These are numbered in sequence with other footnotes. If you are following the newer style of documentation,

place informational footnotes at the bottom of the page or at the end of the essay (preceding the bibliography), signalled by an asterisk or superscript numeral.

Informational footnotes should be used only sparingly to elaborate on a technical aside that would otherwise disrupt continuity of the main text. Never use an informational footnote to introduce a separate topic.

New MLA Style ("In-Text") Documentation Format*

The procedure here is generally simpler. The formatting is easier to handle, especially if you compose on a computer. There's an added bonus, too: Your research writing style is likely to improve. Maintaining a smooth, readable style is enough of a problem without having to interrupt yourself every few minutes with a footnote citation. Also, the new style allows for greater stylistic flexibility in introducing outside sources.

Your main concern is to provide just enough in-text information to allow your readers to locate the source quickly in the bibliography. Naturally, then, a bibliography of works cited is essential when using the newer-style documentation format.

Pattern A

When author of work is mentioned in the sentence. Place the following in parentheses, not necessarily at the end of the sentence: page number(s); act, scene, and line numbers (when alluding to a play);[†] or section and line numbers (when alluding to a long poem).

Example #1

As Frederick Isaac asserts in his article, "Librarian, Scholar, or Author: The Librarian's New Dilemma," it is a serious mistake to segregate librarians from the rest of the scholarly academic community (219).

---

*This is the format used in the model research papers in Chapter 11, pp. 224–233 and 236–245.

[†]If there are no scene divisions, give the act plus the line or page number.

Example #2

As Frederick Isaac asserts in his article, "Librarian, Scholar, or Author: The Librarian's New Dilemma," (219), it is a serious mistake to segregate librarians from the rest of the scholarly academic community.

Example #3

"The Devil is alive in Salem," Reverend Hale proclaims with double-edged irony in Arthur Miller's *The Crucible* (II.69).

Example #4

In Lear's eyes, children's rebellion against their father is a perversion of nature: "You unnatural hags," he shouts (II.iv.281) at Goneril and Regan after they betray his trust in them.*

Example #5

Throughout *The Prelude*, Wordsworth dramatizes the influence of nature upon the poet's imagination:

From nature doth emotion come, and moods
Of calmness equally are nature's gift,
This is her glory; these two attributes
Are sister horns that constitute her strength. (XII.1–4)

Pattern B

When author of work is not mentioned in the sentence. Place author's surname and page number(s) in parentheses at end of sentence. No comma separates the two, and no *pp.* abbreviation is used.

Example #1

One of the most provocative aspects of Yeats's "Leda and the Swan" is the way in which it creates a "fine balance between human and divine, concrete and abstract" (Hargrove 235).

Pattern C

When quoting from a part of the work other than the main text (introduction, preface, afterword, appendix, and so forth). Place this information in the

---

*The author has established earlier in the essay that the play in question is Shakespeare's *King Lear*.

full citation of the work on the "Works Cited" page; it may also be alluded to in the citation.

Example #1

In his introduction to *The Myth of the Birth of the Hero and Other Writings*, Otto Rank regards myth as a dream of the masses of people (9).*

Example #2

In *The Myth of the Birth of the Hero*, Otto Rank regards myth as a dream of the masses of people (9).†

Bibliography ("Works Cited") Format

Bibliographies are always arranged in alphabetical order by author's surname, or by title when no author is given. After you have arranged your bibliography cards in alphabetical order, make sure that you have all the necessary data for each entry before you begin typing out the list.

Also remember: The only entries belonging in your bibliography are those you have actually made reference to in the text of your essay. Any other books or articles you wish to mention belong on a separate sheet entitled "Additional Readings." Here is the basic format for bibliography entries:

1. Author's name is presented last name first. When there are two or more authors, only the first author's name is reversed.

2. The first line is not indented, but subsequent lines in that same entry are indented. This allows the author's name to stand out conspicuously, thus enabling readers to locate the works quickly.

3. Name, article title, book title, editor or translator, edition (if other than first), number of volumes comprising the work (if more than one), and publication data are separated from each other by periods, not commas. Within the publication data, the city of publication is given first, (colon), followed by the name of the publisher, (comma), followed by the copyright date. The publication data are not enclosed in parentheses.

---

*Many prefaces and introductions are paginated in lowercase Roman numerals (iv, xviii, etc.). If this is the case, use these numerals.

†The "Works Cited" citation would then read as follows: Rank, Otto. Introduction. *The Myth of the Birth of the Hero and Other Writings*. New York: Vintage Books, 1959.

4. When listing articles from books, magazines, journals, or newspapers, all the pages on which the article appears are cited following the publication data. The abbreviation *p.* or *pp.* is not used. When listing articles from magazines and journals, a colon precedes the page numbers.

5. Volume numbers for journals follow the title without any intervening punctuation. Always give volume number in Arabic numerals, even when the journal prints it in Roman numerals. The volume year is given in parentheses. *Note*: Some journals number their issues continuously through all the issues in the volume. Other journals number each issue separately; that is, each issue will begin with page 1. When citing an article from a separately paginated journal, add the *issue* number following the volume number and a decimal point.

Books

Format #1: Books with One Author

Sontag, Susan. *On Photography*. New York: Farrar, Straus, and Giroux, 1977.

Format #2: Books with Two or Three Authors; Edition Other Than First

Strunk, William Jr., and E. B. White. *The Elements of Style*. 3rd ed. New York: Macmillan, 1979.

Format #3: Books with Four or More Authors; Multivolume Work

Witt, Mary Ann Frese, et al. *The Humanities: Cultural Roots and Continuities*. 2 vols. Lexington, Mass.: D. C. Heath and Company, 1980.

Format #4: Translated Book

Mann, Thomas. *Doctor Faustus*. Trans. H. T. Lowe-Porter. New York: Alfred A. Knopf, 1948.

Short Work from Edited Anthology

Cole, J. R. "The Language of American Presidents." *The State of the Language*. Eds. Leonard Michaels and Christopher Ricks. Berkeley: University of California Press, 1980. 421–31.

Article from Weekly or Biweekly Magazine

Andrews, Lori B. "Mind Control in the Courtroom." *Psychology Today*, March 1982: 67–73.

Article from a Journal with Continuous Pagination

Wresch, William. "Computers in English Class: Finally Beyond Grammar and Spelling Drills." *College English* 44 (1982): 483–90.

Article from a Journal with Separate Pagination

Bold, Kathryn. "Western Technology: Will It Work for Africa?" *The Owl* 68.2 (1981): 2–4.

Article from Daily Newspaper

Format #1: Article with By-Line

Petit, Charles. "Scary Report on a Bay Area Quake." *San Francisco Chronicle* 13 Oct. 1982, late city ed.: A2.

Format #2: Article without By-Line

"Teens Write Own Ticket for Fun and Profit." *San José Mercury*, 25 March 1982, morning final ed.: F1.

Format #3: Editorial

"Police Corruption Can Damage Us All." Editorial. *USA Today*, 17 July 1984: A10, col. 1.

Article from an Encyclopedia

Altback, Philip G. "University Reform." *International Encyclopedia of Higher Education*. 1977 ed.

Government Publication

United States Bureau of the Census. *Statistical Abstract of the United States*. 102nd ed. Washington: GPO, 1981.

Review

Format #1: Review with By-Line

Miles, Jack. "An Inventor Visits Nature to Reinvent His Life." Rev. of *The Pathless Way: John Muir and American Wilderness*, by Michael P. Cohen. *Los Angeles Times*, 19 Aug. 1984, book review section: 1–3.

Format #2: Review without By-Line

"Exploring a Lost Continent." Rev. of the Waverly Consort. *Time*, 18 Feb. 1980: 57–58.

Format #3: Untitled Review without By-Line

Rev. of *Max Perkins: Editor of Genius*, by A. Scott Berg. *New Yorker*, 31 July 1978: 79.*

Letter

Format #1: Published Letter

Hemingway, Ernest. "To Lillian Ross." 28 July 1948. In *Ernest Hemingway: Selected Letters, 1917–1961*. Ed. Carlos Baker. New York: Scribner's, 1981. 646–49.

Format #2: Personally Received Letter

Vonnegut, Kurt. Letter to the author. 1 June 1985.

Format #3: Unpublished Letter in Estate or Library Archive

Berryman, John. Letter to Ralph Ross. 15 April 1954. John Berryman Papers. University of Minnesota Library, Minneapolis.

Interview

Format #1: Published Interview

Auel, Jean M. " The *West* Interview: Jean M. Auel." With Abby Goldman. *West Magazine* [*San José Mercury News*]. 19 Feb. 1984: 3.

---

*This entry would be alphabetized under "R."

Format #2: Broadcast or Recorded Interview

Armstrong, Neil. Interview. *Celebrity Watch*. KRKR TV, Oceanville, Calif. 10 Jan. 1970.

Format #3: Personally Conducted Interview

Armstrong, Neil. Personal Interview. 10 Jan. 1970.

Armstrong, Neil. Telephone Interview. 10 Jan. 1970.

Lecture

Berkenkotter, Carol. "A Context-Based Theory of Revision." Conference on College Composition and Communication. New York, 30 March 1984.

Information Service Document

Duke, Charles R. "Language Play and the Teaching of Poetry," 1970. ERIC ED 178 915.

Computer Software

Jones, George. *Sentence Tutor*. Computer software. Microlab Engineering, 1980. IBM PC/356KB.

A Brief Note on APA Style

It is unlikely that you will be asked to use a documentation style other than MLA for papers you write in freshman composition. Outside of English studies, however, APA format (the system adopted by the American Psychological Association) is commonly used.

APA format is very similar to new MLA format. The principal differences are as follows:

1. Year of publication is given greater emphasis; it is placed in parentheses immediately after the author's surname:

   Johnson (1986) has been among the first to measure the long-range effects of acid rain upon topsoil.

2. When quoting or paraphrasing include author's surname, comma, year, comma, and the page number(s), preceded by "p." or "pp." immediately following the quotation:

> He discovered that "considerable increases in soil acidity—enough to damage most crops—can occur after one season of acid rainfall" (Johnson, 1986, p. 88).

3. Author and year may be stated before a quotation, with the page reference stated at the end of the quotation:

> Johnson (1986) discovered that "considerable increases in soil acidity—enough to damage most crops—can occur after one season of acid rainfall" (p. 8).

4. The bibliography at the end of the paper is titled "References," not "Works Cited."

5. In every bibliography entry, the year of publication (in parentheses) is the first item that follows name(s) of author(s):

> Johnson, John J. (1986). *Long-range effects of acid rainfall.* New York: Granger Press.

Note that the title of the book is italicized, but unlike MLA format, only the first word of the title is capitalized. For journal articles, likewise, only the first word in the title is capitalized; also, quotation marks are not used:

> Edwards, Ellen. (1986) Schizophrenic behavior among preadolescent children. *Journal of Abnormal Behavior, 34,* 60–68.

Note that in the above example, the volume number is italicized and that "p." or "pp." abbreviations are not used. These abbreviations *are* used to indicate pages from weekly or monthly magazines, for which volume numbers are not recorded:

> Tape, Walter. (1985, June). The topology of mirages. *Scientific American,* pp. 120–29.

For a complete account of APA format consult the *Publication Manual of the American Psychological Association,* 3rd Edition (Washington, D.C.: American Psychological Association, 1983).

Reference Works in Major Subject Areas

This guide lists reference works useful in fact-gathering for any kind of writing project and in establishing a foundation for more specialized research. For convenience, and not to indicate hard-and-fast disciplinary boundaries, these works are categorized according to major subject areas in the fine arts, social sciences, physical sciences, philosophy, and literature. A general category is also included.

The works in each of the discipline categories are grouped according to type: bibliography, abstract, dictionary, encyclopedia, index, and miscellaneous subject-specific works.

Because virtually all of these reference works are valuable resources for all college students, they are worth examining for their intrinsic merits.

General Reference Works

Almanacs (Multidisciplinary Fact Books)

Facts on File. New York: Facts on File. [weekly]

Information Please Almanac. New York: Simon and Schuster. [annual]

The World Almanac and Book of Facts. New York: Newspaper Enterprise Association. [annual]

General Bibliographies

Bibliographic Index: A Cumulative Bibliography of Bibliographies. New York: H. W. Wilson, 1937–current.

Books in Print. New York: R. R. Bowker, 1948–current. [annual supplements]

Guide to Reference Books. 9th ed. Ed. Eugene P. Sheehy. Chicago: American Library Association, 1976. [often referred to as "Sheehy's"]

Paperbound Books in Print. New York: R. R. Bowker, 1955–current.

Ulrich's International Periodical Directory, 22nd ed. 2 vols. New York: R. R. Bowker, 1983.

Language Dictionaries

Unabridged Dictionaries

The Oxford English Dictionary [OED]. 13 vols. plus supplements. Oxford: Oxford University Press, 1933. [avail. in 2-vol. microprint ed.]

Webster's Third New International Dictionary. Springfield, Mass.: G. and C. Merriam Company, 1981.

Abridged Dictionaries

The American Heritage Dictionary. 2nd college ed. Boston: Houghton Mifflin, 1982. [*Note*: The 1st edition (New College edition) of this dictionary is also valuable; it contains an appendix of Indo-European roots not included in the 2nd edition.]

The Random House Dictionary of the English Language. College ed. New York: Random House, 1968.

Webster's New World Dictionary. 2nd college ed. New York: Simon and Schuster, 1982.

Webster's Ninth New Collegiate Dictionary. Springfield, Mass.: G. and C. Merriam Company, 1983.

Specialized Language Dictionaries

Byrne, Josefa Heifetz. *Mrs. Byrne's Dictionary of Unusual, Obscure, and Preposterous Words.* Secaucus, N.J.: Citadel, 1974.

A Dictionary of American Slang. Second Supplemented Edition. Ed. Harold Wentworth and Stuart B. Flexner. New York: Thomas Y. Crowell, 1975.

Evans, Bergen, and Cornelia Evans. *A Dictionary of Contemporary American Usage.* New York: Random House, 1957.

Morris, William, and Mary Morris. *Harper Dictionary of Contemporary Usage.* 2nd ed. New York: Harper and Row, 1985. [lively discussion of usage differences by Usage Panel]

Oxford Dictionary of English Etymology. Ed. C. T. Onions. Oxford: Oxford University Press, 1966.

Roget's International Thesaurus. 4th ed. Ed. Rev. Robert L. Chapman. New York: Thomas Y. Crowell, 1977.

Room, Adrian. *Room's Dictionary of Differences.* New York: Everest House, 1981. [a small dictionary that distinguishes between words of similar but distinct meanings]

Biographical Dictionaries

American Biographies

Dictionary of American Biography. 21 vols. New York: Charles Scribner's Sons, 1974. [occasional supplements]

Notable American Women, 1607–1950. 3 vols. Cambridge: Harvard University Press, 1971.

Who's Who Among Black Americans. 2nd ed. Northbrook, Ill.: Who's Who Among Black Americans, 1978.

Who's Who in America. Chicago: A. N. Marquis, 1899–current.

British Biographies

Dictionary of National Biography. 22 vols. Oxford: Oxford University Press, 1922; supplements through 1970.

Who's Who. London: A. and C. Black, 1849–current.

International Biographies

Chambers Biographical Dictionary. Revised ed. New York: St. Martin's Press, 1969.

Current Biography. New York: H. W. Wilson, 1940–current. [monthly supplements]

International Who's Who. London: Europa Publications, 1935–current. [annual supplements]

General Encyclopedias

Encyclopedia Americana. 30 vols. New York: Americana Corp., 1978.

The New Columbia Encyclopedia. 1 vol. New York: Columbia University Press, 1975.

The New Encyclopaedia Britannica. 30 vols. Chicago: Encyclopaedia Britannica, 1981.

The World Book Encyclopedia. 22 vols. New York: World Book Childcraft Int'l., 1978.

General Indexes

Book and Periodical Indexes

Biography Index. New York: H. W. Wilson, 1946–current.

Essay and General Literature Index, 1900–1933. New York: H. W. Wilson, 1934. [annual supplements]

Journal and Magazine Indexes

British Humanities Index. London: Library Assoc., 1962–current.

General Science Index. New York: H. W. Wilson, 1978–current.

Humanities Index. New York: H. W. Wilson, 1974–current.

International Index. New York: H. W. Wilson, 1907–1965. [humanities and social sciences; later indexes entitled *Social Sciences and Humanities Index*, *Humanities Index*, and *Social Sciences Index*, all listed in this section]

Nineteenth Century Readers' Guide to Periodical Literature, 1890–1899. New York: H. W. Wilson, 1944.

Readers' Guide to Periodical Literature. New York: H. W. Wilson, 1900–current.

Social Sciences and Humanities Index. New York: H. W. Wilson, 1965–1974.

Social Sciences Index. New York: H. W. Wilson, 1974–current.

Newspaper Indexes

Newspaper Index. Wooster, Ohio: Bell and Howell, 1972–current. [covers the *Chicago Tribune*, the *Los Angeles Times*, the *New Orleans Times-Picayune*, and the *Washington Post*]

The New York Times Index. New York: New York Times Book Co., 1913–current.

The Times Index. London: The Times, 1906–current.

Government Publication Indexes

Monthly Catalog of United States Government Publications. Washington, D.C.: Government Printing Office, 1895–current.

Monthly Checklist of State Publications. Washington, D.C.: Government Printing Office, 1910–current.

Reference Works in Philosophy, Psychology, Religion [Library of Congress Classification Prefix: B; Z for Bibliographies]

Bibliographies and Abstracts

A Bibliographical Survey for a Foundation in Philosophy. Lanham, Md.: University of America Press, 1978.

A Bibliography of Philosophical Bibliographies. Ed. Herbert Guerry. Westport, Conn.: Greenwood Press, 1977.

Psychological Abstracts. Lancaster, Penna.: American Psychological Assn., 1927–current.

Dictionaries

Bowden, Henry W. *Dictionary of American Religious Biography.* Westport, Conn.: Greenwood Press, 1977.

Brugger, Walter. *Philosophical Dictionary.* Trans. Kenneth Baker. Spokane: Gonzaga University Press, 1972.

Buttrick, George A., and Keith R. Crim. *The Interpreter's Dictionary of the Bible.* 5 vols. Nashville: Abingdon Press, 1976.

Flew, Antony. *Dictionary of Philosophy.* New York: St. Martin's Press, 1980.

Runes, Dagohert D., ed. *Dictionary of Philosophy.* New York: Philosophical Library, 1983.

Wolman, Benjamin B., ed. *Dictionary of Behavioral Science.* New York: Van Nostrand Reinhold, 1974.

Encyclopedias

Edwards, Paul, ed. *Encyclopedia of Philosophy*. 8 vols. New York: Macmillan and The Free Press, 1967.

Eysenck, H. J., et al. *Encyclopedia of Psychology*. 2nd ed. 3 vols. New York: Seaburg Press, 1979.

Goldenson, Robert M. *The Encyclopedia of Human Behavior*. 2 vols. Garden City, N.Y.: Doubleday, 1970.

Harre, Rom, and Roger Lamb, eds. *The Encyclopedic Dictionary of Psychology*. Cambridge, Mass.: The MIT Press, 1983.

Hastings, James, ed. *Encyclopedia of Religion and Ethics*. 13 vols. New York: Charles Scribner's Sons, 1928.

MacCulloch, Canon John Arnott, ed. *The Mythology of All Races*. 13 vols. New York: Cooper Square Publishers, 1964.

Man, Myth, and Magic: The Illustrated Encyclopedia of Mythology, Religion, and the Unknown. 12 vols. New York: Marshall Cavendish, 1983.

Meagher, O'Brien, and S. S. J. Aherne, eds. *Encyclopedic Dictionary of Religion*. Washington, D.C.: Corpus Publications, 1979.

Melton, J. Gordon. *The Encyclopedia of American Religions*. 2 vols. Wilmington, N.C.: McGrath Publishing Co., 1978.

Indexes

Index to Religious Periodical Literature. Chicago: American Theological Library Association, 1976.

The Philosophers' Index. Cumulative Edition. Bowling Green, Ohio: Philosophy Documentation Center, 1979.

Psychological Index. Princeton: Psychological Review Co., 1895–1936.

Miscellaneous Subject-Specific Works

Alexander, Franz G., and Sheldon T. Selesnick. *The History of Psychiatry: An Evaluation of Psychiatric Thought and Practice From Prehistoric Times to the Present*. New York: Harper and Row, 1966.

Bettenson, Henry, ed. *Documents of the Christian Church*. 2nd ed. London: Oxford University Press, 1963.

Burr, John R., ed. *Handbook of World Philosophy*. Westport, Conn.: Greenwood Press, 1980.

Copleston, Frederick, S. J. *A History of Philosophy*. 8 vols. Westminster, Md.: Newman Press, 1946.

DeGeorge, Richard T. *The Philosopher's Guide*. Lawrence, Kans.: Regents Press, 1980.

Reference Works in History
[Library of Congress Prefixes: C,D,E,F; Z for Bibliographies]

Bibliographies

Bibliographies in American History. New York: H. W. Wilson, 1942.

Bibliography of British History. 3 vols. Oxford: Oxford University Press, 1928–1970.

Graves, Edgar B. *Bibliography of English History to 1485.* Oxford: Oxford University Press, 1975.

Guide to Historical Literature. New York: Macmillan, 1961.

International Bibliography of Historical Sciences. New York: H. W. Wilson, 1930–current.

Panofsky, Hans E. *A Bibliography of Africana.* Westport, Conn.: Greenwood Press, 1975.

Pouiton, Helen J. *The Historian's Handbook: A Descriptive Guide to Reference Works.* Norman, Okla.: University of Oklahoma Press, 1972.

Woods, Richard D. *Reference Materials on Mexican Americans: An Annotated Bibliography.* Metuchen, N.J.: Scarecrow Press, 1976.

Dictionaries

Dictionary of American History. Revised ed. 8 vols. New York: Charles Scribner's Sons, 1976.

Steinberg's Dictionary of British History. 2nd ed. New York: St. Martin's Press, 1971.

Encyclopedias

Delpar, Helen, ed. *Encyclopedia of Latin America.* New York: McGraw-Hill, 1974.

Illustrated Encyclopedia of the Classical World. New York: Harper and Row, 1975.

Index to Book Reviews in Historical Periodicals. Metuchen, N.J.: Scarecrow Press, 1972–current.

Langer, William, ed. *An Encyclopedia of World History: Ancient, Medieval, and Modern.* 5th ed. Boston: Houghton-Mifflin Co., 1972.

Miscellaneous Subject-Specific Works

The Cambridge Ancient History. 3rd ed. 10 vols. Cambridge: Cambridge University Press, 1975.

Documents of American History. 9th ed. Ed. Henry Steele Commanger. New York: Appleton-Century-Crofts, 1973.

McCoy, F. N. *Researching and Writing in History: A Practical Handbook for Students.* Berkeley: University of California Press, 1974.

The New Cambridge Modern History. 14 vols. Cambridge: Cambridge University Press, 1965.

Reference Works in Geography, Anthropology, the Social Sciences, and Economics [Library of Congress Classification Prefixes: G,H; Z for Bibliographies]

Bibliographies and Abstracts

Bibliographic Guide to Business and Economics. Boston: G. K. Hall, 1975–current.

Hoggart, Keith. *Geography and Local Administration: A Bibliography.* Monticello, Ill.: Vance Bibliographies, 1980.

International Bibliography of Social and Cultural Anthropology. London: UNESCO, 1955–current.

Mark, Charles. *Sociology of America: A Guide to Information Sources.* Detroit: Gale, 1976.

Sociological Abstracts. New York: Sociological Abstracts, 1952–current.

White, Carl M. *Sources of Information in the Social Sciences.* 2nd ed. Chicago: American Library Association, 1973. [covers social sciences literature; history; geography, economics, and business administration; sociology; anthropology, psychology, education, and political science]

Dictionaries

Ammer, Christine, and Dean S. Ammer. *Dictionary of Business and Economics.* New York: The Free Press, 1977.

Fairchild, Henry Pratt, ed. *Dictionary of Sociology and Related Sciences.* Totowa, N.J.: Littlefield, Adams and Co., 1977.

Leach, Maria, ed. *Funk and Wagnall's Standard Dictionary of Folklore, Mythology, and Legend.* New York: Funk and Wagnall's, 1972.

Monkhouse, F. J. A. *Dictionary of the Natural Environment.* Revised ed. New York: Halsted, 1977.

Pearce, David. *Dictionary of Modern Economics.* Cambridge, Mass.: MIT Press, 1981.

Webster's New Geographical Dictionary. Springfield, Mass.: G. and C. Merriam Co., 1980.

Winick, Charles. *Dictionary of Anthropology.* Totowa, N.J.: Littlefield, Adams and Co., 1975.

Encyclopedias

Greenwald, Douglas. *Encyclopedia of Economics.* New York: McGraw-Hill, 1981.

Hunter, David E. *Encyclopedia of Anthropology.* New York: Harper and Row, 1976.

Sills, David L., ed. *International Encyclopedia of the Social Sciences.* 17 vols. New York: Macmillan and The Free Press, 1968.

Indexes

Business Periodicals Index. New York: H. W. Wilson, 1958–current.

Economics Information Resources Directory. Detroit: Gale, 1984–current.

Social Sciences Index. New York: H. W. Wilson, 1965–current. [For pre-1965 citations consult the *Social Sciences and Humanities Index.*]

Thompson, Stith. *Motif Index of Folk Literature.* Revised ed. 6 vols. Bloomington, Ind.: Indiana University Press, 1958.

Miscellaneous Subject-Specific Works

Berenson, Conrad, and Raymond Colton. *Research and Report Writing for Business and Economics.* New York: Random House, 1970.

Ferman, Gerald S., and Jack Levin. *Social Science Research: A Handbook.* Cambridge: Schrenkman, 1977.

Hammond Medallion World Atlas. Maplewood, N.J.: Hammond, 1982.

Negley, Glenn. *Utopian Literature: A Bibliography, With a Supplementary List of Works Influential in Utopian Thought.* Lawrence, Kans.: University of Kansas Press, 1977.

Times Atlas of the World. 6th ed. London: Times Books Ltd., 1980.

Times Atlas of World History. Revised ed. Ed. Geoffrey Barraclough. Maplewood, N.J.: Hammond, 1984. [a geographical background to world history]

Wright, John W. *The American Almanac of Jobs and Salaries.* Revised ed. New York: Avon Books, 1984.

Reference Works in Political Science
[Library of Congress Classification Prefix: J; Z for Bibliographies]

Bibliographies

Harmon, Robert B. *Political Science Bibliographies.* 2 vols. Metuchen, N.J.: Scarecrow Press, 1976.

International Bibliography of Political Science. Chicago: Aldine, 1953–current.

Dictionaries

Laqueur, Walter Z., ed. *A Dictionary of Politics.* Revised ed. New York: The Free Press, 1974.

Plano, J. C. *American Political Dictionary.* 6th ed. New York: Holt, Rinehart and Winston, 1982.

Encyclopedias

Worldmark Encyclopedia of Nations. 5th ed. 5 vols. New York: John Wiley and Sons, 1976.

Worldmark Encyclopedia of the States. New York: Harper and Row, 1981.

Indexes

ABC Political Science. Santa Barbara: ABC-Clio, 1969–current.

Miscellaneous Subject-Specific Works

Barone, Michael, and Grant Ujifusa. *The Almanac of American Politics 1984.* Washington, D.C.: National Journal, 1983.

Cook, Chris, and John Paxton. *European Political Facts, 1918–1973.* New York: St. Martin's Press, 1975.

Greenstein, Fred I., and Nelson W. Polsby. *Handbook of Political Science.* 9 vols. Reading, Mass.: Addison-Wesley, 1975.

Stoffle, Carla, et al. *Materials and Methods for Political Science Research.* New York: Neal-Schuman, 1979.

Reference Works in Education
[Library of Congress Classification Prefix: L; Z for Bibliographies]

Bibliographies and Abstracts

Berry, Dorthea. *Bibliographic Guide to Educational Research.* 2nd ed. Metuchen, N.J.: Scarecrow Press, 1980.

Resources in Education [ERIC]. Washington, D.C.: United States Government Printing Office, 1966–current. [abstracts of articles in education, all levels, available through ERIC]

Richmond, W. Kenneth. *The Literature of Education: A Critical Bibliography, 1945–1970.* London: Methuen, 1972.

Dictionaries

Good, Carter V., ed. *Dictionary of Education.* 3rd ed. New York: McGraw-Hill, 1973.

Rowntree, Derek. *Dictionary of Education.* New York: Harper and Row, 1981.

Encyclopedias

Encyclopedia of Education. New York: Macmillan, 1971.

Encyclopedia of Educational Research. 5th ed. 4 vols. New York: The Free Press, 1982.

The International Encyclopedia of Higher Education. 10 vols. San Francisco: Jossey-Bass, 1977.

Indexes

Current Index to Journals in Education. New York: Macmillan, 1969–current.

Education Index. New York: H. W. Wilson, 1929–current.

Miscellaneous Subject-Specific Works

Avy, Donald, et al. *Introduction to Research in Education.* 2nd ed. New York: Holt, Rinehart and Winston, 1979.

Good, Carter V. *Essentials of Educational Research: Methodology and Design.* Englewood Cliffs, N.J.: Prentice-Hall, 1972.

Reference Works in Music and the Visual Arts [Library of Congress Prefixes: M, N; Z for Bibliographies]

Bibliographies

Eheresmann, Donald L. *Fine Arts: A Bibliographic Guide to Basic Reference Works, Histories and Handbooks.* 2nd ed. Littleton, Colo.: Libraries Unlimited, 1979.

Horn, David. *The Literature of American Music in Books and Folk Music Collections: A Fully Annotated Bibliography.* Metuchen, N.J.: Scarecrow Press, 1977.

Karpel, Bernard, ed. *Arts in America: A Bibliography.* 4 vols. Washington, D.C.: Smithsonian Institution Press, 1979.

Mixter, K. E. *General Bibliography for Music Research.* 2nd ed. Detroit: Information Coordinators, 1975.

Western, Dominique C. *A Bibliography of the Arts of Africa.* Waltham, Mass.: African Studies Association, 1975.

Dictionaries

Anderson, Ruth. *Contemporary American Composers: A Biographical Dictionary.* Boston: G. K. Hall, 1976.

Apel, Willi. *Harvard Dictionary of Music.* 2nd revised ed. Cambridge: Harvard University Press, 1969.

Cummings, Paul. *Dictionary of Contemporary American Artists.* 3rd ed. New York: St. Martin's Press, 1977.

Fleming, John, and Hugh Honour. *Dictionary of the Decorative Arts.* New York: Harper and Row, 1977.

Grove, Sir George. *Dictionary of Music and Musicians.* 5th ed. 10 vols. plus supplements. New York: St. Martin's Press, 1955.

Meyers, Bernard S., and Shirley D. Myers. *Dictionary of Twentieth-Century Art.* New York: McGraw-Hill, 1974.

Picerno, Vincent J. *Dictionary of Musical Terms.* Brooklyn: Haskell, 1976.

Encyclopedias

Daniel, Howard. *Encyclopedia of Themes and Subjects in Painting: Mythological, Biblical, Historical, Literary, Allegorical, and Topical.* New York: Harry N. Abrams, 1971.

Encyclopedia of World Art. 15 vols. New York: McGraw-Hill, 1959–68.

International Encyclopedia of Women Composers. New York: R. R. Bowker, 1981.

Praeger Encyclopedia of Art. 5 vols. New York: Praeger, 1971.

Rugoff, Milton, ed. *Britannica Encyclopaedia of American Art.* Chicago: Encyclopaedia Britannica, 1973.

Thompson, Oscar. *International Encyclopedia of Music and Musicians.* 10th revised ed. New York: Dodd, Mead and Co., 1975.

Indexes

Art Index. New York: H. W. Wilson, 1929–current.

Music Index. Detroit: Information Service, 1950–current.

Popular Music Periodicals Index. Metuchen, N.J.: Scarecrow Press, 1973–current.

Miscellaneous Subject-Specific Works

Charles, Sydney R. *Handbook of Music and Music Literature.* New York: The Free Press, 1972.

Ekdahl, Janis. *American Sculpture: A Guide to Information Services.* Detroit: Gale, 1977.

Goldman, Bernard. *Reading and Writing in the Arts: A Handbook.* Revised ed. Detroit: Wayne State University Press, 1978.

Grount, Donald J. *A History of Western Music.* Revised ed. New York: W. W. Norton and Co., 1973.

Rowland, Benjamin. *The Harvard Outline and Reading Lists for Oriental Art.* 3rd ed. Cambridge: Harvard University Press, 1967.

Reference Works in Language, Literature, Theater, Film
[Library of Congress Prefix: P; Z for Bibliographies]

Bibliographies and Abstracts

Baldensperger, Fernand, and Werner P. Friedrich. *Bibliography of Comparative Literature.* New York: Russell and Russell, 1960.

Fairbanks, Carol, and Eugene A. Engeldinger. *Black American Fiction: A Bibliography.* Metuchen, N.J.: Scarecrow Press, 1978.

MLA International Bibliography of Books and Articles on Modern Languages and Literatures. New York: Modern Language Association, 1921–current.

New Cambridge Bibliography of English Literature. 5 vols. Cambridge: Cambridge University Press, 1977. [covers period from ca. A.D. 600 to mid-twentieth century]

Schweik, Robert C., and Dieter Riesner. *Reference Sources in English and American Literature: An Annotated Bibliography.* New York: W. W. Norton and Co., 1977.

Stensland, Anna Lee. *Literature By and About the American Indian: An Annotated Bibliography.* 2nd ed. Urbana: N.C.T.E., 1979.

Dictionaries*

Bede, Jean-Albert, and William Edgerton, eds. *Columbia Dictionary of Modern European Literature.* 2nd ed. New York: Columbia University Press, 1980.

Holman, C. Hugh. *A Handbook to Literature.* 4th ed. Indianapolis: Bobbs-Merrill, 1980. [a dictionary of literary terms and periods]

MacNicholas, John, ed. *Twentieth-Century American Dramatists.* 2 vols. Detroit: Gale, 1980.

Rush, Theressa Gunnels, et al. *Black American Writers Past and Present: A Biographical and Bibliographical Dictionary.* 2 vols. Metuchen, N.J.: Scarecrow Press, 1975.

---

*See pp. 508–509 for English language dictionaries.

Encyclopedias

Bronner, Edwin. *Encyclopedia of American Theatre, 1900–1975.* South Brunswick, N.J.: Barnes and Noble, 1980.

Encyclopedia of World Literature in the Twentieth Century. 2nd ed. 3 vols. New York: Frederick Ungar, 1981.

Preminger, Alex, ed. *Princeton Encyclopedia of Poetry and Poetics.* Enlarged ed. Princeton: Princeton University Press, 1974.

Indexes

Book Review Index. Detroit: Gale, 1965–current.

Essay and General Literature Index. New York: H. W. Wilson, 1900–current.

Film Literature Index. Albany, N.Y.: Filmdex, 1973–current.

Granger's Index to Poetry. 7th ed. New York: Columbia University Press, 1982.

Short Story Index. New York: H. W. Wilson, 1980 plus supplements. [covers period from 1900 onward]

Miscellaneous Subject-Specific Works

American Theatre Annual. Detroit: Gale, 1977–current.

Magill's Survey of Cinema. First and Second Series. 10 vols. Englewood Cliffs, N.J.: Salem Press, 1980, 1981.

Smith, Curtis, ed. *Twentieth-Century Science Fiction Writers.* New York: St. Martin's Press, 1981. [biographies, critical essays, bibliographies]

Spiller, Robert. *Literary History of the United States.* 4th ed. 2 vols. New York: Macmillan, 1974.

Tucker, Martin, ed. *Moulton's Library of Literary Criticism of English and American Authors.* 4 vols. New York: Frederick Unger Publishing Co., 1966.

Reference Works in the Sciences and Technology [Library of Congress Prefixes: Q, T; Z for Bibliographies]

Bibliographies and Abstracts

Biological Abstracts. Philadelphia: Biological Abstracts, 1926–current.

Brief Guide to Sources of Scientific and Technical Information. 2nd ed. Arlington, Va.: Information Resources, 1980.

Chemical Abstracts: Key to the World's Chemical Literature. Easton, Penna.: American Chemical Society, 1907–current.

Ferguson, Eugene S. *Bibliography of the History of Technology.* Cambridge, Mass.: MIT Press, 1968.

Gaffney, M. P. and L. A. Steen, eds. *Annotated Bibliography of Expository Writing in the Mathematical Sciences.* Washington, D.C.: Mathematics Association, 1976.

Malinowsky, Harold R., and Jeanne Richardson. *Science and Engineering Literature.* 3rd ed. Littleton, Colo.: Libraries Unlimited, 1980.

Owen, Dolores B., and Marguerite Hanchey. *Abstracts and Indexes in Science and Technology: A Descriptive Guide.* Metuchen, N.J.: Scarecrow Press, 1974.

Rees, Alan, and Blanche Young. *Consumer Health Information Source Book.* New York: R. R. Bowker, 1981.

Walters, LeRoy, ed. *Bibliography of Bioethics.* 9 vols. Detroit: Gale, 1980–81; New York: The Free Press, 1980–83.

Dictionaries

Abercrombie, M., C. J. Hickman, and M. L. Johnson. *A Dictionary of Biology.* 6th ed. Middlesex: Penguin Books, Ltd., 1973.

Dictionary of Scientific Biography. 16 vols. New York: Charles Scribner's Sons, 1980.

Hawley, Gessner G. *The Condensed Chemical Dictionary.* 9th ed. New York: Van Nostrand Reinhold, 1977.

McGraw-Hill Dictionary of Scientific and Technical Terms. 2nd ed. New York: McGraw-Hill, 1978.

Thewlis, James. *Concise Dictionary of Physics and Related Subjects.* 2nd ed. New York: Pergamon Press, 1979.

Weik, Martin H. *Standard Dictionary of Computers and Information Processing.* 2nd ed. Rochelle Park, N.J.: Hayden Publishing Co., 1977.

Whitten, D. G. A. *Penguin Dictionary of Geology.* Baltimore, Md.: Penguin Books, 1976.

Encyclopedias

Belzer, Jack. *Encyclopedia of Computer Science and Technology.* 14 vols. New York: Dekker, 1981.

Encyclopedia of Bioethics. 4 vols. New York: Macmillan, 1978.

Gatland, Kenneth. *Illustrated Encyclopedia of Space Technology.* New York: Harmony Books, 1981.

Lerner, Rita, and George Trigg. *Encyclopedia of Physics.* Reading, Mass.: Addison-Wesley, 1981.

McGraw-Hill Encyclopedia of Science and Technology. 5th ed. 15 vols. New York: McGraw-Hill, 1982.

Indexes

Applied Science and Technology Index. New York: H. W. Wilson, 1958–current.

Biological and Agricultural Index. New York: H. W. Wilson, 1947–current.

General Science Index. New York: H. W. Wilson, 1978–current.

Miscellaneous Subject-Specific Works

Asimov, Isaac. *Words of Science and the History Behind Them.* Boston: Houghton-Mifflin Co., 1959.

Beveridge, W. I. B. *The Art of Scientific Investigation.* New York: Random House, 1957.

Gordon, Arnold J., and Richard A. Ford. *The Chemist's Companion: A Handbook of Practical Data, Techniques, and References.* New York: John Wiley and Sons, 1972.

Kirk, Thomas G., Jr. *Library Research Guide to Biology: Illustrated Search Strategy and Sources.* Ann Arbor, Mich.: Pierian Press, 1978.

ACKNOWLEDGMENTS

Pages 23–24, "Fear and Trembling and Sick of English" by Christine Long, *The Santa Clara*, Oct. 29, 1982. Reprinted by permission of the author.

Page 25, from "Why I Write" in *Such, Such Were the Joys* by George Orwell, copyright © 1953 by Sonia Brownell Orwell; renewed 1981 by Mrs. George K. Perutz, Mrs. Miriam Cross, Dr. Michael Dickson, Executors of the Estate of Sonia Brownell Orwell. Reprinted by permission of Harcourt Brace Jovanovich and of A. M. Heath & Company Ltd. Published by Martin Secker and Warburg, Ltd.

Page 35, from *Writing the Natural Way* by Gabriele Lusser Rico. Copyright © 1983 by Gabriele Lusser Rico. Reprinted by permission of J. P. Tarcher, Inc., Houghton Mifflin Company, and Lavelle Leahey.

Page 35, Prose reconstruction of "Airplane" cluster by Lavelle Leahey. Reprinted by permission of the author.

Pages 4–49, from "Learning Years" by Beth Doxsee. Reprinted by permission from Spring 1983 *America*. Copyright © 1983 by 13–30 Corporation, 505 Market Street, Knoxville, TN 37902.

Page 49, from "Advice for Would-be Wayfarers" by Denise Graveline. Reprinted by permission from Spring 1983 *America*. Copyright © 1983 by 13–30 Corporation, 505 Market Street, Knoxville, TN 37902.

Page 52 (photo), *His First Refusal*, Anonymous. Courtesy of the Library of Congress.

Page 53 (photo), *The Unmade Bed*, 1957. Copyright © by The Imogen Cunningham Trust.

Page 59, from *Anne Frank: The Diary of a Young Girl*. Copyright © 1952 by Otto H. Frank. Reprinted by permission of Doubleday and Company, Inc.

Pages 67–68, "The Video Game Player" by Joanne Lambkin. Unpublished essay. Reprinted by permission of the author.

Pages 72–73, from "Lost Worlds: The Plains of Mars" by Mark Ingebretsen. Reprinted by permission from Spring 1984 *America*. Copyright © 1984 by 13–30 Corporation, 505 Market Street, Knoxville, TN 37902.

Page 75, from *A Romantic Education* by Patricia Hampl. Copyright © 1984 by Patricia Hampl. Reprinted by permission of the author.

Pages 77–78, "Confessions of a Doorman" by Thomas Hogendijk. Unpublished essay. Reprinted by permission of the author.

Pages 79–80, from "Flight" in *Pigeon Feathers and Other Stories* by John Updike. Copyright © 1962 by John Updike. Reprinted by permission of Alfred A. Knopf, Inc.

Pages 81–82, "Social Nibbling" by Ellen Goodman. Copyright © 1980 by The Boston Globe Newspaper Company/Washington Post Writers Group. Reprinted by permission.

Pages 93–94, from *The Story of Jazz* by Marshall W. Stearns. Copyright © 1956 by Oxford University Press, Inc. Reprinted by permission.

Page 96, from "Pocket Money" by Russell Baker in *So This Is Depravity*. Copyright © 1980 by Congdon and Lattes. Used by permission of Congdon and Weed, Inc.

Pages 101–102, from "The Essence of Charm" by Laurie Lee in *I Can't Stay Long*. Copyright © 1975 by Laurie Lee. Reprinted by permission of Atheneum Publishers, Inc.

Pages 105–107, "How to Figure 'Fuelishness'" by Kim Garretson in *Better Homes and Gardens* Magazine. Copyright © 1979 by Meredith Corporation. All rights reserved.

Page 109, "How to Make a Speech" by George Plimpton. Reprinted by permission of International Paper Company.

Pages 111–112, "The Salinity Problem in Crop Irrigation" by Evan Elliott. Unpublished essay. Reprinted by permission of the author.

Pages 113–114, "Learning to Drive a Manual Transmission" by Marie Noble. Unpublished essay. Reprinted by permission of the author.

Pages 115–118, "Cooling Burnout" by David Stansbury in *Nutshell*, Spring 1984. Reprinted by permission of the author.

Page 148, "How Does a Small Boy Cope with Cerebral Palsy and Become a Psychology Professor?" Reprinted by permission of the United Cerebral Palsy Association, Inc.

Pages 139–140, "Ban This Poison Before It Poisons Us." Editorial in *USA TODAY*, Sept. 20, 1983. Copyright © 1983 by *USA TODAY*. Reprinted with permission.

Pages 141–142, "How Do I Rate Thee? Let Me Count the Ways" by Anita Lee. Unpublished essay. Reprinted by permission of the author.

Pages 149–150, from "Television: The Splitting Image" by Marya Mannes. Copyright © 1970 by *Saturday Review*. Reprinted by permission.

Page 151, "Workhorses." Reprinted by permission of Altos Marketing Services.

Page 152, "Stop: Even on Ice." Reprinted by permission of ITT Corporation.

Page 153, "My personal advice is . . ." Reprinted by permission of Heublein, Inc.

Page 154, "Smart Sets." Reprinted by permission of Zenith Electronics Corporation.

Page 155, "Leonardo da Vinci Gave Us a Great Idea for Bucket Seats." Reprinted by permission of General Motors Corporation.

Page 158, Letter to the Editor by L. Moore in the *San José Mercury*, August 18, 1982. Reprinted by permission of the *San José Mercury News*.

Pages 159–160, "The Problem with Soccer Is . . ." by Andy Rooney in the *San José Mercury*, July 20, 1982. Reprinted by permission of Andrew C. Rooney.

Pages 162–167, "To Draft or Not To Draft . . ." by James Fallows. Reprinted by permission of the author. First published in *The Atlantic*, April 1980.

Pages 167–169, from "Drugs" by Gore Vidal in *Homage to Daniel Shays: Collected Essays 1952–1972*. Copyright © 1970 by Gore Vidal. Reprinted by permission of Random House, Inc.

Pages 170–171, "Who Killed Benny Paret?" by Norman Cousins. Reprinted by permission of the author.

Pages 172–174, from *The Poet and the World* by Denise Levertov. Copyright © 1973 by Denise Levertov Goodman. Reprinted by permission of New Directions Publishing Co.

Pages 175–176, "Breast Feeding in Public Gets a Nod" by Elise Chisholm in the *San José Mercury*, October 10, 1982. Reprinted by permission of *The Baltimore Evening Sun*.

Pages 178–179, "The Nightmare and the Dream," by Paul Gray, a review of E. L. Doctorow's *Loon Lake* in *Time*, September 22, 1980. Copyright © 1980 by Time, Inc. All rights reserved. Reprinted by permission of *Time*.

Pages 180–181, "The Fantasy Film as Final Exam" by Richard Corliss in *Time*, December 17, 1984. Copyright © 1984 by Time, Inc. All rights reserved. Reprinted by permission of *Time*.

Pages 181–183, "Martin Landau's *Dracula* Could Use a Mild Transfusion" by Tom Gough in *The Santa Clara*, January 17, 1985. Reprinted by permission of *The Santa Clara*.

Pages 185–186, "Arnold: 'Dover Beach'" by James Dickey in *Master Poems of the English Language*. Copyright © by Trident Press. Reprinted by permission of Washington Square Press, a division of Simon & Schuster, Inc.

Page 199, from "Endangered Species." U.S. Fish and Wildlife Service, Department of Interior, Washington, D.C. 1981.

Pages 206–208, "The *West* Interview: Jean M. Auel" by Abby Goldman. Originally appeared in *West Magazine* (*San José Mercury News*). Reprinted by permission of the author.

Pages 220–221, "How to 'Write' Programs" in *Time*, January 13, 1983. Copyright © 1983 by Time, Inc. All rights reserved. Reprinted by permission of the author.

Pages 224–233, "Structured Programming: Its Development and Importance" by Jeff Brown. Unpublished paper. Reprinted by permission of the author.

Pages 236–245, "Gradually Adjusting to Retirement: Facing the Change" by Ron K. Rock, Jr. Unpublished paper. Reprinted by permission of the author.

Pages 247–253, from *The Image of the Indian and the Black Man in American Art* by Elwood Perry, 1974. Reprinted by permission of George Braziller, Inc.

Page 250, *The Banjo Lesson* (1893) by Henry Ossawa Tanner. Oil on canvas, 48 x 35 inches. Hampton Institute, Hampton, Virginia, Gift of Robert Ogden, 1894.

Page 296, from *London in the Age of Chaucer* by A. R. Meyers. Copyright © 1972 by the University of Oklahoma Press. Reprinted by permission.

Page 301, from *Beyond Freedom and Dignity* by B. F. Skinner. Copyright © 1971 by B. F. Skinner. Reprinted by permission of Alfred A. Knopf, Inc.

Pages 303–305, "Baby's Baldness at 18 Months Is a Growing Concern" by Dixie Brown in the *San José Mercury News*, August 2, 1983. Reprinted by permission of the author.

Pages 315–316, "Tell It to the Marines" by William Safire in *The New York Times*, April 17, 1983. Copyright © 1983 by the New York Times Company. Reprinted by permission.

Page 327, "Potassium" by Isaac Asimov in *Words of Science*. Copyright © 1959 by Isaac Asimov. Reprinted by permission of Houghton Mifflin Company.

Page 332, from *The Soul of a New Machine* by Tracy Kidder. Reprinted by permission of Little, Brown and Company.

Pages 339–340, "'Just' a Word Makes All the Difference" by Nickie McWhirter in the *San José Mercury*, March 8, 1982. Reprinted by permission of *The Detroit Free Press*.

Pages 348–351, "Confessions of a Doorman" by Thomas Hogendijk. Unpublished essay. Reprinted by permission of the author.

Page 360, from "The Danger Zones: El Salvador Journal" by Don Ballew in *The Santa Clara*, January 10, 1985. Reprinted by permission of *The Santa Clara*.

INDEX

A, an, 437
Abbreviations, 327–28
   dictionary, 327–28
   note-taking, 327–28
Absolute phrase, 382
Abstract diction, 382
Accent marks, 475
   acute, 475
   grave, 475
Accept, except, 438
Acronym, 383
Active voice. *See* Voice
Adapt, adept, 438
Ad hominem fallacy, 136
Adjective, 383, 408, 411, 473
   coordinate, 473
   cumulative, 473
   function of, 407, 408
   possessive pronominal, 411
   predicate, 411
   See also Demonstrative
Ad miseracordiam fallacy, 136
Adept, adopt, 438
Ad populum fallacy, 136
Adverb, 384
   conjunctive, 423
   function of, 408
Advertisement, elements of an, 147–49
Advertising, 147–55
   appeals in, 147, 149
Advice, advise, 439
"Advice for Would-be Wayfarers," 49
Advisory feature, writing an, 104–106
Affect, effect, 439
Affirming the consequent (fallacy), 133–34
Agreement, 384–85
All ready, already, 439
All right, alright, 440
All together, altogether, 440
Allusion, illusion, delusion, 440
Alt, David, *A Roadside Geology of Northern California*, 92

Alumna, alumnae, alumnus, alumni, 440
Alvarez, Julia, "El Doctor," 61
Ambiguity, 268, 385–86
Among, between, 443
Analogy, 92, 93, 94, 130, 386–87
   flawed, 130
Analysis, 91–93
Analytical feature, writing an, 111–12
Angelou, Maya, *I Know Why the Caged Bird Sings*, 281–83
Antecedent (in a syllogism), 133
Apostrophe, 469–70
   with contractions, 469–70
   with figures, 470
   with possessives, 469–70
Appeals, Aristotelian (ethos, pathos, logos), 123, 126–27, 416
Appositive, 387
Apostle, disciple, 441
Approximately, 441
Argument, 121, 127–43, 161–62, 169–70
   building an effective, 138–43
   definition of, 121
   framework, 138–39, 161–62, 169–70
   problems in, 127–28
   vs. opinion, 127–28
Aristotle, 123, 416
Arnold, Matthew, "Dover Beach," 184–86
Art of Loving, The (Fromm), 91
Article, definite, indefinite, 387, 408
Article, nonfiction, 388
As, like, 456
Asimov, Isaac, *Words of Science*, 326–27
Audience, 2, 45–46, 92
   and purpose, 2
   awareness of, 2
   communicating to, 2
Auel, Jean M., 206–208

Authority, arguing from, 125, 126, 149
A while, awhile, 441
Awkward writing. *See* Writing

"Baby's Baldness at 18 Months Is a Growing Concern" (Brown), 303–305
Background reading, 42, 99–100
   See also Research
Bacon, Francis, "Of Suspicion," 215–16
Bad, badly, 442
Bain, Alexander, 417
Baker, Russell, *So This Is Depravity*, 96
Baldwin, James, "Equal in Paris," 59–60
Ballew, Don, "The Danger Zones," 360
Bandwagon fallacy, 136–37
"Ban This Poison Before It Poisons Us," 139–40
Basic drives (advertising appeal), 147
Basin and Range (McPhee), 283–84
Being that, 442
Beside, besides, 442
Between, among, 443
Between you and me, between you and I, 443
Beyond Freedom and Dignity (Skinner), 301
Bibliography, 202, 222–23, 500–504, 505
   preparation of "Works Cited" page (MLA), 500–504
   preparation of "References" page (APA), 505
   working, 222–23
Bibliography card, 204
"Big Two-Hearted River" (Hemingway), 274
Biographies, collective, 192
Book of Greek Myths (Graves), 6

Book review, writing a. *See* Review
Borrow, lend, 443
Braces, 470
   single, 470
   double, 470
Brackets, 470–71
   with interpolated words, 470
   with parenthetical expressions, 471
Brainstorming, 34–38, 388
"Breast Feeding in Public Gets a Nod" (Chisholm), 175–76
Britton, James, 19, 417
Brown, Dee, *Bury My Heart at Wounded Knee,* 200–201
Brown, Dixie, "Baby's Baldness at 18 Months Is a Growing Concern," 303–305
Brown, Jeff, "Structured Programming," 220, 222–33
Bruner, Jerome, 417
Buffon, 420
Burke, Kenneth, 417
Bury My Heart at Wounded Knee (Brown), 200–201

Call numbers, 190
Campbell, George, *Grammatical Man,* 416–17
Campbell, Jeremy, 95
Can, may, 443
Can hardly, can't hardly, 444
Capital, Capitol, 444
Capital letters, 471–72
   with dates, 472
   with days of the week, 472
   with deity, 471
   with first word in dialogue, 471
   with first word in a sentence, 471
   with holidays, 471
   with months of the year, 472
   with names and titles, 471
Card catalogue, library, 192–93
Case, 388–89
   accusative, 388
   dative, 388
   genitive (possessive), 388
   nominative (subjective), 388
Castle of Otranto (Walpole), 81
Cause and effect, 92
Cedilla, 475
Character sketch, 74–76
Childish, childlike, 444
Chisolm, Elise T., "Breast Feeding in Public Gets a Nod," 175–76
Christensen, Erwin O., *A Pictorial History of Western Art,* 88

Christmas, Xmas, 445
Circumflex, 475
Christensen, Francis, 284
Cicero, 29, 416
Clarity, 312–19
   in diction, 312–19
   in relation to complexity, 312–13
Classification, 85, 87–88, 394
   and division, 394
   of parts of speech, 325, 407–408
Clause, 260–61, 277n, 283, 389–90, 404, 415
   dependent (subordinate), 261, 283, 390
   elliptical, 390
   independent, 260, 389, 390
   nonrestrictive, 415
   noun, 404
   relative, 277n
   restrictive, 415
   truncated subordinate, 283
Cliché, 322–24, 390
   defined, 322
   and metaphor, 338
Clue, cue, 445
Clustering, 34–37
Cluttering, 265–66, 298–99
   in paragraphs, 298–99
   in sentences, 265–66
Coherence, 267–71, 294–95, 390
   defined, 267, 390
   external coherence, 295
   in paragraphs, 294–95
   in sentences, 267–71
   internal, 295
Colon, 472–73
   with series, 472
   with time divisions, 472
Column (newspaper), 157, 159
Comma, 473–74
   with appositives, 473
   with coordinate adjectives, 473
   with dates, 474
   with dialogue, 474
   with independent clauses, 473
   with introductory elements, 474
   with nonrestrictive clauses, 473–74
Compare to, compare with, 445
Comparison, 90–91, 93
Complement, 390–91
   predicate adjective, 391
   predicate noun, 391
Complement, compliment, 445
Complex, complicated, 446
Computers, 219–20; 371–73
   composing on, 271–73
   topic for research, 219–20

Concave, convex, 446
Conciseness, 317–18
   See also Wordiness
Conclusion, 139, 161
Conscience, conscientious, conscious, self-conscious, 446–47
Conference-tutorial, 363–65
   preparing for, 364–65
"Confessions of a Doorman" (Hogendijk), 76–78, 348–51
   first draft, 348–51
   final draft, 76–78
Conjunction, 391, 408
   coordinating, 391
   correlative, 391
   function of, 408
   subordinating, 274, 391
Conjunctive adverbs, 423
Connotation, 310–12, 392
   See also Denotation
Consequent (in a syllogism), 133
Continually, continuously, 447
Contrast. *See* Comparison
Convex, concave, 446
"Cooling Burnout" (Stansbury), 115–18
Corliss, Richard, "The Fantasy Film as Final Exam" (Review of *Dune*), 180–81
Could care less, couldn't care less, 448
Could have, could of, could've, 448
Cousins, Norman, "Who Killed Benny Paret?" 170–71
Credible, credulous, 448
Criteria, criterion, 448
Critical reader, role of, 368
Critique list (for in-class workshops), 368–69
Critiquing procedure (for in-class workshops), 369
Cue, clue, 445
Curve-ball fallacy. *See* Evading the issue fallacy

D'Aulaire, Ingri and Edgar, *Book of Greek Myths,* 6
"The Danger Zones" (Ballew), 360
Dash, 474–75
Database, computer, 212–14
Davis, Jefferson, Speech of Resignation, 329
Deadwood. *See* Wordiness
"The Death of the Moth" (Woolf), 279–80
Deduction, 123–24
Definition, 85, 86–87, 93, 94, 100–104, 392

Definition (*continued*)
  categorical, 86, 93, 94, 392
  extended, 100–104
  lexical, 87, 392
  operational, 87, 94, 392
  stipulative, 86, 392
Delusion, allusion, illusion, 440
Demonstrative (adjective), 392–93
Denotation, 310–12, 392
Denying the antecedent (fallacy), 134
  See also Affirming the consequent
Description, 61–66, 67, 71–76, 86, 89–91
  as picture language, 67
  extended, 71–76
  in explanatory context, 89–91
  sensory impact of, 66
Details, use of, 393
Development, 9, 57–67, 85–95, 100–109, 111–13, 121–43, 157–74, 183–86, 368
  of an advisory or instructional feature, 104–109
  of an analytical feature, 111–13
  of an explication, 183–86
  of expressive writing, 57–67
  of an extended definition, 100–104
  of informative writing, 85–95
  of a narrative, 76–78
  of an opinion essay, 157–60
  of persuasive writing, 121–43
  of a problem-solving essay, 167–74
  of a pro-con essay, 160–67
  of a research paper, 217–52
  of a review, 177–81
Dewey Decimal Classification, 194
Diacritical marks, 475–76
  accent marks, 475
  cedilla, 475
  circumflex, 475
  diaeresis, 475
  haček, 476
  tilde, 476
  umlaut, 476
Diaeresis, 475
DIALOG (database), 212
Dialogue, 393
Diary (Nin), 63
Diary of a Young Girl (Frank), 59
Dickey, James, "Matthew Arnold, 'Dover Beach,'" 185–86
Dickinson, Emily, 338–39
Dickinson, G. Lowes, *The Greek View of Life*, 196–97
Diction, 393
  See also Word choice

Dictionary, 191–92, 324–32
  for definitions, 325–26
  for grammar, usage, 327
  for parts of speech, 325
  for pronunciation, 325
  for spelling, 325
  for syllabication, 325
  kinds of dictionaries, 324
  unabridged, 191–92
  ways to use, 325–27
Didion, Joan, "Why I Write," 63
Different from, different than, 448
Dilemma, problem, 448
Dinner, lunch, supper, 449
Direct object. *See* Object
Disciple, apostle, 441
Discourse, 394
  direct, 394
  indirect, 394
Discreet, discrete, 449
Disinterested, uninterested, 449
Distributed term, 132–33
Dived, dove, 450
Divided brain theory of consciousness, 35
Division, 86, 88–89
  See also Classification
Doctorow, E. L., *Loon Lake*, 177–79
Documentation formats, 493–505
  APA style, 505
  footnotes, 494–98
  MLA style, 498–504
  References page (APA), 505
  Works Cited page (MLA), 500–504
Dominant, dominate, 450
Double negative, 394
Doublespeak, 323, 341
Dived, doved, 450
"Dover Beach" (Arnold), 184–86
Doxsee, Beth, "Learning Years," 47–49
Drama in narrative writing, 61
Drowned, drowned, 450
"Drugs" (Vidal), 167–69
Due to the fact that, 450
Dune (film review of), 180–81

"Easier to Start a War Than Consult a Dictionary" (Safire), 315–16
Echoes of Ancient Skies (Krupp), 288
Editor, becoming your own, 364, 367
Editorial writing, 139–40
Effect, affect, 439
Einstein, Albert, *Relativity: The Special and General Theory*, 92
Eiseley, Loren, *The Unexpected Universe*, 5

Either-or fallacy. *See* False dichotomy
Elbow, Peter, *Writing With Power*, 39
Elliot, Evan, "The Salinity Problem in Crop Irrigation," 112
Elipses, 476
Embedding, 272–73, 284, 394
Emerson, Ralph Waldo, "Gifts," 307–308, 336
Emig, Janet, 417
Emotion in writing, 58
Encyclopedias, general, 191
Ensure, insure, 450
Enthused, enthusiastic, 450
"Equal in Paris" (Baldwin), 59–60
Essay exams, 375–78
  preparing for, 377–78
  principles of, 375–76
Essays, kinds of, 46–50, 395
Etc., 451
Ethos, 123, 159
Etymology, 326, 395
Euphemism, 322–24, 395
Evading the issue fallacy, 135–36
Evaluative essay. *See* Review
Evidence, 122, 138, 161
Evidence, proof, 451
Evoke, invoke, 451
Except, accept, 438
Exclamation mark, 476–77
Exposition, 395
Expression, 9, 10
Expressive writing, 58, 63–66
  range of, 58
  problems in, 63–66
  See also Development
Extended definition, writing an, 100–104

Facts, 122
Fallacies, 129–38
Fallows, James, "To Draft or Not to Draft . . . ," 162–67
False dichotomy, 131
"The Fantasy Film as Final Exam" (review of *Dune* by Corliss), 180–81
Fantasy and intrigue (advertising appeal), 149
Farther, further, 451–52
Faulty deductive reasoning, 131–36
Faulty generalizing, 129–31
"Fear and Trembling and Sick of English" (Long), 22–24
Fewer, less, 452
Figuratively, literally, 452
Figures of speech, 395–96
  hyperbole, 396

Figures of speech (*continued*)
  litotes, 396
  metaphor, 396
  periphrasis, 396
  pun, 396
  synecdoche, 396
Fitzgerald, F. Scott, 347, 359
Five-paragraph essay, 8
Five senses (advertising appeal), 149
5 W's and the H Grid, 40–42
Flashback, 59–60
Flaunt, flout, 452–53
Flawed comparison. See Analogy, flawed
Fletcher, Colin, *The Man Who Walked Through Time*, 301
"Flight" (Updike), 79–80
Formatting, manuscript, 487–90
  indentation, 487
  line spacing, 488
  margins, 488
  page layouts, 488–90
  pagination, 490
Four terms fallacy, 134–35
Fragment, 260, 397
France and England in North America (Parkman), 90
Frank, Anne, *Diary of a Young Girl*, 59
Free Writing, 38–39
From Bauhaus to Our House (Wolfe), 80
Fromm, Erich, *The Art of Loving*, 91
Further, farther, 451–52

Gardner, John, 29
Garretson, Kim, "How to Figure Fuelishness," 105–107
Generality, levels of, 295–96
Generalization, 129–31, 326
  faulty, 129–31
Gerund, 397
Gift From the Sea (Lindbergh), 269
"Gifts" (Emerson), 336
Glance, Glimpse, 453
Goldman, Abby (interview with Jean Auel), 206–208
Goodman, Ellen, "Social Nibbling," 81–82
Gough, Tom, "Martin Landau's *Dracula* Could Use a Mild Transfusion" (theater review), 181–83
"Gradually Adjusting to Retirement: Facing the Change" (Rock), 235–45
Graduated, graduated from, was graduated, 453

Grammar, 398
  defined, 398
  morphology, 398
  parts of speech, 398
  syntax, 398
Grammatical Man, 95
Graveline, Denise, "Advice for Would-Be Wayfarers," 49
Graves, Robert, *Book of Greek Myths*, 6
Gray, Paul, "The Nightmare and the Dream" (book review of *Loon Lake*), 177–79
Greek Myths, The (Graves), 6
Greek View of Life, The (Dickinson), 196–97

Hacek, 476
"Haleakala National Park, Hawaii," 72–73
Hampl, Patricia, *A Romantic Education*, 75
["Handguns"] (Moore), 158
Hanged, hung, 453
Helping verb. See Verb, auxiliary
Hemingway, Ernest, "Big Two-Hearted River," 274
["Henry Ossawa Tanner"] (Perry), 247–52
Heuristics, 34–42
  background reading, 42
  brainstorming, 34–38
  5 W's and the H Grid, 40–42
  free-writing, 38–39
  gathering and planning, 40–42
  talk-writing, 39–40
Hogendijk, Thomas, 76–78, 348–51
Hopefully, it is hoped, 454
Hopkins, Gerard Manley, 63
Horney, Karen, M.D., *The Neurotic Personality of Our Time*, 103–104
"How Do I Rate Thee? Let Me Count the Ways" (Lee), 141–42
How-to feature, writing a, 104–106
"How to Drive a Manual Transmission" (Noble), 113–14
"How to Figure Fuelishness" (Garretson), 105–107
"How to Make a Speech," 108–109
"How to 'Write' Programs," 220–21
Huxley, Anthony, *Plant and Planet*, 89
Hyndman, Donald, *A Roadside Geology of Northern California*, 92
Hyphen, 474–75
Hypostatization, 137

Idiom, 398
"I Have a Dream" (King), 320
I Know Why the Caged Bird Sings (Angelou), 281–83
Image-reversal, 149
Imply, infer, 454
Indentation, 487
Indexes, periodical, 192
Induction, 123–24
Infinitive, 399–420
  split, 420
Inflection, 399
Illusion, allusion, 440
Information, 85–86, 211–12
  attributable, 211–12
  common knowledge, 211
  factual, 211
  interpreted, 211
  presenting, 85–86
Information-gathering, 196–200
Information sources outside the library, 210–11
-ing word. See Gerund; Participle
Insure, ensure, 450
Intelligent Life in the Universe (Sagan and Shlovskii), 7
Interjections, 476
Interviewing, 205–208
Invention, 33–42
  See also Heuristics
Inventory sheet, 195–96
Invisible writing, 53
Irony, 399
Irregardless, regardless, 454
Irregular verb. See Verb, irregular
Irving, Washington, 95–96
Italics, 477
It is hoped, hopefully, 454
It's, its, 454–55

James, Henry, "London," 67; "Portraits of Places," 80, 359
Jargon, 332
  as metaphor, 332
  as obscure or evasive language, 332n
  as specialized information, 332
Jastrow, Robert, *Until the Sun Dies*, 6–7
"Jazz and West African Music" (Stearns), 93–94
Johnson, Mark, *Metaphors We Live By*, 321

Journals, 30, 62–63, 357–62
  as scrapbook, 358
  as secret book, 358
  for prewriting activities, 357
  suggestions for entries, 360–61
  suggestions for maintaining, 358–59
  using a computer for keeping, 361–62
" 'Just' a Word Makes All the Difference" (McWhirter), 339–40

Keller, Helen, 279
Keywords (Williams), 104
Kidder, Tracy, *The Soul of a New Machine*, 332
King, Martin Luther, Jr., "Letter from Birmingham Jail," 270; "I Have a Dream," 320
Kinneavy, James, 417
Knowledge and Wonder (Weisskopf), 270
Koestler, Arthur, 417
Krupa, Gene, *Situational Writing*, 113
Krupp, Dr. E. C., *Echoes of Ancient Skies*, 288

Lakoff, George, *Metaphors We Live By*, 321
Lambkin, JoAnn, ["Videogame Player"], 67–68
"The Landscape and the Dream" (Gray), 177–79
Lao Tzu, 371
Lay, lie, 455
Lead, led, 456
Leahey, Lavelle, 34–35
"Learning Years" (Doxee), 47–49
Lee, Anita, "How Do I Rate Thee? Let Me Count the Ways," 141–42
Less, fewer, 452
Lehmann, Phyllis, "More Than You Ever Thought You Would Know About Food Additives," 302
Lend, borrow, 443
"Letter from Birmingham Jail" (King), 270
Letters to the editor, 157–58
Levertov, Denise, "The Obligation of the Poet," 172–74
Librarian assistance, 205
Library of Congress Classification, 194–95

Library of Congress Subject Headings, 201–202
Lie, lay, 455
Lindbergh, Anne Morrow, *Gift from the Sea*, 269
Literally, figuratively, 452
Like, as, 456
Loose, lose, 456
Linguistics, 399–400
  defined, 399–400
  dialectology, 400
  historical, 400
  orthography, 400
  phonology, 400
  psycholinguistics, 400
  semantics, 400
  sociolinguistics, 400
  structural, 400
Linking verb. See Verb, linking
Linnaeus, Carolus, 88
Logos, 123
Logic, 127, 128–38
  See also Reasoning
"London," 67
London in the Age of Chaucer (Meyers), 296
Long, Christine, "Fear and Trembling and Sick of English," 22–24
Loon Lake (Doctorow), 177–79
-ly (as suffix for ordinal numbers), 456

McPhee, John, *Basin and Range*, 283–84
McWhirter, Nickie, " 'Just' a Word Makes All the Difference," 339–40
"Magic" (Yeats), 198
Malapropism, 316–17
The Man Who Walked Through Time (Fletcher), 301
Mannes, Marya, "Television: The Splitting Image," 149–50
Margins, 488
"Martin Landau's *Dracula* Could Use a Transfusion" (Gough), 181–83
Masterful, masterly, 457
May, can, 443
May, Rollo, *The Courage to Create*, 21
Media, medium, 457
Melville, Herman, *Moby Dick*, 337
Metaphor, 319–22
  dormant, 319n
  free association with, 321–22
  kinds of, 321–22

  mixed, 401
  orientational, 321
  origin of the term, 32
  structural, 321
  thinking in, 321
Metaphors We Live By (Lakoff and Johnson), 321
Meyers, A. L., *London in the Age of Chaucer*, 296
Middle term, 132–33
Middleman, Louis, 421
Missing premise fallacy, 135
Moby Dick (Melville), 337
Modifier, 267–68; 401–402
  dangling, 267–68, 401
  misplaced, 267, 401–402
  squinting, 402
Moffett, James, 417
Montaigne, Michel de, "On the Art of Conversing," 143–44
Mood, 402, 418
  declarative, 418
  imperative, 402, 418
  indicative, 402
  interrogative, 418
  subjunctive, 402
Moon of the Caribbees, The (O'Neill), 329
Moore, L. ["Handguns"], 158
Morphology, 398
  See also Grammar, Linguistics
Morley, Christopher, 319
"More Than You Ever Thought You Would Know About Food Additives" (Lehmann), 302
Mortal Lessons: Notes on the Art of Surgery (Selzer), 319–20
The Mountains of California (Muir), 21–22
Muir, John, 21–22

Narration, 59–61, 76–78, 89, 94, 138, 139, 402–403
  in an explanatory context, 89
  in a persuasive context, 138, 139
  narrative buildup, 60
  personal experience narrative, 402–403
The Neurotic Personality of Our Time (Horney), 103–104
New, newly, 457
"The Nightmare and the Dream" (review of *Loon Lake* by Gray), 177–79
Nin, Anais, *Diary*, 63
Noble, Marie, "How To Drive a Manual Transmission," 113–14

Nominative, function of, 407, 408
Nominalization, 403
Nostalgia (advertising appeal), 149
Note-taking, 196–200
Note-taking abbreviations. *See* Abbreviations
Note-taking marks, 491–92
   See also Proofreading marks
Noun, 397, 403, 407–408, 412
   function of, 408
   generic, 397
   predicate, 412
Noun clause. *See* Clause
Noun cluster, 404
Noun phrase. *See* Phrase
Nucleus word, 34
Numbers, 484
   spelling out, 484
   using numerals, 484

Object, 404–405
"The Obligation of the Poet" (Levertov), 172–74
Observation, 62
Obsolete, obsolescent, 457–58
Obsolete words, 328
O'Connor, Flannery, 34
"Of Suspicion" (Bacon), 215–16
Oftentimes, 458
O'Neill, Eugene, *The Moon of the Caribbees*, 329
On Photography (Sontag), 278
"On the Art of Conversing" (Montaigne), 143–44
Opinion essay, 157–60
Opinion vs. argument, 127–28
Organization, 21, 42–44, 107, 368–69
Orwell, George, "Why I Write," 25
Outline, 43–44, 405–406
   finished, 405
   method of doing an, 43–44
   scratch, 43, 405
Overgeneralizing, 128–29
Oxford English Dictionary, 192

Palm Sunday (Vonnegut), 329
Paragraph, 197–99, 293–305, 406
   amplification of, 298
   cluttering, 298
   coherence, 294–95
   common problems with, 297–300
   context-bound, 294
   dialogue paragraphs, 293
   and discourse aim, 299

and discourse mode, 300–303
experimenting, 303–305
fragment paragraphs, 293–94
method, 197–99
parentheses, 478
Parkman, Francis, *France and England in North America*, 90
Parallelism, 269–71, 406
   defined, 269
   excessive, 269
   incomplete, 270
   inter-sentence, 270–71
   within the sentence, 269–70
Participle, 407
   origin of the term, 293
   past, 407
   perfect, 407
   present, 407
   support sentences in, 295–96
   topic sentence in, 295–96
Parts of speech, 398, 407–409
   See also Adjective, Adverb, Conjunction, Noun, Preposition, Pronoun, Verb
Passive voice. *See* Voice
Passed, past, 458
Pathos, 123
Period, 478
   with abbreviations, 478
   with decimals, 478
   with letters, 478
   with numbers, 478
   with sentences, 478
Perry, Ellwood, ["Henry Ossawa Tanner"], 247–52
Person, 409
   first, 409
   second, 409
   third, 409
Persecute, prosecute, 458
Personal pronoun. *See* Pronoun
Person shift, 409
Personal experience narrative, 76–78
Personification, 326
Persuasion, 121, 123–38, 149–55
   common problems, 127–38
   goal of argument, 121
   mass-media, 149–55
   and reasoning, 123–27
Phrase, 261, 409–10
   gerund phrase, 262
   infinitive phrase, 261
   noun phrase, 409
   participial phrase, 261
   prepositional phrase, 410
   verb phrase, 410
Piaget, Jean, 417

A Pictorial History of Western Art (Christensen), 88
Plagiarism, 211–12, 410
   avoiding, 211–12
   causes of, 211–12
   defined, 211, 410
Plant and Planet (Huxley), 89
Plato, 416
Plimpton, George, "How to Make a Speech," 108–109
Plus, 458
Point of view, 9, 10, 410
Portraits of Places (James), 80
Possessive, 411
Post hoc fallacy, 129–30
Precede, proceed, 458
Predicate adjective, 411
Predicate noun, 412
Prefixes, 333–36
   Greek, 333–34
   Latin, 335–36
   See also Roots
Prejudice, prejudiced, 459
Premise, 124, 131–32
Preposition, 407, 408, 412–13
   function, 407, 408
Prepositional phrase. *See* Phrase
Prewriting, 34, 44
   See also Heuristics
Principal, principle, 459
Problem-solving essay, 167–71
"The Problem With Soccer . . ." (Rooney), 159–60
Proceed, precede, 458
Pro-con essay, 160–67
Pronoun, 408, 413–14, 417
   absolute, 413
   definite, 413
   demonstrative, 413
   possessive, 413
   reflexive, 414
   relative, 413, 417
Pronunciation key (in dictionaries), 325
Proof, evidence, 451
Proof, indisputable vs. sufficient, 122
Proofreading, 46, 347–48
   defined, 46
   in revising, 347–48
Proofreading marks. *See* Notetaking marks
Prosecute, persecute, 458
Proposal. *See* Prospectus
Prospectus (for a research paper), 203–204; 222–23
Pun, 396
Punctuation, reasons for, 469
Purpose in writing, 2

Qualification of thesis, 139
Question-begging, 128
Question mark, 478–79
Questionnaire, 208–210
Quite, 459
Quotation marks, 479–80
  with dialogue, 479
  within a quotation, 479
  with title of a short work, 479
  with unconventional use of a word, 479
  with a word discussed as such, 479
Quotation, quote, 459
Quotations, incorporating, 200–201
Quoting, verbatim, 196

Raise, rise, 460
Ramus, Petrus, 416
Readability, 200, 218
Real, really, 460
Rearrangement, 346
  See also Revision
Reasoning, 123–38
  authority-based, 124–25, 126
  classification of, 123–27
  deductive, 123–24
  defined, 123
  emotion-based, 124–25, 126
  inductive, 123–24
  logic-based, 123–24, 126
  problems in, 127–38
Reason is because, reason is that, 460
Recommendations, 139
Red herring, 135–36
Redundancy, 65, 414
Reference books, 324–28, 507–23
  in anthropology, 514–16
  in art, 518–19
  in business, 514–16
  in economics, 514–16
  in geography, 514–16
  in history, 513–14
  in language and literature, 324–28, 508–509, 520–21
  in music, 518–19
  in philosophy, 511–12
  in political science, 516–17
  in psychology, 511–12
  in religion, 511–12
  in science and technology, 521–23
  in social sciences, 514–16
  in theater and film, 520–21
"References" page. *See* Bibliography
Reflexive pronoun, 414
Refutation, 138, 161

Regardless, irregardless, 454
Relative pronoun, 417
Relativity: The Special and General Theory (Einstein), 92
Research, 99, 189–214, 219–23, 235, 246
  computers in, 212–14
  in the fine arts, 246
  in the sciences, 219–23
  in the social sciences, 235
  research outside the library, 205–11
Research, informal. *See* Background reading
Research paper, 217–52
  defined, 217
  interdisciplinary nature of, 218
  models, 224–33, 236–45, 427–56
  motives for writing, 218
  outline for, 223, 236–37
  prospectus for, 222
  uses, 218
Reperception, 346–47
  See also Revision
Restrictive clause, 415
Reviews, 177–81, 415
Revision, 15, 45–46, 343–51, 416
  as addition, 345
  as deletion, 344–45
  as proofreading, 347–48
  as rearrangement, 346
  as reperception, 346–47
  as substitution, 345–46
  on the computer, 15
  stage of the composing process, 45–46
Rhetoric, 416–17
Rhetorical question, 417
Rhetorical situation, 19
Rico, Gabriele, *Writing the Natural Way*, 34
Rise, raise, 460
A Roadside Geology of Northern California (Alt and Hyndman), 92
Rock, Ron K., Jr., "Gradually Adjusting to Retirement: Facing the Change," 235–45
Rogerian argument, 139, 140–42
Rogers, Carl, 139, 417
Role playing, 19–20
Rohmann, D. Gordon, 417
A Romantic Education (Hampl), 75
Rooney, Andy, "The Problem with Soccer . . . ," 159–60
Roots, 335–36
  Greek, 334–35
  Latin, 336
  See also Prefixes

Roughing It (Twain), 276–77, 330–31
Rouse, W.H.D., 420
["Running in the Foothills"] (White), 65–66

Safire, William, 315–16
Sagan, Carl, *Intelligent Life in the Universe*, 6–7
"The Salinity Problem in Crop Irrigation" (Elliot), 112
Saving the Whooping Crane (United States Fish and Wildlife Service), 199–200
Schatzman, E. L., 96
Search-request form (for database search), 212
The Second Sin (Szasz), 130
Selzer, Richard, *Mortal Lessons: Notes on the Art of Surgery*, 319–20
Semicolon, 480–81
Sensory language, 66
  See also Description
Sensual, sensuous, 460
Sentence, 10–11, 259–89, 295–96, 417–18
  balanced, 264
  cluttered, 265–66
  coherence, 265, 267–71
  combining, 284–89
  complex, 418
  compound, 274, 418
  compound-complex, 277, 418
  construction, 10–11
  coordination, 273–74
  cumulative, 264
  defined, 260
  development, 265, 272–75
  elliptical, 260
  fragments, 260, 261
  fused, 262
  interrogatory, 277
  length, 279–80
  periodic, 264
  rhythm in, 276
  run-on, 262, 419
  simple, 274, 417
  support, 295
  topic, 295–96
  topic-support relationship, 296
  transitional expressions in, 280
  types of, 417–18
  variety, 265, 276–81
  varying word order in, 279
  See also Clause, Phrase
Serendipity, 204
Set, sit, 460–61

Sexist language, 337, 419–20
Shakespeare, William, 317
Shall, *will*, 461
Shaughnessy, Mina, 417
Sheridan, Richard, 316
Shlovskii, I. S., *Intelligent Life in the Universe*, 6–7
Sic, 197
Situational Writing (Krupa), 113
The Sketch Book (Irving), 95–96
Skinner, B. F., *Beyond Freedom and Dignity*, 301
Slang, 327–28, 332, 424
Slash, 481
So, 461
   as adverb, 461
   as expletive, 461
   as implicit subordinator, 461
"Social Nibbling" (Goodman), 81–82
Sontag, Susan, *On Photography*, 278
So This Is Depravity (Baker), 96
The Soul of a New Machine (Kidder), 332
Soundness vs. validity of an argument, 132
Spay, *spayed*, *spayded*, 461
Spelling, 325, 483–86
   consulting the dictionary for, 325
   of plurals, 484
   of words carelessly pronounced, 484
   of words containing silent letters, 483
   suggestions for improving, 483–86
Split infinitive. *See* Infinitive
Spooner, Reverend William A., 420
Spoonerism, 420
Springboards for generating essay ideas, 28
Squinting modifier. *See* modifier
Stansbury, David, "Cooling Burnout," 115–18
Stationary, *stationery*, 461–62
Stearns, Marshall, "Jazz and West African Music," 93–94
Stereotyping, 129
The Structure of the Universe (Schatzman), 96
Style, 2, 10, 281, 303, 369, 420–21
Subheads, 107
Subject (of a sentence), 421
Subordination, 274–75
Subjunctive mood. *See* Mood
Subordinate clause. *See* Clause
Subordinate conjunction. *See* Conjunction
Summary, 105, 199–200, 421

Swift, Jonathan, 420
Syllabication, 325
Syllogism, 131–36
Symbol, 422
Syntax, 398, 422
   See also Sentence
Szasz, Thomas, *The Second Sin*, 130

Talk-writing, 39
Tenor, 319
   See also Metaphor
Tense, 314, 422–23
   shifts in, 314, 422–23
Than, *then*, 462
That, *which*, 462
That, *who*, 462
Their, *they're*, *there*, 463
Theirselves, *themselves*, 463
Then, *than*, 462
Thesis, 138–39, 158, 161
This kind, *these kind*, 463
Thoreau, Henry David, *Walden*, 62
Thus, *thusly*, 463
Tilde, 476
Till, *until*, 463
Time of day, expressing, 472
   colon with, 472
   spelling out, 472n
Tone. *See* Voice
"[To Draft or Not to Draft:] Why This Country Needs It" (Fallows), 162–67
Topic sentence, 295–96
Transition, 280, 423
Transitive relationship, 132
Trope. *See* Figures of Speech
Twain, Mark, *Roughing It*, 276–77, 330–31

Umlaut, 476
Undistributed middle fallacy, 132–33
Uninterested, *disinterested*, 449
Unique, 463
The Unexpected Universe (Eiseley), 5
United States Fish and Wildlife Service, *Saving the Whooping Crane*, 199–200
Unity, 423. *See also* Coherence
Until the Sun Dies (Jastrow), 6–7
Until, *till*, 463
Updike, John, "Flight," 79–80
Usage, 313, 328–31, 424
   consistency of, 313
   formal, 328, 329, 424
   extremely formal, 328, 329, 424
   informal, 424

   extremely informal, 424
   standard vs. nonstandard, 330–31
Use, *utilize*, 463

Validity vs. soundness of an argument, 132
Valid-but-unsound fallacy, 131–32
Valla, Laurentius, 416
Values, 122
Vehicle, 319
   See also Metaphor
Venn diagram, 133
Venn, John, 133n
Verb
   auxiliary (helping), 425
   intransitive, 327
   irregular, 425–26
   linking (copulative), 411, 426
   predicating, 426
   transitive, 327
   using strong verbs, 345–46
Vidal, Gore, "Drugs," 167–69
Viewpoint. *See* Point of View
Vocabulary building, 333–36, 337
Voice, 318, 426
   active, 426
   passive, 318, 426
   tone of, 426
Vonnegut, Kurt, Jr., 329

Wade, Tom ["Working in a Service Station"], 113
Walden (Thoreau), 62
Walpole, Horace, *The Castle of Otranto*, 81
Weather, *whether*, 464
Weisskopf, Victor F., *Knowledge and Wonder*, 270
What Is Poetry? (Wheelock), 329
Wheelock, John Hall, *What Is Poetry?*, 329
Which, *that*, 462
White, Mike ["Running in the Foothills"], 65–66
Who, *that*, 462
Whoever, *whomever*, 464–65
"Who Killed Benny Paret?" (Cousins), 170–71
Who, *whom*, 464
Who's, *whose*, 465
"Why I Write" (Didion), 63
"Why I Write" (Orwell), 25
Wilde, Oscar, 175
Williams, Raymond, *Keywords*, 104
Will, *shall*, 461

Wolfe, Tom, *From Bauhaus to Our House*, 80
Woolf, Virginia, "The Death of the Moth," 279–80
Wordiness, 65–66, 344–45, 427
  See also Redundancy
Words, 10, 92, 309–37
  accurate choice of, 314–15
  and analysis, 92
  clarity in using, 312–19
  conciseness in using, 317–19
  connotation of, 310–12
  and context, 310
  definitions of, 309
  denotation of, 310–12
  dialect, 327
  dictionary definitions of, 309
  and experience, 337
  general and specialized, 331–32
  and imagination, 336–37
  and meanings, 309
  metaphorical use of, 310
  obsolete, 328
  and reality, 337
  sexist, 337, 419–20
  slang, 327
  usage, 313, 328, 329, 424
  vivid, 10
Words of Science (Asimov), 326–27
Working bibliography, 222–23
["Working in a Service Station"] (Wade), 113
Works Cited page. *See* Bibliography
Workshop, in-class, 367–69
Writer's block, 34, 45, 427
Writing
  awkward, 388
  in business, 12
  as communication, 17–18, 21
  elements of good, 7–9
  emotion in, 58
  essay-exam, 18, 375–78
  first draft, 44–45
  habit of, 30
  and learning, 18
  method of, 29–46
  and personal relationships, 18
  as recreation and "re-creation," 21, 22, 62
  and role playing, 19–20
  and speaking, 18
  and thinking, 1, 2, 7
Writing the Natural Way (Rico), 34
Writing rituals, 31
Writing process, 32–50
Writing With Power (Elbow), 39
Wrong authority, 137

Xmas, Christmas, 445

Yeats, W. B., "Magic," 198
You, 465
Young, Richard, 417
Your, you're, 465

Editing Abbreviations and Symbols

These marks, which your instructor will make in the margins of your drafts, will help you with the surface elements of a revision. Study the pages indicated before beginning to revise.

ABS	Language is unnecessarily abstract; make concrete. (382)
ADJ	Use an adjective (or adjectival form of word used). (383)
ADV	Use an adverb (or adverbial form of word used). (384)
AGR	Error in subject-verb or pronoun-antecedent agreement. (384–385)
AMB	Expression is ambiguous in this context. (385–386)
AWK	Passage is awkward (stylistically uneven). (276–282)
CAP	Capitalize this word; or, this word should not be capitalized. (471–472)
CAS	Wrong case. (388–389)
COH	Problem with coherence in this sentence or paragraph or between these sentences or paragraphs. (267–271, 390)
COL	Error in colon use; or, colon needed. (472–473)
COM	Error in comma use. (473–474)
CONJ	Use a conjunction or a different conjunction. (391)
CS	Comma splice (similar to run-on sentence). (473)
D	Problem with diction (word choice); use clearer, stronger, or more precise word. (310–317, 345–346)
FMT	Error in manuscript format. (487–490)
FRAG	Sentence fragment (grammatically incomplete sentence). (397)
MM	Mixed metaphor. (401)
MOD	Revise to eliminate dangling or misplaced modifier. (267–268, 401–402)
NOM	Nominalization; change to verb phrase. (403)